Guide to ISLAM

The Asian Philosophies and Religions Resource Guide

Guide to ISLAM

DAVID EDE

and

Leonard Librande, Donald P. Little,
Andrew Rippin, Richard Timms, and Jan Weryho

G.K.HALL &CO.
70 LINCOLN STREET, BOSTON, MASS.

Library of Congress Cataloging in Publication Data
Main entry under title:

Guide to Islam.

Bibliography: p.
Includes index.
1. Islam—Bibliography. 2. Civilization, Islamic—Bibliography. I. Ede, David.
Z7835.M6G84 1983 016.297 83-6134
[BP161.2]
ISBN 0-8161-7905-0

This publication is printed on permanent/durable acid-free paper
MANUFACTURED IN THE UNITED STATES OF AMERICA

Project on Asian Philosophies and Religions

Sponsoring Organizations

Center for International Programs and Comparative Studies of the New York State Education Department/University of the State of New York

Council for Intercultural Programs, Inc.

Steering Committee

Kenneth Morgan	Emeritus, Colgate University *Chairman*
Wing-tsit Chan	Chatham College Emeritus, Darmouth College
David J. Dell	Foreign Area Materials Center Columbia University *Project Manager, 1975–77*
Edith Ehrman	Foreign Area Materials Center *Project Manager, 1971–74*
Robert McDermott	Baruch College, City University of New York
Bardwell Smith	Carleton College
H. Daniel Smith	Syracuse University
Frederick J. Streng	Southern Methodist University

Editorial Coordinators

David J. Dell

Edward S. Haynes

Preparation of this series of guides to resources for the study of Asian philosophies and religions was made possible by a grant from the National Endowment for the Humanities, supplemented through the Endowment's matching funds scheme, with additional financial support from the Ada Howe Kent Foundation, C. T. Shen, and the Council on International and Public Affairs, Inc. None of the above bodies is responsible for the content of these guides, which is the responsibility of those listed on the title page.

This project has been undertaken by the Foreign Area Materials Center, State Education Department, University of the State of New York, under the auspices of the Council for Intercultural Studies and Program, 60 East 42nd Street, New York, NY 10017.

IN MEMORY OF
EDITH EHRMAN
1932-1974

Straightway I was 'ware
So weeping, how a mystic shape did move
Behind me, and drew me backward by the hair
And a voice said in mastery while I strove, . . .
'Guess now who holds thee?—'Death', I said, but there
The silver answer rang . . . 'Not Death, but Love.'

Elizabeth Barrett Browning

Contents

Series Preface

Asian Philosophies and Religions and the Humanities in America

This guide is one of a series of books on resources for the study of Asian philosophies and religions. The series includes volumes on Chinese, Indian, Islamic, and Buddhist philosophies and religions. Since the preparation of the series has been undertaken as a contribution to advancing humanistic learning in America, it is important to place the study of these traditions in that larger context.

Humanistic scholarship and teaching in America has understandably concentrated on Western civilization, of which we are a part. Yet Western civilization has historically drawn significantly upon the humanistic accomplishments of other traditions and has interacted with these traditions. Given the increasing mobility of scholars and students in the second half of the twentieth century and the rapidly advancing technological capacity for communicating ideas in the modern world, this interaction is accelerating as we approach the twenty-first century.

Liberal education for American students in the 1980s and 1990s must reflect not only our human heritage in all of its diversity as it has accumulated through past centuries but also the nature of the future in its intellectual and cultural as well as economic, social, and political dimensions. By the year 2000, a logical future reference point for today's college students who will spend most of their adult lives in the next century, four out of five human beings will live in the Third World of Asia, Africa, and Latin America, which we study least in our colleges and universities today.

Numerical distribution of humanity is certainly not the only criterion that should determine the content of humanistic learning in our institutions of higher education. But when orders of magnitude achieve the proportions that, according to most demographic projections, will exist in the year 2000, geographical location of humanity is certainly one criterion that will be applied by today's students in assessing the "relevance" of their undergraduate education to the real world of the future.

The argument becomes all the more compelling when the qualitative aspects of civilization other than our own are considered. Western man can claim no corner on creative accomplishment, as Hubert Muller has rightly recognized in this passage from The Uses of the Past.

> Stick to Asia, and we get another elementary lesson in humility. Objectively its history looks more important than the history of Europe. . . . It has produced more civilizations, involving a much greater proportion of mankind, over a longer period of time, on a higher level of continuity. As for cultural achievement, we have no universal yardstick; but by one standard on which Western Christendom has prided itself, Asia has been far more creative. It has bred all the higher religions, including Christianity.*

There is little doubt that the rapid growth of student interest in the study of these traditions is the result in part of their search for new value systems in contemporary society. But this interest is also a recognition of other civilizations as being intrinsically worthy of our attention.

Origins of the Project on Asian Philosophies and Religions

The project was initiated in response to this growth of student interest, which began in the 1960s and has persisted in the 1970s, notwithstanding a current general decline in the exponential growth rates in American colleges and universities. Faculty members with specialized training in Asian philosophical and religious traditions, however, are still limited in number and most courses in these subjects are being taught by nonspecialists. While the proportion of those with specialized training has certainly increased in recent years, the situation is unlikely to improve greatly due to the ceilings on faculty size that many institutions have imposed because of financial stringency.

The need for a series of authoritative guides to literature in these fields for use in both

*The Uses of the Past, New York: New American Library, 1954, p. 314.

undergraduate and beginning graduate study of Asian philosophies and religions, which first prompted us to seek support from the National Endowment for the Humanities for the project in 1971, remains just as compelling as the project draws to a close.

Organization of the Project

The project on Asian philosophies and religions was conceived from the beginning as a cooperative venture involving scholars and teachers of these subjects. The key element in the organization of the project has been the project team or working group, a deliberately informal structure with its own leader, working autonomously but within a general conceptual framework developed early in the project by all of those who were involved in the project at that time.

The individual working groups have been linked together by a project steering committee, which has been concerned with the overall organization and implementation of the project. The members of the project steering committee, working group leaders, and other key project personnel are as follows:

Kenneth Morgan, Emeritus, Colgate University (Chairman of the Project Steering Committee)

Wing-tsit Chan, Chatham College and Emeritus, Dartmouth College (Member, Project Steering Committee; Leader of Working Group on Chinese Philosophy and Religion)

Bardwell Smith, Carleton College (Member, Project Steering Committee and Working Group on Buddhist Religion)

H. Daniel Smith, Syracuse University (Member, Project Steering Committee and Working Group on Hinduism)

Robert McDermott, Baruch College, City University of New York (Member, Project Steering Committee and the Working Group on Hinduism)

Thomas Hopkins, Franklin and Marshall College (Leader of the Working Group on Hinduism)

David Ede, Western Michigan University and McGill University (Leader of the Working Group on Islamic Religion)

Karl Potter, University of Washington (Leader of the Working Group on Indian Philosophy)

Frank Reynolds, University of Chicago (Leader of the Working Group on Buddhist Religion)

Kenneth Inada, State University of New York at Buffalo (Leader of the Working Group on Buddhist Philosophy)

Frederick J. Streng, Southern Methodist University (Member, Project Steering Committee and Working Groups on Buddhist Religion and Philosophy)

David Dell (Project Manager, 1975-78 and a Member of the Working Group on Hinduism)

Two characteristics of the project's organization merit mention. One has been the widespread use of other scholars and teachers, in addition to the members of the project steering committee and working groups, in the critical review of preliminary versions of the guides. Reviewers were asked to comment on both commissions and omissions, and their comments were used by the compilers in making revisions. A far more extensive exercise than the customary scholarly review of manuscripts, this process involved well over 200 individuals who contributed immeasurably to improving the quality of the end product.

A similar effort to enlarge participation in the project has been made through discussions at professional meetings about the project among interested scholars and teachers while it was in progress. Over the past four years a dozen such sessions, involving over 300 participants, have been held at both national and regional meetings of the American Academy of Religion and the Association for Asian Studies.

The Classification Scheme and Criteria of Selection for the Guide

Early in the project a conference of most of the key project personnel mentioned above, as well as other members of the project working groups, was held in New York City in June 1972 to develop a common classification scheme and criteria for inclusion of materials in the resource guides.

This task generated lively and intense debate because underlying any classification scheme are the most fundamental issues of conceptualization and periodization in the study of religious and philosophical traditions. The classification schemes for guides in religion and in philosophy have generally been followed by each working group, although there have been inevitable variations. Each of the traditions included in the project has distinctive qualities and characteristics, which makes it difficult to fit all aspects of all traditions into the same set of categories.

The objective of developing a common set of categories was to facilitate examinations of parallel phenomena across traditions. We believe this objective has been at least partially achieved through this series, although we recognize the need for continued refinement before a common set of categories compatible with all the traditions being covered can be evolved.

If developing categories to span diverse religious and philosophical traditions has been difficult, definition and reasonably uniform application of criteria for inclusion of material in the guides has been no easier. The project's basic objective, as originally elaborated at the June 1972 working conference, has been to provide an authoritative guide to the literature, both texts in translation and commentary and analysis, for teachers and advanced undergraduate and beginning graduate students who are not specialized scholars with access to primary texts in their original languages. Because of the limited number of teachers in American colleges and universities who have the necessary language skills, particularly outside their own primary field of scholarly interest, it was expected that the guides would be useful to those teaching in the field who, even though they might have a high level of scholarly specialization in one tradition, would often find it necessary to deal with other traditions in their teaching.

We also sought to achieve some consistency in annotations of entries in the guides. The objective has been to provide short, crisp, critical annotations that would help the user of the guide in identifying material pertinent to his or her interest or most authoritative in its coverage of a particular topic. We recognize, of course, that we have not achieved this objective throughout the entire series of guides encompassing more than 12,000 individual entries.

Because of the difficulties in applying a common set of categories and subcategories to the diverse traditions being covered by the guides, not all categories have been covered in each guide, and in some cases, they have been grouped together as seemed appropriate to the characteristics of a particular tradition. Extensive cross-referencing has been provided to guide the user to related entries in other categories.

The Problem of Availability of Resources in the Guide and the Microform Resource Bank

We realized from the beginning that a series of guides of this character would have little value if the users could not acquire materials listed in the guides. We therefore sought the cooperation of the Institute for Advanced Studies of World Religions, which is engaged in a major effort to develop a collection of resources for the study of world religions in microform, and through the Institute, have established a microform resource bank of material in the guides not readily available from other sources.

Subject to the availability of the material for microfilming and depending upon its copyright status, the Institute is prepared to provide in microform any item included in any of the guides that is out-of-print or otherwise not readily available, in accordance with its usual schedule of charges. Where an item is already included in the Institute's microform collection, those charges are quite modest, and an effort is being made by the Institute to increase its holding of materials in the guides. Material can also be provided in hard xerographic copy suitable for reproduction for multiple classroom use at an additional charge.

Under the terms of a project agreement with the Institute, the Institute is undertaking the microfilming of some 30,000 pages of material included in these guides. In addition, the Institute already has in its microform collection a substantial number of titles in the fields of Buddhist and Chinese philosophy and religion.

The Institute will from time to time issue lists of material in microform from the guides available in its collections, but as its microform collections are continually being expanded, users are urged to contact the Institute directly to see if a particular title in which they are interested is available:

Institute for Advanced Studies of World
Religions
Melville Memorial Library
State University of New York
Stony Brook, New York 11794

Acknowledgments

An undertaking of this scope and magnitude, involving such widespread participation, is bound to accumulate a long list of those who have contributed in one way or another to the project. It would be impossible to identify by name all of those who have contributed, and it is hoped that those who are not so identified will nonetheless recognize themselves in the categories that follow and understand that their help, interest, and support are also appreciated.

To begin with, primary thanks must be extended to the members of the project steering committee, the leaders of the various project working groups, and the members of each of the groups. Those responsible for each guide in the series are separately listed on the title page of that volume.

Thanks should also be expressed to the large number of scholars and teachers who served as critical reviewers of preliminary versions of the guides and the many who participated in sessions at regional and national meetings where the guides were subject to further scrutiny and where many constructive suggestions for their improvement were made.

We wish to acknowledge with grateful thanks the generous financial support of the National Endowment for the Humanities and, through its matching fund scheme, additional support from the Ada Howe Kent Foundation, C. T. Shen, and Council for International and Public Affairs, Inc. The patience and understanding of the Endowment's Education Division during the long and protracted period of completion of this project has been particularly noteworthy.

Many institutions have provided support to the project indirectly by making possible participation of their faculty in the various project working groups. In addition, both the South Asia Center at Columbia University and the Institute for Advanced Studies of World Religions have provided special assistance.

The project has been undertaken under the auspices of the Council for Intercultural Studies and Programs by the Foreign Area Materials Center, a project office of the Center for International Programs and Comparative Studies, State Education Department, University of the State of New York. The last-named institution, acting as the agent of the Council for Intercultural Studies and Programs, has been responsible for administering the National Endowment for Humanities grant and other financial support received for the project and has contributed extensively out of its own resources throughout the project, particularly in the concluding months, to assure its proper completion. Without the interest and support of key officials in the Center for

International Programs and the New York State Education Department, the project could not have been completed.

A particular word of appreciation is in order for Norman Abramowitz of the Center, who succeeded me as Project Director after my resignation from the directorship of the Center in October 1976 and to whom fell the unenviable task of overcoming administrative and financial obstacles in the final three years of the project. Appreciation should also be expressed to G. K. Hall and Company, the publishers of this series, and to its editorial staff. Their forbearance, as the manuscripts have been completed over a far longer time than we anticipated, has been exemplary.

Last but certainly not least are the project managers who have carried responsibility from day to day for implementing the project. Perhaps the most difficult and demanding role has been played by David J. Dell, who came into the project at mid-stream and who struggled to assure its orderly completion. He and Edward Haynes have shared responsibility for final preparation of manuscripts for publication as editorial coordinators for the series, with the former handling two (Chinese Philosophy and Hindu Religion) and the latter, the remaining five titles in the series.

Different, but in many ways no less difficult, was the task confronting the interim project director, Josephine Case, whose services were kindly made available to the project by the New York Public Library in 1974 and 1975. She responded with dignity and sensitivity to the demands of this task.

But in many ways the most important figure in the project is one who is no longer with us. Edith Ehrman was the Manager of the Foreign Area Materials Center from its inception in 1963, a key figure in the conceptualization of this project, and its manager from the beginning until her untimely death in November 1974. She was the moving spirit behind the project during its first three years. It is to her memory that this series of guides is dedicated by all those involved in the project who witnessed the extraordinary display of courage borne of her life during her last difficult illness.

Ward Morehouse, Chairman
Editorial and Publications Committee

Preface

The purpose of this bibliography is to introduce the English-language reader to significant publications on Islam as a religion and a civilization. This reference work is intended to aid both undergraduate and graduate students as well as college teachers who offer courses on Islam but are not specialists in Islamic Studies. While the vast majority of the 2962 entries are books and journal articles in English, a few basic French and German studies have been included.

With few exceptions, the bibliography does not cite works published after 1976. This may appear to some readers as an unfortunate limitation since an enormous amount of work has been published in all areas of Islamic Studies, both analytic works and translations, during the last seven years. This is especially true of studies on contemporary Islam, which have expanded greatly since the Islamic Revolution in Iran. Also appearing in the more recent literature on Islam are numerous studies that raise critical questions regarding the methods, approaches, and theoretical assumptions of Western studies on Islam, the most important and controversial being Edward Said's Orientalism (New York: Pantheon, 1978). We should like to note that a supplemental volume that will include works published since 1976 is already under way.

The categories that divide the annotated material of this guide represent seven out of twelve categories devised by members of the Project on Asian Philosophies and Religions. Four of those categories (Authoritative Texts; Ideal Beings; Mythology, Cosmology, and Basic Symbols; and Soteriological Experience and Processes) are not found in this Guide, not because they were considered invalid as categories for the study of religion but because they did not adequately represent the focus or subject matter of most of the books and articles on Islamic Studies.

Each of the categories was prepared by individual authors. The largest and most comprehensive is "Historical Development," by Donald P. Little, McGill University. This section of the bibliography reveals the enormous geographical realm that constitutes the Islamic world and points out a fundamental characteristic of Islam, namely, that it is both a religion and a civilization.

"Religious Thought," by David Ede, Western Michigan University, covers introductions to Islam and studies on key elements in Islamic intellectual life that are crucial to Islamic beliefs and practices. Philosophy as a separate category is not included in this volume because the project on Asian Philosophies and Religions initially envisioned a separate work for Islamic philosophy. Although that work has not yet been realized, many studies on Islamic philosophy and translations of philosophical texts are included under "Religious Thought," especially in the areas of philosophical theology and mystical philosophy.

"Religious Practices" and "Sacred Places," by Andrew Rippin, University of Alberta, devote attention to studies on the standard, universally accepted rituals, festivals, popular practices, and holy places. The short supply of works here indicates that the field of Islamic Studies has devoted little attention to Islamic practices, especially popular Islam, when compared with studies of the "high tradition" as formulated in the texts on theology, law, and mysticism.

"Institutions," by Leonard Librande, Carleton University (Ottawa), illuminates once again the central character of Islam as a civilization, and shows that a major focus of studies of Islam is on politics and law.

"Art and Architecture," by the late Richard Timms, University of Michigan, covers the key elements on the artistic side of Islamic culture. Although Richard Timms completed the work on art and architecture before his untimely death, several additions and some revisions have been made by Julie Badiee and Merriame Timko.

"Research Aids," by Jan Weryho, McGill University, provide the resources for further investigation into all areas of Islamic Studies, for both the beginning and advanced student. Citations in this section include series titles where applicable.

The author and subject indexes are arranged alphabetically and include concepts and proper names. Each entry is numbered and references in the indexes are to the entry numbers. The indexes include cross-references by entry number for authors and subjects. The subject index enables the reader to pursue a wide variety of topics that are not separately identified in the detailed table of contents.

It will be noticed that some books, especially collected essays, have been annotated more than once. Full bibliographical data are given only once, with a shortened form appearing in subsequent citations. Reference is always given in the shortened form to the initial entry bearing the complete bibliographical data.

The transliteration (romanization) system used in the annotations is based on the Library of Congress system. The citations, however, follow the transliteration forms that appear on the title page of the published books and articles. In a few cases, where names of authors have been transliterated differently in different publications, a single form is used.

Besides the contributors mentioned above, we would like to thank especially Linda Northrup, McGill University, who prepared the section on Education; Cemal Kafadar and Ahmet Karamustafa, McGill University, who brought to light valuable sources in Islamic social history; and Gerhard Böwering, University of Pennsylvania, who suggested numerous studies on Sufism. We appreciate also the comments of several people who helped to improve this bibliographical study when it was in the form of a preliminary draft, especially the valuable criticisms and suggestions of Annemarie Schimmel, Harvard University, and Jere Bacharach, University of Washington. Our thanks go to Karin Kiewra and Ara Salibian of G.K. Hall, who along with Edward Haynes, contributed greatly to the preparation of the manuscript for publication. We would also like to thank Dolores Condic, Pamela Grath, and Violette Masse for typing sections of the manuscript. Appreciation and thanks are extended to Marilyn Page for her assistance in the preparation of the indexes.

David Ede
Western Michigan University

Historical Development

GENERAL STUDIES (A.D. 600 TO PRESENT)

BIBLIOGRAPHIES

1 Birnbaum, Eleazer. Books on Asia from the Near East to the Far East: A Guide for the General Reader. Toronto: University of Toronto Press, 1971, 341 pp.

Devotes ninety-six pages to Islamic history. Useful for beginners, since the selections are designed to suit the "general reader." The annotations are brief.

2 Bolton, A.R. Soviet Middle East Studies: An Analysis and Bibliography. London: Royal Institute of International Affairs, 1959.

A selective bibliography of 281 Soviet articles and books on various aspects of the Arab world. Includes summaries of content.

3 Ettinghausen, R. A Selected and Annotated Bibliography of Books and Periodicals in Western Languages Dealing with the Near and Middle East, with Special Emphasis on Medieval and Modern Times. Washington: Middle East Institute, 1952, 111 pp. Supplement, 1954.

Annotated entries on various aspects of ancient, medieval, and modern civilization in the Near and Middle East, with substantial sections on Islamic civilization--mainly books in English and French, but some in other languages as well. Although compiled more than twenty years ago, it is still useful for Ettinghausen's identification of important sources and his comments on them.

4 Hopwood, Derek, and Diana Grimwood-Jones, eds. Middle East and Islam: A Bibliographic Introduction. Zug, Switzerland: Inter-Documentation, 1972, 368 pp.

A collection of thirty-one bibliographies compiled as basic books for an Islamic studies library in a faculty of arts. The bibliographies, some annotated, cover general reference works, aspects of Islamic civilization, specific regions (Indonesia, North Africa), and Arabic language and literature. A most useful reference.

5 Howard, Harry N., et al. Middle East and North Africa: A Bibliography for Undergraduate Libraries. Williamsport, Penn.: Bro-Dart, 1971, 80 pp.

Twelve hundred entries, topical and regional, graded according to their suitability for undergraduate libraries.

6 Pearson, J.D. Index Islamicus, 1906-1955: A Catalogue of Articles on Islamic Subjects in Periodicals and Other Collective Publications. Cambridge: W. Heffer, 1958, 897 pp. Supplements to date.

Invaluable as an exhaustive index of all articles in Western languages, on virtually every aspect of Islamic civilization.

7 Sauvaget, J. Introduction to the History of the Muslim East: A Bibliographical Guide. Berkeley: University of California Press, 1965, 252 pp.

Indispensable as an introduction to the sources for Islamic history and secondary scholarship (published until 1964) based upon them. There are brief but informative chapters on Islamic languages, archaeology, archives, ethnography, and other subjects about which it is difficult to obtain elementary information elsewhere. The bibliographies are arranged by dynasties and areas, and include both books and articles. The survey encompasses the history of the Ottoman Empire through the eighteenth century; the modern period of Islamic history is outside the scope of the work.

8 Smith, Reuben W. Islamic Civilization in the Middle East: Course Syllabus. Chicago: Committee on Near Eastern Studies, University of Chicago, 1965, 121 pp.

A syllabus for teachers who have no experience in courses on Middle Eastern history, using a "civilization" approach.

SURVEYS AND REFERENCES RELATING TO MUSLIM PEOPLE AS A WHOLE

9 Arberry, A.J. Religion in the Middle East: Three Religions in Concord and Conflict. Vol. 1, Judaism and Christianity, 595 pp. Vol. 2, Islam, 750 pp. Cambridge: Cambridge University Press, 1969.

Volume 1 should by no means be neglected by Orientalists since it contains such important essays as "The Jews of Yemen" (Goitein), "The Coptic Church" (Meinardus), and "The Armenian Church" (Sarkessian). Volume 2 contains nineteen essays on Islam in almost all areas except China, plus nine on the content of Islam--doctrinal, legal, sociopolitical, and cultural. Intended for beginners, the essays are not profound, but are still useful to specialists, who can no longer hope to master many of the diverse local and temporal manifestations of Islam.

10 Armajani, Yahya. Middle East, Past and Present. Englewood Cliffs, N.J.: Prentice-Hall, 1970, 432 pp.

Apparently contains the author's classroom lectures from an introductory course on Middle Eastern history, from the origin of Islam to modern times. Little more than an outline, it is more elementary than most such books and not as reliable. There are vitually no notes and only short bibliographies of works in English.

11 Arnold, Sir Thomas. The Preaching of Islam: A History of the Propagation of the Muslim Faith. Lahore: Shirkaj-Qualam, n.d., 502 pp. Reprint of 2d ed., 1913.

Arnold surveys the spread of Islam through conquest, but focuses on conversion by peaceful ("missionary") means in all parts of the Islamic world, including such neglected areas as China and Malaya. This is a standard work that should be revised and updated in the light of subsequent scholarship. See also 1330.

12 Ashtor, E. A Social and Economic History of the Near East in the Middle Ages. Berkeley, Los Angeles, and London: University of California Press, 1976, 384 pp.

The economic history of this area under Muslim domination is still in its infancy. Of necessity, therefore, this survey, which reaches from the Arab conquests through the fifteenth century, is very general but provides a useful summary of the work that has been done in this field so far.

13 Bacharach, Jere L. A Near East Studies Handbook. Seattle: University of Washington Press, 1976, 158 pp.

Deals in outline with the Near East from A.D. 570 to 1974. Contains atlas, chronological tables, dynastic lists, genealogies, calendars for conversion, and index.

14 Bosworth, C.E. The Islamic Dynasties: A Chronological and Genealogical Handbook. Edinburgh: Edinburgh University Press, 1967, 245 pp.

A concise, accurate chronology of the principal Muslim dynasties, accompanied by brief historical outlines of each. An indispensable reference, it supersedes Lane-Poole's The Mohammadan Dynasties (see 2750).

15 Brockelmann, Carl. History of the Islamic Peoples. Translated by J. Carmichael and M. Perlmann. New York: Capricorn, 1960, 582 pp. Orig. pub. by G.P. Putnam, 1947.

One of the classics of Western historical writing on Islam by the great German Orientalist, Semiticist, and Arabist. Mainly political, the history is pedestrian, difficult to read, but useful as a handy reference work, since, unlike most single-volume and single-author works on Islamic history, it is not restricted in time or place. The translators have added a helpful essay entitled "Review of Events, 1939-1947."

16 Brown, Leon Carl, ed. From Madina to Metropolis: Heritage and Change in the Near Eastern City. Princeton, N.J.: Darwin, 1973, 343 pp.

Papers on the relationship of urban development and planning to the structure and dynasties of the Muslim city of the past. See also 2000, 2487.

17 Cook, M.A., ed. Studies in the Economic History of the Middle East: From the Rise of Islam to the Present Day. London: Oxford, 1970, 526 pp.

Contains twenty-seven articles and two introductory essays on Middle Eastern economic history, in three phases: the Middle Ages, the sixteenth to the eighteenth centuries, and the nineteenth and twentieth centuries. These are either historiographical or historical in character. Most, especially those in the first two sections, are aimed at summarizing the present stage of research and the direction future scholarship should take. Excellent as an introduction to the problems involved in reconstructing the economic history of the Islamic world. See also 38.

18 Fisher, Sydney Nettleton. The Middle East: A History. 3d ed. rev. & enl. New York: Knopf, 1979, 811 pp.

After a few introductory chapters on medieval Islamic history, Fisher reaches the core of the book--the history of the Ottoman Empire and its modern successors. For the Ottoman period in particular it is quite effective as an introductory text for undergraduates. The sections on the Arabs, Turks, and Iranians in modern times are also quite good, especially concerning the role of the major powers in the area. The brief chapter on Palestine is sympathetic to Israel.

19 Freeman-Grenville, G.S.P. The Muslim and Christian Calendars, Being Tables for the Conversion of Muslim and Christian Dates from the Hijra to the Year A.D. 2000. London: Oxford, 1963, 87 pp.

This is indispensable for converting dates.

20 Gibb, H.A.R., ed. The Encyclopaedia of Islam. New ed. Leiden: E.J. Brill, 1960.

Over four volumes have appeared so far, covering all aspects of Islamic civilization from the beginning until the present time, often superseding, sometimes only supplementing, the first edition. Absolutely indispensable for students and scholars alike.

21 Gibb, H.A.R. "An Interpretation of Islamic History." Journal of World History 1 (1953): 39-62. Reprint. Studies on the Civilization of Islam (see 23), pp. 3-33.

A brilliant attempt to trace the development of "rhythms" or themes of Islamic history from the beginnings until the fall of Baghdad in 1258. Gibb focuses on the efforts of the "orthodox" to maintain the unity and universalism of Islamic civilization and culture in the course of the spread of Islam among increasingly diversified areas and groups. Essential as an interpretive survey of main currents of Islamic history.

22 Gibb, H.A.R., and J.H. Kramers, eds. Shorter Encyclopedia of Islam. Leiden: E.J. Brill, 1961, 671 pp.

A reprint of those articles in the first edition of the encyclopedia that deal with "religious" subjects only (see 32).

23 Gibb, H.A.R. Studies on the Civilization of Islam. Edited by S.J. Shaw and W.R. Polk. Boston: Beacon Press, 1962, 369 pp.

An anthology of essays, by the greatest of English Orientalists, on medieval Islamic history, Islamic thought and institutions, and modern intellectual history. Some of the essays are technical ("The Armies of Saladin") and one is in Arabic, but all are beautifully written and stimulating. Especially valuable for historians are "An Interpretation of Islamic History" and "Ta'rīkh," which together present a masterful survey of medieval Islamic history and the historians who wrote it. See also 24, 1925, 1975, 1976, 2365.

24 _____. "Ta'rīkh." In Supplement to the Encyclopaedia of Islam. Edited by M. Th. Houtsma et al. Leiden: E.J. Brill, 1938, pp. 233-45. Reprint. In Studies on the Civilization of Islam (see 23), pp. 108-37.

Still the best introductory survey of the development of Muslim historical writing in Arabic and Persian.

25 Grunebaum, G.E. von. Islam: Essays in the Nature and Growth of a Cultural Tradition. 2d ed. London: Routledge & K. Paul, 1961, 266 pp.

A collection of von Grunebaum's essays on various aspects of Islamic civilization in medieval and modern times. Of special interest to the historian are the suggestive "Profile of Muslim Civilization" and, on a favorite theme developed more fully in modern Islam, "Attempts at Self-Interpretation in Contemporary Islam," as well as the essays on Arabic culture. See also 2001.

26 _____, ed. Unity and Variety in Muslim Civilization. Chicago: University of Chicago Press, 1955, 385 pp.

Contains papers from a conference designed to explore regional adaptations and variations of the mainstream of Islamic culture in an attempt to apply the Chicago concept of the Great and Little Traditions of cultural anthropology. Begins with a set of general essays on universal aspects of Islamic civilization followed by articles on the development of Islam in specific regions. An interesting conceptualization that transcends the more mundane study of Islamic history based on conventional periodization. See also 2078, 2356.

27 Hazard, H.W. Atlas of Islamic History. 3d ed. Princeton, N.J.: Princeton University Press, 1954, 49 pp.

A historical atlas illustrating changes in Islamic political boundaries at one-hundred-year intervals. Includes notes, chronological and dynastic tables.

28 Hitti, Philip K. The Near East in History: A 5000 Year Story. Princeton, N.J.: Van Nostrand, 1961, 574 pp.

A historical account of the Near East since the earliest times up to the present age. The scope of the work is much too ambitious for its size, and hence the description tends to be sketchy. Useful for nonspecialized reading. Each chapter is followed by a short bibliography.

29 Hodgson, Marshall G.S. The Venture of Islam: Conscience and History in a World Civilization. Vol. 1, The Classical Age of Islam, 532 pp. Vol. 2, The Expansion of Islam in the Middle Periods, 609 pp. Vol. 3, The Gunpowder Empires and Modern Times, 469 pp. Chicago and London: University of Chicago Press, 1974.

This monumental work constitutes the first attempt by a single scholar to survey the entire development of Islamic civilization, in all its components, in the context of world history. As such, it is the one basic study of Islamic history that should be read by all students of Islam. With a brilliant interpretation by the author, based on a wide knowledge of primary and secondary sources, it will be immensely rewarding to the dedicated scholar. See also 1120, 1332, 1670.

30 Holt, P.M. et al., eds. The Cambridge History of Islam. 2 vols. Cambridge: Cambridge University Press, 1970, 1:815 pp., 2:966 pp.

A comprehensive (600-1950) and at the same time detailed history of Islamic civilization, the work of a group of Western and Muslim authorities. The main body consists of chapters of narrative political history, conventionally structured in terms of areas and periods, but including such neglected subjects as Indonesia and Central Asia. These chapters, as might be expected, are uneven in interest though not necessarily in authority: a high standard of accuracy has been maintained. Many, if not most, suffer from an unrelieved tediousness in style: the facts are presented with little attention to interpretation. The best chapters are topical ones devoted to extrapolitical aspects of Islamic civilization: religion, culture, art, literature, philosophy, science, warfare. The entire work suffers from a thinness of documentation, which was doubtlessly dictated by economic considerations. See also 1136, 1262, 1932, 2079, 2292.

31 Hourani, Albert. "Islam and the Philosophers of History." Middle Eastern Studies 3 (1967):206-68.

An excellent survey and interpretation of the role assigned to Islamic civilization in world history by major Western historians and philosophers of history, along with Hourani's diagnosis of the present state of Western research on Islamic history. Important for an understanding of the biases and preconceptions implicit in Western scholarship on Islam.

32 Houtsma, M.T. et al, eds. The Encyclopaedia of Islam: A Dictionary of the Geography, Ethnography, and Biography of the Muhammadan Peoples, Prepared by a Number of Leading Orientalists. 4 vols. Leiden: E.J. Brill, 1913-1936. Supplement, 1938.

Authoritative and definitive at the time of its completion, the work is now being completely rewritten and is slowly appearing in a new edition (see 20).

33 Lapidus, Ira, ed. Middle Eastern Cities: A Symposium on Ancient, Islamic, and Contemporary Middle Eastern Urbanism. Berkeley: University of California Press, 1969, 206 pp.

One of two collections of papers presented to conferences on the structure and organization of cities in the Middle East. Three of the essays in this volume concern the Islamic city and challenge previously accepted descriptions of urban organization; the papers are especially interesting for the new light they cast on whether there were guilds in medieval Islamic cities. Three essays on modern cities in the Muslim world, utilizing economic and sociological data. See also 2004, 2488.

34 Levy, Reuben. The Social Structure of Islam: Being the Second Edition of the Sociology of Islam. Cambridge: Cambridge University Press, 1957, 536 pp.

Levy was so universally criticized for naming the first edition of this book a sociology that he changed the title to "Social Structure" in the subsequent edition. Actually it is a summary of what selected Muslim authors have said on such subjects as "classes," women and children, law, morality, science, and--chiefly--government and the army. It has no sociological pretensions of the American variety whatsoever and is quite useful as an introduction to Muslim literature on the subjects listed. The introductory chapter is an excellent, succinct survey of Islamic expansion. See also 1791, 1927, 2073, 2100, 2268.

35 Lewis, Bernard, and P.M. Holt, eds. Historians of the Middle East. London: Oxford, 1962, 519 pp.

Contains forty-one articles and a summary-introduction on the literary sources for Islamic history and the use to which they have been put by later historians in the East and West. For a characterization of the types of Islamic historiography and identification of the principal historians within these types, as well as the ways in which they have been used and abused, this is a first-rate study.

36 Lewis, Bernard, ed. Islam and the Arab World: Faith, People, Culture. New York: Knopf, 1976, 360 pp.

Published in England (Thames & Hudson, 1976) as The World of Islam, which is the more meaningful but perhaps less commercial title, this book is a sumptuously illustrated survey of Islamic civilization under Arabs, Persians, Indians, and Turks by an international group of scholars. Meant for the coffee table, it deserves to be read as an excellent introduction to Islamic civilization. See also 2291, 2489.

37 Lewis, Bernard. Islam in History: Ideas, Men and Events in the Middle East. New York: Library Press, 1973, 349 pp.

An anthology of twenty-one essays by the brilliant English Orientalist on Muslim historiography and Western approaches to it, Muslim-Jewish relations, Turks and Mongols, and change, including heresy and revolution in Islam. As noted elsewhere, Lewis is a master of English prose; even his most erudite efforts are not only comprehensible but elegant as well. Most of these essays are of general rather than technical interest, but are nonetheless valuable to specialists.

38 _____. "Sources for the Economic History of the Middle East." In Studies in the Economic History of the Middle East (see 17), pp. 78-92.

A discussion of the availability of source materials for the various periods of Islamic history that also explains why economic aspects have been neglected. Useful for indicating the most promising areas for future research within this field.

39 McNeill, William H., and Marilyn R. Waldman, eds. The Islamic World. New York: Oxford, 1973, 468 pp.

Includes previously translated texts on the history of Islamic civilization from the formative years (600-750) through the crisis of modernization in the nineteenth and twentieth centuries. The strength of this anthology lies in its comprehensiveness; it includes selections from Arabic, Persian, Indian, and Turkish sources as well as passages from European travelers. The introductions are skimpy.

40 McNeill, William H. The Rise of the West: A History of the Human Community. Chicago: University of Chicago Press, 1963, 829 pp.

This renowned world history contains stimulating chapters (9-13) on Islam from the beginning until modern times, set in a world context. This is a most refreshing view of Islam, which is almost always seen as a closed world outside the tides of universal history. Also refreshing is a nonexpert's mastery of the main currents of Islamic history.

41 The Muslim World: A Historical Survey. Translated by F.R.C. Bagley. Pt. 1, The Age of the Caliphs, by B. Spuler, 1960, 138 pp. Pt. 2, The Mongol Period, by B. Spuler, 1969, 125 pp. Pt. 3, The Last Great Muslim Empires, by H. Kissling et al., 1969, 302 pp. Leiden: E.J. Brill, 1960-1969.

The first two volumes are models of outline history: concise and to the point, they cover the most salient aspects of their periods in an easily digestible form. With excellent maps and dynastic tables, they are outstanding as introductory and reference books. The last volume contains seven articles by as many scholars (one by Spuler) on the Ottomans, the Ṣafavids, the Mughals, Northwest and sub-Saharan Africa, Egypt, and Central Asia. A final volume will presumably cover the rest. These essays are more comprehensive and detailed than Spuler's work, and measure up to the standards of German scholarship. The three form an excellent introduction to Islamic history.

42 Philips, Cyril Henry, ed. Handbook of Oriental History. London: Office of the Royal Historical Society, 1951, 265 pp. Section on Near and Middle East, pp. 3-46.

This section contains useful data on Arab-Muslim names, terminology, and dating. See also 2746.

43 Planhol, Xavier de. The World of Islam. Ithaca, N.Y.: Cornell University Press, 1959, 142 pp.

Planhol attempts to explore the geographical implications of the development of Islam in this highly original interpretation of the spread of religion.

44 Roolvink, R. Historical Atlas of the Muslim Peoples. London: G. Allen & Unwin, 1957, 40 pp.

An indispensable collection of maps based on the dynastic history of the Muslim world from Spain to Indonesia, showing trade and invasion routes as well as changing political boundaries.

45 Savory, R.M., ed. Introduction to Islamic Civilization. Cambridge: Cambridge University Press, 1976, 204 pp.

Eighteen articles by Canadian scholars, originally broadcast as radio talks, on various components of Islamic civilization: faith, law, literatures, art, science, and relations with the Christian West. An excellent introductory survey for beginners.

46 Turner, Bryan S. Weber and Islam: A Critical Study. London and Boston: Routledge & Kegan Paul, 1974, 212 pp.

The author is forced to reinterpret and reformulate Weber's thought in order to find a logical place in it for his views on Islam.

47 Watt, W. Montgomery. Islam and the Integration of Society. Routledge & Kegan Paul, 1961, 293 pp.

A not very successful attempt at socio-economic analysis of aspects of Islamic history, with such murky chapters as "The Role of Ideation" and "The Integration of the Psyche." Much of this is a rehashing in social science jargon of Watt's two-volume study of Muḥammad, with additional material on the Shīʿah and the Khawārij, and the process of Islamization in Iran and West Africa.

48 Young, T. Cuyler, ed. Near Eastern Culture and Society: A Symposium on the Meeting of East and West. Princeton, N.J.: Princeton University Press, 1951, 250 pp.

The first half of this work surveys Western progress in the academic study of Islamic art, archaeology, literature (Persian and Arabic), science, and religion, and suggests avenues of further research. The second half surveys the interaction of Islamic and Western thought in Turkey, Iran, and the Western world, and the foreign affairs of these three areas. The first part is still valuable to students looking for research possibilities, and a concluding essay by Gibb states incisively the purpose of Islamic studies in the West, its virtues and its shortcomings.

The Arab World

The East

49 Gabrieli, Francesco. The Arabs: A Compact History. Translated by Salvator Attansio. New York: Hawthorn, 1963, 215 pp.

An Italian counterpart to Bernard Lewis's The Arabs in History (see 56), also covering the entire history of the Arabs from the earliest to modern times. Well written and authoritative, it has no notes, a tiny bibliography, and is no more than an outline.

50 Gibb, H.A.R. Arabic Literature: An Introduction. 2d rev. ed. Oxford: Clarendon, 1963, 182 pp.

A concise yet comprehensive history of Arabic literature in terms of the periods of its development, within the framework of Gibb's view of Arab political, religious, and cultural history. It should be used to supplement the standard political histories of the Arabs, which, for cultural history, rarely include more than a list of authors. It is more analytical and suggestive than Nicholson's larger, more detailed work on the same subject (see 57) and is much more important than its size would indicate, as is the case with almost all Gibb's writings. See also 1115.

51 Goitein, S.D. Jews and Arabs: Their Contacts through the Ages. New York: Shocken, 1964, 247 pp.

Takes the establishment of the state of Israel in the midst of Arab territory as its point of departure for a study of the role and status of Jews in all aspects of Arab-Islamic civilization. Includes a chapter on the Arab-Israeli conflict.

52 Hitti, Philip K. History of the Arabs from the Earliest Times to the Present. 8th ed. New York: St. Martin's, 1964, 822 pp.

The standard history of the Arabs by the pioneer in Arabic studies in North America. Though not an inspired historian, Hitti is indefatigable; he has gone through the original sources with a fine-toothed comb and has faithfully recorded the facts found in them. A useful introduction and reference book and stronger on political history than cultural, but tends to be encyclopedic in organization and style.

53 _____. Lebanon in History from the Earliest Times to the Present. London: Macmillan, 1957, 548 pp.
A great deal of the material in History of Syria Including Lebanon and Palestine (see 54) is, of necessity, repeated, but the emphasis is different, and there is more data pertaining to Lebanon in particular, especially during the modern period.

54 _____. History of Syria Including Lebanon and Palestine. 2d ed. London: Macmillan, 1957, 750 pp.
An encyclopedic survey of the history of "Greater Syria" from the Stone Age through independence in 1943, with the stress on political history. Much of the material on the Arab period is a rewriting of the same author's History of the Arabs (see 52), with a slightly different emphasis. There is no work of comparable scope and value.

55 _____. Syria: A Short History. London: Macmillan, 1959, 271 pp.
An abridged version of History of Syria Including Lebanon and Palestine (see 54), without footnotes and documentation. Without these, the text seems superficial, and the reader is advised to use the larger work.

56 Lewis, Bernard. The Arabs in History. 4th ed. London: Hutchinson's, 1966, 200 pp.
By far the best interpretive study of the history of the Arabs from pre-Islamic to modern times, based primarily on Western scholarship, but well grounded in the original Arab sources. It has all the virtues of a first-rate introduction to a difficult subject, including accuracy and readability, concision and comprehensiveness. No footnotes, but a good bibliography listing the works from which Lewis's interpretation is derived.

57 Nicholson, Reynold Alleyne. A Literary History of the Arabs. Cambridge: Cambridge University Press, 1969, 506 pp. Orig. pub. in 1907.
Invaluable for its account of the development of Arabic literature from the beginning up to modern times, presented against the background of Arab political history. It is superbly written, though dated in its interpretations, and is useful both as a reference work and as "leisure" reading in Arabic culture. See also 1129.

58 Reichert, Rolf. A Historical and Regional Atlas of the Arabic World: Maps and Chronological Survey. Translated by Phyllis Goetsch and Jose Luis Magalhaes. Salvador de Bahia, Brazil: Centro de Estudos Afro-Orientals, Universidade Federal, 1969, 204 pp.
Contains sixty-eight maps of various parts of the Arab world from the seventh to the twentieth century, with commentary in both Spanish and English. Dynastic tables are also included.

59 Ronart, Stephan, and Nandy Ronart. Concise Encyclopaedia of Arabic Civilization. Vol. 1, The Arab East. New York: Praeger, 1960, 589 pp.
Actually a history of Arabic civilization in encyclopedia format, with entries on the principal dynasties, political and intellectual movements, modern states, leading figures, institutions, etc. The articles are concise and reliable and suffer only from the lack of reference to their sources.

Northwest Africa

60 Abun-Nasr, J.M. A History of the Maghrib. Cambridge: Cambridge University Press, 1971, 416 pp.
Surveys the history of North Africa, including Libya, from the Phoenicians until the independence of the modern states, with emphasis on the eighteenth and nineteenth centuries and on political history in particular. A useful introduction to a subject for which there are few studies in English, but it suffers from lack of documentation.

61 Conover, Helen F. North and Northeast Africa: A Selected, Annotated List of Writings, 1951-57. New York: Greenwood, 1957, 182 pp.
Includes 346 entries, with detailed annotations that summarize the content of each book or article. Useful mainly for the modern period.

62 Julien, Ch. A. History of North Africa: Tunisia, Algeria, Morocco, from the Arab Conquest to 1930. Translated by J. Petrie and edited and revised by R. Le Tourneau. London: Routledge & K. Paul, 1970, 446 pp.
By consensus the best history of Islamic North Africa currently available in English. Though the basic work is Julien's original edition, it also represents the considerable revision made by Le Tourneau for the second edition. What we have then is an authoritative synthesis of the state of scholarship on North African history in 1952. Few changes have been made for this edition other than the addition of maps and an updating of the bibliography.

63 Ronart, Stephan, and Nandy Ronart. Concise Encyclopaedia of Arabic Civilization. Vol. 2, The Arab West. New York: Praeger, 1966, 410 pp.
A history of western Islamic civilization, i.e. North Africa and Spain, with articles on states, institutions, movements, literature, persons, etc. These are summaries of unspecified but surprisingly reliable sources. Helpful for students who find it difficult to use the more formidable and authoritative Encyclopaedia of Islam (see 20).

Iran

64 Arberry, J.J., ed. The Legacy of Persia. Oxford: Clarendon, 1968, 421 pp.

Thirteen essays, of which only two relate to Persia in pre-Islamic times; the rest deal with various aspects of Iranian culture and history, from religion to carpets and gardens. This is still quite good as an introduction to Persian Islamic civilization. See also 2310, 2456, 2613, 2661.

65 Armajani, Yahya. Iran. Englewood Cliffs, N.J.: Prentice-Hall, 1972, 182 pp.

An outline of Iranian history from ancient times to the present, unavoidably superficial, but useful as an elementary survey for students with no previous knowledge of Iran. There are few notes, but an annotated bibliography.

66 Browne, Edward G. A Literary History of Persia. 4 vols. Cambridge: Cambridge University Press, 1951-1953. Orig. pub. in 1928.

Browne, Nicholson, and Arberry form a trio of English Orientalists who studied Islamic civilization through the Arabic and Persian languages and literatures, translating the classics of these two languages and comparing, in marvelous King James prose, literary histories of the Persians and Arabs. Browne's four-volume history of Persian-Islamic literature is a splendid introduction to the Islamic culture of Iran, filled with fact and picturesque detail, weak perhaps on theory, but always close to the primary sources and generous with examples. Equally interesting for medieval and modern times, it is a stunning scholarly achievement. See also 1401.

67 Elgood, Cyril. A Medical History of Persia and the Eastern Caliphate, from the Earliest Times until the Year A.D. 1932. Cambridge: Cambridge University Press, 1951, 617 pp.

An encyclopedia of information on physicians and medical theory and practice during Islamic times.

68 Elwell-Sutton, L.P. A Guide to Iranian Area Study. Ann Arbor, Mich.: J.W. Edwards, 1952, 235 pp.

Short introductory chapters on the history, geography, government, culture, economy, etc., of Iran are followed by annotated bibliographies to each field.

69 Fisher, W.B., ed. The Cambridge History of Iran. Vol. 1, The Land of Iran. Cambridge: Cambridge University Press, 1968, 784 pp.

This introductory volume to the projected eight-volume history of Iran is a collection of essays on geography and geology (including zoology), demographic history, and economics. This background material will be followed by six volumes on history and a final volume on bibliography.

70 Frye, Richard N. The Heritage of Persia. Cleveland: World Publishing, 1963, 301 pp.

Although most of this survey of Iranian history and culture is devoted to pre-Islamic Iran, the final chapter, entitled "The Persian Conquest of Iran," emphasizes the continuity of the whole of Iranian history in a way which few other books do. It is therefore of considerable value.

71 _____. Iran. New York: H. Holt, 1953, 126 pp.

An outline of Persian history since Achaemenid times, by a leading authority.

72 Lambton, A.K.S. Landlord and Peasant in Persia: A Study of Land Tenure and Land Revenue Administration. London: Oxford, 1953, 459 pp.

A survey from the Arab conquests through modern times of the land system in Iran, period by period, including the development of the iqṭā' ("fief") system. The section on the modern period is naturally fuller and better documented than the earlier sections, and carefully examines the economic basis of the social system in Iran. An essential work.

73 Levy, Reuben. Persian Literature: An Introduction. London: Oxford, 1948, 112 pp.

It is surprising how much information on principal trends and individual authors Levy manages to pack into this outline of the history of Persian literature.

74 Lockhart, Laurence. Famous Cities of Iran. Brentford, England: W. Pearce, 1939, 115 pp.

Historical description of sixteen of the principal cities of Islamic Iran.

75 Rypka, Jan. History of Iranian Literature. Translated by Karl Jahn. New York: Humanities Press, 1968, 928 pp.

Rypka's approach to Iranian literature, including that produced by Muslims in India, emphasizes social and political background; the book consequently contains much of value to the historian of both medieval and modern times. The section on folk literature and the many references to recent scholarship, including many Persian and Russian works, make the work especially valuable for Anglophones. See also 1403.

76 Wickens, G.M.; R.M. Savory; and W.J. Watson, eds. Persia in Islamic Times: A Practical Bibliography of Its History. Montreal: Institute of Islamic Studies, McGill University, 1964, 57 pp.

A basic bibliography of 701 Western and Persian sources and scholarship, with hardly any annotation.

77 Wilber, Donald N. Iran, Past and Present. Princeton, N.J.: Princeton University Press, 1958, 312 pp.

A third of this survey covers prehistoric times; the remainder is concerned with modern Pahlavi Iran and is not so much a history as a description of the state, the people, natural resources, and the economy. It is standard as an introduction to Iranian history and society, but lacks footnotes.

78 Wilson, Sir Arnold T. A Bibliography of Persia. Oxford: Clarendon, 1930, 253 pp.
The arrangement of this list of articles and books, in alphabetical order by author, is not very helpful, since there are no annotations, but it does serve as a checklist for materials gleaned elsewhere.

Turkey

79 Birge, J.K. A Guide to Turkish Area Studies. Washington: American Council of Learned Societies, 1949, 240 pp.
Though prepared twenty-five years ago, this is still an indispensable bibliographical aid for Turkish studies. It covers art, religion, education, and intellectual life as well as more mundane aspects of Turkey, i.e., geography, history, political structure, transportation, communication, etc. Besides the annotated bibliography, there is a detailed chronology of Turkish history.

80 Davison, Roderic H. Turkey. Englewood Cliffs, N.J.: Prentice-Hall, 1968, 181 pp.
An introductory survey of the history of Turkey, incorporating modern research, with the emphasis on modern Turkey. A reliable outline for undergraduates of the main political, social, and economic trends.

81 Luke, Sir Harry. The Old Turkey and the New: From Byzantium to Ankara. London: G. Bles, 1955, 243 pp. New & rev. ed. of The Making of Modern Turkey, 1936.
A popular survey of Turkish history by a British civil servant, which dwells on the modern period and the author's impressions of Turkish society. There is no documentation.

India

82 Ahmad, Aziz. An Intellectual History of Islam in India. Edinburgh: Edinburgh University Press, 1969, 226 pp.
Like many, though not all, of the volumes in this series, this one is superficial, attempting the almost impossible task of digesting incredibly complex materials for a wide readership. It is little more than an outline of the Muslim religious literature produced in India, with brief chapters on belles-lettres and fine arts. As an outline, it is useful, but in no way representative of this scholar's incisive work on Islam in India in medieval and modern times. See also 2072.

83 _____. Studies in Islamic Culture in the Indian Environment. Oxford: Clarendon, 1966, 311 pp.
A collection of articles on medieval and modern Islam in the Indian subcontinent, by a leading authority. Concentrates on the relationship of India to the rest of the Islamic world (710-1947) and Muslim-Hindu relations (710-1830). One of the few really first-rate works on Indian Islam as a whole, despite its selective and therefore fragmentary character. See also 1965.

84 Chand, Tara. The Influence of Islam on Indian Culture. Allahabad: Indian Press, 1936, 327 pp.
Instructive for the way in which Hindus have viewed the role and impact of Islam in India, but the focus is on Hinduism and the effect Islam had on its development.

85 De Bary, Wm. Theodore et al., eds. and comps. Sources of Indian Tradition. 2 vols. New York: Columbia University Press, 1958. 1:535 pp., 2:384 pp.
Selections from original sources in translation with introductory background materials. The essays "Islam in Medieval India" (P. Hardy) and "Modern India and Pakistan" (I.H. Qureshi and S.N. Hay) are well coordinated with the readings from original texts. The opportunity to read about Islam in the context of the non-Muslim experience in India should not be missed. See also 1413, 1722.

86 Hollister, J.N. The Shiʿa of India. London: Luzac, 1953, 440 pp.
A useful study of the history of Shīʿism in India, with introductory material on the background of the Shīʿah elsewhere. It includes a summary of doctrines and a characterization of the various branches of the Shīʿah. Covering medieval and modern times, it is good as an introductory reference on an important but often neglected aspect of Indian Muslim history.

87 Ikram, S.M., and A.T. Embree, eds. Muslim Civilization in India. New York: Columbia University Press, 1964, 325 pp.
An introductory survey of the political and cultural history of the Indian subcontinent from the Arab invasion through British colonial rule. Somewhat elementary, it is good as a beginning for those with no knowledge of Muslim India.

88 Ikram, S.M. Muslim Rule in India and Pakistan (711-1858 A.D.): A Political and Cultural History. Lahore: Star Book Depot, 1966, 637 pp.
A political and, to a lesser extent, religious history of Islamic India. Detailed but readable.

89 Lambrick, H.T. Sind: A General Introduction. Hyderabad: Sindhi Adabi Board, 1964, 274 pp.
A study of the influence of geographical and climatic influences on the history of Sind, the book includes considerable material on the Muslim period.

90 Lane-Poole, Stanley. Medieval India under Mohammedan Rule (A.D. 712-1764). London: T. Fisher Unwin, 1906, 449 pp.
A very readable survey of the history of Muslim India, which Lane-Poole has drawn from original sources; the emphasis is on political and military activities.

91 Moreland, W.H., and A. Chatterje. A Short History of India. 3d ed. London: Longmans, Green, 1953, 580 pp.
One of the better general histories of India, by a British colonial official and his Hindu collaborator. Essentially a popular work, it is nevertheless solidly based on Moreland's own scholarly studies. The later section reflects the British point of view, which Moreland unabashedly defends.

92 Mujeeb, M. The Indian Muslims. London: G. Allen & Unwin, 1967, 590 pp.
In his attempt to synthesize the Muslim experience in India from the beginning until recent times, Mujeeb discusses the political system, orthodoxy, Sufism, literature and the arts, and social life, in three phases of Indian Muslim history. Such an ambitious attempt was bound to be somewhat encyclopedic and sketchy, but it is nonetheless valuable as an overall view by a prominent Indian Muslim scholar.

93 _____. Islamic Influence on Indian Society. Delhi: Meenakshi Prakashan, 1972, 204 pp.
An analysis of the political, economic, social, and religious impact of Islam on India from the conquests through modern times, including Gandhi.

94 Philips, C.H. Historians of India, Pakistan, and Ceylon. London: Oxford, 1961, 504 pp.
Contains several interesting articles on both medieval and modern Indian Muslim historiography, as well as on European and nationalist writings. Along with several recent monographs, it lays the foundation for a more objective approach to Indian Muslim history than those of Muslim and Hindu nationalists and British colonial officers.

95 Qureshi, I.H. The Muslim Community of the Indo-Pakistan Subcontinent. The Hague: Mouton, 1962, 334 pp.
A historical analysis of the development of Islam in India from the conquests to the rise of Muslim nationalism, based on primary and up-to-date secondary sources. Concise but well written, and digestible by beginners.

96 Schimmel, Annemarie. Classical Urdu Literature from the Beginning to Iqbāl. Wiesbaden: Otto Harrassowitz, 1975, 261 pp.
An excellent outline of the main trends and principal figures in the history of Urdu literature.

97 _____. Islamic Literatures of India. Wiesbaden: Otto Harrassowitz, 1973, 60 pp.
Survey of the most important literary trends, covering only works in Arabic, Persian, and Turkish produced in Indo-Pakistan.

98 Smith, Vincent. The Oxford History of India. Pt. 2, India in the Muhammadan Period. Oxford: Clarendon, 1920, 468 pp.
This offprint from the Oxford history is an outline of the Islamic history of India from the twelfth through the eighteenth centuries and is representative of the retired Indian Civil Service school of British historiography on India.

99 Spear, Percival. India: A Modern History. Rev. ed. Ann Arbor: University of Michigan Press, 1972, 530 pp.
Almost half the book is devoted to ancient, medieval, and Mughal India, and even the chapter on British India is set apart from "modern" India. Intended as an introduction for general readers, it has no critical apparatus.

100 Titus, Murray T. Islam in India and Pakistan. Rev. ed. Calcutta: YMCA Publishing House, 1959, 328 pp.
A religious history of Muslim India dealing with the Muslim conquests, Muslim religious system and organizations, Muslim-Hindu interaction, Muslim modernism, and partition. Titus is not without his own point of view. See also 1566.

China

101 Broomhall, Marshall. Islam in China: A Neglected Problem. London: Morgan & Scott, 1910, 332 pp.
Islam in China is unfortunately still a problem neglected by Western historians and is likely to remain so, given the present orientation of Sinology. This book, written from a Christian missionary point of view, summarizes very briefly a few historical and travel accounts and describes some Chinese-Muslim monuments as an attempt to present a short history of Islam in China. Most of the book relates modern observations on Chinese Muslims, including the author's own. Recommended only in the absence of anything else.

102 Forbes, Andrew D.W. "Survey Article: The Muslim National Minorities of China." Journal of Religion and Religions 6 (1976):67-87.
A comprehensive, critical bibliographical essay on books and articles in Western languages, with a few in Arabic, Chinese, and Japanese, on the Muslims of China. The study is organized according to the following subjects: general bibliography; pre-Islamic Sino-Arabian contacts; the coming of the Muslims to China; the Muslims of Yunnan; Islam in China under the Ch'ing Dynasty; the nature of Chinese Islam; Islam in China during the nationalist period, 1911-1949; and Islam in China under the communists. The eighty books and articles reviewed are listed in alphabetical order at the end of the essay. An indispensable source for materials on Islam in China.

103 Leslie, Donald Daniel. "Islam in China to 1800: A Bibliographic Guide." Abr-Nahrain 16 (1975-76):16-48.
A very detailed analysis of all existing literature in Chinese, Japanese, Arabic, Persian, and the European languages. Sinkiang and Uighur-Turkish sources not covered.

104 Pickens, Claude L., Jr. Annotated Bibliography of Literature on Islam in China. Hankow: Society of Friends of the Moslems in China, 1950, 72 pp.
Not exhaustive, it nevertheless indicates the paucity of material available on this significant subject. Christian missionaries provide much of what there is, such as this slim pamphlet.

Other Areas

105 Allen, W.E.D. A History of the Georgian People: From the Beginning down to the Russian Conquests in the Nineteenth Century. London: K. Paul, Trench, & Trubner, 1932, 429 pp.
Contains a great deal of valuable information on Georgian-Muslim relations, especially during periods of Muslim expansion.

106 Fraser-Tytler, W.K. Afghanistan: A Study of Political Developments in Central Asia. London: Oxford, 1950, 330 pp.
A history of Afghanistan from 500 B.C. through 1948 by a former officer in the Indian army and a member of the British diplomatic service, based on English sources and the writer's own experience in the area. It is somewhat old-fashioned, complete with a chapter entitled "The Lessons of History."

107 Hall, D.G.E. History of South East Asia. London: Macmillan, 1955, 807 pp.
Wedged into this history of a vast and diverse area are scattered pages on the role of Islam in the area, but these are few. A notable exception is the chapter on Malacca and the spread of Islam in the fifteenth century. Otherwise, the reader must search the index.

108 Hambly, Gavin et al. Central Asia. London: Weidenfeld & Nicolson, 1969, 388 pp.
A collaborative history of Central Asia from Achaemenid times until the present day by a team of eight scholars, in the course of which Islam figures prominently, but Tibetan and Buddhist civilization is also covered. This is the most recent and readable introduction to a complex subject of great importance in Islamic history.

109 Krader, Lawrence. Peoples of Central Asia. Uralic and Attaic Series, no. 26. Bloomington: Indiana University Press, 1963, 319 pp.
A survey of various aspects of the inhabitants of Central Asia--language, physical types, history, religion, society, and demography--as well as of changes brought about in their traditional cultures. An excellent reference work.

110 Pijper, G.F. Islam and the Netherlands. Leiden: E.J. Brill, 1957, 38 pp.
No more than an outline of Dutch interest, scholarly and otherwise, in Islam, primarily in Islam in Indonesia.

111 Playfair, Robert L. A History of Arabia Felix or Yemen from the Commencement of the Christian Era to the Middle of the XIX Century, Including an Account of the British Settlement of Aden with Introductory Chapters on the Geographical Development and the Different Regions of Yemen. Amsterdam: Phila Press, 1970, 193 pp. Reprint of 1859 ed.
A summary of primary literary sources.

112 Wilber, Donald N. Annotated Bibliography of Afghanistan. New Haven: Human Relations Area Files, 1956, 220 pp.
A basic bibliography on Afghan history, culture, and society that should be supplemented by reference to other works.

MEDIEVAL ISLAMIC HISTORY (A.D. 600-1500)

EARLY: PRE-ISLAMIC, MUḤAMMAD, THE UMAYYAD CALIPHATE

113 Abbott, Nabia. Aishah, the Beloved of Mohammed. Chicago: University of Chicago Press, 1942, 230 pp.
An expert reconstruction of the significant role played by the favorite wife of Muḥammad in early Islamic history. Meticulously researched, like all of Abbott's books, it sticks close to the sources and is valuable for its emphasis on a frequently neglected aspect of the Prophet's career. Should be supplemented by the article "ʿĀʾisha" in the new edition of the Encyclopaedia of Islam (see 20).

114 _____. Studies in Arabic Literary Papyri. Vol. 1, Historical Texts, 1957, 123 pp. Vol. 2, Qurʾanic Commentary and Tradition, 1967, 293 pp. Chicago: University of Chicago Press, 1957-1967.
Volume 1 is an important contribution to early Islamic historiography, consisting of an analysis of the significance of a handful of papyri, the texts of which Abbott has edited and summarized. Volume 2 provides a meticulous study of the relationship of early Islamic papyri to Qurʾānic interpretation and ḥadīth. The evidence here suggests that previous theories on the recording and transmission of certain material significant for the early history of Islam should be revised. Abbott's work is highly technical but of great significance for Muslim historiography. Volume 3 covers the early development of Arabic grammar and literature. See also 1224.

115 Andrae, Tor. Mohammed: The Man and His Faith. Translated by T. Menzel. London: G. Allen & Unwin, 1936, 274 pp.
The significance of this work by one of the first Western scholars to write an unbiased biography of Muḥammad is its attempt to view the Islamic prophet in terms of the psychology of religious personalities and the continuity of the religious tradition in the Middle East. Though more recent studies tend to give greater emphasis to the importance of economic factors, Andrae's biography is still helpful for its broader frame of reference.

116 Arberry, A.J. The Seven Odeṣ: The First Chapter in Arabic Literature. London: G. Allen & Unwin, 1957, 258 pp.
A translation of the most renowned examples of pre-Islamic poetry, along with Arberry's wonderfully erudite and entertaining introductions. Together the translation and the commentary provide a "feel" for a period for which

hard data are lacking. Also instructive for Arberry's discussion of the problem of the authenticity of these poems and their validity as examples of pre-Islamic literature.

117 Balādhurī, Aḥmad b. Yaḥyā. The Origins of the Islamic State: A Translation of Kitāb Futūḥ al-buldān. 2 vols. Translated by P.K. Hitti and F.C. Murgotten. New York: Columbia University Press, 1970, 1:519 pp.; 2:299 pp. Reprint of the 1916-1924 ed.

An accurate but somewhat pedestrian translation of the ninth-century Arabic work that records the course of the early Arab conquests. Hitti's title is a somewhat imaginative translation of what can be more literally and accurately rendered as "Conquests of the Lands." Nevertheless, there is some material included on the way in which the Arabs tried to administer the conquered lands and thus organize an "Islamic state."

118 Bell, Richard. The Origin of Islam in Its Christian Environment. London: Macmillan, 1926, 224 pp.

Reflects an approach that is no longer fashionable or even reputable among present-day Islamicists--the attempt to find Christian sources for Islam. Although it is probably more productive to stress, as most scholars now do, the originality of the Muslim experience and to trace its roots to the Mecca and Madīnah milieu, there is no denying the presence of Christian elements in Islam, and Bell's work is still useful for his analysis of them.

119 Bosworth, C.E. Sistan under the Arabs, from the Islamic Conquest to the Rise of the Saffarids (30-250/651-864). Rome: Istituto Italiano per il Medio ed Estremo Oriente, 1968, 145 pp.

An excellent monograph on the history of western Persia from the seventh through the ninth centuries, covering the Arab occupation, sectarian strife, political and religious uprisings, and the rise of vigilante movements, culminating in the establishment of the Ṣaffārid state.

120 Butler, A.J. The Arab Conquest of Egypt and the Last Thirty Years of the Roman Domination. Oxford: Clarendon, 1902, 563 pp.

A dated but still usable history of the period, valuable chiefly for its combination of the Byzantine and Arab periods and the detail on both. There is an informative preface, which lists Greek, Coptic, Arabic, and other sources.

121 Dennett, D.C. Conversion and the Poll Tax in Early Islam. Cambridge, Mass.: Harvard University Press, 1950, 136 pp.

This influential but still controversial study of the relationship between conversion to Islam and the taxes imposed by the Arabs on the areas they conquered demonstrates that no uniform policy was adopted by the Arabs and that preexistent systems were maintained and adapted in various areas.

122 Dermenghem, Emile. Muhammed and the Islamic Tradition. Translated by J.M. Watt. New York: Harper & Brothers; London: Longmans, 1958, 191 pp.

A popular introduction to early Islam, presenting a brief biographical and historical sketch, which is accompanied by translations from selected Islamic texts.

123 Faris, Nabih Amin, ed. The Arab Heritage. Princeton, N.J.: Princeton University Press, 1946, 279 pp.

Nine articles on various aspects of medieval Islamic history and culture; the essays "Pre-Islamic Arabia" and "Islamic Origins: A Study in Background and Foundation" are superb introductions to the origins of Islam in an Arab-Christian-Jewish environment. See also 130, 1132, 1284, 2354.

124 Gabrieli, Francesco. Muhammad and the Conquests of Islam. Translated by Virginia Luling and R. Linell. New York: McGraw-Hill, 1968, 256 pp.

A survey of Islamic history from its beginning through the Arab conquests of the seventh and eighth centuries. Although it appears in a popular series, this book rests on solid scholarship and a thorough knowledge of primary and secondary sources; it constitutes the best summary of what is known about the conquests in English. The opening chapter, "Muhammad in History," is excellent for its unsentimental yet accurate assessment of the historical reputation of the Prophet in the West, and the concluding chapter, "The Achievements of Arab Islam," is also commendable for its objectivity and soundness. There are no footnotes but an excellent bibliography; the text, translated from Italian, is beautifully illustrated.

125 Gibb, H.A.R. The Arab Conquests in Central Asia. New York: AMS Press, 1970, 102 pp. Orig. pub. by the Royal Asiatic Society, 1923.

Gibb's master's thesis, still the standard version of this phase of the Arab conquests: a critical summary of the Arabic sources on this subject.

126 Glubb, John B. The Great Arab Conquests. London: Hodder & Stoughton, 1964, 384 pp.

Valuable for Glubb's insights into military tactics and his knowledge of some of the areas involved; based on his firsthand experiences as head of the Arab Legion. Excellent maps.

127 Goldziher, Ignaz. Muslim Studies. 2 vols. Translated by C.R. Barber and S.M. Stern. London: Allen & Unwin, 1967-1971, 1:254 pp.; 2:378 pp.

Invaluable to historians for its study of the importance of tribalism as a key element of early Islamic history and the unreliability of tradition (ḥadīth) as a source for that history. Goldziher's work was pioneering and is still fundamental for an understanding of Western writing on Islamic history. The updating of the documentation by Stern is valuable. See also 1116, 1227, 1863, 1881, 1888, 2070.

128 Hamdānī, al-. The Antiquities of South Arabia, Being a Translation from the Arabic with Linguistic, Geographic, and Historic Notes of the Eighth Book of al-Hamdani's "al-Iklil." Reconstructed from al-Karmali's Edition and an MS in the Garrett Collection, Princeton University Library. Translated by Nabih Amin Faris. Princeton, N.J.: Princeton University Press, 1938, 119 pp.

A reconstruction and translation of a tenth-century work on Yemen: its public buildings, inscriptions, buried treasures. This is one of the earliest surviving Arabic works on southern Arabian civilization.

129 Ibn Isḥāq. The Life of Muhammad: A Translation of (Ibn) Isḥāq's Sīrat Rasūl Allāh. Translated by A. Guillaume. London: Oxford, 1955, 815 pp.

The earliest surviving biography of the Prophet in modern translation; this is one of the basic sources for early Islamic history, along with the Qur'ān, the ḥadīth, and the annals of the tenth-century historian, al-Ṭabarī. The last two are still, by and large, untranslated.

130 Levi della Vida, G. "Pre-Islamic Arabia." In The Arab Heritage (see 123), pp. 25-57.

By far the most sensible and realistic discussion of pre-Islamic history of Arabia, because it is limited to what can be known in terms of the archaeological and literary data available to us. Though it needs to be updated by reference to still-sparse studies of south Arabian inscriptions, it still provides an essential introduction to the field.

131 Løkkegaard, Frede. Islamic Taxation in the Classic Period with Special Reference to Circumstances in Iraq. Copenhagen: Branner & Korch, 1950, 286 pp.

One of two studies of early Muslim tax policy, its relation to pre-Islamic practice and land and fiscal policy. A pioneering work like Dennett's (see 121), it is not completely foolproof, but is firmly based on Muslim sources, some of which are at present being interpreted in a different way. A useful compendium of material.

132 Moscati, Sabatino. Ancient Semitic Civilizations. London: Elek, 1957, 254 pp.

Moscati sketches the history of the various peoples and kingdoms of the Semitic language group: Babylonians, Assyrians, Canaanites, Hebrews, Aramaeans, Arabs, and Ethiopians. Useful for viewing the Arabs in a wider framework than that in which they are usually presented, stressing the continuity of Semitic civilizations. See also 1127.

133 Mufaḍḍal, ibn Muḥammad al-. The Mufaḍḍalīyāt: An Anthology of Ancient Arabian Odes. 2 vols. Translated and edited by Charles James Lyall. Oxford: Clarendon, 1918-1921, 1:892 pp.; and 2:389 pp.

An anthology of pre-Islamic odes, containing the original Arabic along with Lyall's translations and notes; an important source for the cultural history of pre-Islamic Arabia.

134 Muir, Sir William. The Life of Mohamet from Original Sources. 3d ed. London: Smith, Elder, 1894, 536 pp.

Useful primarily for the long and detailed discussion of the sources that are available for a biography of the Prophet. Otherwise, this book is the longest, most faithful résumé of the sources on the life of Muḥammad in English, written in a smooth narrative style. Muir is sometimes criticized for writing on Islam from the point of view of a Victorian Christian, but he could hardly have done otherwise; what traces there are of prejudice or condescension can surely be read out by the critical reader.

135 O'Leary, De Lacy. Arabia before Muhammad. London: K. Paul, Trench, & Trubner; New York: Dutton, 1927, 234 pp.

A sketch of Arabia in the ancient world, its international relations and political, religious, and economic organization. It is of necessity very general and to a great extent outmoded by more recent studies.

136 Rodinson, Maxime. Mohammed. Translated by A. Carter. London: A. Lane, Penguin Press, 1971, 361 pp.

An attempt to interpret the traditional biography of the Prophet in modern ideological and psychological terms, which entails a great deal of attention to social and economic factors as well as to Muḥammad's psyche. Interesting, though speculative. The documentation is minimal.

137 Rostovtzeff, M. Caravan Cities. Translated by D. Rice and T. Talbot Rice. Oxford: Clarendon, 1932, 232 pp.

A sketch of caravan cities in the ancient Near East and descriptions of the principal centers: Petra, Jerash, Palmyra, and Dura. It is helpful in studying trade routes during the Islamic era.

138 Salem, Elie Adib. Political Theory and Institutions of the Khawarij. Baltimore: Johns Hopkins Press, 1956, 117 pp.

Salem combed Arabic primary sources to find data on the political and social theory of one of the earliest politico-religious sects in Islam, which is of enormous importance in Umayyad history.

139 Shaban, M.A. The ʿAbbāsid Revolution. Cambridge: Cambridge University Press, 1970, 181 pp.

A controversial new study of the first century of Islamic history culminating in the overthrow of the Umayyads in A.D. 749. The bulk of the work is devoted to an analysis of Arab tribal history in conquered Khurāsān (in which the anti-Umayyad movement arose), which runs counter to the traditional interpretation given by Wellhausen and others. A final chapter insists on the key role played by the Khurāsānī Arabs, as opposed to that of the Persians. Much of the evidence is inferential and not altogether convincing.

140 _____. Islamic History A.D. 600-750 (A.H. 132): A New Interpretation. Cambridge: Cambridge University Press, 1971, 197 pp.

The "old" interpretation enshrined in Wellhausen and all historians following him is that Arab tribal conflicts are the key factor to an understanding of early Islamic history, an interpretation that Shaban challenges on the basis of his own reading and interpretation of recently discovered or reedited texts. While his theories are bold and stimulating, his documentation for them is exceedingly thin and his dismissal of his predecessors' theories cavalier. This book, along with its sequel, The ʿAbbāsid Revolution (see 139), should be regarded only as a supplement to existing literature until such time as Shaban's theories are developed more convincingly.

141 Shoufani, Elias. Al-Riddah and the Muslim Conquest of Arabia. Toronto: Toronto University Press, 1973, 180 pp.

An analysis of the period of the "wars of apostasy" that followed the death of Muḥammad. The author rejects the traditional view that these wars were military efforts to re-Islamize certain Arab tribes; rather, they were expansionist wars of the Madīnah community against non-Muslim tribes and were part of the early Arab conquest movement.

142 Torrey, C.C. The Jewish Foundation of Islam. New York: Jewish Institute of Religion Press, 1933, 164 pp.

A counterpart to Bell's Origin of Islam in Its Christian Environment (see 118), reflecting the largely abandoned attempt "to explain" Islam as the imitation of or a derivation from an earlier religion. It is still relevant, however, to study the affinity between Islam and Judaism, and the possibility of borrowing; this book serves as a good introduction.

143 Watt, W. Montgomery. Muhammad at Mecca. Oxford: Clarendon, 1953, 192 pp.

This and the companion volume, Muhammad at Medina (see 144), are interesting from several points of view. Written by a Protestant clergyman, these works nevertheless represent the most thorough attempt by a Western biographer to view the career of Muḥammad in a sympathetic light, even to the extent that the approach sometimes seems apologetic. Mixed with this is a curious flavor of Marxism in Watt's emphasis on economic factors as a formative element in earliest Islam, which reflects the theories of an earlier French Jesuit scholar, H. Lammens. Watt's reading of the original sources is strangely colored by these two considerations. Be that as it may, the two books are now regarded as the standard biography of the Prophet in English and have been enormously influential in recent scholarship.

144 _____. Muhammad at Medina. Oxford: Clarendon, 1956, 418 pp.

In contrast to its companion volume (see 143), here the emphasis is more on tribal dynamics than on economics. The social analysis is recapitulated; it was later extended to other phases of Islamic history (see 47). The work is useful for Watt's detailed analysis of Muḥammad's political achievements in winning over the tribesmen, the Meccans, and the Madīnans to Islam and in organizing them within an Islamic community. The concluding chapter, "The Man and His Greatness," leans over backward to judge "the alleged moral failures" sympathetically.

145 _____. Muhammad, Prophet and Statesman. London: Oxford, 1961, 250 pp.

A condensation and popular version of the two-volume biography (see 143, 144), and useful as an introduction to it. It is deceptively oversimplified because it lacks the documentation and scholarly apparatus of the main work.

146 Wellhausen, Julius. The Arab Kingdom and Its Fall. Translated by M.G. Weir. Beirut: Khayats, 1963, 592 pp. Orig. pub. in 1927.

One of the standard studies of early Islamic history by a great Orientalist, the book was regarded as virtual scripture until recently, when it was attacked by Shaban (see 140). Wellhausen's thesis, based on a painstaking analysis of the early Arabic sources available to him at the time, is that the Umayyads failed to integrate Arab tribes and Persian converts into a viable Islamic state and were ultimately destroyed by the frictions this failure engendered. The second half of the book is detailed and offers tough but rewarding reading. See also 2234.

ʿABBĀSID CIVILIZATION

General Survey

Political

147 Arnold, Sir Thomas Walker. The Caliphate. Rev. ed. New York: Barnes & Noble, 1966, 266 pp. Orig. pub. by Oxford, 1924.

The standard survey in English of the Sunnī caliphate as a political-religious institution from earliest to modern times. Appendixes cover the "heterodox," i.e., Shīʿī and Khārijī caliphates, as well as questions of terminology. This work has been superseded in many respects by E. Tyan's two-volume study of the caliphate, Institutions du droit public musulman (2 vols. Paris: Siney, 1954-1957).

148 Barthold, V.V. Turkestan down to the Mongol Invasion. Translated by T. Minorsky. London: Luzac, 1968, 573 pp.

Though detailed and tedious, and therefore not for beginners, this work is nevertheless a definitive study of Turkish Central Asia, filled with information that is not readily accessible elsewhere in English. See also 291.

149 Belyaev, E.A. Arabs, Islam and the Arab Caliphate in the Early Middle Ages. Translated by A. Gourevitch. New York: Praeger, 1969, 264 pp.

Though universally condemned by Western scholars as the official Soviet-Marxist interpretation of early (through the tenth century) Arab-Islamic history, the work is interesting as an example of an approach that would otherwise be unavailable to those without a knowledge of Russian. The author stresses "class" factors as the key element in understanding Arab-Islamic history, an interpretation for which there is unfortunately too little evidence in the original sources.

150 Bishai, Wilson B. Islamic History of the Middle East. Boston: Allyn & Bacon, 1968, 399 pp.

A survey of Arab-Islamic history up to the Mongol conquest of Baghdad, designed for beginners. The interpretations do not always reflect the latest scholarship, but Bishai's definition of terms at the end of each section is definitely helpful to novices.

151 Grunebaum, G.E. von. Classical Islam: A History 600-1258. Translated by Katharine Watson. London: Allen & Unwin, 1970, 243 pp.

"Straight" history was not von Grunebaum's forte, and this straightforward summation lacks the excitement of his more interpretive, imaginative works. Nevertheless, there are few who have written so authoritatively on this segment of Islamic history and whose work can be consulted and used as a textbook with complete confidence.

152 Ibn al-Ṭiqṭaqā. Al-Fakhrī, on the Systems of Government and the Moslem Dynasties, Composed by Muḥammad, son of ʿAlī, Son of Ṭabaṭaba, Known as the Rapid Talker, May God Have Mercy on Him. Translated by C.E.J. Whitting. London: Luzac, 1947, 326 pp.

A translation of a thirteenth-century discussion of Islamic statecraft and government and a history of the caliphate.

153 Lane-Poole, Stanley. A History of Egypt in the Middle Ages (600-1500). 2d rev. ed. London: Methuen, 1914, 382 pp.

An excellent history of medieval Egypt based on the original sources available to Lane-Poole at the time. Still unsurpassed and unrivaled as a one-volume history of the period. Focuses on politics, with a few remarks on architecture.

154 Levy, Reuben. A Baghdad Chronicle. Cambridge: Cambridge University Press, 1929, 279 pp.

A narrative history of Baghdad from its founding until the Mongol conquest in 1258, in the form of a careful summary of Arabic and Persian sources. As such, it presents a useful and reliable outline of the main trends in the history of the ʿAbbāsid caliphate.

155 Muir, Sir William. The Caliphate, Its Rise, Decline and Fall, from Original Sources. Beirut: Khayats, 1963, 628 pp. Orig. pub. in 1915.

Unfortunately this reprint is not of the edition that included the fullest documentation. Nevertheless, it is the most detailed history of the caliphate readily available in English, based ultimately on original sources (mainly al-Ṭabarī) and others through G. Weil's Geschichte der Chalifen, 5 vols. (Mannheim: F. Bassermann, 1846-1802).

156 Nöldeke, Theodor. Sketches from Eastern History. Translated by John Sutherland Black. London: A. & C. Black, 1892, 288 pp.

This is the only work of the important nineteenth-century Orientalist available in English and includes his studies on the ʿAbbāsid caliph Manṣūr, the Black Rebellion in Iraq, and the dynasty of Yaʿqūb the Coppersmith in eastern Persia, three studies of ʿAbbāsid history that are rare, detailed summaries of primary sources. See also 1184.

157 Omar, Farouk. The Abbasid Caliphate 132/750-170/786. Baghdad: National, 1969, 418 pp.

A study of the first three decades of the ʿAbbāsid dynasty based on a careful reading of Arabic sources, several of them still in manuscript form. Omar has compiled a great deal of data on such important questions as ʿAbbāsid propaganda, the role of Abū Muslim, the growth of Shīʿī aspirations, and developments in the provinces. Originally a dissertation, this is not for beginners, but would be useful after the more general works have been digested.

158 Saunders, J.J. A History of Medieval Islam. London: Routledge & K. Paul, 1965, 219 pp.

A popular but not vulgar history of Islam from the beginnings through the Mongol invasions of the thirteenth century. Though recent, it is curiously dated in many of its interpretations, which may mean that Saunders is not familiar with current scholarship. Von Grunebaum's Classical Islam (see 151) covers more or less the same territory with greater authority.

159 Shaban, M.A. Islamic History, A.D. 750-1055 (A.H. 132-448): A New Interpretation. Vol. 2. Cambridge: Cambridge University Press, 1976, 221 pp.

A continuation of this scholar's two earlier works (see 139, 140), covering ʿAbbāsid history up to the Saljūq invasions. What is "new" is not fully substantiated, but this is a useful summary nevertheless.

160 Watt, W. Montgomery. The Majesty That Was Islam: The Islamic World 661-1100. London: Sidgwick & Jackson, 1974, 276 pp.

A sketch of the main developments in Islamic political and religious history from the beginning through the Saljūq conquest, attempting to trace the interaction between religion and politics, sects and dynasties, theologians and rulers. Though such a study is certainly a desideratum, this particular one, superficial and undocumented, does little to meet the need.

161 Wiet, Gaston. Cairo, City of Art and Commerce. Translated by Seymour Feiler. Norman: University of Oklahoma Press, 1964, 170 pp.

A brief, superficial summary of Egyptian Islamic history as reflected in the development of Cairo, along with chapters on medieval social life in the city.

Economic and Social

162 Aghnides, Nicolas P. Mohammedan Theories of Finance with an Introduction to Mohammedan Law and a Bibliography. Lahore: Premier Book House, 1961, 532 pp.

An introductory section of one hundred fifty pages describes fiqh--Islamic jurisprudence. A second section summarizes in systematic form the material that can be found in fiqh books on taxes, finance, revenue, and land. For those who do not read Arabic, this is a very useful compendium of data on a very complicated subject, though interpretation of the data is minimal.

163 Ben Shemesh, A., trans. Taxation in Islam. Vol. 1, Kitāb al-Kharāj, by Yaḥyā b. Ādam, 1958, 172 pp. Vol. 2, Kitāb al-Kharāj, by Qudāma b. Jaʿfar, 1965, 146 pp. Vol. 3, Kitāb al-Kharāj, by Abu Yūsuf, 1969, 143 pp. Leiden: E.J. Brill, 1958-1969.

Partial translation of three early Islamic texts on taxation, representing the theoretical formulation by legists more than the actual practice, but nevertheless of great significance for this vexing subject within the history of the expansion of Islam and the conversion of the conquered peoples.

164 Chau Ju-Kua. Chau Ju-Kua: His Work on the Chinese and Arab Trade in the Twelfth and Thirteenth Centuries, Entitled Chu-fan-chi. Translated by Friedrich Hirth and W.W. Rockhill. St. Petersburg: Printing Office of the Imperial Academy of Sciences, 1911, 288 pp.

Notes on foreign trade and merchandise by a Chinese inspector of foreign trade.

165 Fahmy, Aly Mohamed. Muslim Seapower in the Eastern Mediterranean, from the Seventh to the Tenth Century, A.D. London: Don Bosco, 1950, 194 pp.

Fahmy has culled Arabic historical and geographical works for data on Muslim navies. Most of his findings relate to arsenals and naval centers in Egypt, Syria, Africa, and Crete, the organization of the navy, and the materials and structure of Muslim warships.

166 Fischel, Walter J. Jews in the Economic and Political Life of Medieval Islam. London: Royal Asiatic Society of Great Britain and Ireland, 1968, 139 pp.

A study of representative Jewish figures under the ʿAbbāsid and Fāṭimid caliphates and under the Il-khāns, designed to show the role and status of Jews under Muslim rulers.

167 Havighurst, Alfred F., ed. The Pirenne Thesis: Analysis, Criticism, and Revision. Boston: Heath, 1958, 109 pp.

In view of the bottles of scholarly ink that have been spilled on the Pirenne thesis, this sampling of essays by various experts on medieval history helps enormously in putting Pirenne's work into some sort of meaningful perspective. Should be read along with Mohammed and Charlemagne (see 175), for few students have the necessary data to evaluate either the validity or the significance of Pirenne's conclusions.

168 Hourani, Albert, and S.M. Stern, eds. The Islamic City: Papers Delivered at the Meetings of the Near Eastern History Group in Oxford, 1965. Oxford: B. Cassirer, 1970, 222 pp.

One of the clichés of medieval Islamic history is that Islamic civilization is an urban civilization. Only recently has this been seriously challenged by scholars, as, for example, in this collection of essays on the medieval city in Islam, which examines both its physical and administrative structure. Stern's and Cahen's articles are important for the question of guilds. See also 1938, 1947, 2002, 2006, 2007, 2009.

169 Hourani, George Fadlo. Arab Seafaring in the Indian Ocean in Ancient and Early Medieval Times. Princeton, N.J.: Princeton University Press, 1951, 131 pp.

A study of trade routes through the Indian Ocean and the Red Sea before and after the Muslim conquests, based on classical sources and Arabic histories and geographies. It is a useful supplement to Pirenne. There is also a chapter on ships and life at sea.

170 Huzayyin, S.A. Arabia and the Far East, Their Commercial and Cultural Relations in Graeco-Roman and Irano-Arabian Times. Cairo: Royal Geographic Society, 1942, 319 pp.

An excellent study of contact between the Middle and Far East during two periods of history, based on original Arabic and European sources, through the seventeenth century. It also provides information on Islam in Central Asia.

171 Lane, Edward William. Arabian Society in the Middle Ages: Studies from the Thousand and One Nights. London: Chatto & Windus, 1883, 283 pp.

An edition of Lane's explanatory notes to his translation of Thousand and One Nights, which were based largely on Lane's own experience in Cairo in the early nineteenth century as well as on extracts from late medieval historians. The book is crowded with data on subjects ranging from suckling babes to grave clothes.

172 Lewis, A.R. Naval Power and Trade in the Mediterranean. Princeton, N.J.: Princeton University Press, 1951, 271 pp.

An attempt to explore in depth the implications of Pirenne's thesis (see 175) on the closing of the Mediterranean as a result of the Arab conquests, this was one of the first studies to look at the Mediterranean trade as a whole rather than at a localized part of it. It is helpful in putting Muslim expansion into the Mediterranean in a broad frame of reference and is well documented.

173 Lombard, Maurice. The Golden Age of Islam. Translated by Joan Spencer. New York: American Elsevier Publishing Co., 1975, 259 pp.
A study of Islamic history through the tenth century, focusing on trade and money. Not profound, it is nonetheless valuable as an introduction to economic aspects of Islamic history of this period.

174 Mann, Jacob. The Jews in Egypt and Palestine under the Fatimid Caliphs: A Contribution to Their Political and Communal History Based Chiefly on Genizah Material Hitherto Unpublished. 2 vols. Oxford: Oxford University Press, 1969, 1:280 pp.; 2:427 pp.
The first volume is a reconstruction of Jewish history in Egypt from the Arab conquest in A.D. 969 through the period of Maimonides, at the beginning of the thirteenth century, based on materials found in a depository in a Cairo synagogue. The second volume contains the texts of the materials themselves and Mann's commentaries on them. The work is extremely important for the life of minority religions under the Fāṭimids.

175 Pirenne, Henri. Mohammed and Charlemagne. Translated by Bernard Miall. London: Allen & Unwin, 1954, 293 pp.
One of the great synthesizing works of this century, embodying the famous "Pirenne thesis" that the Arab conquest broke the unity of Mediterranean civilization and shifted the center to the north, away from the Mediterranean. For revisions of the thesis by other scholars, see the essays edited by Havighurst (see 167).

176 Rahmatallah, Maleeha. The Women of Baghdad in the Ninth and Tenth Centuries as Revealed in the History of Baghdad. Baghdad: Baghdad University, 1963, 78 pp.
Since the status of women in medieval Muslim society is virtually an unexplored field, this compilation of data from a biographical dictionary is useful if only to show what type of source material is available.

177 Richards, D.S., ed. Islam and the Trade of Asia: A Colloquium. Oxford: Cassirer, 1970, 266 pp.
A collection of fifteen papers on various aspects of Muslim trade, it deals with China, East Africa, Indonesia, India, Persia, and the Ottoman Empire, and also includes general studies on Muslim commercial practice and technical studies on archaeological findings. The period covered is from ancient, pre-Islamic times until the middle of the nineteenth century. This work represents the merest beginning of serious scholarly study of Islamic economic history. See also 2368.

178 Siddiqi, S.A. Public Finance in Islam. Lahore: Saikh Muhammad Ashrai, 1952, 250 pp.
Designed as a guide in Islamic principles of finance for modern Muslim financiers, this book is based on Aghnides's Mohammedan Theories of Finance, which it supplements with data from original sources not used or fully exploited by Aghnides (see 162).

179 Tritton, A.S. The Caliphs and Their Non-Muslim Subjects: A Critical Study of the Covenant of ʿUmar. London: Oxford University Press, 1930, 240 pp.
The subtitle is misleading, since only one chapter is devoted to this subject. Other chapters based on primary sources deal with aspects of various Muslim rulers' policy toward the dhimmīs (non-Muslim subjects).

Cultural

180 Aḥmad, Nafīs. Muslim Contribution to Geography. Lahore: Muhammad Ashraf, 1947, 180 pp.
A brief survey of the principal Muslim geographers and cartographers writing in Arabic and Persian during the Middle Ages.

181 Aḥmed, Munīr-ud-Dīn. Muslim Education and the Scholars' Social Status up to the Fifth Century Muslim Era in the Light of Taʾrīkh Baghdād. Zurich: Verlag "Der Islam," 1968, 290 pp.
The author has combed through al-Khaṭīb al-Baghdādī's Taʾrīkh Baghdād to compile data on medieval Muslim education, including the curricula, types of educational institutions, and the social background of teachers and students. He has made a great deal of inaccessible data available in a convenient form, though his source is not so rich on the subject as might have been hoped.

182 Arberry, A.J. Aspects of Islamic Civilization as Depicted in the Original Texts. London: Allen & Unwin, 1964, 408 pp.
An excellent collection from Arberry's extensive translations of Islamic texts, Arabic and Persian, medieval and modern, which can be used to acquaint the student with Muslim intellectual history at firsthand. The introductions are disappointingly brief, but the translations themselves are impeccably accurate and eminently readable. The criterion for selection seems to have been broader than that used for similar anthologies; hence, a greater variety of subject matter is evident. See also 1108, 1412.

183 _____. Classical Persian Literature. London: G. Allen & Unwin, 1958, 464 pp.
A one-volume summary and updating of the first three volumes of Browne's Literary History of Persia (see 66), with snatches of Arberry's translations of representative samples. See also 1400.

184 _____. Shiraz: Persian City of Saints and Poets. Norman: University of Oklahoma Press, 1960, 177 pp.
Rather than attempt a systematic history of the city, Arberry chose to write sketches of prominent citizens: two Ṣūfīs (Ibn Khafīf and Ruzbihan) and two poets (Saʿdī and al-Ḥāfiẓ). These superficial sketches are preceded by a description of Shirāz, taken from travel accounts, and an outline of its history.

185 Arnold, Thomas, and A. Guillaume. The Legacy of Islam. Oxford: Clarendon, 1931, 416 pp.
A collection of thirteen essays surveying the achievements in various fields of Islamic civilization, e.g., art and architecture, literature, philosophy, science, and music, and their influence on European civilization. Many of the essays now seem dated, and a new edition of this work has been prepared (see 207). See also 2103.

186 Barthold, V.V. Mussulman Culture. Translated by S. Suhrawardy. Calcutta: University of Calcutta, 1934, 146 pp.
An outline of the components of Islamic culture as it evolved in history. Barthold first analyzes Christian influences, then turns to Arab and Persian contributions before examining the impact of the Mongols and the loss of cultural leadership to the West. Although such compartmentalization of the phases of cultural development is now out of fashion, this conceptualization of the great Russian Orientalist is still stimulating.

187 Daniel, Norman. Islam and the West: The Making of an Image. Edinburgh: University Press, 1960, 443 pp.
A survey of Christian attitudes toward and misconceptions of Islam during the twelfth to fourteenth centuries, which is important for the history of Muslim-Christian relations and the underlying causes of lingering misapprehensions in the West. It provides detailed summaries and incisive analysis. See also 479.

188 Dodge, Bayard. Muslim Education in Medieval Times. Washington: Middle East Institute, 1962, 119 pp.
A compilation from Arabic sources of material on Muslim educational activities and institutions and the subjects taught. Although Dodge has been somewhat uncritical in his approach to his sources, it is very useful to have these data available in English in one volume.

189 Dunlop, D. Arab Civilization to A.D. 1500. London: Longmans, 1971, 368 pp.
An introductory chapter of twenty-five pages outlines Arab history to 1500. This is followed by chapters on various aspects of Arab civilization: literature, history, geography, philosophy, science, and famous women. It is unavoidably encyclopedic.

190 Farmer, Henry George. A History of Arabian Music to the Thirteenth Century. London: Luzac, 1967, 264 pp.
Farmer has abstracted all the information he could find on music and musicians in Arabic primary sources and arranged it in chronological order, beginning with the Jāhiliyyah. Although the result is not, strictly speaking, a "history," it is a useful compilation of what can be learned from the sources, and is relevant to many aspects of Islamic social history.

191 Ferdausi. The Epic of the Kings: Shah-Nama, the National Epic of Persia. Translated by Reuben Levy. Chicago: University of Chicago Press, 1967, 423 pp.
Reuben Levy, along with Arberry, was one of the foremost English scholars of his generation on Iranian literature. One of many proofs is this abridged translation of the great Persian epic. Unfortunately, there are no notes to elucidate the text, which is central to the Persian cultural experience.

192 Grunebaum, G.E. von. Medieval Islam: A Study in Cultural Orientation. Chicago: University of Chicago Press, 1953, 378 pp.
Von Grunebaum was unique among Orientalists, combining the rigors of a traditional German education with a mastery of Islamic languages and literature and, finally, exposure to cultural anthropological studies at the University of Chicago. All this is reflected in his scholarship, by which he has almost singlehandedly lifted a somewhat parochial discipline into the wider stream of European and North American academic life. This particular book grew out of a series of lectures on "the cultural orientation of the Muslim Middle Ages," which present a wide-ranging analysis of the intellectual milieu of eastern Islam at that time. See also 1783, 1953, 2096.

193 Ḥarīrī, al-. The Assemblies of al-Ḥarīrī, Translated from the Arabic with Notes, Historical and Grammatical. Vol. 1, translated by Thomas Chenery. London: Williams & Norgate 1867, 540 pp. Vol. 2, translated by F. Steingass. London: Royal Asiatic Society, 1898, 395 pp.
A translation of the Maqāmāt, eleventh-century Arabic poems that are a monument to the erudition and linguistic virtuosity of the author and a compendium of medieval urban lore.

194 Ibn Khaldūn, ʿAbd al-Raḥmān b. Muḥammad. The Muqaddimah: An Introduction to History. 3 vols. Translated by F. Rosenthal. London: Routledge & K. Paul, 1958.
Rosenthal's meticulous, somewhat literal, translation of one of the monuments of medieval Islamic civilization by its most original thinker. Though famous for its cyclic analysis of tribal history, it also provides an introduction to most aspects of Islamic culture in the Middle Ages. It contains an exhaustive introduction, bibliography, and notes, which are missing in the one-volume adaptation by N.J. Dawood, The Muqaddimah: An Introduction to History (London: Routledge & K. Paul, 1967, 465 pp.). See also 1979.

195 Khalidi, Tarif. Islamic Historiography: The Histories of Masʿudi. Albany: State University of New York Press, 1975, 180 pp.
A discussion of the philosophy of history of the tenth-century "Herodotus of the Arabs," which demonstrates the indebtedness of Masʿūdī's school to Greek, Indian, and Persian forebears.

196 Lewis, Bernard, ed. and trans. Islam from the Prophet Muhammad to the Capture of Constantinople. Vol. 1, Politics and War, 266 pp. Vol. 2, Religion and Society, 310 pp. New York: Harper & Row, 1974.

A wide-ranging selection of original sources that traces the development of the Muslim empires and the growth of Islamic institutions through the observations of contemporary writers. Readable and well organized for beginners and advanced students alike.

197 Mahdi, Muhsin. Ibn Khaldūn's Philosophy of History: A Study in the Philosophic Foundation of the Science of Culture. Chicago: University of Chicago Press, 1957, 325 pp. Reprint. Chicago: Phoenix, 1964, 1971.

An analysis of the philosophy of the Arab historian best known in the West and regarded by some as "one of the fathers of modern social science and cultural history."

198 Margoliouth, D.S. Lectures on Arabic Historians. Calcutta: University of Calcutta, 1930, 160 pp.

Contains eight lectures, four on general topics (pre-Islamic history, the beginnings of Arabic historiography, poetry as history) and four on the main historians of various periods. This is a very general survey and should be followed by the works of Rosenthal (see 206) and Gibb (see 21-24) as well as specialized studies.

199 Masʿūdī, al-. El-Masʿūdī's Historical Encyclopaedia Entitled "Meadows of Gold and Mines of Gems." Translated by A. Sprenger. London: Oriental Translation Fund, 1841, 464 pp.

The only part of Masʿūdī's universal history available in English, this volume is the geography of the world known to the tenth-century historian and illustrates what has been called his anthropological approach to history. The entire work has been translated into French by Pariet de Corteille and Barbur de Maynard, Les prairies d'or par Macoudi (Paris, 1861-1877). A corrected version of this translation by Charles Pellat is underway (Paris: Société Asiatique, 1962-).

200 Myers, Eugene A. Arabic Thought and the Western World in the Golden Age of Islam. New York: F. Unger, 1964, 156 pp.

A brief outline of the major Muslim thinkers whose works have had some impact upon Western consciousness and the persons who were involved in the translation movement whereby works of antiquity were transmitted through Syriac and Arabic to the Latin West.

201 Nakosteen, M. History of Islamic Origins of Western Education, 800-1350, with an Introduction to Medieval Muslim Education. Boulder: University of Colorado Press, 1964, 361 pp.

The author has compiled a great deal of data on medieval Muslim education from primary sources of difficult access. He has tried to relate these to the medieval Western curricula.

202 Nasr, Seyyid Hossein. Science and Civilization in Islam. Cambridge, Mass.: Harvard University Press, 1968, 384 pp.

Nasr's thesis is that Islamic culture is not merely the filter through which Greek learning passed to the West but is an independent development. Whether or not one accepts this argument, Nasr's survey of the history of Islamic civilization is instructive, based on wide reading in the original sources.

203 Nicholson, Reynold A. Translations of Eastern Poetry and Prose. Cambridge: Cambridge University Press, 1922, 200 pp.

A tantalizingly brief anthology of samples of Arabic and Persian belles-lettres and history, from the sixth to the fifteenth century.

204 Pellat, Charles. The Life and Works of Jāḥiẓ: Translations of Selected Texts. Translated by D.M.Hawke. London: Routledge & K. Paul, 1969, 286 pp.

An excellent study of Jāḥiẓ, the celebrated littérateur of ninth-century Iraq, through representative selections from his works, covering theology, politics, rhetoric, science, manners, love, society. These, along with Pellat's short introduction, paint a portrait of a sophisticated Muslim intellectual who was of considerable importance in the development of Arabic culture. See also 1617.

205 Peters, F.E. Allah's Commonwealth: A History of Islam in the Near East 600-1100 A.D. New York: Simon & Schuster, 1973, 800 pp.

A very useful, popular intellectual history of Islam in its "classical" period. The attempt to provide a summary of political history as scaffolding is minimal; what is important in this book is the characterization of the main intellectual trends in Islam and the sketches of the individuals who embodied them. Especially valuable for Peters's discussion of the role of Hellenism in the evolution of Islam.

206 Rosenthal, Franz. A History of Muslim Historiography. Leiden: E.J. Brill, 1968, 653 pp.

In his basic study of the development of Islamic historical writing, Rosenthal devotes the first part to a survey of the various genres of historiography, and in parts 2 and 3 translates various texts on historiography by medieval Muslim authors.

207 Schacht, Joseph, and C.E. Bosworth. The Legacy of Islam. 2d ed. Oxford: Clarendon Press, 1974, 530 pp.

An evaluation of the contributions of Islam to world civilization and its contacts with other cultures. It has little in common with the first edition (see 185) except the title, since all the articles are new. See also 1567, 1983, 2077, 2290, 2293.

208 Schroeder, Eric. Muhammad's People: A Tale by Anthology. Portland, Ore.: Band Wheelwright, 1955, 838 pp.

A study of medieval Islamic civilization as embodied in translations of Arabic sources, including selections on history, literature, science, and religion; all have been translated previously and Schroeder has recast them into his own style. Many find this book exasperating because of the vague identification of the sources, but it is Schroeder's purpose to shift the emphasis from the authors to their texts for the sake of continuity. Taken on its own terms, the book is instructive and entertaining.

209 Tanūkhī, ʻAlī b. al-Muḥassin al-. The Table-Talk of a Mesopotamian Judge. Translated by D.S. Margoliouth. London: Royal Asiatic Society, 1922, 300 pp.

A tenth-century collection of anecdotes on a wide variety of subjects meant to be amusing but nonetheless informative to students of intellectual history. The stories Margoliouth considered obscene have been, unfortunately, expurgated.

210 Watt, W. Montgomery. The Influence of Islam on Medieval Europe. Edinburgh: University of Edinburgh Press, 1972, 125 pp.

A series of lectures on the Islamic impact on Europe through conquest, trade, science, and philosophy. Superficial, it is useful only as an introduction to the main trends, works, and personages.

211 Williams, John Alden, ed. Themes of Islamic Civilization. Berkeley: University of California Press, 1971, 382 pp.

A useful collection of translations, some of which have been published elsewhere and some original, documenting Islamic intellectual history. The focus is on Islam as a religion, the approach topical. The commentary is expert. See also 1851.

212 Yāqūt. The Introductory Chapters of Yāqūt's Muʻjam al-Buldān. Translated by Wadie Jwaideh. Leiden: E.J. Brill, 1959, 79 pp.

A translation of the introduction to the great twelfth-century compendium of geographical and historical knowledge, which sets forth the significance of such studies and the author's general conception of the universe.

Topography and Travels

213 Ibn Baṭṭūṭa. Travels in Asia and Africa 1325-1354. Translated by H.A.R. Gibb. London: Routledge & K. Paul, 1929, 398 pp.

Gibb's translation of selections from Ibn Baṭṭūṭa, later translated in toto. The introduction to this volume is fuller in historical detail than that of the larger work.

214 _____. The Travels of Ibn Baṭṭūṭa, A.D. 1325-1354. 3 vols. Translated by H.A.R. Gibb. Cambridge: Cambridge University Press, 1958-1971, 771 pp.

Gibb's superb translation of the travel memoirs of a fourteenth-century scholar from the Maghreb who journeyed from Tangiers to China and back to Fās, with copious notes on the places he saw and people he met. This is an invaluable supplement to the contemporary chronicles and biographies. Gibb's notes are excellent.

215 Ibn Jubayr. The Travels of Ibn Jubayr. Translated by R.J.C. Broadhurst. London: J. Cape, 1952, 430 pp.

A translation of the travel notes of a twelfth-century official of the court of Granada, which give a fascinating picture of the Mediterranean world from Spain to Palestine as well as the mentality of a twelfth-century Muslim.

216 Lassner, Jacob. The Topography of Baghdad in the Early Middle Ages, Text and Studies. Detroit: Wayne State University Press, 1970, 324 pp.

A study and translation of al-Khaṭīb al-Baghdādī's description of Baghdād (Ta'rīkh Baghdād), along with several of the author's articles on various aspects of ʻAbbāsid Baghdād. This is one of the most detailed studies of a medieval Islamic city available in English.

217 LeStrange, Guy. Baghdad during the Abbasid Caliphate from Contemporary Arabic and Persian Sources. London: Oxford, 1900, 381 pp.

A study of the layout, principal quarters, streets, and buildings of Baghdād during the medieval period. Good for reference.

218 _____. The Lands of the Eastern Caliphate: Mesopotamia, Persia, and Central Asia from the Moslem Conquest to the Time of Timur. Cambridge: Cambridge University Press, 1905, 536 pp.

A summary of medieval Arab, Persian, and Turkish geographers on the areas listed in the subtitle, this is an invaluable reference work for descriptions of places that frequently occur, without identification, in medieval Islamic history.

219 _____. Palestine under the Moslems: A Description of Syria and the Holy Land from 650-1500. London: A.P. Watt, 1890, 604 pp.

This collection of data from Arab geographies on Muslim Syria and Palestine during the Middle Ages is indispensable as a reference work for place names. See also 1913.

Specialized Studies

Specific Caliphs and Their Reigns

220 Abbott, Nabia. Two Queens of Baghdad: Mother and Wife of Harun al-Rashid. Chicago: University of Chicago Press, 1946, 277 pp.

Ostensibly a study of two important women at Ḥarūn's court, it is also the best, most detailed study of the reign of this most famous of ʻAbbāsid caliphs. Conservative, every word based on a primary source, it represents a careful model of history based upon the reconstruction of literary sources.

221 Bowen, Harold. The Life and Times of ʻAlī ibn ʻĪsā, the Good Vizier. Cambridge: Cambridge University Press, 1928, 420 pp.

A narrative history, closely following primary sources, of the ʻAbbāsid state from A.D. 892 to 946. Focusing on the role of the vizier and fiscal policy, it unfolds the structure of the ʻAbbāsid bureaucracy and the process of governmental corruption endemic to the medieval Islamic state. Important as one of the few really detailed studies of ʿAbbāṣid history available in English, it is also quite readable.

222 Mason, Herbert. Two Statesmen of Mediaeval Islam: Vizier Ibn Hubayra (499-560 AH-1105-1165 AD) and Caliph an-Nāṣir li-Dīn Allāh (553-622 AH/1158-1225 AD). The Hague: Mouton, 1972, 146 pp.

Two monographs on medieval Islamic theory and practice of politics and the attempt to restore the ʿAbbāsid caliphate to its earlier status. The second, on al-Nāṣir, is a tentative study for a future work; the first is complete. Both represent an ingenious exploitation of diverse types of source material, including poetry, and constitute useful contributions to the history of a period of considerable importance in the evaluation of the caliphate.

223 Philby, H. St. John. Harun al-Rashid. New York: Appleton-Century, 1934, 141 pp.

A popular biography of the most famous caliph in the West. It is based on secondary sources and has little, if any, historical value.

224 Ṭabarī, Muḥammad b. Jarīr al-. The Reign of al-Muʿtaṣim (833-842): A Partial Translation of Ta'rīkh, al-rusūl wa-al-mulūk. Translated by E. Marin. New Haven, Conn.: American Oriental Society, 1951, 142 pp.

A translation of short sections of al-Ṭabarī's Annals, giving a sample of the work of one of the most important Islamic historians who wrote in Arabic. More is forthcoming.

Persian and Turkish Dynasties

225 Bosworth, C.E. The Ghaznavids: Their Empire in Afghanistan and Eastern Iran, 994-1040. Edinburgh: University of Edinburgh Press, 1963, 331 pp.

An absolutely first-rate study of the dynasty based in Afghanistan and of great importance in the political and cultural history of Iran and India. Basing his work on a close reading of primary sources, Bosworth focuses on the structure of the Ghaznavid state, its administration of Khurāsān, and its conflict with the Saljūq Turks. Important for an understanding of the military-slave state prominent throughout medieval Islamic history. See also 1921.

226 Boyle, J.A., ed. The Cambridge History of Iran. Vol. 5, The Saljuq and Mongol Periods. Cambridge: Cambridge University Press, 1968, 761 pp.

One of four volumes to be devoted to the history of Iranian Islam, this consists of ten chapters by various authorities. The approach is topical, with introductory essays on political history followed by analyses of Saljūq and Mongol institutions, religion, art, and literature. Of particular importance is the Russian Petrushevsky's article "The Socio-Economic Condition of Iran under the Il-Khans," one of the few indications to non-Russian readers of the state of research on Islam in the Soviet Union. All in all, this work maintains a high level of scholarship and is of great use to students and professors alike. See also 1499, 2312.

227 Bulliet, Richard W. The Patricians of Nishapur: A Study in Medieval Islamic Social History. Cambridge, Mass.: Harvard University Press, 1972, 287 pp.

A pioneering attempt to analyze the social structure of a medieval Muslim city during the period of Saljūq dominion. Also important for the author's use of biographical dictionaries as primary source material. See also 2238.

228 Cahen, Claude. Pre-Ottoman Turkey: A General Survey of the Material and Spiritual Culture and History 1071-1330. Translated by J. Jones-Williams. London: Sidgwick & Jackson, 1968, 458 pp.

A history of the Saljūqs and Mongols in Anatolia by France's foremost historian of Islam. Although it fills a gap and is, because of Cahen's reputation, authoritative, it is somewhat disappointing because of his tendency to generalize and the complete lack of footnotes. Nevertheless, the book is important as a summary of what is currently known about Anatolia during this period and represents a synthesis of a massive amount of material.

229 Frye, Richard N. Bukhara, the Medieval Achievement. Norman: University of Oklahoma Press, 1965, 209 pp.

A convenient, easy summary of the history of Central Asia in Islamic times concentrating on the Sāmānid period (ninth and tenth centuries). Political and cultural history are covered competently, if briefly.

230 _____, ed. The Cambridge History of Iran. Vol. 4, From the Arab Invasion to the Saljuqs. Cambridge: Cambridge University Press, 1975, 734 pp.

A recapitulation of Umayyad and ʿAbbāsid history from the standpoint of Persia. Half of the twenty articles by various Western and Iranian scholars cover the dynastic history of Iran; the rest are devoted to literature, art, science, philosophy, and religion. Although the value of the contributions is uneven, the work as a whole provides an authoritative and convenient introduction to the subject. See also 1496.

231 Frye, Richard N. The Golden Age of Persia: The Arabs in the East. London: Weidenfeld & Nicolson, 1975, 290 pp.

An attempt to trace the continuity of Iranian traditions throughout the period of the Arab caliphate, through Saljūq times. What evidence there is (and much of it is philological) is cogently presented.

232 Ghazālī, al-. Ghazālī's Book of Counsel for Kings (Nasīhat al-Mulūk). Translated by F.R.C. Bagley. London: Oxford University Press, 1964, 197 pp.

A prime example of the "Mirror for Princes" literature, popular during the medieval period, which reflects the persistence of a pre-Islamic tradition of rulership throughout Islamic history.

233 Ḥabīb, Moḥammad. Sultan Mahmud of Ghaznin: A Study. Aligarh: Aligarh Muslim University, 1927, 108 pp.

This essay on the Ghaznavids, emphasizing the reign of Maḥmūd, to some extent tries to counteract the Indian Muslim exaltation of the ṣultān. The shortage of documentation robs the work of any real value, and it has been superseded by Bosworth's books and articles on the Ghaznavids.

234 Ibn Iskandar, Kai Kā'ūs. A Mirror for Princes, the Qabus Nama by Kai Ka'us ibn Iskandar, Prince of Gurgan. Translated by Reuben Levy. London: Cresset, 1951, 265 pp.

A translation of a late eleventh-century manual for a Persian prince, valuable for its description of how a provincial Muslim prince should lead the good life.

235 Ibn al-Nadīm. The Fihrist of al-Nadīm: A Tenth Century Survey of Muslim Culture. 2 vols. Edited and translated by Bayard Dodge. New York: Columbia University Press, 1970. 1:570 pp., 2:579 pp.

A monumental translation of Ibn al-Nadīm's "Index" of Arabic authors and books known to him, along with his annotations. An invaluable compendium of knowledge on Islamic culture of the tenth century.

236 Kabir, Mafizullah. The Buwayhid Dynasty of Baghdad (334/946-447/1055). Calcutta: Iran Society, 1964, 248 pp.

The only book-length study of the Būyids available in English, this work is a faithful recapitulation of primary Arabic sources, covering the political history of the Būyids and discussing religion, culture, finances, and the military during their rule. Although the book is not very strong on interpretation, the summary of the sources is competently done.

237 Makdisi, George. "The Sunni Revival." In Islamic Civilization: 950-1150 (see 244), pp. 155-68.

Important for its English summary of Makdisi's reinterpretation of the nature and significance of the Saljūq era in the development of the caliphate and Islamic religion. Also significant for its emphasis on the role of schools of jurisprudence in medieval political and religious history.

238 Mez, Adam. The Renaissance of Islam. Translated by S. Khuda Bakhsh and D.S. Margoliouth. London: Luzac, 1937, 537 pp.

The book is mistitled: the subject is Islam in the tenth century, and the book consists of twenty-nine essays on various aspects of Islamic civilization at the time: government, religion, classes, literature, geography, fiscal organization, commerce, etc. Encyclopedic in style, with a wealth of data culled from primary sources, this is a valuable reference work on Arab-Islamic civilization at one of its peak periods. See also 1958, 1990, 2123.

239 Miskawaihi. The Concluding Portion of the Experiences of the Nations by Miskawaihi. 2 vols. Translated by D.S. Margoliouth. Oxford: B. Blackwell, 1921.

A contemporary history of the caliphate under Būyid domination by an official at the Būyid court. See also 245.

240 Narshakhi. The History of Bukhara: Translated from a Persian Abridgment of the Arabic Original by Narshakhi. Translated by Richard Frye. Cambridge, Mass.: Mediaeval Academy of America, 1954, 178 pp.

The Arabic original was written in the mid-tenth century. The translator's notes are full and informative.

241 Nāẓim, Muḥammad. The Life and Times of Sultan Maḥmūd of Ghazna. Cambridge: Cambridge University Press, 1931, 271 pp.

A summary of Maḥmūd's campaigns from primary sources, with a sympathetic sketch of his life and achievements.

242 Niẓām al-Mulk. The Book of Government or Rules for Kings: The Siyāsat-nāma or Siyar al-Mulūk. Translated by Hubert Darke. London: Routledge & K. Paul, 1960, 259 pp.

This eleventh-century manual of statecraft by the vizier of the Saljūq sulṭān demonstrates very neatly the enormous influence of the pre-Islamic Persian tradition on the evolution of Muslim governments.

243 Rice, Tamara Talbot. The Seljuks in Asia Minor. London: Thames & Hudson, 1961, 280 pp.

Actually a history of Saljūq art in Anatolia, the book does contain sections on Saljūq political and social history, largely superseded by Cahen's Pre-Ottoman Turkey (see 228).

244 Richards, D.S., ed. Islamic Civilization 950-1150. Oxford: B. Cassierer, 1973, 284 pp.

Contains fifteen papers that attempt to depict and explain the transformation of Islamic civilization during the specified time span. Many focus on the results of the Saljūq invasions and significantly change the traditional view. One paper looks at the activities of the Berbers in the Maghreb at the time. Makdisi's article, "The Sunni Revival" (see 237), is of great importance for a summary of most of his scholarship, previously available only in French.

245 Rudhrawarī, Abu Shujāʿ, and Helal Ibn Muhassin. Continuation of the Experiences of the Nations: Reign of Ta'i' and Quadir. 7 vols. Translated by D.S. Margoliouth. Oxford: B. Blackwell, 1921.

A continuation of Miskawayhī's history of the caliphate under the Būyids (see 239).

246 Vryonis, Speros. The Decline of Medieval Hellenism in Asia Minor and the Process of Islamization from the Eleventh through the Fifteenth Century. Berkeley: University of California Press, 1971, 532 pp.

Vryonis is one of the few scholars with equal competence in Greek and Turkish sources; his decision to study the transformation of Byzantium into Islamic civilization in Anatolia was natural--though courageous, given the magnitude of the task. His superbly documented study is one of the most significant works on the history of the Middle East published in recent years and should serve as a model for studies of the process of Islamization in other parts of the Muslim world.

Fāṭimid and Ayyūbid Egypt and Syria: The Ismā'īlīs (See also 1494-1519)

247 Ehrenkreutz, Andrew S. Saladin. Albany: State University Press, 1972, 290 pp.

A provocative study of the career of Ṣalāḥ al-dīn, based on exhaustive research in the Arabic sources and Western secondary studies of the Ayyūbids and the Crusaders. Of necessity dwelling long on military campaigns, the author reviews such recent economic and religious data as are available and ends with a surprisingly negative estimate of Ṣalāḥ al-dīn's achievements viewed against the needs of Egypt.

248 Gibb, H.A.R. The Life of Saladin from the Works of 'Imād ad-Dīn and Bahā' ad-Dīn. Oxford: The Clarendon Press, 1973, 76 pp.

A close construction of the life of Ṣalāḥ al-dīn from two contemporary histories that were favorably disposed to him.

249 _____. Saladin: Studies in Islamic History. Edited by Yusuf Ibish. Beirut: Arab Institute for Research and Publishing, 1974, 210 pp.

A collection of eight of Gibb's articles published in journals on Ṣalāḥ al-dīn and his descendants, the Ayyūbids. These, with Gibb's Life of Saladin (see 248), constitute the "standard" interpretation of Ṣalāḥ al-dīn in contrast to Ehrenkreutz's iconoclastic version (see 247).

250 Goitein, S.D. A Mediterranean Society: The Jewish Communities of the Arab World as Portrayed in the Documents of the Cairo Geniza. Vol. 1, Economic Foundations, 550 pp. Vol. 2, The Community, 633 pp. Berkeley: University of California Press, 1967-1971.

These volumes, the first in a series, derive their enormous importance from the source material on which they are based, i.e. documents found in a Cairo synagogue. Although the documents are fragmentary and limited to the Jewish communities and their contacts with the Muslims, Goitein in a tour de force has been able to reconstruct the social and economic conditions during the Fāṭimid and Ayyūbid periods.

251 Hitti, Philip K. The Origins of the Druze People and Religion with Extracts from Their Sacred Writings. New York: Columbia University Press, 1928, 80 pp.

A short monograph on the Druzes, outlining their history and beliefs, with an emphasis on their racial origins. A serviceable introduction to this obscure Lebanese sect. See also 1555.

252 Hodgson, M.G.S. The Order of the Assassins: The Struggle of the Early Nizārī Ismā'īlīs against the Islamic World. The Hague: Mouton, 1955, 352 pp.

The standard history of the rise of the Assassins from the Ismā'īlī movement through Mamlūk times, with an analysis of their doctrines; it is one of the fullest and most competent studies of any branch of the Shī'ah. See also 1500.

253 Ivanow, W. Ismaili Tradition concerning the Rise of the Fatimids. London: Oxford, 1942, 337 pp.

A review of Ismā'īlī sources on the disputed question of the genealogy of the Fāṭimids that refutes Bernard Lewis's views on this subject (see 256). A useful summary of the Ismā'īlī position by a sympathetic observer. The texts and translations of relevant sources are included.

254 Lane-Poole, Stanley. Saladin and the Fall of the Kingdom of Jerusalem. Beirut: Khayats, 1964, 416 pp.

A more or less faithful summary of the Arabic and Western sources for the career of the most famous of medieval Muslim military and political leaders. See also 247.

255 Lewis, Bernard. The Assassins: A Radical Sect in Islam. London: Weidenfeld & Nicolson, 1967, 166 pp.

A popular version of Lewis's earlier work on the Shī'ah (see 256). Though not as scholarly as his other efforts, it is still an excellent study of the sect and its role in the development of Shī'ism and medieval Islamic history.

256 _____. The Origins of Ismā'īlism. Cambridge: Heffer, 1940, 114 pp.

A brilliant but controversial interpretation of a decisive moment in the history of the Shī'ah. Though rejected by the Ismā'īlīs themselves, this work laid the foundation for Lewis's reputation in Islamics and, if nothing else, graphically demonstrates the complexity of Shī'ī history and the incredible difficulty in reconstructing it. Lewis's thesis was challenged by Ivanow (see 253).

257 Mamour, Prince P.H. Polemics on the Origin of the Fatimi Caliphs. London: Luzac, 1934, 230 pp.

A survey of the arguments on the genealogy of the Fāṭimids, and Mamour's conclusions that their claim to descent from 'Alī and Fāṭimah is verifiable.

258 O'Leary, De Lacy. A Short History of the Fatimid Caliphate. New York: Dutton, 1923, 267 pp.

A summary of Fāṭimid history based to a large extent on later Arab historians unsympathetic to Ismā'īlī Shī'ism. Dated in other respects as well, it should be supplemented by Canard's article "The Fāṭimids" (see 1483). Still the fullest study of the Fāṭimids available in English.

259 Rabie, Hassanein. The Financial System of Egypt--A.H. 564-741/A.D. 1169-1341. London: Oxford, 1972, 242 pp.

A reconstruction of the organization and function of the financial-land bureaucracy during Ayyūbid and Mamlūk times, based on an exhaustive reading of a wide variety of sources. In this pioneering study Rabie has assembled an enormous amount of information on the land, taxation, and monetary systems and on the financial administration, providing a starting point for scholars interested in other times and areas.

260 Slaughter, Gertrude. Saladin (1138-1193): A Biography. New York: Exposition Press, 1955, 304 pp.

An undocumented popular version; the author consulted Arabic texts through translation.

261 Stern, S.M. Fatimid Decrees: Original Documents from the Fatimid Chancery. London: Faber, 1964, 188 pp.

Translation of and commentary on ten decrees dating from the Fāṭimid period of Egyptian history.

262 Vatikiotis, P.J. The Fatimid Theory of State. Lahore: Orientalia, 1957, 223 pp.

An important contribution to Fāṭimid history because of the author's careful effort to distinguish between the writings of hostile Sunnī polemicists and those of the Fāṭimids themselves. Though he did not completely resolve the historiographical difficulties, Vatikiotis went as far as possible, given the sources available to him at the time.

The Crusades

263 Atiya, Aziz S. The Crusade: Historiography and Bibliography. Bloomington: University of Indiana Press, 1962, 170 pp.

This is a companion volume to Atiya's Crusade Commerce and and Culture (Bloomington: University of Indiana Press, 1962), a readable but somewhat superficial history of the Crusades. The bibliographical section is especially useful for Arabic sources on the Crusades, often neglected in European histories, and together with Gabrieli's Arab Historians of the Crusades (see 265) gives a good introduction to Arab writing on this subject.

264 _____. The Crusade in the Later Middle Ages. 2d ed. New York: Kraus, 1970, 604 pp.

This work is important for its refusal to abide by the usual periodization of the Crusades, which proclaims their end with the fall of the kingdoms of the Levant. Atiya rightly includes the later attacks of Christendom against Islam--literary as well as military--as a continuation of the Crusading impulse.

265 Gabrieli, Francesco, ed. Arab Historians of the Crusades. Translated by E.J. Castello. Berkeley and Los Angeles: University of California Press, 1969, 362 pp.

Translations of Arab historians on the Crusades, with a short introduction and brief notes. Excellent for showing how the Muslims viewed the Crusades and as an antidote to the one-sided historiography on the subject.

266 Ibn al-Qalanisi. The Damascus Chronicle of the Crusades. Translated by H.A.R. Gibb. London: Luzac, 1965, 368 pp.

As valuable as this eyewitness account of Syria may be, it is Gibb's superb introductory essay outlining the complex political situation in Syria on the eve of the Crusades that gives this book its considerable significance.

267 Mayer, Hans E. The Crusades. Translated by John Gillingham. London: Oxford, 1972, 339 pp.

A very useful summary of the present state of scholarship on the Crusades, incorporating research published since the standard works by Runciman (see 268) and Setton (see 269).

268 Runciman, S. A History of the Crusades. Vol. 1, The First Crusade and the Foundation of the Kingdom of Jerusalem, 377 pp. Vol. 2, The Kingdom of Jerusalem, 523 pp. Vol. 3, The Kingdom of Acre and the Later Crusades, 530 pp. London: Penguin, 1965. Orig. pub. by Cambridge, 1951-1958.

An outstanding work of scholarship, the definitive narrative history of the Crusades in any language. Based largely on Western (i.e., non-Arabic) sources and written with a palpable Byzantine bias, it by no means neglects the Muslim side, which Runciman manages to cover quite competently with the aid of translations and secondary sources. Superbly written, it is a rare example of the kind of work that satisfies scholars and the public alike.

269 Setton, K.M., ed. A History of the Crusades. Vol. 1, The First Hundred Years, 707 pp. Vol. 2, The Later Crusades, 1189-1311, 871 pp. Vol. 3, The Fourteenth and Fifteenth Centuries, 813 pp. Vol. 4, The Art and Architecture of the Crusader States, 414 pp. Madison: University of Wisconsin Press, 1969-1977.

A massive cooperative effort by an international team of scholars to produce the definitive history of the Crusades. These volumes are valuable for Islamic history, containing articles by such authorities as Gibb, Cahen, and Lewis on various aspects of the Crusades from Islamic sources. Those based on Western sources are equally informative and authoritative. Two more volumes remain to be published.

270 Stevenson, W.B. The Crusaders in the East: A Brief History of the Wars of Islam with the Latins in Syria during the Twelfth and Thirteenth Centuries. Cambridge: Cambridge University Press, 1907, 387 pp.

A concise history, which is still of interest if only because it takes the Arabic histories into account.

271 Usāmah Ibn-Munqidh. Memoirs of an Arab-Syrian Gentleman, or an Arab Knight in the Crusades: Memoirs of Usāmah Ibn-Munqidh (Kitāb al-I'tibār). Translated by Philip K. Hitti. Beirut: Khayats, 1964, 265 pp. Orig. pub. in 1927.

Translation of the memoirs of a Syrian Arab who fought in the Crusades against the Franks and whose memoirs are a rare and invaluable source for twelfth-century Syrian and Palestinian social history as well as for the mentality of a minor military figure of the time.

Mamlūk Egypt and Syria

272 Anṣarī, ʿUmar b. Ibrāhīm al-Awsī al-. A Muslim Manual of War, Being Tafrīj al-Kurūb fī Tadbīr al-Ḥurūb. Edited and Translated by George T. Scanlon. Cairo: American University at Cairo Press, 1961, 227 pp.

Translation of a Mamlūk treatise on the principles and tactics of warfare, representative of a genre.

273 Ayalon, David. Gunpowder and Firearms in the Mamluk Kingdom. London: Valentine, Mitchell, 1956, 154 pp.

A closely argued and documented monograph showing that the Ottomans defeated the Mamlūks because the latter refused to adapt their traditional cavalry-based warfare to new weaponry, considering the use of artillery a violation of the ethos of their culture. The significance of this work is thus much broader than its title indicates and the work is essential for an understanding of the late medieval military attitude. See also 1920.

274 Fischel, Walter J. Ibn Khaldun in Egypt; His Public Functions and His Historical Research: A Study in Islamic Historiography. Berkeley: University of California Press, 1967, 217 pp.

Valuable as a summary of the biographical data available on Ibn Khaldūn for this phase of his career, his historical writing on contemporary Egypt, and his discussion of monotheistic religions: neither of these two latter subjects is usually dealt with in scholarly treatments of Ibn Khaldūn's "philosophy of history." Contains an exhaustive bibliography.

275 Ibn Taghrībirdī. History of Egypt (1382-1469 A.D.). 8 vols. Translated by William Popper. Berkeley: University of California Press, 1954-1963.

Translations of Arabic annals of Egyptian and Syrian history under the Mamlūks, 1382-1469; an invaluable primary source for this period.

276 Lapidus, I.M. Mulsim Cities in the Later Middle Ages. Cambridge, Mass.: Harvard University Press, 1967, 307 pp.

A seminal study on Islamic urban structure and society. Not as broad in scope as the title indicates, it is limited to Cairo, Damascus, and Aleppo during the Mamlūk period (1250-1517) and is useful mainly for its analysis of the dynamics of the society of these cities. It is marred by an impossibly complex critical apparatus, which makes it difficult to test Lapidus's interpretation.

277 Latham, J.D., and Paterson, W.F. Saracen Archery: An English Version and Exposition of a Mameluke Work on Archery (ca. A.D. 1368). London: Holland Press, 1970, 219 pp.

An outstanding monograph on the nature, role, and significance of archery in Muslim warfare, in the form of an expert translation and exposition of a fourteenth-century text on archery.

278 Little, Donald P. An Introduction to Mamlūk Historiography: An Analysis of Arabic Annalistic and Biographical Sources for the Reign of al-Malik an-Nāṣir Muḥammad ibn Qalā'ūn. Wiesbaden: F. Steiner Verlag, 1970, 154 pp.

A study of the nature of the sources for fourteenth-century Egyptian and Syrian history and an attempt to determine the originality of various historians and the interrelationships among them.

279 Muir, Sir William. The Mameluke or Slave Dynasty of Egypt, 1260-1517. London: Smith, Elder, 1896, 245 pp.

This brief history of the Malūks is based in the main on the last two volumes of G. Weil's Geschichte der Chalifen, 5 vols. (1846-1862) which is itself a summary of primary Arabic sources. This work is a serviceable outline of the political events of the reign of each of the Mamlūk sulṭāns, but Lane-Poole accomplishes the same thing with a better sense of proportion and perspective in his work (see 153).

280 Poliak, A.N. Feudalism in Egypt, Syria, Palestine, and the Lebanon, 1250-1900. London: Royal Asiatic Society, 1939, 87 pp.

An attempt to pour the Muslim iqṭā' system into a Western European feudal mold. Although Poliak is the acknowledged pioneer in the field of Muslim "fiefs" and in spite of the fact that he based his study on original sources, much of his work suffers from a tendency toward hasty generalization. This is still a basic work, if only for its compilation of material from primary Arabic sources.

281 Popper, William. Egypt and Syria under the Circassian Sultans, 1382-1468 A.D.: Systematic Notes to Ibn Taghrī Birdī's Chronicles of Egypt. 2 vols. Berkeley: University of California Press, 1955-1957, 1:120 pp.; 2:123 pp.

Invaluable notes on administrative and military terms and offices, the geography and topography of the Mamlūk empire, weights and measures, coinage and prices.

India

282 Bīrūnī, al-. Alberuni's India: An Account of the Religion, Philosophy, Literature, Geography, Chronology, Astronomy, Customs, Laws and Astrology of India, about A.D. 1030. 2 vols. Translated by Edward C. Sachau. Lahore: Government of West Pakistan, 1962, 1:543 pp.; 2:606 pp.

A translation of an eleventh-century Muslim's description of India and Hindu society, illustrating the great scientific and literary achievements of medieval Islamic civilization.

283 Habibullah, A. The Foundation of Muslim Rule in India. 2d rev. ed. Allahabad: Central Book Depot, 1961, 389 pp.

A history of the conquest of India and the sultanate of Delhi (1206-1290) that closely follows the primary sources. It is primarily military and political history, with short chapters on the arts and society.

284 Haig, Sir T.W., ed. The Cambridge History of India. Vol. 3, Turks and Afghans. Cambridge: Cambridge University Press, 1928, 752 pp.

A collaborative effort by British and Hindu historians that reflects the British view of the precolonial period and the benefits that accrued from colonization. Straightforward narrative in the main, stressing, however, the authoritarian and unstable quality of life in Muslim India.

285 Hardy, P. Historians of Medieval India. London: Luzac, 1960, 146 pp.

An excellent historiographical analysis of the pre-Mughal period that characterizes the works of the principal historians and outlines the pitfalls involved in using them. This work should accompany the reading of straightforward histories of Muslim India, almost all of which are uncritical of the sources upon which they are based.

286 Majumdar, R.D., ed. The History and Culture of the Indian People. Vol. 6, The Delhi Sultanate (1300-1526 A.D.). Bombay: Bharatiya Vidya Bhavan, 1960, 882 pp.

Primarily a narrative account of the political history of the sultanate with chapters on religion and culture; this Hindu version of the sultanate should be compared with the Muslim one by Habibullah (see 283).

287 Moreland, W.H. The Agrarian System of Moslem India: A Historical Essay with Appendices. Delhi: Oriental Books, 1968, 296 pp.

Moreland has tried to trace the history of the peasantry, the bottom layer of Mulsim society in India, and its relationship to the state, from the thirteenth through the eighteenth centuries. Because of the nature of the sources, much of this is administrative history, but this is a refreshing change from the monotonous repetition of political events found in most histories of medieval India.

288 Nizami, K.A. Some Aspects of Religion and Politics in India during the Thirteenth Century. Aligarh: Department of History, Aligarh Muslim University, 1961, 421 pp.

One of the most interesting studies of Islamic religious life in medieval India, with special emphasis on mysticism and the relationship of ʿulamāʾ and Ṣūfīs to the state. It also includes a section on thirteenth-century political history. Nizami has been criticized for exaggerating the role of the Ṣūfīs in India, but this is a refreshing contrast to the many works that dwell exclusively on political and military history with only cursory attention to religious factors.

289 Qureshi, I.H. The Administration of the Sultanate of Delhi. Lahore: Sh. Muhammad Ashraf, 1942, 313 pp.

This outline of the structure of the state and army relies too heavily on theory, which did not always accurately reflect practice. A curious combination of Cambridge political science, Islamic apologetics, and communalism, it is nonetheless a notch above much historical writing on medieval India and provides the basic material for comparing the military "slave" state in India with the same phenomenon elsewhere in the Islamic world. See also 1959.

290 Srivastava, Ashirbadi Lal. The Sultanate of Delhi (Including the Arab Invasion of Sindh), 711-1526 A.D. Agra: Shiva Lal Agarwala, 1953, 419 pp.

A summary of the Muslim history of India from original sources; most of the text is devoted to political events of the sultanate period. There are also short chapters on culture and administration.

The Mongols and Central Asia

291 Barthold, V.V. Four Studies on the History of Central Asia. 3 vols. Translated by V. Minorsky and T. Minorsky. Leiden: E.J. Brill, 1956-1962, 1:183 pp.; 2:200 pp.; 3:187 pp.

Volume 1 contains "History of the Semire-Chye" and "A Short History of Turkestan," the latter being a welcome summary of Barthold's long and difficult magnum opus, Turkestan down to the Mongol Invasion (see 148). Volume 2 is a study of "Ulugh Beg," grandson of Tīmūr (Tamerlane), ruler of Transoxiana in the fifteenth century. Volume 3 contains a study of Mīr ʿAlī Shāh, the fifteenth-century poet and patron, and a history of the Turkman people from earliest times to the nineteenth century.

292 Boyle, J.A., ed. The Cambridge History of Iran. Vol. 5, The Saljuq and Mongol Periods (see 226).

293 Bretschneider, E.V. Medieval Researches from Eastern Asiatic Sources: Fragments towards the Knowledge of the Geography and History of Central and Western Asia from the Thirteenth to the Seventeenth Century. 2 vols. New York: Barnes & Noble, 1967, 1:334 pp.; 2:352 pp. Orig. pub. in 1887.

Some of these essays give information on the history of Islamic Central Asia from Chinese sources.

294 Clavijo, Ruy Gonzalez de. Narrative of the Embassy to the Court of Tamerlane at Samarcand A.D. 1403-1406. Translated by Clemenes R. Markham. New York: B. Franklin, n.d., 200 pp.

A translation of the journal of a fifteenth-century Spanish ambassador to Samarqand, with impressions of places and persons en route.

295 Davy, Major William, trans. Institutes Political and Military Written Originally in the Mogul Language by the Great Timour, Improperly Called Tamerlane. Oxford: Clarendon, 1783, 408 pp.
The memoirs of Tīmūr, produced in the seventeenth century. They are probably apocryphal, according to E.G. Browne (see 66), though their authenticity is defended by some scholars.

296 DeRachewiltz, I. Papal Envoys to the Great Khans. London: Faber & Faber, 1971, 230 pp.
A summary of the travel literature produced by envoys sent by the Vatican to Mogol courts from the twelfth through the fourteenth centuries. A useful outline of a substantial amount of the original material available on papal attempts to secure an alliance with the Mongols.

297 Hookham, Hilda. Tamburlaine the Conqueror. London: Hodder & Stoughton, 1962, 344 pp.
A popular biography of Tīmūr, but based on a reading of original Persian sources. Its usefulness is somewhat lessened by the paucity of footnotes.

298 Howorth, Henry. History of the Mongols from the Ninth to the Nineteenth Century. 5 vols. London: Longmans, Green, 1876-1927.
The fullest, most detailed history of the Mongols available in English, based on the sources then available to Howorth, often in translation or at secondhand through Constantin M. d'Ohsson's four-volume Histoire des Mongols 2d ed., (Amsterdam: F. Müller, 1852).

299 Ibn ʿArabshāh. Tamurlane, or Timur the Great Amir. Translated by J.H. Saunders. London: Luzac, 1936, 341 pp.
A hostile account of the career of Tīmūr and his son, Shāh Rukh; one of the chief sources for Tīmūr and his dynasty.

300 Juvaini, ʿAtā-Malik. The History of the World-Conqueror. 2 vols. Translated by J.A. Boyle. Manchester: University of Manchester Press, 1958, 1:361 pp., 2:401.
An expert translation of the thirteenth-century history of the Mongols by a Persian in the service of the Mongols. Along with Rashīd al-Dīn's Jamiʿ al- Tawārīkh (Universal History), this is one of the chief sources for Mongol history. Boyle's introduction is short, but there are copious notes.

301 Komroff, Manuel, ed. Contemporaries of Marco Polo. New York: Boni & Liveright, 1928, 358 pp.
Accounts of life at Mongol courts by Western envoys and travelers.

302 Prawdin, Michael. The Mongol Empire, Its Rise and Legacy. London: G. Allen & Unwin, 1961, 581 pp.
A popular survey of Mongol history, beginning with Čingīz-Khān and ending with twentieth-century Mongolia. No documentation is provided.

303 Rashīd al-Dīn. The Successors of Genghis Khan. Translated by John A. Boyle. New York: Columbia University Press, 1971, 372 pp.
A translation of the section of Rashīd al-Dīn's Jāmiʿ al-Tawārīkh from the death of Čingīz-Khān until 1307, that is, through the reign of Oljeitu, including the establishment of the Golden Horde and the campaigns into eastern Europe. One of four projected volumes on this work, by one of the world's leading authorities on medieval Persian history and literature.

304 Samolin, William. East Turkestan in the Twelfth Century: A Brief Political Survey. The Hague: Mouton, 1964, 100 pp.
Useful to the Islamicist since it is based on Chinese histories supplemented by archaeological material, both of which are normally outside his ken. The section on the Qarakhanids is of special interest.

305 Saunders, J.J. The History of the Mongol Conquests. London: Routledge & K. Paul, 1971, 275 pp.
Saunders follows the traditional interpretation of the conquests as an unmitigated disaster for those upon whom they were inflicted, disregarding recent works that have viewed the contemporary literary accounts as more than slightly exaggerated. Nevertheless, it is useful to have a concise account in English of the traditional view of the whole sweep of the invasions.

306 Smith, John Masson, Jr. The History of the Sarbadar Dynasty, 1336-1381 A.D., and Its Sources. The Hague: Mouton, 1970, 216 pp.
A study of one of the dynasties that ruled Khurāsān after the Il-Khāns, with a detailed analysis of the sources, including coins.

307 Spuler, Bertold. History of the Mongols, Based on Eastern and Western Accounts of the Thirteenth and Fourteenth Centuries. Translated by H. Drummond and S. Drummond. London: Routledge & K. Paul, 1972, 221 pp.
A short introduction to translated passages from contemporary historians of the Mongol invasions. These are, of course, English translations of Spuler's German translations except when English translations already existed. Like other such composite reconstructions, this one is disjointed, but it has the undeniable merit of giving the student a taste of original sources and encouraging sampling.

308 Vernadsky, George. A History of Russia. Vol. 3, The Mongols and Russia. New Haven, Conn.: Yale University Press, 1953, 462 pp.
This book covers the Mongol conquest of Russia and is especially valuable for the history of the Golden Horde (the Muslim Khanate in southern Russia) during the fourteenth and fifteenth centuries.

Yemen

309 Ḥakamī, al-. Yaman: Its Early Medieval History. Translated and edited by Henry Cassels Kay. London: Arnold, 1892, 511 pp.
Translations of original Arabic texts on the medieval history of Yemen.

310 Khazrajī, ʿAlī Ibn Ḥasan al-. The Pearl Strings: A History of the Resūliyy Dynasty of Yemen. 3 vols. Translated by Sir John Redhouse. Leiden: E.J. Brill, 1908.
The first two volumes contain a translation of the fifteenth-century history of Yemen under the Rasūltids, who flourished in the thirteenth and fourteenth centuries. The last volume contains Redhouse's notes.

311 Varthema, Ludovico di. The Travels of Ludovico di Varthema in Egypt, Syria, Arabia Deserta, and Arabia Felix, in Persia, India, and Ethiopia, A.D. 1503-1508. Translated from the 1510 edition by J.W. Jones and edited by C.P. Badger. New York: Burt Franklin, 1963, 320 pp.
The identity of Varthema and the purpose of his travels in the Middle East, other than tourism, are unknown, but these memoirs are a detailed source for sixteenth-century Muslim social history over a wide area.

North Africa

312 Hopkins, J.F.P. Medieval Muslim Government in Barbary until the Sixth Century of the Hijra. London: Luzac, 1958, 169 pp.
Concise presentation of primary source material on the structure of Muslim administration in North Africa until the time of Almohades. Includes analysis of the financial system, the army, judiciary, bureaucracy, dhimmīs, and the Almohade tribal structure. It reads like a dissertation, which it was.

313 Tourneau, Roger Le. The Almohad Movement in North Africa in the Twelfth and Thirteenth Centuries. Princeton, N.J.: Princeton University Press, 1969, 127 pp.
Three lectures, by a leading authority, on the rise, consolidation, and decline of the Almohad Empire, providing an excellent survey, the best in English, of this aspect of North African history.

314 ______. Fez in the Age of the Marinides. Translated by B.A. Clement. Norman: University of Oklahoma Press, 1961, 158 pp.
A short history of Fās, 1331-1348.

Spain

315 Burns, Robert Ignatious. Islam under the Crusaders: Colonial Survival in the Thirteenth-Century Kingdom of Valencia. Princeton, N.J.: Princeton University Press, 1973, 475 pp.
Arguing that the fall of the Muslim kingdom of Valencia in the thirteenth century should be regarded as an integral part of the Crusades and that this episode offers fuller documentation than the campaigns in the East for the effect of Christian incursions on Muslim territory, Burns proceeds to show how and in what form Islamic society survived in Valencia.

316 ______. Medieval Colonialism: Postcrusade Exploitation of Islamic Valencia. Princeton, N.J.: Princeton University Press, 1975, 394 pp.
A companion volume to the same author's Islam under the Crusaders (see 315), this work analyzes the tax structure of thirteenth-century Valencia as a means of depicting the decline and transformation of an Islamic society as a result of the Reconquista. Both works demonstrate Burns's command of his sources and his subject, hitherto neglected by scholars.

317 Chejne, Anwar G. Muslim Spain: Its History and Culture. Minneapolis: University of Minnesota Press, 1974, 559 pp.
The fullest survey of the history of Islam in Spain currently available in English.

318 Dozy, Reinhart. Spanish Islam: A History of the Moslems in Spain. Translated by Francis Griffin Stokes. London: Chatto & Windus, 1913, 747 pp.
A narrative history of Islamic Spain through the eleventh century, this classic has been superseded in many respects by the research of E. Levi-Provencal (Histoire de l'Espagne Musulmane, Paris: G.P. Maisonneuve, 1950-). This volume is still useful, however, for its summation of original Arabic sources.

319 Haines, C.R. Christianity and Islam in Spain, A.D. 756-1031. London: K. Paul, Trench, 1889, 182 pp.
An essay on Muslim-Christian interaction during the height of Islamic culture in Spain, based on Latin sources and such Arabic works as had been translated by the end of the nineteenth century. This is still a useful introduction to a subject that has not generally been explored in depth in surveys.

320 Ḥajjī, ʿAbdurraḥmān ʿAlī al-. Andalusian Diplomatic Relations with Western Europe during the Umayyad Period (A.H. 13-166/A.D. 755-976): An Historical Survey. Beirut: Dar al-Irshad, 1970, 333 pp.
The author has collected all the information that he could find in Arabic sources on Spanish Umayyad relations with the Christians of Spain, the Franks, Vikings, Germans, and Italians, a field heretofore virtually unexplored in English.

321 Hale, Edwyn. Andalus: Spain under the Muslims. London: R. Hale, 1958, 189 pp.
A popular history based entirely on English, Spanish, and French secondary sources, without scholarly apparatus, by a former British consular official.

322 Ibn ʿAbd al-Hakam. The History of the Conquest of Spain. Translated by J.H. Jones. New York: B. Franklin, 1969, 119 pp.
The Arabic text and English translation of a short account of the Muslim conquest of Spain by a ninth-century Egyptian historian. Ends with the year 743 A.D.

323 Imamuddin, S.M. The Economic History of Spain (under the Umayyads, 711-1031 A.D.). Dacca: Asiatic Society of Pakistan, 1963, 537 pp.

An English version of a dissertation submitted to the University of Madrid, the book does not quite live up to its title; it is rather an encyclopedic survey of what can be found in Arabic and other sources on agriculture, mining, industry, trade, and finance. These data, though very useful, have not been synthesized in a very meaningful way, which would admittedly be an enormously difficult task.

324 _____. A Political History of Muslim Spain. Dacca: Najmah, 1969, 431 pp.

A summary of a disparate variety of sources, some original, some secondary, some unfortunately outdated. Though more detailed than Watt's survey (see 329), it is also concise and superficial, more in the nature of an outline than an interpretive study.

325 Lane-Poole, Stanley. The Moors in Spain. London: T. Fisher Unwin, 1887, 285 pp.

A popular summary of R. Dozy's Histoire des Musulmans d'Espagne (see 318), but enlivened by Lane-Poole's pro-Muslim, anti-Catholic bias.

326 Maqqarī, Aḥmad ibn Muḥammad al-. History of the Mohammedan Dynasties of Spain. 2 vols. Translated by Pascual de Gayangos. London: Oriental Translation Fund, 1840-1843.

Translation of a seventeenth-century work on the history of Islamic Spain and the life of the famous historian and vizier Ibn al-Khaṭīb. Though the work is late, it quotes earlier sources. The translator's notes are helpful.

327 Monroe, J.T. The Shuʿūbiyya in Al-Andalus: The Risāla of Ibn Garcia and Five Refutations. Berkeley: University of California Press, 1970, 105 pp.

Although the Shuʿūbiyyah movement (the movement that challenged Arab cultural and social supremacy in the emerging Islamic empire) has received a great deal of attention for its Eastern manifestations, this is the first, most welcome, study of its development in Spain, written in English. Monroe's introduction to his translation of the tracts provides much information on this subject difficult to obtain elsewhere.

328 Nykl, A.R. Hispano-Arabic Poetry and Its Relations with Old Provencal Troubadors. Baltimore: J.H. Furst Co., 1946, 416 pp.

This approach is conventionally historical: sketches of main historical features introduce the discussion of the major poets of each period, along with samples of their work in English translation.

329 Watt, W. Montgomery. A History of Muslim Spain. Edinburgh: University of Edinburgh Press, 1965, 125 pp.

Given the lack of competent studies of Muslim Spain in English, this brief and superficial book is of necessity widely used. It is little more than an outline of the main periods of Muslim history in Spain, with sections on literature by Pierre Cachia.

Indonesia and Malaysia

330 Fatimi, S.Q. Islam Comes to Malaysia. Edited by Shirlee Gordon. Singapore: Malaysian Sociological Research Institute, 1963, 102 pp.

A useful summation of what is known about the spread of Islam in Malaysia, where large-scale conversions began in the thirteenth century.

331 Van Leur, J.C. Indonesian Trade and Society. The Hague: W. Van Hoeve, 1955, 465 pp.

Some of the articles collected in this volume bear on the role of trade and merchants in the conversion of Indonesia to Islam.

THE LATE MEDIEVAL AND EARLY MODERN EMPIRES (A.D. 1300-1800)

GENERAL

332 Saunders, John J., ed. The Muslim World on the Eve of Europe's Expansion. Englewood Cliffs, N.J.: Prentice-Hall, 1966, 146 pp.

A primer of Islamic history from 1450 to 1500 of the three great empires (Ottoman, Ṣafavid, and Mughal) as well as in Mamlūk Egypt, Southeast Asia, and Black Africa.

333 Stern, S.M., ed. Documents from Islamic Chanceries. Oxford: B. Cassirer, 1965, 254 pp.

Studies of a few of the archival materials that have survived from the late Islamic Middle Ages, along with texts and translations of the documents themselves. Includes commercial and diplomatic documents as well as decrees from the Mamlūk, Ottoman, Ṣafavid, and other chanceries.

THE OTTOMANS

General Studies

Political

334 Aldersen, A.D. The Structure of the Ottoman Dynasty. Oxford: Oxford University Press, 1956, 186 pp.

A reference work, half of which is devoted to indexes and genealogical tables. The introductory chapters cover the circumstances of succession, the role of the harem, marriage, divorce, death. The tables are invaluable.

335 Barber, Noel. Lord of the Golden Horn: The Sultans, Their Harems, and the Fall of the Ottoman Empire. London: Macmillan, 1973, 304 pp.

A popular and vulgar work on the Turks from Sulayman the Magnificent through Atatürk, filled with court and diplomatic gossip about the sulṭāns, with much speculation concerning the power of the harem in Ottoman affairs. Delightful leisure reading, with splendid illustrations, but of dubious scholarly value.

336 Creasy, Edward S. History of the Ottoman Turks: From the Beginning of Their Empire to the Present Time. Beirut: Khayats, 1961, 560 pp. Orig. pub. by Bentley, 1887.

An uncritical summary of J. von Hammer-Purgstall's monumental history of the Ottomans, which was itself an uncritical but more detailed summary of sources. This is still valuable, however, as the most detailed narrative history of the dynasty in English.

337 Eversley, Lord. The Turkish Empire, Its Growth and Decay. London: T. Fisher Unwin, 1917, 392 pp.

The chapters on the history of the empire through the nineteenth century are based by and large on J. von Hammer-Purgstall's Geschichte des osmanischen Reiches (1827-1835) (Graz: Akademische Druck-u. Verlagsenstalt, 1963; reprint of 1827-1835 edition), while the sections on modern "misrule" down to 1914 are based on other secondary sources. A second edition of the work, published in 1923, adds a section by V. Chirol, which brings the history up to 1922. Of little value now other than as a summary of other European works.

338 Gibb, H.A.R., and H. Bowen. Islamic Society and the West. Vol. 1, Islamic Society in the Eighteenth Century. 2 pts. London: Oxford, 1951, 1:386 pp.; 2:285 pp.

This work was conceived as a study of the transformation of Ottoman political, religious, social, and economic institutions under the impact of the West, beginning toward the end of the eighteenth century. This volume, surveying the state of Ottoman society before Western influences began to be a crucial force, during the eighteenth century, was to be only a preliminary volume. Unfortunately, the authors' grant plan was never realized, and this is all we have; it has recently come under attack for the traditional conceptualization of Islamic society as one of static groups and institutions. Nevertheless, this is an important study, compiling a vast amount of information from Turkish and Arabic sources on various aspects of late Ottoman government and society. It has by no means been superseded. See also 1971, 2117, 2118, 2239.

339 Inalcik, Halil. The Ottoman Empire: The Classical Age, 1300-1600. Translated by Norman Itzkowitz and Colin Imber. New York: Praeger, 1973, 258 pp.

The latest and most authoritative short history of the Ottomans (political, social, economic, and religious), based on extensive reading in the primary and secondary sources. The newcomer to Ottoman history should begin here. See also 1954, 2213.

340 Itzkowitz, Norman. Ottoman Empire and Islamic Tradition. New York: A.A. Knopf, 1972, 117 pp.

A brief outline of Ottoman history intended as an introduction for undergraduates.

341 Karpat, Kemal H. The Ottoman State and Its Place in World History. Leiden: E.J. Brill, 1974, 129 pp.

Seven essays on this theme by such eminent authorities as Toynbee and McNeill, representing the world historians, and Inalcik and Karpat, representing the Ottomanists. The brevity of this volume belies its importance.

342 Knolles, Richard. The General Historie of the Turkes. London: A. Islip, 1603, 1152 pp.

The first, and most detailed, general history of the Turks in English, based in part on the author's own experience in Turkey.

343 Lane-Poole, Stanley. Turkey. London: T. Fisher Unwin, 1888, 365 pp.

One of the many summaries in English of J. von Hammer-Purgstall's Geschichte des osmanischen Reiches (1827-1835) (see 337), its main virtues are concision and readability.

344 Lewis, Bernard. Istanbul and the Civilization of the Ottoman Empire. Norman: University of Oklahoma Press, 1963, 189 pp.

Not one of Lewis's major efforts, the book, based on primary sources, is an outline of Ottoman history, government, and culture and describes the Ottoman capital and court.

345 Pitcher, D. An Historical Geography of the Ottoman Empire from Earliest Times to the End of the Sixteenth Century. Leiden: E.J. Brill, 1974, 171 pp.

An atlas of Ottoman history prefaced by a narrative account of the rise and expansion of the Ottomans.

346 Shaw, Stanford J. History of the Ottoman Empire and Modern Turkey. Vol. 1, Empire of the Gazis: The Rise and Decline of the Ottoman Empire, 1280-1808. Cambridge: Cambridge University Press, 1976, 351 pp.

Comprehensive, detailed, well documented from primary and secondary sources, this is an excellent survey.

347 Vucinich, W.S. The Ottoman Empire: Its Record and Legacy. Princeton, N.J.: D. Van Nostrand, 1965, 191 pp.

A book of short readings on various aspects of Ottoman government and society from the empire at its height to the establishment of the Turkish Republic, preceded by the author's own sketch of Ottoman history. Intended as a primer for undergraduate students.

Cultural, Religious, Social

348 Birge, J.K. The Bektashi Order of Dervishes. Hartford, Conn.: Hartford Seminary Press, 1937, 291 pp.

To those hoping for an analysis of the role of the Bektashīs in Ottoman political-religious history, this book will be disappointing; it is devoted in the main to a survey of sources and a summary of beliefs and rites. Be that as it may, much information is valuable and this is the fullest study of the Bektashīs that we have.

349 Davis, Fanny. The Palace of Topkapi in Istanbul. New York: C. Scribners, 1970, 306 pp.

A systematic description of the seat of the Ottoman sultanate, its architecture and art, along with an explanation of the history and purpose of the various parts of the palace complex. Beautifully illustrated with photographs and earlier illustrations, the book is an excellent source on Ottoman court history.

350 Gibb, E.J.W. A History of Ottoman Poetry. 6 vols. London: Luzac, 1900.

Samples of Ottoman poetry up to 1879 with biographical sketches of authors and an outline of the time in which they lived. Though somewhat old-fashioned as literary history, it is still unsurpassed as the basic work in its field.

351 Hasluck, F.W. Christianity and Islam under the Sultans. Edited by Margaret M. Hasluck. 2 vols. Oxford: Clarendon, 1929, 1:877 pp.; 2:360 pp. Reprint. New York: Octagon Books, 1973.

Hasluck's writings on aspects of religious life under Turkish sulṭāns, edited and published by his wife after his death at the height of his career. Volume 1 contains data on Muslim-Christian use and adaptation of each other's sanctuaries and material on Muslim saints and "heterodox" tribes and cults. Volume 2 consists of miscellaneous material, a substantial portion of which relates to the Bektashī dervish order as well as to various holy persons and places.

352 Lewis, Raphaela. Everyday Life in Ottoman Turkey. New York: G.P. Putnam, 1971, 206 pp.

A fine survey, well illustrated, of the life of the Ottomans, mainly the court and religious notables, though chapters on occupations and provincial life are also included. It helps considerably in filling in the background of Ottoman history.

353 Miller, Barnette. Beyond the Sublime Porte: The Grand Seraglio of Istanbul. New Haven, Conn.: Yale University Press, 1931, 281 pp.

Miller compiles data on the political, military, and bureaucratic institutions of the Ottoman Empire through a historical reconstruction of the seraglio. The book has been largely superseded by the recent work of Fanny Davis (see 349).

354 _____. The Palace School of Mehmed the Conqueror. Cambridge, Mass.: Harvard University Press, 1941, 226 pp.

A monograph that assembles the little information available on the school where the members of the sulṭān's palace service received their training. Valuable for its insights into Ottoman statecraft.

355 Pallis, Alexander. In the Days of the Janissaries: Old Turkish Life as Depicted in the Travel-Book of Evliya Chelebi. London: Hutchinson, 1951, 236 pp.

A compilation of excerpts from a seventeenth-century travel book, relating mainly to social history: guilds, dervishes, sports, etc. The passages from Evliya Chelebi are interspersed with Pallis's commentary, which illuminates much of the original material for the student.

356 Runciman, Sir Steven. The Great Church in Captivity: A Study of the Patriarchate of Constantinople from the Eve of the Turkish Conquest to the Great War of Independence. Cambridge: Cambridge University Press, 1968, 455 pp.

Although the bulk of this book is devoted to internal church history, the second half contains sections on the relationship of the church to the Ottoman state, and orthodoxy to Islam.

357 Ware, Timothy. Eustratios Argenti: A Study of the Greek Church under Turkish Rule. Oxford: Clarendon, 1964, 196 pp.

Focuses on an eminent eighteenth-century theologian of Chios and his writings, but these are only of tangential interest. Ware's background chapters on orthodoxy under Islam are concise and helpful.

Specialized Studies

Origins and Early History

358 Barbaro, Nicolo. Diary of the Siege of Constantinople, 1453. Translated by J.R. Jones. New York: Exposition, 1969, 78 pp.

A contemporary account of the siege by a Venetian surgeon resident in Constantinople.

359 Gibbons, Herbert A. The Foundation of the Ottoman Empire: A History of the Osmanlis up to the Death of Bayezid I, 1300-1403. Oxford: Clarendon, 1916, 379 pp.

A political history that follows medieval Muslim historians rather closely. Much has been superseded by recent research.

360 Pears, Edwin. The Destruction of the Greek Empire and the Story of the Capture of Constantinople by the Turks. London: Longmans, Green, 1903, 476 pp.

A rewriting of the history of Byzantium, 1204-1453, on the basis of sources not available to Gibbons. The author's attitude toward the Turks is that of a Byzantinist.

361 Runciman, Steven. The Fall of Constantinople: A Symposium Held at the School of Oriental and African Studies, 29 May 1953. London: School of Oriental and African Studies, 1955, 44 pp.

A collection of speeches on the occasion of the 500th anniversary of the fall of the city by a distinguished group of scholars, including Runciman and Bernard Lewis, attempting to assess the consequences of the defeat on Byzantine, Islamic, and European history. The predictable conclusion is that the results have heretofore been overestimated.

362 ______. The Fall of Constantinople. London: Cambridge University Press, 1955, 256 pp.

A masterful reconstruction of the fall of Byzantium to the Turks, the events that led up to it, and its aftermath. Should be supplemented by Wittek's book (see 363) for the broader consequences of the fall. Runciman's version of the actual fall of the city is marred by his acceptance of a forged eyewitness account, but the book on the whole is authoritative.

363 Wittek, Paul. The Rise of the Ottoman Empire. London: Royal Asiatic Society, 1958, 54 pp.

A significant monograph that argues that the Ottoman Empire grew, not out of a tribal migration, but from frontier warfare conducted by Turkish principalities of Anatolia. This short work overturned previous scholarship and gave a new direction to Turkish studies.

The Sixteenth Century

364 Allen, W.E.D. Problems of Turkish Power in the Sixteenth Century. London: Central Asian Research Centre, 1963, 92 pp.

A monograph on the Ottomans' attempt to control the trade routes of Asia despite challenges from the Portuguese and the Russians.

365 Busbecq, O.G. de. The Turkish Letter of Ogier Ghiselin de Busbecq. Translated by E.S. Forster. Oxford: Clarendon, 1927, 265 pp.

Letters of the ambassador of Charles V at the court of Sulayman, containing a fascinating picture of Turkey and the Ottoman court during the sixteenth century.

366 Cook, M.A. Population Pressure in Rural Anatolia, 1450-1600. London: Oxford, 1972, 118 pp.

Cook adduces new data to verify and expand Fernand Braudel's thesis (The Mediterranean and the Mediterranean World in the Age of Philip II, 2 vols.; trans. S. Reynolds [New York: Harper & Row, 1976]) that the sixteenth century was a time of Ottoman overpopulation and discusses the implication of this thesis for Ottoman social history. His evidence comes from Ottoman fiscal surveys.

367 Fischer-Galati, S.A. Ottoman Imperialism and German Protestantism, 1521-1555. Cambridge, Mass.: Harvard University Press, 1959, 142 pp.

A study of "the nature and extent of the Turkish impact on the German Reformation in the crucial years before the Religious Peace of Augsburg, with the broader framework of East-West relations in the sixteenth century," mainly based, naturally, on German sources.

368 Jenkins, Hester Donaldson. Ibrahim Pasha, Grand Vizier of Suleiman the Magnificent. New York: Columbia University Press, 1911, 123 pp.

A dissertation compiling all the data on Sulayman's vizier that were available to the author, mainly in European sources. There is a section on general biography and chapters on his administrative, diplomatic, and military career. Interesting, given the lack of biographies of secondary figures in medieval Islamic history.

369 Kortepeter, C. Max. Ottoman Imperialism during the Reformation: Europe and the Caucasus. New York: New York University Press, 1972, 278 pp.

A carefully researched study of Ottoman expansion into eastern Europe, Transcaucasia, and the Crimea in the late sixteenth century, based on primary source material (European and Turkish), which explores the "unholy" alliance of Christian powers with the Turks when their mutual interests required it.

370 Lybyer, A.H. The Government of the Ottoman Empire in the Time of Suleiman the Magnificent. Cambridge, Mass.: Harvard University Press, 1913, 349 pp.

The classic study of Ottoman government that had great influence on subsequent studies in conceptualizing the Ottoman state--and even the Islamic state in general--in terms of a ruling institution comprising a slave family, educational system, army, nobility, and government and a Moslem institution concerned with religious affairs. Although this conceptualization has recently come under fire, the book is still a point of departure for students of Ottoman institutions.

371 Merriman, R.B. Suleiman the Magnificent, 1520-1566. Cambridge, Mass.: Harvard University Press, 1944, 325 pp.

Not so much a biography as a chronicle of the diplomacy and military campaigns undertaken during the reign of Sulayman, which means that Sulayman the Lawgiver is neglected. The author relied almost exclusively on works in European languages.

The Empire in the East

372 Baer, Gabriel. Egyptian Guilds in Modern Times. Jerusalem: Israel Oriental Society, 1964, 192 pp.

By "modern," Baer means Ottoman, the only period for which adequate sources for the history of guilds in Egypt are available. Baer's analysis begins with the guild system of the seventeenth century and carries through to its decline and virtual disappearance in the late nineteenth and early twentieth centuries. Like all of Baer's studies of social and economic history of modern Egypt, this monograph is closely argued, well documented, and significant. See also 1937.

373 Bodman, H.L. Political Factions in Aleppo, 1760-1826. Chapel Hill: University of North Carolina Press, 1963, 125 pp.

An analysis of the role of the Janissaries and the provincial notables in the administration of Aleppo during a "reform" period of the Ottoman Empire.

374 Fisher, S.N. The Foreign Relations of Turkey, 1481-1512. Urbana: University of Illinois Press, 1948, 125 pp.

A study of Ottoman foreign affairs during the reign of Bayezid II, including wars with Venice and Persia, and the dynastic entanglements caused by Bayezid's rival, Jem. It is based mainly on Western sources.

375 Heyd, Uriel. Ottoman Documents on Palestine, 1552-1615: A Study of the Firman according to the Mühimme Defteri. Oxford: Clarendon, 1960, 204 pp.

A compilation of translated firmans relating to the Ottoman occupation of Palestine and a discussion of these firmans as historical sources. It is of considerable historiographical interest.

376 Holt, P.M. Egypt and the Fertile Crescent 1516-1922: A Political History. London: Longmans, 1966, 337 pp.

A history of Egypt and Greater Syria during the Ottoman and colonial periods. The earlier sections are extremely useful since there is little material available in English on this subject; the later ones are valuable for their factual, objective treatment. This is an excellent textbook for the modern period because of the stress on continuity from the Ottoman into the "modern" period.

377 Ibn Iyas. An Account of the Ottoman Conquest of Egypt in the Year A.H. 922 (A.D. 1516). Translated by W.M. Salmon. London: Royal Asiatic Society, 1921, 117 pp.

A translation of a contemporary account of the Ottoman invasion of Egypt.

378 Ma'oz, Moshe. Ottoman Reform in Syria and Palestine, 1840-1861. London: Oxford University Press, 1968, 266 pp.

Traces the attempt to implement the Tanzimat reforms and their impact on government and society. Well grounded in archival sources.

379 Rafeq, Abdul-Karim. The Province of Damascus 1723-1783. Beirut: Khayats, 1966, 370 pp.

Rafeq has used Arabic manuscripts and archival material to reconstruct a detailed history of the province of Damascus under the Ottomans in the eighteenth century, when it was transformed into a local despotism by the Azm family. His work is useful in comparing Damascus with other Arab provinces, most notably Egypt.

380 Sanjian, Avedis K. The Armenian Communities in Syria under Ottoman Domination. Cambridge, Mass.: Harvard University Press, 1965, 390 pp.

This history of the "national" Armenian millet (religious community) in Greater Syria under the Ottomans includes a survey of the internal development of the community, its political relation to the Ottoman governors, and its relations with the surrounding subject Muslim population. It is based mainly on Armenian sources and on French and English studies.

381 Serjeant, R.B. The Portuguese off the South Arabian Coast: Hadrami Chronicles with Yemeni and European Accounts of Dutch Pirates off Mocha in the Seventeenth Century. Oxford: Clarendon, 1963, 233 pp.

A collection of source material on South Arabian history during the sixteenth century, focusing on Portuguese activities as recorded by Hadrami chroniclers and on European and Arabic accounts of Dutch piracy in the seventeenth century. Serjeant is an authority on the area and its history and has an expert command of Yemenī and Ḥadramī Arabic, making this a basic work for the period.

382 Shaw, Stanford J. The Budget of Ottoman Egypt 1005-1006/1596-1597. The Hague: Mouton, 1968, 234 pp.

The Turkish text and English translation of the earliest budget for Ottoman Egypt, an example of the several significant documentary sources Shaw has found and made available to historians.

383 _____. The Financial and Administrative Organization and Development of Ottoman Egypt, 1517-1798. Princeton Oriental Studies, no. 19. Princeton, N.J.: Princeton University Press, 1962, 451 pp.

A pioneering work in Ottoman studies, as one of the first systematic attempts to explain the Ottoman archives as the primary source of Ottoman history. The text is almost unreadable, being crammed with statistics and definitions of Ottoman terms, but is nevertheless an invaluable reference work for the day-to-day administration of an Ottoman province. Shaw's introduction, "The Political Structure and Development of Ottoman's Egypt," is brief but informative and reliable.

384 _____. Ottoman Egypt in the Eighteenth Century. Cambridge, Mass.: Harvard University Press, 1962, 81 pp.

An edition and translation of the Niẓām Nāmah-i Misir by Cezzar Aḥmad Pasha, Ottoman governor of Syria, who was sent in 1785 to Egypt to report on the possibility of an invasion to end the tyranny of the Emirs. An interesting firsthand description of eighteenth-century conditions in the government and the military.

385 Stripling, G.W.F. The Ottoman Turks and the Arabs, 1511-1574. Urbana: University of Illinois Press, 1942, 136 pp.

A study of the Ottoman Turks' relation with the Arabs, based entirely on Western sources, culminating in the conquest of Mamlūk Syria, Egypt, and Iraq.

386 Volney, C.F. Travels through Syria and Egypt, in the Years 1783, 1784, and 1785, Containing the Present Natural and Political State of Those Countries, Their Productions, Arts, Manufactures, and Commerce, with Observations on the Manners, Customs, and Government of the Turks and Arabs. 2 vols. London: G.G.J. & J. Robinson, 1787, 1:418 pp.; 2:515 pp. Reprinted in 1972.

An eighteenth-century Frenchman's impressions of Ottoman Egypt and Syria on the eve of the Napoleonic invasion of Egypt.

The Empire in Europe

387 Abbot, G.F. Under the Turks in Constantinople: A Record of Sir John Finch's Embassy, 1674-1681. London: Macmillan, 1920, 418 pp.
This detailed study of a short but typical episode in the history of Anglo-Turkish relations draws heavily upon Finch's letters and papers.

388 Atiya, Aziz Suryal. The Crusade of Nicopolis. London: Methuen, 1934, 234 pp.
A history of the last effort by Western and Eastern Christians to unite against the Turks, which resulted in the battle between the Ottomans and the allied French, Germans, English, and Hungarians at Nicopolis, on the Danube, in 1396. Based on primary sources, both Eastern and Western, this is a definitive study of "the last Crusade."

389 Barker, Thomas M. Double Eagle and the Crescent: Vienna's Second Turkish Siege and Its Historical Setting. Albany: State University of New York Press, 1967, 447 pp.
Barker has written a detailed account of the 1683 Turkish siege of Vienna, utilizing Austrian archival sources but no Turkish materials. Aimed at a more scholarly audience than Stoye's The Siege of Vienna (see 403), it suffers from the same shortcoming--the lack of a Turkish dimension.

390 Birnbaum, Henrik, and Speros Vryonis. Aspects of the Balkans: Continuity and Change; Contributions to the International Balkan Conference Held at UCLA, October 23-28, 1969. The Hague: Mouton, 1972, 447 pp.
Twenty papers on various aspects of Balkan history, several of which deal with the Balkans under the Ottomans and discuss such subjects as historiography, religion, art, and literature.

391 Bohnstedt, John N. The Infidel Scourge of God: The Turkish Menace as Seen by German Pamphleteers of the Reformation Era. Philadelphia: American Philosophical Society, 1968, 58 pp.
A short monograph that adds still another chapter on European attitudes toward the Turks during the early period of the Ottoman threat to Europe (1522-1543).

392 Cassels, Lavender. The Struggle for the Ottoman Empire, 1717-1740. London: J. Murray, 1966, 226 pp.
A popular diplomatic history of the period that culminated in the Peace of Belgrade in 1739; based on German, French, and English sources.

393 Çelebi, Evliya. Narrative of Travels in Europe, Asia, and Africa by Evliya Efendi. Translated by Joseph von Hammer. London: Oriental Translation Fund, 1850, 244 pp.
Travels throughout the seventeenth-century Ottoman Empire, rich in social history and including eyewitness accounts of military engagements by an official of the Ottoman political, military, and religious institutions. See also 1939.

394 Cheu, Samuel C. The Crescent and the Rose: Islam and England during the Renaissance. New York: Octagon, 1965, 583 pp.
This study of English attitudes toward the Levant (mainly the Ottoman and Şafavid empires), is based chiefly on English literature of the time, including travel memoirs. It is useful for the history of Christian-Muslim misconceptions of each other.

395 Coles, Paul. The Ottoman Impact on Europe. New York: Harcourt Brace & World, 1968, 216 pp.
A popular account of the European reaction to the threat and actuality of Ottoman invasions from the fifteenth through the seventeenth centuries. Concise, well written, with many illustrations, the book is a good introduction to Ottoman expansion in Europe, seen from the Western perspective.

396 Haji, Khalifeh. The History of the Maritime Wars of the Turks. Translated by James Mitchell. London: Oriental Translation Fund, 1831, 80 pp.
A monograph of the famous seventeenth-century Ottoman historian on Ottoman naval campaigns; not very detailed but nonetheless useful.

397 Jelavich, Charles, and Barbara Jelavich, eds. The Balkans in Transition: Essays on the Development of Balkan Life and Politics since the Eighteenth Century. Berkeley: University of California Press, 1963, 451 pp.
Thirteen essays by experts on various aspects of Balkan political and social history during the period of Ottoman decline and the rise of nationalism. The articles "The Ottoman View of the Balkans," by Stanford Shaw, and "Some Aspects of the Ottoman Legacy," by Wayne S. Vucinich, are of particular interest to students of Islamic history.

398 McNeill, William H. Europe's Steppe Frontier, 1500-1800. Chicago: University of Chicago Press, 1964, 252 pp.
McNeill's forte is his ability to synthesize and interpret the research of others. In this collection of five lectures, he has attempted to unite the findings of Islamicists and Ottomanists with those of Eastern European historians to explore the history and significance of the borderlands between the Hapsburg, Russian, and Ottoman states.

399 Munson, William B. The Last Crusade. Dubuque, Ia.: W.C. Brown, 1969, 152 pp.
Diplomatic and military relations between the Ottomans and Christian Europe, culminating in the Treaty of Karlowitz, are summarized from Western sources.

400 Schwoebel, Robert. The Shadow of the Crescent: The Renaissance Image of the Turk. New York: St. Martin's, 1967, 257 pp.
A survey of fifteenth-century attitudes toward and conceptions of the Ottoman Turks, which goes far in explaining the military and diplomatic history of the time. Like Daniel's books (see 187, 479), this work is of great value in tracing the history of the Western idea of Islam.

401 Shay, Mary Lucille. The Ottoman Empire from 1720 to 1734 as Revealed in Dispatches of the Venetian Baili. Urbana: University of Illinois Press, 1944, 165 pp. Reprinted from Illinois Studies in the Social Sciences 27, no. 3 (1944).
Reports on the political, economic, and diplomatic affairs of the Ottoman state by Venetian observers, which confirm the judgments of other contemporary Europeans resident in the capital.

402 Stavrianos, L.S. The Balkans since 1453. New York: Holt, Rinehart & Winston, 1961, 970 pp.
By far the fullest, most detailed study of Balkan history under the Ottomans through World War II, based largely on Western secondary sources. The sections on Ottoman ascendancy and decline present an excellent introduction to Ottoman administration of the countries of the area.

403 Stoye, John. The Siege of Vienna. New York: Holt, Rinehart & Winston, 1965, 349 pp.
A more or less popular history of the Turkish siege of Vienna in 1683, based largely on secondary sources. For a full scholarly treatment of the same subject, see Barker's Double Eagle and the Crescent (389).

404 Vaughan, Dorothy M. Europe and the Turk: A Pattern of Alliances, 1350-1700. Liverpool: Liverpool University Press, 1954, 305 pp.
A diplomatic history of Europe's relations with the Ottomans, with chapters on the economic and naval threat posed by the Ottomans to Europe and the role of the Ottomans in the European balance of power. The effect of the counterrevolution on the empire and military campaigns are also studied. Vaughan's extensive research was confined to European sources, but this is a standard work on European-Ottoman relations.

Ottoman Historiography

405 Na'īmā. Annals of the Turkish Empire from 1591 to 1659, of the Christian Era by Niama. Translated by Charles Fraser. London: Oriental Translation Fund, 1832, 467 pp.
A translation of the Turkish chronicle of Na'īmā, an Ottoman historian of the eighteenth century.

406 Reychman, Jan, and Ananiasz Zajaczkowski. Handbook of Ottoman-Turkish Diplomatics. Translated by Andrew S. Ehrenkreutz. The Hague: Mouton, 1968, 232 pp.
Surveys collections of Ottoman documents held in Asia and Europe, discusses the mechanics of Ottoman diplomatic correspondence, and lists various ancillary disciplines relevant to the study.

407 Sari Mehmed Pasha. Ottoman Statecraft, the Book of Counsel for Vizirs and Governors of Sari Mehmed Pasha, the Defterdar, Turkish Text with Introduction, Translation, and Notes. Translated by W.L. Wright, Jr. Princeton, N.J.: Princeton University Press, 1935, 307 pp.
A criticism of Ottoman government and society designed as an administrative handbook by an eighteenth-century official and observer.

408 Thomas, Lewis V. A Study of Niama. New York: New York University Press, 1972, 163 pp.
A biographical sketch of the eighteenth-century Ottoman historian Na'īmā and an outline and analysis of his historical writing. A good introduction to Ottoman historiography of the seventeenth and eighteenth centuries in general, as well as a careful study of one of its most influential practitioners.

THE ṢAFAVIDS AND THEIR SUCCESSORS

409 Barbaro, Josafa, and Ambrogio Contarini. A Narrative of Italian Travels in Persia in the Fifteenth and Sixteenth Centuries. Translated by Charles Grey, William Thomas, and S.A. Roy. New York: B. Franklin, n.d., 229 pp.
Translation of six travel accounts to Iran around the time of the Ṣafavid Shāh Ismā'īl.

410 Busse, Heribert, trans. History of Persia under Qajar Rule: Translated from the Persian of Hasan-e Fasa'i's Farsnama-ye Naseri. New York: Columbia University Press, 1972, 494 pp.
A translation of a Persian history of the Qājār dynasty from its origins until 1882; the original text is a principal source for the period.

411 Chardin, Sir John. Sir John Chardin's Travels in Persia. London: Argonaut, 1927, 287 pp.
Memoirs of travel to Ṣafavid Persia by a jewel merchant of the seventeenth century; rich in details of social life.

412 LeStrange, Guy, trans. Don Juan in Persia: A Shi'ah Catholic, 1560-1604. London: G. Routledge, 1927, 355 pp.
A description of Iran and its war against the Ottoman Turks during the sixteenth century, with a journal of a trip through Europe by a Iranian Muslim convert to Spanish Catholicism.

413 Lockhart, Lawrence. The Fall of the Safavi Dynasty and the Afghan Occupation of Persia. New York: Cambridge, 1958, 584 pp.

A history mainly of Nādir Shāh's military campaigns, based on Persian and European sources, with a brief chapter on Nādir's attainments and personal characteristics. This is a reliable but uninspired summary of the sources.

414 Mazzaoui, Michael M. The Origins of the Safavids: Shīʿism, Sufism, and the Ghulat. Wiesbaden: Franz Steiner Verlag, 1972, 109 pp.

A carefully researched treatment of the historical background from which the Ṣafavids emerged, the development of Shīʿism under the Mongols, and the history of the Ardabīl Ṣūfī order: basic for Ṣafavī history.

415 Minorsky, V., trans. Tadhkirat al-Mulūk: A Manual of Safavid Administration, circa 1137/1725. London: Luzac, 1943, 348 pp.

Minorsky's introduction on Ṣafavid government and administration is excellent, as is his commentary on a difficult technical text.

THE MUGHALS

General Surveys and Studies

416 Burn, Sir R., ed. The Cambridge History of India. Vol. 14, The Mughul Period. Cambridge: Cambridge University Press, 1937, 693 pp.

A summation mainly of political and military history, reflecting the British civil servant's point of view.

417 Edwardes, S.M., and H.L.O. Garrett. Mughal Rule in India. London: Oxford, 1930, 374 pp.

This summary of Mughal history is more readable than most of the genre, though it too sticks close to the translations of medieval chronicles and memoirs of the emperors, as well as to European travel accounts.

418 Elliot, H.M., and J. Dawson. The History of India as Told by Its Own Historians: The Muhammaden Period. 8 vols. London: Trübner, 1867-1877.

A monumental translation of many of the major sources for the history of Muslim India, valuable primarily for its evocation of the spirit of the times and as a sample of the materials with which historians have attempted an analytic reconstruction. Criticism has been lodged against the accuracy of the translations, but this should not preclude their being read.

419 Gascoigne, Bamber. The Great Moghuls. London: J. Cape, 1971, 264 pp.

This is an exceptional coffeetable book, in that its handsome photographs of Mughal monuments and miniatures are accompanied by a text firmly based on (translated) primary sources and travel memoirs, some fifty-five of which are listed in the bibliography, along with modern works. The result is a delightful introduction to the reigns of the emperors through Awrangzīb.

420 Habib, Irfan. The Agrarian System of the Mughal Empire 1556-1707. London: Asia Publishing House, 1963, 453 pp.

A detailed analysis of the Mughal land and revenue system based, insofar as is possible, on primary sources of the period. A useful annotated bibliography of Indian and European sources is given.

421 Ibn Hasan. The Central Structure of the Mughal Empire and Its Practical Working up to the Year 1657. Karachi: Oxford, 1967, 398 pp.

A description of the chief officials and institutions of the Mughals.

422 Maclagan, Sir Edward. The Jesuits and the Great Mogul. London: Burns Oates & Washbourne, 1932, 434 pp.

A history of the Jesuit missions to Akbar, Jahāngīr, Shāh Jahān, and the later Mughals, based on painstaking research into original sources, both European and Indian, with many insights into Mughal religious policy.

423 Rizvi, Syed Athar Abbas. Muslim Revivalist Movements in Northern India in the Sixteenth and Seventeenth Centuries. Agra: Agra University, 1965, 497 pp.

A survey of Ṣūfī and orthodox reform movements under the Mughals. See also 1356.

424 Sarkar, Sir Jadunath. Mughal Administration. Calcutta: Sarkar, 1952, 254 pp.

A sketch of the departments of the Mughal government and their functions, a compilation of data from both primary and secondary sources.

425 Sharma, Sri Ram. A Bibliography of Mughal India (1526-1707 A.D.). Bombay: Karnatak, n.d., 206 pp.

A descriptive essay of the primary sources for the reigns of the six "great" Mughal emperors, Bābur to Awrangzīb (1526-1707). These include histories, letters, and administrative materials.

426 _____. The Religious Policy of the Mughal Emperors. London: Oxford, 1940, 226 pp.

A survey of the policy of the Mughal emperors (Bābur to Awrangzīb).

427 Siddiqi, Nuʿman Ahmad. Land Revenue Administration under the Mughals (1700-1750). Bombay: Asia, 1970, 182 pp.

A study of the land system under the late Mughals, based primarily on chronicles, administrative manuals, and whatever records are available.

428 Srivastava, A.L. The Mughal Empire (1526-1803 A.D.). 3d rev. ed. Agra: Shiva Lal Agarwala, 1959, 614 pp.

A schematic history of the Mughal emperors with detailed political, military, economic, and social data. Since it lacks documentation, its value is limited.

429 Whiteway, R.S. Rise of the Portuguese Power in India. London: Susil Gupta, 1967, 357 pp.

A history of Portuguese military campaigns, viceroyships, and governorships in India during the sixteenth century, utilizing European sources.

Individual Personages and Reigns

430 Abu-l Faẕl ʻAllāmī. Āʼīn-i Akbarī. Translated by H. Blohmann and H.S. Jarrett. Edited by S.L. Goomer. 2d ed. Delhi: Aadiesh Book Depot, 1965, 733 pp. Orig. pub. in 1871.

A compilation of the "Institutes" of Emperor Akbar, with data copied and summarized from the court and administrative records of the Mughal Empire, along with an account of Hinduism under the Mughals.

431 _____. Akbar-nāma. 3 vols. Translated by H. Beveridge. Calcutta: Asiatic Society, 1907-1939.

An exhaustive history of Akbar and his predecessors by the emperor's adviser and companion. Though laudatory, it is, along with the Āʼīn-i Akbarī, a prime source for this period of Mughal history.

432 Ali, M. Athar. The Mughal Nobility under Aurangzeb. Aligarh: Asia, 1966, 294 pp.

A good introduction to the social and economic history of the late Mughals, focusing on the role of the "nobility" in the Mughal state, in the course of which the mansab system is discussed.

433 Bābur, Ẓahīr al-Dīn Muḥammad. The Bābur-nāma in English: Memoirs of Bābur. 2 vols. Translated by A.S. Beveridge. London: Luzac, 1922, 880 pp.

Aside from an introduction on the text and explanatory notes, Beveridge lets the translation speak for itself. The memoirs are surprisingly revealing, filled with details of the emperor's personal life and thoughts, his virtues and vices. There are few portraits of medieval Muslims as intimate as this one.

434 Badāʼūnī, ʻAbd al-Qādir. Muntakhab al-Tawārīkh. 3 vols. Translated by G.S.A. Ranking, W.H. Lowe, and Sir W. Haig. Calcutta: Asiatic Society of Bengal, 1884-1925.

A "secret history" of Akbar's reign by an orthodox Sunnī in the emperor's employ who was scandalized by his impious innovations; this is a useful foil to Abu-l Faẕl's history (see 430).

435 Choudhury, Makhan Lāl Roy. The Din-i-Ilahi or the Religion of Akbar. 2d ed. Calcutta: Das Gupta, 1952, 222 pp.

An interpretation of Emperor Akbar's religious goals and policies by a Hindu scholar.

436 Friedmann, Yohanan. Shaykh Ahmad Sirhindi: An Outline of His Thought and a Study of His Image in the Eyes of Posterity. Montreal: McGill Queen's University Press, 1971, 130 pp.

A reassessment of the role assigned to the seventeenth-century "reformer" by Indian-Mulsim historiography. Though it focuses on Sirhindī's religious thought, it is important for an understanding of religious history under the Mughals between Akbar and Awrangzīb, as well as later writing on the subject designed to serve extra-historical goals. It does, however, overlook some important aspects of Naqshbandī teaching.

437 Guerreiro, Fernao. Jahangir and the Jesuits with an Account of the Travels of Benedict Goes and the Mission to Pegu from the Relations to Father Fernao Guerreiro, S.J. Translated by C.H. Payne. London: Routledge, 1930, 287 pp.

Translation of a seventeenth-century account of missions to the court of Jahāngīr and the Portuguese occupation of Pegu.

438 Gulbadan, Begam. Humayun-nama. Translated by Annette Beveridge. London: Royal Asiatic Society, 1902, 100 pp.

The memoirs of Bābur's daughter, written at Akbar's command as source material for the Akbar-Nāmah. It covers certain aspects of Humāyūn's reign in detail.

439 Haidar, Mirza Muhammad. A History of the Moghuls of Central Asia, Being the Tarikh-i Rashidi of Mirza Muhammad Haidar, Dughlat. Edited and translated by N. Elias and E. Denison Ross. London: Sampson Low, Marston, 1895, 535 pp.

A sixteenth-century history of the Chagatay Khāns and an account of the author's career in the service of the Mughal emperors Bābur and Humāyūn.

440 Hasrat, Bikrama Jit. Dārā Shikūh: Life and Works. Calcutta: Visvabharati Publishing Dept., 1953, 304 pp.

A close summary of what is known from primary sources on the life and works of this Mughal prince, who, though he did not succeed in becoming emperor, was an important figure in Mughal religious history.

441 Jahāngīr. Memoirs of the Emperor Jahangueir. Translated by David Price. London: Oriental Translation Committee, 1829. Reprint. New York: Johnson, 1968, 141 pp.

This forged version of the emperor's memoirs has no introduction and few notes.

442 _____. Tūzuk-i-Jahāngīrī. 2 vols. Translated by Alexander Rogers and edited by H. Beveridge. 2d ed. Delhi: Munshiram Manoharlal, 1968, 1:478 pp.; 2:315 pp.

The journal of the Mughal emperor, covering the years 1605-1624.

443 Jawhar. The Tezkereh al Vakiāt, or Private Memoirs of the Moghul Emperor Humayun Written in the Persian Language by Jouher, a Confidential Domestic of His Majesty. Translated by Major Charles Stewart. London: Royal Asiatic Society, 1832, 192 pp.

Memoirs of Humāyūn (the Tadhkirāt al-wāqiʻāt), written by a personal servant at Akbar's command.

444 Lane-Poole, Stanley. Babur. Oxford: Clarendon, 1909, 206 pp.
A short, readable biography of Bābur based on his own memoirs and other primary sources.

445 Prasad, Beni. History of Jahangir. Allahabad: Indian Press, 1940, 434 pp.
One of the first attempts to use contemporary Persian chronicles for a biography of the Mughal emperor.

446 Saksena, Banarsi Prasad. History of Shahjahan of Dihli. Allahabad: Central Book Depot, 1950, 373 pp.
The author takes the middle ground between the historiographers and detractors of Shāh Jahān in this summary of his career and description of Mughal administration and culture during his reign.

447 Sarkar, Jadunath. A Short History of Aurangzib, 1618-1707. Calcutta: Sarkar, 1954, 478 pp.
Though this biography seems to follow original sources closely, its usefulness is negated by the complete lack of documentation.

448 Smith, Vincent A. Akbar the Great Mogul, 1542-1605. Oxford: Clarendon, 1917, 504 pp.
The fullest biography of Akbar available in English, based on primary literary sources. Smith's views of Akbar's religious policies have been revised by later scholars, most notably Azīz Aḥmad.

MODERN HISTORY (1800-PRESENT)

GENERAL STUDIES

Surveys and Handbooks

449 Adams, Michael, ed. The Middle East: A Handbook. New York: Praeger, 1971, 633 pp.
A collection of articles on all aspects of life in the Middle East. A general introduction outlines Middle Eastern history and Islamic culture together with the most pressing problem of the area today--Palestine. Each country is then surveyed in outline form on geographical, political, and economic features, with more general surveys of economic, social, and cultural affairs. The authors include both British and native residents, all of them experts in their fields.

450 Bonne, Alfred. State and Economics in the Middle East: A Society in Transition. 2d rev. ed. London: Routledge & K. Paul, 1955, 452 pp.
An analysis of Middle Eastern history since 1914 in political-economic terms, based almost entirely on Western secondary studies, supplemented by such statistical data as were available. Interesting chiefly for the attempts to strengthen political analysis with economic data.

451 Clarke, J.I., and W.B. Fisher. Populations of the Middle East and North Africa: A Geographical Approach. London: University of London Press, 1972, 432 pp.
A collection of articles on trends in demographic change in various areas covered by the title (including Cyprus and Israel), based on an exhaustive study of available statistics, and presented against the background of the history and geography of the regions. Up to date and authoritative.

452 Fisher, W.B. The Middle East: A Physical, Social, and Regional Geography. 6th ed. London: Methuen, 1971, 571 pp.
An essential reference work, revised and republished at frequent intervals, with data on physical, social, economic, and regional geography of the Middle East. Many maps and diagrams enhance the obvious value of this work to historians.

453 Kirk, George E. A Short History of the Middle East from the Rise of Islam to Modern Times. New York: Praeger, 1955, 336 pp.
Kirk gives fifty-five pages to the period 600-1517 and two hundred and sixty to the rest; so the book hardly lives up to its title. This work, widely read because of its conciseness and accessibility, is interesting primarily as a Tory view of Western interests in the Middle East. There are many other examples of this genre, but few with Kirk's grasp of the sweep of events in the entire Arab East in modern times.

454 Longrigg, Stephen H. The Middle East: A Social Geography. London: Duckworth, 1963, 291 pp.
A very general survey of the peoples of the Middle East and their organization into states and societies. This is too elementary and impressionistic to be of more than popular, introductory use.

455 Mansfield, Peter. The Ottoman Empire and Its Successors. New York: St. Martin's Press, 1973, 210 pp.
In its introductory chapters the book outlines the decline of the Ottoman Empire and its disintegration. The main portion of the work is devoted to the rise and progress of Arab nation-states in the Middle East as well as in North Africa. Mention is also made of Iran and Turkey. The book is extremely brief, but provides a clear exposition of developments in the modern Arab world.

456 The Middle East: A Political and Economic Survey. 2d ed. London and New York: Royal Institute of International Affairs, 1954, 590 pp.
An introduction traces the political history of the entire area and gives a religious, social, and economic profile. There are separate chapters on the Arab countries (including the Sudan) plus Cyprus, Israel, Persia, and Turkey, in terms of population and society, history and politics, and the economy. Outdated in the main by later works of a similar nature, but still useful.

457 The Middle East and North Africa, 1972-1973. 19th ed. London: Europa, 1972, 931 pp.
An annual survey of the Arab states, as well as Turkey, Cyprus, Iran, Israel, and Afghanistan, with data on geography, history, economy, government officials, education, and articles of timely but more general significance. An indispensable reference work for contemporary history.

458 Peretz, Don. The Middle East Today. New York: Holt, Rinehart & Winston, 1963, 483 pp.
A university-textbook introduction to the modern history of the Middle East: the growth of nationalism, constitutional developments, international affairs--mainly politics. One of the better texts of its type, though it is now dated.

459 Polk, William R., and R.L. Chambers, eds. Beginnings of Modernization in the Middle East: The Nineteenth Century. Chicago: University of Chicago Press, 1968, 427 pp.
Twenty articles on various aspects of modernization in Ottoman Turkey, Egypt and Syria, and the Sudan, including the role of "notables and bureaucrats," "ideological change," "social movements," "foreign intervention," "education," and "problems," plus an introduction that tries to set the theme and the problems attacked in the articles, which were originally presented at a 1966 convention.

460 Sachar, Howard M. The Emergence of the Middle East, 1914-1924. New York: A.A. Knopf, 518 pp.
A popular history of the fragmentation of the Ottoman Empire into Turkey, Syria, Lebanon, Palestine, Iraq, and Arabia, written almost entirely from a European-American point of view and based almost entirely on Western sources. Along with the history of the emergence of new states under Western tutelage, there is a great deal of attention given to Americans and Jews. The main virtue of this work is that it is colorfully written and therefore eminently readable, but the interpretation is narrow and somewhat slanted.

461 _____. Europe Leaves the Middle East, 1936-1954. New York: A.A. Knopf, 1972, 687 pp.
The sequel, with a twenty-two-year lacuna, to the same author's The Emergence of the Middle East (see 460). Here Sachar, with the same verve, describes the struggle among the European powers to establish their presence in the Middle East diplomatically, militarily, politically, economically, and culturally, focusing on World War II and the creation of a Jewish state in Palestine. Strong on European motives, stratagems, and interests, but weak on the effects these had on the peoples of the area. Fascinating reading.

462 Toynbee, Arnold J. Survey of International Affairs, 1925. Vol. 1, The Islamic World Since the Peace Settlement. London: Oxford, 1927, 611 pp.
Toynbee sets this survey of the postwar history of the Middle East and Northwest Africa in the perspective afforded by the secularization movements that followed the abolition of the Ottoman caliphate. Much of it is necessarily based on newspaper reports and other literary sources. Subsequent volumes of the survey should also be consulted.

463 Yale, William. The Near East: A Modern History. Ann Arbor: University of Michigan Press, 1958, 485 pp.
After introductory chapters, this work begins with the early Turkish "reform movement" (1820-1910), continues with the Turkish nationalist movement, Zionism and Palestine, and the establishment of nation-states, and ends with the 1952 revolution in Egypt. It is very general and based largely on secondary sources. Fisher's The Middle East: A History (see 18) does the same thing better.

Political Studies

464 Abboushi, W.F. Political Systems of the Middle East in the 20th Century. New York: Dodd, Mead, 1970, 345 pp.
An outline of the recent political history of Turkey, Iran, some of the Arab states, and Israel, from secondary sources.

465 Davis, Helen Miller, ed. Constitutions, Electoral Laws, and Treatises of the States in the Near and Middle East. Durham, N.C.: Duke University Press, 1947, 446 pp.
A collection of translations of documents relating to political developments (internal and external) in the Arab countries and Iran, Afghanistan, and Turkey prior to 1946; this is a useful source book.

466 Fisher, S.N., ed. The Military in the Middle East: Problems in Society and Government. Columbus: Ohio State University Press, 1963, 138 pp.
Eight papers delivered at a 1961 conference covering Turkey, Iraq, the U.A.R., Egypt, and Israel, as well as papers on the Middle East in general. One of the earliest attempts to set this aspect of modern Middle Eastern history in a broad perspective.

467 Haddad, George M. Revolutions and Military Rule in the Middle East: The Northern Tier. New York: R. Speller, 1965, 251 pp.
Haddad analyzes and compares military coups in Turkey, Iran, Afghanistan, and Pakistan and discusses the relationship of military rule to democracy.

468 Hammond, Paul Y., and Sidney S. Alexander, eds. Political Dynamics in the Middle East. New York: American Elsevier, 1972, 666 pp.
A Rand Corporation study of the "political and social realities" of the Middle East as a background to another study on the economic problems of the area. The inspiration of the book was obviously American-Soviet rivalry in the Middle East and the need to formulate an effective U.S. policy. Almost all the contributors are social scientists, some of them

with a firm grasp of history (e.g., Malcolm Kerr, J.C. Hurewitz, Nadev Safran, P.J. Vatikiotis, and Charles Gallagher), so the level of the articles is generally quite high. The book could be used as an introductory text on the contemporary political history of the Middle East.

469 Hurewitz, J.C. Middle East Politics: The Military Dimension. New York: F.A. Praeger, 1969, 553 pp.
A survey of the role of the military in Middle Eastern states, here a most comprehensive term embracing most of the countries between Pakistan and Algeria, including Israel. After two introductory sections, one on the premodern history of the military in Islamic states, and another on the army in Middle Eastern politics, Hurewitz proceeds to analyze five types of governments and the role of the army in each. In conclusion, there is a section on the effects--social, political, and economic--of the prominent part played by the military. The book originated from a Council on Foreign Relations conference, and begins and ends by setting the theme into the framework of U.S. policy in the Middle East.

470 Karpat, Kemal H., ed. Political and Social Thought in the Contemporary Middle East. New York: Praeger, 1968, 397 pp.
Selections from the political writings, primarily, of modern Arabs, with passages from the writings of Turks and Iranians also, many for the first time in English. There are general surveys for each of three areas, plus introductory data on each of the authors.

471 Kedourie, Elie, ed. Nationalism in Asia and Africa. London: Weidenfeld & Nicolson, 1970, 573 pp.
Kedourie's one-hundred-fifty-page introduction to nationalistic ideology in Asia and Africa is followed by twenty-five samples of its regional variations by the likes of Ziya Gökalp, Shakib Arslan, and Joseph Stalin. Kedourie's theme is that nationalism is very much the same everywhere: "a reaction against European domination" and "salvation through violence." Extremely useful for setting the various local nationalisms within a wider frame of reference than the usual one.

472 Marayati, Abid A. al-. Middle Eastern Constitutions and Electoral Laws. New York: Frederick A. Praeger, 1968, 483 pp.
English translation of constitutions and electoral laws of the east Arab states, Israel, Turkey, and Iran, through 1964.

473 Rosenthal, Erwin I.J. Islam in the Modern National State. Cambridge: Cambridge University Press, 1965, 416 pp.
A study of examples of Islamic political theory and practice in modern states, primarily Turkey and Pakistan, but also Morocco, Tunisia, Iran, and Malaya. One of the few attempts to analyze the function and significance of "classical" Islamic theory over such a wide area in the modern period.

474 Rustow, D.A. Middle Eastern Political Systems. Englewood Cliffs, N.J.: Prentice-Hall, 1971, 113 pp.
A brief comparative survey by a political scientist of governmental systems in Turkey, Iran, the eastern Arab countries, and Israel, in terms of political and social problems, ideology, state mechanisms, and their effectiveness and prospects. A useful introduction to the governments of the area.

475 Sharabi, Hisham B. Government and Politics of the Middle East in the 20th Century. Princeton, N.J.: Van Nostrand, 1962, 296 pp.
One of the best of many introductory surveys of the political organizations of the Middle East (Turkey, Iran, the Arab states, and Israel), designed for undergraduates.

476 Shimani, Yaacov, and Evyatar Lemni. Political Dictionary of the Middle East in the Twentieth Century. Jerusalem: Weidenfeld & Nicolson, 1972, 434 pp.
Includes entries on persons, places, and institutions that have figured in the recent history of the Middle East, and is really more an encyclopedia than a dictionary. The emphasis is on the Arab states, but Israel, Iran, and Turkey are also covered.

477 Spencer, William. Political Evolution in the Middle East. Philadelphia: J.B. Lippincott, 1962, 440 pp.
An elementary text on the modern political history of the states of the Middle East suitable for undergraduates who need a straightforward summary of events with minimal interpretation.

478 Vatikiotis, P.J., ed. Revolution in the Middle East and Other Case Studies. London: G. Allen & Unwin, 1972, 232 pp.
Twelve essays on revolution, five of which concern the Arab world, including the Maghreb, one on Iran, and one on Islamic concepts of revolution. The other essays discuss revolution in general and provide comparative studies from other parts of the world.

International Relations

479 Daniel, Norman. Islam, Europe, and Empire. Edinburgh: University of Edinburgh Press, 1966, 619 pp.
A continuation of Daniel's study (see 187) of Christian understanding and misunderstanding of Muslims and Islam. This volume covers the period of colonial expansion--the late eighteenth and nineteenth centuries--and thus focuses more on political considerations than theology as the key factor in shaping Western attitudes. There are sections on the effects of imperialism and colonialism on the Western image of Islam.

480 DeNovo, John A. American Interests and Policies in the Middle East, 1900-1939. Minneapolis: University of Minnesota Press, 1963, 447 pp.
An excellent, well-documented survey of American cultural, economic, and diplomatic activities in the area before oil became a significant factor, although the struggle to gain

a share of that commodity during the period is not neglected. The accent is on Turkey, but Iran and the Arab states are given some attention as well.

481 Field, James A., Jr. America and the Mediterranean World, 1776-1882. Princeton, N.J.: Princeton University Press, 1969, 465 pp.
A history of American interests in the Mediterranean world, including the Middle East, tracing the impact of business, educational, missionary, and military interests, and stressing the continuity of these interests from a surprisingly early date.

482 Finnie, David H. Pioneers East: The Early American Experience in the Middle East. Harvard Middle Eastern Studies, no. 13. Cambridge, Mass.: Harvard University Press, 1967, 333 pp.
While studies of American interests in the Middle East usually begin with oil and end with ʻAbd al-Nāṣir (Nasser) and Israel, this book traces the little-known history of the earlier American presence in the area, that of archaeologists, missionaries, and diplomats, who contributed quite tangibly to Middle Eastern attitudes toward Americans. It covers Turkey, Persia, and the Arab lands.

483 Foster, Sir William. England's Quest of Eastern Trade. London: A. & C. Black, 1933, 355 pp.
A history of English exploration and trade, with many chapters dealing with Islamic territory.

484 Hurewitz, J.C. Diplomacy in the Near and Middle East: A Documentary Record. 2 vols. Princeton, N.J.: Van Nostrand, 1956, 1:291 pp.; 2:427 pp.
Volume 1 covers documents relating to diplomacy and treaties between 1535 and 1914; volume 2, international relations between 1914 and the date of publication. The documents are allowed to speak for themselves, with only minimal introductory material from the author. A valuable source book.

485 Kirk, George. The Middle East in the War. London: Oxford, 1952, 511 pp.
A chronological, almost journalistic, résumé of the war, mainly in the Arab lands, with some attention to Turkey and Persia. Newspapers are the most frequently cited sources.

486 Kohn, Hans. Nationalism and Imperialism in the Hither East. Translated by Margaret M. Green. London: Routledge, 1932, 339 pp.
Written before the bankruptcy of imperialism and the efflorescence of nationalism, this was one of the first studies of Arab nationalism in its territorial manifestations.

487 _____. Western Civilization in the Near East. Translated by E.W. Dickes. New York: Columbia University Press, 1936, 329 pp.
An early study of the impact of westernization upon the Near East, primarily in political terms. Though neglected now, this book has been influential in formulating the way in which modern Near Eastern history has been studied.

488 Laqueur, Walter Z. Communism and Nationalism in the Middle East. London: Routledge & K. Paul, 1956, 362 pp.
A history of communist activities in the Arab countries, including the Sudan, Israel, and Turkey, from 1919 through the early fifties.

489 _____. The Middle East in Transition: Studies in Contemporary History. New York: F.A. Praeger, 1958, 513 pp.
Contains thirty-six articles on nationalism, in terms of political and social change, and communism and the role of the USSR in the Middle East (including the Soviet Republics). Many of the articles are dated, and several are journalistic, but there are major contributions by Gibb on the importance of social change, S. Haim on Islam and Arab nationalism, and Bernard Lewis on the similarity between Islam and Communism. The articles on Soviet attitudes toward the Middle East are still interesting.

490 _____. The Soviet Union and the Middle East. London: Routledge & K. Paul, 1959, 366 pp.
A survey of Soviet policy toward the Middle East, in particular the Arabs, and including the Northern Tier, based on Russian and Arabic sources.

491 Laqueur, Walter. The Struggle for the Middle East: The Soviet Union and the Middle East 1958-68. London: Routledge & K. Paul, 1969, 360 pp.
A sequel to the same author's earlier books on Soviet policy in the Middle East and the political and social conditions in the various countries toward which it was directed. Covers the Northern Tier, Israel, and the Arabs, then oil, trade, and military considerations, and, finally, ideologies. The appendix includes "documents" that illustrate Laqueur's thesis; the most interesting ones are translations of Russian writers' views on Arab policies.

492 Lenczowski, George. The Middle East in World Affairs. 2d ed. Ithaca, N.Y.: Cornell University Press, 1956, 576 pp.
For many years the standard introductory text in North American universities on the role of Middle Eastern countries (including Afghanistan) in modern international affairs, from the Treaty of Carlowitz (1699) through the early 1950s. The book is systematic and thorough, but based mainly on Western sources.

493 Lewis, Bernard. The Middle East and the West. London: Weidenfeld & Nicolson, 1964, 160 pp.
Six lectures on the impact of the West on the Arabs and Turks primarily, the Persians and Indians to a lesser extent, examining the influence of Western political ideas on Muslim thinkers and the place of the Middle East in international affairs. A lucid introduction to a broad subject, excellent for general trends. Contains good annotated bibliographies.

494 Monroe, Elizabeth. Britain's Moment in the Middle East, 1914-1956. Chatto & Windus, 1963, 254 pp.
Describes British policy and activities from the Arab revolt and the origin of the Palestine question to Suez.

495 Proctor, J. Harris. Islam and International Affairs. London: Pall Mall, 1965, 221 pp.
Articles presented at a symposium on the effect of Islam in formulating political policy, both national and international, in modern times.

496 Ramazani, Rouhollah K. The Middle East and the European Common Market. Charlottesville: University Press of Virginia, 1964, 152 pp.
A study of the effect of the Common Market on the Middle Eastern economy, on exports in particular, and the response of various countries (Israel, Iran, Turkey, and the Arab states). A good example of the increasingly specialized studies of westernization.

497 Searight, Sarah. The British in the Middle East. New York: Atheneum, 1970, 215 pp.
An amusing, copiously illustrated survey of the British presence in the Middle East from the midsixteenth century to 1914, concentrating on British individuals infatuated with the East --mainly travelers, writers, and artists, a welcome change from politicians and soldiers.

498 Spector, Ivar. The Soviet Union and the Muslim World, 1917-1958. Seattle: University of Washington Press, 1959, 328 pp.
Spector discusses Soviet attitudes and policies toward Muslim countries, primarily Turkey, Iran, and Afghanistan. After an introductory survey of Russian expansion in the Muslim world, he begins the core of his study with the Bolshevik Revolution and continues to postwar Soviet foreign policy until 1958. A careful analysis of Russian sources.

499 U.S. National Archives. Materials in the National Archives Relating to the Middle East. Washington: National Archives Publication No. 55-16, 1955, 96 pp.
A description of the U.S. archival holdings on subjects relating to U.S. relations with Iran, Arabia, Iraq, Lebanon, Palestine, Syria, and Turkey.

Religious Studies

500 Arberry, A.J., and Rom Landau, eds. Islam Today. London: Faber & Faber, 1942, 258 pp.
Essays mainly by British authorities, on the state of Islam in 1940 in each Arab country and in Africa, Persia, Afghanistan, India, and Malaysia. Most of the articles are outdated now, but it is still interesting to read what Taha Hussein wrote about modern Egypt, and A.K.S. Lambton about Iran.

501 Atiya, Aziz S. History of Eastern Christianity. Notre Dame, Ind.: University of Notre Dame Press, 1968, 486 pp.
This survey of the development of the eastern Christian churches contains much important material on Muslim-Christian relations and interactions. It is the standard work on the Copts, the Jacobites, the Nestorians, the Armenians, and the Maronites.

502 Gibb, H.A.R. Modern Trends in Islam. New York: Octagon, 1972, 141 pp. Reprint of the 1945 ed.
These lectures on the dilemmas faced by Muslim thinkers and politicians in the modern world have been of such profound influence that one scholar in the same field confesses that everything written since has been footnotes to this study. For better or for worse, Gibb's conceptualization of modern Islam remains the standard one, and this slim book is still the initial step for students. As is usual with Gibb's work, the interpretation is intuitive and persuasive, based on wide reading and experience, only minimally documented.

503 _____, ed. Whither Islam? A Study of Modern Movements in the Moslem World. London: Victor Gallancz, 1932, 384 pp.
A collection of essays by Gibb, Massignon, and lesser lights on Islam in Africa, Egypt and the Fertile Crescent, India, and Indonesia, and two general surveys discussing the situation of Islam in 1930 and the prospects for its future. Widely read at the time, it is dated now, but the chapters by Gibb are, as always, worth reading for his analyses of significant factors.

504 Grunebaum, G.E. von. Modern Islam: The Search for Cultural Identity. Berkeley: University of California Press, 1962, 303 pp.
A collection of eleven of von Grunebaum's essays on modern themes, focusing on the Arab world and the crisis in Arab Islamic culture as a result of the overwhelming influence of the West. There is much Chicago theorizing and German abstraction here, which, for the advanced student with a firm grasp of historical development, is interesting.

505 Keddie, Nikki R. Sayyid Jamāl ad-Dīn 'al-Afghānī': A Political Biography. Berkeley: University of California Press, 1972, 479 pp.
An exhaustive study of the controversial figure who was active in nineteenth-century political and religious movements in many parts of the Muslim world. Since Keddie follows all aspects of his checkered career from Paris to India and points in between, her book serves as a good introduction to many aspects of Islamic politics and religion at a critical point in Muslim history. Many years in preparation and based on primary sources in a number of Oriental and Western languages, this biography is unlikely to be superseded for a long time.

506 _____, ed. Scholars, Saints, and Sufis: Muslim Religious Institutions since 1500. Berkeley: University of California Press, 1972, 401 pp.
Sixteen essays by scholars of widely different specializations on the social role of the 'ulamā' and the Ṣūfīs in the Muslim world since the sixteenth century, important in defining a new direction of research in Islamic history, both medieval and modern. Many of the articles

concern North Africa and Iran, reflecting the relatively advanced stage of research for these areas. See also 1368, 1375, 1703, 1705, 1709, 2243, 2257.

507 Kedourie, Elie. Afghani and Abduh: An Essay on Religious Unbelief and Political Activism in Modern Islam. London: F. Cass, 1966, 97 pp.

A provocative revisionist interpretation of the writings and activities of these two key figures in the pan-Islamic and Islamic modernist movements stressing the religious and political opportunism of both. For a more moderate view, see Nikki Keddie's biography of al-Afghānī (506).

508 Kritzeck, James, ed. Modern Islamic Literature. New York: Holt, Rinehart & Winston, 1970, 310 pp.

One of the few anthologies of this particular phase of Islamic literature available in English translation, it covers a wide range of Muslim areas, from the West to Africa to Indonesia, from about 1800 to the last decade. The usefulness of this collection could have been enhanced by more detail in the introduction and notes, but the variety of the selections included compensates for this minor shortcoming.

509 Kudsi-Zadeh, A. Albert. Sayyid Jamāl al-Dīn al-Afghānī: An Annotated Bibliography. Leiden: E.J. Brill, 1970, 118 pp.

Because the author has tried to include virtually every work touching even tangentially on al-Afghānī, its usefulness goes considerably beyond the specialized field of the individual into that of modern Islamic history in general.

510 Smith, W.C. Islam in Modern History. Princeton, N.J.: Princeton University Press, 1957, 317 pp.

This book is significant as one of the few studies by a Westerner to approach the modern history of the Muslim world from within Islam as a religion, rather than from the viewpoint of political science focusing on nationalism, colonialism, state structure. It is in the tradition of Gibb's Modern Trends (see 502) and is in many ways an amplification of that book. After two general chapters on the Islamic conception of history and the development of Islam in modern history, Smith analyzes four groups of modern Muslims: Arabs, Turks, Pakistanis, and Indians, along with other groups. An influential, widely read study, still useful for the problem of Islam confronted with modernity.

Social and Anthropological Studies

511 Antoun, Richard, and Iliya Harik, eds. Rural Politics and Social Change in the Middle East. Bloomington: Indiana University Press, 1972, 498 pp.

Papers from a 1969 conference of social scientists, dominated by anthropologists, on a much-neglected topic. The most valuable articles survey the state of theory and scholarship and suggest means of improving and directing a still undeveloped branch of Middle Eastern studies of potentially great importance for understanding the history of the area.

512 Ariens-Kappers, C.U., and Leland W. Parr. An Introduction to the Anthropology of the Near East in Ancient and Recent Times. Amsterdam: N.V. Noord-Hollandsche Vit Gever Shaatschappij, 1934, 200 pp.

By "anthropology," the authors mean primarily the study of skulls of various peoples who have inhabited the area. The purpose is to establish racial types.

513 Baer, Gabriel. Population and Society in the Arab East. Translated by H. Szoke. London: Routledge & K. Paul, 1964, 275 pp.

A series of lectures on the demographic and ecological structure of the Arab Middle East, with chapters on general population distribution, the state of women and the family, religious groups, and nomadic, peasant, and rural society. It is very useful as an introduction to Arab society.

514 Coon, Carleton S. Caravan: The Story of the Middle East. New York: Holt, 1951, 376 pp.

One of the first and best anthropological surveys of the area, designed as an introductory text. Useful for beginners in Islamic history who are confused by the diversity of ethnic and linguistic groups and need data on social organization.

515 Cressey, G.B. Crossroads: Land Life in South-West Asia. Chicago: J.B. Lippincott, 1960, 593 pp.

An introductory geography to the Middle East, including Afghanistan and Pakistan, written on a secondary school level.

516 Fisher, S.N., ed. Social Forces in the Middle East. Ithaca, N.Y.: Cornell University Press, 1955, 282 pp.

Fifteen essays on the social structures and dynamics of the area, with specialized chapters on various social types, such as nomads, villagers, farmers, industrial workers, merchants, intellectuals, refugees, and minorities. A good introduction to a subject still in its infancy.

517 Grunebaum, G.E. von. Muhammedan Festivals. New York: H. Schuman, 1951, 107 pp.

A brief description of the rites of pilgrimage, fasting, and saint worship as practiced by the main body of Muslims. There is also a section on the Shīʿī passion play. See also 1784.

518 Lerner, Daniel. The Passing of Traditional Society: Modernizing the Middle East. Glencoe, Calif.: Free Press, 1958, 466 pp.

One of the first genuine social-science studies of the Middle East, attempting to measure the level of modernization attained in Turkey, Lebanon, Egypt, Syria, Jordan, and Iran by means of questionnaires on mass media. The results were predictable, but have the virtue of being based on something concrete. They are useful for gauging the impact of mass communications in the area.

519 Nieuwenhuijze, C.A.O. van. Social Stratification and the Middle East: An Interpretation. Leiden: E.J. Brill, 1965, 84 pp.
An attempt to view Middle Eastern society in terms of socioeconomic classes.

520 _____. Sociology of the Middle East: A Stocktaking and Interpretation. Leiden: E.J. Brill, 1971, 819 pp.
An attempt to conceptualize Middle Eastern society and social institutions in modern sociological terms. The discussion is abstract and somewhat difficult, but this is the only general work of its kind.

521 Rivlin, Benjamin, and Joseph S. Szyliosicz, eds. The Contemporary Middle East: Tradition and Innovation. New York: Random House, 1965, 576 pp.
An anthology of articles on various aspects of politics, society, and culture for the edification of the uninformed general reader.

522 Shiloah, Ailan, ed. Peoples and Cultures of the Middle East. New York: Random House, 1969, 458 pp.
Contains twenty-five articles and extracts from books, designed to introduce the general reader to the culture and society of the Middle East, including the Arab world, Israel, Iran, and Turkey.

523 Sweet, Louise. Peoples and Cultures of the Middle East. Vol. 1, Cultural Depth and Diversity, 437 pp. Vol. 2, Life in the Cities, Town, and Countryside, 438 pp. New York: Natural History Press, 1970.
A book of "anthropological" readings consisting of articles and extracts, presumably with the undergraduate in mind. Areas studied include North Africa, Israel, Turkey, Iran, and Afghanistan as well as the eastern Arab countries, Egypt, and the Sudan.

524 Woodsmall, Ruth Frances. Women and the New East. Washington: Middle East Institute, 1960, 436 pp.
A firsthand report on the status of women in Turkey, Iran, Pakistan, Afghanistan, Indonesia, and India, which permits a comparison of the progress of emancipation in these areas.

Economic Studies

525 Grunwald, Kirt, and Joachim O. Ronall. Industrialization in the Middle East. New York: Council for Middle Eastern Affairs Press, 1960, 394 pp.
The introductory chapters survey the resources of the area--human, natural, and monetary--as resources for industrialization. The remainder of the book traces the history and progress of industrialization in local areas of the Middle East, including Afghanistan, Cyprus, Ethiopia, the Sudan, and everything between.

526 Hershlag, Z.Y. Introduction to the Modern Economic History of the Middle East. Leiden: E.J. Brill, 1964, 419 pp.
A history of economic developments since 1800 in the Ottoman Empire, Egypt, Iran, and the Arab mandate states, based not so much on archives as official publications, newspaper and travel reports, and secondary studies. Important as the first attempt to cover a neglected subject of wide scope.

527 Issawi, Charles, ed. The Economic History of the Middle East, 1800-1914: A Book of Readings. Chicago: University of Chicago Press, 1966, 543 pp.
Selections from primary and secondary sources on the economic history of the Ottoman Empire and the Arab lands of the East, including the Sudan. In the absence of a conventional economic history of the period, this is a useful substitute.

528 Issawi, Charles, and Mohammed Yeganah. The Economics of Middle Eastern Oil. London: Faber & Faber, 1962, 230 pp.
Attempts to supplement studies on the history of the oil industry in the Middle East and its political and social implications by presenting hard data on investment, prices, costs, profits, and effects on local economics.

529 Keen, B.A. The Agricultural Development of the Middle East: A Report to the Director General, Middle East Supply Centre, May 1945. London: His Majesty's Stationery Office, 1946, 126 pp.
This report was undertaken as part of a wartime project of increasing agricultural productivity. It includes a territorial survey of agriculture in the Middle East, poses the problems to be solved in increasing productivity, and suggests solutions. Some of this is dated now, but much is not.

530 Khan, Taufiq M., ed. Middle Eastern Studies in Income and Wealth. London: Bowes & Bowes, 1965, 328 pp.
Contains nineteen papers presented at a 1962 regional conference of the International Association for Research in Income and Wealth. The papers are all by Middle Easterners and deal with one of two general topics: problems of income estimation in the eastern Arab world, Iran, Turkey, and Pakistan, or measurement of capital formation in the same countries.

531 Lenczowski, George. Oil and State in the Middle East. Ithaca, N.Y.: Cornell University Press, 1960, 279 pp.
A fair, balanced study of the development of the oil industry in the Middle East and its relationship to the various governments of the area through the 1956 Suez crisis. In addition to the history of the industry, the book discusses the social and political (nationalistic) effects of industrialization. Although a new, updated edition is obviously needed, this one is very reliable on the situation until about 1960.

532 Longrigg, Stephen H. Oil in the Middle East: Its Discovery and Development. 3d ed. New York: Oxford, 1968, 519 pp.
A history of the growth of the oil industry in the Middle East by an agent of the International Petroleum Company, whose attitude often reflects British petroleum interests and, at

times, his own when he was personally involved as a negotiator. A measure of its timeliness is that Longrigg forecast the predicament the West would find itself in if it did not change its policies in the area. One of the best introductions to the subject.

533 Lubell, Harold. Middle East Oil Crises and Western Europe's Energy Supplies. Baltimore: Johns Hopkins Press, 1963, 233 pp.

Inevitably, and justifiably, a new edition of this extremely timely book will appear, bringing the author's research up to date. It surveys "oil crises" of the 1950s and projects possible crises of the 1960s and analyzes their effects. There are also chapters on alternative sources of oil for the rest of the world and the need to protect Western Europe from Middle Eastern shutdowns.

534 Penrose, Edith. The Growth of Firms, Middle East Oil and Other Essays. London: F. Cass, 1971, 336 pp.

Essays on the international oil industry by an economist with a specialized interest in the Middle East.

535 Schurr, Sam H., and Paul T. Homan. Middle Eastern Oil and the Western World: Prospects and Problems. New York: American Elsevier, 1971, 206 pp.

A recent Rand Corporation attempt to chart and gauge the developing relationship of the Middle East and the West on the basis of increasing Western demand for oil and a changing Eastern attitude toward supply. It all seems dated and academic now in the light of more recent developments, but the major issues are competently analyzed from an international rather than a local perspective.

536 Shwadran, Benjamin. The Middle East: Oil and the Great Powers. 2d rev. ed. New York: F.A. Praeger, 1959, 500 pp.

A history of the development of the oil industry in Iran, Iraq, Saudi Arabia, the Gulf, and the Mediterranean states, well researched and with a firsthand knowledge of the area, designed in part at least to offset Longrigg's official company history. Now somewhat dated--it was written over twenty years ago--it is good for the international politics of the oil industry.

537 Stocking, George W. Middle East Oil: A Study in Political and Economic Controversy. London: Allen Lane, the Penguin Press, 1971, 485 pp.

This book ends with the comforting conclusion that although the Arabs cannot fail to market low-cost oil to the West, such prognostications are hazardous in the light of the possibility of new Arab-Israeli conflict. Includes Iran and the Arab countries.

WORKS ON A SPECIFIC AREA

The Arab World

General Surveys

538 Berger, Morroe. The Arab World Today. New York: Doubleday, 1962, 463 pp.

An American sociologist's survey of Arab societies, social institutions, and social change, based to some extent on observation but mainly on Western secondary sources. More than fifteen years old, it needs updating, but it is useful for data on types of social grouping among the Arabs and the importance of traditions as a determinant in behavior patterns.

539 Berque, Jacques. The Arabs: Their History and Future. Translated by J. Stewart. London: Faber & Faber, 1964, 310 pp.

A quirky, highly personalized study of the eastern Arab states, primarily Lebanon, Iraq, Egypt, and Syria, in modern times in an attempt to define Arab modern identity, in the course of which Berque, a social historian, touches upon economics, class, women, language, the arts, and politics, often in a very stimulating though enigmatic way. "Impressionistic social history" is perhaps the best way to describe it, though "impressionistic" does not mean amateurish in this case.

540 Center for the Study of the Modern Arab World. Arab Culture and Society in Change: A Partially Annotated Bibliography of Books and Articles in English, French, German, and Italian. Beirut: Dar El-Mashreq, 1973, 318 pp.

An outstanding bibliography containing almost five thousand items on acculturation, social organization, women, education, language, politics, law, religion. It is well organized, with pithy annotations.

541 Hottinger, Arnold. The Arabs: Their History, Culture, and Place in the Modern World. London: Thames & Hudson, 1963, 344 pp.

A popular account of the components of "Arabism" as they have evolved in history, in an effort to understand the nature of Arab nationalism.

542 Hourani, A.H. Minorities in the Arab World. London: Oxford, 1947, 140 pp.

The standard description and analysis of religious minority groups in the modern Arab world, with introductory chapters on the development of Islamic attitudes toward these minorities in history; concise but informative.

543 Kerekes, Tibor, ed. The Arab Middle East and Muslim Africa. New York: F.A. Praeger, 1961, 126 pp.

Contains seven articles on various aspects of modern Islam and the Arab world, most of which are concerned with the relationship between Islam and politics in the 1950s.

544 Landau, Jacob M., ed. Man, State, and Society in the Contemporary Middle East. London: Pall Mall, 1972, 532 pp.

Includes thirty-two essays by Western scholars and Middle Easterners on two broad topics: "State and Politics" and "Views of Society and Man," restricted to Israel and the Arab countries (except North Africa). Although it has a political science orientation, it is of interest to students of Arab and Jewish nationalism as well.

545 Ljunggren, Florence, and M. Hamdy, eds. Annotated Guide to Journals Dealing with the Middle East and North Africa. Cairo: American University in Cairo Press, 1964, 107 pp.

Data on periodicals that deal with the Arab world.

546 Ljunggren, Florence, ed. Arab World Index: An International Guide to Periodical Literature in the Social Sciences and Humanities in the Contemporary Arab World, 1960-1964. Cairo: American University in Cairo Press, 1967, 549 pp.

The initial volume of an annual author-and-subject index to seventy Western language journals containing articles on various aspects of the contemporary Arab world.

547 Lutfiyya, A.M., and C.W. Churchill, eds. Readings in the Arab Middle Eastern Societies and Cultures. The Hague: Mouton, 1970, 733 pp.

A collection of fifty-three articles drawn from "various social science disciplines," excluding history, on such topics as social organization, culture, social institutions and cultural change, the family, urban life, and the role of communication. This is a useful background book for the modern history of the Arab world.

548 Rondot, Pierre. The Changing Patterns of the Middle East. London: Chatto & Windus, 1961, 221 pp.

An attempt to trace patterns in political developments in the Arab world and patterns in the attitudes of the participants in these developments, both native and foreign, from the end of World War I through 1958. Good as an outline of the issues and forces that were involved.

549 Thompson, J.H., and Robert D. Reischauer, eds. Modernization of the Arab World. New Perspectives in Political Science, no. 11. Princeton, N.J.: Van Nostrand, 1966, 249 pp.

The theme of these seventeen articles, most published previously, is the Arab attempt to solve the political, economic, and social problems involved in modernization. Half survey these problems in general terms--history, Islam, the army, oil--and half discuss specific areas--Saudi Arabia, Kuwait, Palestine, Israel. Useful as an introductory text. See also 2182.

550 Warriner, Doreen. Land Reform and Development in the Middle East: A Study of Egypt, Syria, and Iraq. 2d ed. London: Oxford, 1962, 238 pp.

The first (1948) edition of this work was designed, at least in part, to call attention to the poverty resulting from the feudal ownership of land in the Middle East. This edition repeats the incisive analysis of the landowning system and examines the agrarian reforms and development that were initiated after 1948. Without a grasp of the economic realities this book presents, it is impossible to gain more than a superficial understanding of the strength of nationalism in the contemporary Arab world.

Nationalism and Politics

551 Abu Lughod, Ibrahim. Arab Rediscovery of Europe: A Study in Cultural Encounters. Princeton, N.J.: Princeton University Press, 1963, 188 pp.

Abu Lughod surveys Arab writers from 1798 to 1870 who showed an awareness of the West and formulated a response to the challenge presented by the West. Excellent for its summary of works not available in translation and for the documentation of channels of westernization through the translation of Western works and the publication of Arab travel memoirs.

552 Antonius, George. The Arab Awakening: The Story of the Arab National Movement. London: H. Hamilton, 1938, 471 pp.

This classic version of the rise of Arab nationalism, by a Christian Arab, has recently begun to be criticized for its somewhat romantic reconstruction of what actually happened. Nevertheless, this enormously influential book is still a good starting point for students who need a sympathetic portrayal of the origins of nationalism through the First World War.

553 Be'eri, Eliezer. Army Officers in Arab Politics and Society. New York: Praeger, 1970, 514 pp.

This description of the role of the Arab military begins with 1936 and carries through 1967 and the war with Israel. The history of repeated coups and the ever increasing influence of the military elite is analyzed in terms of Islamic political tradition, social and economic factors, the nature of political leadership. Egypt, Syria, and Iraq receive most of the author's attention.

554 Cleveland, W.L. The Making of an Arab Nationalist: Ottomanism and Arabism in the Life of Sati' al-Husrī. Princeton, N.J.: Princeton University Press, 1971, 211 pp.

An analysis of one of the pivotal figures of nationalism in the Middle East as a convert from Ottomanism to Arabism. There is a biography and an exposition of his thought, both closely documented from original sources.

555 Haim, S.G., ed. Arab Nationalism: An Anthology. Berkeley: University of California Press, 1962, 255 pp.
Contains twenty selections from writings of Arab nationalists in translation, with a long, provocative introduction to Arab nationalism in general and its relationship to Pan-Islam and westernization. An excellent source.

556 Hanna, S.A., and G.H. Gardner, eds. Arab Socialism: A Documentary Survey. Leiden: E.J. Brill, 1969, 418 pp.
A collection of translations from modern Arab political theorists and politicians designed to show that Arab socialism grew out of Islamic roots, forcing the authors to take the curious position that most, if not all, Arab modernists have been socialists. The selections themselves are interesting as examples of political writing as long as the rubric under which they were collected is not taken too seriously.

557 Hourani, Albert. Arabic Thought in the Liberal Age, 1789-1939. London: Oxford, 1962, 403 pp.
A survey of the intellectual history of the Arabs under the influence of the tradition of English and French liberalism. There are introductory sections on the traditional Islamic political system and Ottoman political organization, followed by discussions of various schools of thinkers, with summaries and analyses of the writings of the leading figures in each. The best and most important book on the ideas that inform modern Arab political development. See also 1688.

558 Kerr, Malcolm H. The Arab Cold War, 1958-1970: Gamal ʻAbd al-Nasir and His Rivals. 3d ed. London: Oxford, 1971.
An incisive analysis of attempts at Arab unity in the form of the United Arab Republic, a union involving Syria and Iraq, and the Cairo summit meeting and its aftermath. Kerr is an exemplary political scientist, in that he knows Arabic as well as his field, writes very well without a trace of professional jargon, and has a sense of humor. This is an excellent study of Arab politics.

559 Khadduri, Majid. Arab Contemporaries: The Role of Personalities in Politics. Baltimore and London: Johns Hopkins Press, 1973, 255 pp.
Biographical studies of leading political figures in the modern Arab world, covering the gamut from Luṭfī al-Sayyid to Jamāl ʻAbd al-Nāṣir.

560 _____. Political Trends in the Arab World: The Role of Ideas and Ideals in Politics. Baltimore and London: Johns Hopkins Press, 1970, 298 pp.
Essays on nationalism, constitutionalism, socialism, Islamic revivalism, in the Arab world.

561 Nuseibeh, Hazem Zaki. The Ideas of Arab Nationalism. Ithaca, N.Y.: Cornell University Press, 1956, 227 pp.
An introduction to the content of pre-1956 Arab nationalism (before the time of its radicalization), which traces its roots to the common historical experience of the Arabs. Modern Arab political thought and its medieval antecedents are reviewed, and the impact of nationalism on society is examined. This book is very helpful to beginners.

562 Sayegh, Feyez A. Arab Unity: Hope and Fulfillment. New York: Devin-Adair, 1958, 272 pp.
A definitive statement of Arab self-consciousness in theory, aspiration, and practice, by one of its chief exponents writing in English. The approach is historical, and, in addition to ideology, covers the Arab League and various defense, economic, and cultural pacts.

563 Sharabi, Hisham B. Arab Intellectuals and the West: The Formative Years, 1875-1914. Baltimore: Johns Hopkins Press, 1970, 139 pp.
An outline of the development of "Islamic reformism," "Christian intellectualism," and "Muslim secularism" under the impact of westernization in Egypt and the Fertile Crescent. Sharabi's purpose is to trace the main lines of the development of political-religious thought during this period, not to analyze particular thinkers in detail. A significant contribution to Arab intellectual history.

564 _____. Nationalism and Revolution in the Arab World. Princeton, N.J.: D. Van Nostrand, 1966, 176 pp.
Provides an outline of the history and main components of Arab nationalism along with translations of constitutions, official government and revolutionary statements, political speeches. A primer of Arab nationalism for undergraduates.

565 Zeine, Zeine N. Arab Turkish Relations and the Emergence of Arab Nationalism. Beirut: Khayats, 1958, 156 pp.
A good study based on Arabic, Turkish, and Western sources, on the growth of Arab nationalism in relation to the Arab position in the Ottoman Empire, beginning with 1841. Written by an Arab with an Arab point of view, the work has a sounder appreciation of historical factors than most works on Arab nationalism.

International Relations

566 Afifi, Mohamed El-Hadi. The Arabs and the United Nations. London: Longmans, 1964, 202 pp.
Deals mainly with the role of various U.N. agencies in Arab states and the role of the U.N. in the Arab-Israeli wars.

567 Badeau, John S. The American Approach to the Arab World. New York: Harper & Row, 1968, 209 pp.

In addition to serving as American ambassador under President Kennedy to the U.A.R., in which capacity he was one of the few foreigners to be on intimate terms with ʿAbd al-Nāṣir (Nasser), Badeau served as president of the American University in Cairo and as a missionary. As a result he knows Egypt as few, if any, contemporary Americans do. His book is an authoritative review of what American policy toward the Arabs has been in the past and should be in the future.

568 Busch, Briton C. Britain, India, and the Arabs, 1914-1921. Berkeley: University of California Press, 1971, 522 pp.

Documents the struggle between the various factions within the British government over policy toward the Arabs.

569 Copeland, Miles. The Game of Nations. London: Weidenfeld & Nicolson; New York: Simon & Schuster, 1969, 272 pp.

Describes the role of the CIA, by a former participant, in the 1949 Ḥusnī al-Zaʿīm coup in Syria and the 1952 coup in Egypt and the subsequent rise to power of ʿAbd al-Nāṣir (Nasser); it confirms the most cynical views of American ineptness in the Middle East.

570 Fitzsimons, M.A. Empire by Treaty: Britain and the Middle East in the Twentieth Century. Notre Dame, Ind.: University of Notre Dame Press, 1964, 235 pp.

The point of departure for this study of a familiar subject is Britain's attempt to work its will in the Arab East through treaties. The bulk of the book is concerned with the post-World War II era. Most of the sources are secondary.

571 Hirszowicz, Lukasz. The Third Reich and the Arab East. Toronto: University of Toronto Press, 1966, 403 pp.

A detailed, factual survey of German-Arab relations and German campaigns in the Arab lands, country by country.

572 Kedourie, Elie. The Chatham House Version and Other Middle Eastern Studies. New York: Praeger, 1970, 488 pp.

A collection of Kedourie's distinctly original essays on modern Arab history, focusing on the role that Britain and the Chatham House group, led by Toynbee and Gibb, had in influencing British policy in the Arab world. Because Kedourie's views invariably challenge the prevailing interpretation of things, they demand either categorical dismissal or, more reasonably, a fresh look at cherished clichés and dogmas.

573 _____. England and the Middle East: The Destruction of the Ottoman Empire, 1914-1921. London: Bowers & Bowes, 1956, 236 pp.

A critical analysis of British policy in the Middle East during World War I and through 1921, centering on the Sykes-Picot Agreement and the creation of mandates in Syria and Mesopotamia. This is a stimulating study, in which the author's own opinion and interpretations loom large but not so argumentatively as in his later works.

574 Khalil, Muhammed. The Arab States and the Arab League: A Documentary Record. 2 vols. Beirut: Khayats, 1962, 1:705 pp.; 2:1019 pp.

A massive collection of documents relating to the history of the Arab League, translated into English or French. Volume 1 covers constitutional developments, and volume 2, international affairs.

575 Klieman, Aaron S. Foundation of British Policy in the Arab World: The Cairo Conference of 1921. Baltimore: Johns Hopkins Press, 1970, 322 pp.

Whereas most books on British-Arab relations attempt to survey this vast topic as a whole on the basis of memoirs of British administrators, this book sensibly focuses instead on a limited but significant aspect. More importantly, it is based almost entirely on archival research, resulting in a first-rate monograph; more of this kind of work is needed before a general history of the role of the British in the Arab world can be written with any degree of authority.

576 Lawrence, T.E. Revolt in the Desert. New York: G.H. Doran Co., 1927, 335 pp.

Lawrence's abridgment of Seven Pillars of Wisdom (see 577); he reduced the original text by half in this version. If Lawrence is to be read, his magnum opus should be tackled.

577 _____. Seven Pillars of Wisdom: A Triumph. London: Jonathan Cape, 1955, 700 pp. First private printing, 1926.

One of the most phenomenally popular books of the century, in which Lawrence gives his intensely personal and highly political version of the Arab revolt and his role in it, all of which is still a matter of debate and public interest. It is equally interesting as documentation of Western ambivalence toward the Arabs.

578 Macdonald, Robert W. The League of Arab States: A Study in the Dynamics of Regional Organization. Princeton, N.J.: Princeton University Press, 1965, 407 pp.

Macdonald attempts to assess the success of the Arab League in attaining its goal of regional and political integration, examining the structure and dynamics of the organization in the process. No Arab sources were used.

579 Mikesell, Raymond F., and Hallis B. Chenery. Arabian Oil: America's Stake in the Middle East. Chapel Hill: University of North Carolina Press, 1949, 201 pp.

A petroleum engineer and an expert on the Middle East collaborated on this handy description of the oil industry in Arabia, twenty-five years ago, and its importance in formulating American policy in the area.

580 Mousa, Suleiman. T.E. Lawrence: An Arab View. Translated by Albert Butrus. New York: Oxford, 1966, 301 pp.

Almost everyone else who has written a book on Lawrence has been a journalist and ignorant of Arabic. This is the only work that checks Lawrence's claims against Arab memories of the episodes in which he was involved. Although Mousa overstates his case in belittling Lawrence's role in the Arab revolt, his work is an instructive corrective and is useful to the historian more interested in Lawrence's historical significance than his psychological quirks.

581 Nevakivi, Jukka. Britain, France, and the Arab Middle East, 1914-1920. New York: Oxford, 1969, 284 pp.

One of the first books based on the new material made available by the opening of the British archives, it suffers from an embarrassment of riches: too many undigested documents with too little interpretation. Interesting for bringing to light data on British and French policy heretofore only guessed at.

582 Page, Stephen. The USSR and Arabia: The Development of Soviet Policies and Attitudes toward the Countries of the Arabian Peninsula, 1955-1970. London: Central Asian Research Centre, 1971, 152 pp.

A monograph on Russian policy toward Saudi Arabia, the Gulf states, and Yemen; makes extensive use of Russian sources.

583 Polk, William R. The United States and the Arab World. 2d rev. ed. Cambridge, Mass.: Harvard University Press, 1969, 375 pp.

Two-thirds of this book focuses on the Arab world, with a review of recurrent themes in Arab-Islamic history and the encounter with the West in the eighteenth and nineteenth centuries, all as background to a final section that analyzes U.S. policy in the area, conditioned by the special American interests in Israel. The historical approach of this study gives it a depth that others on the same subject lack.

584 Roosevelt, Kermit. Arabs, Oil, and History: The Story of the Middle East. London: V. Gollancz, 1949, 271 pp.

Because Roosevelt was the CIA troubleshooter for the Middle East, this book is of some interest as a reflection of the way in which that agency viewed the problems of the area and the mission of the United States in solving them.

585 Sayegh, Feyez A., ed. The Dynamics of Neutralism in the Arab World: A Symposium. San Francisco: Chandler, 1964, 275 pp.

A discussion by Arab participants of nonalignment as a program in international relations for the Arab world.

586 Sayegh, Kamal S. Oil and Arab Regional Development. New York: F.A. Praeger, 1968, 357 pp.

Given the fact of the exhaustibility of Arab oil, how can the oil industry best be exploited for long-term Arab advantage? This well-documented work is connected with regional planning.

587 Speiser, E.A. The United States and the Near East. Rev. ed. Cambridge, Mass.: Harvard University Press, 1952, 283 pp.

Despite the title, the book is actually an outline of eastern Arab history since World War I. Only the last chapter takes up the question of American interests in the Arab world since the forties.

588 Stevens, Georgiana G., ed. The United States and the Middle East. Englewood Cliffs, N.J.: Prentice-Hall, 1964, 182 pp.

Contains six papers on modernization, politics, and the Arab-Israeli conflict (with only one chapter, despite the title, on U.S. policy in the area), as seen in the early sixties. The papers are dated and have no documentation, but do manage to set forth some basic considerations involved in U.S. interest in the area.

589 Trevelyan, Humphrey. The Middle East in Revolution. London: Macmillan, 1970, 275 pp.

One of the most recent in a long series of memoirs published during this and the last century by British diplomats posted in the Middle East, this book covers Trevelyan's tours of duty in Cairo, Baghdad, and Aden in the fifties and sixties. Especially fascinating on ʿAbdul Karīm Qāsim and his erratic conduct of Iraq's affairs, as well as on Britain's final moments of dominance in the Arab world.

590 Williams, Ann. Britain and France in the Middle East and North Africa, 1914-1967. New York: St. Martin's, 1968, 194 pp.

A history of British and French policy in the Arab countries, stressing accidental elements as opposed to conscious planning. It is brief and necessarily superficial, using Arabic sources.

The Palestine Problem

591 Abu-Lughod, Ibrahim, ed. The Arab-Israeli Confrontation of June 1967: An Arab Perspective. Evanston, Ill.: Northwestern University Press, 1970, 201 pp.

Contains nine essays by Arab-American scholars in which the 1967 conflict is a point of departure for discussions of the whole Palestine problem (both local and international aspects) from an Arab perspective. Given this frank statement of orientation, the book is a valuable contribution to a literature in which purposes are not always so clearly expressed.

592 _____. The Transformation of Palestine: Essays on the Origin and Development of the Arab-Israeli Conflict. Evanston, Ill.: Northwestern University Press, 1971, 522 pp.

A review of the growth of Zionism, its impact on Palestine, the conflicts between Israel and the Arab states, and the international implications of the problem, designed to document the Arab point of view.

593 Buehrig, Edward H. The UN and the Palestinian Refugees: A Study in Nonterritorial Administration. Bloomington: Indiana University Press, 1971, 215 pp.
A study of the United Nations Relief Works Agency's attempt to handle the problem of the refugees from the Palestine wars.

594 Burns, E.L.M. Between Arab and Israeli. London: G.G. Harrap, 1962, 336 pp.
Memoirs of the chief of staff of the U.N. Truce Supervision Organization and commander of the U.N. Emergency Force, 1954-1957.

595 Cohen, Abaron. Israel and the Arab World. London: W.H. Allen, 1970, 576 pp.
A recapitulation of the history of the Zionist movement and the reaction of Palestinian and other Arabs to it, set against the background of relations between Arabs and Jews in the past. The author is himself a prominent Zionist.

596 Crossman, Richard. Palestine Mission: A Personal Record. London: Hamilton, 1947, 256 pp.
Crossman was a British member of the Anglo-American Committee of Enquiry Regarding the Problems of European Jewry and Palestine, formed in 1945. This is his report on the activities of the committee, his analysis of the problems it investigated, and his estimate of the persons and issues involved.

597 Dodd, C.H., and M.E. Sales, eds. Israel and the Arab World. London: Routledge & K. Paul, 1970, 247 pp.
A compilation of source material--documents as well as extracts from memoirs and histories--designed to introduce the uninformed reader or student to the problems involved and to prepare him to discuss these problems intelligently.

598 Esco Foundation. Palestine: A Study of Jewish, Arab, and British Policies. 2 vols. New Haven, Conn.: Yale University Press, 1947, 1380 pp.
One of the first "in-depth" studies of the Palestine problem, prior to partition, by a committee of scholars. Still useful for the vast body of data compiled.

599 Gabbay, Rony E. A Political Study of the Arab-Jewish Conflict: The Arab Refugee Problem (A Case Study). Geneva: Librairie E. Droz, 1959, 611 pp.
Although the material on the Palestinian refugees is plentiful, most of it is buried in journalistic or tendentious works. This scholarly, well-documented study of the problem, though dated now, is still useful.

600 Geddes, Charles L. The Arab-Israeli Dispute: An Annotated Bibliography of Bibliographies. A.I.I.S. Bibliographic Series, no. 7. Denver, Colo.: American Institute of Islamic Studies, 1973, 8 pp.
Covers twenty-seven bibliographies in Arabic, Hebrew, Russian, and Western languages. Indispensable in view of the large number of books written on this subject.

601 Gendzier, Irene L., ed. A Middle East Reader. New York: Pegasus, 1969, 477 pp.
One of many collections of articles centering on the Arab world and Israel, this one takes as its unifying theme the potentiality and actuality of social change in the respective states, as a means of deepening the reader's understanding of the Arab-Israeli conflict. The introduction enunciates the theme and puts the various authors' opinions into perspective.

602 Great Britain, Palestine Royal Commission. Report. London: His Majesty's Stationery Office, 1946, 304 pp. Orig. pub. in 1937.
The report of a royal commission assigned to determine the causes of the 1936 "disturbances" within the context of the implementation of the British mandate over the area. In effect, it is a history of the mandate with a concluding section on the possibility of a settlement. Excellent for its reflection of the views of the British toward the problem.

603 Harkaby, Y. Arab Attitudes to Israel. Jerusalem: Israel Universities Press, 1971, 527 pp.
The author surveyed recent Arabic writings on Israel in an effort to define Arab attitudes toward Israel and the reasons for them.

604 Howard, Harry N. The King-Crane Commission: An American Inquiry in the Middle East. Beirut: Khayats, 1963, 369 pp.
The scope of this book is broader than the title indicates, in that it covers the whole problem of Allied interest in the fate of the Ottoman Empire, with emphasis on the American role following the Paris Peace Conference. It should be read with the same author's The Partition of Turkey (see 950), to which this book is a footnote.

605 Hurewitz, J.C. The Struggle for Palestine. New York: Greenwood, 1968, 404 pp. Reprint of 1950 ed.
A well-documented study of the campaign from 1936 to 1948 to establish a Jewish state in Palestine, based on Hebrew and Arabic sources as well as European and American.

606 Ingrams, Doreen, ed. Palestine Papers 1917-1922: Seeds of Conflict. London: J. Murray, 1972, 198 pp.
A compilation of British government papers on the Palestine question, connected by the author's brief commentary and notes.

607 John, Robert, and Sami Hadawi. The Palestine Diary. Vol. 1, 1914-1945, 425 pp. Vol. 2, 1945-1948, 421 pp. Beirut: Palestine Research Center, 1970. 2d ed. New York: New World Press, 1972.
Curiously mistitled, the book is a history of the Palestine controversy from its inception in World War I through partition, told from a pro-Palestinian point of view, with the aim of educating the American public. Many documents are included.

608 Khalidi, Walid, ed. From Haven to Conquest: Readings in Zionism and the Palestine Problem until 1948. Beirut: Institute for Palestine Studies, 1971, 914 pp.

This is one of the bulkiest anthologies of writings on Zionism and the Palestine problem, even though it stops at 1948 and even though the criterion of selection was admittedly slanted to put Zionism in an unfavorable light. The selections, from a wide variety of sources, along with the author's own lengthy history of the problem, constitute perhaps the most thorough and accessible presentation of the Arab attitude toward Zionism yet published.

609 Khouri, Fred J. The Arab-Israeli Dilemma. Syracuse, N.Y.: Syracuse University Press, 1968, 436 pp.

Consists of a history of the political, diplomatic, and military conflict over Palestine, through the 1967 war, ending with consideration of proposals for reconciling the conflict. Though more sympathetic to the Arabs than most books on this problem, Khouri's analysis is not propagandistic and is well documented from UN publications.

610 Kirk, George. The Middle East, 1945-1950. London: Oxford, 1954, 338 pp.

Valuable for its account of the decline of British influence in Palestine, the creation of the state of Israel, and the first Arab-Israeli war, as well as for developments in Egypt, Persia, and Turkey.

611 Landau, Jacob M. The Arabs in Israel: A Political Study. New York: Oxford, 1969, 300 pp.

An analysis of the political activities and organizations of the Arab minority in Israel and their participation in Israeli political life, based on Arabic and Hebrew press reports, Israeli-Arabic literature, documents, and interviews: the most important and useful documentation concerns voting patterns. It covers only the period 1948-1967, but not the June 1967 war, and focuses on the political adaptation of the Arabs to the Israeli state.

612 Peretz, Don. Israel and the Palestine Arabs. Washington: Middle East Institute, 1958, 264 pp.

Although this book is now dated in some respects, it is still a useful analysis of the main components of the problem: refugees, repatriation, the Arab minority in Israel, compensations, and the role of the U.N. committee.

613 Polk, William R.; David M. Stamler; and Edmund Asfur. Backdrop to Tragedy: The Struggle for Palestine. Boston: Beacon, 1957, 399 pp.

A collaborative attempt to see the creation of Israel against a broad historical background, from Biblical times through the mandate period. In addition to the historical survey, there are separate essays on Jewish and Arab interests in Palestine, plus an analysis of economic aspects of the problem, often neglected in other works of a similar nature.

614 Quandt, William B. et al. The Politics of Palestinian Nationalism. Berkeley: University of California Press, 1974, 234 pp.

A study of the political struggle of Palestinian Arabs before and after the establishment of Israel. It traces the growth of Palestinian nationalism as a reaction to political Zionism, gives a description of the various Palestinian organizations, and discusses the present state of the Palestinian movement. A Rand Corporation research study.

615 Safran, Nadev. From War to War: The Arab-Israeli Confrontation, 1948-1967. New York: Pegasus, 1969, 464 pp.

This is as good as any and better than most of the studies of this never-ending struggle. Written by a political scientist whose best work has been in intellectual history, it combines a historical approach with statistical analysis of the aims and acquisitions of each side. There are also journalistic views from Tel Aviv and Cairo, and editorial prognostications, all making for a very readable book.

616 Sharabi, Hisham [Bashir]. Palestine and Israel: The Lethal Dilemma. New York: Pegasus, 1969, 224 pp.

The book, by a prominent Arab-American political scientist, is revealing for its expression of increased hostility toward U.S. policy in the Middle East and increased resentment toward Arab politicians and their propaganda following the Arab defeat in 1967.

617 Stein, Leonard. The Balfour Declaration. London: Vallentine, Mitchell, 1961, 681 pp.

An exhaustive study of the events leading up to the declaration, namely, the Zionist movement and its relationship to the British government and World War I, and the reaction to it by the various parties concerned. In addition to published works, Stein had access to papers of several of the British and Zionist principals. The book is somewhat weak on the Arab attitude.

618 Sykes, Christopher. Cross Roads to Israel. London: Collins, 1965, 479 pp.

A popular account, based largely on published sources, of the history of the Zionist movement, concentrating on Britain's involvement and the Palestine mandate. Less obviously biased than most books on the same subject, this is a readable introduction to a most complex and emotional matter.

619 United Nations, Special Committee on Palestine. Report to the General Assembly: Lake Success, 1947. 4 vols. Official Records, Second Session, Supplement no. 11.

An exhaustive survey of the background and development of the Palestine problem, containing the recommendations for partition and federal statehood. A subsequent volume, published in 1948 as Supplement no. 1, reviews the failure of the U.N. decision taken in 1947.

620 Vatikiotis, P.J. Conflict in the Middle East. London: G. Allen & Unwin, 1971, 224 pp.
Against the background of Islam, Arab nationalism, and Western influences, the author examines the Arab-Israeli conflict--the June 1967 war, in particular--as symptomatic of the underlying conflict in the area.

621 Zurayk, Qustantin. The Meaning of the Disaster. Translated by R. Bayly Winder. Beirut: Khayats, 1956, 74 pp.
One of the few analyses of the creation of Israel in 1948 that are both critical of the role played by the Arabs themselves and available in an English translation. It is also one of the few available English works to show any significant insight into the underlying causes of malaise in the modern Arab world.

Specific Countries

Arabia

622 American Geographical Society. Bibliography of the Arabian Peninsula. New Haven, Conn.: Human Relations Area Files, 1956, 256 pp.
A topical bibliography covering a wide variety of subjects, from geography to ethnology to international affairs.

623 Burckhardt, John Lewis. Travels in Arabia, Comprehending an Account of Those Territories in Hedjaz Which the Mohammadans Regard as Sacred. London: F. Cass, 1968, 478 pp. Reprint of the 1829 ed.
The celebrated memoirs of travels in holy Arabia by a European in disguise, with descriptions of the pilgrimage and the sacred cities.

624 Burton, Sir Richard T. Personal Narrative of a Pilgrimage to al-Madinah and Meccah. 2 vols. New York: Dover, 1964, 1:436 pp.; 2:479 pp. Reprint of the Memorial Edition, 1893.
A record of the pilgrimage made in disguise by the most renowned of British explorer-Orientalists, to the holy cities of Arabia. It is filled with the curious and erudite lore Burton specialized in.

625 Dickson, H.R.P. The Arab of the Desert: A Glimpse into Badawin Life in Kuwait and Saudi Arabia. London: Allen & Unwin, 1949, 648 pp.
One of the many eyewitness accounts of Bedouin life by Englishmen. Dickson's father was British consul at Damascus, and Dickson gained his entree into tribal life at an early age through a Bedouin wet nurse. Excellent not just for the usual descriptions of food, hospitality, and honor but for those of prostitution, hawking, wildlife, sickness, and disease. If it is true that Bedouin life has not appreciably changed in past centuries, the value of such works as sources ancillary to history is obvious.

626 Doughty, Charles M. Travels in Arabia Deserta. New York: Random House, 1936, 696 pp. Reprint of 1st ed., 1888.
Memoirs of journeys through Arabia, crammed with details of life in the desert, which are hard to come by in academic studies of the Arabian peninsula. See also 1680, 1824.

627 Hogarth, David George. The Penetration of Arabia: The Development of Western Knowledge concerning the Arabian Peninsula. Khayats Oriental Reprint, no. 22. Beirut: Khayats, 1966, 359 pp.
A survey of Western exploration of the Arabian peninsula. A summary, actually, of Western travel literature on the area, which gives a good idea of the character of the land and the type of Westerner it has attracted.

628 Hopwood, Derek, ed. The Arabian Peninsula: Society and Politics. S.O.A.S. Studies on Modern Asia and Africa, no. 8. London: G. Allen & Unwin, 1972, 320 pp.
Contains fourteen articles on the history, political development, society, economy, and culture of the peninsula, including the Gulf states, which as a whole add up to an excellent introduction to the modern history of the area. There is also a good bibliographical chapter.

629 Howarth, David. The Desert King: A Life of Ibn Saud. London: Collins, 1964, 252 pp.
A popular account.

630 Inayatullah, Shaikh. Geographical Factors in Arabian Life and History, Being an Inquiry into the Influence of Physico-Geographical Environment upon Arabian Life and Institutions. Lahore: Sh. Muhammad Ashraf, 1942, 158 pp.
A survey of the determinants of life in the Arabian peninsula--environment, food, domestic animals, economy--and their effect on Arabian history, derived from literary sources rather than from personal experience, but still interesting.

631 Kiernan, R.H. The Unveiling of Arabia: The Story of Arabian Travel and Discovery. London: G.G. Harrap, 1937, 360 pp.
A summary of the various memoirs of travelers and explorers in the Arabian peninsula, in the course of which Kiernan records much material on the geography, history, and anthropology of the area.

632 Landau, Jacob M. The Hejaz Railway and the Muslim Pilgrimage: A Case of Ottoman Political Propaganda. Detroit: Wayne State University Press, 1971, 294 pp.
Translation of, and commentary on, an Arabic propaganda pact on the Hijāz railway that the Ottomans directed at the Arabs.

633 Lipsky, George A. et al. Saudi Arabia: Its People, Its Society, Its Culture. Survey of World Cultures, no. 4. New Haven, Conn.: HRAF Press, 1959, 367 pp.
A general survey of Arabian society, economy, and culture by a team of researchers.

634 Macro, Eric. Bibliography of the Arabian Peninsula. Coral Gables, Fla.: University of Miami Press, 1958, 80 pp.
Almost twenty-five hundred entries, arranged in alphabetical order. See also 2863.

635 Philby, H. St. J.B. Arabia of the Wahhabis. London: Constable, 1928, 422 pp.
Memoirs of Philby's 1917-1918 experience in Arabia, much of it in the company of Ibn Saʿūd, who was embarking on his policy of Wahhābī expansion in Arabia during this time.

636 _____. Arabian Jubilee. London: R. Hale, 1952, 280 pp.
An informal history of the Saʿūdīs from the turn of the century to 1950, based largely on the author's own experience as adviser to King Ibn Saʿūd.

637 _____. A Pilgrim in Arabia. London: R. Hale, 1946, 198 pp.
One of the most recent descriptions of the pilgrimage to Mecca written by a Westerner. Philby went, not in disguise, but as a convert.

638 Thesiger, Wilfred. Arabian Sands. New York: Dutton, 1958, 326 pp.
One of the latest in a series of memoirs of travelers in the Arabian peninsula, with much useful information on topography and social life.

639 Twitchell, K.S. Saudi Arabia, with an Account of the Development of Its Natural Resources. 2d ed. Princeton, N.J.: Princeton University Press, 1953, 231 pp.
A survey of the geography and economy of Arabia and its position in world trade drawing on Twitchell's extensive experience in the country and his acquaintance with leading Saʿūdīs. It is now dated, of course, by the new oil diplomacy.

640 Winder, Richard Bayly. Saudi Arabia in the Nineteenth Century. New York: St. Martin's, 1965, 312 pp.
The standard political history of the Arabian peninsula, including the Gulf States, from 1818; based on Arabic and Turkish, as well as Western, works.

The Gulf States

641 Abū-Ḥākima, Aḥmad M. History of Eastern Arabia, 1750-1800. Beirut: Khayats, 1965, 213 pp.
A history of the ʿUtūb states, the forerunner of the present-day states of Kuwait and Bahrain, based on Arabic sources, many unpublished, as well as Western travel accounts.

642 Albaharna, Husain M. The Legal Status of the Arabian Gulf States: A History of Their Treaty Relations and Their International Problems. Manchester: Manchester University Press, 1968, 351 pp.
Essentially an analysis of conflicting territorial claims and boundary problems in the context of treaty relations between the Gulf states and Britain.

643 Belgrave, Sir Charles. The Pirate Coast. London: G. Bell, 1966, 200 pp.
A study of Britain's suppression of Arab "piracy," or the expansion of British naval power in the Gulf during the early nineteenth century, based on the diary of a British commander who participated. Belgrave was a British agent in the Gulf, and his bias is obvious from the title he selected, but his work is worthwhile as an authoritative account of British interest in the Gulf from an early date.

644 Busch, Briton C. Britain and the Persian Gulf, 1894-1914. Berkeley: University of California Press, 1967, 432 pp.
A well-documented study of British policy in the twenty years before World War I. It draws heavily on Foreign Office and India Office archives.

645 Dickson, H.R.P. Kuwait and Her Neighbors. London: G. Allen & Unwin, 1956, 627 pp.
The author had a long career in the area as a British military and political officer and representative of the Kuwait Oil Company; on this basis he wrote these memoirs, which include an informal history of Kuwait.

646 El-Mallakh, Ragei. Economic Development and Regional Cooperation: Kuwait. Publications of the Center for Middle Eastern Studies, no. 3. Chicago: University of Chicago Press, 1968, 265 pp.
Based on firsthand research in Kuwait, the book attempts to analyze the economic development of a small but economically important Middle Eastern state and to use Kuwait as a case study for economists without Middle Eastern expertise. Obviously, it is of timely significance in understanding the present oil crisis.

647 Hay, Sir Rupert. The Persian Gulf States. Washington: Middle East Institute, 1959, 160 pp.
A very elementary survey of the states--society, politics, and economy--based upon the author's experience in the area in various political and military capacities.

648 Hewing, Ralph. A Golden Dream: The Miracle of Kuwait. London: W.H. Allen, 1963, 318 pp.
A popular, journalistic, and entertaining account of the ruling family of Kuwait and Kuwaiti history by an author who specializes in biographies of wealthy men.

649 Kelly, J.B. Britain and the Persian Gulf, 1795-1880. New York: Oxford, 1968, 911 pp.
A history of the beginnings of Britain's power in the Persian Gulf in the nineteenth century until the agreement of 1880 between Britain and Bahrain, based on British archives and written from a British point of view.

650 _____. Eastern Arabian Frontiers. London: Faber & Faber, 1964, 319 pp.
A history of the "Buraimi oasis dispute," involving the conflict between the Saʿūdīs, the British, and various Gulf states over their frontiers and the oil that lies within them. Kelly sets the problem in a broader context, so

that his book is in many ways a history of the area since 1800, including the rise of the Wahhābīs.

651 Kumar, Ravinder. India and the Persian Gulf Region, 1858-1907: A Study in British Imperial Policy. New York: Asia, 1965, 259 pp.
On the basis of government of India and Foreign Office papers, the author reviews such subjects as the Wahhābī revival, the Berlin-Baghdad railroad, and Ottoman-Persian activity in the Gulf in the light of Britain's imperial interests.

652 Landen, Robert Garan. Oman since 1856: Disruptive Modernization in a Traditional Arab Society. Princeton, N.J.: Princeton University Press, 1967, 488 pp.
Landen attempts to fill the gap between 1850 and 1914 with a history of the critical period when Omani culture was transformed under British influence. Extensive research into archives and documents lies at the core of his solid book.

653 Lorimer, J.G. Gazetteer of the Persian Gulf: ʿOmān, and Central Asia. 6 vols. Calcutta: Government Printing Office, 1915. Reprint. New York: Gregg, 1970.
This historical and geographical survey issued by the government of India, but restricted to official use until the 1950s, is a monumental reference work on the history of the area since the time of British involvement.

654 Marlowe, John. The Persian Gulf in the Twentieth Century. London: Cresset Press, 1962, 280 pp.
A history of the Gulf, including Iran, based only on sources in English and limited even further by the lack of footnotes.

655 Miles, S.B. The Countries and Tribes of the Persian Gulf. 2d ed. London: Cass, 1966, 643 pp.
Miles's history, mainly of Oman, and his description of the tribes and the economy of the area grew out of his experience as political agent in the Persian Gulf and his travels in the area. It is still a standard source for history and ethnography.

656 Phillips, Wendell. Oman: A History. London: Longmans, 1967, 246 pp.
A history of Oman from ancient to modern times, combining Phillips's own archaeological research and personal experience in the area. In spite of the author's bias, reflecting his friendship with one tribal faction in Oman politics and his position as economic adviser and representative for the king of Oman and its dependencies, the book is on the whole a valuable study of a subject on which little scholarship is otherwise available.

657 Ramazani, Rouhollah K. The Persian Gulf: Iran's Role. Charlottesville: University Press of Virginia, 1972, 157 pp.
A history of Iran's activities in the Gulf and an analysis of its present political and economic claims and interests there. Both Persian and Arabic sources have been utilized.

658 Salil-ibn-Razik. History of the Imams and Seyyids of ʿOman. Translated by George Percy Badger. New York: B. Franklin, n.d., 435 pp. Orig. pub. by the Hakluyt Society.
A translation of a history of Oman from early Islamic times through the first half of the nineteenth century.

659 Wilson, Sir Arnold T. The Persian Gulf: An Historical Sketch from the Earliest Times to the Beginning of the Twentieth Century. Oxford: Clarendon, 1928, 327 pp.
Wilson draws largely on published Western sources, ancient and modern. He is at his best when discussing British involvement in the area, since he was himself an executor of British policy.

South Arabia

660 Hickinbotham, Sir Tom. Aden. London: Constable, 1958, 242 pp.
An informal sketch of the country and people of the colony by a British official who draws heavily upon his own experience in the area.

661 Little, Tom. South Arabia: Arena of Conflict. New York: Praeger, 1968, 196 pp.
A journalistic account of recent South Arabian history, focusing on the British colony and the independence movement as reflected in British press reports.

662 Macro, Eric. Bibliography on Yemen and Notes on Mocha. Coral Gables, Fla.: University of Miami Press, 1960, 62 pp.
Contains almost nine hundred entries on Yemen and a brief sketch of the history and situation of the port of Mocha.

663 _____. Yemen and the Western World since 1571. New York: Praeger, 1968, 150 pp.
A history of European interest in southwestern Arabia since the sixteenth century, by a British officer with experience in the area. Although many details of commercial dealings are presented, the absence of a systematic scholarly apparatus reduces the value of the book.

664 Marston, Thomas E. Britain's Imperial Role in the Red Sea Area, 1800-1878. Hamden, Conn.: Shoe String Press, 1961, 550 pp.
Marston has made an assiduous study of the India Office and Foreign Office documents relating to the activities of the British in Arabia, Yemen, Aden, Abyssinia, and the Somali Coast. It is one of the best documented studies of British policy in the Middle East that we have.

665 Schmidt, Dana Adam. Yemen, the Unknown War. New York: Rinehart & Winston, 1968, 316 pp.
A journalistic account of the Yemeni civil war, beginning with the coup d'état of 1962 and the Egyptian withdrawal of 1967. No documentation is given, though the author did visit the scene of the hostilities and interview participants.

666 Wenner, Manfred W. Modern Yemen. Baltimore: Johns Hopkins Press, 1967, 257 pp.
One of the few books in English (or in any other European language) on Yemen, this is useful mainly for its review of the tangled political events that have taken place in Yemen in the twentieth century. A pioneering study, it has been criticized for the author's lack of first-hand experience in the country, but for political scientists this is very hard to come by in one of the most isolated countries in the world.

Syria and Lebanon

General

667 Abouchdid, Eugenie Elic. Thirty Years of Lebanon and Syria (1917-1947). Beirut: Sader-Rihani, 1948, 614 pp.
A history of the mandate, written by a Lebanese in a journalistic format and including many documents.

668 Cumming, Henry H. Franco-British Rivalry in the Post-War Near East: The Decline of French Influence. London: Oxford, 1938, 229 pp.
A review of the contest between the French and the British interests in the area, focusing on treaties, conferences, and secret agreements, which ultimately left the British with the Palestine problem and the French with a cultural presence but little else.

669 Hopwood, Derek. The Russian Presence in Syria and Palestine, 1843-1914. Oxford: Clarendon, 1969, 232 pp.
One of several books published about this time on Russian penetration of the area through the Orthodox Church and its mission, this one reflects the increased attention given to the new Russian thrust into the Arab world via Syria rather than the intrinsic significance of the subject.

670 Hourani, Albert. Syria and Lebanon: A Political Essay. London: Oxford, 1946, 402 pp.
The emphasis here is on the westernization of Syria and Lebanon in the twentieth century, with full treatment of the entanglement of the area in international politics, but also with attention to Syrian intellectual history under the influence of the West and the growth of Arab nationalism. The reader is bound to be disappointed that this excellent study ends with 1945, and that no historian of Hourani's stature has written a sequel of equal quality.

671 Longrigg, Stephen H. Syria and Lebanon under the French Mandate. London: Oxford, 1958, 404 pp.
A history of the French mandate in Syria by an official of the British mandate in Iraq. Though detailed and thorough, it is limited to European sources; consequently the author's assessment is by no means comprehensive. Nevertheless, it is the fullest treatment of the subject yet published.

672 Tibawi, A.L. A Modern History of Syria including Lebanon and Palestine. London: Macmillan, 1969, 441 pp.
The more useful half of this work is the section on Syria under the Ottomans if only because relatively little has been written on this phase of Syrian history. The section on Syria during World War I and thereafter is a competently written but familiar story.

673 Ziadeh, Nicola A. Syria and Lebanon. London: Ernest Benn, 1957, 312 pp.
This book summarizes the modern history through the mandate and independence and analyzes political and economic factors at work in the area. Hourani's Syria and Lebanon (see 670) covers much the same subject more authoritatively.

Syria

674 Abu Jaber, Kemal S. The Arab Baʿth Socialist Party: History, Ideology, and Organization. Syracuse, N.Y.: Syracuse University Press, 1966, 218 pp.
A history of the development of one of the most important political parties in the Arab East and an analysis of its organization and ideology, based on a thorough study of the relevant Arabic texts within the framework of Western political science.

675 Asfur, E. Syria: Development and Monetary Policy. Harvard Middle Eastern Monographs Series, no. 1. Cambridge, Mass.: Harvard University Press, 1959, 158 pp.
Includes a survey of the Syrian economy as background to an analysis of the role of monetary institutions and policy in the development of the economy from 1950 to 1958.

676 Husri, Sati. The Day of Maysalun: A Page from the Modern History of the Arabs. Translated by Sidney Glazer. Washington: Middle East Institute, 1966, 187 pp.
A translation of an account of the French defeat of the Arabs in 1920, when the last hope for an Arab state in Syria was destroyed with the banishment of Faisal I. A significant document in the history of Arab nationalist feeling in the Fertile Crescent in the postwar period.

677 International Bank for Reconstruction and Development. The Economic Development of Syria. Baltimore: Johns Hopkins Press, 1955, 486 pp.
A compilation by a team of economists whose aim was to survey Syrian economic resources and to formulate a program of development. Although no experts on Syria were included and the team remained in Syria only three months, they managed to collect an impressive amount of data on the Syrian economy and its potentialities.

678 Petran, Tabita. Syria. New York: Praeger, 1972, 284 pp.
A competent history of recent Syrian politics, concentrating on the short-lived union with Egypt and why it failed, but continuing to 1971. Petran is a Western journalist who knows Arabic.

679 Saab, Hassan. The Arab Federalists of the Ottoman Empire. Amsterdam: Djambatan, 1958, 322 pp.
An excellent, well-documented study of the Arabs under Ottoman domination and their attempts, beginning in the late eighteenth century, to extricate themselves from the empire. The last chapter is original and significant, devoted to the formation of secret societies and their role in the growth of Arab nationalism.

680 Seale, Patrick. The Struggle for Syria: A Study of Post-war Arab Politics, 1945-1948. London: Oxford, 1965, 344 pp.
An excellent narrative and analysis of the events of this period, utilizing Arabic sources, newspapers, broadcasts, Western studies, interviews and letters, it is as detailed a review of this complex and confusing period in modern history as has appeared so far.

681 Tibawi, A.L. American Interests in Syria, 1800-1901: A Study of Educational, Literary, and Religious Work. Oxford: Clarendon, 1966, 333 pp.
A study of American missionary efforts in Syria during the century against the background of European mission activities in the area. Since little significant progress was made in conversion, Tibawi gives a great deal of attention to the missionaries' role in the Arabic renaissance, concluding that it has been exaggerated.

682 Torrey, Gordon H. Syrian Politics and the Military, 1945-1958. Columbus: Ohio State University Press, 1964, 438 pp.
This was published a year before Seale's book on the same subject (see 680) and is based on much the same sources, except that Torrey does not seem to have drawn as heavily on personal contacts with participants. The difference is mainly in style--Seale is generally more detailed and concrete--but both works should be consulted.

683 Yamak, Labib Zuwiyya. The Syrian Social Nationalist Party: An Ideological Analysis. Cambridge, Mass.: Harvard University Press, 1966, 177 pp.
An interpretation of the ideology of the SSNP, largely on the basis of the writings of Aṭūn Saʿadah, this is one of the most detailed studies of an Arab political party's view of itself.

684 Zeine, Zeine N. The Struggle for Arab Independence: Western Diplomacy and the Rise and Fall of Faisal's Kingdom in Syria. Beirut: Khayats, 1960, 297 pp.
Presents British and French policies toward the Arabs and the Arab reaction to them during and after World War I. This study is based on primary sources, both European archives and Arabic memoirs, in an attempt to find "the facts" beneath the biases and misunderstandings.

Lebanon

685 Gulick, John. Social Structure and Cultural Change in a Lebanese Village. New York: Johnson, 1964, 191 pp. Orig. pub. in 1955.
One of the early attempts by a trained American anthropologist to conduct field research in a Middle Eastern village, this book describes such aspects of village life as subsistence, religion, recreation, and values, against a background of environmental and population factors and in the context of cultural stability and change.

686 _____. Tripoli: A Modern Arab City. Cambridge, Mass.: Harvard University Press, 1967, 253 pp.
An attempt to analyze the political, social, and economic structure of Tripoli, limited by the author's difficulty in obtaining hard data on all segments of the society of the town. It is interesting, nonetheless, for its material on Lebanon a step removed from the capital and on the more general problem of Middle Eastern urbanism.

687 Harik, Iliya. Politics and Change in a Traditional Society: Lebanon, 1711-1845. Princeton, N.J.: Princeton University Press, 1968, 324 pp.
A well-documented study of Lebanon under the Shihābī emirate, based partly on archival studies, with valuable information on Christian-Muslim relations, the land and social system, and the role of the Maronite Church in Lebanese politics and culture. An excellent contribution to the history of modern Lebanon by a political scientist.

688 Hudson, Michael C. The Precarious Republic: Political Modernization in Lebanon. New York: Random House, 1968, 364 pp.
An analysis of political institutions in Lebanon with an estimate of their effectiveness and suggestions for improvement. The value of this study lies less in the recording of new data than in the presentation of material in a format useful to those with a political scientist's frame of reference.

689 Kerr, Malcolm H., trans. Lebanon in the Last Years of Feudalism, 1840-68: A Contemporary Account by Aṭūn Ḍāhir al-ʿAqīqī, and Other Documents. Beirut: American University of Beirut, 1959, 159 pp.
A discussion of a transitional period in Levantine history based on contemporary sources.

690 Mills, Arthur E. Private Enterprise in Lebanon. Beirut: American University of Beirut, 1959, 154 pp.
Mills analyzes the role of the environment, management, and state policy in the recent development of Lebanese private enterprise. The author, long resident in Lebanon, has used French and English materials.

691 Polk, William R. The Opening of South Lebanon, 1788-1840: A Study of the Impact of the West on the Middle East. Cambridge, Mass.: Harvard University Press, 1963, 299 pp.

A study of southern Lebanon before and after inroads of westernization brought about by Muḥammad ʻAlī's invasion in 1832, in terms of politics, economy, and fiscal and social organization. One of the few works that attempt to measure westernization concretely, it is based on British, French, American, and Lebanese (including Turkish) archives and sources.

692 Qubain, Fahim. Crisis in Lebanon. Washington: Middle East Institute, 1961, 243 pp.

A study of the 1958 crisis, in which the loose consolidation of political, social, and religious forces in Lebanon came apart, leading to U.S. military intervention.

693 Salibi, Kamal S. The Modern History of the Lebanon. Asia-Africa Series of Modern Histories, no. 6. London: Weidenfeld & Nicolson, 1965, 228 pp.

A history of Lebanon from the seventeenth century through 1960, based on original sources and what little secondary scholarship there is available. A standard, authoritative work.

694 Sayigh, Yusif A. Entrepreneurs of Lebanon: The Role of the Business Leader in a Developing Economy. Harvard Middle Eastern Studies, no. 7. Cambridge, Mass.: Harvard University Press, 1962, 181 pp.

A case study of the role of entrepreneurship in development, using Lebanese entrepreneurs as an example.

695 Suleiman, Michael W. Political Parties in Lebanon: The Challenge of a Fragmented Political Culture. Ithaca, N.Y.: Cornell University Press, 1967, 326 pp.

An excellent description of nineteen Lebanese political parties and an analysis of their function in Lebanese political, economic, and social life. In the process of showing that parties in Lebanon do not fulfill the functions they are expected to perform in the West, Suleiman traces a useful sketch of Lebanese political life in general.

Jordan

696 Abdullah. Memoirs of King Abdullah of Transjordan. Edited by Philip P. Graves. London: J. Cape, 1950, 278 pp.

This is of great interest for the relationship of the Hāshimī family to the Turks and the British and the role of the Arabs in World War I.

697 Abidi, Aqil Hyder Hasan. Jordan: A Political Study, 1948-1957. London: Asia, 1965, 251 pp.

A summary of the political history of Jordan since its creation as a state, with detailed documentation drawn from official British and Jordanian publications as well as secondary studies.

698 Aruri, Naseer H. Jordan: A Study in Political Development (1921-1965). The Hague: Nijhoff, 1972, 206 pp.

Although the author concentrates on politics, he has grounded his study firmly in social and economic conditions. Based on archival and other primary sources, this is the one indispensable book on Jordan.

699 Glubb, Sir John Bagot. A Soldier with the Arabs. London: Hodder & Stoughton, 1957, 460 pp.

Glubb Pasha's memoirs of his years as commander of the Jordan Legion from 1939 until his dismissal in 1956, reflecting his dual loyalty to the Arabs and the British. An essential source for the period.

700 Harris, George L. et al. Jordan: Its People, Its Society, Its Culture. New York: Grove, 1958, 246 pp.

An introduction to Jordan--society, government, economy, and culture--for general readers. Has no documentation.

701 Hussein. Uneasy Lies the Head: An Autobiography of H.M. King of Jordan. London: Heinemann, 1962, 233 pp.

Popular memoirs that bring out the formative influence of the British on the education and outlook of the king.

702 International Bank for Reconstruction and Development. The Economic Development of Jordan. Baltimore: Johns Hopkins Press, 1957, 488 pp.

A report on the potential for economic development in Jordan and recommendations on how to achieve it, by a team of economists of the International Bank.

703 Patai, Raphael. Golden River to Golden Road. 2d ed. Philadelphia: University of Pennsylvania Press, 1967, 560 pp.

A revised edition of Society, Culture, and Change in the Middle East, a somewhat traditional anthropological survey of social groupings in the Middle East under the impact of westernization and modernization. Patai has been criticized for his condescending attitude toward Middle Eastern culture and his biased perspective; if this is taken into account, the book can be useful as a survey of day-to-day life in the area and the pressures to which it is being subjected.

704 _____. The Kingdom of Jordan. Princeton, N.J.: Princeton University Press, 1958, 315 pp.

A profile of Jordanian government, culture, economy, and society with emphasis on people and the Jordanian way of life. Although Patai lays claim to "comprehensiveness," this is true of his range of subjects rather than of the thoroughness and rigor of his method: the book is a general introduction for laymen.

705 Shwadran, Benjamin. Jordan: A State of Tension. New York: Council for Middle Eastern Affairs Press, 1959, 436 pp.
Although the bulk of the book concerns the area since it became a state in 1921, there is background discussion of the role of the area in Middle Eastern history, beginning in the Bronze and Iron ages. This is one of the best-documented books on political events in Jordan. It contains an extensive bibliography.

706 Vatikiotis, P.J. Politics and the Military in Jordan: A Study of the Arab Legion, 1921-1957. New York: Praeger, 1967, 169 pp.
This detailed case study of the role of the army in Arab politics examines the history of the Arab Legion--its formation, structure, composition, equipment, campaigns--and its relationship to Jordanian politics, society, and economy, up to 1957, with an epilogue on the 1967 war with Israel. More monographs like this one are needed before meaningful generalizations on the significance of the military in the Middle East can be made.

Iraq

707 Birdwood, Christopher Bromhead. Nuri as-Said: A Study in Arab Leadership. London: Cassell, 1959, 306 pp.
A sympathetic biography of the dominant figure in Iraqī politics in this century.

708 Blunt, Anne. Bedouin Tribes of the Euphrates. London: Cass, 1968, 445 pp. Orig. pub. in 1879.
A journal of a journey made by Lady Anne with her husband, Wilfred, from Iskandarūn to Baghdad, with many nineteenth-century observations on Bedouin life.

709 Dann, Uriel. Iraq under Qassem: A Political History. New York: Praeger, 1969, 405 pp.
As detailed a study of the brief period as any in print, this is largely based (unfortunately but probably unavoidably) on press accounts. Interesting for its account of a crucial episode in modern Iraqī history and also for the data it provides for a comparative study of military coups d'états in the Arab world generally.

710 The Economic Development of Iraq: Report of a Mission Organized by the International Bank for Reconstruction and Development at the Request of the Government of Iraq (see 713).

711 Gallman, Waldemar J. Iraq under General Nuri: My Recollections of Nuri al-Said, 1954-1958. Baltimore: Johns Hopkins Press, 1964, 241 pp.
Gallman was American ambassador to Iraq during this period: his memories of the premier, Nūrī al-Saʻīd, are fond ones.

712 Harris, George L. et al. Iraq: Its People, Its Society, Its Culture. New Haven, Conn.: HRAF Press, 1958, 350 pp.
An introduction to Iraq for the general reader interested in its government, economy, and society; undocumented and dated.

713 International Bank for Reconstruction and Development. The Economic Development of Iraq. Baltimore: Johns Hopkins Press, 1952, 463 pp.
A report on the economic resources of Iraq and their potentialities for development, prepared by a team of economists, who spent three months in Iraq compiling the data.

714 Ireland, Philip Willard. Iraq: A Study in Political Development. New York: Russell & Russell, 1970, 510 pp. Orig. pub. in 1937.
This is the best-documented history of Iraq in the modern era, from the time of British hostilities with the Turks in Arabia through the termination of the British mandate. Ireland is one of the few writers to have used both British and Iraqī archives in addition to interviews with leading figures, again, on both sides.

715 Jalal, Ferhang. The Role of Government in the Industrialization of Iraq, 1950-1965. London: F. Cass, 1972, 142 pp.
A history of the Iraqī government's attempt to develop the economy of Iraq, written by the director-general of the Industrial Bank of Iraq.

716 Khadduri, Majid. Independent Iraq, 1932-1958: A Study in Iraqi Politics. 2d ed. London: Oxford, 1960, 388 pp.
A history of "independent" Iraq by an Iraqī scholar, based on original records and primary literary sources as well as interviews with many leading political figures, both Iraqī and British. Devoted exclusively to political developments and recurrent coups d'état, it stops short of the overthrow of the monarchy in 1958, which is treated in the sequel. Long on summary of events, short on interpretation.

717 ____. Republican Iraq: A Study in Iraqi Politics since the Revolution of 1958. London: Oxford, 1969, 318 pp.
The sequel to the author's Independent Iraq (see 716), covering the ten years following the decisive 1958 revolution. Like the earlier work, this one is a competent résumé of the course of events, but conservative in its interpretation of them.

718 Langley, K.M. The Industrialization of Iraq. Cambridge, Mass.: Harvard University Press, 1961, 313 pp.
An economic history of modern Iraq through 1958, with an emphasis on the growth of industry but also, of necessity, involving other aspects of the Iraqī economy, including agriculture, banking, and development.

719 Longrigg, Stephen H. Four Centuries of Modern Iraq. Oxford: Clarendon, 1925, 378 pp.
A history of Iraq from the sixteenth through the nineteenth centuries, or during the Ottoman occupation, based on original literary chronicles, travelers' reports, and the author's own experience in the area, with a distinctly dim view of the end result of the whole process. Longrigg supports the thesis that the Turks are responsible for the decline and decay of Arab Iraq.

720 Marayati, ʻAbid Amīn al-. A Diplomatic History of Modern Iraq. New York: Speller, 1961, 222 pp.
Contains original work on Iraq's participation in the League of Nations and the United Nations, whose papers the author has used.

721 Qubain, Fahim I. The Reconstruction of Iraq: 1950-1957. London: Atlantic, 1958, 277 pp.
Qubain surveys the development program for Iraq formulated by the Nūrī al-Saʻīd regime before its overthrow in 1958, including agriculture, industry, and human resources. Since the book was completed before the revolution, it seems dated but is nevertheless valid as an analysis of the development scheme.

722 Shwadran, Benjamin. The Power Struggle in Iraq. New York: Council for Middle Eastern Affairs Press, 1960, 90 pp.
A short journalistic account of the two years following the 1958 coup led by Qāsim against the Nūrī al-Saʻīd regime and the Hāshimī monarchy.

723 Wilson, Sir Arnold T. Loyalties: Mesopotamia 1914-1917: A Personal and Historical Record. London: Oxford, 1930, 340 pp.
Wilson, British High Commissioner in Iraq, regarded it as his "pious obligation" to record the progress of the civil and military campaign to occupy and administer Iraq. The result is this set of memoirs, which may be read as a defense of British policy in Iraq, in which efficiency and British interests were the primary consideration.

724 _____. Mesopotamia 1917-1920: A Clash of Loyalties, a Personal and Historical Record. London: Oxford, 1931, 420 pp.
A continuation of Loyalties (see 723).

Egypt

General Surveys and Studies

725 Abu Lughod, Janet L. Cairo: 1001 Years of the City Victorious. Princeton, N.J.: Princeton University Press, 1971, 284 pp.
By far the most complete study of the history of any Muslim city. By a sociologist with historical awareness. See also 1998.

726 Ayrout, Henri. The Egyptian Peasant. Translated by J.A. Williams. Boston: Beacon, 1963, 166 pp.
A description of the timelessness of life in the Egyptian village and a portrait of the eternal Egyptian peasant by an Egyptian priest. The short introduction by the American sociologist Morroe Berger helps to set Ayrout's description in the context of the efforts by ʻAbd al-Nāṣir to reform and improve the peasant's lot. Since the peasant rarely appears on the pages of the political histories of Egypt, but is always standing beyond them, this is a welcome contribution to Egyptian studies.

727 Berger, Morroe. Islam in Egypt Today: Social and Political Aspects of Popular Religion. Cambridge: Cambridge University Press, 1970, 138 pp.
An outline of religious organizations in Egypt: mosques, schools, waqfs (religious endowments), Ṣūfī orders, and benevolent societies. The documentation is thin.

728 Berque, Jacques. Egypt: Imperialism and Revolution. Translated by Jean Stewart. London: Faber & Faber, 1972, 736 pp.
A comprehensive study of the British presence in Egypt, its impact on rural and urban life, the rise of nationalism, its economic and social implications, and the role of classes in the new political society. Like all of Berque's work, this book is stimulating, but very personal and intuitive--difficult and challenging.

729 Collins, R.O., and R.L. Tignor. Egypt and the Sudan. Englewood Cliffs, N.J.: Prentice-Hall, Inc., 1967, 180 pp.
A general outline of the intermingling of Egyptian and Sudanese history, focusing on the modern period but with three chapters on earlier developments. Intended as an introduction for students and general readers, the book is based on an expert reading of up-to-date scholarship and provides an excellent summary of the subject.

730 Farnie, D.A. East and West of Suez: The Suez Canal in History, 1854-1956. Oxford: Clarendon, 1969, 860 pp.
An exhaustive study of the canal in Egyptian and world history with an excellent bibliography of works in Western languages, to which the research was confined.

731 Geddes, Charles L. An Analytical Guide to the Bibliographies on Modern Egypt and the Sudan. Denver, Colo.: American Institute of Islamic Studies, 1972, 78 pp.
An annotated list of monographs, articles, and library catalogs on the history of Egypt since 1789.

732 Harris, C.P. Nationalism and Revolution in Egypt: The Role of the Muslim Brotherhood. The Hague: Mouton, 1964, 276 pp.
One of several studies of the Muslim Brotherhood of Egypt, this one takes a historical approach, attempting to set the movement in the general background of modern Egyptian history. Based on both Arabic and Western sources, it is a competent history.

733 Holt, P.M., ed. Political and Social Change in Modern Egypt: Historical Studies from the Ottoman Conquest to the United Arab Republic. London: Oxford, 1968, 400 pp.
Contains twenty-four articles on sources, history from 1517 to 1798, and nineteenth- and twentieth-century history. The first section is outstanding, accurately depicting the nature and availability of the sources and the problems involved in using them. The second section covers the political history of the period, with three articles on land revenue, popular movements, intellectual life; the third section deals mainly

with social and economic history and less with politics. Most of the articles try to suggest lines of future research. See also 2233, 2247.

734 Husaini, Ishak Musa al-. The Moslem Brethren: The Greatest of Modern Islamic Movements. Translated by John F. Brown and John Racy. Beirut: Khayats, 1956, 186 pp.

Though largely superseded by Mitchell's The Society of the Muslim Brothers (see 739), this work is still interesting in its expression of sympathy for the aims of the movement.

735 Issawi, Charles. Egypt in Revolution: An Economic Analysis. London: Oxford, 1963, 343 pp.

Actually this is a third, completely revised, edition, of Egypt: An Economic and Social Analysis (1947) and Egypt at Mid-Century (1954). An economic history of Egypt from the time of the Napoleonic invasion through the first decade of the ʿAbd al-Nāṣir revolution. This is the standard general work on the subject, solidly researched and documented, an authoritative reference work, and the best introduction to this field.

736 Lacouture, Jean, and Simonne Lacouture. Egypt in Transition. Translated by F. Scarfe. London: Methuen, 1958, 532 pp. Orig. pub. in French, 1956.

A fine example of the contribution journalists can make to the understanding of contemporary history, provided they are as well educated and sophisticated in outlook as the Lacoutures. The background chapters on the history of modern Egypt are less interesting than those that reflect the authors' own observations of political, economic, social, and cultural life in Egypt shortly after the revolution. The value of the book lies in the authors' attempt to set the revolutionary movement in the context of "Egyptianness."

737 Little, Tom. Modern Egypt. New York: F.A. Praeger, 1967, 300 pp.

A journalist's history of modern Egypt, based almost entirely on secondary sources in English and on his own experience in the country. It will serve as a readable introductory outline of the subject, but then so will the much more authoritative work by Vatikiotis, The Modern History of Egypt (see 740) or the more stimulating Egypt in Transition by the Lacoutures (see 736).

738 Marlowe, John. A History of Modern Egypt and Anglo-Egyptian Relations, 1800-1956. 2d ed. Hamden, Conn.: Archon Books, 1965, 468 pp. Orig. pub. in 1954.

Marlowe has put together his own summary-synthesis of the standard secondary works on this subject available in English, which is pleasant to read but of little help to scholars, since there is no acknowledgment of what has been borrowed from whom.

739 Mitchell, Richard P. The Society of Muslim Brothers. London: Oxford, 1969, 349 pp.

An excellent history of the fundamentalist Egyptian reform movement, active in recent politics until outlawed by ʿAbd al-Nāṣir. There are also chapters on the organization and ideology of the brotherhood, which are grounded in Mitchell's wide reading in primary Arabic sources.

740 Vatikiotis, P.J. The Modern History of Egypt. London: Weidenfeld & Nicholson, 1969, 512 pp.

A conventional history of Egypt since 1800, emphasizing the dominant theme of westernization and the stresses to which it has led in Egyptian society, politics, religion, and culture. Although Vatikiotis knows Arabic well, this book is in the main a summary of Western secondary studies. There is a somewhat perfunctory attempt to insist upon the continuity of Egyptian history, but very little space is given to it. The book is strongest on the process of westernization and the transformation of Egyptian society.

741 Wakin, Edward. A Lonely Minority: The Modern Story of Egypt's Copts. New York: Morrow, 1963, 178 pp.

A firsthand account of "the Coptic question" by an American journalist. Aimed at a general, rather than scholarly, readership, the book succeeds in presenting the Coptic point of view on minority life in revolutionary Egypt.

742 Ziadeh, Fahat J. Lawyers, the Rule of Law and Liberalism in Modern Egypt. Stanford, Calif.: Hoover Institution on War, Revolution and Peace, Stanford University, 1968, 177 pp.

An interesting reading of Egyptian history in terms of the westernization of a powerful and influential element of Egyptian political, social, and economic life, it traces the rise and fall of lawyers in the governments from the time of Muḥammed ʿAlī through ʿAbd al-Nāṣir (Nasser) and their role in Egyptian nationalism and as a government elite. Well documented from primary sources.

Prerevolution

743 Adams, Charles C. Islam and Modernism in Egypt: A Study of the Modern Reform Movement Inaugurated by Muhammad Abduh. London: Oxford, 1933, 283 pp.

The book consists of a biography of Muḥammad ʿAbduh and an exposition of his doctrines, to which is appended a study of his principal disciple, Rashīd Riḍā. It is still basic for the intellectual history of modern Egypt.

744 Ahmed, J.M. The Intellectual Origins of Egyptian Nationalism. London: Oxford, 1960, 135 pp.

A short but authoritative history of the development of modern political thought in Egypt, culminating in Aḥmad Luṭfī al-Sayyid. Not nearly as detailed as Safran's Egypt, it covers much the same material from a different point of view. See 772.

745 Amin, Osman. Muhammad ʿAbduh. Translated by Charles Wendell. Washington: American Council of Learned Societies, 1953, 103 pp.

Memoirs of Amin on ʿAbduh rather than a formal biography, but useful for a contemporary's impressions of this influential Egyptian thinker.

746 Baer, Gabriel. A History of Landownership in Modern Egypt, 1800-1950. Middle Eastern Monographs, no. 4. London: Oxford, 1962, 252 pp.

A detailed study of land in Egypt, beginning with Muḥammad ʿAlī and stopping short of the 1952 revolution. Originally a dissertation, it is abundantly documented with statistics and follows a century-by-century chronology for the distribution of iltizām (tax-farm) lands, which were abolished by Muḥammad ʿAlī. There are separate discussions of waqf (religiously endowed) lands, state, and public domain.

747 _____. Studies in the Social History of Modern Egypt. Chicago: University of Chicago Press, 1969, 259 pp.

A collection of twelve of Baer's articles on various aspects of Egyptian history outside the main flow of political events in Cairo covered by the chronicles (and the secondary histories based on them) but of great importance in understanding the evolution of modern Egypt. Almost single-handedly, Baer has reconstructed what we now know about guilds, slavery, village organization, waqfs, land ownership, and the like. As yet, there are no studies of equal authority and clarity on other parts of the modern Islamic world.

748 Blunt, Wilfred Scawen. Secret History of the English Occupation of Egypt: Being a Personal Narrative of Events. New York: Knopf, 1922, 416 pp.

A personal, rather than a secret, account, which, the author claims, was read and approved by no less an authority than Muḥammad ʿAbduh. Useful primarily for the detailed discussion of the ʿUrabī uprising.

749 Brinton, Jasper Y. The Mixed Courts of Egypt. Rev. ed. New Haven, Conn.: Yale University Press, 1968, 416 pp.

An account by an American member of the courts established to handle cases involving foreign nationals in Egypt. So far the standard source on an institution that was representative of the colonization of Egypt.

750 Cromer, the Earl of. Abbas II. London: Macmillan, 1915, 84 pp.

A sequel to Modern Egypt (see 751) and concerned with Egyptian political history up to the death of Tawfīq in 1892.

751 _____. Modern Egypt. 2 vols. London: Macmillan, 1908, 1:594 pp.; 2:600 pp.

A history of Egypt from 1876 to 1898, drawing on the author's own experience as British consul-general and his access to Foreign Office archives and leading personalities. Part 1 is a narrative history; part 2 surveys certain aspects of Egyptian society and government.

752 Dodwell, Henry. The Founder of Modern Egypt: A Study of Muhammad Ali. Cambridge: Cambridge University Press, 1931, 276 pp.

The best biography of this figure to date, by a historian of British India. The shortcoming of this book is that the author has relied on British consular reports to the exclusion of other, including Arabic, sources, but it will have to serve until a more broadly based biography is written. It is stronger on military campaigns and objectives than on internal measures.

753 Ghorbal, Shafik. The Beginners of the Egyptian Question and the Rise of Mehemet Ali: A Study in the Diplomacy of the Napoleonic Era Based on Researches in British and French Archives. London: Routledge, 1928, 318 pp.

An excellent history of the Napoleonic expedition and the rise of Muḥammad ʿAlī, set against the background of European interest and rivalry in Egypt. It is somewhat curious that an Egyptian historian should neglect Arabic sources, but Ghorbal's reading of the British and French archives gave him a solid base for his interpretation, and his work is still a standard source for the period today.

754 Herold, J. Christopher. Bonaparte in Egypt. London: H. Hamilton, 1962, 424 pp.

A quite competent and readable popular version of Marquis de la Jonquière's five-volume account of Napoleon's invasion of Egypt. The French translation of al-Jabartī's historical work was also consulted, making this book the fullest version of the course of the campaign and occupation so far published in English.

755 Heyworth-Dunne, James. An Introduction to the History of Education in Modern Egypt. London: Luzac, 1938, 503 pp.

Considerably broader in scope than the title suggests, the book traces the process by which Western culture was introduced into Egypt from the time of the French occupation, through the reign of Tawfīq Pasha under the British, until 1883. It is based on a firm grasp of Arabic sources and experience in Egypt and underlies much of what has been written about the westernization of Egypt.

756 _____. Religious and Political Trends in Modern Egypt. Washington: published by the author, 1950, 126 pp.

Despite its general title, this is a pioneering study of the Muslim Brotherhood of Egypt and its founder, Ḥasan al-Bannāʾ, based on the author's own experience in Egypt and his reading of Brotherhood writings. A basic study of this political-religious movement that has not been altogether superseded by more recent studies.

757 Hussein, Taha. The Future of Culture in Egypt. Translated by Sidney Glazer. Washington: American Council of Learned Societies, 1954, 164 pp.

Translation of an eminent Egyptian intellectual's program for the development of Egyptian culture toward integration with the

Mediterranean tradition from which he believes it comes: a statement typical of a certain phase of Egyptian liberal nationalism, now outdated.

758 Khalid, Khalid M. From Here We Start. Translated by Ismā'īl R. Al-Fārūqī. Washington: American Council of Learned Societies, 1953, 165 pp.
This translation is an influential analysis of the need to purge Egyptian society of a corrupt "priesthood" and to construct a society based on "socialist" principles.

759 Landau, Jacob M. Jews in Nineteenth-Century Egypt. New York: New York University Press, 1969, 354 pp.
A collection of documents from archives, newspapers, travel memoirs, in Hebrew, Arabic, and European languages, on various aspects of the subject. More useful is the introductory essay, which describes the status of the Jewish community in Ottoman Egypt.

760 _____. Parliaments and Parties in Egypt. Tel Aviv: Israel Oriental Society, 1953, 212 pp.
One of the earliest attempts to describe the composition of political parties in Egypt and their function in governmental institutions before the 1952 revolution. A solid piece of work, written from a historian's point of view.

761 Landes, David S. Bankers and Pashas: International Finance and Economic Imperialism in Egypt. Cambridge, Mass.: Harvard University Press, 1958, 354 pp.
A study of the European economic penetration of Egypt based on the correspondence between an international financier and the private banker to the viceroy of Egypt.

762 Lane, E.W. An Account of the Manners and Customs of the Modern Egyptians. London: J.M. Dent, 1954, 630 pp.
An illustrated survey of nineteenth-century social life in Egypt, based on the author's own immersion in it. There is information recorded here on the details of everyday life that can be found nowhere else. See also 1333, 1867, 2628.

763 Lloyd, G.A.L. Egypt since Cromer. 2 vols. London: Macmillan, 1933, 1:300 pp.; 2:418 pp.
A sequel to Cromer's Modern Egypt (see 751), by a British high commissioner, who narrates events up until 1930 with "a deep faith in the imperial destiny of [Britain] . . . and in her capacity to benefit mankind." Though it lacks the authority of Cromer, it is still invaluable as a statement of the British point of view.

764 Luṭfī al-Sayyid, 'Afāf. Egypt and Cromer: A Study in Anglo-Egyptian Relations. London: Murray, 1968, 236 pp.
The daughter of Luṭfī al-Sayyid attempts to determine the extent to which personalities affected the course of Egyptian history during the Cromer period. Based on Arabic as well as English sources and on interviews, the book provides fascinating portraits not only of Cromer but of some of the leading figures in the development of Indian nationalism. Lest it be thought that the book consists of biographical sketches, it should be pointed out that it is an analysis of events in terms of the persons who were involved and provides a very incisive interpretation of the period.

765 Marlowe, John. Cromer in Egypt. New York: Praeger, 1970, 332 pp.
This volume should be read along with 'Afāf Luṭfī al-Sayyid's Egypt and Cromer and Cromer's Modern Egypt (see 764, 751). The former is a well-balanced presentation of both British and Egyptian interests, whereas Marlowe's book, based almost exclusively on British sources, is a fuller explanation of Cromer's and his government's point of view, written for a general, rather than a scholarly, audience.

766 Murray, G.U. Son of Ishmael: A Study of the Egyptian Bedouin. London: G. Routledge, 1935, 334 pp.
A compendium of firsthand data on the life of the desert nomads of Egypt, a subject neglected in political histories of Egypt except when the Bedouin rose against the government.

767 Owen, E.R.J. Cotton and the Egyptian Economy, 1820-1914: A Study in Trade and Development. Oxford: Clarendon, 1969, 416 pp.
A study of the dominant feature of the Egyptian economy during the nineteenth century and based, rightly enough, on French and English records, this is one of a number of expert economic studies of modern Egypt that add a new, hitherto unrecorded dimension to the history of the period.

768 Quraishi, Zaheer M. Liberal Nationalism in Egypt: Rise and Fall of the Wafd Party. Delhi: Alwaz, 1967, 245 pp.
A history of the rise and fall of the prototype of Egyptian political parties (1918-1953). Based on literary and oral Arabic sources, it focuses on the internal structure and membership of the party with some attempt to place it in the economic and social history of Egypt. Valuable as the most detailed study of a single Egyptian political party so far published in English.

769 Rifaat Bey, M. The Awakening of Modern Egypt. London: Longmans, Green, 1947, 242 pp.
Since this history of the foreign occupation of Egypt beginning with the 1798 Napoleonic invasion was originally a series of lectures, it is not as well documented as it should be. Nevertheless, it is significant as an Egyptian historian's reading of events that were of great moment in the emergence of an autonomous state.

770 Rivlin, H.A.B. The Agricultural Policy of Muhammad Ali in Egypt. Cambridge, Mass.: Harvard University Press, 1961, 393 pp.

An attempt to determine whether or not Muḥammad ʿAlī had an agricultural policy, and if so, to analyze it, as part of a scholarly effort to find the truth behind the Muḥammad ʿAlī legend. Rivlin used no unpublished archival material and only a few Middle Eastern sources, but the research into various aspects of Muḥammad ʿAlī's land policy constitutes the most important work on this key figure since the publication of Heyworth-Dunne's History of Education (see 755).

771 Rowlatt, Mary. Founders of Modern Egypt. London: Asia, 1962, 188 pp.

A history of Egypt from 1866 to 1911, focusing on the role of ʿUrabī in the development of Egyptian nationalism, it is based on both Arabic and Western sources, including interviews with the author's grandfather, who witnessed the events. One of the fullest accounts of the ʿUrabī episode available in English.

772 Safran, Nadev. Egypt in Search of Political Community: An Analysis of the Intellectual and Political Evolution of Egypt, 1804-1952. Cambridge, Mass.: Harvard University Press, 1961, 298 pp.

A superb intellectual and political history of modern Egypt that examines the writings of the major figures involved in that history. Besides giving an authoritative view of Egyptian history of this period, it also serves as a representative case study for other areas of the Muslim world that have gone through the conflict of traditionalism versus modernity.

773 Tignor, Robert L. Modernization and British Colonial Rule in Egypt: 1882-1914. Princeton, N.J.: Princeton University Press, 1966, 417 pp.

An account of British objectives in Egypt, the concrete means they employed to achieve them, the interplay of personalities of the colonizers and the colonized, all based on British and Egyptian papers and memoirs. As objective as any of the many histories of the most successful period of the British occupation, and more so than most of the British apologies on the subject.

774 Wendell, Charles. The Evolution of the Egyptian National Image from Its Origins to Ahmad Lutfi al-Sayyid. Berkeley: University of California Press, 1972, 329 pp.

Wendell sees the origins of the Egyptian national image in the community (ummah) founded by the Prophet Muḥammad in Madīnah, to which he devotes an initial chapter summarizing secondary scholarship. The bulk of the book is an intellectual history of Egypt in the eighteenth and nineteenth centuries, concentrating on political thinkers and culminating in the press writings of Luṭfī al-Sayyid on Egyptian nationhood. The last section, analyzing Luṭfī's work, is valuable, and the preceding sections help in placing his work in historical perspective.

775 Wilson, Sir Arnold T. The Suez Canal: Its Past, Present, and Future. 2d ed. London: Oxford, 1939, 224 pp.

A history of the canal valuable for its exposition of the British interest, up to 1933. Farnie's work (see 730) takes a broader view and is more detailed and better documented.

Under Jamāl ʿAbd al-Nāṣir (Nasser)

776 Abdel-Malek, A. Egypt: Military Society, the Army Regime, the Left, and Social Change under Nasser. Translated by C.L. Markmann. New York: Random House, 1968, 458 pp.

A study of the left in Egypt by an Egyptian leftist, with an analysis of "the social character of the military regime" and the search for "a national ideology." Given the identity of the author, this is the most authentic discussion of the state as conceived by ʿAbd al-Nāṣir and the new "revolutionary" society available in English. It is especially valuable for the discussion of the place of the intellectual in this society.

777 Dekmejian, R. Hrair. Egypt under Nasir: A Study in Political Dynamics. Albany: State University of New York Press, 1971, 368 pp.

In the absence of competent scholarly studies of the regime of ʿAbd al-Nāṣir, this political scientific analysis, based on primary Arabic sources, is a welcome contribution to Egyptian history, though much of it is couched in social scientific jargon and pseudomathematical formulas that at times obscure the author's interpretations.

778 Eden, Sir Anthony. The Suez Crisis of 1956. Boston: Beacon, 1968, 242 pp.

Eden's account of the affair that discredited him and drove him from office.

779 Heikal, Mohamed. Nasser, the Cairo Documents. London: New English Library, 1972, 328 pp.

Heikal, who was editor of al-Ahram and ʿAbd al-Nāṣir's confidante, gives his firsthand version of ʿAbd al-Nāṣir's relationship or confrontation with eleven major world figures, from Dulles to Guevara. Most interesting for the Egyptian, semiofficial view of ʿAbd al-Nāṣir's foreign policy ventures.

780 Lacouture, Jean. Nasser, a Biography. Translated by D. Hofstadter. New York: Knopf, 1973, 399 pp.

One of the best of many journalistic biographies of ʿAbd al-Nāṣir, finished shortly after his death, and therefore complete.

781 No entry.

782 Nutting, Anthony. Nasser. London: Constable, 1972, 492 pp.

There is as yet no scholarly biography of ʿAbd al-Nāṣir, but, rather, many journalistic pastiches. This one is based on the author's own recollections during his career in the British Foreign Service and his personal acquaintance with leading Egyptian political personalities, although much of it also comes from the press. As an informed personal interpretation, it will be an important source for biographers.

783 _____. No End of a Lesson: The Story of Suez. New York: Clarkson N. Potter, 1967, 205 pp.
A critical account of England's role in the Suez affair of 1956 by an official of the Foreign Office who resigned in protest.

784 O'Brien, Patrick. The Revolution in Egypt's Economic System: From Private Enterprise to Socialism, 1952-1965. London: Oxford, 1966, 354 pp.
A book on the transformation of the Egyptian economy since ʻAbd al-Nāṣir, which can be read profitably along with Saab's study (see 785) on agrarian reform during almost the same period. Although the scope of the book is limited, O'Brien has adapted a historical approach to his material, which takes him back into the economic measures of Muḥammad ʻAlī, giving his work somewhat greater utility than the title would indicate.

785 Saab, Gabriel S. The Egyptian Agrarian Reform, 1952-1962. New York: Oxford, 1967, 236 pp.
A survey of the Egyptian agrarian and land system before and after the 1952 revolution, with detailed discussion of the technical aspects of reform and a considered judgment of the success attained in reaching social and economic goals.

786 Vatikiotis, P.J., ed. Egypt since the Revolution. London: Allen & Unwin, 1968, 195 pp.
A collection of conference papers on the accomplishments and significance of the revolution in Egypt between 1952 and 1966, treating such aspects as politics and foreign policy, the economy, and cultural life, by such authorities as Malcolm Kerr, Roger Owen, and Vatikiotis. Dated, it nonetheless provides an interesting interim report.

787 Vatikiotis, P.J. The Egyptian Army in Politics: Pattern for New Nations? Bloomington: Indiana University Press, 1961, 300 pp.
Traces the development of "a military establishment" in Egypt and its transformation into a ruling elite. These historical chapters are followed by a political, scientific, theoretical analysis that takes Islam and varieties of nationalism into consideration. Based largely on Arabic sources, this is one of the best studies of its type.

788 Wheelock, Keith. Nasser's New Egypt: A Critical Analysis. London: Stevens, 1960, 326 pp.
This is the best of many journalistic accounts of Egypt under ʻAbd al-Nāṣir. Although Wheelock did not use Arabic sources and relied largely on Western press reports, he did have the cooperation of the Egyptian government, including ʻAbd al-Nāṣir himself, and his manuscript was checked by several scholars. It also has the virtue of footnotes.

The Sudan

789 Abbas, Mekki. The Sudan Question: The Dispute over the Anglo-Egyptian Condominium, 1884-1951. London: Faber & Faber, 1952, 201 pp.
Concise and well documented, the book is based on archival material and letters, as well as the standard secondary sources.

790 ʻAbd al-Raḥīm, Muddathir. Imperialism and Nationalism in the Sudan: A Study in Constitutional and Political Development. Oxford: Clarendon, 1969, 275 pp.
An analysis of British policy in the Sudan, and Sudanese response to it, in the form of collaboration, uprisings, the growth of nationalism, political organization, and relations with Egypt.

791 Barbour, K.M. The Republic of the Sudan: A Regional Geography. London: University of London Press, 1961, 292 pp.
An excellent description of the land and the people.

792 Bedri, Yousef, and George Scott, trans. The Memoirs of Babikr Bedri. Vol. 1. London: Oxford, 1969, 250 pp.
One of four volumes of the autobiography of a Sudanese educator, this one is especially interesting for its eyewitness account of the Mahdiyyah movement and the Battle of Omduran.

793 Beshir, M.O. The Southern Sudan: Background to Conflict. New York: Praeger, 1968, 192 pp.
The history of southern Sudan, told from the point of view of a northern Sudanese Arab, with extensive use of documents and archives.

794 Fabunmi, L.A. The Sudan in Anglo-Egyptian Relations: A Case Study in Power Politics, 1800-1956. London: Longmans, 1960, 466 pp.
A general history, utilizing British, Egyptian, Sudanese, and U.N. archival materials.

795 Henderson, K.D.D. Sudan Republic. London: E. Benn, 1965, 256 pp.
The author has synthesized secondary studies in this description of present-day Sudanese government and society, with occasional discussions of historical matters.

796 Hill, Richard Leslie. A Bibliography of the Anglo-Egyptian Sudan from the Earliest Times to 1937. London: Oxford, 1939, 213 pp.
An exceptional book in that it includes listings on such neglected topics as health, meteorology, hydrography, and forestry, in addition to the more conventional topics expected from such bibliographies.

797 _____. A Biographical Dictionary of the Anglo-Egyptian Sudan. Oxford: Clarendon, 1951, 392 pp.
Contains almost two thousand biographical sketches of persons prominent in nineteenth- and twentieth-century history of the Sudan.

798 _____. Egypt in the Sudan, 1820-1881. London: Oxford, 1959, 188 pp.
The standard work on the Egyptian occupation of the Sudan.

799 Holt, P.M. The Mahdist State in the Sudan, 1881-1898: A Study of Its Origins, Development, and Overthrow. Oxford: Clarendon, 1958, 264 pp.
A study of the Maḥdiyyah movement in its Sudanese and Islamic context, the first to exploit the Khartoum archives.

800 _____. A Modern History of the Sudan from the Funj Sultanate to the Present Day. London: Weidenfeld & Nicolson, 1961, 242 pp.
A concise but authoritative survey of Sudanese political history from the Arab conquest, concentrating on developments since the nineteenth century.

801 MacMichael, H.A. A History of the Arabs in the Sudan and Some Account of the People Who Preceded Them and of the Tribes Inhabiting Darfūr. 2 vols. Cambridge: Cambridge University Press, 1922, 1:347 pp.; 2:488 pp.
Provides data on Arab tribes in the Sudan from Arabic and other sources.

802 Nasri, Abdul Rahman el-. A Bibliography of the Sudan, 1928-1958. London: Oxford, 1962, 171 pp.
A supplement to Hill's bibliography (see 796).

803 Shibeika, Mekki. British Policy in the Sudan, 1882-1902. London: Oxford, 1952, 439 pp.
Closely documented from archival sources, this is a detailed study of the Maḥdī and Gordon and subsequent British policy and campaigns.

804 Trimingham, John Spencer. Islam in the Sudan. London: Oxford, 1949, 280 pp.
A history of the spread of Islam in the Sudan and a description of Sudanese Islamic beliefs and practices.

805 Wingate, Major F.R. Mahdism and the Egyptian Sudan, Being an Account of the Rise and Progress of Mahdism, and of Subsequent Events in the Sudan to the Present Time. London: Macmillan, 1891, 617 pp.
A history of the Maḥdiyyah movement from the vantage point of an officer in the British army in Egypt, later governor-general of the Sudan.

Libya

806 Evans-Pritchard, E.E. The Sanusi of Cyrenaica. Oxford: Clarendon, 1949, 240 pp.
An excellent history of the Sanūsī order of dervishes with an analysis of its relationship to tribes, religion, and politics; it is also good on the Turkish administration of Cyrenaica as well as the Italian military campaign. Combining an anthropological (field) and historical approach, it is one of the best books on the area that is now Libya.

807 Khadduri, Majid. Modern Libya: A Study in Political Development. Baltimore: Johns Hopkins Press, 1963, 404 pp.
Like many of the works on the Middle East by American political scientists, this book has been outdistanced by the course of events subsequent to its publication. Distinctly sympathetic toward the monarchy, Khadduri dwells on state making, the structure of the government, and the constitution, most of which is now of antiquarian interest; the concluding chapter, "Prospects of Reform," is also outdated.

808 Kubbah, Abdul Amir Q. Libya: Its Oil Industry and Economic System. Baghdad: Arab Petro-Economic Research Centre, 1964, 274 pp.
Since Kubbah describes himself as a "former petroleum economist" to the Libyan Ministry of Petroleum, his description of the Libyan oil industry and its place in the economy should be authoritative.

809 Norman, John. Labor and Politics in Libya and Arab Africa. New York: Bokman, 1965, 219 pp.
A description of labor institutions in Libya and analysis of their relationship to the government and to Arab nationalism. Norman's data come from interviews, the press, and U.N. publications.

810 Pelt, Adrian. Libyan Independence and the United Nations: A Case of Planned Decolonization. New Haven, Conn.: Yale University Press, 1970, 1016 pp.
Pelt was the U.N. commissioner in Libya in 1950-1951 who supervised the transition from an Italian colony to independence. He is thus well qualified to write this massive study of the process.

811 Ziadeh, Nicola A. Sanūsīyah: A Study of a Revivalist Movement in Islam. Leiden: E.J. Brill, 1958, 148 pp.
Though more recent than Evans-Pritchard's work (see 806), it does not supersede but rather supplements the earlier one with material on "leaders, philosophy, and organization."

Northwest Africa

General

812 Abun-Nasr, Jamil M. The Tijaniyya: A Sufi Order in the Modern World. Middle Eastern Monographs, no. 7. London: Oxford, 1965, 204 pp.
In addition to a history of the Ṣūfī order and a summation of its doctrines, this book contains chapters on its political role in Northwest Africa.

813 Ashford, D.E. National Development and Local Reform: Political Participation in Morocco, Tunisia, and Pakistan. Princeton, N.J.: Princeton University Press, 1967, 439 pp.
A study of local government in three countries of the Muslim world, based almost entirely on English and French sources. It is interesting for its attempt to describe a level of political life that has only recently been treated in works by Western, mainly American, political scientists.

814 Barbour, Nevill, ed. A Survey of Northwest Africa (The Maghrib). 2d ed. London: Oxford, 1962, 411 pp.
The standard survey in English of all the countries of North Africa except Egypt, it includes data and statistics on the history and political, social, and economic conditions of each country. Useful primarily as a reference work for the modern period.

815 Berque, Jacques. French North Africa: The Maghrib between Two World Wars. Translated by J. Stewart. London: Faber, 1967, 422 pp.
An analysis, rather than a history, of Maghreb society during the twenties and thirties by a French sociologist. It is a stimulating survey of Maghreb political and social organization, and also includes the author's observations on such subjects as sex, "street scenes," mentality, and neighborhoods. Although it is highly impressionistic, the impressions are sound, based on long experience and study and a high intelligence.

816 Bovill, E.W. The Golden Trade of the Moors. 2d ed. London: Oxford, 1968, 293 pp.
The standard history of the Sahara as the intermediate zone of commerce and culture between North Africa and the western Sudan, from ancient times through the nineteenth century, the time of the kingdoms of West Africa.

817 Brace, Richard M. Morocco--Algeria--Tunisia. Englewood Cliffs, N.J.: Prentice-Hall, 1964, 184 pp.
A general outline of the modern history of the Maghreb, intended as an introductory survey for general readers or college undergraduates; quite good within these limitations.

818 Briggs, Lloyd Cabot. Tribes of the Sahara. Cambridge, Mass.: Harvard University Press, 1960, 295 pp.
A description of the desert and the peoples who inhabit it, drawn from personal experience and wide reading in the literature.

819 Brown, L. Carl, ed. State and Society in Independent North Africa. Washington: Middle East Institute, 1966, 332 pp.
Contains fifteen papers delivered at a 1964 conference on various aspects of the recent history of North Africa, including politics (domestic and foreign), culture (religion and language), sociology (urbanization, trade unions, rural development), and economies (oil, planning). Expert, and still timely in many respects.

820 Fasi, ʻAllal. The Independence Movements in Arab North Africa. Translated by H.Z. Nuseibeh. American Council of Learned Societies, Near Eastern Translation Program, no. 8. Washington: American Council of Learned Societies, 1954, 414 pp.
"A comprehensive treatise on the resistance movement of the North Africans in its manifold diplomatic, military, and political aspects." It covers Algeria, Tunisia, and Morocco, and is a valuable statement of nationalist aspirations in North Africa by a leading exponent of the movement.

821 Fisher, Sir Godfrey. Barbary Legend: War, Trade, and Piracy in North Africa, 1415-1830. Oxford: Clarendon, 1957, 349 pp.
A history of English relations with Ottoman Barbary (Algiers, Tunis, and Tripoli) and Morocco, concentrating on the struggle for naval supremacy in the Mediterranean. It draws exclusively on Western sources, including archives, but absolves the states of the noteriety the West has assigned to them.

822 Gallagher, Charles. The United States and North Africa: Morocco, Algeria, and Tunisia. American Foreign Policy Library, no. 16. Cambridge, Mass.: Harvard University Press, 1963, 275 pp.
Surely the best concise history of the Maghreb available in English, and of far wider scope and utility than the title would indicate. The work has no footnotes and thus can be used only as an introduction, but it is nonetheless an excellent one.

823 Gellner, Ernest, and Charles Micaud. Arabs and Berbers: From Tribe to Nation in North Africa. London: Duckworth, 1972, 448 pp.
Contains twenty-three essays on tribalism and tribal structure in Morocco, the growth of Moroccan nationalism and its relation to the Berber tribes, social change, the role of the tribes in the 1971 coup, along with the editors' introduction and conclusion. Excellent, in the main, on the modern history of Morocco from a variety of viewpoints, particularly anthropology and political science.

824 Gordon, D.C. North Africa's French Legacy, 1954-1962. Cambridge, Mass.: Harvard University Press, 1962, 121 pp.
A study of France's mission civilisatrice in Tunisia, Morocco, and Algeria, its partial rejection by nationalists, the attempt at Arabization. Though based on French sources, it is quite an objective analysis of the impact of French culture on the Maghreb.

825 Liebesney, Herbert J. The Government of French North Africa. Philadelphia: University of Pennsylvania Press, 1943, 130 pp.
A survey of the French administration of its North African dependencies, Morocco, Algeria, and Tunisia; concise and factual.

826 Ortzen, Len, ed. and trans. North African Writing. London: Heinemann, 1970, 131 pp.
Contains samples of Algerian and Moroccan fiction in translation, which illustrates more the universal isolation of the intellectual than anything specific about North African intellectual life.

827 Zartman, I. William. Government and Politics in Northern Africa. New York: Praeger, 1963, 205 pp.
This survey of the political systems of eight states of North Africa, including all those on the Mediterranean, with the Sudan,

Ethiopia, and Somalia, also contains an introductory chapter on democracy and independence, and a concluding one on unity and strategy. It is a good outline.

Tunisia

828 Brown, L. Carl. The Surest Path: The Political Treatise of a Nineteenth-Century Muslim Statesman. Cambridge, Mass.: Harvard University Press, 1967, 182 pp.
A translation of the introduction to Khayr al-dīn al-Tunisī's tract on problems of political philosophy that reflects the ideas of nineteenth-century Ottoman reformers.

829 _____. The Tunisia of Ahmad Bey, 1837-1855. Princeton, N.J.: Princeton University Press, 1974, 409 pp.
A history of the modernization of Tunisia's political elite, focusing upon the career of its leader. Well written and fully documented.

830 Ling, Dwight L. Tunisia: From Protectorate to Republic. Bloomington: Indiana University Press, 1967, 273 pp.
A short outline of Tunisian history during the French protectorate and the struggle for independence. Vividly written, it will serve as an easily digestible introduction to modern Tunisian history.

831 Marsden, Arthur. British Diplomacy and Tunis, 1875-1902: A Case Study in Mediterranean Policy. Edinburgh: Scottish Academic Press, 1971, 276 pp.
Marsden has exploited recently available sources, both archives and private papers, to research a topic heretofore neglected. His book is significant for filling out the picture of Britain's diplomatic interests in an area less vital to its concerns than Egypt and Mesopotamia.

832 Micaud, C.A. et al. Tunisia: The Politics of Modernization. New York: 1964, 205 pp.
Leon Carl Brown and Clement Henry Moore have joined with Micaud to write three chapters on the process of modernization in Tunisia: Brown discusses the early stages, beginning with the initial contacts with the West, and Moore starts with the period of the Neo-Destour and one-party democracy. Micaud recapitulates social and economic modernization. By and large, these are interpretive essays with minimal documentation.

833 Moore, Clement Henry. Tunisia since Independence: The Dynamics of One-Party Government. Berkeley: University of California Press, 1965, 230 pp.
One of the best studies of North Africa by a political scientist, notable because it is free of social science jargon and schematization. Moore's analysis is well documented and penetrating.

834 Ziadeh, Nicola A. Origins of Nationalism in Tunisia. Beirut: American University of Beirut, 1962, 167 pp.
Besides a review of Tunisia under the French protectorate, this monograph analyzes the anonymous book La Tunisie martyre: ses revindications and its role in the growth of Tunisian nationalism.

Algeria

835 Barnby, H.G. The Prisoners of Algiers: An Account of the Forgotten American Algerian War, 1785-1797. London: Oxford, 1966, 343 pp.
A narrative account of the events surrounding the seizure of American ships and enslavement of American seamen by the Bey of Algiers. Based mainly on the letters and diary of one of the prisoners, it is good on this phase of Barbary history, given the lack of other works in English.

836 Behr, Edward. The Algerian Problem. London: Hodder & Stoughton, 1961, 256 pp.
A journalistic history of Algeria, focusing on the French occupation, the rise of nationalism, and the subsequent struggle with France. There is no documentation, other than a short list of works in French.

837 Clark, Michael K. Algeria in Turmoil: A History of the Rebellion. New York: F.A. Praeger, 1959, 466 pp.
A journalist's account of the revolution of 1930-1958, more detailed than most others available in English.

838 Confer, V. France and Algeria: The Problem of Civil and Political Reform, 1870-1920. Syracuse: Syracuse University Press, 1966, 148 pp.
A study of the "middle period" of French occupation of Algeria, when, under French civilian control, an alternative policy was available to France but was not taken. It is a study of French policy toward Algeria, based on French sources.

839 Gordon, D.C. The Passing of French Algeria. London: Oxford, 1966, 265 pp.
An analysis of the Algerian liberation movement from 1930 to 1965, when Ben Bella was removed from office by Boumedienne, emphasizing the French identity of Algeria. Somewhat journalistic in style, it is nevertheless solidly researched and documented and is a reliable, unbiased account. A companion volume to the same author's North Africa's French Legacy (see 824).

840 Morgan, J. A Complete History of Algiers, to Which is Prefixed an Epitome of the General History of Barbary from the Earliest Times: Interspersed with Many Curious Passages and Remarks, Not Touched on by Any Writer Whatever. New York: Negro Universities Press, 1970, 680 pp. Reprint of 1731 ed.
An eighteenth-century account based, in turn, on Spanish histories of Algiers, it is mainly of curiosity value.

841 Ottaway, David, and Marina Ottaway. Algeria: The Politics of a Socialist Revolution. Berkeley: University of California Press, 1970, 322 pp.
A history of the Algerian revolution under Ben Bella and Boumedienne, stressing the political behavior of the leading personalities who were, and are, involved. The material was collected during a three-year sojourn in Algeria.

842 Quandt, William B. Revolution and Political Leadership: Algeria, 1954-1968. Cambridge, Mass.: M.I.T. Press, 1969, 313 pp.
A study of Algerian political elite factions produced by the revolution. On the basis of five different categories of leadership, Quandt analyzes the course of events in Algeria during the period designated in the title.

843 Tully, Richard. Letters Written during a Ten Years' Residence at the Court of Tripoli, Published from the Originals in the Possession of the Family of the Late Richard Tully, esq., the British Consul: Comprising the Authentic Memoirs and Anecdotes of the Reigning Bashaw, His Family, and Others Persons of Distinction; Also an Account of the Domestic Manners of the Moors, Arabs, and Turks. Edited by Seton Deardon. London: A. Barker, 1957, 381 pp. 1st ed., 1816.
A collection of the letters of a British consul, 1783-1793.

Morocco

844 Ashford, D.E. Political Change in Morocco. Princeton, N.J.: Princeton University Press, 1961, 432 pp.
A political scientist's study of the independence movement in Morocco, with an analysis of the development of political institutions, the labor movement, interest groups, based largely on press reports and interviews. Though not definitive, it is a useful introduction in English to the progress of nationalism in Morocco.

845 Barbour, Nevill. Morocco. London: Thames & Hudson, 1965, 239 pp.
Though Barbour provides a popular presentation of Moroccan history, he is certainly an authority on the subject, and this book is an easy introduction to it.

846 Bernard, Stephane. The Franco-Moroccan Conflict, 1943-1956. New Haven, Conn.: Yale University Press, 1968, 680 pp.
A sociologist's study of the decisive phase of "decolonization" in Morocco, divided into three parts: a history of the conflict, "its sociological mechanism," and the role of the institutions and social groups involved.

847 Burke, Edmund. Prelude to Protectorate in Morocco: Precolonial Protest and Resistance, 1860-1912. Chicago: University of Chicago Press, 1976, 306 pp.
A study of patterns and causes of change in Morocco in the precolonial period based mainly on European archival and literary sources.

848 Geertz, Clifford. Islam Observed: Religious Development in Morocco and Indonesia. New Haven, Conn.: Yale University Press, 1968, 136 pp.
Lectures by an anthropologist on Muslim experience at opposite ends of the Islamic world; very suggestive for elements of unity and variety in Islamic civilization and for the use of history by anthropology.

849 Gellner, Ernest. Saints of the Atlas. London: Weidenfeld & Nicolson, 1969, 317 pp.
An anthropological study of Berber tribal government led by hereditary saints. See also 1381.

850 Halstead, John P. Rebirth of a Nation: The Origins and Rise of Moroccan Nationalism, 1912-1944. Cambridge, Mass.: Harvard University Press, 1967, 323 pp.
A study of Moroccan politics and society since 1900 through the rise of nationalism, based on Arabic and French sources, with careful and balanced analysis of the major policies, institutions, and persons involved on both the Moroccan and French sides. Well grounded in the modern history of the area, this book is broader in scope and therefore more useful than many recent studies of the Maghreb by political scientists.

851 Hoffman, Bernard G. The Structure of Traditional Moroccan Rural Society. The Hague: Mouton, 1967, 223 pp.
A useful reference work on the various components of Moroccan rural society (Berber, Arabic, European, Jewish, and other) and their ethnic interrelationships, with an analysis of social organizations and institutions.

852 Landau, Rom. Moroccan Drama, 1900-1955. San Francisco: American Academy of Asian Studies, 1956, 430 pp.
A general history of Morocco, including the Spanish zone, during the first half of the twentieth century, it attempts to describe and evaluate foreign occupation and the movement toward nationalism and independence. For a long time, Landau held a virtual monopoly on Moroccan studies in English, and his books are still useful as a journalistic account of modern Moroccan history.

853 Maxwell, Gavin. Lords of the Atlas: The Rise and Fall of the House of Glaoua, 1893-1956. London: Longmans, Green, 1966, 318 pp.
A popular account of the modern history of a Moroccan Arab tribe used by the French to pacify the tribes of the Atlas and the south. It is based largely on French sources and has no footnotes.

854 Mikesell, Marvin W. Northern Morocco: A Cultural Geography. Berkeley: University of California Press, 1969, 135 pp.
A survey of the ethnic, social, and economic life of Morocco, as well as a geographical description of the area.

855 Montagne, Robert. The Berbers: Their Social and Political Organisation. Translated by David Seddon. London: F. Cass, 1973, 93 pp. 1st French ed., 1931.

A summary of Montagne's research on Berber society, collected firsthand in Morocco, published as Les Berberes et le Makkzen. The value of this outline of Berber political and social structure is considerably enhanced by Seddon's translation, which puts the work of British and French "colonial scholars" in perspective.

856 Waterbury, John. The Commander of the Faithful: The Moroccan Political Elite--A Study in Segmented Politics. London: Weidenfeld & Nicolson, 1970, 368 pp.

A study of Moroccan politics since independence, focusing upon the structure and background of the political elite and its relationship to the monarchy.

857 Zartman, I. William. Destiny of a Dynasty: The Search for Institutions in Morocco's Developing Society. Columbia: University of South Carolina Press, 1964, 108 pp.

Zartman examines the nature of the monarchy in a state that is moving toward a parliamentary system.

858 _____. Problems of New Power: Morocco. New York: Atherton, 1964, 276 pp.

An analysis of five problems that confronted independent Morocco: evacuation of American bases, organizing the army, agrarian reform, Arabization of education, and organizing elections. As a whole, the essays give a good introduction to the functioning of a new Maghrib state.

Iran

General Surveys and Studies

859 Avery, Peter W. Modern Iran. London: E. Benn, 1965, 527 pp.

A straightforward political history of Iran during the nineteenth and twentieth centuries from a British point of view.

860 Browne, Edward G. The Press and Poetry of Modern Persia, Partly Based on the Manuscript Work of Mirza Muhammad ʻAli Khan 'Tarbiyat' of Tabriz. Cambridge: Cambridge Press, 1914, 362 pp.

In addition to an annotated list of Persian newspapers, there are samples of political and patriotic poetry, which provide excellent reading for the growth of Iranian nationalism.

861 Cottam, Richard W. Nationalism in Iran. Pittsburgh: University of Pittsburgh Press, 1964, 332 pp.

A study of the rise of nationalism and nationalisms in Iran and the conflicts engendered by them. It is reliable in the main, though the documentation could have been much fuller. Good for its inclusion of local and minority groups as well as of the mainstream of nationalism.

862 Curzon, George N. Persia and the Persian Question. 2 vols. London: Longmans, Green, 1892, 1:369 pp.; 2:653 pp.

Curzon toured Iran for six months in 1889 as a correspondent to the Times (London). This is a compilation of the data he gathered on the various cities and regions he visited, supplemented by information culled from three hundred books on the area in European languages.

863 Elwell-Sutton, L.P. Modern Iran. London: G. Routledge, 1941, 239 pp.

This is one of the best of many short introductory surveys of the whole of Iranian civilization written for laymen. Although there is no documentation and only a skeletal bibliography, Elwell-Sutton was and is an authority on the subject, and his summary of scholarship is reliable, though now thirty years out of date.

864 Hass, William S. Iran. New York: Columbia University Press, 1946, 273 pp.

One of many general surveys of modern Iran in terms of history, population, religion, politics, psychology, economy, suitable only as a readable introduction. No notes and no bibliography.

865 Kamshad, H. Modern Persian Prose Literature. Cambridge: Cambridge University Press, 1966, 226 pp.

A continuation of E.G. Browne's Literary History of Persia (see 66), which ended with 1924. Kamshad describes the work of the leading Iranian authors of the past fifty years and sets them against the political, social, and cultural background of the time. Kamshad is no Browne, but he certainly succeeds in writing a readable introduction to recent Iranian literature and cultural life.

866 Upton, Joseph M. The History of Modern Iran: An Interpretation. Harvard Middle Eastern Monographs, no. 2. Cambridge, Mass.: Harvard University Press, 1960, 163 pp.

No Persian works are cited for this interpretation of Iran's history from 1800 to 1958 in terms of modern "disunifying pressures." The book is better, therefore, for its analysis of foreign interventions than for the Iranian attitude and response to these.

867 Wilber, Donald N. Contemporary Iran. London: Thames & Hudson, 1963, 224 pp.

A rewriting and updating of the same author's Iran, Past and Present (see 77), omitting the survey of pre-Pahlavi Iran and analyzing contemporary Iranian history in terms of historical patterns and challenges to those patterns. The book, intended for general readers, has no documentation.

868 Wilson, Sir Arnold T. Persia. London: E. Benn, 1932, 400 pp.

One of the first of many general surveys of Iranian society, government, economy, and culture written by a Western observer during this century, the book is interesting both for the picture of contemporary Iran and for what it reveals of the official British attitude toward the country.

869 Wulff, Hans E. The Traditional Crafts of Persia, Their Development, Technology, and Influence on Eastern and Western Civilizations. Cambridge, Mass.: M.I.T. Press, 1966, 404 pp.
Contains a detailed description of Iranian crafts--metalworking, woodworking, building, textile making, leather working, and agriculture--as practiced today, along with notes on their historical development. Of obvious importance for the economic history of Iran. See also 2315.

Political-Religious History

870 Algar, Hamid. Mirza Malkum Khan: A Study in the History of Iranian Modernism. Berkeley: University of California Press, 1973, 237 pp.
A study of a key figure in the development of modern Iran in the nineteenth century, and an attempt to reconstruct the intellectual history of the period from primary sources. As such, it goes deeper into one aspect of material covered by the same author in his Religion and State in Iran (see 871). Both works are indispensable for an understanding of the modern history of Iran.

871 _____. Religion and State in Iran, 1785-1906: The Role of the Ulama in the Qajar Period. Berkeley: University of California Press, 1970, 286 pp.
An outstanding book on the function of religious scholars in modern Iranian politics, which can serve as a model for research on the same topic in other Islamic states. Algar's own research is both exhaustive and painstaking in terms of the works that he has consulted, lucid and convincing in presentation. The theme itself, the interaction of religion and politics, is of central significance in both medieval and modern history, and has rarely been expounded so competently for any period of Islamic history.

872 Arasteh, A. Reza. Education and Social Awakening in Iran, 1850-1968. 2d ed. Leiden: E.J. Brill, 1969, 237 pp.
After an introductory chapter on ancient and medieval education in Iran, the author surveys the educational system of modern Iran and describes its role as an instrument of social change in the Pahlavi period. Not very critical or analytical.

873 Banani, Amin. The Modernization of Iran, 1921-1941. Stanford, Calif.: Stanford University Press, 1961, 191 pp.
A study of the reforms instituted in Iran by Riza Shah, following some of the guidelines of Western secondary sources but based primarily on Persian language sources, including interviews. An excellent, well-documented study of the attempt to westernize an Islamic society.

874 Binder, Leonard. Iran: Political Development in a Changing Society. Berkeley: University of California Press, 1962, 362 pp.
A political scientist's interpretation of Iranian politics and how they operate, written for other political scientists.

875 Browne, E.G. The Persian Revolution of 1905-1909. Cambridge: Cambridge University Press, 1910, 470 pp.
The classic British version of the early Iranian nationalist movement by a sympathetic English Orientalist and Iranophile. Although much of Browne's interpretation has been and is being revised by later scholars, it is still the point of departure for study of the period in question because of Browne's thorough knowledge of Persian sources and wide acquaintance with Iranians.

876 Keddie, Nikki R. Religion and Rebellion in Iran: The Iranian Tobacco Protest of 1891-1892. New York: Humanities Press, 1966, 163 pp.
An analysis of a crucial episode in the Iranian constitutional movement, based on British Foreign Office papers, Persian and European literary sources, and, mainly, diplomatic documents. It focuses on political developments in Iran against the background of Anglo-Russian rivalry.

877 Riza Shah Pahlavi, Mohammed. Mission for My Country. London: Hutchinson, 1961, 336 pp.
An autobiography of the Shāh, with the assistance of Donald Wilhelm, a political scientist. Needless to say, the development of Iran under Pahlavi leadership is cast in the best possible light, but it is useful to have this official revision of recent Iranian history available, along with an explicit statement of future goals.

878 _____. The White Revolution. Tehran: Imperial Pahlavi Library, 1967, 177 pp.
The official statement of Riza Shāh's plans for a bloodless revolution in Iran, including land reform, electoral reform, the literacy and health corps, industrial profit sharing, and foreign policy. Excellent for the regime's image of itself and its aims.

879 Yar-Shater, Ehsan, ed. Iran Faces the Seventies. New York: Praeger, 1971, 391 pp.
Contains fifteen papers presented at a 1968 conference on Iranian politics, economy, society, and culture during the sixties. The book is valuable for the articles by Lambton and Issawi, which sum up their longer works on land and the economy, and for the wide range of the other articles, covering such subjects as the bazaar, modern painting, and music. There is very little criticism of the government or its policies.

880 Zabih, Sepehr. The Communist Movement in Iran. Berkeley: University of California Press, 1966, 279 pp.
The book has a dual purpose: to study how communism as a doctrine evolves in an Eastern country and to see how the Iranian environment affects the evolution of communism. The approach is basically historical and is based on Persian and some Russian sources.

Diplomatic and International Relations

881 Fatehi, Nasrollah Saifpour. Diplomatic History of Persia, 1917-1923: Anglo-Russian Power Politics in Iran. New York: R.F. Moore, 1952, 331 pp.

Fatehi relies rather heavily on press reports for a detailed reconstruction of the diplomacy of this period, though he also cites Persian and British documents.

882 Greaves, Rose Louise. Persia and the Defense of India, 1884-1892: A Study in the Foreign Policy of the Third Marquis of Salisbury. London: University of London, 1959, 301 pp.

Primarily British, but also Austrian and American, archives, as well as the private papers of Gladstone and others, were consulted for this analysis of an important phase of British policy toward Persia in the late nineteenth century.

883 Hamzavi, A.H. Persia and the Powers: An Account of Diplomatic Relations, 1941-1946. London: Hutchinson, 1946, 125 pp.

A pamphlet written by the Iranian press attaché in London, attacking Soviet interference in Iranian affairs.

884 Kazemzadeh, Firuz. Russia and Britain in Persia, 1864-1914: A Study in Imperialism. New Haven, Conn.: Yale University Press, 1968, 711 pp.

The most detailed and authoritative work on this aspect of Iranian history published so far, this is a diplomatic history of Russian and British activities in Iran during the fifty years preceding the First World War, based on Russian, Persian, and English sources.

885 Lenczowski, George. Russia and the West in Iran, 1918-1948: A Study in Big-Power Rivalry. Ithaca, N.Y.: Cornell University Press, 1949, 383 pp.

A detailed history of British and Russian diplomacy and military activities in Iran after World War I. Much of this has been superseded by Ramazani's Foreign Policy of Iran, 1500-1944 (see 888), which has a wider and firmer command of Persian sources, but Lenczowski is still a valuable supplement, since he approaches the subject from the opposite direction and is uniformly objective.

886 Millspaugh, A.C. The American Task in Persia. New York: Century, 1925, 322 pp.

An account of Shuster's mission to Persia in the twenties (see 889), when he was made administrator general of the finances of Persia in an effort to revive Persian finances and economy.

887 _____. Americans in Persia. Washington: Brookings Institution, 1946, 293 pp.

Focuses on Millspaugh's second mission to Iran, in the forties, when he experienced many of the same difficulties as Shuster (see 886, 889) in an attempt to organize Iranian finances independent of foreign control.

888 Ramazani, R.K. The Foreign Policy of Iran, 1500-1944: A Developing Nation in World Affairs. Charlottesville: University Press of Virginia, 1966, 330 pp.

The broad span of time taken as a subject for study indicates that Ramazani believes that there are certain key factors in Iranian history that have influenced Iran's relations with foreign powers. Actually, however, most of the book deals with nineteenth- and twentieth-century diplomacy, and only an introductory chapter is devoted to "the traditional foreign policy, 1500-1905." Half the book, furthermore, is given to a discussion of the changes introduced by Riza Shāh.

889 Shuster, W. Morgan. The Strangling of Persia: The Story of the European Diplomacy and Oriental Intrigue That Resulted in the Denationalization of Twelve Million Mohammedans, a Personal Narrative. New York: Century, 1920, 423 pp.

Shuster, an American, was engaged as treasurer-general of Iran in 1911 to reorganize Iranian finances, but was forced to leave by the Russians. The subtitle nicely sums up the scope and tone of the book.

890 Yeselson, Abraham. United States-Persian Diplomatic Relations, 1883-1921. New Brunswick, N.J.: Rutgers University Press, 1956, 243 pp.

A short survey of United States policy in Persia, based on U.S. State Department archives.

Economic Studies

891 Bharier, Julian. Economic Development in Iran, 1900-1970. London: Oxford, 1971, 314 pp.

A detailed study of economic policy in the light of Iranian resources--agriculture, industry, transport, and finances--based on five years' research in Iran.

892 Elwell-Sutton, L.P. Persian Oil: A Study in Power Politics. London: Lawrence & Wishart, 1955, 343 pp.

One of the most readable books on the petroleum industry, it is also an authoritative history of the Anglo-Iranian Oil Company in Iran, with emphasis on the Mosaddeq crisis.

893 Ford, Alan W. The Anglo-Iranian Oil Dispute of 1951-1952: A Study of the Role of Law in the Relations of States. Berkeley: University of California Press, 1954, 348 pp.

Written by a student of international law, this book is useful for the discussion of the negotiations and adjudication involved in the dispute.

894 Issawi, Charles, ed. The Economic History of Iran, 1800-1914. Publications of the Center for Middle Eastern Studies, no. 8. Chicago: University of Chicago Press, 1971, 404 pp.

Contains articles and extracts from documents and books that treat the economic history of Iran but have not been published previously in English and are not readily available elsewhere. There is an epilogue by the editor, which describes the economy from 1914 to 1971, as well as introductory chapters on the geographical and historical background and social structure of Iran.

895 Lambton, A.K.S. The Persian Land Reform 1926-66. New York: Oxford, 1969, 386 pp.
An outgrowth of the same author's Landlord and Peasant in Persia (see 72), this volume examines the actual measures that constituted the "reform" and, more importantly, their impact on the Iranian economy and society. Her conclusions tend to support the government's claim that reform has been effective in improving the lot of the Iranian peasantry in particular and Iranian agriculture in general.

Turkey

General

896 Berkes, Niyazi. The Development of Secularism in Turkey. Montreal: McGill University Press, 1964, 537 pp.
This is a profound study of Turkish history from 1718 to 1939, which, unlike so many works on the modern Islamic world, has a unifying theme: the secularization of a religiously inspired society and state. With a firm command of Turkish sources, Berkes is able to trace from within the full impact of change brought about partially, but by no means completely, under Western influence. Religion and politics, political and religious history, are all given careful attention in this comprehensive work.

897 Gökalp, Ziya. The Principles of Turkism. Translated by R. Devereux. Leiden: E.J. Brill, 1968, 141 pp.
A translation of one of the key works by a theorist of the Atatürk revolution, summarizing his main ideas.

898 ______. Turkish Nationalism and Western Civilization: Selected Essays of Ziya Gökalp. Translated by Niyazi Berkes. London: G. Allen & Unwin, 1959, 336 pp.
Selections on Turkish nationalism and its relation to Islam and the West, from the writings of an influential twentieth-century Turkish thinker. Berkes's introduction places Gökalp within the political and intellectual history of his time.

899 Heyd, Uriel. The Foundations of Turkish Nationalism: The Life and Teachings of Z. Gökalp. London: Luzac, 1950, 174 pp.
The biography of Gökalp is quite short; most of the book consists of an analysis of his thought under the following topics: "Philosophical Foundation," "Sociological Concepts," "Westernization," "Islam," and "Turkism." The volume, used with translations from Gökalp's writings, serves as a full introduction to this influential thinker.

900 Lewis, Bernard. The Emergence of Modern Turkey. London: Oxford, 1961, 511 pp.
Along with Berkes's Development of Secularism in Turkey (see 896), this is a major study of the growth of a modern, secularized Turkey out of the Ottoman Empire. The approaches to the material and the material itself are so complex that both books need to be read and consulted frequently.

901 Lewis, G.C. Turkey. London: E. Benn, 1955, 222 pp.
An account of Turkish history from the nineteenth century, along with a survey of the population and economy, aimed at the general reader.

902 Price, M. Phillips. A History of Turkey from Empire to Republic. 2d ed. of 1956 ed. London: Allen & Unwin, 1961, 237 pp.
A superficial account of Turkish history, primarily of the twentieth century, with background chapters on the Ottoman Empire, based on secondary European sources and the author's travels in Turkey.

903 Shaw, Stanford J., and Ezel Kural Shaw. History of the Ottoman Empire and Modern Turkey. Vol. 2, Reform, Revolution, and Republic: The Rise of Modern Turkey, 1808-1975. Cambridge: Cambridge University Press, 1976, 518 pp.
An authoritative summation, not so analytical as Berkes's and Lewis's works (see 896, 900).

904 Toynbee, Arnold J., and Kenneth P. Kirkwood. Turkey. New York: Scribner's, 1927, 329 pp.
Although both authors spent time in Turkey, their book is based on European sources. It is a popular, undocumented account of the Kemalist revolution up to 1926.

905 Tugay, Emine Foat. Three Centuries: Family Chronicles of Turkey and Egypt. London: Oxford, 1963, 324 pp.
Fascinating memoirs of Ottoman "upper-class" life in Turkey and Egypt by a granddaughter of Khedive Ismail.

906 Ward, R.E., and D.A. Rustow, eds. Political Modernization in Japan and Turkey. Princeton, N.J.: Princeton University Press, 1964, 502 pp.
A collection of essays that attempt to compare the experience of two traditional societies in the process of westernization and modernization under such headings as economics, education, the media, and the military. Very interesting for its insights into Turkish history through comparison and contrast with the Japanese example, and an obvious choice for a course in non-Western comparative politics.

Prerevolution

907 Ahmad, Feroz. The Young Turks: The Committee of Union and Progress in Turkish Politics, 1908-1914. Oxford: Clarendon, 1969, 205 pp.
This book has received considerable attention since it was submitted as a dissertation at the University of London, and justifiably so, for it shows the author's firm grasp of political studies and his extensive reading in Turkish sources. By a careful analysis of the events between 1908 and 1914, he challenges the view that the Committee of Union and Progress monopolized political power in Turkey after 1908.

908 Anderson, M.S. The Eastern Question, 1774-1923. New York: St. Martin's, 1966, 436 pp.
An attempt to update Sir J.A.R. Marriott's Eastern Question (see 921) as an undergraduate text; for the diplomatic history of the collapse and division of the Ottoman Empire, it is a reliable detailed presentation of European scholarship on the subject, which fulfills the author's intention. Russian sources were used, but no Turkish or Arabic ones.

909 Bailey, Frank Edgar. British Policy and the Turkish Reform Movement: A Study in Anglo-Turkish Relations, 1826-1853. Cambridge, Mass.: Harvard University Press, 1942, 312 pp.
Bailey analyzes the influence of Western nations on the reform movement, particularly in Britain, using British archival sources.

910 Blaisdell, Donald C. European Financial Control in the Ottoman Empire: A Study of the Establishment, Activities, and Significance of the Ottoman Public Debt. New York: Columbia University Press, 1929, 243 pp.
Blaisdell used archival material available in Berlin and Istanbul for this study of the Public Debt Council as a typical instance of European "financial imperialism."

911 Bullard, Sir Reader. Britain and the Middle East, from Earliest Times to 1952. London: Hutchinson's, 1952, 196 pp.
Although Bullard, British minister and ambassador to Tehran, begins with British pilgrims and Crusaders, his emphasis is on the Eastern question and the dissolution of the Ottoman Empire, and the role that Britain played in the successor states.

912 Davison, Roderic H. Reform in the Ottoman Empire, 1856-1876. Princeton, N.J.: Princeton University Press, 1973, 483 pp. Orig. pub. in 1963.
A study of Ottoman politics and administration during the Tanzimat period, based on Turkish as well as Western sources. So far this is still the standard work on the attempt to reform the structure of Ottoman government and society under the threat of foreign intervention.

913 Devereux, Robert. The First Ottoman Constitutional Period: A Study of the Midhat Constitution and Parliament. Baltimore: Johns Hopkins Press, 1963, 310 pp.
A history of the first attempt to establish a parliamentary system of government in Turkey (1875-1877): the events leading up to the promulgation of the constitution, the structure of the constitution, the structure and activities of the parliament, and the results of the parliamentary movement. It is well documented from Turkish sources.

914 Djemal Pasha. Memories of a Turkish Statesman--1913-1919. London: Hutchinson, 1922, 302 pp.
Recollection of Turkey during World War I by a member of the triumvirate that was ruling at the time.

915 Earle, Edward Meade. Turkey, the Great Powers, and the Baghdad Railway: A Study in Imperialism. New York: Macmillan, 1923, 364 pp.
The construction of the railway is used as a case study of European economic imperialism. Although there are few notes, Earle seems to make extensive use of papers related to the enterprise.

916 Grabill, Joseph L. Protestant Diplomacy and the Near East: Missionary Influence on American Policy, 1810-1927. Minneapolis: University of Minnesota Press, 1971, 395 pp.
Grabill has been indefatigable in tracking down unpublished sources to establish his thesis that the Protestant missionaries were of prime importance in formulating American policy toward the late Ottoman Empire, before the advent of the era of oil diplomacy.

917 Holland, Thomas Erskine, ed. The European Concern in the Eastern Question: A Collection of Treaties and Other Public Acts. Oxford: Clarendon, 1885, 366 pp.
Documents relating to Greece, Samos and Crete, Egypt, Lebanon, the Balkans, Turkey, Australia, and Russia (1826-1885).

918 Joseph, John. The Nestorians and Their Muslim Neighbors: A Study of Western Influence on Their Relations. Princeton Oriental Studies, no. 20. Princeton, N.J.: Princeton University Press, 1961, 281 pp.
A history of the Nestorians in nineteenth-century Iraq as an Ottoman millet (religious community), their entanglement in the Kurdish problem, British involvement, and the Iraqi massacre. This is an excellent study of Ottoman and, later, Iraqi policy toward a particular minority community and the various factors affecting that policy.

919 Luke, Sir Harry. Cyprus under the Turks, 1571-1878: A Research Based on the Archives of the English Consulate in Cyprus under the Levant Company and After. London: C. Hurst, 1969, 281 pp. Reprint of 1921 ed.
Luke uncovered ten thousand documents in seven languages relating to the history of Cyprus under the Turks. Over half of the book consists of specimens of these, preceded by a brief history.

920 Mardin, Şerif. The Genesis of Young Ottoman Thought: A Study in the Modernization of Turkish Political Ideas. Princeton, N.J.: Princeton University Press, 1962, 456 pp.

By "Young Ottomans," Mardin means a group of Turkish intellectuals who thrived during the Tanzimat period (1839-1878), particularly during its last decade. He sets this group of thinkers into an Ottoman and Islamic and then more immediate, biographical context; finally, he analyzes the thought of six representative figures. This is a basic work for the development of modern Turkey.

921 Marriott, J.A.R. The Eastern Question: An Historical Study in European Diplomacy. Oxford: Clarendon, 1963, 602 pp. Reprint of 4th ed., 1940. 1st ed., 1917.

The classic study of European interests in subjugating and dividing the Ottoman Empire, based upon, and reflecting, English sources. Updated by Anderson in The Eastern Question (see 908) and others.

922 Midhat, Ali Haydar. The Life of Midhat Pasha: A Record of His Services, Political Reforms, Banishment, and Judicial Murder, Derived from Private Documents and Reminiscences by His Son. London: J. Murray, 1903, 292 pp.

An informed account of the activities of a key figure in the late nineteenth-century Ottoman reforms.

923 Miller, William. The Ottoman Empire and Its Successors, 1801-1927, with an Appendix, 1927-1936, Being a Revised and Enlarged Edition of "The Ottoman Empire, 1801-1913." Cambridge: Cambridge University Press, 1929, 616 pp.

The emphasis is on the Balkans, especially Greece, and on diplomatic history. Makes extensive use of primary sources in European languages.

924 Nalbandian, Louise. The Armenian Revolutionary Movement: The Development of Armenian Political Parties through the Nineteenth Century. Berkeley: University of California Press, 1963, 247 pp.

Describes the struggle of the Armenians against the Ottoman government; the years from 1862 to 1896 are analyzed in terms of the formulation of societies and parties. There is full documentation.

925 Pears, Edwin. Life of Abdul Hamid. New York: H. Holt, 1917, 365 pp.

A distinctly biased biography of the sulṭān and his reign, which reflects the contemporary attitude of the British toward the Ottomans. Pears was a barrister in Istanbul during the period of the book.

926 Puryear, Vernon John. France and the Levant from the Bourbon Restoration to the Peace of Kutiah. Berkeley: University of California Press, 1941, 252 pp.

Discusses French diplomatic and economic policy in the Ottoman Empire, 1814-1833, based on French archival sources.

927 _____. International Economics and Diplomacy in the Near East: A Study of British Commercial Policy in the Levant, 1834-1853. Stanford, Calif.: Stanford University Press, 1935, 264 pp.

An analysis of economic factors involved in the Eastern question, based largely on archival materials in English, French, German, and Russian.

928 _____. Napoleon and the Dardanelles. Berkeley: University of California Press, 1951, 437 pp.

A readable discussion of Napoleon's policy in the Near East, focusing on the question of the Straits and their importance in his designs on Russia; based on French archival sources.

929 Ramsaur, E.E. The Young Turks: Prelude to the Revolution of 1908. Princeton, N.J.: Princeton University Press, 1957, 180 pp.

A straightforward account, based on Turkish and European sources, of the formation and activities of the groups constituting the Young Turk movement and their attempts to launch a revolution in the Ottoman Empire. Should be supplemented by the more recent book by Feroz Ahmad (see 907).

930 Seton-Watson, R.W. Disraeli, Gladstone, and the Eastern Question: A Study in Diplomacy and Party Politics. New York: Barnes & Noble, 1962, 590 pp. Reprint of 1935 ed.

British, Austrian, and Russian archives provided the material for this analysis of the factors that influenced British policy toward the Ottoman Empire during the late nineteenth century.

931 Shaw, Stanford J. Between Old and New: The Ottoman Empire under Sultan Selim III, 1789-1807. Cambridge, Mass.: Harvard University Press, 1971, 535 pp.

A detailed, painstaking reconstruction of the events of this period, drawn from primarily Turkish and European archival sources. The emphasis is on military and diplomatic history and Selim's administrative reforms.

932 Shotwell, James T., and Francis Deak. Turkey at the Straits: A Short History. New York: Macmillan, 1940, 196 pp.

An outline of the role of the Turkish Straits in European diplomatic history from the Treaty of London (1840) to the Franco-British-Turkish Mutual Assistance Pact (1939).

933 Sousa, Nasim. The Capitulatory Regime of Turkey, Its History, Origin, and Nature. Johns Hopkins University Studies in Historical and Political Science, n.s., no. 18. Baltimore: Johns Hopkins Press, 1933, 378 pp.

Although there are introductory chapters on the origin and history of the principle of extraterritoriality in Islamic law and the Ottoman Empire, the book is mainly concerned with the modern period, with World War I as the crucial point. Careful documentation from European sources.

934 Temperley, Harold J. England and the Near East: The Crimea. Hamden, Conn.: Archon Books, 1964, 548 pp. Reprint of 1936 ed.
Intended as the first volume of a history of the British presence in the Near East, this work covers the years 1808-1854. Though it concentrates on the Crimean War, it reviews Ottoman political and diplomatic history of the time and the role the European powers played in it.

935 Toynbee, Arnold J. The Western Question in Greece and Turkey: A Study in the Contact of Civilizations. Boston: Houghton Mifflin, 1922, 420 pp.
Toynbee traveled through Greece and Turkey in 1921 for the Manchester Guardian to research this analysis of the Greek-Turkish conflict, which he sets in historical perspective.

936 Trumpener, Ulrich. Germany and the Ottoman Empire, 1914-1918. Princeton, N.J.: Princeton University Press, 1968, 433 pp.
A history of Ottoman Turkey's involvement in World War I as an ally of Germany, focusing on German policy toward the Ottoman and the nature of the Committee of Union and Progress Party as rulers of the empire from 1913 to 1918. Based largely on German archival material, few Turkish sources.

937 Weber, F.G. Eagles on the Crescent: Germany, Austria, and the Diplomacy of the Turkish Alliance, 1914-1918. Ithaca, N.Y.: Cornell University Press, 1970, 284 pp.
One of several recently published works based on research in German and Austrian archives, tracing the diplomatic relations of these two countries with the Ottoman Empire from the time of the Balkan wars to the Armistice of Mudros. A highly specialized contribution to the position of the Ottomans in early twentieth-century international relations.

938 Yalman, Ahmed Emin. Turkey in the World War. New Haven, Conn.: Yale University Press, 1930, 310 pp.
An eyewitness account of the war period and its aftermath by a Turkish professor and editor closely associated with prominent Turkish politicians.

Since Atatürk

939 Allen, Henry Elisha. The Turkish Transformation: A Study in Social and Religious Development. Chicago: University of Chicago Press, 1935, 251 pp.
An early attempt to gauge the effects of the Kemalist reforms in Turkey, in which the author draws upon his reading of modern Turkish writers, his observations of life in Turkey, and his research into primary and secondary sources. The book has not had the use or recognition that it deserves.

940 Armstrong, H.C. Gray Wolf: An Intimate Study of a Dictator. London: Arthur Baker, 1933, 352 pp.
A distinctly popular biography of Atatürk, without documentation, but interesting if only because ʻAbd al-Nāṣir (Nasser) is claimed to have said, "This has been the most important book in my life." The author is not sympathetic to the subject.

941 Atatürk, Ghazi Mustapha Kemal. A Speech Delivered by Ghazi Mustapha Kemal, President of the Turkish Republic, October, 1927. Leipzig: K.T. Koehler, 1929, 724 pp.
Surely one of the longest speeches on record, this address took six days to deliver before the deputies of the Republican Party. It traces the course of the revolutionary movement led by Atatürk and the principles for which he was fighting.

942 Bisbee, Eleanor. The New Turks: Pioneers of the Republic, 1920-1950. Philadelphia: University of Pennsylvania Press, 1951, 298 pp.
A profile of the Turkish people and Turkish affairs under the republic, derived from the author's experience in Turkey as teacher and her wide circle of acquaintances among the Turks.

943 Edib, Halide. Memoirs of Halide Edib. New York: Century, 1926, 472 pp.
This volume covers the period preceding World War I--the Constitutional Revolution of 1908, the American question, Pan-Turanism--and the early war years.

944 _____. Turkey Faces West: A Turkish View of Recent Changes and Their Origins. New Haven, Conn.: Yale University Press, 1930, 273 pp.
An enthusiastic account of the course of the Turkish revolution by a participant.

945 _____. The Turkish Ordeal: Being the Further Memoirs of Halide Edib. London: Century, 1928, 407 pp.
A sequel to her memoirs, covering her activities in "the underground," the organization of the Anatolian News Agency, and her close association with Atatürk.

946 Eren, Nuri. Turkey Today--and Tomorrow: An Experiment in Westernization. London: Pall Mall, 1963, 276 pp.
A Turkish diplomat's analysis of the effects of the Kemalist revolution on Turkish politics, economy, culture, and diplomacy.

947 Evans, Laurence. United States Policy and the Partition of Turkey, 1914-1924. Baltimore: Johns Hopkins Press, 1965, 437 pp.
A supplement to Howard's general history of the same subject (see 950), based on U.S. State Department documents and papers of Wilson and his representatives. Turkish sources were not consulted.

948 Frey, F.W. The Turkish Political Elite. Cambridge, Mass.: M.I.T. Press, 1965, 483 pp.
An analysis of the various political institutions of the Turkish Republic, the Grand National Assemblies, the cabinets, and political parties, in terms of the education and social background of the membership, voting patterns, etc.

949 Hershlag, Z.Y. Turkey: The Challenge of Growth. Rev. ed. Leiden: E.J. Brill, 1961, 406 pp.
A study of the economic development of Turkey since the establishment of the republic, divided into chronological periods, through the sixties. The data are based on Turkish and U.N. documents and sources, as well as recent scholarship on the subject.

950 Howard, Harry N. The Partition of Turkey: A Diplomatic History, 1913-1923. Norman: University of Oklahoma Press, 1931, 486 pp.
A study of the diplomacy of the world powers in dismembering the Ottoman Empire, based exclusively on non-Turkish sources. Quite thorough and competent within the limits set by the author and the sources available to him at the time; should be supplemented by reference to more recent, specialized studies.

951 Karpat, K.H. Turkey's Politics: The Transition to a Multi-Party System. Princeton, N.J.: Princeton University Press, 1959, 522 pp.
Concentrates on the 1946-1950 or postwar period, when the one-party system of the Turkish Republic was replaced with a multiparty system, which the author views as a further step toward westernization and modernization in politics and political participation. Has detailed documentation from Turkish sources both for party ideology and activities and the effect on Turkish government.

952 Kerr, Stanley Elphinstone. The Lions of Marash: Personal Experiences with American Near East Relief, 1919-1922. Albany: State University of New York Press, 1973, 318 pp.
The author's recollections of the Kemalist policy toward the Armenians of Marash.

953 Kinross, Lord. Ataturk: The Rebirth of a Nation. London: Weidenfeld & Nicolson, 1964, 532 pp.
A long narration of the events in the life of Kemal Atatürk and his efforts to establish a modern, secular state in Turkey; it reads almost like a novel and completely lacks documentation. Still, it is the best biography of the Ghazi in English, and the bibliography, which includes many contemporary Turkish sources, commands respect.

954 Mears, E.G., ed. Modern Turkey: A Politico-Economic Interpretation, 1908-1923 Inclusive, with Selected Chapters by Representative Authorities. New York: Macmillan, 1924, 779 pp.
Mears served in Turkey and the Levant as a commercial representative of the U.S. government and the Chamber of Commerce, and on the basis of that experience he wrote many of the chapters on the Turkish economy at the end of World War I. Articles by other authors on aspects of Turkish government and society are also included.

955 Orga, Irfan. Portrait of a Turkish Family. London: V. Gollancz, 1950, 303 pp.
These detailed memoirs of life in Turkey (mainly Istanbul) during World War I and the revolution help offset much of the general and abstract writing about the period.

956 _____, and Margarete Orga. Ataturk. London: M. Joseph, 1962, 304 pp.
A popular biography of Atatürk that draws heavily on Turkish sources.

957 Robinson, Richard D. The First Turkish Republic: A Case Study in National Development. Cambridge, Mass.: Harvard University Press, 1963, 367 pp.
Robinson is interested in modern Turkish history as an instance of accelerated development guided by westernized leaders. The interpretation is based mainly on secondary sources.

958 Sterling, Paul. Turkish Village. London: Weidenfeld & Nicolson, 1965, 316 pp.
An anthropological study of the structure, organization, and dynamics of village life in Anatolia, based on field research.

959 Thornburg, Max Weston; Graham Spry; and George Soule. Turkey: An Economic Appraisal. New York: Twentieth Century Fund, 1949, 324 pp.
A survey of the Turkish economy, undertaken to make recommendations regarding American foreign aid to Turkey. These recommendations are included. In addition to data on Turkish agriculture, energy, communications, mining, and banking, the book also reveals much about American policy in the area.

960 Trask, Roger R. The United States Response to Turkish Nationalism and Reform, 1914-1939. Minneapolis: University of Minnesota Press, 1971, 280 pp.
A well-written diplomatic history from the American side, limited to non-Turkish sources, primarily State Department and missionary records.

961 Walker, Warren S., and Ahmet E. Uysal. Tales Alive in Turkey. Cambridge, Mass.: Harvard University Press, 1966, 310 pp.
Translations of forty-one Turkish folk tales, humorous, moralistic, supernatural, collected from oral informants throughout Turkey, admirably reflecting the Turkish rural mentality. With introductions and notes by the editors.

962 Webster, Donald Everett. The Turkey of Ataturk: Social Process in the Turkish Reformation. Philadelphia: American Academy of Political and Social Science, 1939, 337 pp.
The first two parts of this book are a summary history of Turkey and Kemalism. The third, most valuable part is an examination of "contemporary Kemalism" (i.e., in the thirties), based on the author's experience in Turkey and his reading in Turkish sources.

963 Weiker, W.F. The Turkish Revolution, 1960-1961: Aspect of Military Politics. Washington: Brookings Institution, 1963, 172 pp.
An interpretation of the military role in Turkish politics through a case study of the military overthrow of the Menderes regime, based on Turkish sources and intended as a background paper for the formulation of American policy. Besides the actual events and their political implications, the book also covers the impact on education, the constitution, and political parties.

The Kurds

964 Arfa, Hassan. The Kurds: An Historical and Political Study. London: Oxford, 1966, 178 pp.
The author has spent much time living among the Kurdish tribes and also fighting them as chief of staff of the Iranian army. It is his experience that gives this short study its interest.

965 Bois, Thomas. The Kurds. Translated by M.W.M. Willand. Beirut: Khayats, 1966, 159 pp.
An introduction to Kurdish social, political, and cultural life.

966 Edmonds, C.J. Kurds, Turks and Arabs: Politics, Travel and Research in North-Eastern Iraq, 1919-1925. London: Oxford, 1957, 457 pp.
Edmonds has woven observations from his experience as political officer into this diplomatic history of the Mosul dispute involving Great Britain and Turkey.

967 Kinnane, Derk. The Kurds and Kurdistan. London: Oxford, 1964, 85 pp.
A short sketch of Kurdish history and the attempts of the Kurds to free themselves from the domination of the countries they have inhabited.

968 O'Ballance, Edgar. The Kurdish Revolt: 1961-1970. London: Faber & Faber, 1973, 196 pp.
A journalistic account of the Kurdish revolt in Iraq and the measures taken by the Iraqī government to suppress it.

Central Asia

969 Allworth, Edward, ed. Central Asia: A Century of Russian Rule. New York: Columbia University Press, 1967, 552 pp.
A collection of articles surveying the "Russianization" of the Islamic territories of Central Asia. Although the emphasis is on political history, there are interesting chapters on cultural change, including art and architecture, literature, and music. A good introductory survey to the more specialized studies on the same subjects that have recently begun to appear.

970 Allworth, Edward. Nationalities of the Soviet East, Publications and Writing Systems: A Bibliographical Directory and Transliteration Tables for Iranian and Turkic Language Publications, 1818-1945, Located in U.S. Libraries. Modern Middle East Series, no. 3. New York: Columbia University Press, 1971, 440 pp.
Gives locations for over three thousand books and periodicals in Turkic and Iranian languages on a wide variety of subjects, from anthropology through art, economics through philosophy. Also has valuable transliteration tables.

971 Becker, Seymour. Russia's Protectorates in Central Asia: Bukhara and Khiva, 1865-1924. Cambridge, Mass. Harvard University Press, 1968, 416 pp.
A study of the Russian conquest, "benign" neglect, and ultimate "modernization" of two of the principal Muslim states of Central Asia. This is an incisive case study of Russian policy toward Central Asia and the effects of this policy on Islamic states.

972 Bennigsen, Alexandre, and Chantal Lemercier-Quelquejay. Islam in the Soviet Union. New York: F.A. Praeger, 1967, 272 pp.
A study of Islam during various phases of Russian history: prerevolution, revolution, Bolshevik triumph, sovietization, and postwar, based primarily on Russian sources but with a firm grasp of Islam. An excellent introduction.

973 Kaushik, Devendra. Central Asia in Modern Times: A History from the Early 19th Century. Moscow: Progress, 1970, 271 pp.
A book on sovietization of Central Asia by an Indian who earned a doctorate in the USSR and whose views are favored by Soviet academicians. Polemical, it refutes "the false thesis peddled by British and American 'Sovietologists'" that Central Asia was revolutionized by force or under pressure.

974 Kazemzadeh, Firuz. The Struggle for Transcaucasia, 1917-1921. Oxford: Ronald, 1951, 356 pp.
A history of Transcaucasia, which after the Russian revolution was divided into three republics that soon were sovietized--Azerbayjan, Armenia, and Georgia. It is based on archives and memoirs (many in Russian), supplemented by European secondary sources.

975 Khalfin, N.A. Russia's Policy in Central Asia, 1857-1868. Translated by Hubert Evans. London: Central Asian Research Centre, 1964, 107 pp.
A condensed translation of a Russian study of the dissolution of Turkestan.

976 Park, Alexander G. Bolshevism in Turkestan, 1917-1927. New York: Columbia University Press, 1957, 428 pp.
The policies and methods (political, religious, economic, and cultural) of the early Bolsheviks in Central Asia.

977 Pierce, Richard A. Russian Central Asia, 1867-1917: A Study in Colonial Rule. Berkeley: University of California Press, 1960, 359 pp.
A survey of Russian rule in Central Asia up to the revolution, with analysis of methods of administration and organization in the cities and countryside and economic development, using Russian sources.

978 Rakowska-Harmstone, T. Russia and Nationalism in Central Asia: The Case of Tadzhikistan. Baltimore: Johns Hopkins Press, 1970, 325 pp.
A case study of the sovietization of the Russian "Islamic" states, which includes a good summary of the pre-Soviet history of the area and an analysis of the Islamic political system. The remainder of the book treats the process by which this system was transformed. This gives an excellent idea of an important aspect of westernization of the Islamic world that is not usually included in works restricted to Western European influence.

979 Wheeler, Geoffrey. The Modern History of Soviet Central Asia. London: Weidenfeld & Nicholson, 1964, 272 pp.
A survey of nineteenth- and twentieth-century history of Central Asia under Russian domination, with an emphasis on "social, cultural, and intellectual developments," rather than political and economic history. A very useful summary of the sovietization of the area as a whole.

980 Winner, Thomas G. The Oral Art and Literature of the Kazakhs of Russian Central Asia. Durham, N.C.: Duke University Press, 1958, 269 pp.
A social history of Kazakh oral art and literature from early folklore through twentieth-century writings under Soviet rule. There is an introductory chapter on the components of Kazakh culture and society.

Afghanistan

981 Adamec, Ludwig W. Afghanistan, 1900-1923: A Diplomatic History. Berkeley: University of California Press, 1967, 245 pp.
Based largely on archival sources in India, London, and Bonn, as well as on Afghan newspapers and reference works, this book covers the Afghan foreign policy response to European imperialism in the first quarter of the twentieth century. It is one of several recently published books on Afghanistan to have abandoned the repetition of secondary authorities to explore original sources.

982 Elphinstone, Mountstuart. An Account of the Kingdom of Caubul, and Its Dependencies in Persia, Tartary, and India, Comprising a View of the Afghaun Nation, and a History of the Dooraunee Monarchy. 2 vols. New & rev. ed. London: Richard Bentley, 1842, 1:422 pp.; 2:440 pp. 1st ed. 1815.
These are findings of a mission sent to Afghanistan by the British government to collect data on the geography, ethnography, and government of the area; still useful to students of Afghan history.

983 Fletcher, Arnold. Afghanistan, Highway of Conquest. Ithaca, N.Y.: Cornell University Press, 1965, 325 pp.
A general history of modern Afghanistan from 1747 to the 1960s. The documentation is minimal, and the sources cited are mainly Western travel-military memoirs or secondary sources, though the author also interviewed "Afghan leaders."

984 Grassmuck, George, and Ludwig W. Adamec, with Francis H. Irwin. Afghanistan: Some New Approaches. Ann Arbor: University of Michigan, Center for Near Eastern and North African Studies, 1969, 405 pp.
A useful supplement to Wilber's bibliography on Afghanistan (see 112), with many entries on Russian publications. In addition, there are five essays on various aspects of modern Afghan history and culture, one a translation of a Russian study on Afghan ethnography.

985 Gregorian, Vartan. The Emergence of Modern Afghanistan: Politics of Reform and Modernization, 1880-1946. Stanford, Calif.: Stanford University Press, 1969, 586 pp.
One of the first really scholarly works on modern Afghanistan, incorporating material from original Persian, Russian, and Turkish sources. Focusing on Amīr ʿAbd al-Raḥmān Khān and his successors in their attempt to keep the British and Russians at bay, Gregorian traces the simultaneous process by which a tribal society was gradually restructured, a process still underway today.

986 Griffiths, John C. Afghanistan. New York: F.A. Praeger, 1967, 179 pp.
A popular outline version of recent Afghan history and a sketch of contemporary politics and society, this is short and superficial, with no documentation.

987 Newell, Richard S. The Politics of Afghanistan. South Asian Political Systems, no. 3. Ithaca, N.Y.: Cornell University Press, 1972, 236 pp.
A general introduction to modern Afghan government, politics, and economy, based largely on secondary sources and the author's own experience in the area. It has an annotated bibliography, but no notes.

India, Pakistan, and Bangladesh

General

988 Aḥmad, Azīz, and G.E. von Grunebaum, eds. Muslim Self-statement in India and Pakistan, 1857-1968. Wiesbaden: Harrassowitz, 1970, 240 pp.
An anthology of Indo-Muslim statements of self-identity from Sayyid Aḥmād Khan to Muḥammad Ayub Khān, some translated for the first time. Contains a valuable "bio-bibliographical survey" and brief notes. A companion volume to Aḥmad's Islamic Modernism in India and Pakistan (see 989), complementing that book's exposition and

analysis with representative samples of the thought of the key figures in the development of the Muslim community in the subcontinent. See also 1717.

989 Aḥmad, Azīz. Islamic Modernism in India and Pakistan, 1857-1964. London: Oxford, 1967, 294 pp.

A survey of the role of the principal figures in the development of modern Islam in the Indian subcontinent, including Sayyid Aḥmad Khān, Muḥammad Iqbāl, Abū'l-Kalām Āzād, and various other lesser persons and groups. The emphasis is on summarizing various views against the background of historical events. Translated selections from the writings themselves are to be found in the author's companion volume (see 988); together they form one of the best modern intellectual histories of a Muslim area now available.

990 Aziz, K.K. The Historical Background of Pakistan, 1857-1947: An Annotated Digest of Source Material. Karachi: Pakistan Institute of International Affairs, 1970, 626 pp.

An annotated bibliography of 9,244 items (letters, diaries, trial reports, memorabilia, dissertations, and fiction), all in English, from the Mutiny to partition.

991 Edwardes, Michael. British India, 1772-1947: A Survey of the Nature and Effects of Alien Rule. London: Sidgwick & Jackson, 1967, 396 pp.

A popular history that has the virtue of readability.

992 Hardy, Peter. The Muslims of British India. Cambridge: Cambridge University Press, 1972, 306 pp.

Outstanding for its use of Persian and Urdu sources and its analysis of the Muslims as a separate entity in India rather than a single component of British policy in the subcontinent. Represents a new point of departure for British and Western studies of Indian Islam in the colonial period. Includes an excellent annotated bibliography on Muslim India.

993 Hodson, H.V. The Great Divide: Britain--India--Pakistan. London: Hutchinson, 1969, 543 pp.

An account of the Mountbatten viceroyship by a member of his government who had access to the Mountbatten papers.

994 Hoskins, Halford Lancaster. British Routes to India. London: F. Cass, 1966, 494 pp. Reprint of the 1928 ed.

An exposition of the role of the Middle East as a vital link in the trade and communications of the British Empire, essential for an understanding of British policy in the area. The approach is chronological; based on primary sources.

995 Huttenback, Robert A. British Relations with Sind, 1799-1843: An Anatomy of Imperialism. Berkeley: University of California Press, 1962, 161 pp.

An account of British expansion in northeastern India during the first half of the nineteenth century through the activities of the East India Company, based on British archives; concise, but thoroughly documented.

996 Ikram, S.M. Modern Muslim India and the Birth of Pakistan. Lahore: Shaikh Muhammad Ashraf, 1965, 350 pp.

A history of Muslim India from the Mutiny until 1950, with an emphasis on biographies of such major figures as Kalām Āzād, Sir Sayyid Aḥmad Khān, Sir Muḥammad ʻAlī Jinnāh, by one of the more sophisticated Muslim historians of Muslim India. Useful for identifying the chief thinkers who inspired the founding of Pakistan.

997 Ingram, Edward, ed. Two Views of British India: The Private Correspondence of Mr. Dundas and Lord Wellesley: 1798-1801. Bath: Adams & Dart, 1970, 344 pp.

Letters between two officials of the British administration of India during the critical period of Napoleon's expedition to Egypt.

998 Lokhandwalla, S.T., ed. India and Contemporary Islam: Proceedings of a Seminar. Simla: Indian Institute of Advanced Study, 1971, 496 pp.

Contains thirty-nine papers, practically abstracts, almost all by Indian scholars, on a variety of topics relating mainly, but not exclusively, to the subject proclaimed in the title. Most are more interesting as samples of current research on Islam in India than for their content. The discussions that followed the reading of the papers are summarized.

999 Malik, Hafeez. Moslem Nationalism in India and Pakistan. Washington: Public Affairs Press, 1963, 355 pp.

Malik attempts to analyze Indian nationalist movements against the background of Muslim history in India. Useful to compare with British and Hindu versions of the same phenomena, it is one of the more analytical studies of the separatist movement by a Muslim.

1000 Niemeijer, A.C. The Khilafat Movement in India, 1919-1924. The Hague: Martinus Nijhoff, 1972, 263 pp.

Based on English archival sources exclusively, this work analyzes Muslim-Hindu relations during the period when the Khilafat movement was an important issue in Indian politics.

1001 Norris, J.A. The First Afghan War, 1838-1842. Cambridge: Cambridge University Press, 1967, 500 pp.

A new and fresh look at the original British sources on an important episode in British imperialism in India and Afghanistan that revises the standard British account of these four years and shows what can and should be done for the history of Victorian India in general.

1002 Philips, C.H. et al. The Evolution of India and Pakistan, 1858 to 1947: Select Documents. London: Oxford, 1962, 786 pp.
A collection of state and private papers, illustrating the development of governments and nationalisms in British India.

1003 Sharīf, Ja'far. Islam in India, or the Qānūn-i-Islām: The Customs of the Musalmans of India. Translated by G.A. Herklots. New edition by William Crooke. New Delhi: Oriental Books Reprint Corporation, 1974, 374 pp. Reprint of 1921 ed.
A description of Muslim-Indian life and religious practices, intended for the edification of Europeans.

1004 Smith, W.C. Modern Islam in India: A Social Analysis. London: V. Gollancz, 1946, 344 pp.
A pioneering study, independent of British colonialist and Indian nationalist historiography, it focuses on intellectual and political movements, with a section on "organized theological groups," and reflects Smith's deep commitment to religion and progress for the Muslim community in India. Though often misinterpreted and even distorted in the subcontinent, it has been profoundly influential among Muslim intellectuals.

1005 Spear, Percival. India, Pakistan, and the West. 4th ed. New York: Oxford University Press, 1967, 178 pp. 1st ed. 1948.
A concise introduction to the emergence of Pakistan in the framework of Indian history.

Pakistan and Bangladesh

1006 Abbott, Freeland. Islam and Pakistan. Ithaca, N.Y.: Cornell University Press, 1968, 242 pp.
A study of the role of Islam in Pakistan viewed historically, beginning with eighteenth-century Islam in India. Based entirely on English sources and translations, it is nonetheless useful for its emphasis on the political problems posed by Islam as a religion.

1007 Ahmad, Kabir Uddin. Breakup of Pakistan: Background and Prospects of Bangladesh. London: Social Science Publishers, 1972, 147 pp.
A history of East Pakistan and its emergence as Bangladesh; it is not unbiased, but it is as sober an account as any published so far.

1008 Ahmad, Kazi. A Geography of Pakistan. 2d ed. Karachi: Oxford University Press, Pakistan Branch, 1969, 262 pp.
A compact, clear, useful introduction in paperback by a Pakistani geographer.

1009 Ahmad, Nafis. An Economic Geography of East Pakistan. 2d ed. London: Oxford, 1968, 401 pp.
An indispensable book for an understanding of the difficulty in maintaining the two former provinces of Pakistan and the economic impediments to a viable Bangladesh state.

1010 Ali, Tariq. Pakistan: Military Rule or People's Power? London: J. Cape, 1970, 270 pp.
A refreshing Marxist interpretation of the political and social structure of Pakistan, emphasizing neither Islam nor the Pakistan-India conflict as the root of Pakistan's recurrent problems as much as the class structure of the country. Although avowedly polemical in intent, this work by the lately celebrated student activist has a freshness of approach, and the new insights this brings, to recommend it.

1011 Andrus, J. Russell, and Azizali F. Mohammed. Trade, Finance and Development in Pakistan. Karachi: Oxford, 1966, 289 pp.
A description of the commercial and financial system in Pakistan and its role in economic development.

1012 Ashford, D.E. National Development and Local Reform: Political Participation in Morocco, Tunisia, and Pakistan. (See 813.)

1013 Ayub Khan, Mohammed. Friends Not Masters: A Political Autobiography. New York: Oxford, 1967, 289 pp.
A valuable record of Ayūb's conception of the history of Pakistan, its relations with India and the world powers, and his role in shaping Pakistan's destiny. Perhaps of greater interest than this aspect of the book, in the light of events subsequent to 1967, is its embodiment of the philosophy of the soldier saving a country from politicians, a philosophy that obviously is widespread in the Islamic world, but has rarely been set forth in autobiographical form by such a prominent advocate.

1014 Aziz, K.K. The Making of Pakistan: A Study in Nationalism. London: Chatto & Windus, 1967, 223 pp.
Traces the factors--historical, political, religious, cultural, and psychological--that led to the establishment of a Muslim state in the subcontinent. A convenient summary.

1015 Callard, Keith. Pakistan: A Political Study. London: G. Allen & Unwin, 1957, 355 pp.
A political scientist's analysis of the political structure of Pakistan, the role of Islam in the state, the position of religious minorities, foreign affairs, etc. Uncluttered by social scientific jargon, it is a sound study of Pakistan at an early point in its development, long since left behind by recent events.

1016 Feldman, Herbert. Revolution in Pakistan: A Study of the Martial Law Administration. London: Oxford University Press, 1967, 242 pp.
Covers the policies and measures introduced by Ayūb Khān's government in Pakistan from 1958 until 1962 and discusses the problems faced by the Pakistanis in trying to create a nation-state.

1017 Griffin, Keith B. Growth and Inequality in Pakistan. London: Macmillan; New York: St. Martin's Press, 1972, 282 pp.
Ten essays by economists who assess the economic policies of the Pakistan government during its first quarter century in terms of their consequences for group and regional welfare.

1018 Hasan, Said. Pakistan: The Story behind Its Economic Development. New York: Vantage, 1971, 248 pp.
The chief secretary of the Pakistanī Ministry of Economic Affairs in the fifties recounts the story of planning, foreign aid, and economic development in Pakistan.

1019 Lewis, Stephen R., Jr. Pakistan: Industrialization and Trade Policies. London: Oxford, 1970, 214 pp.
A survey of the components of the Pakistani economy and the elements of government economic policy related to commerce and industry.

1020 Philips, C.H., and Mary Doreen Wainwright, eds. The Partition of India: Policies and Perspectives, 1935-1947. Cambridge, Mass.: M.I.T. Press, 1970, 607 pp.
Contains twenty-nine articles that attempt to define the main fields of research in tracing the history of partition. Half of the articles are contributions of persons who were engaged in partition, the other half, by historians. This is by far the fullest study of this momentous phase of Islamic history in the Indian subcontinent.

1021 Symonds, Richard. The Making of Pakistan. 3d ed. London: Faber & Faber, 1950, 227 pp.
One of the earliest accounts of the history of the creation of Pakistan, by a British and U.N. official in the area. There is very little documentation, since most of the material is derived from the author's experience and his interviews with Pakistanis.

1022 Tayyeb, A. Pakistan: A Political Geography. London: Oxford, 1966, 250 pp.
A study of the geographical factors that affect the political organization of Pakistan and its economic activities. The sections on East Pakistan and its relationship to the West are helpful for an understanding of the creation of Bangladesh.

1023 Tinker, H.R. India and Pakistan: A Political Analysis. 2d ed. New York: F.A. Praeger, 1967, 248 pp.
A straightforward, somewhat oversimplified analysis of the two major political entities of the Indian subcontinent during the 1960s. Though dated by the emergence of Bangladesh, it is still useful for basic data. Includes an appendix on Kashmir.

1024 Vorys, Karl von. Political Development in Pakistan. Princeton, N.J.: Princeton University Press, 1965, 341 pp.
Von Vorys examines the governmental policies of Ayūb Khān in the context of alternative policies permitted by the Pakistani government.

1025 Wilber, Donald N. et al. Pakistan: Its People, Its Society, Its Culture. Survey of World Cultures, no. 13. New Haven, Conn.: Human Relations Area Files, 1964, 487 pp.
A survey of Pakistanī politics, society, economy, and culture.

1026 Ziring, Lawrence. The Ayub Khan Era: Politics in Pakistan, 1958-1969. Syracuse, N.Y.: Syracuse University Press, 1971, 234 pp.
Surveys the entire rule of Ayūb Khān, analyzing especially the bureaucratic legacy, the rural power structure, and the role of the urban intelligentsia in Pakistan's politics.

Indonesia

1027 Benda, Harry J. The Crescent and the Rising Sun: Indonesian Islam under the Japanese Occupation, 1942-1945. The Hague: W. van Hoeve, 1958, 320 pp.
In addition to the analysis of the Muslims' response to Japan's policy in Indonesia, the book includes a survey of Indonesian Islam under Dutch colonial rule, so that its scope is considerably broader than the title indicates.

1028 Geertz, Clifford. The Religion of Java. London: Free Press of Glencoe, 1964, 392 pp. Orig. pub. in 1960.
A field anthropological description of religious beliefs, practices, and institutions, along with chapters on the history of Islam in the area. In the conclusion, Geertz discusses the integration of religion in Javanese society. See also 1396.

1029 Hurgronje, C. Snouck. The Achehnese. 2 vols. Translated by A.W.S. O'Sullivan. Leiden: E.J. Brill, 1906, 1:439 pp.; 2:384 pp.
An exhaustive description of life in the kingdom of Acheh in Sumatra, commissioned by the Dutch government in order to determine the role of religion in the politics of the country. Includes much on the nature of Islam in Sumatra.

1030 Nieuwenhuijze, C.A.O. van. Aspects of Islam in Post-Colonial Indonesia: Five Essays. The Hague: W. van Hoeve, 1958, 248 pp.
Contains essays on Islam as a religion and its political and social implications by a former Dutch civil servant and present sociologist.

1031 Van Niel, Robert. The Emergence of the Modern Indonesian Elite. The Hague: W. van Hoeve, 1960, 314 pp.
An interpretive analysis of social change in Indonesia under colonialism, 1900-1927, paying considerable attention to the role of various Islamic components of Indonesian society.

Africa South of the Sahara

1032 Adeleye, R.A. Power and Diplomacy in Northern Nigeria 1804-1906: The Sokoto Caliphate and Its Enemies. London: Longman Group, 1971, 387 pp.
In addition to retracing the history of the caliphate, Adeleye analyzes its relation with colonial powers. This is the fullest study

of the Sokoto Caliphate currently available and, along with the books on the same subject by Hiskett, Johnston, and Last (see 1042, 1045, 1050), provides the deepest analysis of any aspect of the history of Islam in Africa.

1033 Atterbury, Anson P. Islam in Africa: Its Effects--Religious, Ethical and Social--upon the People of the Country. New York: Negro Universities Press, 1969, 208 pp. Reprint of 1899 ed.

One of the first attempts by a Christian missionary to give a "sympathetic" portrayal of African Islam within the context of African and Islamic history. The object of this study was to determine whether it was better to leave the ranges to the Muslims or to undertake a major Christian missionary effort. "The great solution" was to supplant Islam with Christianity.

1034 Baulin, Jacques. The Arab Role in Africa. Middlesex: Penguin Books, 1962, 144 pp.

A journalistic account of the influence of Egyptian and North African Islam and Arab nationalism in sub-Saharan Africa. Little more than an outline, it is nevertheless useful in the absence of more detailed studies.

1035 Bovill, E.W. The Golden Trade of the Moors (see 816).

1036 Bravmann, Rene A. Islam and Tribal Art in West Africa. London: Cambridge University Press, 1974, 190 pp.

Contains valuable information on the impact of Islamization on West Africa not available elsewhere and demonstrates the value of art objects as historical sources when other sources are lacking.

1037 Brelvi, Mahmud. Islam in Africa. Lahore: Institute of Islamic Culture, 1964, 657 pp.

A general and superficial survey, with a strong missionary strain, of the history and geography of African states with a sizable Muslim population.

1038 Fisher, Allen G.B., and Humphrey J. Fisher. Slavery and Muslim Society in Africa: The Institution in Saharan and Sudanic Africa, and the Trans-Saharan Trade. London: C. Hirst (Doubleday), 1970, 182 pp.

A study of the trans-Saharan (as opposed to trans-Atlantic) slave trade designed to meet the demand for slaves from the Muslim countries south of the Sahara. Besides a discussion of the status of slaves in Muslim law, there is description of life and activities of the slave in a Muslim environment. Most of this is based on the accounts of European observers.

1039 Fisher, Humphrey J. Ahmadiyyah: A Study in Contemporary Islam on the West African Coast. London: Oxford University Press, 1963, 206 pp.

A topical and historical account of Islam West Africa, focusing on the development of the Punjabi Aḥmadiyyah sect in West Africa and its influence on orthodox doctrine.

1040 Hampson, Ruth M., comp. Islam in South Africa: A Bibliography. Cape Town: University of Cape Town, School of Librarianship, 1964, 55 pp.

Two hundred thirty annotated entries on history, beliefs and ritual, peoples, and the relationships of Islam and Christianity in South Africa. Though obviously limited, it is nevertheless helpful in the absence of broader bibliographical aids.

1041 Harries, Lyndon. Islam in East Africa. London: Universities Mission to Central Africa, 1954, 92 pp.

This is a handbook for Christian missionaries, designed to familiarize them with the rudiments of Muslim beliefs and of the spread of Islam in Africa. It is interesting to the historian, therefore, as a sample of missionaries' attitudes toward and understanding of Islam.

1042 Hiskett, Mervyn. The Sword of Truth: The Life and Times of Shehu Usuman Dan Fodio. New York: Oxford University Press, 1973, 194 pp.

An excellent popular version of the scholarship on the nineteenth-century jihād that resulted in the establishment of the Sokoto Caliphate; the approach is biographical, emphasizing the intellectual milieu from which the "revolutionary movement" arose.

1043 Hodgkin, Thomas, ed. Nigerian Perspectives: An Historical Anthology. London: Oxford University Press, 1960, 340 pp.

An attempt to portray the social life of the Nigerian peoples through extracts from writings by and about Nigerians. Hodgkin provides an excellent historical introduction. Most of the book is devoted to the Islamic period.

1044 Hogben, S.J., and A.H.M. Kirk-Greene. The Emirates of Northern Nigeria: A Preliminary Survey of Their Historical Traditions. London: Oxford University Press, 1966, 638 pp.

This is a revised edition of Hogben's Muhammadan Emirates of Nigeria (London, 1930). Part 1 surveys the spread of Islam in Africa and the growth of the Islamic empires. Part 2 surveys the history of thirty-nine Islamic emirates. This is a basic reference work for the political history of Islamic states in Africa.

1045 Johnston, H.A.S. The Fulani Empire of Sokoto. London: Oxford University Press, 1967, 312 pp.

Covers much the same territory as Last's book (see 1050), leaning perhaps more heavily, however, on oral Hausa tradition and British colonial sources, although the Arabic sources were also consulted.

1046 Kaba, Lansine. The Wahhabiyya: Islamic Reform and Politics in French West Africa. Evanston, Ill.: Northwestern University Press, 1974, 285 pp.

Analyzes the intellectual role of an Islamic reform movement in the politics of West Africa, 1945-1958. It is based on archives located in Mali and interviews with informants in the area. Helpful on the Islamic component in African nationalism.

1047 King, Noel W. Christian and Muslim in Africa. New York: Harper & Row, 1971, 153 pp.
An informal discussion of the causes of Christianity and Islam in Africa in which the author attempts to assess the transplantation of these two religions into an alien environment. The text is deceptively light; the annotated bibliography is valuable.

1048 Klein, Martin A. Islam and Imperialism in Senegal: Sine-Saloum, 1847-1914. Stanford, Calif.: Stanford University Press, 1968, 285 pp.
A history of two Senegalese states under the impact of colonialism, beginning with French military, missionary, and commercial penetration in the middle of the nineteenth century until the beginning of the First World War. Using primarily European archival sources, the author has tried to supplement these with oral traditions. Although the work consists mainly of political history, it also includes a chapter on social and economic change.

1049 Kritzeck, James, and William H. Lewis, eds. Islam in Africa. New York: Van Nostrand-Reinhold, 1969, 339 pp.
These nineteen articles on the origins and growth of Islam in Africa, the development of Islamic institutions in Africa (marabouts, law, separatism, minorities), and the evaluation of Islam in various regions of Africa constitute probably the easiest and at the same time an authoritative approach to the general subject of African Islam. Though there is no explicit attempt to develop the theme of regional variations on a Pan-African Islam, this is implicit in the structure and organization of the book.

1050 Last, Murray. The Sokoto Caliphate. London: Longmans, Green & Co., 1967, 280 pp.
A carefully documented account of the establishment and development of the Sokoto Caliphate and vizierate, based largely on Arabic sources.

1051 Lewis, I.M. Islam in Tropical Africa: Studies Presented and Discussed at the Fifth International African Seminar, Ahmadu Bello University, Laria, January 1964. London: Oxford University Press, 1966, 470 pp.
Twenty articles by various authorities, both European and African; half treat the introduction and spread of Islam in selected regions of Africa, and half discuss particular aspects of Islam in an African country. Some of the latter are quite specialized (e.g., "Cattle Values and Islamic Values in a Pastoral Population"), so that this collection of essays is probably aimed at a more scholarly readership than is Kritzeck and Lewis's (see 1049).

1052 Low, Victor N. Three Nigerian Emirates: A Study in Oral History. Evanston, Ill.: Northwestern University Press, 1972, 296 pp.
Attempts to reconstruct the history of three nineteenth-century northeastern Nigerian Islamic states from interviews with hundreds of informants. The result is equally interesting from historical and historiographical points of view.

1053 Martin, B.G. Muslim Brotherhoods in Nineteenth-Century Africa. Cambridge: Cambridge University Press, 1976, 267 pp.
A comparative study of seven Ṣūfī brotherhoods in East, North, and West Africa, attempting to determine their contribution and relation to African Islam in general; based primarily on Arabic sources.

1054 McCall, Daniel F., and Norman R. Bennett. Aspects of West African Islam. Boston: Boston University, African Studies Center, 1971, 234 pp.
Twelve articles on the early expansion of Islam in Africa, political, military, and commercial developments in central Muslim Africa during the nineteenth century, and foreign and Islamic influences on the modern history of Africa. Nothing ties these articles together, as the vagueness of the title indicates. Some, especially those in part 1, are very general; others are quite specialized.

1055 Naqar, ʿUmar al-. The Pilgrimage Tradition in West Africa: An Historical Study with Special Reference to the Nineteenth Century. Khartoum: Khartoum University Press, 1972, 160 pp.
Part 1 covers the references to pilgrimage from West Africa to Mecca prior to the nineteenth century; part 2 discusses pilgrimage from the Islamic states in the nineteenth century, for which the documentation is greater. Part 3 assesses the effects of pilgrimage on education, reform, and social attitudes.

1056 O'Brien, Donald B. Cruise. The Mourides of Senegal: The Political and Economic Organization of an Islamic Brotherhood. Oxford: Clarendon Press, 1971, 321 pp.
A description of a Ṣūfī brotherhood in Senegal from a sociological point of view, based upon less than a year's fieldwork. The description focuses on the structure of religious authority within the order, economic aspects, and the present direction of change.

1057 Oded, Arye. Islam in Uganda: Islamization through a Centralized State in Pre-Colonial Africa. New York and Toronto: Wiley, 1974, 381 pp.
A history of the penetration of Islam in Uganda, with emphasis on the process whereby conversion was achieved and Christian-Muslim rivalry for converts. Based on interviews as well as archival and literary sources.

1058 Oloruntimehin, B.O. The Segu Tukulor Empire. London: Longman Group, 1972, 357 pp.
A study of the rise and fall of a West African kingdom from its foundation through revolution (1852-1864) and its conquest by the French (1893). Its history is intimately related to the leadership of the Tijaniyyah Ṣūfī order of West Africa and thus provides an opportunity to analyze the relationship between politics and Islam in West Africa.

1059 Paden, John N. Religion and Political Culture in Kano. Berkeley: University of California Press, 1973, 461 pp.
A study of the role of Islam in the political structure of the Kano Emirate and state with special attention to the Ṣūfī orders and the reform movement.

1060 Stewart, C.C., with E.K. Stewart. Islam and Social Order in Mauritania: A Case Study from the Nineteenth Century. Oxford: Clarendon Press, 1973, 204 pp.
A study of the resurgence of Islam in West Africa through the influence of the Qādirī Ṣūfī order in general and the activities of one of its principal leaders, Shaykh Sidiyyah al-Kabīr, in particular. Important primarily for its thesis that the mystical and legalistic traditions were not polar but complementary and contributed to the distinctive development of the Islamic tradition in West Africa.

1061 Trimingham, John Spencer. A History of Islam in West Africa. London and New York: Oxford University Press, 1962, 262 pp.
Intended as historical background to the same author's Islam in West Africa (see 1066), this book traces the expansion of Islam in the Sahara and the establishment of Islamic "stagnation" in the seventeenth and eighteenth centuries, and the reawakening of Islam in the nineteenth century, followed by the advent of European colonialism. All in all, given the paucity of the sources, this work is commendable for the clear outline of the subject. See also 1391.

1062 _____. The Influence of Islam upon Africa. New York: Praeger, 1968, 159 pp.
An outline of the effects of Islamization on territories and peoples of Africa; useful to readers who do not have time to work through Trimingham's more detailed books.

1063 _____. Islam in East Africa. Oxford: Clarendon Press, 1964, 198 pp.
There is a short chapter on the spread of Islam in East Africa. The remainder of the book is devoted to a description of Islamic beliefs, practices, and social organization. See also 1392.

1064 _____. Islam in Ethiopia. London: Frank Cass, 1949, 299 pp. Reprinted in 1965.
Combines the historical and phenomenological approaches characteristic of Trimingham's work on African Islam. This book is distinguished, however, by its emphases on the conflict between Christianity and Islam and its discussion of the tribal distribution of Islam in the area. It should be noted that Trimingham is a missionary and his work, though scholarly and objective in the Western sense, is not accepted as such by all Africanists and African Muslims.

1065 _____. Islam in the Sudan (see 804).
The first half of this book outlines the history of the Sudan from the Christian kingdoms through the Arab conquests and the condominium; the second half describes "orthodox Islam," faith Islam, and the Ṣūfī orders, and ends with a discussion of the interaction of Islam, paganism, and "Westernism."

1066 _____. Islam in West Africa. Oxford: Clarendon Press, 1959, 262 pp.
A phenomenological study of the religious beliefs and practices of West African Muslims. In addition to a description of theology, ritual, and institutions, Trimingham analyzes the interaction of pre-Islamic with Islamic beliefs and customs, and the impact of Western civilization on African religion and society. Should be read in conjunction with the same author's A History of Islam in West Africa (see 1061).

Religious Thought

INTRODUCTIONS TO ISLAM

1067 Adams, Charles J. "The Islamic Religious Tradition." In Religion and Man. Edited by W. Richard Comstock. New York: Harper & Row, 1971, pp. 553-617.

Of the many short introductions to Islam found in textbooks on the religions of man, this is one of the best. Well written, it consciously directs its attention to the Islamic religious tradition. With the annotated bibliography of basic works, it serves the purpose of introducing the beginner to Islam.

1068 ʻAlī, Syed Ameer. The Spirit of Islam: A History of the Evolution and Ideals of Islam (see 1742).

1069 Arberry, A.J. Aspects of Islamic Civilization as Depicted in the Original Texts (see 182).

1070 ʻAzzām, ʻAbd al-Raḥmān. The Eternal Message of Muḥammad. Translated by C.E. Farah. New York: Devin-Adavi, 1964, 297 pp.

A modern Arab Muslim's interpretation of the Islamic religious tradition. More than a biography of the prophet Muḥammad, this work interprets the meaning of the prophetic message for Muslims. The work may serve as an excellent example of a contemporary Muslim's view of Islam that is shared by many of its followers.

1071 Bishai, Wilson B. Humanities in the Arabic-Islamic World. Dubuque, Ia.: Brown, 1973, 147 pp.

Although not an introduction to the Islamic religious tradition, this book treats various aspects of Islamic culture that the author considers to be "humanistic contributions of the Arabic-Islamic world." Includes excerpts from writings of al-Ghazālī and Ibn Rushd (Averroes), plus chapters on Arabic language and literature and pictorial art, architecture, and music. Glossary of Arabic terms and index.

1072 Christopher, John B. The Islamic Tradition. New York and London: Harper & Row, 1972, 185 pp.

Although this survey of Islam touches upon many aspects of Islamic religion and culture, it is by and large a much too superficial account. It includes, however, chapters on science and arts and literature, two subjects often neglected in most introductions.

1073 Cragg, Kenneth. The Call of the Minaret. New York: Oxford University, 1956, 376 pp.

This is an interpretation of Islam that quite openly seeks to lead its reader (necessarily a Christian reader) to interreligious rapprochement with Islam. This detracts from the book's usefulness as an introduction, as the reader is easily caught up in the ministry Cragg seems to be proclaiming. See also 1778.

1074 _____. The House of Islam. 2d rev. ed. Encino, Calif.: Dickenson Publishing Co., 1975, 145 pp.

A clearly written introduction that is an "essay in interpretation" (preface) of what the author understands to be the key elements in the Islamic religious tradition. Annotated bibliography. Glossary and index.

1075 Dermenghem, Emile. Muhammad and the Islamic Tradition (see 122).

1076 Encyclopaedia Britannica, The (see 2738).

The main articles on Islam together constitute one of the best general introductions to the study of the Islamic tradition that exists. They are: "Islam," "Islam, History of," "Islamic Law," "Islamic Mysticism," "Islamic Myth and Legend," "Islamic Peoples, Arts of," "Islamic Theology and Philosophy" (vol. 9, pp. 911-1025); "Ḥadīth" (vol. 8, pp. 536-38); and Qur'ān" (vol. 15, pp. 341-45). The articles are written by outstanding scholars in their respective fields; the bibliographies that follow each article are selective and briefly annotated. The illustrations that accompany the articles on art are of the highest quality (in color) and well chosen.

1077 Farah, Caesar E. Islam: Beliefs and Observances. Woodbury, N.Y.: Barron's Educational Series, 1968, 306 pp. Chicago: Henry Regnery, Gateway Edition, 1971.

A fairly comprehensive introduction to Islam. The book is perhaps unique with its section on the "Black Muslims." It covers pre-Islamic Arabia, Muḥammad, the Qur'ān, doctrines, obligations, the community, sects, and modern developments. See also 1780.

1078 Fārūqī, Ismā'īl R. al-. "Islam." In Historical Atlas of the Religions of the World. Edited by I. al-Farūqī and D.E. Sopher. New York: Macmillan Co., 1974, pp. 237-81.
A general survey of selected aspects of Islam, from the beginnings to the present, that reflects the author's own interpretations of Islam. Too brief to serve as a comprehensive introduction, it nonetheless is enhanced by the numerous maps and photographs. Short bibliography.

1079 Fyzee, A.A.A. A Modern Approach to Islam (see 1666).

1080 Gardet, L. Mohammedanism. Translated by William Bunidge. London: Burns & Oates, 1961, 176 pp.
A difficult study, this introduction reflects this outstanding French scholar's interest in Islamic thought. Origins of Islam, its history, beliefs, and doctrines, and modern Islam are the topics examined. A good introduction.

1081 Gibb, H.A.R.. Mohammedanism. 2d ed. London, New York, and Toronto: Oxford University, 1962. Reprinted with revisions, 1970.
This "classic" introduction to Islam covers the expansion of Islam, Muḥammad, the Qur'ān, Ḥadith, law, sects, Sufism, and modern Islamic developments. Annotated bibliography and index.

1082 Great Religions of the World. The Story of Man Library. Washington: National Geographic Book Service, 1971, pp. 220-71, 279-81.
The photographs alone make this an invaluable introduction to Islam. The text is good, especially the chapters on the pilgrimage to Mecca.

1083 Guillaume, Alfred. Islam. Baltimore: Penguin, 1954, 210 pp.
This introduction is badly outdated today, but its factual account may be of help to the student. The author's attempt to compare Islam and Christianity by setting Islamic beliefs against the Apostles' Creed is disappointing. Index and glossary.

1084 Hitti, Philip K. Islam: A Way of Life. New York: Humanities, 1971, 241 pp.
Discusses Islam as a religion, a state, and a culture. The work was intended as a popular introduction to the Arab contributions to civilization through Islam. Easy but unrewarding reading. Index and maps. See also 1786.

1085 Hodgson, Marshall G.S. The Venture of Islam (see 29).

1086 Jeffery, Arthur, ed. Islam: Muhammad and His Religion. New York: Liberal Arts, 1958, 252 pp.
Contains translations of Islamic materials on the Prophet, the Qur'ān, the doctrines and duties of Islam, and its practices. Each section has a brief introduction and frequently translations are introduced with explanatory notes and brief bibliographical notices. Glossary. See also 1788.

1087 _____, ed. and trans. A Reader on Islam: Passages from Standard Arabic Writings Illustrative of the Beliefs and Practices of Muslims. The Hague: Mouton, 1962, 687 pp.
A collection of translated materials on various aspects of Islamic beliefs and practices. The translations are excellent as well as the choice of materials. Areas covered are: the Qur'ān, the traditions, law, the biography of Muḥammad, creeds and confessions, theology, and practical piety. A most useful collection of primary texts. Glossary of Arabic terms and bibliography. See also 1220, 1414, 1444, 1789.

1088 Klein, F.A. The Religion of Islam. New York: Humanities, 1971, 241 pp. Reprint of 1906 ed.
Useful for the inclusion of key terms in Arabic script (with English equivalents), but as an introduction the book is outdated and misleading in many areas.

1089 Kritzeck, James, ed. Anthology of Islamic Literature. New York: Holt, Rinehart & Winston, 1964, 379 pp.
A history of literary accomplishments in Islam. The introductory pages to each section are excellent, as are the selections. The translations cover the Qur'ān, pre-Islam, caliphal periods, the Ottoman, Ṣafavid, and Mughal empires, and the modern world.

1090 Lammens, Henri. Islam: Beliefs and Institutions. Translated by Sir E. Denison Ross. London: Frank Cass, 1919, 256 pp.
Outdated. The reader must be warned that the author wrote with a strong bias against the Arab (with his "anarchical temperament") and Islam. Contents include Muḥammad, the Qur'ān, law, sects in Islam, reformists, and modernists. See also 1790.

1091 Levy, Reuben. The Social Structure of Islam: Being the Second Edition of the Sociology of Islam (see 34).

1092 Morgan, Kenneth, ed. Islam--the Straight Path: Islam Interpreted by Muslims. New York: Ronald Press, 1958, 453 pp.
A collection of essays written by several Muslim scholars interested in explaining Islam to Westerners.

1093 Nasr, Seyyed Hossein. Ideals and Realities of Islam. London: Allen & Unwin, 1966, 184 pp.; Boston: Beacon, 1972, 184 pp.
An interpretation of several central aspects of the Islamic religious tradition by a contemporary Muslim. Although the work is apologetic, it draws upon both Western studies on Islam and the traditional sources. A general chapter on Islam is followed by chapters on the Qur'ān, the Prophet, law, and Sufism. The last chapter, on the Sunnīs and Shī'īs, is a useful introduction to the problem of similarities and differences between the two major communities in

Islam. Annotated bibliographies follow each chapter. Index.

1094 Noss, John B. Man's Religions. 5th ed. New York: Macmillan, 1974, pp. 507-57.

A factual account of some important aspects of Islam. The fifth edition has corrected many errors found in previous editions.

1095 Rahman, Fazlur. Islam. New York, Chicago, and San Francisco: Holt, Rinehart & Winston, 1966, 271 pp.; Garden City, N.Y.: Doubleday, 1968, 331 pp.

The best introduction to Islam, written by an outstanding Muslim scholar of Islamic studies. The study includes an examination of issues not often found in English-language introductions, such as a chapter on education and Fazlur Rahman's own brilliant interpretation of the development of the traditions of the Prophet. The book is clearly written but quite difficult in places. Bibliography and index. See also 1229, 2044.

1096 Schimmel, Annemarie. "Islam." In Historia Religionum: Handbook for the History of Religion. Vol. 2. Edited by C.J. Bleeker and George Widengren. Leiden: Brill, 1971, pp. 125-210.

An examination of the entire development of Islam, which takes into account its history, doctrines, religious practices, and present situation. The chapter ends with a look at the history of Islamic studies in the West.

1097 Schroeder, Eric. Muhammad's People: A Tale by Anthology (see 208).

1098 Schuon, Frithjof. Dimensions of Islam. Translated by P.N. Townsend. London: Allen & Unwin, 1970, 167 pp.

A series of eleven essays delving into various major themes of Islamic thought. The essays are marked by frequent reference to other religions, since in fact the topics discussed are universal in nature. This is not a historical introduction but a discussion of basic themes this scholar of comparative religion considers to be shared by many religions.

1099 _____. Understanding of Islam. Translated by D.M. Matheson. Baltimore: Penguin, 1972, 159 pp.

An attempt to explain why Muslims follow Islam through a mystical interpretation of the meaning and contemporary relevance of Islam, the Qur'ān, the Prophet, and Sufism. As with other works by Schuon, this one tries to reveal what the author thinks to be the inner, often hidden, universal truths that underlie a specific religious tradition. The study does presuppose some prior knowledge of Islam. No index or bibliography.

1100 Smart, Ninian. "The Muslim Experience." In The Religious Experience of Mankind. New York: Scribner, 1969, pp. 372-423.

Despite its brevity, a fair introduction. The comparison of Islam with Judaism and Christianity at the end is interesting. Very short bibliography.

1101 Sourdel, Dominique. Islam. Translated by Douglas Scott. New York: Walden, 1962, 155 pp.

An introduction to the religious, historical, social, political, theological, philosophical, artistic, and modern developments of Islam. Dated and superseded by better introductions. Index and tiny bibliography.

1102 Stewart, Desmond, and the editors of Time-Life Books. Early Islam. New York: Time, 1967, 192 pp.

An introduction to basic religious and cultural aspects of Islam, with a readable text accompanied by many excellent photographs, both black and white and in color. The life of the Prophet, basic religious practices, the period of conquest, and achievements in art, philosophy, and science are related by pictures and text. Insufficient as a comprehensive introduction to Islam, it nevertheless is of value because of its emphasis upon important cultural aspects of Islam shown in fine illustrations.

1103 Tritton, A.S. Islam: Belief and Practices. 2d ed. London: Hutchinson's University Library, 1954, 200 pp.

The only merit of this introduction is that it places emphasis upon the popular tradition, thus making it almost unique compared to the other introductions. The chapters on beliefs, sects, and social life and popular ideas make this book particularly valuable. The glossary offers extensive notes on several important Arabic terms.

1104 Watt, W. Montgomery. What is Islam? New York and Washington: Praeger, 1968, 256 pp.

The book falls into two parts: an analysis of the Qur'ān's vision of the universe, which takes into account the historical background, and an analysis of the embodiment of that vision in history, which focuses on Muḥammad's life, later political developments, aspects of the religious intellectual life of the community, Islam's expansion, Islamic worship and piety, and the present situation. The study is based largely upon the author's previous studies on Islam, which, like this one, presuppose a functionalist approach to the study of Islam.

1105 Williams, John A. Islam. New York: George Braziller, 1961, 256 pp.

A selection of translations from Islamic materials woven into a narration by the author on the Qur'ān, tradition, law, Sufism, theology, and sects. Short index. Good, straightforward introduction. See 2082.

1106 Williams, John Alden, ed. Themes of Islamic Civilization (see 211).

1107 Zaehner, R.C., ed. The Concise Encyclopedia of Living Faiths. London: Hutchinson, 1971, pp. 178-208.

A brief introduction by H.A.R. Gibb. Plates included. Demands thoughtful reading.

PRE-ISLAMIC BACKGROUND

1108 Arberry, A.J. "Arabia Deserta." In Aspects of Islamic Civilization as Depicted in the Original Texts (see 182), pp. 19-31.
This chapter presents abridgments of the seven most important pre-Islamic literary sources.

1109 _____. The Seven Odes: The First Chapter in Arabic Literature (see 116).

1110 Bell, Richard. The Origin of Islam in Its Christian Environment (see 118).

1111 Bravmann, M.M. The Spiritual Background of Early Islam. Leiden: Brill, 1972, 336 pp.
The work is mainly a collection of previously published articles on basic ideas of early Islam and their relationship to their pre-Islamic background. Such important concepts as murūwah (manly virtues), dīn (religion), Islam, īmān (faith), ᶜamr (command), sunnah (path), and important themes such as life and death, punishment of crime, the return of the hero, are examined by means of exhaustive philological analysis. Although the title gives the impression that the work is a general study, it is not. The studies are difficult and technical and should not be tackled by the beginner. No subject index; only an index of Arabic terms. See also 1236.

1112 Encyclopaedia of Islam, The (see 20).
The following articles have appeared and are recommended for the pre-Islamic background: "al-ᶜArab," containing a detailed section on the history of the Arabs before Islam (vol. 1, pp. 524-33); "Djazīrat al-ᶜArab," or the geography and ethnology of the Arabian Peninsula (vol. 1, pp. 533-56); "Arabiyya," on language (vol. 1, pp. 561-67); "Badw," Bedouin life (vol. 1, pp. 872-92); and "Kāhin," on the shaman, or diviner (vol. 4, pp. 420-23). The article "Djāhiliyya" (vol. 2, pp. 383-84), although brief, is useful, for its directs the reader to several other articles pertinent to the pre-Islamic period.

1113 Fahd, Toufic. La Divination Arabe: Études religieuses, sociologique et folklorique sur le milieu (motif) de l'Islam. Leiden: E.J. Brill, 1966, 617 pp.
A detailed and comprehensive study of various pre-Islamic magico-religious beliefs and practices that takes into account the numerous functions and sacred instruments of the kāhin (soothsayer, diviner). With extensive notes, exhaustive bibliography, and indexes.

1114 _____. Le Panthéon de l'Arabie centrale à la Veille de l'hégire. Paris: Paul Geuthner, 1968, 321 pp.
The sequel to La Divination Arabe (see 1113), this study examines the chief characteristics of pre-Islamic religion (based on writings of classical Muslim historians), and alphabetically lists and analyzes all known central sacred sanctuaries. With notes, bibliography, and indexes.

1115 Gibb, H.A.R. Arabic Literature: An Introduction (see 50).
The third chapter deals specifically with the pre-Islamic period and its literary forms.

1116 Goldziher, Ignaz. Muslim Studies. Vol. 1 (see 127).
This late nineteenth-century study of the early development of Islam stands today as a classic Western work in Islamic studies. The pre-Islamic background, as well as the religious outlook of the earliest Muslim community, is analyzed. Here, in the first two chapters, Goldziher contrasts the religious outlook of pre-Islamic Arabs with that of Muḥammad by comparing basic attitudes found in pre-Islamic poetry and the Qur'ān. There is also a study of the fundamental differences between the social order of tribal life before Islam and the first teachings of Islam. Two excursuses are particularly relevant: "What is meant by 'al-Jāhiliyya'" and "On the veneration of the dead in paganism and Islam."

1117 Grunebaum, G.E. von. "Growth and Structure of Arabic Poetry, A.D. 500-1000." In The Arab Heritage (see 123), pp. 121-41.
An introduction to Arabic poetry that is particularly useful for understanding its importance at the time of Muḥammad. The appendix contains several examples of poetry that convey the general nature of Arabic verse. Bibliography.

1118 _____. "The Nature of Arab Unity before Islam." Arabica 10 (1963):5-23.
A difficult study on the intriguing question of what kind of unity existed among the Arabs before Islam, which includes a careful look at the complex features of pre-Islamic Arabian culture. It also examines the conditions that allowed Mecca to play a special role among the pre-Islamic Arabs.

1119 Henninger, Joseph. "La religion bedouine preislamique." In L'Antica Società Beduina. Edited by Francesco Gabrieli. Rome: Centro di Studi Semitici, 1959, pp. 115-40.
A summary of beliefs and practices of the Bedouin prior to Muḥammad's day. The article contains a useful survey of key Western studies on the subject.

1120 Hodgson, Marshall. "The World before Islam." In The Venture of Islam. Vol. 1 (see 29), pp. 103-45.
A superb analysis of the period before Muḥammad's time. Despite the author's use of unusual terms (explained in the introduction), the chapter is a remarkable overview of the pre-Islamic setting and studies on it to date.

1121 Ibn al-Kalbī, Hishām. The Book of Idols: Being a Translation from the Arabic of the Kitāb al-Aṣnām. Translated with introduction and notes by N.A. Faris. Princeton, N.J.: Princeton University Press, 1952, 59 pp.
A translation of a unique early Islamic document that describes numerous pre-Islamic sacred objects venerated by Arabs before the rise of Islam.

1122 Kister, M.J. "Al-Ḥīrā': Some Notes on Its Relations with Arabia." Arabica 15 (1968): 143-69.

Kister concludes that the fall of Ḥīrā' to Bedouin raiders coincided with the rise of Mecca. A scholarly and technical inquiry, with conclusions important for understanding the background of the rise of Islam.

1123 _____. "Mecca and Tamīm (Aspects of Their Relations)." Journal of the Economic and Social History of the Orient 8 (1965):113-63.

Based on an exhaustive survey of the sources, this article reveals more than ever before the manner in which Mecca achieved its economic and political position on the trade routes prior to the time of Muḥammad. Difficult, but a basic and essential study.

1124 _____. "Some Reports Concerning Mecca: From Jahiliyya to Islam." Journal of the Economic and Social History of the Orient 15 (1972): 61-93.

A study on the conditions in Mecca and its relations with tribes and vassal kingdoms before and during the initial rise of Islam. The study sheds new light on Mecca and its role as a trade center.

1125 Levi della Vida, G. "Pre-Islamic Arabia." In The Arab Heritage (see 123), pp. 25-57.

1126 Lyall, C.J. Translations of Ancient Arabian Poetry. London: Williams & Norgate, 1930, 142 pp. Reprint of 1885 ed.

This anthology includes an excellent selection of pre-Islamic poetry with a good introduction and sufficient notes. A new printing of this study would be well received.

1127 Moscati, S. "The Arabs." In Ancient Semitic Civilizations (see 132), pp. 181-219.

1128 Mufaḍḍal ibn Muḥammad, al-. The Mufaḍḍalīyāt: An Anthology of Ancient Arabian Odes (see 133).

1129 Nicholson, Reynold Alleyne. A Literary History of the Arabs (see 57).

The first three chapters (pp. 1-140) depict the major characteristics, events, and literature of the pre-Islamic era.

1130 Nöldeke, Theodor. "Arabs (Ancient)." In Encyclopaedia of Religion and Ethics. 13 vols. Edited by James Hastings. New York: Charles Scribner's Sons, 1962, 1:659-73.

First published in 1908, this is a basic study on pre-Islamic religious beliefs and practices current in Muḥammad's milieu. Particular attention is devoted to gods and goddesses, cultic (and other) beliefs and practices, and the pre-Islamic pilgrimage to Mecca.

1131 Obermann, Julian. "Early Islam." In The Idea of History in the Ancient Near East. Edited by Robert C. Dentan. New Haven, Conn.: Yale University Press, 1955, pp. 239-310.

A study of the importance of genealogy in pre-Islamic Arabia and its transformation in early Islam. The author quotes from primary sources, most interesting of which are the poetry passages that reveal the concern for remembering the ways of the ancestors so that tribal solidarity (ʿAṣabiyyah) may be maintained. Brief bibliography.

1132 _____. "Islamic Origins: A Study in Background and Foundation." In The Arab Heritage (see 123), pp. 58-120.

A discussion of Islamic origins in the light of Jewish and Christian influences upon it. General background, theory, and substance of revelation in the Semitic tradition are analyzed. Although dated in some respects, the article is a useful introduction to Islamic origins. Good bibliography.

1133 O'Leary, De Lacy. Arabia before Muhammad (see 135).

1134 Ringgren, Helmer. Islam: 'Aslama and Muslim. Uppsala: C.W.K. Gleerup, 1949, 34 pp.

A study of the word "Islam" and words related to it, taking into account usages found before the rise of Islam, as well as the transformations of them at the time of Muḥammad. A valuable study.

1135 _____. Studies in Arabian Fatalism. Wiesbaden: Otto Harrassowitz, 1955, 255 pp.

A philological analysis of the fatalistic beliefs of the pre-Islamic Arabs. The author examines the early poems (pre-Islamic and early Islamic), the Qur'ān, and some traditions of Muḥammad in order to show the central importance of such beliefs before Islam, as well as the modification of them in Islam.

1136 Serjeant, R.B. "Ḥaram and Hawtah: The Sacred Enclave in Arabia." In Mélanges Taha Husain. Edited by ʿAbdurraḥmān Badawī. Cairo: Dar al-Maaref, 1962, pp. 41-58.

Serjeant was a pioneer in his study of present-day life among Bedouins of the Arabian peninsula and in the comparison of their unchanged practices with the earliest days of Islam. This is an important study of the sacred places and their properties in pre-Islamic Arabia.

1137 _____. "Hūd and Other Pre-Islamic Prophets of Ḥaḍramawt" (see 1893).

1138 _____. The Sayyids of Ḥaḍramawt: An Inaugural Lecture. London: School of Oriental and African Studies, University of London, 1957, 29 pp.

A basic monograph on the holy families of the sacred areas, especially important since one such family was a major opponent to Muḥammad in Mecca.

1139 Shahīd, Irfan. "Pre-Islamic Arabia." In The Cambridge History of Islam. Vol. 1 (see 30), pp. 3-29.

A significant essay on the last period of ancient Arabia that gives attention to Arabia's unique geographical features, traces the political, religious, and economic history of the southern Arabian city-state civilizations in the millennium before Islam, and examines the background of northern and central Arabia just prior to Muḥammad's day.

1140 Smith, Sidney. "Events in Arabia in the Sixth Century." Bulletin of the School of Oriental and African Studies 16 (1954): 425-68.

A careful examination of major events in the century preceding the rise of Islam, based on numerous (including non-Arabic) sources. The author argues that a more exacting analysis of social conditions in sixth-century Arabia is needed. Includes a detailed table of events, plus map.

1141 Smith, W. Robertson. Kinship and Marriage in Early Arabia. Oosterhout: Anthropological Publications, 1966, 324 pp. Reprint of 1907 ed.

A classic study by the nineteenth-century sociologist whose theories on sacrifice, totemism, marriage, and kinship have been influential down to the present day. Readers must place this work in the context of the history of theories of religion and society if they are to benefit from it.

1142 _____. Lectures on the Religion of the Semites: The Fundamental Institutions (see 1894).

1143 Torrey, Charles C. The Jewish Foundation of Islam (see 142).

1144 Watt, W.M. "Belief in a 'High God' in Pre-Islamic Mecca." Journal of Semitic Studies 16 (1971):35-40.

Although no new theory on deity worship in pre-Islamic Mecca is proposed, the article is nonetheless a useful analysis of the relevant Qur'ānic material showing that belief in a high god was widespread in the Mecca milieu at the time of the rise of Islam.

1145 Wendell, Charles. "The Pre-Islamic Period of Sīrat al-Nabī." Muslim World 62 (1972):12-41.

An important study of the formative influence of Muḥammad's environment upon himself examined in light of comparative material. The essay is followed by a critical response to it by M.A. Rauf (pp. 42-48).

1146 Wolf, Eric R. "The Social Organization of Mecca and the Origins of Islam." Southwestern Journal of Anthropology 7 (1951):329-56.

An analysis of the economic, religious, and political factors of Mecca society that helps explain the origin and early success of Islam. The article stresses the central importance of trade and the role it played in the transformation of Mecca society. An excellent study, well documented.

LIFE OF MUḤAMMAD

1147 Andrae, Tor. Mohammed: The Man and His Faith (see 115).

1148 Archer, J.C. Mystical Elements in Mohammed. New Haven, Conn.: Yale University Press, 1924, 87 pp.

A reaction to the view that Muḥammad was an epileptic. The author emphasizes the mystical bent in the Prophet's character and tries to show that Muḥammad sincerely believed himself overcome by the divine. The chapter on Christian monks fails in probing whether Muḥammad ever met or knew of these ascetics of the desert.

1149 Birkeland, Harris. The Legend of the Opening of Muhammad's Breast. Oslo: I Kommisjon Hos Jacob Dybwad, 1955, 60 pp.

A careful, technical, and critical examination of the extant literary material on the famous legend about the election of Muḥammad as a future prophet while still a child.

1150 Bodley, R.V.C. The Messenger. New York: Greenwood, 1969, 386 pp.

Written as a novel, this book contains a good index and some interesting glossaries. It is not a scholarly work, as is clear from the inclusion of the numerous tales of Muḥammad's life, which add color and detail but whose authenticity is questionable.

1151 Brett, Bernard. Mohammed. New York: Collins, 1972, 48 pp.

A most unusual work. Though it appears to be a child's book with brilliantly colored drawings and large print, it is a simply narrated biography of the Prophet and the rise of Islam. Worth inspecting. Index.

1152 Eickelman, Dale F. "Musaylima: An Approach to the Social Anthropology of Seventh Century Arabia." Journal of the Economic and Social History of the Orient 10 (1967):17-52.

An important study of a prophet in the Arabian peninsula who was a contemporary of Muḥammad. The article attempts to learn why prophets arose and how the movement of Musaylima compared to that of Muḥammad.

1153 Gabrieli, Francesco. Muhammad and the Conquests of Islam (see 124).

1154 Glubb, John Bagot. The Life and Times of Muhammad. London: Hodder & Stoughton, 1970, 416 pp.

General Glubb has written many books on subjects related to the Arabian peninsula. This biography is a sympathetic popular account based upon previous Western studies and Glubb's own personal reflections. The only unique feature of the work is that Glubb is the only Western biographer of Muḥammad to have lived a great part of his life with the Bedouins of Arabia. Index and short bibliography.

1155 Haykal, Muḥammad Ḥusayn. The Life of Muḥammad. Translated from the 8th edition by Ismā'īl Rāgī A. Fārūqī. n.p.: North American Trust Publications, 1976, 640 pp.

One of the most influential biographies of the prophet Muḥammad ever written, this work has greatly influenced modern Muslim attitudes toward Islam and ranks as one of the most significant Arabic-language theological writings of modern times. See also 1164.

1156 Ibn Isḥāq. The Life of Muhammad: A Translation of (Ibn) Isḥāq's Sīrat Rasūl Allāh (see 129).

1157 Muir, Sir William. The Life of Mahomet from Original Sources (see 134).

1158 Rodinson, Maxime. "The Life of Muḥammad and the Sociological Problem of the Beginnings of Islam." Diogenes 20 (1975):28-51.

Arguing that the origins of Islam can be understood only when the whole social, political, and religious context is established, the author reviews critically various works on the life of Muḥammad, including M. Watt's studies (see 143, 144).

1159 Sugana, Gabriele Mandel. The Life and Times of Mohammed. Translated by Francis Koval. London: Hamlyn Publishing, 1968, 75 pp.

The merit of this brief account of Muḥammad is found in its excellent illustrations. Photographs of ruins, landscapes, mosques, miniature paintings, and art objects abound. The text, although brief, is well written and informative.

1160 Rodinson, Maxime. Mohammed (see 136).

1161 Watt, W. Montgomery. Muhammad at Mecca (see 143).

1162 _____. Muhammad at Medina (see 144).

1163 _____. Muhammad: Prophet and Statesman (see 145).

1164 Wessels, Antoine. A Modern Arabic Biography of Muḥammad: A Critical Study of Muḥammad Ḥusayn Haykal's Ḥayāt Muḥammad. Leiden: E.J. Brill, 1972, 272 pp.

This is a study of a fascinating modern Muslim biography of Muḥammad (see 1155). Written in the 1930s for the educated Muslim, the biography offers a rigorous defense of Muḥammad (and Islam) against the claims of Orientalists and the teachings of Christian missionaries. Haykal's work exemplifies a Muslim modernist's view of Muḥammad, as well as concern and alarm over the threats to Islam coming from the West. Wessels's study of the biography provides us with a comprehensive analysis of an important work. Good bibliography and index.

THE QUR'ĀN

Selected articles on the Qur'ān do not appear, since virtually all articles (over 800) on various Qur'ānic subjects have been listed in J.D. Pearson's Index Islamicus (see 6). The articles are organized under several subheadings, such as "Readings and Variants," "Recitation," "Commentaries," "Explanation of Single Passages," and "Explanation of Various Topics," thus facilitating the use of this indispensable guide to periodic literature in Islamic studies.

TRANSLATIONS

1165 Ali, ᶜAbdullah Yusuf, trans. The Holy Qur'ān: Text, Translation and Commentary. 2 vols. Washington: American International, 1946, 1:456; 2:512.

A fairly literal translation of the Qur'ān, footnoted extensively with commentary and Arabic text. Brief, factual introduction with an index of sūrahs and subjects. Each sūrah is accompanied by an introduction and summary.

1166 Arberry, A.J., trans. The Holy Koran: An Introduction with Selections. London: Allen & Unwin, 1953, 141 pp.

Selections from the Qur'ān that illustrate its beauty, with a good introduction that describes its literary features.

1167 Arberry, A.J. The Koran Interpreted. 2 vols. London: Allen & Unwin, 1955, 1:350 pp.; 2:358 pp.

The best English translation that exists. The translator has attempted to convey the richness of the Arabic in English verse. The preface includes a brief study of the history of translation of the Qur'ān into English, as well as a discussion of the problems involved in translation.

1168 Bell, Richard, trans. The Qur'ān: Translated with a Critical Re-arrangement of the Surahs. 2 vols. Edinburgh: Clark, 1937, 697 pp.

A critical translation that is fairly literal and encumbered by "ye" and "hath." The traditional order of the Qur'ān has also been abandoned for a chronological arrangement of the verses arrived at by Bell on the basis of criteria described in his Introduction (see 1178). Each sūrah has a lengthy introduction, dating it and identifying its parts. Subject index and index of Arabic names.

1169 Dawood, N.A., trans. The Koran. Baltimore: Penguin Books, 1961, 427 pp.

A readable translation but difficult to use, since the translator has arranged the contents chronologically without explanation.

1170 Palmer, E.H., trans. The Qur'ān. 2 vols. Sacred Books of the East, edited by Max Müller, vols. 6 and 9. Delhi: Motilal Banarsidass, 1965, 1:268 pp.; 2:362 pp. Orig. pub. in 1880.

One of the oldest English translations still in use today. Reliable and fairly readable.

1171 Pickthall, Muhammad M. The Glorious Koran: A Bilingual Edition with English Translation, Introduction and Notes. Albany: State University of New York Press, 1976, 826 pp. Reprint of 1938 ed.

One of the most widely read translations of the Qur'ān and one that Muslim scholars find to be an acceptable rendition of the Arabic text, by a convert to Islam and an English literary figure.

1172 Rodwell, J.M., trans. The Koran. London: Dent, 1909, 506 pp.

A versified translation of the Qur'ān that uses old Biblical forms of address. The sūrahs are arranged chronologically.

COMMENTARIES

1173 Āzād, (Mawlānā) Abū'l-Kalām. The Tarjumān al-Qur'ān (see 1755).

1174 Bayḍāwī, al-. Baidāwī's Commentary on Surah 12 of the Qur'ān: Text, Accompanied by an Interpretive Rendering and Notes. Translated by A.F.L. Beeston. Oxford: University Press, 1963, 97 pp.

A brief selection (on sūrah 12) from the classical Muslim commentary by al-Bayḍāwī (d. 1260?).

1175 _____. Chrestomathia Baidawiana: The Commentary of al-Baidawi on Sura III Translated and Explained for the Use of Students of Arabic. Translated by D.S. Margoliouth. London: Luzac, 1894, 21 pp.

Like the preceding entry, this brief selection is from the same classical commentary. See also 1852.

1176 Paret, Rudi. Der Koran: Kommentar und Konkordanz. Stuttgart: V.M. Kohlhammer, 1971, 559 pp.

The best Western scholarly commentary and concordance of the Qur'ān that is available. Meant to accompany Paret's German translation of the Qur'ān, it is a basic resource for the serious student of the Qur'ān. The concordance is the first of its kind, listing identical verses, closely related verses, and verses related comparatively.

1177 Watt, W. Montgomery. Companion to the Qur'ān. London: Allen & Unwin, 1967, 355 pp.

Very limited in scope, this commentary attempts to provide the reader with the basic background material needed for understanding the Qur'ān. Based upon Arberry's translation of the Qur'ān (see 1167), the book gives explanatory notes on problematic verses. Often reference is made to other sūrahs and verses. Useful index of proper names in the Qur'ān, as well as an index to the commentary.

STUDIES ON THE QUR'ĀN

General Studies

1178 Bell, Richard. Bell's Introduction to the Qur'ān. New ed. Rev. and enlarged by W.M. Watt. Edinburgh: Edinburgh University Press, 1970, 258 pp.

The best general Western study of the Qur'ān that exists in English. Though quite technical in many instances, it relates pertinent facts about the Qur'ān in an accurate and clear style. The chapters touch on the historical context out of which the Qur'ān arose, Muḥammad's experience, the history of the text, its external form, its literary style, the formation of the written Qur'ān, chronology of the verses, the names of the sūrahs, the Qur'ānic doctrines, and Muslim and Western study of the Qur'ān. See also 1168.

1179 Buhl, F. "Al-Ḳur'ān." In Shorter Encyclopedia of Islam (see 22), pp. 273-87.

A comprehensive introduction to the critical study of the Qur'ān that is somewhat dated and employs some unfortunate terminology, such as "Muhammadans." Useful if Bell's Introduction (see 1178) is not available.

1180 Cragg, Kenneth. The Event of the Qur'ān: Islam in Its Scripture. London: Allen & Unwin, 1971, 208 pp.

A personal and subjective inquiry into the meaning of the Qur'ān. The author tries to "get inside" the Qur'ān and view its interaction with the "pagan" background. Index.

1181 _____. The Mind of the Qur'ān. London: Allen & Unwin, 1973, 209 pp.

A companion volume to The Event of the Qur'ān (see 1180), this one also mirrors the personal reflections of the author. The underlying concern of the book "is with inter-religious converse and responsibility in the contemporary world" (preface). The chapter on exegetical tradition is recommended; it examines three important classical commentators, with examples. Index.

1182 Geiger, Abraham. Judaism and Islam. New York: KTAV Publishing House, 1970, 170 pp. Reprint of 1898 ed.

A pioneering work (written in Latin in 1832) that concludes that Jewish sources (including Biblical, exegetical, and other post-Biblical materials) were appropriated by Muḥammad by means of oral communication. This work has had enormous influence upon later Western Qur'ān studies.

1183 Margoliouth, D.S., and A. Mingana. "Qur'ān." In Encyclopaedia of Religion and Ethics (see 1130).

A brief introduction to the Qur'ān reflecting late nineteenth-century Western approaches to the study of the Qur'ān.

1184 Nöldeke, Theodor. "The Koran." In Sketches from Eastern History (see 156), pp. 21-59.
Originally published in the Encyclopaedia Britannica (9th ed.), this is still a useful introduction to the study of the Qur'ān.

1185 Rahman, Fazlur. Major Themes of the Qur'ān. Chicago and Minneapolis, Minn.: Bibliotheca Islamica, 1980, 180 pp.
A brilliant, original examination of the contents of the Qur'ān that diverges significantly from previous studies, both Muslim and Western. Rahman shows, through his synthetic exposition of fundamental themes ("God," "Man as Individual," "Man in Society," "Nature," "Prophethood and Revelation," "Eschatology," and "Satan and Evil,") that the Qur'ān offers a cohesive outlook on life and the Universe. A basic study.

1186 Stanton, H.A. Weitbrecht. The Teachings of the Qur'ān: With an Account of Its Growth and a Subject Index. New York: Biblo & Tannen, 1969, 136 pp. Reprint of 1919 ed.
The summary of Qur'ānic teachings is superficial and superseded by better introductions (see 1178), but the subject index (pp. 75-110) to the Qur'ān is still useful.

Specific Studies

1187 Bakker, Dirk. Man in the Qur'ān. Amsterdam: Drubberij Holland, 1965, 219 pp.
The image of man, man's creation, his role in the world, and his relation to his fellow men and to God are themes that receive careful exegetical study. Extensive notes, bibliography, and index.

1188 Birkeland, Harris. The Lord Guideth: Studies on Primitive Islam. Oslo: I Kommisjon Hos H. Aschehoug & Co. (W. Nygaard), 1956, 140 pp.
An exacting exegetical study of five early sūrahs (93, 94, 108, 105, and 106) that share the common theme of divine guidance. Much of the work is a critical examination of the Muslim exegesis of the sūrahs, both in the traditions (ḥadīth) and theological commentaries (tafsīr) writings. A technical study, not for the beginner.

1189 _____. Muslim Interpretation of Surah 107. Oslo: I Kommisjon Hos H. Aschehoug & Co. (W. Nygaard), 1958, 56 pp.
An examination of Muslim exegesis of one of the earliest sūrahs as formulated in the traditions (ḥadīth) and theological commentaries (tafsīr writings). A technical study.

1190 Izutsu, Toshihiko. Ethico-Religious Concepts in the Qur'ān. Rev. ed. Montreal: McGill University, 1966, 284 pp. Orig. pub. as The Structure of Ethical Terms in the Koran. Tokyo: Keio University, 1959.
This is a basic study of key ethical concepts (unbelief, faith, good, bad, hypocrisy) in the Qur'ān. The study examines the Qur'ānic transformation of pre-Islamic values and analyzes carefully a variety of Arabic terms demonstrating the richness and profundity of ethical concepts in the Qur'ān. Subject index and index of Arabic terms. A valuable study.

1191 _____. God and Man in the Koran: Semantics of the Koranic Weltanschauung. Tokyo: Keio Institute of Cultural and Linguistic Studies, 1964, 242 pp.
Through the application of semantic analysis, the author attempts to reveal the structure of the God-man relationship in the Qur'ān. The study examines the ontological relation, the linguistic and nonlinguistic communicative relation, and the ethical relation between God and man. A difficult study. Index of Arabic terms.

1192 Jeffery, Arthur. The Foreign Vocabulary of the Qur'ān. Baroda: Oriental Institute, 1928, 311 pp.
A dictionary of non-Arabic words found in the Qur'ān. The introduction is particularly valuable for the entire subject of non-Arabic terms used in the Qur'ān. Indexes of loan words.

1193 Jeffery, A. Materials for the History of the Text of the Qur'ān. Leiden: E.J. Brill, 1937, 609 pp.
A listing of the known differences distinguishing some twenty-eight codices of the Qur'ān. The entire problem of variant readings is discussed in the introduction, as is the desirability of a scholarly study of the Qur'ān through its variant readings. A technical study.

1194 _____. The Qur'ān as Scripture. New York: Russell Moore, 1952, 103 pp.
The nature of the sacred book, prophecy, inspiration, the relation of the Qur'ān to earlier scriptures, and the textual history of the Qur'ān are the subjects of this important study.

1195 Katsh, A.I. Judaism in Islam: Biblical and Talmudic Backgrounds of the Koran and Its Commentaries. New York: Bloch, 1954, 265 pp.
A detailed study of sūrahs 2 and 3, which cites various verses and the tafsīr literature on the verses and establishes parallels in Jewish literature. On this basis the author claims to prove the Jews of Arabia in Muḥammad's time were highly educated and in touch with their literary tradition.

1196 O'Shaughnessy, Thomas. The Development of the Meaning of Spirit in the Kur'an. Rome: Pontifical Institute, 1953, 75 pp.
In assessing the term "rūḥ" in the Qur'ān, the author is led to believe that gnostic influences were particularly active in the formation of the meaning of this term.

1197 _____. The Koranic Concept of the Word of God. Rome: Pontificio Instituto Biblico, 1948, 69 pp.
An attempt to analyze the Qur'ānic concept of the word of God as it applies to the Qur'ānic view of Christ. The book examines the

concept in the Qur'ān, some classical commentators' interpretations of it, and investigates the origins of the concept and what it meant to Muḥammad.

1198 _____. Muhammad's Thoughts on Death: A Study of Qur'anic Data. Leiden: E.J. Brill, 1969, 90 pp.
A scholarly study on death in the Qur'ān.

1199 Parrinder, Geoffrey. Jesus in the Qur'an. New York: Barnes & Noble, 1965, 187 pp.
Written for "the general public as well as students of theology and the comparative study of religion" (preface), comparative religionist Parrinder shows what the Qur'ān says about Jesus, along with parallels from the Bible.

1200 Rahbar, Daud. God of Justice: A Study in the Ethical Doctrine of the Qur'an. Leiden: E.J. Brill, 1960, 446 pp.
This is not a critical exegetical study of ethics in the Qur'ān, but rather an examination of key words relating to the free-will problem and the problem of divine mercy. The author tries to show that the God of the Qur'ān does not predetermine human action by examining the "original sense" and "contextual significance" of innumerable verses. One half of the book (appendixes) lists verses relevant to key words.

1201 Raisanen, Heibbi. The Idea of Divine Hardening: A Comparative Study of the Notion of Divine Hardening, Leading Astray and Inciting to Evil in the Bible and the Qur'an. Helsinki: Finnish Exegetical Society, 1972, 108 pp.
An exegetical study of Qur'ānic and Biblical material on the problem of predestination. The section on the Qur'ān represents careful exegesis of the important texts. The author concludes that the "negative predestination" found in the Qur'ān is explained by the bitter experience of the Mecca opposition to Muḥammad and his message. Includes a survey of Western literature on the subject.

1202 Roberts, Robert. The Social Laws of the Qur'ān. London: Williams & Norgate, 1925, 126 pp.
Although dated in many respects, this book is still a useful summary of Qur'ānic regulations concerning marriage, divorce, slavery, inheritance, criminal acts, commercial transactions, food restrictions. See also 2102.

1203 Torrey, Charles C. The Commercial-Theological Terms in the Koran. Leiden: E.J. Brill, 1892, 51 pp.
An analysis of a number of Qur'ānic terms whose origin lies in the commercial vocabulary of Muḥammad's day. The author argues that these trade terms shape and characterize the "theology" of the Qur'ān, creating an atmosphere in which the "commercial spirit" is the central feature of Muḥammad's religious outlook. Technical terms and phrases are not transliterated, and in many cases are left untranslated.

1204 Wagtendonk, K. Fasting in the Koran. Leiden: E.J. Brill, 1968, 154 pp.
An excellent study on the origin and significance of fasting in the Qur'ān. Fasting in pre-Islamic Arabia, the origin of Ramaḍān, and exegetical analysis of various texts are all carefully laid out, making this a basic study on the fast. Index of verses, names, and subjects.

1205 Watt, W. Montgomery. Islamic Revelation in the Modern World. Edinburgh: Edinburgh University Press, 1969, 143 pp.
This is not an "objective" study of the Qur'ān and theories of Islamic revelation, but Muslim apologetics by a Christian theologian. The scholarly Watt is here, but his primary aim is to present Islam in the best light possible to "both the religiously minded and the secular in outlook." The secondary aim is to show that Western scholarship is "not necessarily hostile to Islam as a religion."

STUDIES ON THE COMMENTARIES OF THE QUR'ĀN

1206 Baljon, J.M.S. Modern Muslim Koran Interpretation (1800-1960). Leiden: E.J. Brill, 1961, 135 pp.
An examination of modern Muslim exegesis of the Qur'ān. The introduction treats the major exegetes and their lives and work. The main chapters explore the various modes of interpretation and the major issues modern exegetes treat.

1207 Birkeland, Harris. Old Muslim Opposition against Interpretation of the Koran. Oslo: I Kommisjon Hos Jacob Dybwad, 1955, 42 pp.
A technical study on the negative reaction of the early traditionalists to the exegetical activity of the first generation of Muslim commentators of the Qur'ān.

1208 Carra de Vaux, B. "Tafsīr." In Shorter Encyclopedia of Islam (see 22), pp. 558-59.
A brief and sketchy discussion of the "science" of the interpretation of the Qur'ān.

1209 Gatje, Helmut. The Qur'ān and Its Exegesis: Selected Texts with Classical and Modern Muslim Interpretations. Translated and edited by Alford T. Welch. Berkeley and Los Angeles: University of California Press, 1976, 313 pp.
The only study of its kind in English, this is a collection of exegetical writings on selected Qur'ānic texts from the pens of key Muslim commentators. The work is arranged according to these topics: "Revelation," "Muḥammad," "Salvation History," "Islam," "The 'Book Religions' and Paganism," "God," "Angels, Spirits, and Mankind," "Eschatology," "Duties and Prohibitions," "Dogmatics," "Mystical and Philosophical Qur'anic Exegesis," "Shī'ite Qur'anic Exegesis," and "Modern Qur'anic Exegesis." With notes, annotated bibliography, and indexes.

1210 Goldziher, Ignaz. Die Richtungen der Islamischen Koranauslegung. 2d ed. Leiden: Brill, 1970, 392 pp. Reprint of 1920 ed.
The only comprehensive study of a Muslim Qur'ānic commentary in a Western language.

1211 Jansen, J.J.G. The Interpretation of the Koran in Modern Egypt. Leiden: Brill, 1974, 114 pp.
An attempt to study the nature of modern Muslim exegesis of the Qur'ān by examining commentaries written by the most important Egyptian commentators.

1212 Schimmel, Annemarie. "Translations and Commentaries of the Qur'ān in Sindhi Language." Oriens 16 (1963):224-43.
A useful descriptive study of the extant translations and commentaries of the Qur'ān in Sindhi, with examples from the commentary of the eighteenth-century mystic ʿAbdurraḥīm Girhōrī.

1213 Smith, Jane I. An Historical and Semantic Study of the Term "Islam" as Seen in a Sequence of Qur'an Commentaries. Missoula, Mont.: Scholars Press, 1975, 247 pp.
By examining one Qur'ān commentary for each century (fourteen in all), the author attempts to show the development of the concept "Islam" in both its personal and communal aspects. Helpful introductory notes on each exegete and his exegetical method serve as a good introduction to Qur'ān commentaries.

HADĪTH (TRADITIONS OF THE PROPHET)

TRANSLATIONS

1214 Baghawī, Abū Muḥammad al-Ḥusayn al-. Mishkāt al-Masābīh. Translated by James Robson. Lahore: Sh. Muh. Ashraf, 1963-1965, 1453 pp.
This translation of al-Baghawī's (d. 1122) collection of ḥadīth brings to the English reader all of the authentic traditions found in the classical Sunnī hadīth manuals, except the isnads (chain of authorities). Expertly translated, this monumental collection is preceded by an excellent introduction that treats the history of such collections, as well as technical works on the hadīth.

1215 Bukhārī, Muḥammad ibn Ismāʿīl al-. A Manual of Hadith. Translated by Muḥammad ᶜAlī. 2d ed. Lahore: Ahmadiyyah Anfuman Ishā'at Islam, 1951, 408 pp.
A selection of translated ḥadīth material.

1216 _____. Les Traditions islamiques. 4 vols. Translated by O. Houdas. Paris: Imprimerie Nationale, 1903-1914, 1:682 pp.; 2:649 pp.; 3:700 pp.; 4:676 pp.
Complete French translation, with notes, of the best-known collection of canonical ḥadīth, that of al-Bukhārī (d. 870).

1217 _____. The Translation of the Meanings of Sahiḥ al-Bukhārī. 2 vols. Translated by Muḥammad Muḥsin Khān. Gujranwala Cantt., West Pakistan, 1971, 1:461 pp.; 2:478 pp.
A translation of 1,655 traditions set alongside the Arabic. The chain of authorities (isnād) for the traditions have been excluded from both the Arabic text and the translation.

1218 _____. "Appendix B: Translation of 'Kitābu-l-Qadar' from the Ṣaḥīḥ of al-Bukharī." In The Traditions of Islam (see 1228), pp. 171-78.
Translation of the chapter on predestination. See also 1601.

1219 _____. "Appendix." In The Concept of Belief in Islamic Theology (see 1587), pp. 235-50.
Contains the Book of Faith (Kitāb al-Īmām), translated by W.P. McLean.

1220 Jeffery, Arthur, ed. and trans. A Reader on Islam (see 1087), pp. 79-248.
The section on tradition contains a fine selection of ḥadīth material. The Book on Fasting, from the collection of al-Bukhārī, one-half of the chapter on "appropriate clothing," from Abū Dā'ūd's collection, the forty traditions of al-Nawawī, the accounts of creation, the fall of Adam, death and the hereafter, and the repentance of Satan, all from a variety of collections, make this set of translations the best available.

1221 Nawawī, Muhyī al-Dīn. Gardens of the Righteous: Riyadh as Salihin of Imam Nawawi. Translated by Muḥammad Zafrulla Khan. London: Curzon Press, 1975, 332 pp.
The translation of one of the most important compilations of selected ḥadīth by the famous scholar of Islamic Law, Yaḥyā b. Sharaf al-Dīn al-Nawawī (d. 1278).

1222 _____. "The Forty (Two) Traditions of al-Nawawī." Translated by E.F.F. Bishop. Moslem World 29 (1939):153-77.
A discussion of the earlier collectors of these traditions precedes the translation.

1223 Samarqandī, Abū Layth al-. "The Creation of Man and Angels in the Eschatological Literature (Translated Excerpts from an Unpublished Collection of Traditions)." Translated by J. Macdonald. Islamic Studies 3 (1964): 285-308.

_____. "The Angel of Death in Late Islamic Tradition." Islamic Studies 3 (1964): 485-519.

_____. "The Twilight of the Dead." Islamic Studies 4 (1965):55-102.

_____. "The Preliminaries to the Resurrection and Judgment." Islamic Studies 4 (1965):137-79.

_____. "The Day of Resurrection." Islamic Studies 5 (1966):129-97.

______. "Paradise." Islamic Studies 5 (1966):331-83.

A translation in five parts of the ḥadīth material compiled by Abū Layth al-Samarqandī (d. 983). The collection provides a good insight into popular eschatological beliefs.

STUDIES ON THE ḤADĪTH

General Studies

1224 Abbott, Nabia. Studies in Arabic Literary Papyri. Vol. 2 (see 114).

The most recent major work on the development of the traditions and the question of their authenticity. Basing her work on midsecond-century Islamic papyri fragments, Professor Abbott studies the procedures and opinions of the early transmitters. From her findings on their methods and the care taken by major transmitters, she concludes that the majority of traditions are authentic. She also has some interesting ideas on the problem of the numbers of traditions and variants. The principal work on tradition to date.

1225 Amīn, Hassan al-. The Islamic Shi'ite Encyclopaedia. Vol. 2 (see 2752), pp. 94-107.

The only easily available listing of Shī'ī authors on the hadīth. It lists the mamor collections of the fourth and fifth centuries, as well as editions in print and reviews on other collections and commentaries up to the fourteenth century. The author concludes with a list of technical manuals on tradition.

1226 Azmi, M.M. Studies in Early Ḥadīth Literature. Beirut: Khayats, 1968, 342 pp.

The book presents the traditional Muslim view of tradition and attacks Joseph Schacht's studies on ḥadīth (see 1233).

1227 Goldziher, Ignaz. Muslim Studies. Vol. 2 (see 127).

The basic Western study on ḥadīth. Based on a particular interpretation of Umayyad times, the work is critical of the authenticity of most traditions.

1228 Guillaume, Alfred. The Traditions of Islam. Oxford: University Press, 1924, 184 pp.

The author begins with a history of tradition based mainly on the work of Ignaz Goldziher (see 1227). He then gives some criticisms of traditions by Muslims themselves, a chapter on Christian and Jewish borrowings, two chapters on Muḥammad and the caliphate in ḥadīth literature, and a chapter in which he translates the Book of Qadar (Predestination) of al-Bukhārī (see 1218). Includes a glossary of technical terms.

1229 Rahman, Fazlur. "The Origins and Development of Tradition." In Islam (see 1095), pp. 43-74.

This chapter is a general review and criticism of Western views on tradition. The author presents his own understanding of the development of tradition into a religious science, an approach that takes into account the Western studies on ḥadīth and yet preserves the integrity of the important concept of the Sunnah (way) of the Prophet.

1230 Robson, James. "Ḥadīth." In EI2. Vol. 3 (see 20), pp. 23-28.

An introductory article on the most important aspects of ḥadīth literature based on present research. The article includes the development of tradition, collections of tradition, criticism of tradition, and study and transmission of tradition.

1231 ______. "Ḥadīth Ḳudsī." In EI2. Vol. 3 (see 20), pp. 28-29.

A brief and informative article on divine traditions as distinguished from prophetic traditions.

1232 Schacht, Joseph. "Ahl al-Ḥadīth." In EI2. Vol. 1 (see 20), pp. 258-59.

Schacht explains that the "partisans of tradition" is a term for certain members of the legal schools who placed a special emphasis on the traditions. He notes that these people are not to be taken as traditionists (muḥaddithīn).

1233 ______. The Origins of Muhammadan Jurisprudence (see 2107).

A fundamental study on Islamic law, much of which is a critical examination of the legal traditions of the Prophet and their chains of transmitters (isnād). Schacht concludes, as did Goldziher, (see 1227) that the legal traditions are the product of a long development occurring well after the death of Muḥammad.

1234 Siddiqi, M. Zubayr. Hadith Literature. Calcutta: Calcutta University Press, 1961, 187 pp.

A study of ḥadīth from the traditional Muslim point of view.

Specific Studies

1235 Adams, Charles J. "The Authority of Ḥadīth in the Eyes of Some Modern Muslims." In Essays on Islamic Civilization Presented to Niyazi Berkes. Edited by D.P. Little. Leiden: E.J. Brill, 1976, pp. 27-49.

An examination of the manner in which the Pakistanī reformer Mawdūdī evaluated the ḥadīth so as to preserve its role as a source of guidance for Muslims today. See also 2112.

1236 Bravmann, M.M. "Sunnah and Related Concepts." In The Spiritual Background of Early Islam (see 1111), pp. 122-98.

A philological study on the interpretation of the term "sunnah"; the author argues that "sunnah" originally meant "the procedure that has been introduced into practice by a certain person." A technical discussion.

1237 Graham, William A. Divine Word and Prophetic Word in Early Islam: A Reconsideration of the Sources, with Special Reference to the Divine Saying or Ḥadīth Qudsī. The Hague: Mouton, 1976, 266 pp.

This work challenges the assumption held by many Muslim and Western scholars that there was from early Islam a clear-cut distinction between revelation and the prophet's teaching. Besides shedding new light on concepts of revelation and the nature of ḥadīth qudsī in early Islam, over half of the book contains a collection of ninety "divine sayings" in Arabic with English translation. A valuable study.

1238 Hamidullah, Muhammad. The Earliest Extant Work on the Ḥadīth: Sahifah Hammam Ibn Munabbih. Translated by M. Rahimuddin. Publications of Centre Cultural Islamique, no. 2. Paris, 1961, 143 pp.
An interesting work on the use of written recording methods for traditions in the first centuries of Islam. Should be read in light of Nabia Abbott's work (see 1224).

1239 Hosain, M. Hadayat. "The Development of the Ḥadīth Concordance in Arabic Literature (Ilm al-Atrāf)." Journal of the Asiatic Society of Bengal, n.s. 20 (1924):99-110.
The work lists and describes the various concordances, from the eleventh century to the present, on the major collections of tradition.

1240 _____. "Islamic Apocrypha (Tadlīs)." Journal of the Royal Asiatic Society of Bengal 2 (1936):1-7.
The article describes the "concealment of defects" in the chain of transmitters and in the body of a tradition. It concludes with a list of works on tadlīs.

1241 Juynboll, G.H.A. "Aḥmad Muḥammad Shākir (1892-1958) and His Edition of Ibn Ḥanbal's Musnad." Der Islam 49 (1972):221-47.
A masterful study of a famous orthodox Muslim traditionist's approach to the science of tradition.

1242 _____. The Authenticity of the Tradition Literature: Discussions in Modern Egypt. Leiden: E.J. Brill, 1969, 171 pp.
The study is concerned with attacks and counterattacks on the traditions by modern Muslim scholars and is organized according to the major issues of the controversies. The index gives easy access to the views of a particular author. A unique work.

1243 Kister, M.J. "Ḥaddithū ʿan banī isrāʿila walā haraja: A Study of an Early Tradition." Israel Oriental Studies 2 (1972):215-40.
A detailed study of Muslim discussions on a famous ḥadīth in which Muḥammad tells his followers that it is permissable to narrate stories about the "children of Israel."

1244 _____. "Al-Taḥannuth: An Inquiry into the Meaning of a Term." Bulletin of the School of Oriental and African Studies 31 (1968):223-36.
An analysis of the ḥadīth material in which the term al-Taḥannuth (denoting the ritual of venerating the Kaʿbah and providing for the poor) occurs. Kister shows that Muḥammad was practicing this ancient custom when, according to Muslim tradition, he received his first revelation on Mt. Ḥirā'.

1245 _____. "You Shall Only Set Out for Three Mosques: A Study of an Early Tradition." Le Museon 82 (1969):173-96.
A study describing the manner in which the various mosques of Mecca, Madīnah, and Jerusalem came to be ranked.

1246 Rahman, Fazlur. Islamic Methodology in History. Karachi: Central Institute of Islamic Research, 1965, 208 pp.
In this important work, the author attempts to show the "historical evolution of the application of the four basic principles of Islamic thinking" (preface), which are the Qur'ān, sunnah, ijtihād (original thinking), and ijmāʿ (consensus). This work is a valuable contribution to studies on ḥadīth, law, and Islamic thought as a whole. Difficult and not for the beginner.

1247 Robson, James. "The Material of Tradition." Muslim World 41 (1959):166-80, 257-70.
A discussion of the methods and principles of judging the authenticity of the traditions employed by the canonical authors. There is also a long discussion on the divergence of traditions and the problem of abrogation. The last part treats the topic of Jesus in Muslim tradition and the phenomenon of ḥadīth qudsī (divinely inspired tradition). A fine source of information on some basic issues.

1248 _____. "Standards Applied by Muslim Traditionists." Bulletin of the John Rylands Library 43 (1961):459-79.
A study of the various grades of acceptable and unacceptable traditions according to the transmitters. The methods of transmission are also analyzed.

1249 _____. "Tradition: Investigation and Classification." Muslim World 41 (1951):98-112.
A fascinating article on the criteria employed by the traditionists to weed out spurious traditions and to recognize the unacceptable traditionists.

1250 _____. "Tradition: The Second Foundation of Islam." Muslim World 41 (1951):22-33.
On the development of tradition as a literary form. There is a detailed discussion of the methods of transmission noted by the specialist Ibn al-Salaḥ.

1251 _____. "Traditions from Individuals." Journal of Semitic Studies 9 (1964):327-40.
An important article discussing the various interpretations traditionists have given to the technical terms used to describe solitary traditions.

1252 Schacht, Joseph. "A Revaluation of Islamic Traditions." Journal of the Royal Asiatic Society (1949):143-54.
A summary statement of his views on the traditions, written shortly before the publication of The Origins of Muhammadan Jurisprudence. See 2107.

1253 Siddiqi, M. Zubayr. "Aṭrāf al-ḥadīth." Studies in Islam 8 (1971):17-28.
A survey of the concordances on the traditions since the eleventh century and an examination of the manner in which they are organized.

1254 _____. "The Importance of Hadīth as a Source of Islamic Law." Studies in Islam 1 (1964): 19-25.
An attempt to prove that the recognition of ḥadīth as an authoritative source for the law predates al-Shāfi'ī (d. 820).

1255 Smith, Jane I., and Y.Y. Haddad. "Women in the Afterlife: The Islamic View as Seen from Qur'ān and Tradition" (see 2276).

1256 Speight, R. Marston. "The Will of Sa'd b.a. Waqqāṣ: The Growth of a Tradition." Der Islam 50 (1973):249-67.
A form analysis of a tradition according to which Sa'd was forbidden by the Prophet to bequeath more than one-third of his estate. This study on nineteen versions gives insight into how the traditions served religious needs in the early days of Islam. A pioneering effort matched by the works of M.J. Kister (see 1243-45).

1257 Wensinck, A.J. A Handbook of Early Muhammadan Tradition. Leiden: Brill, 1927, 268 pp.
An English concordance of the traditions in the collections of al-Bukhārī, Muslim, Abū Da'ūd, al-Tirmidhī, al-Nasā'ī, Ibn Māja, al-Darimī, and Mālik b. Anas.

1258 _____. "Sunna." In Shorter Encyclopedia of Islam (see 22), pp. 552-54.
A dated but informative article on this technical term. The various problems of the meaning in light of the Qur'ān and ḥadīth are also raised.

1259 Yusuf, S.M. "The Sunnah--Its Transmission, Development and Revision." Islamic Culture 37 (1963):271-82; 38 (1964):15-25.
A study of sunnah (the practice of the Prophet) and its early history up to al-Shāfi'ī (d. 820). The author examines the changing content of the sunnah through the various historical events in early Islam.

ISLAMIC MYSTICISM (TAṢAWWUF)

GENERAL AND INTRODUCTORY WORKS

1260 Anawati, G., and L. Gardet. La mystique musulmane. Paris: Vrin, 1961, 310 pp.
A study of the development of Ṣūfī thought in its classical formation. One of the best general studies available.

1261 Arberry, A.J. An Introduction to the History of Sufism. London: Longmans, 1942, 84 pp.
The title of this essay is misleading; it is not an introduction to Sufism, but rather three lectures on the development of Ṣūfī studies in Europe from their beginnings up to the time of the Second World War.

1262 _____. "Mysticism." In The Cambridge History of Islam. Vol. 2 (see 30), pp. 604-32.
A brief summary introduction to aspects of mysticism in Islam, with excerpts from the writings of the mystics.

1263 _____. Sufism: An Account of the Mystics of Islam. London: Allen & Unwin, 1950; New York: Harper Torch, 1970, 141 pp.
A basic primer on Islamic mysticism. An introduction to the subject with concise accounts of individual Muslim mystics and selected quotations from Ṣūfī literature as well as a succinct survey of classical and medieval Sufism, but too short and selective to form an authoritative history of Islamic mysticism.

1264 Burckhardt, T. An Introduction to Sufi Doctrine. Lahore: Shraf, 1959, 155 pp.
A study of selected Ṣūfī doctrines with a useful glossary of Arabic terms, with heavy reliance on the teachings of Ibn al-'Arabī (d. 1240). The author approaches Sufism from the "inside" on the basis of intuitive insight and associates Ṣūfī symbols with general esoteric ideas.

1265 Fakhry, Majid. "Three Varieties of Mysticism in Islam." International Journal for Philosophy of Religion 2 (1971):193-207.
An analytical study of types of Islamic mysticism (philosophical, visionary, and unitary) in which the author attempts to show that "failure to discriminate between the diverse possible objects of mystical experience can have far-reaching consequences for the interpretation of the experience in question" (p. 194).

1266 Horten, Max. "Mystics in Islam." Translated by V. June Hager. Islamic Studies 13 (1974): 67-93.
A translation of the section on mysticism from Max Horten's Die Philosophie des Islam (Berlin, 1924). Still a useful survey.

1267 Lings, Martin. What is Sufism? Berkeley: University of California, 1975, 133 pp.
A brief introduction to Sufism that tries to explain and interpret it from the "inside."

1268 Massignon, L. "Ṭarīḳa" and "Taṣawwuf." In Shorter Encyclopedia of Islam (see 22), pp. 573-78, 579-83.
The two articles together constitute an introduction to both the mystical orders (ṭarīqah) and the development of mystical thought (taṣawwuf) in Islam. The article "Tarīḳa" contains a complete list of Ṣūfī orders in Islam. It also includes titles of other Encyclopedia of Islam articles on various important aspects of Islamic mysticism.

1269 Nasr, S.H. Sufi Essays. London: Allen & Unwin, 1972, 184 pp.
A collection of previously published essays (except one) covering a wide range of topics on Sufism. One-third of the book is apologetic in nature, treating some major contemporary

problems facing the modern world in general and Islam in particular, whose solutions lie, according to Nasr, in understanding and applying the principles of Sufism. See also 1419.

1270 Nicholson, R.A. The Idea of Personality in Sufism. Lahore: Ashraf, 1970, 105 pp. Orig. pub. in 1923.

Three general lectures that focus on the problem of union between the human and divine within man's personality as outlined in Ṣūfī writings.

1271 _____. The Mystics of Islam. New York: Shocken Books, 1975, 178 pp.

A useful and succinct introduction to the basic themes and conceptions of Ṣūfī experience. Along with Arberry's Sufism (1263), this is the best introductory treatment of Sufism in English.

1272 _____. "Sufis." In Encyclopaedia of Religion and Ethics. Vol. 12 (see 1130), pp. 10-17.

This article still stands as a solid introduction to Islamic mysticism.

1273 Padwick, Constance E. Muslim Devotions: A Study of Prayer Manuals in Common Use (see 1810).

1274 Palmer, E.H. Oriental Mysticism: A Treatise on Sufistic and Unitarian Theosophy of the Persians. London: Luzac, 1938, 84 pp.

A brief but useful introduction to Sufism based upon a work of the thirteenth-century Persian mystic ʿAzīz Ibn Muḥammad-i Nasafī.

1275 Rice, Cyprian. The Persian Sufis. 2d ed. London: Allen & Unwin, 1969, 104 pp.

A sketchy introduction to Islamic mysticism on the Ṣūfī path and mystical states as depicted in the writings of Persian mystics.

1276 Schimmel, Annemarie. Mystical Dimensions of Islam. Chapel Hill: University of North Carolina Press, 1975, 506 pp.

The most comprehensive historical treatment of Islamic mysticism in English, covering the development of Islamic mysticism, from its origins through the nineteenth century. The work investigates aspects of Sufism not heretofore stressed in historical surveys, such as Turkish popular mysticism and Sufism in Indo-Pakistan. Two appendixes are of special interest: "Letter Symbolism in Sufi Literature" and "The Feminine Element in Sufism." Exhaustive bibliography, indexes of Qur'ānic quotations, prophetic traditions, names and places, and subjects.

1277 Schuon, Frithjof. Dimensions of Islam (see 1098).

1278 _____. Understanding Islam (see 1099).

1279 Shah, Idries. The Way of the Sufi. London: Cape, 1968, 288 pp.

An anthology of Ṣūfī texts and some introductory remarks. Other books by I. Shah (mainly anthologies) include: The Magic Monastery; Wisdom of the Idiots; Oriental Caravan; Caravan of Dreams; The Dermis Probe; Tales of the Dervishes; The Sufis; Thinkers of the East; The Subtleties of the Inimitable Mulla Nasrudin; Exploits of the Incomparable Mulla Nasrudin; Pleasantries of the Incredible Mulla Nasrudin; Reflections; Fables in the Sufi Tradition; The Diffusion of Sufi Ideas in the West.

1280 Valiuddin, Mir. Love of God: The Sufi Approach. New Delhi, 1968, 205 pp.

An attempt to analyze the structure of the Ṣūfī concept of love. The author draws upon innumerable quotations from a variety of mystical writings in order to show the complexity and centrality of the concept in Islamic mysticism.

1281 Williams, L.F.R. Sufi Studies East and West: A Symposium in Honor of Idries Shah's Services to Sufi Studies by Twenty-four Contributors Marking the 700th Anniversary of the Death of Jalaluddin Rumi (A.D. 1207-1273). New York: Dutton, 1973, 260 pp.

An unscholarly collection of twenty-two essays, the majority of which praise Idries Shah for his "services to Ṣūfī studies." Unenlightening.

1282 Zaehner, R.C. Hindu and Muslim Mysticism. London: Athlone, 1960, 234 pp.

Chapters 5 to 8 deal with Sufism and focus on Bisṭāmī (d. 874), al-Junayd (d. 910), and al-Ghazālī (d. 1111). The study does not resolve the problematic relationship between Hindu and Muslim mysticism. The hypothesis of Bisṭāmī's monastic revolution ("Vedanta in Muslim dress") and Junayd's theistic restoration is not founded on a careful analysis of relevant texts.

SPECIFIC STUDIES

Classical Sufism

1283 Amedroz, H.F. "Notes on Some Sufi Lives." Journal of the Royal Asiatic Society (1912): 551-86, 1087-89.

A great variety of information on early Ṣūfīs.

1284 Faris, N.A. "Al-Ghazzali." In The Arab Heritage (see 123), pp. 142-58.

A general introduction to the thought of al-Ghazālī with special attention given to his ethics as depicted in a short tract (The Ten Rules) and an excellent account of his Revival of the Religious Sciences (Iḥyāʾ ʿUlūm al-Dīn). Short bibliography.

1285 Gardet, L. "Dhikr." In EI2. Vol. 2 (see 20), pp. 223-27.

A good essay on the Ṣūfī ritual of dhikr (remembering God), including a description of the ritual and a discussion of its main stages. See also the author's article on "duʿāʾ" (free prayer), another fundamental Ṣūfī practice.

1286 Krymsky, A.E. "A Sketch of the Development of Sufism to the End of the Third Century of the Hijra." Translated by N.S. Doniach. Islamic Quarterly 5 (1959-60):109-25; 6 (1961):79-106.
A survey of early Sufism up to the beginning of the tenth century A.D. that views the rise of Sufism in light of social and economic causes and argues that Islamic mysticism is not the outgrowth of asceticism, but rather develops from non-Islamic influences.

1287 Macdonald, D.B. "The Development of the Idea of Spirit in Islam." Moslem World 22 (1932): 25-42, 153-68.
An exegetical study of rūḥ (spirit) in the Qur'ān and in aspects of later Islamic thinkers, particularly in the thought of certain mystics. Still a basic study.

1288 _____. "Life of al-Ghazzali." Journal of the American Oriental Society 20 (1899): 71-132.
A beautifully written account of the life and thought of al-Ghazālī.

1289 Mackeen, A.M. Mohamed. "The Early History of Sufism in the Maghrib prior to al-Shādhilī (d. 656/1256)." Journal of the American Oriental Society 91 (1971):398-408.
A study of Sufism in Spain and North Africa outlining the chief characteristics of the Ṣūfī movement prior to the establishment of the Ṣūfī orders.

1290 Massignon, L. Essai sur les origines du lexique technique de la mystique musulmane. Paris: Vrin, 1968, 453 pp.
An analysis of Ṣūfī terminology, an investigation into the Islamic roots of Sufism, and an examination of the ascetic movement (eighth century) and of important Ṣūfī mystics of the ninth century. This is a basic work on Islamic mysticism in the classical period and indispensable for a survey study of Sufism.

1291 _____. "Ḥallādj." In EI2. Vol. 3 (see 20), pp. 99-105.
A sketch of the life and thought of the great tenth-century martyr and mystic. The article examines the political and social background of his life, indicating that political factors were a decisive cause for the trial and execution of al-Ḥallāj (d. 922).

1292 _____. La Passion d'al-Hosayn ibn Mansour al-Halladj, martyr mystique de l'Islam. 2 vols. Paris: Gueunthner, 1922, 942 pp.
This important work on the life and thought of al-Ḥallāj not only represents a thorough study of a famous Muslim mystic but also examines the mystical outlook that developed in the Ṣūfī milieu of the ninth century. The work figures among the most valuable studies on Sufism.

1293 Nicholson, R.A. "The Goal of Muhammadan Mysticism." Journal of the Royal Asiatic Society (1913):55-69.
An analysis of the Ṣūfī concept of fanā' (annihilation) based on the study of several Arabic sources, particularly the Kitāb al-Luma' of Abū Nasr al-Ṭūsī al-Sarrāj (d. 988).

1294 _____. "A Historical Enquiry Concerning the Origin and Development of Sufism." Journal of the Royal Asiatic Society (1906):303-48.
The study provides a list of definitions of the terms "ṣūfī" and "taṣawwuf."

1295 Nwyia, Paul. Exégèse Coranique et language mystique: Nouvel essai sur le lexique technique des mystiques musulmans. Beirut: Dar El-Machreq, 1970, 439 pp.
An indispensable study on the development of the technical language of the mystics. The first part is an analysis of the exegetical writings of three of the greatest mystical commentators of the Qur'ān; the second part examines the structure and vocabulary of the mystical experience; and the last part analyzes the images and symbols born of the experience itself. One of the most important studies on Sufism, with indexes of citations from the Qur'ān, proper names, and technical terms.

1296 Samarrai, Q. The Theme of Ascension in Mystical Writings. Baghdad: National, 1968, 308 pp.
A study of the Ṣūfī theme of mystical ascent, based on the writings of al-Qushayrī (d. 1074).

1297 Schimmel, Annemarie. "The Origin and Early Development of Sufism." Journal of the Pakistan Historical Society 8 (1959):55-67.
An investigation into the early phase of Islamic mysticism that argues that the important ideas of early Sufism come from the Qur'ān and that it is only later that outside influences have a bearing on the development of Sufism.

1298 _____. "Some Aspects of Mystical Prayer in Islam." Die Welt des Islams, n.s. 2 (1952): 112-25.
By examining the works of numerous Muslim mystics, the author brings to the reader the meaning and function of prayer (du'ā') in Islamic mysticism. The essay contains many quotations gleaned from a variety of Ṣūfī authors.

1299 Sharma, Arvind. "The Spiritual Biography of al-Ghazālī." Studies in Islam 9 (1972): 65-85.
A study of al-Ghazālī's life based largely on his Deliverance from Error (see 1439), as well as other sources. A good, concise summary, based entirely on previous studies.

1300 Shehadi, Fadlou. Ghazali's Unique and Unknowable God. Leiden: E.J. Brill, 1964, 132 pp.
An analysis of al-Ghazālī's conception of God that includes an examination of mystical approaches as well as the theological and philosophical arguments set forth by the great Muslim thinker.

1301 Smith, Margaret. An Early Mystic of Baghdad. London: Sheldon, 1935, 311 pp.
A study of the life, works, and teachings of al-Muḥāsibī (d. 857), the famous Ṣūfī theologian of Baghdād. The work has been superseded by J. van Ess, Die Gedankenwelt des Harit Al-Muhasibi, anhand von Ubersetzungen aus seinen dargestellt und erlautert (Bonn, 1961).

1302 _____. Al-Ghazali, the Mystic. London: Luzac, 1944, 247 pp.
A study of the life and personality of al-Ghazālī (d. 1111) together with an account of his mystical teaching and an estimate of his place in the history of Islamic mysticism.

1303 _____. Rabiʻa the Mystic and Her Fellow Saints in Islam. Cambridge: Cambridge University Press, 1928, 220 pp.
A fundamental study on the life and teachings of Rābiʻah al-ʻAdawiyyah, an eighth-century Ṣūfī, one of the earliest mystics in Islam and the first Ṣūfī to fully develop the theme of mystical love in the context of early ascetic practices. The work also deals with the role of women in Sufism.

1304 Valiuddin, M. The Qur'anic Sufism. Delhi: Asia House, 1959, 221 pp.
The author views Sufism as based directly on the Qur'ān and attempts to show the Qur'ānic contribution to the development of Islamic mysticism.

1305 Watt, W. Montgomery. Muslim Intellectual: A Study of al-Ghazali (see 1645).

1306 Wensinck, A.J. "On the Relation between Ghazali's Cosmology and His Mysticism." Akadamie Van Wetten-Schappen Mededeeling, Ser. A., 75 (1933):183-209.
A philological study of three terms (mulk, malakūt, and jabarūt) that figure significantly in the esoteric cosmological theories of numerous mystical philosophers in Islam, as well as of al-Ghazālī.

1307 Zarrinkoob, A.H. "Persian Sufism in Its Historical Perspective." Iranian Studies 3 (1970):139-208.
A collection of lectures of a general introductory nature on various aspects of Islamic mysticism.

Theosophical and Philosophical Mysticism

1308 Affifi, A.E. "Ibn ʻArabī." In A History of Muslim Philosophy. Vol. 1 (see 1574), pp. 398-421.
An introduction to the life and thought of Ibn al-ʻArabī (d. 1240).

1309 _____. The Mystical Philosophy of Muhyid-Dīn Ibnul-ʻArabi. Cambridge: Cambridge University Press, 1939, 213 pp.
A systematic presentation of the mystical views of Ibn al-ʻArabī. Indispensable for understanding his mysticism.

1310 Corbin, Henry. Avicenna and the Visionary Recital (see 1442).

1311 _____. Creative Imagination in the Sufism of Ibn ʻArabī. Translated by R. Manheim. Bollingen Series, no. 91. Princeton, N.J.: Princeton University Press, 1969, 406 pp.
A study of the mystical imagery and spiritual symbolism in the writings of Ibn al-ʻArabī in which the author attempts to reveal the universal aspects of the mystical message of the great theosopher.

1312 _____. En Islam iranien: Aspects spirituels et philosophiques. Vol. 2, Sohrawardī et les platoniciens de Perse (see 1480).
Contains essays on the mysticism of Suhrawardī Maqtūl, including translations and commentaries of The Recital of the Empurpled Archangel and the Recital of the Occidental Exile.

1313 Fakhry, Majid. "Post-Avicennian Developments: Illumination and the Reaction against Peripateticism." In A History of Islamic Philosophy (see 1568), pp. 326-47.
Contains brief outlines of the mystical philosophy of Suhrawardī (d. 1191) and Mullā Ṣadrā (d. 1641).

1314 Hawi, Sami S. Islamic Naturalism and Mysticism: A Philosophic Study of Ibn Ṭufayl's Ḥayy ibn Yaqẓān. Leiden: E.J. Brill, 1974, 282 pp.
An attempt to offer "a systematic exposition, interpretation, and critical appraisal" (introduction) of Ibn Ṭufayl's philosophic novel. Although the book contains some interesting observations by the author, it is not a coherent, systematic treatment of the document under study.

1315 Hourani, G.F. "The Principle Subject of Ibn Ṭufayl's Ḥayy ibn Yaqẓān." Journal of Near Eastern Studies 15 (1956):40-46.
In the process of correcting some conclusions made by L. Gauthier (Ibn Thofail, sa vie, ses oeuvres, Paris, 1909), Hourani offers his views concerning the central subject of Ibn Ṭufayl's philosophic romance.

1316 Izutsu, Toshihiko. A Comparative Study of the Key Philosophical Concepts in Sufism and Taoism. Vol. 1. Tokyo: Keio Institute of Cultural and Linguistic Studies, 1966, 272 pp.
An examination of the mystical philosophy of Ibn al-ʻArabī based upon an analysis of the major ontological concepts in the Fuṣūṣ al-Ḥikam. one of the most influential mystical writings in Islam.

1317 _____. The Concept and Reality of Existence. Tokyo: Keio Institute of Cultural and Linguistic Studies, 1971, 167 pp.
The essay "An Analysis of Waḥdat al-Wujūd" (Unity of Being) (pp. 35-55) is especially relevant. Here the author examines the ontological structure of this important concept in Islamic mystical philosophy.

1318 _____. "Creation and the Timeless Order of Things: A Study in the Mystical Philosophy of ʿAyn al-Quḍāt." Philosophical Forum 4 (1972):124-40.

A study of ʿAyn al-Quḍat al-Hamadhānī's (d. 1131) view of creation. The study is one of the very few analytical investigations into the thought of this important Ṣūfī who preceded Ibn al-ʿArabī and has received little attention by Western students of Islamic mysticism.

1319 _____. "Mysticism and the Linguistic Problem of Equivocation in the Thought of ʿAyn al-Quḍāt al-Hamadhānī." Studia Islamica 31 (1970):153-70.

A linguistic analysis of al-Hamadhānī's use of equivocation.

1320 Landau, Rom. The Philosophy of Ibn Arabi. New York: Macmillan Co., 1959, 126 pp.

A useful introduction to aspects of Ibn al-ʿArabī's thought, containing quotations from his works plus a translated selection from the Tarjumān al-Ashwāq. See also 1446.

1321 Landolt, Hermann. "Simnānī on Waḥdat al-Wujūd." In Collected Papers on Islamic Philosophy and Mysticism. Edited by M. Mohaghegh and H. Landolt. Tehran: Wisdom of Persia Series, 1971, pp. 93-114.

A valuable study of an important but little studied mystic who criticized Ibn al-ʿArabī's doctrine of the "unity of being." This is a shortened version of the author's "Der Briefwechsel zwischen Kāšānī und Simnānī über Waḥdat al-Wuǧūd," Der Islam 50 (1973):29-81.

1322 Meier, Fritz. "The Mystery of the Kaʿba: Symbol and Reality in Islamic Mysticism." In The Mysteries: Papers from the Eranos Yearbooks. Edited by R. Manheim. New York: Pantheon Books, 1955, pp. 149-69.

An examination of the preamble to Ibn al-ʿArabī's great mystical writing, the Meccan Revelations (Al-Futūḥāt al-Makkiyyah). The preamble describes Ibn al-ʿArabī's own mystical transformation through a recollection of several visions and esoteric discourses focusing on the symbolism of the rite of the circumambulation of the Kaʿbah.

1323 Nasr, S.H. Three Muslim Sages. Cambridge, Mass.: Harvard University Press, 1964, 185 pp.

Essays on Ibn Sīnā (d. 1037), Suhrawardī (d. 1191), and Ibn al-ʿArabī (d. 1240), with emphasis on their mystical thought.

1324 _____. "Ṣadr al-Dīn Shirāzī (Mullā Ṣadra)." In A History of Muslim Philosophy. Vol. 2 (see 1574), pp. 932-61.

A sketch of Ṣadrā's life, works, and thought.

1325 _____. "Shihāb al-Dīn Suhrawardī Maqtūl." In A History of Muslim Philosophy. Vol. 1 (see 1574), pp. 372-98.

An introductory article on the life and thought of the Iranian theosopher and father of the Ḥikmat al-Ishrāq (illuminative wisdom) tradition in Islamic mystical thought. This article is one of the very few sources in English on the great thinker.

1326 Nicholson, R.A. Studies in Islamic Mysticism. Cambridge: Cambridge University Press, 1967, 282 pp. Reprint of 1921 ed.

An examination of the mystical doctrines and practices of Abū Saʿīd b. Abiʾl-Khayr (d. 1049), a discussion of the Ṣūfī idea of the perfect man on the basis of a treatise by ʿAbd al-Karīm al-Jīlī (d. 1415), an analysis and partial translation of the mystical odes of Ibn al-Fāriḍ (d. 1235), and some remarks on the Fuṣūṣ al-Ḥikam, by Ibn al-ʿArabī. One of the most valuable studies on Islamic mysticism. See also 1448.

1327 Rahman, Fazlur. "Dream, Imagination and ʿAlam al-Mithāl." Islamic Studies 3 (1964): 167-80. In The Dream and Human Societies. Edited by G.E. von Grunebaum. Berkeley: University of California Press, 1966, pp. 409-19.

An analysis of the "realm of images," a doctrine that the author shows to be a product of medieval Islamic mysticism. The origin and development of this doctrine is traced, with special emphasis on Ibn al-ʿArabī's formulation of it.

1328 _____. The Philosophy of Mullā Ṣadrā. Albany: State University of New York Press, 1975, 277 pp.

The first comprehensive, critical treatment of Ṣadrā's thought, based on a careful study of his major work, the al-usfār al-Arbaʿah (The Four Journeys). This study reveals the important role of mysticism in one of Islam's most original thinkers.

1329 _____. Selected Letters of Shaikh Aḥmad Sirhindī. Karachi: Iqbal Academy, 1968, (English) 81 pp.; (Persian) 274 pp.

The first part of the study is a superb analysis of the doctrine of the God-world relationship in Ibn Sīnā, Suhrawardī, and Ibn al-ʿArabī. The remainder of the English section attempts to show the originality of Aḥmad Sirhindī's thought in light of the preceding trends in Islamic mysticism to which Aḥmad Sirhindī reacted critically.

Ṣūfī Saints and Orders

General Studies

1330 Arnold, Sir Thomas. The Preaching of Islam (see 11).

A classic study on the spread of Islam to all parts of the Islamic world, emphasizing the role the Ṣūfīs played in the propagation of Islam.

1331 Farah, C.E. "Rules Governing the Shaykh-Murshid's Conduct." Numen 21 (1974):81-96.

A worthwhile analysis of what constitutes the proper mode of behavior, or appropriate etiquette (adab), of the Ṣūfī masters vis-à-vis their disciples, based upon numerous Arabic sources.

1332 Hodgson, M.G.S. "The Sufism of the Tariqah Orders." In The Venture of Islam. Vol. 2 (see 29), pp. 201-54.
A general survey of the development of the Ṣūfī orders from the middle of the tenth century to 1273, stressing the social and intellectual roles of Sufism.

1333 Lane, Edward William. An Account of the Manners and Customs of the Modern Egyptians (see 762).
An account of popular Islam as it was viewed by Lane, with information on Ṣūfī saints and their followers.

1334 Meier, Fritz. "The Transformation of Man in Mystical Islam." In Man and Transformation: Papers from the Eranos Yearbooks. Translated by R. Manheim. Bollinger Series, no. 30, 5. New York: Bollinger Foundation, 1964, pp. 37-69.
Drawing upon numerous writings of the Ṣūfīs, Meier examines the relationship of Ṣūfī shaykh (master) and novice and the processes involved in transforming an ordinary person into one who has gained mystical knowledge. Excellent study.

1335 Trimingham, J. Spencer. The Sufi Orders in Islam. Oxford: Oxford University Press, 1971, 333 pp.
The most comprehensive study of the Ṣūfī orders available. The work serves as a useful introduction to the organizational aspects of Sufism, as well as offering a sketch of all the Ṣūfī orders in Islam. Helpful glossary and bibliography.

Central Asia, Iran, and Indo-Pakistan

1336 Ahmad, Aziz. "Political and Religious Ideas of Shah Walī-Ullāh of Delhi" (see 1725).

1337 _____. "The Sufi and the Sultan in Pre-Mughal Muslim India." Der Islam 38 (1963): 142-53.
An analysis of the interaction and conflict in pre-Mughal India. The author argues that with the weakening of the orders, most notably the Chishtī, came the weakening of Indian Islam.

1338 Algar, Hamid. "The Naqshbandi Order: A Preliminary Survey of Its History and Significance." Studia Islamica 44 (1976): 123-52.
Examines the origin, spread, political role, and important leaders of this widespread Ṣūfī order. The study includes a brief critique of the view that organized Sufism is a degenerative form of Islam, a view held by some Western and Muslim scholars alike. See also 1364.

1339 Ali, S.M. Saints of East Pakistan. Oxford: Oxford University Press, 1971, 61 pp.
Accounts of some Ṣūfī saints in what is now Bangladesh.

1340 Anwarul Haq, M. The Faith Movement of Mawlānā Muḥammad Ilyās. London: Allen & Unwin, 1972, 210 pp.
A study of a Ṣūfī revivalist movement in twentieth-century India that attempted to dissociate religion from politics, a rare occurrence in Islamic history. Useful for information on popular religion.

1341 Arnold, Sir Thomas. "Saints and Martyrs (Muhammadan in India)." In Encyclopaedia of Religion and Ethics. Vol. 11 (see 1130), pp. 63-73.
A brief sketch of the most important Indian Ṣūfī masters, their orders, their shrines, and the worship of saints. Given the lack of concise information on these aspects of Sufism, this article is recommended as a good place to begin.

1342 Eaton, R.M. "Sufi Folk Literature and the Expansion of Indian Islam." History of Religions 14 (1974):117-27.
An excellent analysis of the role of Sūfī folk literature, as contrasted to the Great Tradition expressed in mystical treatises, in the conversion of Hindu non-elites to Islam in Deccan society. The author has also published a major work on the social roles of Ṣūfīs in India, from 1300 to 1700, entitled The Sufis of Bijapur (Princeton, N.J.: Princeton University Press, 1978).

1343 Faruqi, Bashir Ahmad. The Mujaddid's Conception of Tawhid. Lahore: Ashraf, 1940, 192 pp.
A study of the idea of God's oneness as propounded by Aḥmad Sirhindī (d. 1624), a Naqshbandī Ṣūfī of northern India. The author's approach to the subject is influenced by a strong orthodox Muslim point of view.

1344 Friedmann, Y. Shaykh Ahmad Sirhindi: An Outline of His Thought and a Study of His Image in the Eyes of Posterity (see 436).

1345 Hourani, A. "Shaikh Khalid and the Naqshbandi Order." In Islamic Philosophy and the Classical Tradition: Essays Presented to R. Walzer on His Seventieth Birthday. Edited by S.M. Stern. Columbia: University of South Carolina Press, 1972, pp. 89-103.
A study on the life of the founder of the modern branch of the Naqshbandī order, a Ṣūfī brotherhood that resisted European conquest in the Caucasus. See also 1592.

1346 Makdisi, George. "Ibn Taymiyya: A Ṣūfī of the Qadariya Order." American Journal of Arabic Studies 1 (1973):118-29.
An attempt to show, through an analysis of original sources, that Ibn Taymiyyah was not an enemy of Ṣufism, but rather a moderate Ṣūfī himself. See also 1659.

1347 Margoliouth, D.S. "Contributions to the Biography of ʿAbd al-Nādir Jilan." Journal of the Royal Asiatic Society (1907):267-310.
A biographical sketch of ʿAbd al-Qādir al-Jilānī (d. 1165), the founder of the Qādirī order.

1348 Meier, F. Die Fawā'iḥ al-Gamāl wa-Fawātiḥ al-Ǧalāl Naqmuddīn al-Kubrā. Wiesbaden: Steiner, 1957, 425 pp.
A masterly study and basic work on the structure of Muslim mystical experience as represented by Najm al-Dīn al-Kubrā (d. 1221), the founder of the Kubrawī order, as well as a thorough inquiry into the various facets of mystical union and the nature and modes of Ṣūfī experience.

1349 Meier, Fritz. "The Problem of Nature in the Esoteric Monism of Islam." In Spirit and Nature: Papers from the Eranos Yearbooks. Translated by R. Manheim. Bollingen Series, no. 30, 1. New York: Bollingen, 1954, pp. 149-204.
A study of the mystical thought of ʻAzīz Ibn Muḥammad-al-Nasafī, a Persian mystic of the thirteenth century and a leading Ṣūfī of the Kubrawī order.

1350 Nizami, K.A. "Early Indo-Muslim Mystics and Their Attitudes towards the State." Islamic Quarterly 22 (1948):387-98; 23 (1929):13-21, 162-70, 312-21; 24 (1950):60-71.
An inquiry into the relationship of Indian Suhrawardī and Chishtī Ṣūfīs with Muslim rulers and sulṭāns of thirteenth- and fourteenth-century India. See also the author's articles "Čishtī" and "Čishtiyya," in EI2, vol. 2 (see 20), pp. 49-56.

1351 _____. The Life and Times of Shaikh Farid-ud-Din Ganj-i-Shakar. Delhi: Idarah-i Adabiyat-i Delli, 1955, 144 pp.
A monograph on the important Chishtī Bābā Farīd (d. 1265), his life, teachings, and practices.

1352 _____. "Naqshbandi Influence on Mughal Rulers and Politics." Islamic Culture 39 (1965):41-52.
A study of the role played by certain Naqshbandīs, particularly that of Shaykh Aḥmad Sirhindī and Shāh Walī Allāh, in shaping the religious outlook of Mughal rulers.

1353 _____. "Some Aspects of Khanqah Life in Medieval India." Studia Islamica 8 (1957): 51-69.
An essay describing in detail the khanqah (convent) organization, with special attention devoted to the khanqahs of the Chishtī and Suhrawardī orders. The article is particularly useful for its concrete descriptions of various aspects of the social and cultural life of the members of these famous Ṣūfī organizations.

1354 Nizami, Khaliq Ahmad. Some Aspects of Religion and Politics in India during the Thirteenth Century (see 288).
Includes an excellent historical account of the impact of the Suhrawarī and Chishtī orders on Muslim India in the thirteenth century.

1355 Rahman, Fazlur. Selected Letters of Shaikh Aḥmad Sirhindī (see 1329).

1356 Rizvi, Syed Athar Abbas. Muslim Revivalist Movements in Northern India (see 423).
A study of Sufism in India during the sixteenth and seventeenth centuries, with special emphasis on the Naqshbandī order and Aḥmad Sirhindī.

1357 Salik, S.A. The Saint of Jilan. Lahore: Ashraf, 1961, 111 pp.
An account of the life of ʻAbd al-Qādir al-Jīlānī (d. 1166), the founder of the Qādirī order.

1358 Schimmel, Annemarie. "The Martyr-Mystic Hallāj in Sindhī Folk-Poetry." Numen 9 (1962):161-200.
A study of the impact al-Hallāj has had upon Sindhi mystical folk literature. The author examines several mystical symbols associated with al-Hallāj that are found in Sindhi poetry.

1359 _____. Pain and Grace: A Study of Two Mystical Writers of Eighteenth-Century Muslim India. Studies in the History of Religions, no. 36. Leiden: E.J. Brill, 1976, 310 pp.
A detailed work on the life and writings of Mīr Dard and ʻAbdu'l Laṭīf of Bhit, replete with translated excerpts from their writings. The introductory chapters traces Ṣūfī development in eighteenth-century India.

1360 _____. "Shāh ʻInāyat Shadīd of Jhōk: A Sindhī Mystic of the Early 18th Century." In Liber Amicorum: Studies in Honour of C.J. Bleeker. Leiden: E.J. Brill, 1969, pp. 151-70.
An interesting article on the life and later estimation of a Sindhi mystic, hitherto unknown to students of Islamic mysticism. As is the case with many martyr-mystics, Shāh ʻInāyat was killed for his sociopolitical attitudes rather than for esoteric, pantheistic ideas.

1361 Sharib, Z.H. Khawaja Gharib Nawaz. Lahore: Ashraf, 1961, 162 pp.
A sketch of the life and teachings of Muʻīn al-dīn Ḥasan Chishtī (d. 1236), the founder of the Chishtī order.

1362 Sorley, H.T. Shah Abdul Latif of Bhit: His Poetry, Life and Times. Lahore: Ashraf, 1966, 432 pp. Reprint of 1940 ed.
A study of this eighteenth-century mystical poet of Sind with translations of some of his poems and an examination of the social and political background.

1363 Subhan, J.A. Sufism, Its Saints and Shrines: An Introduction to the Study of Sufism with Special Reference to India and Pakistan. 2d rev. ed. Lucknow: Lucknow Publishing, 1960, 423 pp. Reprint of 1938 ed.
This book presents a wealth of information on a variety of Indian and Pakistanī Ṣūfīs and their orders. Particular emphasis falls on the Chishtī, Qādirī, Suhrawardī, and Naqshbandī orders and their Ṣūfī masters.

Ottoman Turkey

1364 Algar, Hamid. "Some Notes on the Naqshbandī Tarīqat in Bosnia." Die Welt des Islam, n.s. 13 (1971):168-203. In Studies in Comparative Religion 9 (1975):69-97.
A superb study that traces the development of the West Turkish branch of this famous order from its beginnings to present times, including a vivid description of a dhikr ceremony witnessed by the author in a village near Sarajevo. The author argues that this order provides the element of continuity with traditional Islam and Muslims of other countries. An appendix offers examples of dhikr utterances in Turkish, with English translation. See also 1338.

1365 Birge, J.K. The Bektashi Order of Dervishes (see 348).

1366 Brown, J.P., and H.A. Rose. The Dervishes or Oriental Spiritualism. London: Cass, 1968, 496 pp. Reprint of 1868 ed.
A survey study of Ṣūfī orders in Turkey, first published in 1868, edited with notes by H.A. Rose. Although dated in many respects, the work contains much useful, detailed information on Ṣūfī practices among the brotherhoods of Ottoman Turkey.

1367 Faroqhi, Suraiya. "The Tekke of Haci Bektash: Social Position and Economic Activities." International Journal of Middle Eastern Studies 7 (1976):183-208.
A valuable study, since examinations of social and economic aspects of Ṣūfī organizations are hard to find. The author shows how the central convent (dergāh) of the Bektashī order maintained its economic life in medieval times.

1368 Martin, B.G. "A Short History of the Khalwati Order." In Scholars, Saints, and Sufis (see 506), pp. 275-307.
A historical account of the Khalwatī order, which reached its zenith in the Ottoman Empire during the sixteenth and seventeenth centuries.

Africa

1369 Abun-Nasr, J.M. The Tijaniyya: A Sufi Order in the Modern World (see 812).

1370 Andrezejewski, B.J. "The Veneration of Sufi Saints and Its Impact on the Oral Literature of the Somali People and on Their Literature in Arabic." African Language Studies 15 (1974):15-53.
A fascinating study, based on original sources, on the veneration of Ṣūfī saints among the Somalis and the place of Ṣūfī saint stories in the oral and literary traditions. The article contains numerous illustrations of this type of literature.

1371 Barklay, H.B. "A Sudanese Religious Brotherhood: Al-Ṭarīqa al-Hindīya." Muslim World 53 (1963):127-37.
A brief description of the social organization and rituals of a small Ṣūfī order of the Sudan, founded by Yūsuf Muḥammad al-Amīn al-Hindī (d. 1942).

1372 Behrman, Lucy C. Muslim Brotherhoods and Politics in Senegal. Cambridge, Mass.: Harvard University Press, 1970, 224 pp.
An examination of the political role of Ṣūfī organizations in present-day Senegal analyzing their interrelationships and their relationships with various political parties, the government, and the Muslim reform movement in Senegal. The author argues that the brotherhoods are a key factor in Senegalese politics. Extensive bibliography and index.

1373 Berger, Morroe. Islam in Egypt Today: Social and Political Aspects of Popular Religion (see 727).
A report on various aspects of religious behavior and organization in present-day Egypt. The chapter "Aspects of Sufi Organization and Activity" (pp. 62-89) is of great value, since there are few studies on present-day orders.

1374 Crapanzano, V. The Hamadsha: A Study in Moroccan Ethnopsychiatry. Berkeley and Los Angeles: University of California, 1973, 242 pp.
An anthropological study of a Moroccan urban Ṣūfī order in which psychosomatic healing plays an important role. This is a basic work, not only because it is an exhaustive study on one modern order but because it raises important questions about the relationship between the outlook of the members of orders and the traditional teachings of the Ṣūfīs.

1375 _____. "The Hamadsha." In Scholars, Saints, and Sufis (see 506), pp. 327-48.
A study of the Moroccan urban brotherhood popular among the poor urban masses. The essay points out that very often there is little connection between the practice of the orders and the teachings of the Ṣūfīs.

1376 DeJong, F. "Cairene Ziyara-Days: A Contribution to the Study of Saint Veneration in Islam." Die Welt des Islam, n.s. 17 (1976-77):26-43.
An extremely valuable descriptive study of the ritual of saint veneration (ziyārah), based upon the firsthand observations of the author, who attended numerous saint veneration days in Cairo, from 1972 to 1973. With copious notes.

1377 Dermenghem, E. Le culte des saints dans l'Islam Maghrabin. 6th ed. Paris: Gallimard, 1954, 351 pp.
The best descriptive study of saint worship in North Africa.

1378 Eickelman, Dale F. Moroccan Islam: Tradition and Society in a Pilgrimage Center. Modern Middle East Series, no. 1. Austin and London: University of Texas Press, 1976, 303 pp.
A socioanthropological study of Islam as formulated and understood in one specific region of western Morocco, with attention devoted to one Ṣūfī (marabout) pilgrimage center. The work outlines development of Islam in Morocco, the

growth and domination of marabout Islam, then analyzes the economic and social institutions of Boujad (the most important pilgrimage center in western Morocco) and the important role of the center in the life of the people. With glossary of technical terms, extensive bibliography, and index.

1379 Evans-Pritchard, E.E. The Sanusi of Cyrenaica (see 806).

1380 Gellner, Ernest. "Doctor and Saint." In Scholars, Saints, and Sufis (see 506), pp. 307-26.
An interesting sociological study of the Ṣūfī saint and his holy lineage among the Berbers. Gellner argues that although holy lineages of tribal peoples have something in common with urban mystical orders, they often are distinct in nature and function, and that one cannot understand the role of saint and his lineage in the tribal context by referring it to "the diffusion of Ṣūfī ideas."

1381 _____. Saints of the Atlas (see 849).
A socioanthropological study of the religious and political life of the Berbers of the central High Atlas of Morocco that provides an invaluable account of popular Islamic religious practices and the functional role of the saint and Ṣūfī lodges in tribal society.

1382 Gilsenan, Michael. Saint and Sufi in Modern Egypt: An Essay in the Sociology of Religion. Oxford: Clarendon, 1973, 248 pp.
A sociological investigation into the twentieth-century Egyptian branch of the Shādhilī order founded by Shaikh Salamah (d. 1939), which includes a translation of the "laws" or rules of practice and conduct of the order.

1383 _____. "Some Factors in the Decline of the Ṣūfī Orders in Modern Egypt." Muslim World 57 (1967):11-18.
A concise examination of why Ṣūfī brotherhoods are declining. The author concludes that although they have weakened, they persist, appealing to the peasants and urban artisans.

1384 Haas, W.S. "The Zikr of the Rahmaniya Order in Algeria." Moslem World 33 (1943):16-28.
An interesting psychophysiological analysis of the dhikr ritual as practiced among the members of the Raḥmāniyyah branch of the Khalwatī order.

1385 Kennedy, J.G., and Hussein Fahim. "Nubian Dhikr Rituals and Cultural Change." Muslim World 64 (1974):205-19.
A descriptive analysis of two dhikr performances in Egyptian Nubia. The authors contend that the decline of dhikr rituals corresponds to the general decline of Ṣūfī orders in Egypt.

1386 Lewis, I.M. "Sufism in Somaliland: A Study in Tribal Islam." Bulletin of the School of Oriental and African Studies 17 (1955): 581-602; 18 (1956):145-60.
A socioanthropological study of Ṣūfī organization that emphasizes the role of Sufism in the social structure of tribal Islam. An excellent study with detailed bibliography.

1387 Lings, M. A Sufi Saint of the Twentieth Century. 2d rev. ed. Berkeley and Los Angeles: University of California, 1971, 242 pp.
A study of the spiritual heritage and legacy of Shaykh Aḥmad al-ʿAlawī, a North African Ṣūfī (d. 1934) who was a master in the Shādhilī order. The study offers a spiritual biography of the shaykh, an analysis of his mystical thought and practice, and neglected aphorisms and poems. An interesting feature of this study is the chapter entitled "The Symbolism of the Letters of the Alphabet." Index.

1388 Mackeen, A.M. Mohamed. "The Rise of al-Shādhilī (d. 656/1258)." Journal of the American Oriental Society 91 (1971):477-86.
An examination of the life of the founder of the Shādhilī order of North Africa.

1389 Martin, B.G. Muslim Brotherhoods in Nineteenth-Century Africa (see 1053).

1390 Stewart, C.C., and E.K. Stewart. Islam and Social Order in Mauritania (see 1060).

1391 Trimingham, J.S. A History of Islam in West Africa (see 1061), pp. 88-100.
Chapter 4, "Institutional Islam," contains a concise section on Ṣūfī orders.

1392 _____. Islam in East Africa (see 1063), pp. 76-112.
Chapter 3, "Islamic Organization," contains useful information on Ṣūfī practices.

1393 Ziadeh, N.A. The Sanusiyya: A Study of a Revivalist Movement in Islam (see 811).

Indonesia and Malaysia

1394 Attas, Syed Naguib al-. The Mysticism of Hamzah Fanṣūrī. Kuala Lumpur: University of Malaya, 1970, 556 pp.
A comprehensive study of the mystical teachings of Hamzah Fanṣūrī, a sixteenth-century Ṣūfī of Sumatra who is considered the greatest representative of Malay Sufism.

1395 _____. Some Aspects of Sufism as Understood and Practiced Among the Malays. Singapore: Malaysian Sociological Research Institute, 1963, 104 pp.
The study includes a brief outline of Sufism in general, followed by an examination of Malayan Ṣūfī orders and their rituals.

1396 Geertz, Clifford. "Mysticism" and "The Mystical Sects." In The Religion of Java (see 1028), pp. 309-55.
An anthropological study of the role and function of mysticism in Javanese society.

1397 Hadiwijono, Harun. Man in the Present Javanese Mysticism. Baarn: Bosh & Keuning, N.V., 1967, 271 pp.

An attempt to trace the history of mysticism in Java by examining the concept of man reflected in the pre-Islamic (i.e., Hindu) mystical literature, Sumatran Islamic literature, and nineteenth- as well as twentieth-century Javanese literature.

1398 Ibn Faḍli'llāh, Muḥammad. The Gift Addressed to the Spirit of the Prophet. Translated by A.H. Johns. Canberra: Australian National University, 1965, 225 pp.

A critical edition and translation of a Javanese version of a seventeenth-century Arabic-Indian work by Muḥammad Ibn Faḍli'llāh (d. 1620), which presents the orthodox justification and interpretation of Ṣūfī ideas. The work also includes the Arabic text.

1399 Johns, A.H. Malay Sufism. London: Luzac, 1957, 111 pp.

A study of Malay Sufism as represented by a collection of anonymous Ṣūfī tracts from northern Sumatra of the seventeenth century.

Persian Mystical Poetry

General Studies

1400 Arberry, A.J. Classical Persian Literature (see 183).

A history of classical Persian literature written for the beginning student of Persian literature, containing many examples of Persian mystical poems. Bibliography, no index.

1401 Browne, E.G. A Literary History of Persia (see 66).

A monumental study in English of Persian literature, this work is an invaluable guide and reference work for all Persian literary forms, including mystical poetry.

1402 Gibb, E.J.W. A History of Ottoman Poetry (see 350).

Volume 1 contains an introduction to mystical poetry.

1403 Rypka, Jan. History of Iranian Literature (see 75), pp. 69-353.

The section "History of Persian Literature up to the Beginning of the 20th Century" contains a great deal of information on Persian poetry and the influence of Sufism. The stress of the study is on the literary aspects of Persian poetry.

Specific Studies

1404 Bausani, A. "The Religious Thought of Maulana Jalaludin Rumi." Iqbal 13 (1965): 61-86.

A brief and lucid discussion of the literary form of Rūmī's greatest work, the Mathnawī and the basic outlines of his religious thought, divided into the following subjects: God, creation, world, and man.

1405 Chelkowski, Peter J. The Scholar and Saint: Studies in Commemoration of Abu'l-Rayhan al-Bīrūnī and Jalal al-dīn al-Rūmī. New York: New York University Press, 1975, 306 pp.

Six of the fourteen essays are devoted to Rūmī (pp. 169-306). They are: "Rūmī and the Ṣūfī Tradition" (S.H. Nasr); "A Philosophical Interpretation of Rūmī's Mystical Poetry: Light, the Mediator, and the Way" (P. Morewedge); "The Turk in Mawlānā/Mawlānā in Turkey" (T.S. Halman); "A Spring-day in Konya according to Jalāl al-Dīn Rūmī" (Annemarie Schimmel); "The Style of Jalāl al-Dīn Rūmī" (R.M. Rehder); and "Mawlavī as a story teller" (G.H. Yousofi).

1406 Friedlander, Ira. The Whirling Dervishes: Being an Account of the Sufi Order Known as the Mevlevis and Its Founder the Poet and Mystic Mevlana Jalalu'ddin Rumi. New York: Macmillan, 1975, 159 pp.

A popular account of Jalāl al-Dīn Rūmī's life, and the history of the Mawlawī order, with photographs of a staged performance of the dance ceremony. Also there is a brief sketch of Mevlevi music.

1407 Izutsu, Toshihiko. "The Paradox of Light and Darkness in the Garden of Mystery of Shabistarī." In Anagogic Qualities of Literature. Edited by J.P. Strelka. University Park: Pennsylvania State University Press, 1971, pp. 228-308.

An analysis of two key concepts in Sufism, "light" and "darkness," as they appear in the Gulshan-e Rāz of Maḥmūd Shabistarī (d. 1320) and as they are philosophically commented upon by Muḥammad Gīlānī Lāhījī (d. 1506). See also 1477.

1408 Meier, Fritz. "The Spiritual Man in the Persian Poet ʻAṭṭār." In Spiritual Disciplines: Papers from the Eranos Yearbooks. Translated by R. Manheim. New York: Bollingen Foundation, 1960, pp. 267-304.

An excellent study of Farīd al-Dīn ʻAṭṭār's mystical view of man, including a description of one of his most important works, the Ilāhī Nāmah See also 1464.

1409 Ritter, Helmut. Das Meer der Seele. Leiden: E.J. Brill, 1955, 777 pp.

A basic study of fundamental Ṣūfī conceptions concerning God and man on the basis of the Sufism of ʻAṭṭār (thirteenth century). The work includes invaluable information about the first six centuries of Sufism. Extremely useful analytical index; extensive bibliography and notes. Emphasis on the Ṣūfī theme of love of God. One of the best studies on Sufism.

1410 _____. "Muslim Mystics' Strife with God." Oriens 5 (1952):1-15.

A fascinating account of tales by beggars, fools, and Ṣūfīs from the poems of Farīd al-Dīn ʻAṭṭār (d. 1200). The study is full of examples of Ṣūfī stories that reflect a pessimistic yet humorous outlook on the meaning of life, death, and creation.

1411 Schimmel, Annemarie. "The Symbolic Language of Maulanā Jalāl al-Dīn Rūmī." Studies in Islam 1 (1964):26-40.
A sensitive analysis of some of the main lines of symbolism in Rūmī's poetry, with special attention devoted to one of the central symbols of his poetry, the sun.

TRANSLATIONS OF MYSTICAL WRITINGS

General Anthologies

1412 Arberry, A.J. Aspects of Islamic Civilization as Depicted in the Original Texts (see 182).
Chapter 8 and parts of other chapters contain translated excerpts from the writings of Ṣūfīs.

1413 De Bary, Wm. Theodore et al., eds. and comps. Sources of Indian Tradition (see 85), pp. 411-35, 436-63.
Chapter 15, "The Mystics," contains excerpts from the writings of Indian Muslim mystics of the thirteenth century. The selections, although short, together constitute a picture of Ṣūfī practice and thought in pre-Mughal India. Chapter 16, "Religious Tension under the Mughals," contains brief excerpts from the writings of Shāh Walī Allāh, the most important eighteenth-century Indian Muslim thinker.

1414 Jeffery, Arthur, ed. and trans. "Practical Piety." In A Reader on Islam (see 1087), pp. 519-669.
Contains many excerpts from mystical writings on such topics as prayer, duties of Muslims, popular accounts of the Prophet, and stories about famous mystics.

1415 Smith, Margaret. Readings from the Mystics of Islam. London: Luzac, 1950, 144 pp.
An anthology of passages drawn from the writings of nearly fifty Persian and Arab mystics, covering the period from the eighth to the middle of the nineteenth century. Each passage is preceded by a brief biographical sketch of the Ṣūfī author.

1416 _____. The Ṣūfī Path of Love. London: Luzac, 1954, 154 pp.
An anthology of two hundred short selections from Ṣūfī texts, with an introductory chapter on the nature and origins of Sufism by sixteen Western Orientalists.

Classical Sufism

1417 Hujwīrī, al-. The Kashf al-Maḥjūb: The Oldest Persian Treatise on Ṣūfism by al-Hujwīrī. Translated by R.A. Nicholson. Leiden: E.J. Brill, 1959, 443 pp.
A translation of an early Persian treatise on Sufism by ʿAlī ibn ʿUthmān al-Hujwīrī (d. 1077), which divides the Ṣūfīs into schools and explains their thought and practices. This work counts as one of the most valuable extant treatises on Islamic mysticism.

1418 Ibn ʿAbi'l-Dunyā, and Aḥmad Ghazālī. Tracts on Listening to Music. Translated by James Robson. London: Royal Asiatic Society, 1938, 192 pp.
Arabic text and English translation of treatises by Ibn ʿAbi'l Dunyā (d. 894) and Aḥmad Ghazālī (d. 1126) concerning the Ṣūfī practice of listening to music that induces mystical experience.

1419 Ibn Abi'l-Khayr. "The Spiritual States in Sufism." Translated by S.H. Nasr. In Sufi Essays (see 1269), pp. 68-84.
Contains a translation of Abū Saʿīd Ibn Abi'l Khayr's (d. 1049) Forty Stations (Maqāmāt-i ʿArbaʿīn), which depicts the spiritual stations the Ṣūfī passes through on his way to union with God.

1420 Ibn al-Jawzī. "The Devil's Delusion." Translated by D.S. Margoliouth. Islamic Culture 9 (1935):1-21, 187-308, 377-99, 533-77; 10 (1936):20-39, 169-92, 339-68, 633-47; 11 (1937):267-73, 382-92, 529-33; 12 (1938):109-18, 235-40, 352-64, 447-58; 19 (1945):69-81, 171-88, 272-89, 376-83; 20 (1946):58-71, 181-90, 297-310, 408-22; 21 (1947):73-79, 174-83, 394-402; 22 (1948): 75-86.
A translation of Talbīs Iblīs, an Arabic polemical treatise by the Ḥanbalī theologian ʿAbd al-Raḥmān Ibn al-Jawzī (d. 1200), directed against "eccentric" Ṣūfī beliefs and practices.

1421 Junayd, al-. The Life, Personality and Writings of al-Junayd. Gibb Memorial Series, n.s., no. 22. Translated by A.H. Abdel-Kader. London: Luzac, 1962, 245 pp.
Edition and translation of some extant writings of Abū'l-Qāsim Muḥammad al-Junayd (d. 910) with a sketch of his life and a summary treatment of his main ideas. Unsatisfactory comparison of al-Junayd and Plotinus.

1422 Kalābādhī, al-. The Doctrine of the Ṣūfīs. Translated by A.J. Arberry. Cambridge: Cambridge University Press, 1935, 189 pp.
A complete translation of the Kitāb al-taʿarruf by Abū Bakr Muḥammad Kalābādhī (d. 990), which is a compilation of sayings on central doctrines of early Ṣūfī thought and practice.

1423 Khārrāz, al-. Kitāb aṣ-Ṣidq: The Book of Truthfulness. Edited and translated by A.J. Arberry. Oxford: University Press, 1937, 154 pp.
Edition and translation of the Arabic text Kitāb aṣ-Ṣidq by Abū Bakr al-Khārrāz (d. 899), a Ṣūfī of Baghdād and one of al-Junayd's masters, who is accounted by tradition as the first to discuss the theory of fanā' (annihilation) and baqā' (remaining in God).

1424 Niffarī, al-. The Mawāqif and Mukhāṭabāt of Muḥammad Ibn ʿAbdi'l-Jabbār al-Niffarī, with Other Fragments. Translated by A.J. Arberry. Gibb Memorial Series, n.s., no. 9. London: Luzac, 1935, 495 pp.
Edition and translation of these two main works by Muḥammad b. ʿAbd i'l-Jabbār al-Niffarī (d. 965), with a short introduction about his

life and his mystical outlook. Central to this outlook, as revealed by these texts, is the recollection (dhikr) of God through prayer. These works were of great influence upon later Ṣūfīs.

1425 Tirmidhī, al-. "A Ṣūfī Psychological Treatise." Translated by N. Heer. Muslim World 51 (1961):25-36, 83-91, 163-72, 244-58.
A translation of the elucidation of the difference between the breast, the heart, the inner heart, and the intellect, by Muḥammad ibn ʻAlī al-Ḥakīm al-Tirmidhī (d. 932?).

Abū Ḥamīd al-Ghazālī (d. 1111) (For theological works, see 1632-45)

1426 Ghazālī, al-. Worship in Islam, Being a Translation, with Commentary and Introduction, of al-Ghazali's Book of the Iḥyā' on the Worship. Translated by E.E. Calverley. 2d ed. London: Luzac, 1957, 242 pp.
Translation with commentary on al-Ghazālī's book on worship, from his major work, The Revival of the Religious Sciences.

1427 _____. The Book of Knowledge, Being a Translation with Notes of the Kitāb al-ʻIlm of al-Ghazzālī's Iḥyā' ʻUlūm al-Dīn. Translated by N.A. Faris. Lahore: Ashraf, 1962, 242 pp.
Book 1, volume 1 (40 books in 4 volumes) of The Revival of the Religious Sciences, al-Ghazālī's magnum opus. In this work, al-Ghazālī writes as a spiritual reformer, casting aside the theological and juridical formulations of Islam in favor of a more mystical interpretation of Muslim beliefs and practices. Addressing himself to the ordinary Muslim, he attacks the jurists and theologians from many angles in the attempt to change certain attitudes toward Islam. This volume sets the tone for the whole work.

1428 _____. The Foundations of the Articles of Faith, Being a Translation with Notes of the Kitāb Qawā'id al-ʻAqā'id of al-Ghazzālī's Iḥyā' ʻUlūm al-Dīn. Translated by N.A. Faris. Lahore: Ashraf, 1963, 144 pp.
The second book of the first volume of The Revival of the Religious Sciences deals with an exposition of the Shahādah (There is no God but God, and Muḥammad is His Messenger), an analysis of what constitutes proper religious instruction, and the meaning of īmān (faith).

1429 _____. "Ghazzali's 'Epistle of the Birds': A Translation of the Risālat aṭ-Ṭayr." Translated by N.A. Faris. Moslem World 34 (1944):46-53.
A short treatise modeled after one written by Ibn Sīnā having the same title (see 1442). Instead of writing a philosophical-mystical allegory, al-Ghazālī sets forth a religious-mystical tract on the salvation of man. See also Farīd al-Dīn ʻAṭṭār's Manṭiq al-Ṭayr. (See 1463.)

1430 _____. The Mysteries of Almsgiving: A Translation from the Arabic, with Notes, of the Kitāb Asrār al-Zakāh of al-Ghazzālī's Iḥyā' ʻUlūm al-Dīn. Translated by N.A. Faris. Beirut: American University of Beirut, 1966, 96 pp.
Book 5 of the first volume of The Revival of the Religious Sciences, on zakāt (almsgiving), one of the "five pillars" of Islam.

1431 _____. The Mysteries of Purity, Being a Translation with Notes of the Kitāb Asrār al-Tahārah of al-Ghazzālī's Iḥyā' ʻUlūm al-Dīn. Translated by N.A. Faris. Lahore: Ashraf, 1966, 96 pp.
Book 3, volume 1 of The Revival of the Religious Sciences. This is a practical treatise on the importance of cleanliness and methods of ablution, along with a brief definition of purification.

1432 _____. Al-Ghazālī's Mishkāt al-Anwār (The Niche for Lights). Translated by W.M.T. Gairdner. London: Royal Asiatic Society, 1924, 98 pp. Lahore: Ashraf, 1952, 175 pp.
The Mishkāt al-Anwār, the most esoteric treatise of al-Ghazālī in translation, is a commentary on the famous Qur'ānic "light verse" (24:35) and a certain tradition of the Prophet. The work has had great influence on later Ṣūfī thought. The translation is preceded by a good introduction.

1433 _____. On the Duties of Brotherhood. Translated by Muhtar Holland. Woodstock: Overlook Press, 1976, 95 pp.
Spiritual advice and counsel on the subjects of brotherhood, from the Iḥyā'.

1434 _____. "Emotional Religion in Islam as Affected by Music and Singing, Being a Translation of a Book of the Iḥyā' ʻUlūm ad-Dīn of al-Ghazzali with Analysis, Annotation, and Appendices." Translated by D.B. Macdonald. Journal of the Royal Asiatic Society (1901): 195-253; (1902):1-28.
Al-Ghazālī's examination of the pros and cons of singing and listening to music. Here he explains the function of music and argues that it has a worthy place in the life of the Muslim. A moderate Ṣūfī view of music.

1435 _____. The Book of Fear and Hope. Translated by W. McKane. Leiden: E.J. Brill, 1962, 104 pp.
The third book of the fourth volume of The Revival of the Religious Sciences. Here al-Ghazālī is neither philosopher nor theologian, but rather spiritual counselor, anxious to communicate ways of spreading an authentically "religious" Islam. "Hope" and "fear" are defined and employed in the religious life as positive, therapeutic instruments to keep the soul pure. The treatise is practical and directed to ordinary believers; here one is made aware of the mystical spirituality that underlies The Revival of the Religious Sciences. Indexes.

1436 _____. Ghazali on Prayer. Translated by Kōjirō Nakamura. Tokyo: University of Tokyo Press, 1973, 143 pp.
A critical translation of one book from al-Ghazālī's Iḥyā' ʻUlūm al-Dīn, entitled The Book of Invocations and Supplications. The

translation is preceded by a brief sketch of al-Ghazālī's life, plus a good analysis of the mystical concepts of dhikr (invocation, or recollection of God) and du'ā' (supplication) in al-Ghazālī's thought. For a bibliography covering works in European, Japanese, Arabic, Persian, and Turkish languages, see Nakamura's "A Bibliography on Imām al-Ghazālī," Orient 13 (1977): 119-34.

1437 _____. "Al-Risālat al-Laduniyya, by Abū Ḥāmid Muḥammad al-Ghazālī." Translated by Margaret Smith. Journal of the Royal Asiatic Society 19 (1938):177-200, 353-74.

An important treatise on al-Ghazālī's religious philosophy, which includes his theory of knowledge (mystical), the origin of the human soul, and his mystical view of the unity of the universe. With notes and introduction.

1438 _____. Ninety-Nine Names of God in Islam: A Translation of the Major Portion of al-Ghazālī's al-Maqsad Al-Asnā. Translated by R.C. Stade. Ibadan: Daystar, 1970, 138 pp.

This work falls in line with writings on Ṣūfī practice and is a spiritual guide for understanding the meaning of the names of God.

1439 _____. The Faith and Practice of al-Ghazālī. Translated by W.M. Watt. London: Allen & Unwin, 1952, 155 pp.

A translation of Al-Munqidh Mīna'd-Ḍalāl (Deliverance from Error), the "autobiography" of al-Ghazālī. One of the most interesting works yet translated, it describes his turn to the study (and acceptance) of Sufism, after having become dissatisfied with philosophy and theology. It is a simple account of the great thinker's intellectual and spiritual struggle for certainty. Also translated is his Bidayāt al-Hidāyah (The Beginning of Guidance), an essay on religious practices.

1440 _____. Book XX of al-Ghazālī's Iḥyā' 'Ulūm al-Dīn. Translated by L. Zolondek. Leiden: E.J. Brill, 1963, 77 pp.

Book 20 of The Revival of the Religious Sciences on the conduct of life as exemplified by the Prophet. A vivid portrayal of the manners and customs of Muḥammad, set forth as a model for life. The treatise illustrates clearly al-Ghazālī's middle-of-the-road mysticism.

Theosophical Writings

1441 'Ayn al-Quḍāt al-Hamadhānī. A Sufi Martyr. Translated by A.J. Arberry. London: Allen & Unwin, 1969, 101 pp.

Translation of the Shakwa al-Gharīb, an apologia by the Ṣūfī 'Ayn al-Quḍāt al-Hamadhānī (d. 1131), with an introduction and notes. This is a remarkable defense of his love-mysticism in light of orthodox Islam.

1442 Corbin, Henry. Avicenna and the Visionary Recital. Translated by W.R. Trask. Bollingen Series, no. 46. New York: Bollingen, 1960, 423 pp.

A study of various mystical aspects of Ibn Sīnā's (d. 1037) thought and a translation of his work Ḥayy ibn Yaqẓān, with analysis, as well as a translation and analysis of The Recital of the Birds (Risālah al-Ṭayr). Part 2 contains the translation of a Persian commentary on Ḥayy ibn Yaqẓān, including extensive notes by Corbin. A difficult but essential study of the mystical side of Ibn Sīnā.

1443 _____. Spiritual Body and Celestial Earth: From Mazdean Iran to Shī'ite Iran. Translated by Nancy Pearson. Princeton, N.J.: Princeton University Press, 1977, 351 pp.

The second part contains translations from the writings of Suhrawardī, Ibn al-'Arabī, Mullā Ṣadrā, and other Ṣūfī philosophers generally unknown to Western readers.

1444 Ibn al-'Arabī. "Instructions to a Postulant." In A Reader on Islam (see 1087), pp. 640-55.

A translation of a short tract advising the novice (murīd) Ṣūfī on the qualities and attributes needed for attaining unity with God. A simple but beautiful essay of advice and counsel.

1445 _____. Sufis of Andalusia: The Rūḥ al-Quds and Durrat al-Fākhirah. Translated by W.J. Austin. London: Allen & Unwin, 1971, 173 pp.

Translations from two treatises by Ibn al-'Arabī (d. 1240) with an introduction to his life and work. The translations are biographical sketches of minor Ṣūfī masters who lived in Muslim Spain during the twelfth and thirteenth centuries.

1446 _____. The 'Tarjumān al-Ashwāq': A Collection of Mystical Odes by Muhiu'ddin Ibn al-'Arabī. Edited and translated by R.A. Nicholson. London: Royal Asiatic Society, 1911, 155 pp.

Translation of The Interpreter of Longing, a mystical poem that is one of the best introductions to the thought of Ibn al-'Arabī. See also 1320.

1447 _____. "Ibn al-'Arabī's Shajarat al-Kawn." Translated by A. Jeffery. Studia Islamica 11 (1959):43-77, 113-60.

Translation of a mystical treatise on the doctrine of the person in Muḥammad. Here Ibn al-'Arabī expounds upon the unique relationship Muḥammad shares with God, mankind, and the universe as a whole.

1448 Ibn al-Fāriḍ. Studies in Islamic Mysticism (see 1326).

Chapter 3 is the best introduction to the thought of Ibn al-Fāriḍ (d. 1235) and includes a partial translation of his great mystical poem the Ta'iyyah.

1449 Ibn Sīnā. Avicenna on Theology. Translated by A.J. Arberry. London: Murray, 1951, 82 pp.

A collection of translated excerpts from the writings of Ibn Sīnā (d. 1037) that includes his autobiography, short selections on predestination, prophecy, prayer, the afterlife, the nature of God, and a mystical poem on the soul.

1450 _____. "A Treatise on Love." Translated by E.L. Fackenheim. Medieval Studies 7 (1945): 208-28.
Translation of Ibn Sīnā's Risālah fī'l-'ishq, a mystical work based upon his theories on the nature of the soul.

1451 Ibn Ṭufayl. Ibn Ṭufayl's Ḥayy ibn Yaqẓān. Translated by Lenn E. Goodman. New York: Twayne Publishers, 1972, 246 pp.
The authoritative English translation of Ibn Ṭufayl's philosophic romance, preceded by a lengthy introduction or essay on the life and thought of Ibn Ṭufayl. Extensive notes accompany the translation.

Ṣūfī Masters Associated with Orders

1452 Darqāwī, al-. Letters of a Sufi Master. Translated by T. Burckhardt. London: Perennial Books, 1973, 38 pp.
Translation of the aphorisms of Mulay al-'Arabī al-Darqāwī (d. 1823), founder of the Darqāwī branch of the Shādhilī order.

1453 Ibn 'Aṭā' Allāh. "Counsels of a Sufi Master." Studies in Comparative Religion 5 (1971):207-15.
A translation of sixty-five mystical sayings (ḥikam) intended as spiritual guidance for disciples, by Ibn 'Aṭā' Allāh al-Iskandarī (d. 1309). For a complete translation of the Kitāb al-Hikam, see 1454-55.

1454 _____. Ibn 'Aṭa' Allāh's Sūfī Aphorisms (Kitāb al-Ḥikam). Translated by V. Danner. Leiden: E.J. Brill, 1973, 88 pp.
A translation of the Kitāb al-Ḥikam, a compilation of mystic maxims by the Egyptian Ṣūfī Ibn 'Aṭa' Allāh (d. 1309), an important master in the Shādhilī order. These aphorisms are among the most famous and widely recited sayings in Sufism. The translation is preceded by a study of Ibn 'Ata' Allāh's life and works. With introduction and glossary.

1455 _____. Ibn 'Atā' Allāh et la naissance de la confrérie sādilite. Translated by Paul Nwyia. Beirut: Dar el-Machreq, 1952, 107 pp.
An excellent translation in French of the Kitāb al-Ḥikam; much closer to the original than that of Danner (see 1454), who gives his own personal interpretation of the Arabic text.

1456 Kāshānī, al-. The 'Awārif-u'l-Ma'ārif. Translated by H. Wilberforce-Clarke. New York: Weiser, 1970, 168 pp.
Abridged English rendering of the Misbah al-Hidāyah, a Persian Ṣūfī treatise by 'Izz al-Dīn Maḥmūd al-Kāshānī (d. 1335), which is modeled on the 'Awārif al-Ma'ārif by Abū Hafs 'Umar al-Suhrawardī (d. 1234), a treatise on Ṣūfī theories and practices.

1457 Shādhilī, al-. Illumination in Islamic Mysticism. Translated by E. Jurji. Princeton, N.J.: Princeton University Press, 1938, 130 pp.
A translation of the Qawānīn Ḥikām al-Ishrāq by Abu'-l Ḥasan 'Alī al-Shādhilī (d. 1258), a collection of Ṣūfī sayings on mystical illumination. With introduction and notes.

1458 _____. "Prayers of al-Shādhilī." Translated by E.H. Douglas. In Middle Eastern Studies in Honor of Aziz Suryal Atiya. Edited by Sami A. Hanna. Leiden: E.J. Brill, 1972, 106-22.
Translation of Ṣūfī prayers ascribed to Abū'l-Ḥasan 'Alī al-Shādhilī, the Moroccan Ṣūfī. They are devotional recitations (dhikr), invocations, expressions of praise, etc.

1459 Shallabear, W.G., trans. "A Malay Treatise on Popular Ṣūfī Practice." In Macdonald Presentation Volume. New York: Books for Libraries Press, 1968, pp. 351-70. Reprint of 1933 ed.
A translation of a short treatise that explains the bay'ah (covenant with Ṣūfī masters) and the practice of dhikr of the Qādirī and Naqshbandī orders.

1460 Suhrawardī, al-. A Sufi Rule for Novices: Kitāb Ādāb al-Murīdīn of Abū al-Najīb al-Suhrawardī. Translated by M. Milson. Cambridge, Mass., and London: Harvard University Press, 1975, 93 pp.
An abridged translation of one of the most popular and widely read practical manuals for the aspiring Ṣūfī, by the founder of the first major Ṣūfī order in Islam, the Suhrawardiyyah. The manual was intended not only for novices but also for laypersons interested in the Ṣūfī way. Includes introduction, glossary of technical terms, and bibliography.

1461 Walī Allāh, Shāh. A Mystical Interpretation of Prophetic Tales by an Indian Muslim: Shāh Walī Allāh's 'Ta'wīl al-ḥādīth'. Translated by J.M.S. Baljon. Leiden: E.J. Brill, 1973, 67 pp.
A partial translation of an early work of one of India's greatest Muslim mystics; an example of esoteric elaborations on the lives of prophets. With notes and glossary.

Persian Poetry

Farīd al-Dīn 'Aṭṭār (d. 1220)

1462 'Aṭṭār. Muslim Saints and Mystics: Episodes from the Tadhkirat al-auliyā' (Memorial of the Saints) by Farīd al-Dīn 'Aṭṭār. Translated by A.J. Arberry. Chicago: University of Chicago Press, 1966, 392 pp.
An abridged translation of 'Aṭṭār's hagiographical work that vividly characterizes various episodes in the lives of numerous well-known Ṣūfīs. Each biography includes a brief introduction and bibliography by the translator.

1463 _____. The Conference of the Birds. Translated by C.S. Noth. London: Janus, 1954, 147 pp. Berkeley, Calif.: Shambala, 1971.
Translation of the Mantiq al-Tayr, an allegory of the mystic's journey to God, rendered into English from the French translation of the original by Garcin de Tassy (Paris, 1863). See also 1429.

1464 _____. The Ilāhi-Nāma or Book of God of Farīd al-Dīn ʿAṭṭār. Translated by John A. Boyle. Manchester: Manchester University Press, 1976, 392 pp.

One of the greatest mystical works in Islam, this is the great epic about a king's sons who wanted to gain power and pleasure. To each stated wish, the king responds by telling his sons numerous stories that illustrate the futility of striving to attain their stated desires. See also 1408.

Mawlānā Jalāl al-Dīn Rūmī (d. 1273)

1465 Rūmī. Discourses of Rumi. Translated by A.J. Arberry. London: Murray, 1961, 276 pp.

Translation of instructive stories and fables.

1466 _____. More Tales from the Mathnawī. Translated by A.J. Arberry. London: Allen & Unwin, 1963, 252 pp.

A continuation of tales from the Mathnawī. Another one hundred stories culled from the last three books of Rūmī's greatest work, Mathnawī-i Maʿnawī. See also 1472.

1467 _____. Mystical Poems of Rumi. Translated by A.J. Arberry. Chicago: University of Chicago Press, 1968, 203 pp.

Two hundred lyrical poems by Rūmī, with notes.

1468 _____. Tales from the Mathnawi. Translated by A.J. Arberry. London: Allen & Unwin, 1961, 300 pp.

One hundred extracts from the first three books of the Persian Mathnawī, focusing on themes of Ṣūfī life and doctrines as illustrated by stories and fables.

1469 _____. Sun of Tabriz. Translated by C. Garbett. Cape Town: Beerman, 1956, 77 pp.

Translations of selected poems of Rūmī, with illustrations.

1470 _____. Rumi: Poet and Mystic. Translated by R.A. Nicholson. London: Allen & Unwin, 1950, 190 pp.

Selections from Rūmī's writings, translated from the Persian, with introduction and notes.

1471 _____. Selected Poems from the Divan-i Shams-i Tabriz. Translated and edited by R.A. Nicholson. Cambridge: Cambridge University Press, 1952, 422 pp. Reprint of 1898 ed.

Devotional lyrics of Rūmī addressed to his master, Shams al-Dīn Tabrīzī (d. 1248).

1472 _____. The Mathnawī-i maʿnawī. 8 vols. Edited and translated by R.A. Nicholson. Gibb Memorial Series, n.s., no. 4. London: Luzac, 1925-1940.

Edition and translation of the Mathnawī with notes and commentary. Vols. 1, 3, and 5 contain the Persian text; vols. 2, 4, and 6, the English translation; vols. 7 and 8, commentary. This work stands as one of the most significant and influential mystical writings in Islam as well as one of the greatest poetical works in the history of the world's literatures.

1473 _____. The Teachings of Rumi: The Masnawī of Maulāna Jālalu-'d'dīn Muhammad Rūmī. Translated by E.H. Whinfield. New York: Dutton, 1975, 330 pp.

Abridged translation of Rūmī's major work.

Others

1474 Anṣarī, ʿAbdullāh-i. "Ansari's Prayers and Counsels." Translated by A.J. Arberry. Islamic Culture 10 (1936):369-89.

Translation of the Persian prayers and spiritual counsels of ʿAbdullāh-i Anṣarī (d. 1089) of Herat.

1475 Ḥāfiẓ. Fifty Poems of Hafiz. Translated by A.J. Arberry. Cambridge: Cambridge University Press, 1947, 187 pp.

Texts and translations of the Persian poems of Muḥammad Shams al-dīn Ḥāfiẓ (d. 1389), many of which are mystical.

1476 Jāmī, al-. Lawāʾiḥ. Translated by E.H. Whinfield. London: Royal Asiatic Society, 1928, 61 pp.

A translation of The Lightshafts by ʿAbd al-Raḥmān al-Jāmī (d. 1492), the famous Ṣūfī of Herat. This work became one of the most widely read prayer manuals of later Sufism, and is modeled after ʿAbdullāh-i Anṣarī's Munājāt-ū Nasāʾih.

1477 Shabistarī, Maḥmūd ibn ʿAbd al-Karīm al-. Gulshan-i raz: The Mystic Rosegarden of Saʿd ad-din Mahmud Shabistari. Translated by E.H. Whinfield. London: Trubner, 1880, 172 pp.

Translation of the Persian Ṣūfī poem The Rose Garden of Mystery by Saʿd al-Dīn Maḥmūd al-Shabistarī (d. 1320), with notes from the commentary of Lāhījī (d. 1506), one of the most influential mystical works in Islam. See also 1407.

1478 Saʿdī. Kings and Beggars. Translated by A.J. Arberry. London: Luzac, 1945, 100 pp.

Translation of two chapters from the Gulistān of Muṣliḥ al-Dīn Saʿdī (d. 1292).

1479 Sanāʾī. The First Book of the Hadīqatu' l-Haqīqat, or the Enclosed Garden of the Truth of the Ḥakīm Sanāʾi of Ghazan. Edited and translated by Major J. Stephenson. New York: Samuel Weiser, 1972, 297 pp. Reprint of 1980 ed.

Translation of the major work of the Persian poet Abūʾl-Majd Majdūd Sanāʾī (d. 1131). The ten chapters treat a variety of subjects, including mystical themes and the practical life and experiences of the Ṣūfī.

SHĪʻAH

GENERAL STUDIES

1480 Corbin, Henry. En Islam iranien: Aspects spirituels et philosophiques. Vol. 1, Le Shīʻisme duodecimain, 332 pp. Vol. 2, Sohrawardī et les platoniciens de Perse, 384 pp. Vol. 3, Les fidèles d'amour, Shīʻisme et Soufisme, 355 pp. Vol. 4, L'école d'Ispahan; l'école shaykkie; le douzième Imām, 567 pp. Paris: Editions Gallimard, 1971-1972.
Four volumes containing seven separate studies on Persian-Islamic thought, by the French phenomenologist of Iranian Islam. All volumes, with the exception of volume 3, deal specifically with Shīʻī religious thought. Volume 1 treats Ithnā ʻAsharī (Twelver) Shīʻism, not historically, but "theosophically." Volume 3 develops the controversial thesis that Sufism and Shīʻism not only have a common source but that "true" Sufism springs from Shīʻism. Volume 4 treats seventeenth-century Shīʻī philosophy (especially Mullā Ṣadrā), nineteenth-century developments, and includes a final study that is more the reflections of Corbin than anything else. As is the case with many of Corbin's works, these volumes reveal a great deal of the author's own sympathetic views on Iranian Islam. An English translation of all four volumes is forthcoming. See also 1312.

1481 _____. Histoire de la philosophie islamique. Paris: Gallimard, 1964, 380 pp.
This is not a comprehensive history of Islamic philosophy but rather a study of the development of religious and philosophical thought in Islam to the death of Ibn Rushd (Averroes, d. 1198); the work stresses important aspects of Shīʻī thought.

1482 Donaldson, Dwight M. The Shiite Religion: A History of Islam in Persia and Iraq. London: Luzac, 1933, 393 pp.
A general study on the origin and development of the Shīʻah and their doctrines viewed from the perspective of the later orthodox Shīʻī writings. The interpretation of the early Shīʻī developments is inadequate, but there is much information on popular religious practices and beliefs. See also 1918.

1483 The Encyclopaedia of Islam (see 20).
The following articles on the Shīʻah have appeared and are recommended: "Ahl-i Ḥaḳḳ" (V. Minorsky, vol. 1, pp. 260-63); "Alids" (B. Lewis, vol. 1, pp. 400-403); "Bāṭiniyya" (M.G.S. Hodgson, vol. 1, pp. 1098-1100); "Bohorās" (A.A.A. Fyzee, vol. 1, pp. 1254-55); "Fāṭimids" (M. Canard, vol. 2, pp. 850-64); "Ghulāt" (M.G.S. Hodgson, vol. 2, pp. 1093-95); "Ḥashīshiyya" (B. Lewis, vol. 3, pp. 267-68); "Ismāʻīliyya" (W. Madelung, vol. 4, pp. 198-206); "Imāma" (W. Madelung, vol. 3, pp. 1163-69). Many more articles on Shīʻī events, places, and personages may be found in this edition as well as in Shorter Encyclopedia of Islam (see 22).

1484 Hollister, J.N. The Shiʻa of India (see 86).

1485 Kohlberg, E. "The Development of the Imāmī Shīʻī Doctrine of Jihād." Zeitschrift der Deutschen Morgenlandischen Gesellschaft 126 (1976):64-86.
A study on aspects of the Shīʻī doctrine of jihād (struggle) as depicted in various Shīʻī legal writings, from earliest times to the nineteenth century. Based on original sources, this analysis is the first attempt to set forth in some detail the doctrine of jihād in Shīʻī thought.

1486 Nasr, S.H. Ideals and Realities of Islam (see 1093).

1487 Tabāṭabāʼī, ʻAllāmah Sayyid Muḥammad Ḥusayn al-. Shiʻite Islam. Translated by S.H. Nasr. Albany: State University of New York, 1975, 253 pp.
A general historical survey of the religious beliefs of the Shīʻah written by a contemporary Iranian scholar. The book is not an exhaustive, critical study, but it is worth investigating, since it is the only English language compendium of Shīʻī beliefs set forth by a living representative of the main branch (Ithnā ʻAsharī) of the Shīʻah.

1488 Shorter Encyclopedia of Islam (see 22).
The following articles relate to Shīʻī thought and movements. "Ḳarmaṭian" (L. Massignon, pp. 218-23); "Khodjas" (W. Ivanow, pp. 256-57); "al-Mahdī (D.B. Macdonald, pp. 310-13); "Nuṣairī" (L. Massignon, pp. 453-56; "Shīʻa" (R. Strothmann, pp. 534-41; "Taḳīha" (R. Strothmann, pp. 561-62); "Al-Zaidīya" (R. Strothmann, pp. 651-63).

EARLY DEVELOPMENTS

1489 Hodgson, M.G.S. "How Did the Early Shīʻah Become Sectarian." Journal of the American Oriental Society 75 (1955):1-13.
A fundamental study on the formation of the Shīʻah as a distinct and separate Islamic religious movement.

1490 Watt, W. Montgomery. "The Muslim Yearning for a Savior: Aspects of Early ʻAbbāsid Shīʻism." In The Savior God: Comparative Studies in the Concept of Salvation Presented to E.O. James. Edited by S.G.F. Brandon. New York: Barnes & Noble, 1963, pp. 191-204.
A brief analysis of the early political history of the Shīʻah covering the period A.D. 750-925.

1491 _____. "The Rāfidites: A Preliminary Study." Oriens 16 (1963):110-21.
An investigation into an early politico-religious group of the Shīʻī movement based upon a critical use of heresiographical literature and historical materials. The article is technical, but it is useful for the student interested in the politico-religious history of early Islam.

1492 _____. "The Reappraisal of Abbasid Shīʻism." In Arabic and Islamic Studies in Honor of H.A.R. Gibb. Edited by G. Makdisi. Leiden: E.J. Brill, 1965, pp. 638-55.
By critically evaluating heresiographical as well as historical materials, Watt argues Imamate Shīʻism did not establish its definite character until shortly before 900. The essay includes a useful summary of the most important features of early ʻAbbāsid Shīʻism.

1493 _____. "Shīʻism under the Umayyads." Journal of the Royal Asiatic Society (1960): 158-72.
An illuminating article on Shīʻī opposition to the Umayyads; the author combines the results of his study of historical and heresiographical materials in order to shed more light on the early Shīʻah.

ISMAʻĪLĪS (See also 247-62)

1494 Corbin, Henry. "Cyclical Time in Mazdaism and Ismailism." In Man and Time: Papers from the Eranos Yearbooks. Translated by R. Manheim. Bollingen Series, no. 30, 3. New York: Bollingen Foundation, 1957, pp. 115-73.
A comparative study of various notions of time in pre-Islamic Zoroastrian and Ismāʻīlī thought. As with some other works by Corbin, this one reflects his own esoteric interpretation of the materials.

1495 _____. "Divine Epiphany and Spiritual Birth in Ismailian Gnosis." In Man and Transformation: Papers from the Eranos Yearbooks. Translated by R. Manheim. Bollingen Series, no. 30, 5. New York: Bollingen Foundation, 1964, pp. 69-161.
A study on aspects of Ismāʻīlī cosmology, angelology, and the central role of the Imām in Ismāʻīlī thought including an analysis of Ismāʻīlī cosmology, angelology, and the central role of the Imām in Ismāʻīlī mystical thought.

1496 _____. "Nāṣir-i Khusraw and Iranian Ismāʻīism." In The Cambridge History of Iran. Vol. 4, From the Arab Invasion to the Saljuqs (see 230), pp. 520-32.
A brief study of the life and works of Naṣīr-i Khusraw (d. 1072-1077?), one of the greatest thinkers of the Ismāʻīlīs. The article is by no means detailed, but given the lack of study in English on this great Iranian, it is recommended.

1497 Dodge, Bayard. "Al-Ismāʻīliyyah and the Origin of the Fāṭimids." Muslim World 49 (1959):296-305. "The Fāṭimid Legal Code." Muslim World 50 (1960):30-38. "The Fāṭimid Hierarchy and Exegesis." Muslim World 50 (1960):130-41. "Aspects of the Fāṭimid Philosophy." Muslim World 50 (1960):182-92.
These articles contain a great deal of information on the origins, legal system, missionary activities, and intellectual outlook of the Ismāʻīlī Fāṭimids.

1498 Hamdani, H.F. "A Compendium of Ismāʻīlī Esoterics." Islamic Culture 11 (1937): 210-20.
A discussion of the contents of an important Ismāʻīlī work entitled Zahr al-Maʻānī, a compendium of Ismāʻīlī beliefs, covering theology, cosmology, anthropology, and eschatology, by a Yamanite missionary (dāʻī), Idrīs ʻImād al-Dīn, from the fourteenth century.

1499 Hodgson, M.G.S. "The Ismaʻili State." In The Cambridge History of Iran. Vol. 5, The Saljuq and Mongol Periods (see 226), pp. 422-82.
An account of the Ismāʻīlī movement in Iran.

1500 _____. The Order of the Assassins: The Struggle of the Early Nazārī Ismāʻīlīs against the Islamic World (see 252).
Two appendixes are of particular importance here: the first contains a translation of a tract on the popular appeal of the qiyāmah (resurrection) entitled Haft Bāb-i Baba Sayyid-nā (The Seven Chapters of Bābā Sayyid-na, i.e., Ḥasan-i Ṣabbāḥ); the second is a translation of the section on Nizārīs from the heresiography of al-Shahrastānī (d. 1153), entitled Kitāb al-Milal wa'l-Niḥal. See also 1546.

1501 Ivanow, W. Ismaili Tradition Concerning the Rise of the Fatimids (see 253).

1502 _____. "An Ismailitic Work by Nasiru'd-din Tusi." Journal of the Royal Asiatic Society (1931):557-564.
A summary review with notes of the Rawḍat al-Taslīm by Naṣīr al-Dīn al-Ṭūsī (d. 1274), one of the greatest theologians in Islam. The work that is summarized contains a concise exposition of Ismāʻīlī theology; given the lack of mateials on Ismāʻīlī thought, this study should not be overlooked. For a translation of the text, see 1516.

1503 _____, trans. Kalāmi Pīr: A Treatise on Ismaili Doctrine. Bombay: Islamic Society, 1955, 93 pp.
Edition and translation of a text setting forth Ismāʻīlī religious beliefs held in the post-Alamūt period (post thirteenth century A.D.).

1504 _____. True Meaning of Religion. Bombay: Islamic Research Association, 1933, 65 pp. Reprinted in 2 vols. Bombay: Ismaili Society, 1947.
Text and translation of Risālāt dar Haqīqat-i Dīn, by Shihāb al-Dīn Shāh (d. 1885), heir to the Agha Khan.

1505 Levy, R. "The Account of the Ismaʻili Doctrines in the Jamiʻ al-Tawarikh of Rashid al-din Faḍlallah." Journal of the Royal Asiatic Society (1930):509-36.
Arabic text and translation of the discussion on Ismāʻīlī doctrines as expounded by Rashīd al-Dīn (d. 1318) in his history (Jāmiʻ al-Tawārīkh). See 303.

1506 Lewis, B. The Assassins: A Radical Sect in Islam (see 255).

1507 Lewis, Bernard. The Origins of Ismaʿilism (see 256).

1508 Lewis, B. "An Ismaʿili Interpretation of the Fall of Adam." Bulletin of the School of Oriental and African Studies 9 (1937-39): 691-704.
A summary view of a small part of an Ismāʿīlī compendium of responses on theological subjects to twenty-five questions. Lewis summarizes the contents of one question, on Adam and his fall. Included is the Arabic text of the section summarized.

1509 Makarem, Sami Nassib, trans. Ash-Shāfiya (The Healer): An Ismāʿīlī Poem Attributed to Shihāb ad-dīn Abū Firās. Beirut: American University of Beirut, 1966, 260 pp.
A translation with extensive notes plus the Arabic text of a thirteenth-century compendium of Ismāʿīlī beliefs.

1510 Makarem, Sami Nassib. "The Philosophical Significance of the Imām in Ismāʿīlism." Studia Islamica 27 (1967):41-53.
An analysis based on original sources of the Ismāʿīlī concept of Imām (the authoritative guide of the believers), which demonstrates the neoplatonic influence upon this, the most central concept of Shīʿī thought. The author argues that the Imām is conceived to be both the embodiment of the Word of God and His will in Ismāʿīlī thought.

1511 Salisbury, E.E., trans. "Translation of an Unpublished Arabic Risāleh, by Khālid Ibn Zeid al-Juʿfy." Journal of the American Oriental Society 3 (1852):165-93.
An exposition of "moderate" Ismāʿīlī doctrines designed for those who deviated from the "true" path. A useful source for understanding Ismāʿīlī religious doctrines.

1512 _____. "Translation of Two Unpublished Arabic Documents Relating to the Doctrines of the Ismāʿīlīs and Other Bātinian Sects." Journal of the American Oriental Society 2 (1851):257-324.
A translation with introduction and notes of two undated and unidentified documents. The first is an attack against the Ismāʿīlīs and the second presents the Ismāʿīlī system of cosmology, religious beliefs, a mystical interpretation of these beliefs, and a statement of Imamate doctrine from the Ismāʿīlī point of view. Salisbury thinks that the second document is essentially a collection of sermons of the type that Ismāʿīlī missionaries delivered.

1513 Stern, S.M. "The Early Ismāʿīlī Missionaries in North-West Persia and in Khurāsān and Transoxania." Bulletin of the School of Oriental and African Studies 23 (1960):56-90.
A study of the propagation of Ismāʿīlī thought by the dāʿīs (missionaries) to areas where the Ismāʿīlīs failed to gain a large popular following. The author gives tentative conclusions as to why this mission failed when others were successful.

1514 Tritton, A.S. "Theology and Philosophy of the Ismaʿilis." Journal of the Royal Asiatic Society (1958):178-88.
A brief outline sketch of the theological doctrines of the Ismāʿīlīs. The article is weakened by a complete lack of reference to sources.

1515 Ṭūsī, Naṣīr al-dīn Muḥammad Ibn Muḥammad al-. The Nasirean Ethics. Translated by G.M. Wickens. London: Allen & Unwin, 1964, 352 pp.
An English translation of one of the most important religio-philosophical ethical writings in Islam, the Akhlāq-i Naṣīrī, written by the great Ismāʿīlī philosopher-theologian, al-Ṭūsī (d. 1274). The translation is preceded by an excellent introduction to al-Ṭūsī's thought.

1516 Ṭūsī, Naṣīr ad-dīn al-. Rawḍat at-Taslīm or Taṣawwurāt. Edited and translated by W. Ivanow. Ismaili Society Series A, no. 4. Leiden: E.J. Brill, 1950, 497 pp.
An exposition of Nizārī Ismāʿīlī doctrine. See also 1502.

1517 Walker, Paul E. "Cosmic Hierarchies in Early Ismāʿīlī Thought: The View of Abū Yaʿqūb al-Sijistānī." Muslim World 66 (1976): 14-28.
An analysis of Ismāʿīlī cosmology as depicted in the writings of the famous tenth-century Ismāʿīlī theologian. The author shows that both Neoplatonism and the Ismāʿīlī tradition contributed to theories of cosmic hierarchies of being.

1518 _____. "An Ismaili Answer to the Problems of Worshiping the Unknowable, Neoplatonic God." American Journal of Arabic Studies 2 (1974): 7-21.
An analysis of Abū Yaʿqūb al-Sijistānī's (d. 971) theological conception of God, which the author examines in light of Plotinus's conception of God.

1519 _____. "The Ismaili Vocabulary of Creation." Studia Islamica 40 (1974):75-87.
A study of the Ismāʿīlī Neoplatonic theory of creation based largely on an analysis of some of Abū Yaʿqūb al-Sijistānī's important works.

The Epistles of the Brethren of Purity

1520 Fakhry, Majid. A History of Islamic Philosophy (see 1568), pp. 184-204.
Chapter 5 contains a useful analysis of the religio-philosophical doctrines of Epistles of the Brethren of Purity, which stresses the mathematical, cosmological, and psychological ideas of these supposed Ismāʿīlī writings.

1521 Fārūqī, Ismāʿīl R. al-. "On the Ethics of the Brethren of Purity." Muslim World 50 (1960):109-21, 193-98; 51 (1961):18-24.
An exposition of the ethical theory of the Ikhwān al-Ṣafā' based upon an analysis of their writings. The last section of the study attacks

the view that these writings and their authors were part of the Ismā'īlī sect or any other Shī'ī movement.

1522 Ikhwān al-Ṣafā'. Arabische Philosophie und Wissenschaft in der Enzyklopadie: Kitāb Ikhwānas-safā' (III), Die Lehre von Seele und Intellect. Translated by Suzanne Diwald. Wiesbaden: Otto Harrassowitz, 1975, 641 pp.

The German translation of the Neoplatonic Brethren of Purity treatises on the soul and intellect. This volume will be followed by two others, which together will constitute a complete translation of the entire corpus of treatises. The present volume includes an exhaustive bibliography.

1523 Marquet, Y. "Ikhwān al-Ṣafā." EI2. Vol. 3 (see 20), pp. 1071-76.

A detailed study that takes into account the sources of ideas, composition, contents, form, and the purpose for writing the epistles. The controversial issue of their authorship is also raised.

1524 Nasr, S.H. An Introduction to Islamic Cosmological Doctrine. Cambridge, Mass.: Harvard University, 1964, 312 pp.

A large section of this work (part 1, pp. 25-107) analyzes the cosmological views of the epistles. The study also contains an exhaustive bibliography on the epistles.

1525 Ṭibawi, A.L. "Ikhwān Aṣ-Ṣafā and Their Rasā'il: A Critical Review of a Century and a Half of Research." Islamic Quarterly 2 (1956):28-46.

An analysis of studies on the Brethren of Purity and their writings (the Rasā'il), plus suggestions for future research. The article is technical, but sets forth clearly the major difficulties regarding the study of one fundamentally important aspect of Islamic thought.

ITHNĀ 'ASHARĪ (TWELVERS)

1526 Eliash, J. "On the Genesis and Development of the Twelver Shī'ī Three-Tenet Shahādah." Der Islam 47 (1971):265-72.

A discussion of the origin and development of the three-tenet Shahādah (personal witness to Islam): "I bear witness that there is no God but God, that Muḥammad is the Messenger of God, and that 'Alī is the Wālī of God."

1527 Eliash, Joseph. "The Ithnā 'Asharī-Shī'ī Juristic Theory of Political and Legal Authority." Studia Islamica 29 (1969):17-30.

A discussion of Islamic doctrines that have direct bearing on the problem of the authority of the Imām (authoritative guide for believers) in this branch of Shī'ī Islam.

1528 Ḥillī, Ḥasan Ibn Yūsuf al-. Al Bāb al-Ḥadī 'Ashar. Translated by W.M. Miller. Oriental Trust Fund, n.s., no. 29. London: Luzac, 1958, 104 pp.

Translation of a Shī'ah creed written by one of the great Shī'ī theologians of medieval Islam (d. 1325). This creed is considered to be an authoritative statement of the beliefs of the Ithnā 'Asharī (Twelver) branch of the Shī'ah.

1529 Ibn Bābawayh. A Shī'ite Creed. Translated by A.A.A. Fyzee. Bombay: Islamic Research Association, 1942, 144 pp.

A translation, with introduction and notes, of the Risālat al-I'tiqādāt (Treatise on the Tenets of Faith) by Ibn Bābawayh (d. 991), one of the foremost Ithnā 'Asharī (Twelver) followers. Given the paucity of primary materials on the Shī'ah, this work stands as a basic source for understanding early Shī'ī religious thought.

1530 King, N.Q., and S.A. Rizvi. "The Khoja Shia Ithna-Ashariya Community in East Africa." Muslim World 64 (1974):194-204.

A general description of the history of Ithnā 'Asharī Shī'ism in East Africa, plus a look at particular jamā'āts (congregations).

1531 Kohlberg, Eton. "Some Imāmī-Shī'ī Views on Taqiyyah." Journal of the American Oriental Society 95 (1975):395-403.

An attempt to reexamine the idea that Taqiyyah (dissimulation of belief) is the distinguishing mark of Ithnā 'Asharī Shī'ism. The author argues that Shī'ī views on Taqiyyah are complex and underwent modifications and changes.

1532 Mazzaoui, Michael M. The Origins of the Safavids: Shī'ism, Sufism, and the Ghulat (see 414).

1533 Millward, G.W. "Aspects of Modernism in Shī'a Islam." Studia Islamica 37 (1973): 111-28.

The author argues that "there has been and will continue to be evidence of trends towards modernism and adaptation in Ithnā 'Asharī Shī'ī Islam which have hitherto passed largely unnoticed," and sets forth some reasons as to why Shī'ī Islam has not, as yet, had a "modernist" movement comparable to those found in other parts of the Islamic world. As a case study for modernist tendencies, the author examines writings of the present-day Iranian scholar 'Allāmah Tabāṭabā'ī. See also 1487.

1534 Nasr, S.H. "Ithnā 'Asharī Shī'īsm and Iranian Islam." In Religion in the Middle East. Vol. 2 (see 9), pp. 96-118.

A very superficial treatment of Islam in Iran that touches upon the pre-Islamic background, Sufism, religious institutions, popular beliefs, and religious practices. Bibliography.

1535 Tritton, A.S. "Popular Shi'ism." Bulletin of the School of Oriental and African Studies 13 (1951):829-39.

A summary of popular Shī'ī beliefs by Ibn Bābawayh. It is difficult to know whether Tritton has offered a paraphrase in certain parts, a translation, or a concise summary, since there are no notes or bibliographical data whatsoever.

ZAYDIYYAH

1536 Khan, M.S. "The Early History of Zaydi Shiʿism in Daylaman and Gilan." Zeitschrift der Deutschen Morgenlandischen Gesellschaft 125 (1975):301-15.
A historical account of Zaydī beginnings in Iran.

1537 Kohlberg, E. "Some Zaydī Views on the Companions of the Prophet." Bulletin of the School of Oriental and African Studies 39 (1976):91-98.
This study explores the various attitudes of several Zaydī authors on the Prophet Muḥammad's companions.

1538 Serjeant, R.B. "The Zaydis." In Religion in the Middle East. Vol. 2 (see 9), pp. 285-302.
The best general account in English of the origin and development of the Zaydiyyah, a modderate Shīʿī sect of Yemen. The study includes an assessment of the contemporary situation. Good bibliography.

SECTS

GENERAL STUDIES

1539 Laoust, Henri. Les schismes dans l'Islam. Paris: Payot, 1965, 466 pp.
Since no comprehensive English language study on Islamic sectarianism exists, this classic study is recommended. The study examines not only various sects but also analyzes divergent systems of political, legal, and theological thought in Islam.

1540 Lewis, Bernard. "Some Observations on the Significance of Heresy in the History of Islam." Studia Islamica 1 (1953):43-63. In Islam in History: Ideas, Men and Events in the Middle East (see 37), pp. 217-37.
An examination of some technical terms used by classical Muslim writers that have been interpreted to mean "heresy" by Western Orientalists. Lewis argues that the Greco-Christian concept of heresy has no exact counterpart in Islam because of the absence of an apostolic tradition, and he concludes that the Islamic term normally translated as "unbelief" comes closest in meaning to the Christian term "heresy."

HERESIOGRAPHIES

1541 Baghdādī, al-. Moslem Schisms and Sects. Translated by R.C. Seeyle. Columbia University Oriental Studies, vol. 15. New York: Ams, 1966, 224 pp. Reprint of 1920 ed.
A translation of one of the famous classical heresiographies, the Al-Farq Bayn al-Firaq, by Abū Manṣūr ʿAbd al-Qāhir al-Baghdādī (d. 1037), with introduction and notes. The introduction is particularly useful, for it contains a table of sects mentioned and examined by al-Baghdādī.

1542 Ibn Ḥazm. "The Heterodoxies of the Shiites in the Presentation of Ibn Ḥazm." Translated by I. Friedlander. Journal of the American Oriental Society 28 (1907):1-80; 29 (1908): 1-183.
A translation of the section on Shīʿism from Ibn Ḥazm's (d. 1064) famous heresiographical work, the Kitāb al-Milal wa'l-Niḥal (Book on Religion and Sects), with extensive commentary by Friedlander. Includes translation (vol. 28) and commentary (vol. 29).

1543 Shahrastānī, al-. "The Muʿtazilites." Translated by A.K. Kazi and J.C. Flynn. Abr-Nahrain 8 (1968-69):36-68.
A translation of the section on the Muʿtazilah from the classical heresiography al-Milal wa'l-Niḥal, by al-Shahrastānī (d. 1153).

1544 _____. "The Jabarites and the Ṣifātīya." Translated by A.K. Kazi and J.C. Flynn. Abr-Nahrain 9 (1969-70):81-107.
A translation of the sections on the Jabariyyah and Ṣifātiyyah, two "schools" or, more precisely, theological positions (the first relating to the problem of free will and determinism, the second to the problem of God's attributes), from the Al-Milal wa'l-Niḥal.

1545 _____. "The Kharijites and the Murji'ites from Shahrastānī's Kitāb al-Milal wa'l Niḥal." Translated by A.K. Kazi and J.C. Flynn. Abr-Nahrain 10 (1970-71):49-76.
Containing translation of the sections on two early politico-theological sects.

1546 _____. "Shahrastānī's Kitāb al-Milal wa'l-Niḥal: The Shiʿites." Translated by A. Kazi and J.C. Flynn. Abr-Nahrain 15 (1974-75): 50-98.
A translation of the section on the Shīʿah from Shahrastānī's heresiographical work. See also 1500.

THE KHAWĀRIJ (KHARIJITES) AND IBĀḌIYYAH

1547 Lewicki, T. "The Ibadites in Arabia and Africa." Journal of World History 13 (1971): 51-130.
The best English language analysis of the only surviving branch of the Khawārij (Kharijites), the earliest politico-religious sect in Islam. The author traces the history of the Ibāḍiyyah from their beginnings in Baṣra through their origins and development in North Africa, where they played an important role in the conversion of Berber tribes. Detailed notes. See also Lewicki's article, "al-Ibāḍiyya," in EI2. Vol. 3 (see 20), pp. 648-60.

1548 Rubinacci, Roberto. "The Ibadis." In Religion in the Middle East. Vol. 2 (see 9), pp. 302-18.
An examination of the only surviving branch of the Khawārij, the oldest sect in Islam. Good introduction to the subject. Bibliography.

1549 Salem, Elie Adib. Political Theory and Institutions of the Khawarij (see 138).

1550 Watt, W. Montgomery. "Kharijite Thought in the Umayyad Period." Der Islam 36 (1961): 215-31.
A study of the politico-religious thought of the Khawārij in the first century of Islam based upon an analysis of certain heresiographical writings in light of the historical background.

1551 ______. "The Kharijites." In The Formative Period of Islamic Thought (see 1576), pp. 9-38.
An excellent starting point for learning about the first "sect" in Islam. Watt concentrates only on the earliest phase of the Khawārij movement. With copious notes.

DRUZE

1552 Assaad, S.A. The Reign of al-Hakim bi Amr Allah. Beirut: Arab Institute for Research and Publishing, 1974, 209 pp.
A study on the political history of the reign of the Fāṭimid ruler al-Ḥākim (996-1021 A.D.) including a chapter on the origin of the Druze movement. Extensive notes and bibliography.

1553 Bryer, D. "The Origins of the Druze Religion." Der Islam 52 (1975):47-84, 239-62; 53 (1976):5-27.
Divided into four chapters, the study examines the Ismāʿīlī origins; the rise of the Druze religion; the religious thought of the true founder of the faith, Ḥamza ibn ʿAlī; and the relationships of Ḥamza's doctrine to Ismāʿīlism.

1554 Hirschberg, J.W. "The Druzes." In Religion in the Middle East. Vol. 2 (see 9), pp. 330-49.
A brief examination of the Druze beliefs and a sketch of the history and organization of Druze society. Bibliography.

1555 Hitti, Philip K. The Origins of the Druze People and Religion with Extracts from Their Sacred Writings (see 251).
This study has been superseded by Bryer's "The Origins of the Druze Religion" (see 1553). The value of this account is found in the appendix, where a few excerpts from Druze texts are translated.

1556 Hodgson, Marshall G.S. "Al-Darazi and Ḥamza in the Origin of the Druze Religion." Journal of the American Oriental Society 82 (1962):5-20.
A superb study on the origin of the Druze faith that analyzes the roles of Ḥamza ibn ʿAlī and al-Darazī in the formation of that community. Hodgson concludes that the Druze sect bears clearly the genius of Ḥamza in its fundamental religious outlook and its independence of Islam. See also "Durūz," in EI2, vol. 2 (see 20), pp. 631-37.

1557 Makārim, Sāmī Nasīb. The Druze Faith. Delmar, N.Y.: Caravan, 1974, 153 pp.
Written by a Druze, this study examines the historical background of the movement and the belief system of this little understood and often misinterpreted religion. Detailed notes, glossary of technical terms, appendixes, bibliography, and index accompany the text.

1558 Toftbek, E. "A Shorter Druze Catechism." Muslim World 44 (1954):38-42.
A translation of an abridged Druze catechism written at the end of the nineteenth century.

AḤMADIYYAH

1559 Addison, J.T. "The Ahmadiyyah Movement and Its Western Propaganda." Harvard Theological Review 22 (1929):1-32.
A review of the origins and teachings of Qadian and Lahore branches of the Aḥmadiyyah plus examination of their missionary approaches among Western Christians.

1560 Ahmad, Aziz, and G.E. von Grunebaum. Muslim Self-statement in India and Pakistan, 1857-1968 (see 988), pp. 77-85.
Chapter 5 contains a selection of translated excerpts from the writings of Mīrza Ghulām Aḥmad and Mīrzā Bashīr al-Dīn Maḥmūd, the founder of and successor to the Aḥmadiyyah.

1561 Fisher, Humphrey J. Ahmadiyyah: A Study in Contemporary Islam on the West African Coast (see 1039).

1562 Ghulam Aḥmad, Hazrat Mirza. Triumph of Islam. Translated by Mirza Maʿsum Bey. Lahore: Raheel Art, 1968, 188 pp.
An abridgment of Ghulām Aḥmad's Barahin-i-Aḥmadiyyah, published in 1880, which contains homiletic essays on the Prophet, Qur'ān, God's existence, and His attributes.

1563 Hazrat Mirza, Bashiruddin Mahmud Ahmad. Ahmadiyyat or True Islam. 2d ed. Washington: American Fazl Mosque, 1951, 246 pp.
An exposition of Aḥmadiyyah teachings by the successor to Ghulām Aḥmad, the founder of the movement.

1564 Robson, James. "The Aḥmadīs." In Religion in the Middle East. Vol. 2 (see 9), pp. 349-62.
A concise treatment of the life of the founder of the Aḥmadiyyah movement, Ghulām Aḥmad (d. 1908) and the Qadian and Lahore branches of the sect. Bibliography.

1565 Smith, W.C. "Aḥmadiyya." In EI2. Vol. 1 (see 20), pp. 301-03.
A survey of the life and thought of the founder of the Aḥmadiyyah as well as a description of the Aḥmadiyyah community. Bibliography.

1566 Titus, Murray T. Islam in India and Pakistan (see 100), pp. 256-72.
Contains a survey of the teachings of the founder of the Aḥmadiyyah movement.

CLASSICAL AND MEDIEVAL THEOLOGY (ʿILM AL-KALĀM)

GENERAL AND INTRODUCTORY STUDIES

1567 Anawati, G.S. "Philosophy, Theology and Mysticism." In The Legacy of Islam (see 207), pp. 350-92.
A splendid introduction to three thought systems of Islam with analysis of their origins, basic characteristics, their connections with each other, and the influence they have exerted on the Christian West. Good bibliography.

1568 Fakhry, Majid. A History of Islamic Philosophy. New York: Columbia, 1970, 427 pp.
This book is misnamed; it should be titled "A History of Islamic Thought," since it includes investigations into things theological and mystical, even political and social. It is useful for an overview of some aspects of early political and religious controversies, Islamic theology (kalām), mysticism, later theological reaction, and modern trends. Bibliography and index. See also 1313, 1520.

1569 Gardet, L. "ʿIlm al-kalām." In EI2. Vol. 3 (see 20), pp. 1141-50.
A survey of the origin, development, main trends, and important thinkers of Islamic theology. Bibliography.

1570 Macdonald, D.B. The Development of Muslim Theology, Jurisprudence, and Constitutional Theory. Khayat's Oriental Reprint Series, no. 10. New York: Scribners, 1903, 386 pp.
Although largely out of date, part 3 on theology, continues to serve as a useful introduction to Islamic theological and mystical thought. The volume's importance is enhanced by the appendix, which contains translations of excerpts from Muslim writings, the most important being three short creeds by al-Ashʿarī, al-Ghazālī, and al-Nasafī. See also 2074.

1571 _____. "Kalām." In Shorter Encyclopedia of Islam (see 22), pp. 210-14.
For years a basic introduction to the study of theology, this article has now been surpassed by more recent studies, such as L. Gardet's article "ʿIlm al-kalām" (see 1569).

1572 _____. "An Outline of the History of Scholastic Theology in Islam." Muslim World 15 (1925):140-55.
A reprint of the article on kalām (Islamic theology) in Shorter Encyclopedia of Islam (see 1571).

1573 Seale, Morris S. Muslim Theology: A Study of Origins with Reference to the Church Fathers. London: Luzac, 1964, 137 pp.
This study attempts to establish the influence of the Greek church fathers on the teachings of the Qadariyyah, Muʿtazilah, and Murji'ah, three theological movements in early Islam. The study is problematic because of its method, which is to set side by side writings of Christian theologians (Clement of Alexandria, Origen, and John of Damascus) and their Muslim counterparts. Rash conclusions about origins of and influences on early Islamic theological thought follow.

1574 Sharif, M.M. A History of Muslim Philosophy: With Short Accounts of Other Disciplines and the Modern Renaissance in Muslim Lands. 2 vols. Wiesbaden: Harrassowitz, 1963-1966, 1792 pp.
A collection of eighty-three articles written by various scholars on a great variety of subjects. Pre-Islamic thought, the teachings of the Qur'ān, theology, mysticism, political thought, art and architecture, music, the sciences, and modern developments, as well as philosophy, are topics covered. The articles in these volumes are of uneven quality. Bibliographies with articles, index with volume 2. See also 1308, 1324, 1325.

1575 Tritton, A.S. Muslim Theology. London: Royal Asiatic Society, 1947, 218 pp.
A general study on the development of Islam theology.

1576 Watt, W. Montgomery. The Formative Period of Islamic Thought. Edinburgh: University of Edinburgh Press, 1973, 424 pp.
The most detailed and comprehensive treatment of the development of early Islamic thought (632-945 A.D.) that exists in the English language. This work, much of which is based upon the author's previous studies on early Islamic sects, shows that Islamic thought emerged from the political-religious upheavals of the Muslim community. The issues, problems, and disputes of thought in the formative period of Islam set the stage for the further development of thought in Islam. The study is essential for understanding this crucial period in Islamic history. The notes are extensive and include bibliography, with index. See also 1551.

1577 _____. Islamic Philosophy and Theology. Edinburgh: University of Edinburgh Press, 1962, 196 pp.
The title of this book is misleading, since Islamic philosophy is not discussed at all. It is a book on early Islamic sects and theology, and as such is a good survey of the early development of Islamic theological thought in the Western Islamic regions. The standard Orientalists' view that the thirteenth century marked the end of creative thought in Islam prevails: part 4, covering the years 1250-1900 A.D., is twenty-seven pages long and entitled "The Period of Darkness."

1578 Wolfson, H.A. The Philosophy of the Kalam. Cambridge, Mass., and London: Harvard University Press, 1976, 779 pp.
A monumental work (the sequel to the author's Philo and the Church Fathers) that systematically examines with great care the origin, structure, and diversity of six central teachings of Islamic theology: divine attributes, Qur'ān, creation, atomism, causality, the freewill problem. Wolfson concludes that although these problems are not new to Islam, each

has an independent development in Islamic theology, and like the previous systems studied, kalām is the attempt to explain scripture in terms of philosophy.

SPECIFIC STUDIES

1579 Arberry, A.J. Revelation and Reason in Islam. London: Allen & Unwin, 1957, 122 pp.
In these lectures (Forwood Lectures for 1956) Arberry considers how theology, philosophy, and mysticism sought to resolve the conflict within Islam between reason and revelation. A useful, but very general, introduction to a fundamental problem of Islamic thought. Notes and index.

1580 Davidson, Herbert A. "Arguments from the Concept of Particularization in Arabic Philosphy." Philosophy East and West 18 (1968): 299-314.
An analysis of an important argument employed by Muslim theologians after al-Ashʿarī to prove the existence of God and to prove the creation of the world. Davidson traces the development of the concept of particularization (takhsīs) by examining the writings of leading Muslim theologians.

1581 _____. "John Philoponus as a Source of Medieval Islamic and Jewish Proofs of Creation." Journal of the American Oriental Society 89 (1969):357-91.
A section of this lengthy study is devoted to an analysis of the Muslim theological proof for creation, which is traced back to the Christian philosopher John Philoponus.

1582 Donaldson, D.M. Studies in Muslim Ethics. London: S.P.C.K., 1963, 304 pp.
The only comprehensive treatment of the subject in English, this study includes an examination of philosophical, theological, and mystical theories on ethics, and of ethical attitudes in the Qur'ān and ḥadīth, as well as a discussion of modern developments. Notes and bibliography.

1583 Fakhry, Majid. "The Classical Islamic Arguments for the Existence of God." Muslim World 47 (1957):133-45.
Fakhry shows why Muslim theologians and philosophers rejected the cosmological argument for God's existence in favor of an argument from the contingency of the world. The major portion of the article analyzes different Muslim thinkers' approaches to the theory of temporality of the world.

1584 _____. Islamic Occasionalism and Its Critique by Averroes and Aquinas. London: Allen & Unwin, 1958, 220 pp.
A study on the transmission of Islamic theological notions of atomism (or occasionalism) to the Latin West plus a survey of the historical development of Islamic atomism, with special attention given to al-Ghazālī's (d. 1111) attack on causality and its defense by Ibn Rushd (Averroes) and Maimonides.

1585 Grunebaum, D.E. von. Theology and Law in Islam. Wiesbaden: Harrassowitz, 1971, 105 pp.
A collection of essays by outstanding scholars of Islam: "Theology and Law in Islam" (J. Schacht), "The Great Community and the Sects" (W.M. Watt), "Historical Consciousness in Islam" (W. Braune), "Law and Traditionalism in the Institutions of Learning of Medieval Islam" (G. Makdisi), "Functional Interdependence of Law and Theology" (F. Rahman).

1586 Hourani, G.F. "Two Theories of Value in Medieval Islam." Muslim World 50 (1960): 269-78.
An excellent discussion of the two main theories of value elaborated by the Muʿtazilah and the followers of al-Ashʿarī theory over that of the Muʿtazilah.

1587 Izutsu, Toshihiko. The Concept of Belief in Islamic Theology. Tokyo: Keio Institute of Cultural and Linguistic Studies, 1965, 258 pp.
A semantic analysis of those concepts in Sunnī theology that relate to belief and its objects. Although one of the objectives of the work is to "present a detailed description of the historical process" out of which the concept of belief emerged, it does not. The study is difficult and not recommended for the beginner; for the advanced student, however, this study is basic. The appendix includes a translation of the chapter on faith from the ḥadīth collection of al-Bukhārī (see 1219). Indexes of persons, sects, and Arabic words.

1588 Kassem, Hammond. "The Idea of Justice in Islamic Philosophy." Diogenes 79 (1972): 81-108.
A very general introductory treatment of the problem of justice in Islamic theology, in the thought of Ibn Rushd (Averroes) and Ibn al-ʿArabī, with a comparison to the Western philosopher Leibniz.

1589 Rahman, Fazlur. Prophecy in Islam: Philosophy and Orthodoxy. London: Allen & Unwin, 1958, 118 pp.
Although the title might lead readers to expect a general study of prophecy in Islam, this book examines Muslim philosophers' formulations of prophetic revelation (as influenced by the Hellenistic philosophers) and how Muslim orthodoxy responded to it. It is a study of medieval Islamic philosophical psychology wherein the Muslim philosophers' theory of the intellect is analyzed. Clearly written, with copious notes. Index.

1590 Rosenthal, Franz. Knowledge Triumphant: The Concept of Knowledge in Medieval Islam. Leiden: Brill, 1970, 356 pp.
A comprehensive study on the concept of knowledge as it has been understood and expressed in various branches of Islamic thought and literature. A partly philosophical, partly historical investigation, this work reveals the central importance of the concept of knowledge in Islamic civilization. The author argues that

the concept of knowledge was dominant over all aspects of Muslim intellectual, spiritual, and social life and that, because of this, Islamic civilization made everlasting contributions to mankind. Index.

1591 Schacht, J. "New Sources for the History of Mohammadan Theology." Studia Islamica 1 (1953):23-42.
Although many of the "new sources" examined twenty-five years ago now have been edited and some translated, the article is still useful because it discusses important historical problems of Islamic theology that still remain, such as non-Islamic influences, the background of the freewill problem, the precedents of Ashʻariyyah theology, and the emergence of a "popular" orthodoxy.

1592 Swartz, Merlin. "Acquisition (Kasb) in Early Kalām." In Islamic Philosophy and the Classical Tradition: Essays Presented to R. Walzer on His Seventieth Birthday (see 1345), pp. 355-89.
A philological analysis of a central concept (kasb) related to the freewill problem in early Islamic theology. The author examines the significance of the term from pre-Islamic poetry through Muʻtazilī and Ashʻarī theologians. A technical article, not for the beginner. Extensive notes, including bibliography.

1593 The Encyclopaedia of Islam (see 20).
Among the numerous articles that have appeared to date, these few are cited: "Aḳīda" (M.W. Watt), (vol. 1, pp. 333-36); "Akhlāḳ" (R. Walzer), (vol. 1, pp. 325-29); "Allāh" (L. Gardet), (vol. 1, pp. 406-17); "ʻĀlam" (L. Gardet), (vol. 1, pp. 349-52); "ʻAmal" (L. Gardet), (vol. 1, pp. 427-29); "Dīn" (L. Gardet) (vol. 2, pp. 293-96); "Ḥaḳīḳa" (L. Gardet) (vol. 2, pp. 75-76); "Islām" (L. Gardet) (vol. 4, pp. 171-77); "al-ḳadāʼ wa'l-ḳadar" (L. Gardet) (vol. 4, pp. 365-67).

1594 Shorter Encyclopedia of Islam (see 22).
For theological ideas, movements, and theologians, consult "Dogmatics" under "Register of Subjects."

1595 Tritton, A.S. "The Speech of God." Studia Islamica 36 (1972):5-23.
Summaries of positions held by famous Muslim theologians (from earliest times to the nineteenth century) on the important issue of the relationship between God's attribute of speech and His essence; that is, Is His speech eternal or created? Interesting for those studying the problem of God's attributes.

1596 Van Ess, J. "The Logical Structure of Islamic Theology." In Logic in Classical Islamic Culture. Edited by G.E. von Grunebaum. Wiesbaden: Harrassowitz, 1970, pp. 21-51.
A fascinating but technical discussion on the kind of logic employed by Muslim theologians. The author analyzes systematically the nature of theological argument showing, among other things, that Stoic influence was greater than that of Aristotle. See also 2093, 2136.

1597 Watt, W. Montgomery. Free Will and Predestination in Early Islam. London: Luzac, 1948, 181 pp.
A study on aspects of the freedom-determinism controversy of the first three centuries of Islam. On the basis of a thorough examination of heresiographical writings and theological works, Watt "reconstructs" the early development of this central problem of Islam, arguing that the controversy arose within Islam and did not originate because of foreign (Christian) influences.

1598 _____. "The Origin of the Islamic Doctrine of Acquisition." Journal of the Royal Asiatic Society (1943):234-47.
An investigation into the idea of acquisition (kasb), a key concept in the freedom-determinism controversy, that shows that the notion was introduced into theological discussions long before al-Ashʻarī. For essentially the same treatment, see 1597.

1599 _____. "Some Muslim Discussions of Anthropomorphism." Transactions of the Glasgow University Oriental Society 13 (1947-49):1-10.
An analysis of key arguments formulated by Muslim theologians on the central problem of anthropomorphism (tashbīh). The study focuses on the doctrine that it is permissible to use anthropomorphism predicates of God, without explaining how they apply (bi-lā kayf) to Him.

EARLIEST DEVELOPMENTS (See also 1489-93, 1541-46)

1600 Frank, R.M. "The Neoplatonism of Ǧahm Ibn Ṣafwān." Le Museon 78 (1965):395-424.
An attempt to analyze the basic structure of Jahm Ibn Ṣafwān's thought in light of its Neoplatonic source, concluding that the school of thought (Jahmiyyah) founded by this early eighth-century thinker, in terms of its origins and its spirit, was "altogether incompatible with the basic spirit of Sunnī Islam, not only to those of the Ḥanbalī school but also to most of the systems of kalām" (p. 424).

1601 Guillaume, A. "Some Remarks on the Free Will and Predestination in Islam, Together with a Translation of the Kitabu-l Qadar from the Sahih of al-Bukhari." Journal of the Royal Asiatic Society (1924):43-63.
Useful for the translation of The Chapter on Qadar (predestination) from one of the canonical collections of the traditions of the Prophet. The position in this chapter, as in the other collections of ḥadīth, is thoroughly deterministic: God is the sole author of man's actions and decrees man's destiny before his existence. See also 1228.

1602 Madelung, W. "Early Sunni Doctrine concerning Faith as Reflected in the Kitāb al-Īmān of Abū ʻUbayd al-Qāsim b. Sallām (d. 224/839)." Studia Islamica 32 (1968):233-54.
A detailed examination of a document that sets forth one important early Muslim theory about faith, namely, that good actions should accompany intellectual assent and verbal confession. The study is a descriptive analysis of

the theory, and while of great value to the more advanced student, it is too difficult for the beginner.

1603 Obermann, J. "Political Theology in Early Islam: Ḥasan al-Baṣrī's Treatise on Qadar." Journal of the American Oriental Society 55 (1935):138-62.

An analysis of the earliest extant theological treatise in Islam, the famous epistle of al-Ḥasan al-Baṣrī to the caliph ʿAbd al-Malik (c. 700), in which he argues that humans are responsible for their acts.

1604 Pessagno, J.M. "The Murji'a, Īmān and Abu ʿUbayd." Journal of the American Oriental Society 95 (1975):382-94.

A brief study of the Murji'ah conception of faith based on heresiographical writings, with special attention given to the use of the word maʿrifah (knowledge) in Murji'ah terminology.

1605 Sahas, D.J. John of Damascus on Islam: The 'Heresy of the Ishmaelites.' Leiden: Brill, 1972, 171 pp.

A welcome study on the life of the great Christian theologian, John of Damascus (d. 750), written from the point of view of his contacts with Muslims, with an analysis of his attributed writings pertinent to Islam, including an examination of the section on the Muslim heresy from the De Haeresibus, with translation. Also translated (with Greek text) is the famous Disputatio Saraceni et Christiani. Extensive bibliography. Index.

1606 Schacht, J. "An Early Murci'ite Treatise: The Kitāb al-ʿAlim wa'l-Mutaʿallim." Oriens 17 (1964):96-117.

The article, although partly a technical discussion of textual problems, contains a very nice summary of the contents of a popular creed of the Murji'ah. This summary is interesting, because there are very few works in English that show the popular religious attitudes of early Islam.

1607 Schwarz, Michael. "The Letter of al-Ḥasan al-Baṣrī." Oriens 20 (1967):15-30.

An analysis of the treatise of al-Ḥasan al Baṣrī on the freewill problem. This study is useful because it examines the treatise (not yet published in English) in detail and argues that some major issues of later Islamic theology are discussed in this early theological writing.

1608 Van Ess, Josef. "The Beginnings of Islamic Theology." In The Cultural Context of Medieval Learning: Proceedings of the First International Colloquium on Philosophy, Science, and Theology in the Middle Ages, September 1973. Boston: D. Reidel, 1975, pp. 87-104.

An attempt to show that Islamic theology existed as early as the first century of Islam. The recorded discussion appended to the article raises important questions about the problem of the definitions of theology and kalām.

1609 _____. "Umar II and His Epistle against the Qadarīya." Abr-Nahrain 12 (1971-72):19-26.

A brief analysis of a letter written by ʿUmar Ibn ʿAbd al-ʿAzīz (d. 720) attacking those who upheld the freewill position in the freedom-determinism controversy. The study sheds light on a central theological controversy that had its beginnings in first-century Islam.

1610 Watt, W. Montgomery. "The Conception of Īmān in Islamic Theology." Islam 43 (1967):1-10.

An examination of the significance of īmān (faith) in early Islamic thought, particularly that of the Khawārij, Murji'ah, and the followers of al-Ashʿarī. With extensive notes and excellent summary.

1611 Wensinck, A.J. The Muslim Creed: Its Genesis and Historical Development. Cambridge: Cambridge University Press, 1932; London: Cass, 1962, 304 pp.

A classic study on early theological developments in Sunnī Islam by the Dutch scholar of ḥadīth literature. Wensinck analyzes the earliest discussions on faith, works, the "five pillars," eschatology and the meaning of Islam, using the canonical collections of the traditions of the Prophet as his basic source. After discussing key aspects of the theological enterprise (kalām), he turns to an analysis (translation and commentary) of three early creeds. One of the most important studies in Islamic theology, but outdated in some respects. The work should be read in light of Watt's The Formative Period of Islamic Thought (see 1576).

THE MUʿTAZILAH

1612 Frank, R.M. "The Divine Attributes according to the Teaching of Abū'l-Hudhayl al-ʿAllāf." Le Museon 82 (1969):451-506.

Like the majority of Frank's works, this one on divine attributes is a basic study on a very central problem in Islamic theology. The author gives attention to one significant early Muʿtazilī theologian whose thought was to become the most prominent and influential among all of the Muʿtazilah. This is not an introduction to the subject. It is difficult, technical, yet of great value for the advanced student interested in this fundamental problem of the kalām.

1613 _____. The Metaphysics of Created Being according to Abū l-Hudhayl al-ʿAllāf. Leiden: Nederlands Historisch-Archaeologisch Instituut in het Nabije Costen, 1966, 53 pp.

A technical exposition of an early Muʿtazilī theologian's (d. 841?) ontology of created being. The work is significant because it is one of the very few careful studies of the metaphysical system of the early kalām. It is a basic and essential study for those who are interested in Islamic theology as a theological system.

1614 _____. "Several Fundamental Assumptions of the Basra School of the Muʿtazilah." Studia Islamica 33 (1971):25-62.

A superb but difficult analysis of the idea held by certain Muʿtazilah that universally binding moral principles are known to all persons. The study is based upon the Mughnī of ʿAbd al-Jabbār (d. 1025).

1615 Hourani, George F. "Islamic and Non-Islamic Origins of Muʿtazilite Ethical Rationalism." International Journal of Middle Eastern Studies 7 (1976):59-87.
A critical assessment of non-Islamic systems of thought (Zoroastrianism, Manichaeism, Christianity, and Greek philosophy) that might have influenced early Islamic theological thought (here, Muʿtazilī views on ethics), plus an examination of the background of the Muʿtazilah movement itself. The author concludes that the Muʿtazilah chose whatever doctrines suited their views inside Islam, but were never overwhelmed by non-Islamic systems.

1616 Hourani, G.F. Islamic Rationalism: The Ethics of ʿAbd al-Jabbar. Oxford: Clarendon, 1971, 158 pp.
The basic analytical study on ethical theory in Islamic thought to date, this work is the first attempt to set out sytematically the ethics of ʿAbd al-Jabbār (d. 1025), the famous Muʿtazilī theologian. This reconstruction of the ethics of ʿAbd al-Jabbār alters our previous understanding of the Muʿtazilah and their place in Islamic thought. One feature of this study is the intriguing comparison of Muʿtazilī ethics with modern British intuitionism. Extensive notes and index.

1617 Jāḥiẓ, ʿAmr ibn Bahr al-. The Life and Works of Jāḥiẓ (see 204).
Included among the texts translated from the pen of the writer and Muʿtazilah theologian al-Jāḥiẓ (d. 868) are excerpts from his theological works.

1618 Nader, Albert. Le Système Philosophique des Muʿtazila. Beyrouth: Les Lettres Orientales, 1956, 354 pp.
Since no comprehensive study of Muʿtazilī thought exists in English, this work is cited; it covers the main theological arguments of the Muʿtazilah, casting some light on the teachings of the most notable thinkers of this important theological movement.

1619 Nyberg, H.S. "al-Mutazila." Shorter Encyclopedia of Islam (see 22), pp. 421-27.
On the origins, political background, and ideas of this major theological school in Islam. The article stresses the political history of the Muʿtazilah, but gives a good deal of attention to the central problems of Islamic theology as it sets forth Muʿtazilī doctrine.

1620 Peters, J.R.T.M. God's Created Speech: A Study of the Speculative Theory of the Muʿtazilī Qaḍī l-Quḍāt Abū l-Ḥasan ʿAbd al-Jabbār ibn Aḥmad al-Hamadānī. Leiden: E.J. Brill, 1976, 447 pp.
A systematic analysis of a central problem in Islamic theology based on the study of ʿAbd al-Jabbār's great work, the Mughnī. Much of the study is devoted to an exposition of this theologian's entire thought.

1621 Pines, Shlomo. "A Note on an Early Meaning of the Term Mutakallim." Israel Oriental Studies 1 (1971):224-40.
A thought-provoking study on the function of the early Muʿtazilī theologians (mutakallimin) that proposes a new working hypothesis: the discovery of the role of reason in establishing religious truths was due to the fact that some of the early Muʿtazilah "directed their attention to the technique of the debates in which they engaged with their Moslem and non-Moslem opponents, and in this way came to value both intuitive and discursive reason, not only as an instrument of insuring victory, but for its own sake" (p. 233).

1622 Schwarz, Michael. "Some Notes on the Notion of Iljāʾ in Muʿtazilite Kalām." Israel Oriental Studies 2 (1972):413-27.
A study of a key argument employed by the Muʿtazilah to meet the charge that they denied God's omnipotence when they argued that God does not will the evil actions of humans. A difficult but valuable study on one aspect of a central problem in Islamic theology.

1623 Tritton, A.S. "Some Muʿtazili Ideas about Religion, in Particular about Knowledge Based on General Report." Bulletin of the School of Oriental and African Studies 14 (1952): 612-22.
A summary of the contents and abridged translation of one section of a manuscript on the doctrines of the Muʿtazilah.

1624 Watt, W. Montgomery. "The Political Attitudes of the Muʿtazilah." Journal of the Royal Asiatic Society (1963):38-57.
A study of the origins of the Muʿtazilah based upon a critical evaluation of heresiographical writings and Muʿtazilī sources.

AL-ASHʿARĪ TO AL-GHAZĀLĪ

1625 Allard, M. Le Problème des attributs divins dans la doctrine d'al-Ashʿari et de ses premiers grands disciples. Recherches publiées sous la direction de l'Institut de Lettres Orientales de Beyrouth, tom 28. Beyrouth: Imprimerie Catholique, 1965, 450 pp.
The subject of analysis is the central problem of divine attributes in al-Ashʿarī through al-Juwaynī (d. 1085), which the author sets against the intellectual background of the time.

1626 Ashʿarī, Abu'l-Ḥasan al-. Al-Ibānah ʿan Usūl ad-Diyānah (The Elucidation of Islam's Foundation). Translated by W.C. Klein. New Haven, Conn.: American Oriental Society, 1940, 143 pp.
A translation of one of the earliest and most important dogmatic works in Islam, containing an exposition of beliefs followed by chapters on specific questions that al-Ashʿarī answers in light of the views of his opponents. The translation is preceded by a lengthy introduction on early Islamic theology.

1627 Ash'arī, al-. The Theology of al-Ash'arī: The Arabic Texts of al-Ash'arī's Kitāb al-Luma' and Risālat Istiḥsān al-Khaw fī 'Ilm al-Kalām. Translated by R.J. McCarthy. Beyrouth: Imprimerie Catholique, 1953, 284 pp.

A translation of two fundamental works by al-Ash'arī (d. 935), highlights of the Polemic against Deviators and Innovators, and A Vindication of the Science of Kalām, plus the Arabic texts. The appendixes are of special note: a defense (translated) of al-Ash'arī's position by Ibn 'Asakir (d. 1176); a list of works attributed to al-Ash'arī; and the translation of two creeds written by al-Ash'arī. One of the most important sources available for the study of Sunnī theology. Indexes.

1628 Baghdādī, al-. "The Logical Basis of Early Kalam." Translated by W.M. Watt. Islamic Quarterly 6 (1961):3-10; 7 (1963):13-39.

A translation with commentary of the first chapter of the Kitāb Uṣūl al-Dīn (Foundations of Religion) by 'Abd al-Qāhir al-Baghdādī (d. 1037), an Ash'arī theologian. The subject of the chapter is truth and knowledge in general and in particular, and the theory of knowledge expounded therein reflects the outlook of the Sunnī theologians before al-Ghazālī.

1629 Frank, R.M. "The Structure of Created Causality according to al-Ash'arī." Studia Islamica 25 (1966):13-75.

An analysis of the problem of human causality formulated by al-Ash'arī (d. 935) in his Kitāb al-Luma' (see 1630), which involves an examination of the terms and structure of the problem as al-Ash'arī formulated it and an elaboration of the "philosophical structure of his solution to it" (p. 16).

1630 Hourani, G. "Juwayni's Criticism of Mu'tazilite Ethics." Muslim World 65 (1975): 161-73.

A study on aspects of ethical theory in Islamic theology. Here the author carefully analyzes al-Juwaynī's (d. 1085) critique of his opponents' (the Mu'tazilah) arguments that challenged his voluntarist theory ("which relates the value of acts directly and entirely to attitudes of God as expressed in revelation" [p. 162]).

1631 Makdisi, G. "Ash'arī and the Ash'arites in Islamic Religious History." Studia Islamica 17 (1962):37-80; 18 (1963):19-39.

A study on the relationship between al-Ash'arī (d. 935) and Ash'arī orthodoxy; the author shows that the importance of so-called Ash'arī orthodoxy in the history of Islamic theology has been exaggerated and, consequently, the place of traditionalism in Islamic thought has been overlooked.

AL-GHAZĀLĪ (See also 1283-1307, 1426-40)

1632 Ghazālī, al-. Ghazālī's Book of Counsel for Kings (see 232).

1633 _____. Al-Ghazalī on Divine Predicates and Their Properties: A Critical and Annotated Translation of These Chapters in al-Iqtiṣād fī'l-i'tiqād. Translated by 'Abd-r-Raḥmān Abū Zayd. Lahore: S.M. Ashraf, 1970, 115 pp.

Although this is not a "critical and annotated translation," it is an English rendering of one part of a most important theological handbook, which represents the culmination of Ash'arī philosophical theology. The section translated is on divine attributes and their relation to God's essence.

1634 _____. Tahāfut al-Falāsifah, or Incoherence of the Philosophers. Translated by S.A. Kamali. Lahore: Pakistan Philosophical Congress, 1958, 267 pp.

Al-Ghazālī's most important philosophical-theological writing and one of the seminal works in the history of Islamic thought. Born out of a religious concern, the study attacks three (among others) basic philosophical propositions: the world is eternal; God knows universals only; resurrection of the dead is impossible. This work is of great significance for the study of the conflict between philosophy and theology in Islam.

1635 _____. "Al-Ghazalī's Tract on Dogmatic Theology." Edited and translated by A.L. Tibawi. Islamic Quarterly 9 (1965):65-122.

A brief examination of al-Ghazālī's stay in Damascus and Jerusalem, plus a translation of a treatise (al-Risālah al-Qudsiyyah) on the fundamentals of Islam. The purpose of the treatise is to uphold Sunnī orthodoxy by attacking the "innovations" (bid'ah) of the Mu'tazilah.

1636 _____. "Ghazālī on Ethical Premises." Translated by Michael Marmura. Philosophical Forum 1 (1968):393-403.

A translation of the section on ethical premises (premises that are not certain and are unusable in demonstrations) from al-Ghazālī's Mi'yār al-'Ilm (The Standard for Knowledge), preceded by an excellent introduction stating the problem.

1637 Goodman, L.E. "Ghazālī's Argument from Creation." International Journal of Middle East Studies 2 (1971):67-85, 168-88.

A clearly written analysis of al-Ghazālī's proofs for the existence of God with a discussion of the conflict of al-Ghazālī and Ibn Rushd over the problem of the creation of the world; the study is one of the few that examines carefully the key arguments of this central issue of Islamic theology and philosophy.

1638 Hourani, G.F. "The Chronology of Ghazali's Writings." Journal of the American Oriental Society 79 (1959):225-33.

A listing, in chronological order, of the works assumed to be authentic. The article is technical but useful for the nonspecialist who would like to get a bird's-eye view of the voluminous writings of al-Ghazālī.

1639 _____. "The Dialogue between al-Ghazālī and the Philosophers on the Origin of the World." Muslim World 48 (1958):183-91, 308-14.

A successful attempt to summarize and clarify the arguments employed by the Muslim philosophers and al-Ghazālī in the central debate on whether the world is eternal or not.

1640 Hourani, George F. "Ghazālī on the Ethics of Action." Journal of the American Oriental Society 96 (1976):69-89.

An analysis of one aspect of al-Ghazālī's ethical system (the ethics of conduct) based upon a study of the problem in three major writings of al-Ghazālī. The author argues that these writings reveal a consistent ethical theory of conduct.

1641 Marmura, Michael. "Ghazālī and Demonstrative Science." Journal of the History of Philosophy 3 (1965):183-204.

An analysis of al-Ghazālī's critique of causality and his defense of demonstrative science based upon his philosophical and theological writings.

1642 Quasem, M. Abul. "Al-Ghazālī's Conception of Happiness." Arabica 22 (1975):153-62.

After examining various passages on the notions of happiness and misery in al-Ghazālī's writings, the author attempts to establish al-Ghazālī's theory of happiness.

1643 Shehadi, Fadlou. Ghazali's Unique and Unknowable God (see 1300).

1644 Sherif, Mohamed Ahmed. Ghazālī's Theory of Virtue. Albany: State University of New York Press, 1975, 205 pp.

The only comprehensive analysis of al-Ghazālī's ethical system, based upon an examination of his major writings. The author shows that ethics is of capital importance in al-Ghazālī's entire system of thought, then sets out to examine the most important aspects of his ethical theory. He argues convincingly that al-Ghazālī blended philosophical, religious, and mystical elements together to form a coherent ethical system. An important contribution to the study of al-Ghazālī's thought.

1645 Watt, W. Montgomery. Muslim Intellectual: A Study of al-Ghazali. Edinburgh: Edinburgh University Press, 1963, 215 pp.

A general study of the life and times of al-Ghazālī. The book has considerable merit in that it relates the thinker to his own social context. Its weakness lies in the fact that the author gives a rather cursory and superficial treatment of the thought of one of Islamic civilization's greatest minds.

POST-AL-GHAZĀLĪ

1646 Fakhry, Majid. "Philosophy and Scripture in the Theology of Averroes." Medieval Studies 30 (1968):78-89.

An attempt to show that although Ibn Rushd (Averroes) was affiliated deeply with the philosophical tradition in Islam, on the specific problem of the relationship of philosophy and the Qur'ān he developed a method whereby he distinguished clearly between the spheres of philosophy and theology. Fakhry argues that Ibn Rushd has not been given the credit due to him as a systematic theologian.

1647 Hourani, G. "Averroes on Good and Evil." Studia Islamica 16 (1962):14-40.

An analysis of Ibn Rushd's theory of value based upon a reconstruction of it from those writings wherein he addressed himself to questions of good and evil. Hourani treats the theological problem of evil in Ibn Rushd and his theory of ethics.

1648 Ibn al-Nafīs. The Theologus Autodidactus of Ibn al-Nafīs. Edited and translated by M. Meyerhof and J. Schacht. Oxford: University Press, 1968, 148 pp.

This is a partial, free translation of a thirteenth-century theological allegory about a man called Perfect, a mythical prophet-scientist who discovers by himself the main tenets of Islam, the life story of the last prophet, and the fate of his community. It is a counterpart to Ibn Ṭufayl's Ḥayy ibn Yaqẓān, wherein a mythical figure discovers by himself philosophical and mystical truths. See also 1451.

1649 Ibn Rushd. Averroes: On the Harmony of Religion and Philosophy. A Translation, with Introduction and Notes, of Ibn Rushd's Kitāb Faṣl al-Maqāl, with Its Appendix and an Extract from Kitāb al-Kashi ʿan Manāhij al-Adilla. Translated by G. Hourani. London: Luzac, 1967, 128 pp. Gibb Memorial Series, n.s., no. 21.

The most direct and exhaustive harmonization of religion and philosophy that has survived from medieval Islam. Here Ibn Rushd (Averroes) defends philosophy, not as a philosopher, but as a jurist-scholar trying to prove that philosophy is sanctioned by the Qur'ān and that contradictions between the two are reconcilable. It is an excellent source for understanding the tension and conflict between philosophy on the one hand and law and theology on the other, as well as for gaining a good grasp of what a Muslim philosopher conceived philosophy to be. Superb introduction by Hourani.

1650 _____. Averroes' Tahāfut al-Tahāfut. 2 vols. Translated by Simon van der Bergh. London: Luzac, 1954, 1:374 pp.; 2:219 pp.

Volume 1 is the translation of Ibn Rushd's refutation of al-Ghazālī's critique of certain claims of philosophers (see 1634); volume 2 contains van der Bergh's exhaustive notes.

1651 Ījī, al-. Die Erkenntnislehre des ʿAdudaddin al-Īcī, Übersetzung und Kommentär des ersten Buches seiner Mawāqif. Translated by J. van Ess. Wiesbaden: Franz Steiner Verlag, 1966, 510 pp.

The most detailed, thorough, and exhaustive study on Islamic theology to date. The work is more than a translation and commentary of al-Ījī's (d. 1355) theological writing (Kitāb al-Mawāqif fī ʿIlm al-Kalām); it investigates through lengthy digressions theological issues pertinent to the study of Islamic theology as a whole. Massive indexes along with the most extensive bibliography on Islamic theology to the time of publication.

1652 Maimonides, Moses. The Guide of the Perplexed. Translated with an introduction and notes by Saloman Pines. Introductory essay by Leo Strauss. Chicago: University of Chicago Press, 1963, 658 pp.

The authoritative English translation of the great Jewish thinker's (d. 1204) philosophical work containing expositions on the thought of Muslim theologians. He argues against many of the claims of the theologians while supporting others, including an exposition of atomism (occasionalism) according to kalām theology. The introduction by Pines is an excellent survey of the important Muslim philosophers and theologians who contributed to Maimonides's thought. Glossary of technical Arabic terms.

1653 Rāzī, al-. A Study of Fakhr al-Dīn al-Rāzī and His Controversies in Transoxiana. Translated by Fahallah Khaleif. Beirut: Dar el-Machreq, 1966, 297 pp.

A translation and commentary of Fakhr al-Dīn al-Rāzī's Munāẓarāt (The Controversies), a type of autobiography in which the author examines sixteen questions that arose during his travels. Although much of the text deals with difficult problems of law, he addresses himself to problems of Islamic theology, such as the question of God's attributes. The translation is valuable, since it is the only work that we have of this celebrated theologian in English. The commentary to the text is helpful, but the introduction is much too brief. Bibliography and index.

1654 Taftāzānī, al-. A Commentary on the Creed of Islam: Saʿīd ad-din al-Taftāzānī on the Creed of Naim al-din al-Nasafi. Translated by E.E. Elder. New York: Columbia, 1950, 187 pp.

A translation, with introduction and notes, of a commentary by al-Taftāzānī (d. 1389) on the creed of Abu'l-Muʿīn al-Nasafī, with a discussion of al-Taftāzānī's accommodation of al-Nasafī to Ashʿarī theology.

ANTISPECULATIVE THOUGHT

1655 Goldziher, Ignaz. The Ẓāhirīs: Their Doctrine and Their History. Translated by W. Behn. Leiden: E.J. Brill, 1971, 227 pp.

This is the authoritative study of the legal-theological school, the Ẓāhiriyyah, first published in German in 1884. In it Goldziher examines critically and in detail the basic tenets of jurisprudence and theology in one of the central traditionalist, antispeculative movements of early medieval Islamic thought. The study reveals that the Ẓāhirīs were not simple-minded literalists but rigorous systematic thinkers who were concerned with preserving the authority of the Qur'ān. This work is fascinating and rewarding, but as with most of Goldziher's books, slow-going. Bibliography (1884 vintage) and index.

1656 Ibn Qudāma. Censure of Speculative Theology: An Edition and Translation of Ibn Qudāma's Taḥrīm an-Nazar fī Kutub Ahl al-Kalām, with Introduction and Notes; A Contribution to the Study of Islamic Religious History. Translated by George Makdisi. London: Luzac, 1962, 129 pp.

Ibn Qudāma (d. 1223), a Ḥanbalī theologian, attacks all manner of speculation about religious belief and views kalām (speculative theology) as a basic evil. The treatise illuminates one of the most basic controversies in Islamic theological thought, namely, the use of allegorical interpretation of Qur'ānic verses pertaining to divine attributes. Ibn Qudāma writes against that position, affirming a literal interpretation of the verses as they stand. Good introduction and notes.

1657 Ibn al-Jawzī. Kitāb al-Quṣṣāṣ wa'l Mudhakkirīn. Translated by Merlin J. Swartz. Beyrouth: Dar al-Machrez, 1971, 437 pp.

Ibn al-Jawzī was a twelfth-century Muslim of Baghdād who was famous as an eloquent preacher and wrote what is perhaps the earliest manual on the art of "religious storytelling" (quṣṣāṣ), or preaching. This recent translation, with an excellent introduction and notes, is a basic source for understanding more of the religious history of medieval Islam. This aspect of Muslim religious history has been given little attention by Western scholars, thus making Swartz's study and translation crucially important. Detailed bibliography of basic sources.

1658 Ibn Taymiyyah. "A Seventh-Century (A.H.) Sunnī Creed: The ʿAqīda Wāṣitīya of Ibn Taymiyyah." Translated by Merlin Swartz. In Humaniora Islamica: An Annual Publication of Islamic Studies and the Humanities 1 (1974): 91-131.

A brief sketch of the life and thought of Ibn Taymiyyah, plus a translation of his famous creed setting forth orthodox beliefs, with extensive notes.

1659 _____. Ibn Taymiyyah's Struggle against Popular Religion: With an Annotated Translation of his Kitāb iqtiḍā' as-ṣirāṭ al-mustaqīm mukhālafat aṣḥāb al-jaḥīm. Translated by Muhammad Umar Memon. The Hague: Mouton, 1976, 423 pp.

A study of the reformist Ḥanbalī theologian-jurist's attack against what he considered to be "heretical novelties" (bidʿāt) in the thought and practice of Islam, especially in popular Sufism. The largest portion of the book (pp. 89-375) contains the translation of Ibn Taymiyyah's The Necessity of the Straight Path against the People of Hell. With extensive notes, bibliography, and a glossary of Arabic terms.

1660 Laoust, H. "Aḥmad b. Ḥanbal." In EI2. Vol. 1 (see 20), pp. 272-77.
The best general survey in English of the great traditionalist and founder of one major school of law, covering his life, works, and doctrines.

1661 Patton, W.M. Aḥmad b. Ḥanbal and the Miḥna. Leiden: E.J. Brill, 1897, 208 pp.
Still an important study on the great theologian-jurist and traditionalist of ninth-century Baghdad and his role in the famous controversy over the problem of the authority of the Qur'ān that led to the short-lived Mu'tazilī Inquisition (Miḥna). A reprint would be well received.

1662 Tritton, A.S. "Ibn Hazm: The Man and the Thinker." Islamic Studies 3 (1964):471-84.
A concise essay on important aspects of the thought of Ibn Ḥazm (d. 1064), based largely on his heresiographical work, Kitāb al-Fiṣal fī'l-Milal wa'l-Niḥal.

MODERN ISLAM

GENERAL STUDIES

1663 'Azzām, 'Abd-al-Raḥmān. The Eternal Message of Muḥammad (see 1070).

1664 Charnay, Jean-Paul. Islamic Culture and Socio-Economic Change. Social, Economic and Political Studies of the Middle East, vol. 4. Leiden: E.J. Brill, 1971, 81 pp.
A series of lectures of a theoretical nature on social and economic aspects of Islamic culture; the author attempts to identify the enduring trends of thought and action in the evolution of Islam. See also 2064.

1665 Cragg, Kenneth. Counsels in Contemporary Islam. Edinburgh: University of Edinburgh Press, 1965, 255 pp.
A good, solid introduction to the important religious movements and key personages of contemporary Islam that takes into account the Arab East, Turkey, Pakistan, and India. Excellent bibliographies for each of the twelve chapters.

1666 Fyzee, A.A.A. A Modern Approach to Islam. Bombay: Times of India, 1963, 127 pp.
Four essays setting forth a reinterpretation of Islam by the outstanding contemporary modernist Muslim scholar of Islamic law. The first essay is a good outline of the modern interpretation of Islam as expressed by the Indian modernist Muslim author Abū'l-Kalām Āzād (d. 1958). The second defines and distinguishes religion and law in Islam, while the third describes the contribution of some important Indian thinkers to Islamic law and theology. The final essay is the author's own interpretation of Islam.

1667 Geertz, Clifford. Islam Observed: Religious Development in Morocco and Indonesia (see 848).

1668 Gibb, H.A.R. "The Heritage of Islam in the Modern World." International Journal of Middle East Studies 1 (1970):221-37; 2 (1972): 129-47.
An analysis of the heritage of Islam (understood here as a socio-politico-religous system) in the modern world. Gibb offers an interpretation of the modern significance of the caliphate in relation to constitutional theory, the social orders in Islam (special attention is devoted to the role of Ṣūfī brotherhoods), Islamic law and modern times, social institutions (particularly marriage), religious organization, and education.

1669 _____. Modern Trends in Islam (see 502).

1670 Hodgson, M.G.S. The Venture of Islam. Vol. 3 (see 29), pp. 165-441.
Book 6, "The Islamic Heritage in the Modern World," is a comprehensive study of modern Islam covering Turkey, the Arab world, Iran, Russia, India, and Pakistan. Highly recommended.

1671 Keddie, Nikki R., ed. Scholars, Saints, and Sufis (see 506).

1672 Leiden, Carl, ed. The Conflict of Traditionalism and Modernism in the Middle East. Austin: University of Texas, 1966, 160 pp.
Of the eleven essays presented on various problems related to the modern Middle East, three are relevant here: "Some Aspects of Religious Reform in the Muslim Middle East" (Osman Amin), "Remarks on Traditionalism in Islamic Religious History" (George Makdisi), and "Some Recent Constructions and Reconstructions of Islam" (G.E. von Grunebaum).

1673 Merad, A. et al. "Iṣlāḥ." In EI2. Vol. 4 (see 20), pp. 141-71.
Discusses the dynamics of reform in the Arab world, Iran, Turkey, India, Pakistan, and Central Asia by examining the principal doctrinal tenets of key reformists, both modernists and so-called revivalists.

1674 Rahman, Fazlur. "Islam and the Problem of Economic Justice." Pakistan Economist (1974):14-36.
A thought-provoking essay that proposes a reformulation of Islamic principles of social and economic justice that would enable Muslim peoples to create an economic system independent of capitalism and communism. The central focus of this study is "a discussion of the principle and conceptual instruments given by the Qur'ān and other Islamic sources explicitly or implicitly for economic creativity and equitable distribution of wealth" (pp. 22-23).

1675 _____. "Islamic Modernism: Its Scope, Method, and Alternatives." International Journal of Middle East Studies 1 (1970): 317-33.
An excellent analysis that explores the various types of modernist approaches to Islam and offers a critical appraisal of each.

1676 Rodinson, Maxime. Islam and Capitalism. Translated by Brian Pearce. New York: Pantheon, 1973, 308 pp.
A fascinating Marxist analysis (explained in the foreword) of Islam and capitalism, theoretical in nature and polemical in intent. Rodinson asks (and attempts to answer) questions such as: Does Islam (past and present) favor capitalism, socialism, or feudalism? Or is it neutral to such economic systems? Is there implied in Islam some new economic system? Why have many Muslim countries accepted capitalism? What are the connections between economic, political, and religious systems? Extensive notes and bibliography.

1677 Rosenthal, E.I.J. Islam in the Modern National State (see 473).

1678 Smith, W.C. Islam in Modern History (see 510).

THE ARAB WORLD

The Wahhābiyyah

1679 Burckhardt, John Lewis. Notes on the Bedouins and Wahabys Collected during His Travels in the East. Vol. 2. London: Coulbourn & Bentley, 1831, pp. 95-391. Reprint. Johnson Reprint, 1967.
A vivid description of Wahhābī beliefs and various aspects of the political, social, and economic life of early nineteenth-century Wahhābī Arabia by one of the great travelers of the last century.

1680 Doughty, Charles M. Travels in Arabia Deserta (see 626).
Scattered throughout this famous report of a traveler's journey through Arabia are narratives about different aspects of the Wahhābī movement at the turn of the century.

1681 Laoust, H. "Ibn ʿAbd al-Wahhab." In EI2. Vol. 3 (see 20), pp. 677-79.
A brief sketch of the life of the founder of the Arabian Wahhābī movement.

1682 Margoliouth, D.S. "Wahhābīya." In Shorter Encyclopedia of Islam (see 22), pp. 618-21.
Analysis of the history and doctrines of the Wahhābīs of Arabia, plus a short account of the movement in India. Bibliography.

1683 Musil, Alois. Northern Negd. American Geographical Society--Oriental Explorations and Studies, no. 5. New York: Statni Tisharna, 1928, 368 pp.
Contains an account of the Wahhābīs of Arabia with particular emphasis upon the role of the Ikhwān communities in reviving the religious doctrines of the Wahhābīs.

1684 Phoenix. "A Brief Outline of the Wahabi Movement." Journal of the Central Asian Society 27 (1930):401-16.
A summary account with emphasis on the military role of the Ikhwān (brotherhood) of ʿAbd al-Azīz Ibn Saʿūd (d. 1953).

1685 Rentz, George. "The Wahhābīs." In Religion in the Middle East. Vol. 2 (see 9), pp. 270-85.
A good introductory essay on the Wahhābīs of Arabia with a short summary of the impact of the movement outside Arabia. Bibliography. See also "Ikhwān," in EI2, vol. 3 (see 20), pp. 1064-68.

1686 Voll, John. "Muḥammad Ḥayyā al-Sindī and Muḥammad Ibn ʿAbd al-Wahhāb: An Analysis of an Intellectual Group in Eighteenth Century Madīna." Bulletin of the School of Oriental and African Studies 38 (1975):32-40.
A brief discussion of the life and role of the teacher of Ibn ʿAbd al-Wahhāb.

Jamāl al-Dīn al-Afghānī

1687 Ahmad, Aziz. "Afghani's Indian Contacts." Journal of the American Oriental Society 89 (1969):476-91.
An attempt to assess the actual influence al-Afghānī had on Muslim India by examining, in part, letters to al-Afghānī from his Indian friends. The author argues that al-Afghānī's impact on India was limited until the end of the 1880s and that his influence on Indian Pan-Islamic trends did not fully develop until the twentieth century.

1688 Hourani, Albert. Arabic Thought in the Liberal Age, 1789-1939 (see 557).
Includes two chapters on Jamāl al-Dīn al-Afghānī and Muḥammad ʿAbduh.

1689 Keddie, Nikki R. An Islamic Response to Imperialism: Political and Religious Writings of Sayyid Jamāl ad-Din 'al-Afghānī.' Berkeley: University of California Press, 1968, 212 pp.
The value of this work is found in the translations of certain writings of al-Afghānī, including the famous Refutation of the Materialists, as well as the analysis of his thought.

1690 _____. Sayyid Jamāl ad-Dīn ʿal-Afghānīʾ: A Political Biography (see 505).

1691 Kedourie, Elie. Afghani and Abduh: An Essay on Religious Unbelief and Political Activism in Modern Islam (see 507).

1692 Kudsi-Zadeh, A.A. "Islamic Reform in Egypt: Some Observations on the Role of Afghani." Muslim World 61 (1971):1-12.
An attempt to convey a clear picture of al-Afghānī's reformist role in late nineteenth-century Egypt, particularly in the field of education. See also 509.

Muḥammad ʿAbduh

1693 ʿAbduh, Muḥammad. The Theology of Unity. Translated by Isḥāq Mūsa al-Husaini and Kenneth Cragg. London: Allen & Unwin, 1966, 164 pp.
Muḥammad ʿAbduh's most systematic work and one of the most influential Muslim theological writings of the contemporary period. Written from within the tradition of medieval Islamic

theology, this work sets the example for modern theological writing in Islam. The essentials of ʿAbduh's modernist thought, found scattered in many other writings, are contained in this treatise. Index.

1694 Adams, Charles C. Islam and Modernism in Egypt: A Study of the Modern Reform Movement Inaugurated by Muhammad Abduh (see 743).

1695 Kerr, Malcolm. Islamic Reform: The Political Theories of Muhammad Abduh and Rashid Rida. Berkeley: University of California Press, 1966, 249 pp.

A basic study on Islamic reform that analyzes classical theories of law and government in Islam and the attempts by Muḥammad ʿAbduh and Rashīd Riḍā to reform them. The work contains an excellent summary of Muḥammad ʿAbduh's theories on reason and revelation and his theology of natural law. Extensive notes, bibliography, and index. See also 1981.

al-Ikhwān al-Muslimūn (Muslim Brotherhood)

1696 Delanoue, G. "Al-Ikhwān al-Muslimūn." In EI2. Vol. 3 (see 20), pp. 1068-71.

An outline of the origin and thought of the Muslim Brethren of Egypt.

1697 Harris, C.P. Nationalism and Revolution in Egypt: The Role of the Muslim Brotherhood (see 732).

1698 Heyworth-Dunne, James. Religious and Political Trends in Modern Egypt (see 756).

1699 Husaini, Ishak Musa al-. The Moslem Brethren: The Greatest of Modern Islamic Movements (see 734).

1700 Mitchell, Richard P. The Society of the Muslim Brothers (see 739).

1701 Quṭb, Sayyid. Social Justice in Islam. Translated by J.B. Hardie. Washington: American Council of Learned Societies, 1953, 282 pp.

A translation of a work expounding the basic ideas upon which the policies of the Muslim Brotherhood rest, especially the interpretation of social justice in Islam.

1702 Sibāʿī, Muṣṭafā as-. "Islam as a State Religion: A Muslim Brotherhood View in Syria." Translated by R.B. Winder. Muslim World 44 (1954):215-26.

A translation of an article first published in Arabic in 1950, by one of the leaders of the Syrian branch of the Muslim Brotherhood who argues for the establishment of Islam as the state religion of Syria. A clear exposition of the position of the Brotherhood on a fundamental problem in modern Islam.

IRAN (See also 1526-35)

1703 Algar, Hamid. "The Oppositional Role of the Ulama in Twentieth Century Iran." In Scholars, Saints, and Sufis (see 506), pp. 231-57.

Published in 1972, this is a landmark study that defines the political theory of Ithnā ʿAsharī Shīʿī Islam. "It is the dual purpose of this paper to delineate the chief religious and doctrinal considerations that have inspired the persistent opposition of the ulama to monarchical absolutism, and to examine the expression of that opposition in the present century, particularly in the last decade" (p. 232).

1704 Keddie, Nikki R. "The Origins of the Religious-Radical Alliance in Iran." Past and Present 34 (1966):70-80.

Recognizing that one fundamental characteristic of Iran since 1890 is "the appearance of peculiar alliances between part of the religious leaderships and the liberal or radical nationalist elements of the country in opposition to the government" (p. 70), Keddie attempts to discover how this came about. Readers should consult also the author's Religion and Rebellion in Iran: The Iranian Tobacco Protest of 1891-1892 (see 876) and Sayyid Jamāl ad-Dīn al-ʿAfghānī': A Political Biography (see 505).

1705 Keddie, N.R. "The Roots of the Ulama's Power in Modern Iran." In Scholars, Saints, and Sufis (see 506), pp. 211-29. Studia Islamica 29 (1969):31-53.

A concise analysis of several hypotheses that purport to explain the bases of power among the highest religious authorities (the mujtahids) during the period just before the constitutional revolution. Specifically, the question asked is, "Why have the modern Iranian ʿulamāʾ exercised and retained so much more political power than the ulama of other Middle Eastern countries?" (p. 211).

1706 Lambton, A.K.S. "The Persian ʿUlamā and Constitutional Reform." In Le Shiʿisme Imamite: Colloque de Strasbourg (6-9 mai, 1968). Edited by Toufic Fahd. Paris: Presses Universitaires de France, 1970, pp. 245-69.

A fundamental study analyzing how the ʿulamaʾ became the leaders of the popular movement that contributed greatly to the constitutional revolution of 1905-1906. The study traces key elements in Shīʿī political theory and practice, and examines the relations between the religious classes and the merchants, craft guilds, and peasants. It investigates the causes of discontent (and finally action) among the ʿulamāʾ and nationalists; political and social changes and economic dislocations resulting from foreign exploitation are counted as significant.

1707 _____. "A Reconsideration of the Position of the Marjaʿ al-Taqlīd and the Religious Institution." Studia Islamica 20 (1964):115-35.

An analysis of several papers presented by prominent Shīʿī leaders in 1960-1961 on the subject of the selection and functions of the marjaʿ al-taqlīd (authoritative source of imitation for guidance on spiritual as well as political matters). Authors of papers analyzed include Mehdī Bāzargān, Sayyid Maḥmūd Ṭāliqānī, Murtaḍā Muṭahharī and Sayyid Muḥammad Bihishtī. Lambton's analysis shows clearly that these writers hold that the main function of the marjaʿ al-taqlīd is concerned with social and political issues, not the religious practices of the individual believer. This study should be examined in light of H. Algar's "The Oppositional Role of the Ulama in Twentieth Century Iran" (see 1703).

1708 Millward, G.W. "Aspects of Modernism in Shīʿa Islam" (see 1533).

1709 Thaiss, Gustav. "Religious Symbolism and Social Change: The Drama of Husain." In Scholars, Saints, and Sufis (see 506), pp. 349-66.
A discussion of the place of Ḥusayn's martyrdom at Karbalā' in Shīʿī rituals performed in present-day Iran, based on anthropological fieldwork in the bazaar in Tehran. The author shows that the narrations describing the teachings of Ḥusayn and the sermons on Ḥusayn's struggle against oppressive rule offered by preachers during the rituals convey political meaning that is directly applicable to the sociopolitical situation of the Pahlavi regime.

TURKEY

1710 Berkes, Niyazi. The Development of Secularism in Turkey (see 896).

1711 Gökalp, Ziya. Turkish Nationalism and Western Civilization: Selected Essays of Ziya Gökalp (see 898).

1712 Heyd, Uriel. The Foundations of Turkish Nationalism: The Life and Teaching of Z. Gökalp (see 899).

1713 Lewis, Bernard. "Islamic Revival in Turkey." International Affairs 18 (1952):38-48.
Although dated, this essay is useful for its discussion of the growth of religious revival in Turkey during the 1940s.

1714 Schimmel, Annemarie. "Islam in Turkey." In Religion in the Middle East. Vol. 2 (see 9), pp. 68-95.
A survey of Islam focusing upon the religious life of present-day Turkey, written by one who has lived and taught in that country for a considerable time. Good bibliography.

INDIA, PAKISTAN, AND BANGLADESH

General Studies

1715 Abbott, Freeland. Islam and Pakistan (see 1006).

1716 Ahmad, Aziz. Islamic Modernism in India and Pakistan, 1857-1964 (see 989).

1717 ____, and G.E. von Grunebaum, eds. Muslim Self-statement in India and Pakistan, 1857-1968 (see 988).
This anthology contains selections from the basic writings of Sayyid Aḥmad Khān; Ghirāgh ʿAli Muḥammad Qāsim Nānotawī; Mirzā Ghulām Aḥmad of Qādian; Mirzā Bashīr al-Dīn Maḥmūd; Ṣiddiq Ḥasan Khān; Shiblī Nuʿmānī; Khwāja Alṭāf Ḥusayn Ḥālī; Amīr ʿAlī; Mawlānā Muḥammad ʿAli; Abū'l-Kalām Āzād; Muḥammad Iqbāl; Muḥammad ʿAlī Jinnāh; Abū'l-Aʿlā Mawdūdī; Ghulām Aḥmad Parwēz; Khalīfah ʿAbd al-Ḥakīm; A.A.A. Fyzee; Moḥammad Ayūb Khān; and extracts from the constitution of Pakistan. Chapter 1 contains an indispensable annotated bibliography of the most important Indo-Pakistani thinkers, their writings, and Western studies on them, from the beginning of the eighteenth century to the present.

1718 Hardy, Peter. The Muslims of British India (see 992).

1719 ____. Partners in Freedom and True Muslims: The Political Thought of Some Muslim Scholars in British India, 1912-1947. Scandinavian Institute of Asian Studies, no. 5. Lund: Student Litteratur, 1972, 63 pp.
An essay on the politico-religious ideas of certain Muslim scholars who joined with non-Muslims in the struggle against the British. In particular the study focuses upon Abū'l-Kalām Āzād and members of the Jamʿiyyāt al-ʿUlamā-i Hind and the chief spokesman of that society. In this brief but thoughtful essay, Hardy tries to connect their ideas with the earlier Islamic tradition and examines their views on the role of Islamic law in modern society. Explanatory notes and glossary of Arabic and Sanskrit terms.

1720 Ikram, S.M. Modern Muslim India and the Birth of Pakistan (see 996).

1721 McDonough, Sheila. The Authority of the Past: A Study of Three Muslim Modernists. Chambersburg, Pa.: American Academy of Religion, 1970, 56 pp.
An examination of the thought of Sayyid Aḥmad Khān, Muḥammad Iqbāl, and Ghulām Aḥmad Parwēz on the question of what aspects of the Islamic heritage should be authoritative for Muslims today. Notes and short bibliography.

1722 Qureshi, I.H., and S.N. Hay. "Modern India and Pakistan." In Sources of Indian Tradition (see 85), pp. 739-82, 827-77.
Selected writings from works of nineteenth- and twentieth- century Indian Muslim thinkers with brief introductory comments by Qureshi. Represented are Sayyid Aḥmad Khān, Muḥammad Iqbāl, Muḥammad ʿAlī Jinnah, Mawdūdī, and others.

1723 Rahman, Fazlur. "Muslim Modernism in the Indo-Pakistan Sub-Continent." Bulletin of the School of Oriental and African Studies 21 (1958):82-99.
A study on the origin and development of Islamic modernism in Indo-Pakistan, along with an analysis of the main intellectual trends in modern Indian Islam.

1724 Smith, W.C. Modern Islam in India: A Social Analysis (see 1004).

Individual Thinkers and Movements

Shāh Walī Allāh

1725 Ahmad, Aziz. "Political and Religious Ideas of Shah Walī-Ullāh of Delhi." Muslim World 52 (1962):22-30.
A concise examination of Shāh Walī Allāh's (d. 1762) contribution to modernist thinking in Muslim India.

1726 Jalbani, G.N. Teachings of Shah Waliyullah of Delhi. Lahore: Ashraf, 1967, 199 pp.
A reliable introduction.

1727 Walī Allāh, Shāh. A Mystical Interpretation of Prophetic Tales by an Indian Muslim: Shāh Walī Allāh's 'Ta'wīl al-Aḥādīth' (see 1461).

1728 _____. "Shāh Walī Ullāh and Ijtihād: A Translation of Selected Passages from His 'Iqd al-Jīd Aḥkām al-Ijtihād wa'l-Taqlīd." Translated by Daud Rahbar. Muslim World 45 (1955):346-58.
A translation of passages from a source that reveals his positive attitude toward ijtihād (original thinking in forming legal opinions).

1729 _____. "Shāh Walī Allāh's Last Testament: al-Maqāla al-Waḍiyya fī al-Naṣīḥa wa al-Waṣiyya." Translated by Hafeez Malik. Muslim World 63 (1973):105-18.
Shāh Walī Allāh's (d. 1762) farewell address ("a lucid epistle in advice and counsel"), which highlights his views on Islamic law and mysticism.

Mujāhidīn (Wahhābī Movement of India)

1730 Ahmad, Queyamuddin. The Wahabi Movement in India. Calcutta: K.L. Mukhopadhyay, 1966, 391 pp.
A comprehensive analysis of the politico-religious history of the Wahhābī (Mujāhidīn) movement in nineteenth-century India.

1731 Bari, M.A. "A Nineteenth-Century Muslim Reform Movement in India." In Arabic and Islamic Studies in Honor of H.A.R. Gibb (see 1492), pp. 84-102.
A well-documented study on the Wahhābiyyah of India, with attention devoted to the reformist teachings of its founder, Sayyid Aḥmad Barelawī, in light of the political background.

1732 _____. "The Politics of Sayyid Ahmad Barelwi." Islamic Culture 31 (1957):156-64.
An attempt to show that the nineteenth-century Muslim Indian reformist movement of Sayyid Aḥmad Barelawī, often referred to as the Wahhābī movement of India, was not an offshoot of the eighteenth-century Arabian movement of the same name.

1733 Hunter, W.W. The Indian Musulmans. Lahore: Premier Book House, 1964, 165 pp. Orig. pub. in 1871.
An important source on the Mujāhidīn movement in India. The author, a member of the Bengal civil service, analyzes this "treasonable organization" in detail, as a part of a report to Governor-General Mayo. Aside from much information on this movement, the book sets forth in bold relief the attitudes held by some British colonizers of India regarding their Muslim subjects.

Sayyid Aḥmad Khān

1734 Aḥmad Khān. "Sir Sayyid Aḥmad Khān's 'The Controversy over Abrogation' (in the Qur'ān): An Annotated Translation." Translated by Ernest Hahn. Muslim World 64 (1974):124-33.
A translation of a treatise in which Aḥmad Khān argues that the problem of abrogation (naskh) does not apply to the Qur'ān, but only to previous scriptures.

1735 Baljon, J.M.S. The Reforms and Religious Ideas of Sir Sayyid Ahmad Khan. Leiden: E.J. Brill, 1949, 101 pp. 3d rev. ed. Lahore: Muhammad Ashraf, 1964, 160 pp.
The first biographical study in English of the midnineteenth-century Indian Muslim modernist, this study still stands as an outstanding systematic introduction to the man, his thought, and his background. The study is strengthened by the fact that it is based upon Aḥmad Khān's Urdu writings as well as his English works. Bibliography.

1736 Nizami, K.A. Sayyid Ahmad Khan. Delhi: Government of India, 1966, 184 pp.
An account of the life and thought of Sayyid Aḥmad Khān based upon numerous sources including previously unexamined letters of Aḥmad Khān. Includes a chronology of his life and bibliography.

1737 Rawlinson, H.G. "Sayyid Ahmad Khān." Islamic Culture 4 (1930):386-96.
A glowing biographical sketch of Sayyid Aḥmad Khān.

1738 Shah, Mohammad, ed. Writings and Speeches of Sir Syed Ahmad Khan. Bombay: Nachiketa Publications, 1972, 272 pp.
A collection of writings, from various sources (speeches and letters), by Aḥmad Khān, including some translations from his non-English writing. Accurate quotation of sources is lacking.

1739 Shah, Muhammad. Sir Syed Ahmad Khan: A Political Biography. Meerut, India: Meenakshi Prakashan, 1969, 272 pp.
A biography that attempts to establish that Aḥmad Khān was an Indian nationalist.

1740 Topa, I.N. "Sir Sayyid Ahmad Khan: A Study in Social Thought." Islamic Culture 27 (1953):225-41.
A sympathetic, straightforward analysis of Sayyid Aḥmad Khān's progressive theories of morality, society, and civilization and the role of the individual in regenerating society.

Amīr ʻAlī

1741 ʻAlī, Syed Ameer. "Memoirs." Islamic Culture 6 (1931):509-42; 6 (1932):1-18, 163-82, 333-62, 504-25.
The autobiography of Amīr ʻAlī, fascinating and superbly written.

1742 _____. The Spirit of Islam: A History of the Evolution and Ideals of Islam. London: Chatto & Windus, 1964, 515 pp.
This work, first published in 1891, is a classic study and one of the basic sources for understanding the liberal modernist Muslim interpretation of Islam. Addressed to the non-Muslim English language reader, it defends Islam against the attacks of Western critics. Beautifully written, it is one of the outstanding apologetic works in the history of Islam.

1743 Aziz, K.K. Ameer ʻAli: His Life and Work. Lahore: Publishers United, 1968, 684 pp.
The first part of this work is a biography of Amīr ʻAlī (pp. 1-119) and constitutes the longest biography of this important Indian Muslim. Part 2 (pp. 119-663) is a collection of articles written by Amīr ʻAlī gathered from various journals and newspapers. Bibliography of writings included.

Muḥammad Iqbāl

1744 Dar, Bashir Ahmad. A Study in Iqbal's Philosophy. Lahore: Chulam Ali & Sons, 1971, 329 pp.
Essays on various aspects of Iqbāl's thought, including chapters on his theory of art, thinkers who influenced him, and his theories of society.

1745 Houben, J.J. "The Individual in Democracy and Iqbal's Conception of Khudi." In Crescent and Green: A Miscellany of Writings on Pakistan. London: Cassell, 1955, pp. 142-61.
An illuminating interpretation of Iqbāl's theory of khudī (self-consciousness), which is a central concept in his theories of the individual and society. The study is based upon Iqbāl's Reconstruction of Religious Thought in Islam. See 1749.

1746 Iqbāl, Muḥammad. Javid-Nama. Translated by A.J. Arberry. London: Allen & Unwin, 1966, 151 pp.
A translation of Iqbāl's greatest poem, The Book of Eternity, inspired by Dante's Divine Comedy, and considered to be one of the finest examples of poetry in the Persian language.

1747 _____. The Mysteries of Selflessness. Translated by A.J. Arberry. London: Murray, 1953, 92 pp.
Translation of the Rumūz-i-Bikhūdī, a philosophical poem that continues Iqbāl's conception of individuality, as developed first in the Asrār-i khūdī (see 1750). Here he stresses the relationship between the individual and the state.

1748 _____. Persian Psalms. Pts. 1 and 2. Translated by A.J. Arberry. Lahore: Ashraf, 1948, 127 pp.
Translation of the Zabur-i ʻAjam (Persian Psalms).

1749 _____. The Reconstruction of Religious Thought in Islam. Lahore: Ashraf, 1934, 205 pp.
A summation of the theological-philosophical thought of Muslim India's greatest twentieth-century thinker.

1750 _____. The Secrets of the Self. Rev. ed. Translated by R.A. Nicholson. Lahore: Ashraf, 1940, 148 pp.
Translation of the Persian text (published in 1915) of the Asrār-i khūdī (Secrets of the Self), one of Iqbāl's philosophical poems modeled on the style of Rūmī's Mathnawī. Here Iqbāl develops his idea of the individual in the true Islamic society.

1751 Malik, Hafeez, ed. Iqbal: Poet-Philosopher of Pakistan. New York: Columbia University, 1971, 441 pp.
A collection of high quality essays on the biography, politics, poetry, and religious outlook of Muḥammad Iqbāl, including an essay by Iqbāl's son on his father. The value of these studies is enhanced by an updating, to some extent, of Schimmel's exhaustive bibliography of works by and on Iqbāl (see 1752). An excellent starting point for studies on one of the most original and influential thinkers in modern Islam.

1752 Schimmel, Annemarie. Gabriel's Wing: A Study in the Religious Ideas of Sir Muhammad Iqbal. Leiden: E.J. Brill, 1963, 428 pp.
The definitive study on Iqbāl's religious thought. The author argues that Iqbāl cannot be understood unless the religious background of Muslim India--particularly the mystical thought of India--is taken into account. The work includes a complete bibliography of all of Iqbāl's writings (including those in English) as well as studies on his writings. See also 1794.

1753 Vahid, Syed Abdul. Iqbal: His Art and Thought. London: Murray, 1959, 254 pp.
A standard introduction to Iqbāl's thought as viewed through his poetical writings; a short biography is included.

Abū'l Kalām Āzād

1754 Āzād, (Mawlana) Abūl-Kalām. India Wins Freedom: An Autobiographical Narrative. New York, London, and Toronto: Longmans, Green, 1960, 293 pp.
A classic work relating the story of India's independence by one who played a key role in the negotiations of it, and who, as a Muslim nationalist, regretted deeply the partition of India and the formation of Pakistan.

1755 _____. The Tarjumān al-Qur'ān. 2 vols. Translated by Syed Abdul Latif. London: Asia Publishing, 1962-1967, 1:201 pp.; 2:208 pp.
An exegetical commentary of sūrah fātiḥa (vol. 1) and sūrahs 2-8, translated from Āzād's Tarjumān al-Qur'ān, one of the great modern commentaries of the Qur'ān.

1756 Baljon, J.M.S. Modern Muslim Koran Interpretation 1880-1960 (see 1206).
A study of modern Muslim exegesis of the Qur'ān based in part on the exegetical works of Abū'l-Kalām Āzād and G.A. Parwēz.

1757 Cragg, Kenneth. Counsels in Contemporary Islam (see 1665), pp. 125-39.
Contains a chapter on Abū'l-Kalām Āzād.

1758 Fyzee, A.A.A. A Modern Approach to Islam (see 1666), pp. 1-24.
Chapter 1 offers a clear, comprehensive analysis of Abū'l-Kalām Āzād's religious thought.

Abū'l-A'lā Mawdūdī

1759 Abbott, Freeland. "The Jama'at-i-Islami of Pakistan." Middle East Journal 2 (1957): 37-51.
A good analysis of the Jamā'āt-i-Islāmī, founded and led by Mawdūdī; the article concentrates on the organization as a political party.

1760 _____. "Mawlānā Maudūdī on Quranic Interpretation." Muslim World 48 (1958):6-19.
To fifteen rather specific questions on the interpretation of the Qur'ān posed by the author, Mawdūdī gives answers that reveal his methods of interpreting the Qur'ān.

1761 Adams, Charles J. "The Authority of Ḥadīth in the Eyes of Some Modern Muslims" (see 1235).

1762 _____. "The Ideology of Mawlānā Maudūdī." In Religion and Politics in South Asia. Edited by Donald Smith. Princeton, N.J.: Princeton University Press, 1966, pp. 371-97.
A carefully written exposition on the life of Mawdūdī, the organization he founded (the Jamā'āt-i-Islāmī), and the main tendencies of his thought.

1763 Mawdūdī, Sayyid Abū'l-A'lā. "Economic and Political Teachings of the Qur'ān." In A History of Muslim Philosophy. Vol. 1 (see 1574), pp. 155-78.
An example of Qur'ānic interpretation by Mawdūdī.

1764 _____. First Principles of the Islamic State. Translated and edited by K. Ahmad. Lahore: Islamic Publications, 1960, 72 pp.
Here Mawdūdī outlines his theory of a Pakistani theocracy, whose establishment, along with that of the Jamā'āt-i-Islāmī party, occupied his attention and activity for such a long time.

1765 _____. The Islamic Law and Constitution. Translated and edited by Khurshid Ahmad. 2d ed. Lahore: Islamic Publications, 1960, 439 pp.
The best source in English for the study of Mawdūdī's theories on the Islamic state.

1766 _____. Islamic Way of Life. Rev. ed. Lahore: Islamic Publications, 1965, 116 pp.
Several radio talks put together to form a sketchy picture of Mawdūdī's theories of society, politics, economics, and religion.

1767 _____. Towards Understanding Islam. Translated and edited by K. Ahmad. Lahore: Islamic Publications, 1963, 191 pp.
An elementary study on Islam directed to young Muslim students. The book is interesting for the Western student who wants to get a bird's-eye view of Mawdūdī's interpretation of Islam.

Ghulām Aḥmad Parwēz

1768 McDonough, Sheila. The Authority of the Past: A Study of Three Muslim Modernists (see 1721), pp. 35-54.
The last chapter treats the thought of Parwēz.

1769 Parwez, Ghulam Chaudhri. Islam: A Challenge to Religion. Lahore: Zarreen Art, 1968, 392 pp.
A fascinating interpretation of Islam that expounds the author's peculiar Qur'ānic exegetical method. A basic writing for the English language student on a well-known contemporary Pakistani thinker.

INDONESIA (See also 1027-31)

1770 Bakker, D. "The Struggle for the Future: Some Significant Aspects of Contemporary Islam in Indonesia." Muslim World 62 (1972): 126-36.
A brief survey of religious trends in present-day Indonesia as observed by a Christian theologian.

1771 Boland, B.J. The Struggle of Islam in Modern Indonesia. The Hague: Nijhoff, 1971, 283 pp.
After surveying historically the political developments in Indonesia since 1956 and Islam's role in political life (pp. 1-157), the author examines "the most important activities and problems of the Islamic community in present-day Indonesia" (pp. 157-243). Bibliography.

1772 Federspiel, Howard M. Persatuan Islam: Islamic Reform in Twentieth Century Indonesia. Ithaca, N.Y.: Cornell University Press, 1970, 247 pp.
A detailed study on the background and ideas of the Muslim movement Persatuan Islam that analyzes its political and educational program and compares the movement to other Muslim organizations in Indonesia. Glossary and large bibliography of books and articles.

1773 Nieuwenhuijze, C.A.O. van et al. "Indonesia." In <u>EI2</u>. Vol. 3 (see 20), pp. 1213-35.
A major article on the geography, ethnography, languages, history (Islamic and colonial periods), the role of Islam in Indonesia, and Indonesian literatures, written by a number of specialists in Indonesian studies.

1774 Nieuwenhuijze, C.A. O. van. <u>Aspects of Islam in Post-Colonial Indonesia: Five Essays</u> (see 1030).

1775 Noer, Deliar. <u>The Modernist Muslim Movement in Indonesia, 1900-1942</u>. London and New York: Oxford University, 1973, 390 pp.
The first detailed English language study of the modern Muslim reformist movements of Indonesia (educational, social, and political) and the reactions to them; a welcome study given the paucity of materials in English on Indonesian Islam. Glossary, exhaustive bibliography of books and articles, and index.

<u>AFRICA SOUTH OF THE SAHARA</u> (See 1032-66, 2951-59)

<u>ṢŪFĪS AND ṢŪFĪ ORGANIZATIONS</u> (See 1330-99)

Religious Practices

INTRODUCTORY ACCOUNTS

1776 Abu Bakr Effendi. The Religious Duties of Islam as Taught and Explained by Abu Bakr Effendi. Edited and translated by M. Brandel-Syrier. Pretoria Oriental Series, no. 2. Rev. ed. Leiden: E.J. Brill, 1960, 198 pp.

A translation of a textbook for religious instruction printed about 1874. The text, with interlinear commentary, follows the traditional lawbook (Ḥanafī, in this case) style, covering the legal aspects of purification, prayer, fasting, zakāt, and other rituals.

1777 Arnold, Edwin. Pearls of the Faith, or Islam's Rosary. London: Routledge & Kegan Paul, 1882, 190 pp. Reprint. Lahore: Orientalia, 1954.

A legend, tradition, or prayer illustrates poetically one of the ninety-nine names of God. An attempt to impart the spirit of Islam, but it has little factual material for the student.

1778 Cragg, Kenneth. The Call of the Minaret (see 1073), pp. 105-39.

Chapter 4 covers prayer and the religious life in Islam. Cragg believes Islam holds much for the Christian, in its manifestation of God's ways, and Christianity holds the important element lacking in Islam. This conviction runs throughout his works, sometimes blatantly, sometimes subtly. It appears in this chapter, where one feels the author's sense of appreciation of Islam, yet a condescension toward it. Nevertheless, the chapter is worth reading as an introduction, although Cragg tends to give pronouncements on matters still debated by scholars.

1779 _____. The Dome and the Rock: Jerusalem Studies in Islam. London: Society for Promoting Christian Knowledge, 1964, 262 pp.

The section entitled "Pillars of the House" (pp. 11-79) provides an interesting and in some ways sensitive account of Islam, yet still is consistent with Cragg's aims and views. Major portions of two articles by Cragg on prayers (see also 1823, 1833) are included. Attention should also be paid to the section "Precincts and People" (pp. 139-214) for an account of Muslim customs.

1780 Farah, Caesar E. Islam: Beliefs and Observances (see 1077), pp. 125-50.

Chapter 7, "The Fundamentals of Islam: Obligations," gives a reasonably full introductory account of basic practices; it includes details and Qur'ānic justification for the rituals. A recommended beginning.

1781 Gaudefroy-Demombynes, Maurice. "The Cult" and "Social Life." In Muslim Institutions. Translated by John P. MacGregor. London: George Allen & Unwin, 1950, pp. 70-107, 159-76.

A highly readable and informative introduction, notable especially for its exact use of Arabic terms, which can provide much clarification about what is being discussed.

1782 Grunebaum, Gustav E. von. "Islam: Experience of the Holy and Concept of Man." Diogenes 48 (1964):81-104.

One of the few works that seeks to go beyond the surface of the "five pillars" and explore Muslims' religious motivation and psychology. While by no means an introductory essay, it is for the most part eminently readable and worthwhile.

1783 _____. "The Religious Foundation: Piety." In Medieval Islam (see 192), pp. 108-41.

An introduction to the medieval historical development of worship, with an emphasis on Ṣūfī thought.

1784 _____. Muhammedan Festivals (see 517).

An excellent book that exposes the intricacies of the ḥajj, of Ramaḍān and of the tenth of Muḥarram. Also included is a section on prayer, veneration of saints, and worship of the Prophet.

1785 Hastings, James, ed. Encyclopaedia of Religion and Ethics (see 1130).

The articles here should not be ignored, for they are generally of high quality and often unique in the topic covered; full use should also be made of the index volume. The following articles are recommended: "Birth (Muhammadan)" (S. Lane-Poole, vol. 2, pp. 659-60); "Circumcision (Muhammadan)" (D.S. Margoliouth, vol. 3, pp. 677-79); "Death and Disposal of the Dead

(Muhammadan)" (S. Lane-Poole, vol. 4, pp. 500-502); "Festivals and Fasts (Muslim)" (K. Vollers, vol. 5, pp. 881-84); "Pilgrimage (Arabian and Muhammadan)" (T.W. Juynboll, vol. 10, pp. 10-12); "Prayer (Muhammadan)" (T.W. Juynboll, vol. 10, pp. 196-99); "Preaching (Muslim)" (D.S. Margoliouth, vol. 10, pp. 221-24); "Purification (Muslim)" (W. Popper, vol. 10, pp. 496-500).

1786 Hitti, Philip K. Islam: A Way of Life (see 1084), pp. 25-40.
"The Book: Beliefs and Practices" is the title of the relevant chapter.

1787 Jamali, Mohammad Fadhel. Letters on Islam: Written by a Father in Prison to His Son. London: Oxford University, 1965, 108 pp.
An educated, modern Iraqī statesman tries to give his son religious instruction by letter and reveals his traditional point of view toward the fundamentals of his faith. Not overly enlightening.

1788 Jeffery, Arthur, ed. Islam: Muhammad and His Religion (see 1086).
A collection of translated passages from the Qur'ān and important source materials on Islamic practices.

1789 Jeffery, Arthur, ed. and trans. A Reader on Islam (see 1087).
An excellent selection of passages from classical and modern sources covering the spectrum from prayers to festivals.

1790 Lammens, Henri. "The Qur'ān: The Five Pillars of Islam." In Islam: Beliefs and Institutions (see 1090), pp. 56-64.
Here prayer is discussed in detail, but other practices are given little attention.

1791 Levy, Reuben. "Islamic Jurisprudence." In The Social Structure of Islam (see 34), pp. 150-91.
Includes a study of Islamic worship from the legal point of view. References are provided to major legal and dogmatic texts for ritual requirements.

1792 Macdonald, Duncan Black. The Religious Attitude and Life in Islam. Chicago: University of Chicago, 1909, 317 pp.
The author attempts, with varying success, to examine the emotional side of religion that lies behind the external rituals, primarily through the statements of philosophers and Ṣūfīs. The work, however, is dated in its approach to the subject matter, since Macdonald here is deeply influenced by the popular interest in the "psychology of religion" prevalent at the turn of the century. The reader is advised to examine the preface carefully.

1793 Muhajir, Ali Musa Raza. Islam in Practical Life (The Religion of Islam). Lahore: Sh. Muhammad Ashraf, 1968, 221 pp.
Explains orthodox practices from the Muslim point of view. Valuable as a source of Qur'ānic quotes that support these practices, as well as a representative piece of Islamic apologetics.

1794 Schimmel, Annemarie. Gabriel's Wing: A Study in the Religious Ideas of Sir Muhammad Iqbal (see 1752).
The second chapter examines Iqbāl's views on the "five pillars."

1795 Sell, Edward. The Faith of Islam. London: Society for Promoting Christian Knowledge, 1907, 428 pp.
Chapter 4, "The Practical Duties of Islam," pp. 292-352. Chapter 6, "The Feasts and Fasts of Islam," pp. 353-75. Appendix B, "The Law of Jihād," pp. 406-14. Although a Christian bias permeates this book, a careful reader should have no problem recognizing it when it occurs. The book is primarily a source for details on various aspects of ritual requirements.

1796 Tritton, A.S. Islam: Belief and Practices (see 1103).

1797 Waddy, Charis. The Muslim Mind. London and New York: Longman, 1976, 204 pp.
An introductory work composed in part of quotes from the writings of modern Muslims illustrating aspects of their faith and life.

1798 Watt, W. Montgomery. "Islamic Worship and Piety." In What is Islam? (see 1104), pp. 185-93.
In the space allotted Watt gives the basics of worship in Islam; unfortunately he raises complicated interpretive issues, which he introduces but deals with superficially.

1799 Wensinck, A.J. The Muslim Creed: Its Genesis and Historical Development (see 1611).

THE FIVE PILLARS

THE SHAHĀDAH (CONFESSION OF FAITH)

1800 Eliash, J. "On the Genesis and Development of the Twelver Shīʿī Three-Tenet Shahādah" (see 1526).

1801 Ghazālī, al-. The Foundations of the Articles of Faith (see 1428).

1802 Smith, Wilfred Cantwell. The Faith of Other Men. New York: New American, 1965, 128 pp.
Chapter 4, "Muslims" (pp. 50-62), is an attempt to explain what it means to believe in Islam: it deals mainly with the Shahādah and its meaning to a Muslim. An unusual work, well worth reading.

ṢALĀT (PRAYER) (For Ṣūfī prayer-rituals, see 1285, 1371, 1373, 1384-85, 1458-59)

1803 Borthwick, Bruce M. "The Islamic Sermon as a Channel of Political Communication." Middle East Journal 21 (1967):299-313.
A study of modern governmental use of the Friday khuṭbah (sermon). Examples show the use of traditional Islamic stories and the parallels drawn to modern situations.

1804 Bousquet, G.H. "Ghusl." In EI2. Vol. 2 (see 20), p. 1104.
A brief discussion of general ablution (ghusl), from the legal point of view.

1805 Cragg, Kenneth. Alive to God: Muslim and Christian Prayer. London, New York, and Toronto: Oxford University, 1970, 194 pp.
Primarily a collection of Muslim and Christian inspirational passages drawn from a variety of famous works. The introductory essay is worth reading for its survey on the use of prayer.

1806 Fischer, H.J. "Prayer and Military Activity in the History of Muslim Africa South of the Sahara." Journal of African History 12 (1971):391-406.
This study illustrates the important role of prayer in the Islamic history of tropical Africa, particularly in terms of its function as a means of instilling discipline among military troops.

1807 Goitein, S.D. "The Origin and Nature of Friday Worship." Moslem World 44 (1959): 183-95. In Studies in Islamic History and Institutions. Leiden: E.J. Brill, 1966, pp. 111-25.
This is an important and unique article that should be read in order to appreciate the significance of the jumʿah (Friday) prayer. See also 1808, 1834, 1910.

1808 _____. "Prayer in Islam." In Studies in Islamic History and Institutions (see 1807), pp. 73-89.
Although it sheds little light on prayer's role or its significance to Muslims, this article is interesting, for it does deal with the establishment and subsequent growth of prayer ritual.

1809 Nakamura, Kōjirō. Ghazali on Prayer (see 1436).

1810 Padwick, Constance E. Muslim Devotions: A Study of Prayer Manuals in Common Use. London: Society for Promoting Christian Knowledge, 1961, 313 pp.
A collection of translations from Arabic manuals on prayer, many of which come from the pens of Muslim mystics. The introduction gives an excellent survey of various practices connected with the devotions.

1811 Pederson, J. "Masdjid." In Shorter Encyclopedia of Islam (see 22), pp. 330-53.
A fundamental study on the mosque. Especially relevant here are sections C to G, where religious activities of the mosque are discussed, most notably that of prayer. See also 1899.

1812 Schacht, J. "Wuḍūʾ." In Shorter Encyclopedia of Islam (see 22), pp. 635-36.
A brief description of the ablution ritual, which is performed before prayer.

1813 Schimmel, Annemarie. "Some Aspects of Mystical Prayer in Islam" (see 1298).

1814 Wensinck, A.J. "Ṣalāt." In Shorter Encyclopedia of Islam (see 22), pp. 491-99.
A comprehensive study on the background development and practice of Muslim prayer.

1815 _____. "Tayammum." In Shorter Encyclopedia of Islam (see 22), pp. 588-89.
A brief legal analysis of the practice of using sand instead of water in the performance of ritual ablution.

1816 Zwemer, Samuel M. Heirs of the Prophet: An Account of the Clergy and Priests of Islam. Chicago: Moody Bible, 1946, 137 pp.
Zwemer, editor of Moslem World in its most active missionary period and trainer of missionaries at Princeton, wrote this book for the general Christian public. It examines the mosque and the people associated with it. Even on such an innocent topic Zwemer's crusading doesn't cease. Pederson's article "Masdjid" covers the same material in a far better manner (see 1899). A condensation of the book is in Moslem World 34 (1944):17-39.

1817 _____. "The Pulpit in Islam." Moslem World 23 (1933):217-29.
A study of the minbar, mainly based on C.H. Becker's "Die Kanzel inkultus des alten Islam," Islam Studien (1924):450-71, a work recommended in itself. A historical and functionalist approach is followed.

ḤAJJ (PILGRIMAGE)

1818 Abdullah, ʿAnkawi. "The Pilgrimage to Mecca in Mamluk Times." Arabian Studies 1 (1974): 146-70.
A historical essay emphasizing the role of the pilgrimage and the organization of the travel to Mecca, using primary sources. Demonstrates the importance of the ḥajj to Muslims.

1819 Bell, Richard. "Muhammad's Pilgrimage Proclamation." Journal of the Royal Asiatic Society (1937):233-44.
A discussion of sūrah 9. See also 1820.

1820 _____. "The Origin of the ʿīd al-Aḍḥā." Moslem World 23 (1933):117-20.
Bell, making use of his unique Qurʾānic exegesis method, reconstructs Muḥammad's modification of the pre-Islamic sacrifice of animals during the pilgrimage. For full appreciation, this should be read after the study of Bell's Introduction to the Qurʾān (see 1178).

1821 Burckhardt, John Lewis. Travels in Arabia (see 623).

1822 Burton, Sir Richard T. Personal Narrative of a Pilgrimage to al-Madinah and Meccah (see 624).

1823 Cragg, Kenneth. "Pilgrimage Prayers." Muslim World 45 (1955):269-80.
A translation of a pilgrim's prayer manual. Should be read alongside a detailed description of the ḥajj.

1824 Doughty, Charles M. Travels in Arabia (see 626).
Includes observations on the ḥajj.

1825 Gaudefroy-Demombynes, Maurice. Le Pèlerinage à la Mekka (Contribution à l'étude du pèlerinage de la Mekke). Paris: Paul Geuthner, 1923, 332 pp.
The central study of the ḥajj; the author gathered all the information available to create a solid work of detail and interpretation. It concentrates only on the religious rites and leaves aside any consideration of the historical-political implications of the ḥajj.

1826 Hurgronje, C. Snouck. Mekka in the Latter Part of the Nineteenth Century. Translated by J.H. Monahan. Leiden: E.J. Brill; London: Luzac, 1931, 309 pp.
A result of the author's stay in Mecca in 1884-1885, the book tries to show daily life in the Holy City, including an account of the ḥajj. Social and family life, marriage, and funeral customs constitute much of the work.

1827 Jomier, J. "Le pèlerinage musulman vu du Caire vers 1960." Mélanges d'institut Dominicain d'études orientales du Caire 9 (1967):1-72.
A modern description of the pilgrimage and its practice in contemporary Egypt. Gives outline and analysis of radio talks, broadcast before and during the pilgrimage, that aim at increasing ḥajj participation. A valuable study.

1828 Kamal, Ahmad. The Sacred Journey. New York: Duell, Sloan & Pierce, 1961, 115 pp.
A detailed description of the ḥajj written primarily for Muslims, this is an excellent source for details (including the prayers) of the pilgrimage. Includes a section on Madīna and Jerusalem.

1829 Meulen, D. van der. "The Mecca Pilgrimage and Its Importance to the Netherlands East Indies." Moslem World 31 (1941):48-60.
A dated propaganda piece that lauds the Dutch government's assistance to pilgrims. It contains interesting observations on persons who participate in the pilgrimage.

1830 Wensinck, A.J.; J. Jomier; and B. Lewis. "Ḥadjdj." In EI2. Vol. 3 (see 20), pp. 31-38.
A basic study on the pilgrimage, including full details of the pre-Islamic background and Islamic development. The last section, by Lewis, concentrates on the social, cultural, and economic effect of the pilgrimage. The bibliography should be noted. See also "ʿĪd" and "ʿĪd al-Aḍḥā," by E. Mittwoch, vol. 3, pp. 1007-8; "Iḥrām," by A.J. Wensinck and J. Jomier, vol. 3, pp. 1052-53.

1831 Zwemer, Samuel M. "The Palladium of Islam." Moslem World 23 (1933):109-16.
A short work on the Kaʿbah's black stone.

RAMAḌĀN (SACRED MONTH OF FASTING)

1832 Antoun, Richard T. "The Social Significance of Ramaḍān in an Arab Village." Muslim World 58 (1968):36-42, 95-104.
An anthropological study of social relations in a community during Ramaḍān. Demonstrates very well peoples' involvement with their religion and its practices.

1833 Cragg, Kenneth. "Ramaḍān Prayers." Muslim World 47 (1957):210-23.
A translation of a Shīʿah manual of Ramaḍān prayers with a few explanatory footnotes.

1834 Goitein, S.D. "Ramaḍān--The Muslim Month of Fasting, Its Early Development and Religious Meaning." In Studies in Islamic History and Institutions (see 1807), pp. 90-110.
Revised from the article in Der Islam (18 (1929):184-94), this deals primarily with the establishment of Ramaḍān. It should be carefully compared with K. Wagtendonk's work (see 1204). Goitein ignores the significance, and no account is given, of the ritual and mystic aspects of fasting. It does include a short but worthwhile section on present-day Ramaḍān celebrations. A certain intimacy with Qur'ānic matters is presumed.

1835 Jomier, J., and J. Corbon. "Le Ramadan, au Caire, en 1956." Mélanges d'institut Dominicain d'études orientales du Caire 3 (1956): 1-74.
One of the few modern descriptions of Ramaḍān, this is an excellent study detailing some of the changes that have come about, due to contemporary life, especially in regard to actual fasting. Note should be taken of the section on ʿīd al-fiṭr (pp. 62-64).

1836 Mittwoch, E. "ʿīd" and "ʿīd al-fiṭr." In EI2. Vol. 3 (see 20), pp. 1007-8.
A brief account of the ritual festivals in Islām (ʿīd) and the festival of breaking the fast of Ramaḍan (ʿīd al fiṭr).

1837 Plessner, M. "Ramaḍān." In Shorter Encyclopedia of Islam (see 22), pp. 486-89.
A short description of the practice of Ramaḍān.

1838 Wagtendonk, K. Fasting in the Koran (see 1204).

1839 Wensinck, A.J. Arabic New Year and the Feast of Tabernacles. Amsterdam: Koninklijke Akademie von Wetenschappen, 1925, 41 pp.
Wensinck views Ramaḍān as a modification of the pre-Islamic New Year's rites. Further, he traces parallels between Ramaḍān and the Jewish Feast of Tabernacles. As with Goitein (see 1834), this is a technical matter and should be carefully compared with Wagtendonk (see 1204).

ZAKĀT (WEALTH SHARING)

1840 Ghazālī, al-. The Mysteries of Almsgiving (see 1430).

1841 Hurgronje, C. Snouck. "La Zakat." In Selected Works of/Oeuvres Choisies de C. Snouck Hurgronje. Edited by G.H. Bousquet and J. Schacht. Leiden: E.J. Brill, 1957, pp. 150-70.
For greater detail than introductory works and the Encyclopaedia of Islam article, this French work is virtually the only source on zakāt. It critically studies the Qur'ānic and hadīth material to establish the history and use of this practice.

1842 Schacht, J. "Zakāt." In Shorter Encyclopedia of Islam (see 22), pp. 654-56.
Traces the origin, theory, and practice of zakāt.

JIHĀD (STRUGGLE)

1843 Dajani-Shakeel, Hadia. "Jihād in Twelfth-Century Arabic Poetry: A Moral and Religious Force to Counter the Crusades." Muslim World 66 (1976):96-113.
An analysis of the use of poetry in the struggle against the Crusaders.

1844 Hughes, Thomas Patrick. "Jihād." In A Dictionary of Islam (see 2737), pp. 243-48.
An introduction to jihād that includes a valuable translation of the Ḥanafī legal position on the subject.

1845 Khadduri, Majid. War and Peace in the Law of Islam (see 2143), pp. 51-137.
Book 2, "The Law of war: The Jihād," is a well documented, basic work on jihād from the point of view of the Islamic jurists. Essential reading for this topic.

1846 Kohlberg, E. "The Development of the Imāmī Shī'ī Doctrine of Jihad" (see 1485).

1847 Lambton, A.K.S. "A Nineteenth Century View of Jihād." Studia Islamica 32 (1970):181-92.
Surveys first the development of the Ithnā 'Asharī Shī'ī theory of jihād, showing that it had significant impact on political attitudes of nineteenth-century Iranian religious leaders, then analyzes a treatise written circa 1809 by a religious leader demanding a jihād against Russia.

1848 Peters, Rudolph, trans. Jihad in Mediaeval and Modern Islam. Leiden: E.J. Brill, 1977, 90 pp.
Translations of the chapter on jihād from Averroes' (Ibn Rushd's) Bidāyat al-Mujtahid and of Maḥmūd Shaltūt's Qur'ān and Fighting, demonstrating the development of the concept of jihād.

1849 Siddiqui, Aslam. "Jihād: An Instrument of Islamic Revolution." Islamic Studies 2 (1963):383-98.
Due to frequent attacks on the subject in the past, there is a great collection of modern apologetic material from Muslims on jihād. This article is no particular exception, but it does attempt a view of jihād from a historical perspective.

1850 Tyan, E. "Djihād." In EI2. Vol. 2 (see 20), pp. 538-40.
A comprehensive study of jihād, with an emphasis on legal aspects.

1851 Williams, John Alden. "Struggle: Jihād." In Themes of Islamic Civilization (see 211), pp. 253-303.
A collection of translated passages ranging from the Qur'ān to contemporary writings.

THE QUR'ĀN IN RITUAL

1852 Bayḍāwī, al-. "Bayḍāwī on the Fawātiḥ: A Translation of His Commentary on 'Alif-Lam-Mim,' Sūrah 2." Vol. 1. Translated by P. Cachia. Journal of Semitic Studies 13 (1968):218-31.
Discusses the classical Muslim view of the "mysterious letters." See also 1174, 1175.

1853 Cuperus, W.S. Al-Fātiḥa dans la pratique religieuse musulmane du Maroc. Utrecht: Drukkerij Elinkwijk, 1973, 188 pp.
A study based on ethnologist and traveler reports concerning the ritual use of the first sūrah of the Qur'ān. The main body of the work details the variety of occasions and places in which the prayer is used. With glossary and an extensive bibliography.

1854 Donaldson, Bess Allen. "The Koran as Magic." Moslem World 27 (1937):254-66.
Examines the use of specific sūrahs as well as the entire text of the Qur'ān for the purpose of influencing future events. A study of a common practice.

1855 Jomier, J. "La place du Coran dans la vie quotidienne en Egypte." Institut des Belles Lettres Arabes 57 (1952):131-65.
Introduced by a short survey of the different occasions on which the Qur'ān is used, this article contains a list of Qur'ānic verses (from sūrah 1 to 18) that are employed as prayers, invocations, along with brief comments on their function in everyday life.

1856 Khalifa, Rashad. Miracle of the Qur'ān: Significance of the Mysterious Alphabets. St. Louis: Islamic Productions International, 1973, 200 pp.
The author employed a computer to prove mathematically the divine nature of the Qur'ān by means of a modern variation on the numerical-value-of-the-alphabet theme. The resulting book is a product of modern "magical" uses of the Qur'ān.

1857 Nieuwenhuijze, C.A.O. van. "The Qur'ān as a Factor in the Islamic Way of Life." Der Islam 38 (1962):215-57.
A sociological approach to the function of the Qur'ān as an integrating factor in Islamic society. Mostly devoted to theoretical considerations, it does provide, however, an intellectual framework for further, more practice-oriented studies.

SHĪ'Ī RITUALS

1858 Lane-Poole, Stanley. "The Persian Miracle Plays." In Studies in a Mosque. London: W.H. Allen, 1883, pp. 208-51.
A study of the importance and content of the Miracle Play of Ḥasan and Ḥusayn, which serves as a good introduction before reading the play itself (see 1859). The chapter also displays some of the Shī'ī feelings toward the festival as a whole.

1859 Pelly, Sir Lewis. The Miracle Play of Hassan and Husain Collected from Oral Tradition. 2 vols. London: Wm. H. Allen, 1879, 1:303 pp.; 2:352 pp.
An account of the passion commonly performed over a period of several days during the Shī'ī celebrations in the month of Muḥarram. An important source for popular Shī'ī beliefs and practices.

1860 Robson, J. "The Muharrem Ceremonies." Hibbert Journal 54 (1955-56):267-74.
A review of other people's accounts of the festival and its significance. Introductory.

1861 Strothmann, R. "Ta'zīya." In Shorter Encyclopedia of Islam (see 22), pp. 590-91.
"Ta'zīyah" is the term applied to the mourning for Ḥusayn, as expressed in the passion play, and a term for the play itself. A description is given of the play along with the historical background of the events underlying the story.

OTHER RITUALS

1862 Ghazālī, al-. The Mysteries of Purity (see 1431).

1863 Goldziher, Ignaz. "On Veneration of the Dead in Paganism and Islam." In Muslim Studies. Vol. 1 (see 127), pp. 229-38.
Goldziher's solid scholarship traces rituals connected with death and the dead through pre-Islamic times to official Islamic opinion and popular practice through the ages. Based primarily on ḥadīth material and poetical works, the article provides a historical counterpart to a detailed, descriptive work like Morgenstern's (see 1869).

1864 Granqvist, Hilma. Birth and Childhood among the Arabs: Studies in a Muhammadan Village in Palestine. Helsingfors: Solderstrom, 1947, 289 pp.
This work includes the author's personal observations of rituals connected with birth and circumcision, as well as general anthropological data on birth and early childhood. A mine of information, it is the basis of many later analyses.

1865 _____. Marriage Conditions in a Palestinian Village. Vol. 2. Helsingfors: Societas Scientiarum Fennica, 1931, 200 pp.
All the result of the author's personal research, the first half of volume 2 concentrates on the actual ceremonies and rituals of marriage. Engagement, married life, and divorce, primarily from the female participant's point of view, are also included in the work. Well documented.

1866 _____. Muslim Death and Burial: Arab Customs and Traditions Studied in a Village in Jordan. Helsinki: Societas Scientiarum Fennica, 1965, 287 pp.
A detailed anthropological study of the rites of dying, death, burial, and mourning. Not a book designed for easy reading, it is a tremendous source of data.

1867 Lane, E.W. An Account of the Manners and Customs of the Modern Egyptians (see 762).
Covering rites of birth, marriage, and death, as well as descriptions of popular beliefs and various festivals.

1868 Marx, Emanuel. "Circumcision Feasts among the Negev Bedouins." International Journal of Middle East Studies 4 (1973):411-27.
Circumcision festivals studied for their economic and social implications and their role in forming social relationships.

1869 Morgenstern, Julian. Rites of Birth, Marriage, Death, and Kindred Occasions among the Semites. New York: Ktav, 1973, pp. 320.
On rites that originated as redemptive sacrifices to evil spirits. Extensive use is made of the accounts of eighteenth-century Middle Eastern travelers and ethnologists. Although a useful compendium is formed of those accounts, the interpretations of the rites should be treated with care, for they often rest on antiquated anthropological theories. Further, one should not assume that all Muslims follow these rites.

1870 Rodinson, Maxime. "Ghidhā'." In EI2. Vol. 2 (see 20), pp. 1057-72.
This extensive and excellent article on food, food taboos, and related rituals will probably fulfill almost every need for information on the subject. Many items of bibliography, although few are in English, are included. See also G.H. Bousquet on ritual slaughter: "Dhabīḥa," in EI2, vol. 2 (see 20), pp. 213-14.

1871 Tritton, A.S. "Muslim Funeral Customs." Bulletin of the School of Oriental and African Studies 9 (1937-39):653-61.
A detailed article supplying a complete sketch of the rituals connected with burial, bringing out the variations due to different legal traditions; a valuable study.

1872 Westermarck, Edward. Marriage Ceremonies in Morocco. London: Macmillan, 1914, 422 pp.
A book that presents, and then interprets, the "magical" features of marriage rituals in North Africa. The product of sixteen trips to Morocco by the author.

POPULAR PRACTICES

1873 Andrezejewski, B.J. "The Veneration of Ṣūfī Saints and Its Impact on the Oral Literature of the Somali People and on Their Literature in Arabic" (see 1370).

1874 Arnold, Sir Thomas. "Saints and Martyrs (Muhammadan in India)" (see 1341).

1875 Canaan, Taufik. Mohammedan Saints and Sanctuaries in Palestine. Luzac's Oriental Religions Series, vol. 5. London: Luzac, 1927, 331 pp.
A detailed investigation into rites and practices associated with sanctuaries and their saints. See also 1908.

1876 Crapanzano, V. The Hamadsha: A Study in Moroccan Ethnopsychiatry (see 1374).

1877 DeJong, F. "Cairene Ziyara-Days: A Contribution to the Study of Saint Veneration in Islam" (see 1376).

1878 Donaldson, Bess Allen. The Wild Rue: A Study of Muhammadan Magic and Folklore in Iran. London: Luzac & Co., 1938, 216 pp.
An interesting, sometimes amusing account of popular practices in Shīʿī Islam. The study lacks documentation of most sources and is not based upon sound anthropological methods of investigation. Use with extreme care.

1879 Fahim, Hussein M. "Change in Religion in a Resettled Nubia Community, Upper Egypt." International Journal of Middle East Studies 4 (1973):163-77.
An anthropological study of the effect of economic change and new social influences on popular (and orthodox) religious practices.

1880 Goldziher, Ignaz. "The Appearance of the Prophet in Dreams." Journal of the Royal Asiatic Society (1912):503-6.
A short account, based on literary sources, of the popular belief that the Prophet appears in dreams in order to help in important decisions.

1881 _____. "Veneration of Saints in Islam." In Muslim Studies. Vol. 2 (see 127), pp. 255-341.
An important study that traces historically the veneration of saints, both living and dead, and their functions in rituals. Despite the work's age, it has yet to be replaced by a more thorough examination.

1882 Margoliouth, David S. "Relics of the Prophet Mohammed." Moslem World 27 (1937):20-27.
A short account of some of the items (especially a cloak) popularly held to have belonged to the Prophet.

1883 Sharīf, Jaʿfar. Islam in India, or the Qānūn-i-Islām: The Customs of the Musalmans of India (see 1003).
An account of popular practices in India including a section on Muḥarram rites. Full of details (the index is helpful) and good reading.

1884 Westermarck, Edward. Pagan Survivals in Mohammedan Civilization. London: Macmillan, 1933, 190 pp.
Primarily using the data collected for Ritual and Belief in Morocco (see 1885), Westermarck widens his view to include other parts of the Islamic world in order to describe trends in popular practices. An interesting and stimulating book whose title should not put off the reader.

1885 _____. Ritual and Belief in Morocco. 2 vols. London: Macmillan, 1926, 1:608 pp.; 2:629 pp.
Twenty-one visits from 1898 to 1927 by the author are the basis of this monumental work documenting the often unique Islamic beliefs in North Africa. Rituals of birth and death are included. Exhaustive index.

1886 Zwemer, Samuel M. The Influence of Animism on Islam: An Account of Popular Superstitions. New York: Macmillan, 1920, 246 pp.
The underlying missionary zeal and the belief in the superiority of Christianity render this book suitable for extremely cautious study only. It is a mine of facts (and some worthwhile interpretation), but often it is hard to distinguish fact from the author's prejudices. Sections on the ḥajj and prayer are included. Chapter 3 on animism in prayer, with slight modification, is in Moslem World 8 (1918): 359-75; chapter 5 on the ʿAqīqah sacrifice, with slight modification, in Moslem World 6 (1916): 236-52; chapter 2, in part on the rosary, in an improved version appeared in Moslem World 21 (1931):329-43.

Sacred Places

GENERAL STUDIES (See also Islamic Art and Architecture)

1887 Chelhod, Joseph. Les structures du sacré chez les Arabes. Paris: G.P. Maisonneuve & Larose, 1964, 288 pp.

An important study on the concept of the sacred in Islam. The author believes that the concept reflects the nomadic and commercial way of life in Arabia, rather than an adapted Judeo-Christian idea. The bibliography is extensive, although an article by H. Lammens ("Les sanctuaires pré-islamites dans l'Arabie Occidentale," Mélanges de l'Université Saint-Joseph 9 [1926]:373-91) is an omission that could add valuable material on pre-Islamic Arabia. See also the review of this book by J. Waardenburg, Bibliotheca Orientalis 25 (1968):252-58.

1888 Goldziher, Ignaz. "Veneration of Saints in Islam." In Muslim Studies. Vol. 2 (see 127), pp. 255-341.

This section deals with the relation between sacred spaces and saints on both a theoretical and practical level.

1889 Grunebaum, Gustav E. von. "The Sacred Character of Islamic Cities." In Mélanges Taha Husain (see 1136), pp. 25-37.

An examination of the factors involved in declaring the cities of Mecca, Madīnah, Damascus, and Karbalā' sacred. Informative and stimulating.

1890 Harawī, al-. Guide des lieux de pélerinage. Translated and edited by Janine Sourdel-Thomine. Damascus: Institut français de Damas, 1957, 231 pp.

A translation with many notes and a lengthy introduction of the Kitāb al-Ziyarāt of al-Harawī (d. 1215). The work gives a view of popular religion during the lifetime of the author through surveying Muslim sacred places from Iran to Spain. With extensive bibliography.

1891 Kriss, Rudolph, and Hubert Kriss-Heinrich. Volksglaube im Bereich des Islam: Band I, Wallfahrtswesen und Heiligenverehrung. Wiesbaden: Otto Harrassowitz, 1960, 359 pp.

The title "Popular Belief in the Islamic World: Pilgrimages and Veneration of Sacred Places" indicates the scope of this book; it is a well-illustrated work with an extensive bibliography. The study separates the many Middle Eastern sacred places into geographical categories, giving much detail on them as well as providing a view of how these places fit into the everyday life of Muslims.

1892 Serjeant, R.B. "Ḥaram and Hawtah: The Sacred Enclave in Arabia" (see 1136).

1893 _____. "Hūd and Other Pre-Islamic Prophets of Hadramaut." Le Museon 67 (1954):121-79.

Primarily an account of the supposed tomb of the prophet Hūd in southern Arabia and its history, the article also outlines the rituals (especially the pilgrimage) undertaken to this elaborate shrine. With notes and bibliography.

1894 Smith, W. Robertson. Lectures on the Religion of the Semites: The Fundamental Institutions. New York: Schocken, 1972, 507 pp. Reprint of 1894 ed.

A classic study that sets forth Smith's theories on sacrifice and totemism, from which he attempted to explain the origins of religion. The work is still of great value for students of Islam, because it examines certain pre-Islamic practices that were carried into Islam and gives a great deal of attention to sacred spaces.

1895 Sourdel-Thomine, Janine. "Les anciens lieux de pélerinage Damascains d'après les sources arabes." Bulletin d'études orientales 14 (1952-54):65-85.

Based in part on her translation of al-Harawī's work (see 1890), this article focuses on a description of sacred places in Damascus. Many of the sites are connected with either a prophet or a companion of Muḥammad, which gives them their sanctity.

1896 Wendell, Charles. "Baghdad, Imago Mundi and Other Foundation Lore." International Journal of Middle East Studies 2 (1971):99-128.

Buried within this summary of materials about the founding of Baghdād are valuable hints on popular beliefs associated with the view that Baghdād is the sacred center of the Islamic Empire and a microcosmic symbol of the world. Helpful notes and references.

1897 Wensinck, A.J. "The Ideas of the Western Semites concerning the Navel of the Earth." Verhandelingen der Kininklijke Akademie van Wetenschappen te Amsterdam, Afdeeling Letter-Kunde, nieuwe reeks 17:1 (1916):1-65.
An extremely technical but important and fascinating article on the notion of the center of the world as the place of the origin of creation and the place closest to God, along with other related ideas.

THE MOSQUE

GENERAL STUDIES

1898 Kuban, Doğan. Muslim Religious Architecture. Pt. 1, The Mosque and Its Early Development. Leiden: E.J. Brill, 1974, 31 pp.
A historical-architectural study of mosques that considers the functional aspects of these buildings and their influence on construction and development. Well illustrated, with extensive bibliography. It is to be followed by a second part dealing with other aspects of Muslim religious buildings, such as madrasas and mausoleums.

1899 Pederson, Johs. "Masdjid." In EI1. Vol. 3 (see 32), pp. 316-88.
A basic study on the origins, development, structure, and function of the mosque, along with details on its personnel and education program. "The Mosque in Dutch East Indies (R.A. Kern, pp. 376-78) and "Architecture" (E. Diez, pp. 378-89) both extend the scope of the article into various geographical regions. Also valuable are the following articles: "Miḥrāb" (E. Diez, vol. 3, pp. 485-90), on the niche indicating the direction of prayer; "Minbar" (E. Diez, vol. 3, pp. 499-500), on the "pulpit" in the mosque (both of these articles are illustrated); "Muṣalla" (A.J. Wensinck, vol. 3, p. 746), on this separate location for supplementary prayers; "Zawīya" (E. Lévi-Provençal, vol. 4, p. 1220), on the auxiliary buildings connected to the mosque. For a condensed version of Pedersen's work, see "Masdjid," in Shorter Encyclopedia of Islam (see 1811). See also 2040.

MECCA AND MADĪNAH

1900 Alexander, Grant. "The Story of the Ka'ba." Moslem World 28 (1938):43-53.
A collection of pre-Islamic legends about the Ka'bah, its construction and function.

1901 Buhl, F. "Al-Madīna." In Shorter Encyclopedia of Islam (see 22), pp. 291-98.
An excellent historical survey that details the sanctuaries in the town.

1902 Creswell, K.A.C. "The Ka'ba in 608 A.D." Archaeologia 94 (1951):97-102.
An introductory but detailed account based on original Arabic sources, concerning the rebuilding of the Ka'bah during Muḥammad's lifetime. Creswell sees Ethiopian influence on the style of construction. The article adds some valuable information on the structure and use of the sacred building.

1903 Esin, Emel, and Haluk Doganbey. Mecca the Blessed, Madinah the Radiant (see 2325).

1904 Lammens, Henri, and A.J. Wensinck. "Mecca." In EI1. Vol. 3 (see 32), pp. 437-48.
The section of this article by Lammens, which deals with Mecca up to A.D. 750, is an account of big business in early Mecca, extracted from Lammens's La Mecque à la veille de l'hégire. Wensinck's section, from A.D. 750 on, is a straight historical account. Valuable supplements to this article are found in Wensinck's and Jomier's "Ka'ba" (in EI2, vol. 4 [see 20], pp. 317-22), which gives a full description of the modern building, its history, and its use. Wensinck's "Al-Masdjid al-Ḥarām" (in EI1, vol. 3 [see 32], pp. 389-90) gives a short description and history of the entire sacred area. Gaudefroy-Demombynes' "Shaiba (Banū)" (in EI1, vol. 4 [see 32], pp. 269-71) is a historical study of the Keepers of the Keys to the Ka'bah. Carra de Vaux's "Zamzam" (in EI1, vol. 4 [see 32], pp. 1212-13) is a short account of the sacred well.

1905 Meier, Fritz. "The Mystery of the Ka'ba: Symbol and Reality in Islamic Mysticism" (see 1322).

1906 Zwemer, S.M. "Al-Haramain." Moslem World 37 (1947):7-15.
A very introductory account of the territory and features of the two sacred cities. Note should be taken, however, of "the Mecca certificate" (plates 1-4 preceding page 1) given to pilgrims. It is comprised of a number of sketches of Islamic sacred places.

PALESTINE

1907 Buhl, F. "Al-Ḳuds." In EI1. Vol. 2 (see 32), pp. 1094-1104.
A description of Jerusalem, historically presented, beginning with pre-Islamic times. The following articles are valuable supplements: "Al-Ḥaram al-Sharīf" (by O. Grabar, in EI2, vol. 3 [see 20], pp. 173-75), a general survey of the entire sanctuary region; "Ḳubbat al-Sakhra" (by J. Walker, in EI1, vol. 2 [see 32], pp. 1088-91), a survey of the historical and modern day importance of the Dome of the Rock, with extensive bibliography; "Al-Masdjid al-Aḳsā" (by A.J. Wensinck, in EI1, vol. 3 [see 32], p. 389), mainly deals with the name of this central mosque.

1908 Canaan, Taufik. Mohammedan Saints and Sanctuaries in Palestine (see 1875).
By far the greatest number of studies on Islamic holy places have centered on Palestine. This one studies nine types of sanctuaries, ranging from shrines to single stones, classified from over five hundred examples the author visited or heard about. A full description of each type is given as well as some valuable characterizations of Muslim shrines in general.

1909 Duncan, Alistair. The Noble Sanctuary: Portrait of a Holy Place in Arab Jerusalem. London: Longmans Group, 1972, 80 pp.

A lush presentation of "al-ḥaram al-sharīf," with many stunning photographs and a text providing both history and description of the mosque. The work is a summary of all that is known about the Dome of the Rock, the al-Aqsā Mosque, and related buildings.

1910 Goitein, S.D. "The Sanctity of Jerusalem and Palestine in Early Islam." In Studies in Islamic History and Institutions (see 1807), pp. 135-49.

Based on his articles in Journal of the American Oriental Society (70 [1950]:104-8) and Bulletin of the Palestine Exploration Society (12 [1945-46]:120-26). This study is important for its argument against Goldziher's position (Muslim Studies, vol. 2 [see 127], pp. 44-46) that Jerusalem became sanctified for political reasons only. Goitein argues persuasively for the early establishment of a pilgrimage in the city.

1911 Grabar, Oleg. "The Umayyad Dome of the Rock in Jerusalem" (see 2401).

1912 Hirschberg, J.W. "The Sources of Moslem Tradition concerning Jerusalem." Rocznik Orientalistyczny 17 (1952):34-50.

A detailed article covering three aspects: Muslim views of Jerusalem through history, traditional reports about Jerusalem, and the significance of Muḥammad's ascent into heaven from Jerusalem. (On the last see J.R. Porter's "Muhummad's Journey to Heaven" in Numen 21 [1974]:64-80). Hirschberg's views on the relationship between Muḥammad and the Jews are best (and easily) ignored.

1913 LeStrange, G. Palestine under the Moslems: A Description of Syria and the Holy Land (650-1500) (see 219).

The standard work giving a historical outline along with description of the region. Pages 83-223 are primarily translations of geographical and descriptive texts dealing with Jerusalem. Pages 224-73 provide similar materials on Damascus.

1914 Matthews, C.D. "A Muslim Iconoclast (Ibn Taymiyyah) on the 'merits' of Jerusalem and Palestine." Journal of the American Oriental Society 36 (1936):1-21.

An edition of an Arabic text, prefaced by an interesting discussion of the sanctity of Jerusalem.

1915 Matthews, Charles D. Palestine--Mohammadan Holy Land. Yale Oriental Series--Researches, no. 24. New Haven, Conn.: Yale, 1949, 176 pp.

A translation of two old pilgrim guides that give stories and legends about Jerusalem and tell of gaining merit through the performance of rituals there. Interesting evidence of Islam's legitimizing the use of pre-Islamic rites and sanctuaries.

1916 McCown, Chester C. "Muslim Shrines in Palestine." American School of Oriental Research in Jerusalem, Annual 2 & 3 (1921-22):47-79.

A descriptive account of saints' tombs and sacred trees, with illustrations.

1917 Sivan, Emmanuel. "The Beginning of the 'Faḍā'il al-Quds' Literature." Der Islam 48 (1971):100-110.

Faḍā'il literature, which deals with the merit of a certain place, is a complete genre of Arabic literature virtually uninvestigated. This article serves as an introduction to that literature on Jerusalem.

SHĪʿĪ SACRED PLACES

1918 Donaldson, Dwight M. The Shiite Religion: A History of Islam in Persia and Iraq (see 1482).

Karbalā,' Madīnah, Meshhed, and Baghdād are among the places held especially sacred by the Shīʿīs. Donaldson devotes a chapter to each, giving its history and significance to the sect. Not an overly sympathetic work, it is one of the few in English covering Shīʿī beliefs.

1919 Streck, M. "Meshhed." E. Honigmann, "Messhed Ḥusain." In EI1. Vol. 3 (see 32), pp. 467-77, 477-79.

Meshed, the capital of Khurāsān province, is the greatest place of pilgrimage for Shīʿīs, containing the sanctuary of Imām al-Riḍā. An extensive description of the history and architecture of the buildings is given. Messhed Ḥusayn, the other name for Karbalā', is where Ḥusayn ibn ʿAlī was killed; a full description of the city and its sanctuaries is given.

Islamic Institutions

THE ARMY

1920 Ayalon, David. Gunpowder and Firearms in the Mamluk Kingdom (see 273).
A historical discussion of the appearance and first uses of firearms in Egypt, as well as a social study of the conflict of values precipitated by their introduction. There is a lengthy chapter on various terms used for arms; the bulk of the work is devoted to the attitude of the Mamlūk troops to firearms. Appendix 2, by Paul Wittek, discusses the earliest references to firearms among the Ottoman Turks.

1921 Bosworth, C.E. "Ghaznavid Military Organization." Der Islam 36 (1960):37-77.
A valuable, detailed study of the ninth- and tenth-century Ghaznavid army, drawn from original sources. The author describes the elements forming the army, devoting one section to the uses of slaves, another to the various nationalities. There is also a section on weapons, particularly the elephant, and a most interesting account of the organization that ran the army. For a later revision of this article, see "The Army," in The Ghaznavids (see 225), pp. 98-128.

1922 _____ et al. "Ghulām." In EI2. Vol. 2, pp. 1079-91.
This article, divided into four different sections, on the caliphate, Persia, India, and the Ottoman Empire, deals with the role and significance of young male slaves who served as attendants or guards and formed a component of Islamic armies. Bosworth's article and the article "Djaysh" (see 1924) constitute the best general introduction to the armed forces in Islam.

1923 Bosworth, C.E. "Military Organization under the Būyids of Persia and Iraq." Oriens 18-19 (1965-66):143-67.
A good detailing of Būyid military organization in the tenth century. The author treats in particular the Daylamī and Turkish factions of the Būyid army and also touches on the administrative machinery of the state to pay, supervise, and recruit the army.

1924 Cahen, Calude et al. "Djaysh." In EI2. Vol. 2 (see 20), pp. 504-15.
The article is divided into three parts: the classical period (up to the thirteenth century), the Muslim West, and the modern period (eighteenth and nineteenth centuries). It describes in a general manner the recruitment, training, payment, and organization of the army in Islamic lands. The first and longest section, by Cahen, is the best of the three, as it is more detailed and gives better descriptions. See also 1922.

1925 Gibb, H.A.R. "The Armies of Saladin." Cahiers d'histoire égyptienne 3 (1951): 304-20. In Studies on the Civilization of Islam (see 23), pp. 74-88.
A study of the composition of the army of Ṣalāḥ al-dīn. The article treats the corps from Egypt, those from Syria and Mesopotamia, which had previously served Nūr al-Dīn, and the auxiliary troops of Turks, Kurds, Arabs, and others. The final paragraphs discuss how supplies and arms moved with the army. The article has many informative footnotes.

1926 Levy, Avigdor. "The Officer Corps in Sultan Mahmud II's New Ottoman Army, 1826-39." International Journal of Middle Eastern Studies 2 (1971):21-39. "The Ottoman Ulema and the Military Reforms of Sultan Mahmud II." Asian and African Studies: Annual of the Israel Oriental Society 7 (1971):13-39.
The first article deals with the problems Maḥmūd II faced, such as the opposition against the employment of European officers and instructors, when trying to staff his new army after the annihilation of the janissary corps. The second article reveals how Maḥmūd II, through the promise of material benefits and other concessions, won the Sunnī ʻulamā' over to his cause against the Bektashī janissaries.

1927 Levy, Reuben. "Military Organization in Islam." In The Social Structure of Islam (see 34), pp. 407-57.
The chapter surveys Muslim military groups historically, touching such subjects as non-Muslim recruits, mercenaries, the Turkish elements, chains of command, infantry and cavalry, and tactics and arms as well as treating more specifically the Saljūq, Mamlūk, and Ottoman

armies. It is a good survey of the military organizations in Islam.

1928 Ménage, V.L. "Sidelights on the Devshirme from Idrīs and Saʿduddīn." Bulletin of the School of Oriental and African Studies 18 (1956):181-83. "Some Notes on the Devshirme." Bulletin of the School of Oriental and African Studies 28 (1966):64-78.

The first article consists of a refutation of J. Palmer's thesis (see 1930), a correct rendering of the Idrisian account, and a look at two Ottoman historians' attempt to legitimize the devshirme (forced levy of Christian children for military and administrative service), the practice of which blatantly violates Islamic law. The second article, a review of Basilike Papoulia's exhaustive Ursprung und Wesen der 'Knabenlese' im osmanischen Reich (Südosteuropaische Arbeiten 59, Münich, 1963), deals meticulously with several technical aspects of the institution. For a clear, concise account that gives the general contents of the institution of the devshirme, see Ménage's "Devshirme," in EI2, Vol. 2 (see 20), pp. 210-13.

1929 Mihailovic, Konstantin. Memoirs of a Janissary. Translated by Benjamin Stolz. With commentary and notes by Svat Soucek. Ann Arbor: University of Michigan Press, 1975, 255 pp.

After having served in the Ottoman army as a slave soldier during the reign of Mehmed the Conqueror, Mihailovic fled to Europe, where he wrote his memoirs for Christian propagandistic purposes. Although the author is not very insightful and was quite unable to grasp the general nature of the Ottoman-Turkish culture, his book is very useful because of its authentic details.

1930 Palmer, J.A.B. "The Origin of the Janissaries." Bulletin of the John Rylands Library (1953):448-81.

An analysis of the two main traditions in Ottoman historiography in relation to the origin of the janissary corps, the one situating it in the reign of Orhan, the other in that of Murad I. Palmer's proposed solution that converges the chroniclers' and the Idrisian accounts through literary analysis has been refuted (see 1928); still, the detailed descriptions of the different traditions are highly useful.

1931 Parry, V.J., and M.E. Yapp, eds. War, Technology and Society in the Middle East. London: Oxford University Press, 1975, 448 pp.

A collection of twenty papers by noted authorities; only a few are mentioned here. "The Role of the Camel and the Horse in the Early Arab Conquests" (D.R. Hill); "Preliminary remarks on the Mamlūk Military Institution in Islam" (David Ayalon); "Byzantine and Turkish Societies and Their Sources of Manpower" (S. Vryonis, Jr.); "The Socio-Political Effects of the Diffusion of Firearms in the Middle East" (H. Inalcik); and "The Modernization of Middle Eastern Armies in the Nineteenth Century: A Comparative View" (M.E. Yapp).

1932 Parry, V.J. "Warfare." In The Cambridge History of Islam. Vol. 2 (see 30), pp. 824-50.

A comprehensive essay covering the development of armed forces and weapons and tactics from early Islam down to the Ottoman Empire. Though the article touches upon many facets of warfare, like systems of payment, levels of command, and type of soldiery, some readers will find the discussion of military implements most informative.

1933 Shaw, S.J. "The Origins of Ottoman Military Reform: The Nizam-i Cedid Army of the Sultan Selim III." Journal of Modern History 37 (1965):291-305.

The Nizam-i cedid army (the new order army) represented an important step in the reform of military forces under the Ottomans in the eighteenth century. This corps used the new firearms and weapons of the Europeans--items the older corps had refused to carry. The author reviews the beginning and maturing of the corps. Although it proved itself superior to the older corps, Selim III was forced to keep the new corps in Istanbul, for reasons that are discussed.

1934 Vryonis, S. "Isidore Glabas and the Turkish Devshirme." Speculum 31 (1956):433-43.

A study on a sermon by Isidore Glabas, the archbishop of Thessalonica in the last decade of the fourteenth century, which is the earliest document on the origins of the devshirme. This document makes it possible to establish that the original levy of Christian youths took place no later than A.D. 1395.

1935 Vryonis, Speros. "Seljuk Gulams and Ottoman Devshirmes." Der Islam 41 (1965):224-52.

An excellent source on the system of recruitment used by the pre-Ottomans to furnish "slaves" for their governmental and military institutions. Vryonis, after discussing this practice before the rise of the Ottomans, studies its use under the Ottomans, discussing whether it was an innovation or an adaption of the earlier practice.

GUILDS

1936 Arnakis, G.G. "Futuwwa Traditions in the Ottoman Empire: Akhis, Bektashi Dervishes and Craftsmen." Journal of Near East Studies 12 (1953):232-47.

Arnakis argues that the akhī (craftsmen) associations of thirteenth- and fourteenth-century Anatolia were multifaceted organizations with religious, socioeconomic, and political functions and that by the early fifteenth century their religious functions, along with the special rites associated with them, were taken up by the Bektashīs and to a lesser extent the Mawlawīs and Khalwatīs, while the economic organization continued in the trade guilds of the Ottoman Empire.

1937 Baer, Gabriel. "The Administrative, Economic and Social Functions of the Turkish Guilds." International Journal of Middle Eastern Studies 1 (1970):28-50. "Monopolies and Restrictive Practices of Turkish Guilds." Journal of the Economic and Social History of the Orient 13 (1970):145-65.

These studies constitute a treatment of the functions and practices of guilds under Ottoman rule. Although the titles of his articles lay claim to a wider area, Baer deals primarily with Istanbul. These articles, plus his Egyptian Guilds in Modern Times (see 372), lead to the conclusion that Ottoman guilds functioned more as state administrative bodies under strict government control than as autonomous associations of merchants and producers.

1938 Cahen, Claude, and Franz Taeschner. "Futuwwah." In EI2. Vol. 2 (see 20), pp. 961-69.

Two articles appear under this title. The first article is a summary of much of the authoritative work Cahen has done on this institution. He indicates what scanty information there is on the futuwwah and related groups before the fourteenth century, but spends more time on the reign of the late ʿAbbāsid al-Nāṣir li-Dīn Allāh, when writings on the futuwwah appeared. For further elaboration, see Cahen's "Y a-t-il eu des corporations professionnelles dans le monde musulman classique?", in The Islamic City (see 168), pp. 51-65. The second article, by Franz Taeschner, treats briefly the survival of the court futuwwah after the Mongol invasion, then the popular organizations of Anatolia called akhilik, and finally a longer section on the system of guilds in Islam. This entry is particularly valuable as the best source for the English reader. Good bibliographies. For further elaboration, see Taeschner's "Futuwwa, eine gemeinschaftbildende Idee im mitteralterlichen Orient und ihre verschiedenen Erscheinungsformen," in Schweizerisches Archiv für Volkskunde 52 (1956):122-58.

1939 Çelebi, Evliya. Narrative of Travels in Europe, Asia, and Africa by Evliya Efendi (see 393).

While giving an account of a guild's procession in Istanbul in the middle of the seventeenth century, Evliya presents the whole working population of Istanbul--from artisans to pimps--according to their craft organizations, relating names, numbers, and various tales. This gem constitutes the main source for most of the secondary studies on Ottoman guilds, but unfortunately is used rather uncritically.

1940 Gerber, Haim. "Guilds in Seventeenth Century Anatolian Bursa." Journal of Israel Oriental Society 11 (1976):59-86.

A rare microlevel study of guilds in a single Ottoman town based on Ottoman archival sources. Gerber's findings indicate a higher level of guild autonomy than Baer's studies reveal (see 1937).

1941 Lambton, A.K.S. Islamic Society in Persia. London: Oxford, 1954, 32 pp.

Though this extremely informative monograph ranges beyond our concern here, the portion on urban corporate organizations and the craft guilds is unique and ought not to be overlooked.

1942 Lewis, Bernard. "The Islamic Guilds." The Economic History Review 8 (1937):20-37.

This article treats the various theories concerning the origins of the guilds and dwells on the relation of Sufism, the akhī (craft associations) movement, the fuṭawwah, and the guilds. The author also describes the guilds' structure and speaks of two extant sources for the medieval guilds. Footnotes provide an excellent bibliography of the pertinent French and German literature.

1943 Massignon, L. "Guilds (Mohammedan)." In Encyclopaedia of Social Sciences. Vol. 7. New York: Macmillan, 1932, pp. 214-16.

A brief historical discussion of the guild in Islam from its beginning to modern Turkey. Some of the ideas of Professor Massignon have now been modified by Cahen (see 1938).

1944 _____. "Sinf." In EI1. Vol. 4 (see 32), pp. 436-37.

The brief article is divided into two parts. In the first Massignon provides a brief history, and in the second he mentions various organizational titles of the guild. Massignon's last word on the subject is found in his "La 'Futuwwa' ou 'Pacte d'Honneur Artisanal' entre les Travailleurs Musulmans au Moyen Age," in Opera Minora, vol. 1, Beirut: Dar El Maaref, 1963, pp. 398-421.

1945 Riaz, M. "Caliph al-Nāṣir li-Dīn Allāh and the System of Futuwwat." Journal of the Pakistan Historical Society 18 (1970):180-90.

A brief treatment of the twelfth-century caliph al-Nāṣir's interest in the futuwwah, and of the nature of the futuwwah.

1946 Salinger, G. "Was the Futūwa an Oriental Form of Chivalry?" Proceedings of the American Philosophical Society 94 (1950):481-93.

A detailed discussion of the fraternal Muslim organization called futuwwah during the caliphate of al-Nāṣir li-Dīn Allāh (twelfth century). The author shows that the spirit of this organization is essentially different from that of the chivalry of Western Europe. The article is particularly valuable as a source of information in English on the history of the futuwwah, with a lengthy bibliography. This article should be read in light of an important review by F. Taeschner: Review of Salinger's Article, Oriens 5 (1952):332-36.

1947 Stern, S.M. "The Constitution of the Islamic City." In The Islamic City (see 168), pp. 34-47.

The author seeks to define the character of the guilds, demonstrating that they are distinct in essential aspects from their Western counterpart.

THE BUREAUCRACY

1948 Bjorkman, W. et al. "Diplomatic." In EI2. Vol. 2 (see 20), pp. 301-16.

Four articles treat state documents in general. The first article, introductory in nature, cites the various types of documents included under the title and describes their transmission and multiplication as well as the archives for their storage, and even the materials used to write and to seal these documents. The second article deals with the Maghreb area and the documents found there. H. Busse wrote the third article (perhaps the most important), on Persia, providing much detail on documentary practices. The fourth article discusses the Ottoman Empire and its practices.

1949 Bowen, H. The Life and Times of ʻAlı ibn ʻIsā', the Good Vizier (see 221).

1950 Chandra, Satish. Parties and Politics at the Mughal Court, 1707-1740. Algarh: Muslim University, 1959, 309 pp.

Though this is a wisely accepted study of the nobility of Mughal India, it also provides a clear view of a struggle for the office of wizārah (vizierate) at this time.

1951 Duri, A.A. et al. "Dīwān." In EI2. Vol. 2 (see 20), pp. 323-37.

"Dīwān" first meant "register" and later came to be used for "office." The first article treats the offices of the bureaucracy historically as they developed under the caliphs and under the Imāms of the Fāṭimid state, reaching as far as the end of the Būyid rule in the thirteenth century. The second article, on Egypt, treats the development of the dīwān when Egypt was a province under the Fāṭimids and under the Ayyūbids and Mamlūks. The third article, on Spain and North Africa, is brief and indicates the outstanding dīwāns of the area. The article on Iran, by A.K.S. Lambton, traces the development of offices down to the Qājārs, and the last article covers it in India. All articles are marked by their attempt to trace the development of offices as well as to provide the names and functions of the chief officers.

1952 Goitein, S.D. "The Origin of the Vizierate and Its True Character." Islamic Culture 16 (1942):255-63, 380-92.

An outstanding contribution to the study of the wizārah. The author's intent is to indicate the true origins of that office. Previously, it was taken for granted that the institution was borrowed wholesale from the Persians. The article investigates the foundations laid by al-Manṣūr and finds the model for the practice of al-Manṣūr and his successors in Arab custom.

1953 Grunebaum, G.E. von. "The Body Politic: Law and the State." In Medieval Islam (see 192), pp. 142-69.

The fourth part of this essay is a useful résumé of the various bureaucratic posts in medieval Islamic government. The author has tried to show the cleavage between norm and usage apparent in many of these posts, since the purpose of the essay is to discuss the gradual abandonment of the traditional political theory of al-Māwardī in favor of a more realistic theory.

1954 Inalcik, Halil. The Ottoman Empire: The Classical Age, 1300-1600 (see 339).

Part 3, "The State," provides some chapters that go into great detail on the Ottoman class system and palace organization and on the central administrative and provincial bureaucracy.

1955 Lambton, A.K.S. "The Administration of Sanjar's Empire." Bulletin of the School of Oriental and African Studies 20 (1957): 367-88.

A discussion of the administrators and their offices in the twelfth-century reign of Sanjar in Khurāsān. Based in great part on a new collection of documents from the period, the article is not a simple résumé of the documents but rather an extensive interpretation of the materials' significance.

1956 Lewis, B. "Daftar." In EI2. Vol. 2 (see 20), pp. 77-81.

"Daftar" denotes a booklet of registration, often in use in an administrative office. The history of the register is first pursued up to the eleventh century. The author then turns to various types of daftar, registers for fiscal, military, and diplomatic matters. A brief look at the Saljūq and Mongol, Mamlūk, Ottoman, and Mughal practices follows.

1957 _____. "Dīwān-i Humāyūn." In EI2. Vol. 2 (see 20), pp. 337-39.

This title refers to the Ottoman imperial council, which, until the middle of the seventeenth century, was the central administrative organ of the empire. The entry discusses this "dīwān" under the topics of constitution and procedure, place of meeting, administration, and decline.

1958 Mez, Adam. The Renaissance of Islam (see 238).

Chapters 6-10 treat the bureaucracy of various Islamic states in the tenth century. The author cites the primary sources in his attempt to characterize the various functions of the bureaucracy. Topics covered are the administration, the wazīr, finances, the court, and the nobility.

1959 Qureshi, I.H. The Administration of the Sultanate of Delhi (see 289).

Covers the legal sovereign, the actual sovereign, the royal household, the ministers, finance, the army, justice, ḥisbah (the office of market inspector) and police, religious affairs, education and public works, provincial and local government, the spirit of government. Fifteen appendixes provide further information on various offices and revenues, and the bibliography is fairly complete, although the index is too brief.

1960 Richards, J.F. Mughal Administration in Golconda. Oxford: Clarendon Press, 1975, 350 pp.

A study of the state of Golconda centered in the capital, Hyderabad, in the late seventeenth and early eighteenth centuries. Provides reasons why the Mughals such as Awranzīb did not succeed well in Golconda after its overthrow in 1687. Selected bibliography and index.

1961 Roemer, H.R. "Inshā'. In EI2. Vol. 3 (see 20), pp. 1241-44.

After a brief discussion of the content of the science of inshā', the method of correctly drawing up state documents, papers, or letters, the author traces the history of this science from Muḥammad to the Ottoman Empire. Extensive bibliography.

1962 Sarkar, Sir J. Mughal Administration (see 424).

1963 Savory, R.M. "The Principal Offices of the Safawid State." Bulletin of the School of Oriental and African Studies 23 (1960): 91-105; 24 (1961):65-84.

Savory first treats the principal offices of this Persian dynasty during the rule of Ismā'īl I (1501-1524): the wakīl or vice-regent, the amīr al-umarā', or commander-in-chief, the qurchibashi (a military position), and the ṣadr, or head of the religious institution. In the second part, he describes the principal offices under the next ruler, Tahmasp I, and compares and contrasts these to the ones previously discussed, intending to demonstrate the gradual evolution these offices were undergoing.

THE OFFICES OF CALIPH AND SULṬĀN

1964 Ahmad, A. "An Eighteenth-Century Theory of Caliphate." Studia Islamica 28 (1968):127-33.

The theories of Shāh Walī Allāh (d. 1762) on the caliphate. The author paraphrases the ideas of Walī Allāh from his Izālah, to which the author makes frequent reference.

1965 Ahmad, Aziz. "Delhi Sultanate and the Universal Caliphate." In Studies in Islamic Culture in the Indian Environment (see 83), pp. 3-11.

A cursory study of state and rule in India from A.D. 710 to the partition of India. It discusses the various proposals from the universal caliphate of the early rulers to Pan-Islamism, the mutual influences of Hindus and Muslims, and the resulting separatism movement from 1857 to 1947.

1966 Arnold, Sir T.W. The Caliphate (see 147).

1967 Arnold, T.W. "Khalīfa." In EI1. Vol. 2, pt. 2 (see 32), pp. 881-85.

After a short introduction noting the various uses made of this term in Islam, the article first examines the history of the office of the caliph from its inception to its demise with the abolition of the Ottoman sultanate in 1922. The second part turns to the political theories of the caliphate, discussing al-Māwardī, Ibn Khaldūn, and the doctrine of the Shī'īs and the Khawārij. The article must be updated with more recent material. See "Khalīfa," in EI2, vol. 4 (see 20), pp. 937-53.

1968 Ashraf, K.M. "The 'Sultanate' and Its Reaction on Muslim Society." In Life and Conditions of the People of Hindustan. New Delhi: Munshiram Manoharlal, 1970, pp. 28-72.

In this first chapter of his book on India, Ashraf traces the evolution of the sultanate created on the pattern of the Sassanian emperors. He characterizes the sultanate of India as one based purely on force, so that the sulṭān and the state were "coterminous." The latter half of the chapter deals with the personnel structure of slaves and retainers that served the Indian sulṭān.

1969 Barthold, V.V. "Caliph and Sultan." Translated by N.S. Doniach. Islamic Quarterly 7 (1963):117-35.

Unfortunately, only the first installment of this article has appeared, so that the second, which examines the transfer of power from the caliphate to the sultanate, is not available except to readers of Russian. The study of the political power of the caliphs up to the Saljūqs, outlined in the first installment, is worth reading.

1970 Binder, L. "Al-Ghazālī's Theory of Government." Muslim World 45 (1955):229-41.

A somewhat different approach to this eleventh-century author than that of A.K.S. Lambton (see 1984). Binder intends to show that al-Ghazālī did not oppose former theories of government and in fact "paved the way to the post-'Abbāssid development of Sunnī political theory." He is using a different work of al-Ghazālī from that used by Lambton, whose major concern is indeed the caliphate.

1971 Bowen, H., and H.A.R. Gibb. "Caliphate and Sultanate." In Islamic Society and the West. Vol. 1, pt. 1 (see 338), pp. 26-38.

A brief essay that traces the development of Islamic thought on the caliphate and the sultanate from the earliest days, through the work of the Saljūq vizier Niẓām al-Mulk and the eleventh-century al-Ghazālī, down to the sulṭāns of the Ottoman Empire. The article intends to show how the caliphate and the sultanate to all intents and purposes became synonymous for these sulṭāns.

1972 Busse, M. "The Revival of Persian Kingship under the Būyids." In Islamic Civilization: 950-1150 (see 237), pp. 47-70.

The work, the best source for this topic, by the authority on the Būyids, follows the recorded events, which reveal the growing awareness by the Būyids of their Persian lineage.

1973 Farsakh, A.M. "A Comparison of the Sunnī Caliphate and the Shī'ī Imamate." Muslim World 59 (1969):50-63, 127-41.
A valuable comparison of the Sunnī and Shī'ī ideas of leadership of the Muslim community that discusses how the Imām/caliph is chosen, how an evil ruler is deposed, the personal qualities of the Imām/caliph, and his duties.

1974 Ghazālī, al-. Ghazālī's Book of Counsel for Kings (see 232).

1975 Gibb, H.A.R. "Al-Māwardī's Theory of the Khilāfah." Islamic Culture 11 (1937):291-302. In Studies on the Civilization of Islam (see 23), pp. 151-65.
Gibb examines one section of al-Māwardī's Al-Ahkām al-Sulṭāniyyah, starting with why the work was composed, and offering the suggestion that it was for a caliph and, in fact, to further a political end of the caliph. There is a section on the caliphate in the theory of al-Māwardī and a concluding section on the treatment of the caliphate when political power was seized by force. It is here, in al-Māwardī's appeal to necessity, that Gibb sees the beginnings of the downfall of the juristic theory of the caliphate.

1976 _____. "Some Considerations on the Sunnī Theory of the Caliphate." In Studies on the Civilization of Islam (see 23), pp. 141-50.
The article deals with the relation between Sunnī theory and the work of al-Māwardī. Use this article in conjunction with the entry (1975) on al-Māwardī.

1977 Hurgronje, G. Snouck. "Islam and Turkish Nationalism." In Verspreide Geschriften van C. Snouck Hurgronje. Vol. 6. Leiden: Brill, 1927, pp. 435-52.
A thoughtful essay on the state of the caliphate in the early twenties, the work reflects well the turmoil associated with this office then and records much of the public opinion of the time.

1978 Ibn Hasan. "The King and His Position in the State" and "The King and State Business." In The Central Structure of the Mughal Empire and Its Practical Working up to the Year 1657 (see 421), pp. 54-63, 64-91.
These two chapters attempt to describe the basis of kingship in Mughal India and consider some of the institutions peculiar to Indian rulers.

1979 Ibn Iskandar, Kai Kā'ūs. A Mirror for Princes (see 234).

1980 Ibn Khaldūn. The Muqaddimah (see 194).
The third chapter of volume 1, on dynasties, royal authority, the caliphate, is relevant here.

1981 Kerr, M. Islamic Reform: The Political Theories of Muhammad Abduh and Rashid Rida (see 1695).
Chapters 2 and 5 deal specifically with the caliphate, the former reviewing the classical theory and the latter the ideas of Muḥammad 'Abduh and Rashīd Riḍā.

1982 Kramers, J.H. "Sulṭān." In EI1. Vol. 4, pt. 1 (see 32), pp. 543-45.
Traces the original sense of the term "sulṭān" and its transformation into a title of office in the tenth and eleventh centuries. Kramers discusses the use of this title by the Ghaznavids and the Mamlūks, among others, ending with the Ottomans.

1983 Lambton, A.K.S. "Islamic Political Thought." In The Legacy of Islam (see 207), pp. 404-24.
A short but thorough introduction to the subject. Bibliography.

1984 _____. "The Theory of Kingship in the Naṣīhat ul-Muluk of Ghazālī." Islamic Quarterly 1 (1954):45-55.
The Persian text here treated by Lambton was written for a Saljūq sulṭān of the twelfth century and concerns the practical conduct of the ruler and his authority. The author provides a running exposition of the work, comparing and contrasting it with earlier works of this nature, and emphasizing its particular view of the ruler.

1985 Macdonald, D.B. "The Caliphate." Moslem World 7 (1917):349-57.
Though written some time ago, this essay is accurate and informative, aiming to provide a characterization of the office and various theories proposed in Islam on the caliphate.

1986 Madelung, W. "Imāma." In EI2. Vol. 3 (see 20), 1163-69.
"Imāma" is here used in the general sense of the "supreme leadership" of the Muslim community. The essay begins with its early historical development, placing emphasis on the struggle of Mu'āwiyah and 'Alī ibn Abī Ṭālib in which major factions with differing points of view on the question of Muslim leadership came into existence. The many doctrines of the imamate that gained some ascendancy in Islam are discussed: a) "Sunnism," b) "Mu'tazilism," c) "Shī'ism" (Zaydiyyah, Imāmiyyah, Ismā'īliyyah), and d) "Khawārijism." There are brief mentions of later writers like al-Ghazālī and modern Arab authors and of the directions various Shī'ī groups have taken since the twelfth century.

1987 Margoliouth, D.S. "The Caliphate Historically Considered." Moslem World 11 (1921): 332-43.
Though much of the information has been altered and added to in the last decades, the discussion on the history of the caliphate as an institution remains true. Readers should note that Margoliouth was involved in the early twentieth-century debate over the question of the caliphate's viability in the modern world.

1988 _____. "The Latest Developments of the Caliphate Question." Moslem World 14 (1924): 334-41.
An interesting essay, commenting on the abolition of the caliphate by Mustafa Kemal in Turkey and the shock expressed over this act in other Islamic lands.

1989 _____. "The Sense of the Title Khalifah." In A Volume of Oriental Studies Presented to Edward G. Browne. Edited by T.W. Arnold and R.A. Nicholson. London: Cambridge, 1922, pp. 322-28.

A brief study of the linguistic sense of the title, including a look at similar roots in other languages and some later derivations suggested by Ibn al-ʿArabī and Ibn Khaldūn.

1990 Mez, Adam. The Renaissance of Islam (see 238).

Chapters 1-3 discuss in some detail the caliphate and sultanate in the tenth century.

1991 Niẓām al-Mulk. The Book of Government (see 242).

1992 Ringgren, Helmer. "Some Religious Aspects of the Caliphate." In La Regalita Sacra: The Sacral Kingship; Contributions to the Central Theme of the VIIIth International Congress for the History of Religions (Rome, April 1955). Studies in the History of Religions, supplements to Numen, 4. Leiden: Brill, 1959, pp. 737-48.

Discusses elements of sacred kingship of the ancient Near East found in the caliphate.

1993 Rosenthal, E.I.J. Political Thought in Medieval Islam: An Introductory Outline. Cambridge: Cambridge University Press, 1962, 324 pp.

Part 1 examines juridical theories of the caliphate, the art of government as depicted by the "Mirrors for Princes" literature, and Ibn Khaldūn's philosophy of state. Part 2 offers a concise treatment of political philosophy in Islam, examining the theories of al-Fārābī, Ibn Sīnā, Ibn Bājja, Ibn Rushd, and al-Dawwānī. Exhaustive notes, plus glossary of terms.

1994 Siddiqi, A.H. "Caliphate and Sultanate." Journal of the Pakistan Historical Society 2 (1954):35-50.

A good study of the relation between these two offices, from the time of the Ṣaffārids of Persia to the Mongol invasions. The author points out those events that mark the gradual demise of the caliphate and the rise of the sultanate.

1995 Tyan, E. "Bayʿa." In EI2. Vol. 1 (see 20), pp. 1113-14.

This article on the act "by which one person is proclaimed and recognized as head of the Muslim State" has three parts: etymology of the word, the legal nature of the act, and the effect of the act on the ruler.

1996 Watt, W.M. "God's Caliph: Qur'ānic Interpretations and Umayyad Claims." In Iran and Islam: In Memory of V. Minorsky. Edited by C.E. Bosworth. Edinburgh: University Press, 1971, pp. 565-74.

A semantic study of the development of the Arabic root "kh-l-f" (which is usually in one form translated as "caliph"), traced through the Umayyad period to shed some light on the manner in which the Umayyads justified their rulership.

1997 _____. Islamic Political Thought. Islamic Surveys, no. 6. Edinburgh: University of Edinburgh Press, 1968, 186 pp.

A study of the beginnings and development of Muslim political concepts down to the modern day. Not a study of political theorists such as Niẓām al-Mulk and al-Ghazālī, the book looks instead at key historical documents, such as the constitution of Madīnah, and significant politico-religious movements such as the Shīʿah. The author has restricted himself to the first five centuries of Islam and in his final chapter applies his observations on the political thought of that time to the contemporary situation. With notes and index. The appendix is a translation of the constitution of Madīnah.

THE CITY (See also 2487-89)

1998 Abu Lughod, Janet L. Cairo: 1001 Years of the City Victorious (see 725).

The most authoritative study on Cairo, from its origins to contemporary times, with exhaustive bibliography on the city itself, plus related topics.

1999 Aldridge, James. Cairo. Boston: Little, Brown & Co., 1969, 370 pp.

A popular history of Cairo, written by a novelist who is a self-confessed admirer of the city and its people. Bibliography.

2000 Ettinghausen, Richard. "Muslim Cities: Old and New." In From Madina to Metropolis (see 16), pp. 290-318.

A well-illustrated survey. It attacks a number of clichés about old Muslim cities and points out how new buildings in cities could better preserve a continuity with the past, thereby establishing an artistic relationship between the old and new parts of cities.

2001 Grunebaum, G.E. von. "The Structure of the Muslim Town." In Islam: Essays in the Nature and Growth of a Cultural Tradition (see 25), pp. 141-58.

Here von Grunebaum seeks to define the Muslim town by contrasting it with the Greek or Roman towns, noting in particular the role of the town as a seat of power. The town in Islam, he concludes, was not an "autonomous association of citizens" like the Greek or Roman towns.

2002 Hourani, A.H. "Introduction: The Islamic City in the Light of Recent Research." In The Islamic City (see 168), pp. 9-24.

Hourani examines past research and the articles appearing in this book to characterize anew the typical medieval Islamic city, particularly the relation of the individual to his neighbor. The article is a milestone for knowledge of urban life in Islam.

2003 Lapidus, I.M., ed. Middle Eastern Cities (see 33).

2004 Lapidus, I.M. "Muslim Cities and Islamic Societies." In Middle Eastern Cities (see 33), pp. 47-79.
A study of the city in Islam as part of the larger social, geographic, and religious environment. The author concludes that cities were "modules of population woven into the fabric of a larger society."

2005 _____. Muslim Cities in the Later Middle Ages (see 276).

2006 _____. "Muslim Urban Society in Mamlūk Syria." In The Islamic City (see 168), pp. 195-206.
A study of the sociopolitical stratification of urban society, particularly in fourteenth-century Syria, which deals with three classes: the military elite, the ʿulamā,' and the rest of the population, including shopkeepers, artisans, and workers. Lapidus also discusses the composition of the quarter (or neighborhood) of the city.

2007 Lassner, J. "The Caliph's Personal Domain: The City Plan of Baghdad Re-Examined." In The Islamic City (see 168), pp. 103-18.
A valuable article, since it studies a city specifically created by a Muslim caliph to be the center of his rule. Lassner discusses the topography of Baghdād, pointing to various reasons for its plans.

2008 LeStrange, Guy. Baghdad during the Abbasid Caliphate (see 217).

2009 Scanlon, G.T. "Housing and Sanitation: Some Aspects of Medieval Public Service." In The Islamic City (see 168), pp. 179-94.
The author concludes that the Muslims borrowed from the Romans to solve problems of water and sanitation in the city of Fusṭāṭ in Egypt because of unique problems met there by Muslim architects, who found the area to be on hard rock and subject to problems caused by the flooding of the Nile.

2010 Stern, S.M. "The Constitution of the Islamic City" (see 1947).
Though most great civilizations have cities, Stern seeks to define what peculiarly constitutes the city in Islam. He notes the absence of corporative institutions in general in Islamic urban society and for this reason attacks any attempt to equate the Islamic guilds with Western craft guilds or the madrasah with the Western university.

2011 Wendell, Charles. "Baghdad, Imago Mundi and Other Foundation Lore" (see 1896.

EDUCATION

2012 Ahmad, Aziz. An Intellectual History of Islam in India (see 82), pp. 52-65.
A brief sketch of Muslim educational institutions in medieval and modern India is found in chapter 6.

2013 Aḥmed, Munīr-ud-Dīn. Muslim Education and the Scholars' Social Status up to the Fifth Century Muslim Era in the Light of Taʾrikh Baghdad (see 181).

2014 Akrawi, Matta. "The University Tradition in the Middle East." In The University and the Man of Tomorrow: The Centennial Lectures. Vol. 11. Beirut: American University of Beirut, 1967, pp. 99-125.
Discusses the main features of traditional Arab-Muslim higher education, which was motivated by the idea of the cultivation of knowledge for God's sake, as well as more recent modern university development affected by Western educational ideas, and the influence of the former upon the latter. The author, at the time of writing the article, was professor of education at the American University of Beirut and was formerly president of the University of Baghdād.

2015 Arab Information Center. Education in the Arab States. New York: Arab Information Center, 1966, 306 pp.
A collection of information papers on various Arab countries including Algeria, Iraq, Jordan, Kuwait, Lebanon, Libya, Morocco, Saudi Arabia, Sudan, Syria, Tunisia, U.A.R., and Yemen. In each case an outline of the educational system is given, discussing historical background, particular problems such as influence of colonial rule, levels of education, and various types of educational programs (e.g., technical and professional).

2016 Arasteh, A.R. Education and Social Awakening in Iran, 1850-1968 (see 872).

2017 Benor, J.L. "Arab Education in Israel." Middle Eastern Affairs 1 (1950):224-29.
Discusses changes introduced into the education of Arabs after the Israeli occupation of Palestine in 1948.

2018 Beshir, Mohamed Omer. Educational Development in the Sudan, 1898-1956. Oxford: Clarendon, 1969, 276 pp.
Although the work is a fairly detailed account of educational development in the Sudan from colonial times to independence, it may also be seen as a case study in educational development among countries formerly under colonial control. Contains bibliography, index, appendixes, and tables.

2019 Buchanan, J.R. "Muslim Education in Syria (before the War)." Moslem World 12 (1922): 394-406.
A historical account of educational developments during this period. A seven-year sample curriculum is included.

2020 Center for the Study of the Modern Arab World. Arab Culture and Society in Change . . . A Bibliography (see 540).
Two sections of this bibliography (sections 7 and 12) deal with Islamic and Arab education in a fairly comprehensive way; includes articles in other Western European languages and is partially annotated.

2021 Curle, Adam. Planning for Education in Pakistan: A Personal Case Study. London: Tavistock, 1966, 208 pp.
Educational planning is here discussed in terms of the author's own experience in Pakistan. Education in various regions of Pakistan, problems, the role of the adviser, and Pakistan's planning organization are dealt with. Contains an index, tables, and maps.

2022 Dodge, Bayard. Al-Azhar: A Millennium of Muslim Leaning. Washington: Middle East Institute, 1961, 239 pp.
A history of one of the most famous Muslim institutions of learning, which is still today one of the most influential. The author devotes attention to the ideology of al-Azhar's founders, the Fāṭimids, and traces its development through the Ayyūbid, Mamlūk, and Ottoman periods as well as the period of modern reforms. The book is based on Muslim sources and includes appendixes, bibliography, and index.

2023 _____. Muslim Education in Medieval Times (see 188).

2024 Doolittle, M. "Lessons in Religion and Ethics." In Macdonald Presentation Volume. Princeton, N.J.: Princeton University Press, 1933, pp. 107-17.
This translation of a Muslim textbook in religion for primary schools was prepared as an example of the material presented to Muslim children and of the method used in presenting that material. Should be read in conjunction with the next entry (2025).

2025 _____. "Moslem Religious Education in Syria." Moslem World 18 (1928):374-80.
This article is interesting for the period it discusses (the twenties), though otherwise dated. It includes a description of the available textbooks at that time.

2026 "The Education of Women." Moslem World 8 (1918):395-403.
This translation of an article by an anonymous Muslim author originally appeared in Qibla (Mecca, November 28, 1917/1336 A.H.); it is interesting for its attitude toward women's education and should be compared with more recent articles on the subject.

2027 Goldziher, Ignaz. "Education." In Encyclopaedia of Religion and Ethics. Vol. 5 (see 1130), pp. 198-207.
A basic article, founded on original sources, that deals principally with primary education in the traditional Islamic world, but has some reference to higher education as well as to turn-of-the-century reforms. Sections include: (a) Education in the Early History of Islam, (b) Subjects of Primary Education and Forbidden Books, (c) Status of the Elementary Teacher, (d) Payment of Teachers, (e) School Administration, (f) Education of Girls, (g) Education in Ethical and Political Writings, and (h) Modern Movements toward Reforms. Good bibliography.

2028 Hamiuddin Khan, M. History of Muslim Education. Vol. 1, 712 to 1750 A.D. Karachi: Academy of Education Research, 1967, 260 pp.
Describes Muslim education with particular reference to India, from A.D. 712 to the decline of the Mughals in A.D. 1750. There are chapters on the promotion of learning in Islam, progress of education under the sulṭāns of Delhi and in autonomous states under early and later Mughal rulers, women's education, curricula, development of the arts, system of education and education of Hindus under the Muslims.

2029 Harbi, Muhammad K. Technical Education in the Arab States. Paris: UNESCO, 1965, 57 pp.
A good general description of modern education, including technical education, in the Arab world. Education of the area in general is discussed in addition to education in particular countries. Includes tables.

2030 Heyworth-Dunne. J. An Introduction to the History of Education in Modern Egypt (see 755).

2031 Kazamias, Andreas M. Education and the Quest for Modernity in Turkey. London: Allen & Unwin, 1966, 304 pp.
The study attempts to establish the connections between education and social change, using Turkey as a case study. Information may be found on traditional Islamic education as it existed in Ottoman times, as well as on the present state of education in this Islamic country, which has attempted to modernize and secularize along Western lines. The historical part of the study is based on secondary sources, and the present situation is analyzed on the basis of the author's research. With appendixes and index.

2032 Khan, Muʻid. "The Muslim Theories of Education during the Middle Ages." Islamic Culture 18 (1944):418-33.
Following a very general survey of sources that deal with Muslim education, the author devotes the rest of his article to an explanation of the Ḥanafī and Shāfiʻī theories of education in the Middle Ages. The discussion focuses on early methods of education, definition of Muslim education, classification of subjects, courses of study, and methods of teaching according to the Ḥanafī and Shāfiʻī "schools." Although the article is not well written, it may be useful for its information, which is not found in this form elsewhere.

2033 Khan, Yusif Husain. "The Educational System in Medieval India." Islamic Culture 30 (1956):106-25.
A survey article dealing with major figures and developments in medieval Muslim education in India.

2034 Knight, E.G. "Education in French North Africa." Islamic Quarterly 2 (1955):294-308.
An enlightening article that reveals the disparities and discriminatory practices in the education of North African and French students in North Africa (especially Morocco and Tunisia) under French rule.

2035 Kraemer, J. "Tradition and Reform at al-Azhar University." Middle Eastern Affairs 7 (1956):89-94.

This description of the reforms that have, since the Reform Law was passed in 1930, changed al-Azhar from a medieval to a modern university is based on the author's personal experience as a participant and observer in lectures and conversations with teachers and students.

2036 Laoust, H. "Introduction à une étude de l'enseignement arabe en Égypte." Revue des études islamiques 7 (1933):301-51.

An excellent article describing the development of modern education up to the time of the article and in light of social, political, and economic developments.

2037 Makdisi, G. "Muslim Institutions of Learning in Eleventh Century Baghdad." Bulletin of the School of Oriental and African Studies 24 (1961):1-56.

A reassessment of Ignaz Goldziher's view, as set forth in his Le dogme et la loi de l'Islam, that it was in the Niẓāmiyyah institutions "that the victory of the Ash'arite school was decided in its struggle against Mu'tazilsim on the one hand, and intransigent orthodoxy on the other." Other studies have been based on this view, but Makdisi sees the need for a closer examination of the sources. He sets out to do this by examining educational institutions in Baghdād both before and after the foundation of the Niẓāmiyyah, in order to better determine its role. Thus, information may be gained not only about the Niẓāmiyyah and the theological-political debates of the time but also about Muslim institutions of learning in Baghdād in the eleventh century, an important era in the development of Muslim education.

2038 Matthews, Roderic, and Matta Akraw, I. Education in Arab Countries of the Near East. Washington: American Council on Education, 1949, 584 pp.

A descriptive study of the educational systems of Egypt, Iraq, Jordan, Palestine, Syria, Lebanon. It deals with organization and administration, primary and secondary schools, higher education, educational missions, and teacher training in each country, as well as items of special concern to particular countries. The last chapter is an interpretation of the role of education in cultural and social change. Contains an index, charts, tables, and illustrations.

2039 Nakosteen, M. History of Islamic Origins of Western Education, 800-1350 (see 201).

2040 Pederson, J. "Masdjid." In EI1. Vol. 3, pt. 1 (see 1899), pp. 350-68.

Still one of the most basic writings on traditional Muslim education, the article is divided into sections dealing with: Islamic studies in the mosque to the end of the Fāṭimid period; special educational institutions; origin and spread of the madrasah school; development of the madrasah school and similar institutions; libraries; the subjects taught and methods of instruction; the teachers; the students; and recent reforms in education. Contains a bibliography.

2041 _____. "Some Aspects of the History of the Madrasa." Islamic Culture 3 (1929):525-37.

An excellent, though general, article that deals not only with the history of the madrasah school, as the title would indicate, but also with the institutions of traditional learning in early Islam, prior to the rise and spread of the madrasah school.

2042 Pinto, O. "The Libraries of the Arabs during the Time of the Abbasides." Islamic Culture 3 (1929):210-43.

The important role of books in Muslim culture is emphasized as well as the practice of establishing libraries for the use of all. The author includes a list of all the public libraries he could find mentioned as existing in the "Arab Empire" during the 'Abbāsid caliphate, as well as whatever information as he could find about each.

2043 Qubain, Fahim I. Education and Science in the Arab World. Baltimore: Johns Hopkins Press, 1966, 539 pp.

The main purpose of the study is to survey the science-training establishment and scientific manpower resources in Arab countries. In the process, however, it covers the entire educational system and serves as a good introduction to modern education in Arab countries. Contains tables, bibliography, and index.

2044 Rahman, Fazlur. "Education." In Islam (see 1095), pp. 221-37.

Chapter 11 provides an excellent introduction to the subject.

2045 _____. "The Qur'ānic Solution of Pakistan's Educational Problem." Islamic Studies 6 (1967):315-26.

An interpretation of the Qur'ān's attitude toward education, the Muslim philosophy of education, and what function this attitude and philosophy should play in a modern Muslim nation such as Pakistan.

2046 Rauf, Abdur. Religious Education in West Pakistan. Lahore: West Pakistan Bureau of Education, 1964, 67 pp.

A useful survey of religious education at various levels with some attention given to specialized religious institutions.

2047 Rosenthal, Franz. The Technique and Approach of Muslim Scholarship. Rome: Pontificium Institutum Biblicum, 1947, 74 pp.

The main purpose of the work is to illustrate "the Muslim attitude toward fundamental problems of scholarship and to show the similarities of and differences between Muslim and Western scholarship." As the author notes, the study is incomplete, since it is based on documentation that is fuller for some centuries (ninth, tenth, fifteenth, sixteenth) than for others. Still, it is the only study of its kind thus far produced.

2048 Sadiq, Issa Khan. Modern Persia and Her Educational System. New York: Bureau of Publications, Teachers' College, Columbia University, 1931, 125 pp.
This analysis gives background information on the country, educational traditions, administration of the educational system, school system, and problems and proposals for their solutions. Contains a bibliography.

2049 Sahay, Binode Kumar. Education and Learning under the Great Mughals, 1526-1707 A.D., with Special Reference to Contemporary Literatures. Bombay: New Literature, 1968, 238 pp.
One chapter deals in particular with education under the Mughals. The educational "system" is discussed, as well as the curriculum at different stages, the policy of various emperors, and the principal centers of learning. Bibliography and index.

2050 Sayyidayn, Khwajah Ghulam. The Humanist Tradition in Indian Educational Thought. Bombay: Asia, 1966, 237 pp.
Following a rather lengthy and wordy first chapter (which does, however, provide the reader with a feeling for the "Indian setting") the author endeavors to present the philosophies of education of several thinkers in this field in India. Though not all are Muslim, he does deal with such well-known Muslims as Iqbāl, Mawlāna Abū'l-Kalām Āzād, and Zakir Ḥusain. A useful introduction to these men, who made contributions in educational thought during this century. Index.

2051 Shalaby, Ahmad. History of Muslim Education. Beirut: Dar al-Kashahaf, 1954, 266 pp.
In this study covering the seventh century A.D. until the fall of the Ayyūbid dynasty in Egypt in 648 (A.D. 1250), Shalaby discusses the places of education before the establishment of schools, libraries, teachers, students, founders, endowments, and organization. A supplement to the study deals with Ismā'īlism and education during the Fāṭimid period in Egypt. This is one of the better introductions to Muslim education in early and medieval times. Bibliography, index, and plates.

2052 Sharabi, H.B. "The Syrian University." Middle Eastern Affairs 6 (1955):155-56.
A description of the history, administration, personnel, curriculum, and student body of the Syrian university.

2053 Snider, N. "Mosque Education in Afghanistan." Muslim World 58 (1968):24-35.
The article, which summarizes mosque education in present-day Afghanistan, shows it to be not far removed from medieval Muslim education.

2054 Tibawi, A.L. "Arab Education under the Caliphate." Islamic Review 42 (June 1954): 13-18.
A good introductory article on education in early and medieval Islam. See also Tibawi's later article (2057) and Makdisi's (2037), which do not agree on several points. Unlike most articles of this sort, this one devotes some attention to Muslim education in Spain.

2055 _____. Islamic Education: Its Traditions and Modernization into the Arab National Systems. London: Luzac, 1972, 256 pp.
A very good (perhaps the best to date) introduction to modernization in Muslim education, with one chapter devoted to particular national systems. Bibliography.

2056 _____. "Muslim Education in the Golden Age of the Caliphate." Islamic Culture 28 (1954): 418-38.
Discusses Muslim attitudes toward education as reflected in the Qur'ān and tradition, theories of education presented in Muslim educational literature, and various types of educational institutions, among other matters.

2057 _____. "Origin and Character of al-Madrasah." Bulletin of the School of Oriental and African Studies 25 (1962):225-38.
A critique of assumptions made by G. Makdisi (see 237).

2058 _____. "Philosophy of Muslim Education." Islamic Quarterly 4 (1957):78-89.
A good, concise article on the Muslim philosophy of education. Attention is given as well to several individuals or groups who either have tried to change or in some way have influenced that philosophy.

2059 Tota, Khalil A. The Contribution of the Arabs to Education. New York: Bureau of Publications, Teachers' College, Columbia University, 1926, 105 pp.
Tota has culled the sources for information on early and medieval Islamic education and as a result has produced one of the most comprehensive discussions of the subject. Though new interpretations of the information have been offered by such scholars as Makdisi (see 2037), little information has been added since the completion of this study.

2060 Tritton, A.S. Materials on Muslim Education in the Middle Ages. London: Luzac, 1957, 209 pp.
This volume is a collection of quotations from Muslim sources showing what kinds of information are available. These are divided into chapters dealing with such subjects as elementary education, advanced education, teachers and taught, scholastic life, institutions, classification of studies, Christians and Jews, tradition, the Qur'ān and the law, philosophy, medicine, and books. Little attempt is made at interpretation or analysis. Bibliography and index.

2061 _____. "Muslim Education in the Middle Ages (c. 600-800 A.D.)." Muslim World 43 (1953): 82-94.
Educational attitudes and practices of early and medieval times are illustrated and described from original sources in this interesting and informative article. It suffers, however, from lack of adequate documentation, although the author does cite Ibn al-Ḥajj (d. 1383 A.D.) as a main authority.

2062 Williams, James. Education in Egypt before British Control. Birmingham: F. Juckes, 1939, 83 pp.
Two chapters of this pamphlet deal with education during the Islamic period in Egypt: "Medieval Moslem Education" and "Education under the Khedives." Though the material found therein can be found in greater detail elsewhere, this short pamphlet, based on Muslim sources, is accurate, well written, and interesting.

THE LAW

GENERAL STUDIES

2063 Cardahi, C. "Conflict of Law." In Law in the Middle East. Edited by M. Khadduri and H.J. Liebesney. Washington: Middle East Institute, 1955, pp. 334-48.
The article catalogs various areas of conflict in the law without and within Islam. See also 2080-81, 2116, 2125, 2131, 2138, 2145, 2158, 2168, 2211, 2214.

2064 Charnay, Jean-Paul. Islamic Culture and Socio-Economic Change (see 1664).
Of particular interest here is the final chapter, "Reciprocal Influences between Methodologies of Moslem Law and Western Law."

2065 Coulson, N.J. Conflicts and Tensions in Islamic Jurisprudence. Chicago: University of Chicago Press, 1969, 118 pp.
Six superb lectures given at the University of Chicago Law School. Each is a compact essay on a different point of conflict in the law, liberally illustrated and clearly stated. The first three examine three points of conflict in the development of the law; the last three touch on legal practice and administration. For the beginner the book can identify the nature of Islamic law.

2066 _____. A History of Islamic Law. Edinburgh: University of Edinburgh Press, 1964, 264 pp.
Certainly the most readable authoritative work on the history of the development of Islamic law and its numerous concepts, the book is divided into three parts: genesis, medieval, and modern. It supplies necessary addenda to Schacht's work (see 2076), is well indexed, and has a good glossary of technical terms. Recommended for the first reading on Islamic law.

2067 _____. "The State and the Individual in Islamic Law." International and Comparative Law Quarterly 6 (1957):49-60.
Investigates the status of the individual in the sharīʿah (law) and concludes that, in the eyes of the traditional Islamic jurisprudence, the individual is virtually powerless before the state, and the ruler is limited only by his conscience. Coulson concludes that a present-day attempt of modern Islamic states to guarantee individual liberties is indeed a difficult task, as this is denied by the sharīʿah itself.

2068 Goitein, S.D. "The Birth-Hour of Muslim Law?" Muslim World 50 (1960):23-29.
The author, sifting through various materials from the Prophet, concludes that Islamic law was not born long after his death, but was in fact a conscious concern of the Prophet in his lifetime. The Prophet, Goitein claims, did envisage "law as part of divine revelation."

2069 Goldziher, I. Mohammed and Islam. Translated by K.C. Seeyle. New Haven, Conn.: Yale University Press, 1917, 360 pp.
Chapter 2, "The Development of Law," discusses the initial stages of Islamic law. This translation is not generally available, because the author suppressed it due to some inaccuracies.

2070 Goldziher, Ignaz. Muslim Studies (see 127).
The second volume is mainly concerned with tradition, but the subject of law does come up. See the index under "law" for pertinent sections.

2071 Goldziher, I. "The Principles of Law in Islam." In The Historians' History of the World. Edited by H.S. Williams. New York: Hooper & Jackson, 1908, pp. 294-304.
A brief essay on the development of the law in Islam. Of particular interest is Goldziher's discussion of influences from Roman, Jewish, and Greek sources.

2072 _____, and J. Schacht. "Fiḳh." In EI2. Vol. 2 (see 20), pp. 886-91.
The first article by Goldziher is an examination of various usages of the term; the second examines a "fiqh" in its sense of jurisprudence. There follows a very brief history of the development of jurisprudence. The article presupposes some acquaintance with the law.

2073 Levy, Reuben. "Islamic Jurisprudence." In The Social Structure of Islam (see 34), pp. 150-91.
A good introductory essay on the basic sources for the law, the contribution of al-Shāfiʿī (d. 820), and the so-called four schools of orthodox Islam. An appendix offers synopses of three typical lawbooks.

2074 Macdonald, D.B. "Development of Jurisprudence." In The Development of Muslim Theology, Jurisprudence, and Constitutional Theory (see 1570), pp. 65-118.
A dated portrayal of the development of the law, requiring emendation from the introductions of Schacht (2076) or Coulson (2065).

2075 Ibn Abi Zayd. First Steps in Muslim Jurisprudence. Translated by A.D. Russell and A.M. Suhrawardy. London: Luzac, 1906, 121 pp.
This short work is an edited translation of parts of the legal text of the tenth-century Mālikī jurist, Ibn Abi Zayd. Besides being a firsthand introduction to this school, it is a valuable means of becoming acquainted with technical Arabic legal vocabulary.

2076 Schacht, Joseph. An Introduction to Islamic Law. Oxford: Clarendon, 1964, 304 pp.
This remains the best introduction available. The first fifteen chapters constitute a historical survey of amazing depth, in so brief a space, of Islamic jurisprudence. The next nine chapters treat various subjects related to the law, such as legal procedures and contracts. The final chapter on the nature of Islamic law is an exquisite essay on how Islamic jurisprudence is peculiar to Islam. With an eighty-page bibliography (partially annotated), a calendar of important "legal" dates (from the beginning of the Islamic era to the present day), and an exhaustive glossary of technical terms.

2077 _____. "Islamic Religious Law." In The Legacy of Islam (see 207), pp. 392-403.
Brief, comprehensive introduction to the subject. Bibliography.

2078 _____. "The Law." In Unity and Variety in Muslim Civilization (see 26), pp. 65-86.
A survey of the development of Islamic law to the present day.

2079 _____. "Law and Justice." In The Cambridge History of Islam. Vol. 2 (see 30), pp. 539-68.
The essay presents the history of the development of jurisprudence in Islam from the days of the Prophet to the age of the three great empires (Ottoman, Ṣafavid, Mughal) of the sixteenth century.

2080 _____. "Pre-Islamic Background and Early Development of Jurisprudence." In Law in the Middle East (see 2063), pp. 28-56.
The article outlines in detail, with corroborating evidence, Schacht's now famous theory of the ancient schools of law, and develops the role played by al-Shāfiʿī. This is well worth reading if the author's longer work on jurisprudence is inaccessible or too difficult.

2081 _____. "The Schools of Law and Later Developments of Jurisprudence. In Law in the Middle East (see 2063), pp. 57-84.
A continuation of the previous article (2080), which examines in some detail the role of the qāḍī and the muftī (legal officers) as well as "legal devices." Schacht ends with some general remarks on Western influences on Islamic law.

2082 Williams, John A. "The Law: Fiqh, Sharīʿa." In Islam (see 1105), pp. 78-121.
After a brief introduction, Williams presents various topics such as worship and marriage from the fiqh lawbooks, and provides translations from the original sources to exemplify how each topic was treated in the fiqh literature. Very helpful for beginners.

GREAT LEGALISTS OF ISLAM

2083 Fariz, K.A. "An Early Muslim Judge, Shurayh." Islamic Culture 30 (1956):287-308.
This brief biography is based on original sources and is well documented. Most of the article is devoted to translations or paraphrases of the reports of Shurayh, a midseventh-century judge of Kūfah.

2084 Fyzee, A.A.A. "Ismaʿili Law and Its Founder." Islamic Culture 9 (1935):107-12.
A brief account of the life of the Fāṭimid judge al-Nuʿmān, who is our major source of Fāṭimid law.

2085 Heffening, W. "Al-Shāfiʿī." In Shorter Encyclopedia of Islam (see 22), pp. 512-15.
The article covers the life and the works of this early legalist, who was the first true organizer of Islamic law, but fails to discuss any of his ideas.

2086 _____. "Al-Shaibānī." In Shorter Encyclopedia of Islam (see 22), pp. 518-19.
This describes the life of the great jurist of the late eighth century and mentions his works without any examination of their contents.

2087 Laoust, H. "Aḥmad b. Ḥanbal" (see 1660).

2088 Schacht, Joseph. "Abū Ḥanīfa al-Nuʿmān." In EI2. Vol. 1 (see 20), pp. 123-24.
A brief biography of the eponym of the Ḥanafī school of law. His doctrines and those of his school are not treated here.

2089 _____. "Abū Yūsuf." In EI2. Vol. 1 (see 20), pp. 164-65.
This article traces the life of the eighth-century Abū Yūsuf and examines the modification of attitudes toward traditions that he effected on the nascent Ḥanafī school of law.

2090 _____. "Al-Awzāʾī." In EI2. Vol. 1 (see 20), pp. 772-73.
The article outlines what is known of the life of this early eighth-century legalist, his works, and some of his important ideas. Bibliography.

2091 _____. "Mālik b. Anas." In Shorter Encyclopedia of Islam (see 22), pp. 320-24.
Covers the sources of knowledge on Mālik, his life and works, assesses his role in jurisprudence, and discusses the madhhab (school) that used his name. Bibliography.

SOURCES OF THE LAW

2092 Berque, J. "ʿAmal." In EI2. Vol. 1 (see 20), pp. 427-28.
Contains a discussion of "judicial practice" as a source of law. This is a very brief treatment, but followed by a complete bibliography.

2093 Brunschvig, R. "Logic and Law in Classical Islam." In Logic in Classical Islamic Culture (see 1596), pp. 113-30.
A most enlightening essay on the status of logic in the law. Particularly valuable is the discussion on "analogy." The article raises many questions it does not always seek to answer and introduces much of the technical terminology of the legalists.

2094 Coulson, N.J. "Doctrine and Practice in Islamic Law: One Aspect of the Problem." Bulletin of the School of Oriental and African Studies 18 (1956):211-26.
A study of the conflict common in Islamic jurisprudence between the theory of law proposed by the legalists and the practical necessities of actual court cases and legal intercourse. Coulson has chosen to use the office of the judge (qāḍī) to illustrate his point, as well as the different approaches characteristic of the Malikī and Ḥanafī schools of law.

2095 _____. "Muslim Custom and Case-law." Die Welt des Islam 6 (1959):13-24.
A generally informative essay on the existence of custom and judicial practice as binding in Islam, as opposed to the acclaimed doctrine of the sharīʿah, outside of which custom and case law frequently stand.

2096 Grunebaum, Gustave E. von. "The Body Politic: Law and the State." In Medieval Islam (see 192), pp. 142-69.
The first half of this essay deals with the relation of the theoretical law and actual circumstances. The emphasis on the principle of consensus as the basic instrument in the explication of the law is particularly noteworthy.

2097 Hamidullah, M. "Sources of Islamic Law--A New Approach." Islamic Quarterly 1 (1954): 205-11.
This cursory discussion points out the fact that the four traditionally held sources of the law do not represent all the sources.

2098 Hasan, A. "The Theory of Naskh." Islamic Studies 4 (1965):181-200.
The article examines the classical theory of abrogation, a device that allowed greater flexibility to the legalists. Though the article has much useful information, the reader should be aware of the argument underlying the author's discussion, namely, his denial "that some of the Qur'ānic verses are abrogated."

2099 Hourani, G.F. "The Basis of Authority of Consensus in Sunnite Islam." Studia Islamica 21 (1964):13-60.
An intellectual history of the various arguments adduced for consensus down to modern days. The reader should note that the author intends to demonstrate that there is no sound basis for the traditional doctrine of consensus and that few arguments have been based on consensus. To this end the latter parts of the article treat Western scholarship on consensus in Islamic law.

2100 Levy, Reuben. "Usage, Custom and Secular Law under Islam." In The Social Structure of Islam (see 34), pp. 242-70.
A study of the interaction of Muslim law and local customs or, as in the case of modern Persia and Turkey, of Muslim law and non-Muslim canons. The first part of the chapter, on custom, is the most useful, since in the actual practice of the law's precepts local custom has played a very significant role.

2101 Rahman, Fazlur. Islamic Methodology in History (see 1246).

2102 Roberts, R. The Social Laws of the Qur'an (see 1202).
Though Roberts reads too much into the influence of Jewish materials on Islamic legal thought, he gives an inadequate view of the relation of the law and the Qur'ān and translates numerous passages relevant to the law.

2103 Santillana, D. de. "Law and Society." In The Legacy of Islam (see 185), pp. 284-310.
The article is superficial in its survey of the law and may, unless critically read, mislead the reader concerning the growth of legal principles of Islam.

2104 Schacht, Joseph. "Foreign Elements in Ancient Islamic Law." Journal of Comparative Legislation 32 (1950):9-16.
In the most important work in English on the subject, Schacht gives examples of the influence of Roman and Persian law, the canon law of the Eastern churches, and Talmudic law on the law of Islam. Schacht does not judge the degree of such influence on early Islamic law, but simply cites instances known to him.

2105 _____, and D.B. Macdonald. "Idjtihād." In EI2. Vol. 3 (see 20), pp. 1026-27.
The essay discusses ijtihād (original thinking), a particular methodology for deriving laws, under three headings: early Islam, the classical period, and late medieval times. The historical treatment is too general with little information actually given and no examples to help define the term adequately.

2106 Schacht, Joseph. "Ikhtilāf." In EI2. Vol. 3 (see 20), pp. 1061-62.
A very sketchy discussion on the divergence of opinions among legalists and the literature associated with this subject.

2107 _____. The Origins of Muhammadan Jurisprudence. Oxford: Clarendon, 1950, 348 pp.
This is the most influential Western study of Islamic jurisprudence. By extensive research into the work of the jurist al-Shāfiʿī, Schacht was able to trace the early evolution of Islamic law from the first century A.H. to the flourishing of the schools of law two centuries later. His most astonishing findings concern the relation of the law and its principles, especially ḥadīth (tradition). The work is technical and too difficult for the beginner. See also 1233.

2108 _____. "Taklīd." In Shorter Encyclopedia of Islam (see 22), pp. 562-64.
The article treats the pattern of uncritical adoption of words or actions in its pre-Islamic context, and points out the effects of this kind of uncritical adoption on law in Islam.

2109 Shāfiʻī, al-. Islamic Jurisprudence: Shāfiʻī's Risala. Translated by M. Khadduri. Baltimore: Johns Hopkins Press, 1961, 376 pp.
A translation of a classical work of law, by Muḥammad ibn Idrīs al-Shāfiʻī. The glossary, index, and short bibliography are helpful, and the lengthy introduction to al-Shāfiʻī and his Risālah is the best available.

2110 Vesey-Fitzgerald, S.G. "Nature and Sources of the Shariʻa." In Law in the Middle East (see 2063), pp. 85-112.
A brief discussion of the four sources of the law, as well as the five categories of value. The author also illustrates the nature of the law with examples peculiar to Islamic law.

2111 Weiss, Bernard. "Al-Āmidī on the Basis of Authority of Consensus." In Essays on Islamic Civilization Presented to Niyazi Berkes (see 1235), pp. 342-56.
An analysis of a prominent twelfth-century Shāfiʻī jurist's exposition of the textual basis (Qur'ān and ḥadīth) of the authority of consensus.

2112 Ziadeh, F. "Urf and Law in Islam." In The World of Islam: Studies in Honour of P.K. Hitti. Edited by J. Kritzeck and R.B. Winder. London: Macmillan, 1959, pp. 60-67.
This is a brief study of "custom" in Islam and its relation to the law. Ziadeh notes that the former has often displaced the latter in Islam.

SPECIFIC POINTS OF THE LAW

Administration of the Law

2113 Brunschvig, R. "Bayyina." In EI2. Vol. 1 (see 20), pp. 1150-51.
A clear exposition of the emphasis placed on eyewitness testimony in Islam.

2114 Cohen, C., and M. Talbi. "Ḥisba." In EI2. Vol. 3 (see 20), pp. 485-89.
A general article, introductory in nature, on the duty of every Muslim to promote good and forbid evil. Some detail is given on the office of the muḥtasib (market inspector). With a good bibliography.

2115 Chehata, Chafik T. "Aḳt." In EI2. Vol. 1 (see 20), pp. 318-20.
A detailed discussion of the elements related to the "legal transaction" in Islam.

2116 Gibb, H.A.R. "Constitutional Organization." In Law in the Middle East (see 2063), pp. 3-27.
Gibb demonstrates the place of the ummah (community) in the law and how Muslim theoreticians rationalized the political forms and institutions to maintain and express the law. He translates important paragraphs on this topic from Abd al-Ẓāhir al-Baghdādī, Ibn Khaldūn, al-Ghazālī and Naṣīr al-dīn Ṭūsī.

2117 _____, and H. Bowen. "The Administration of Law." In Islamic Society and the West. Vol. 1, pt. 1 (see 338), pp. 114-33.
This article discusses the role of the jurists, the qāḍīs (judges), and the muftīs (legal advisers). Gibb emphasizes the modus operandi worked out between government and these three officials.

2118 _____. "The Ottoman Empire and the Sacred Law." In Islamic Society and the West. Vol. 1, pt. 1 (see 338), pp. 19-25.
Provides a brief survey of the status of the sharīʻah (Islamic jurisprudence) before the Ottomans and describes the role of the sharīʻah in the Ottoman Empire.

2119 Hamidullah, M. "Administration of Justice in Early Islam." Islamic Culture 2 (1937): 162-71.
Hamidullah notes those legal aspects that are known to have been treated by Muḥammad in his lifetime, thereby constituting early Islamic practice of law.

2120 Hassan, H.I. "Judiciary System from the Rise of Islam to 567 A.H." Islamic Quarterly 7 (1963):23-30.
Though the article is brief and short on evidence, it does mention some of the changing aspects of judgeship in Islam up to the eleventh century.

2121 Heffening, W. "Shāhid." In Shorter Encyclopedia of Islam (see 22), pp. 517-18.
A descriptive article on the legal witness and his qualifications under Islamic law.

2122 Juynboll, T.W. "Ḳāḍī." In Shorter Encyclopedia of Islam (see 22), pp. 201-02.
Short treatment of the office of judge in Islam.

2123 Mez, Adam. "The Qāḍī." In The Renaissance of Islam (see 238), pp. 216-34.
A lively portrayal of the office of the judge in tenth-century Islam, with examples of incidents taken from the sources.

2124 Tyan, E. "Fatwā." In EI2. Vol. 2 (see 20), pp. 866.
This article traces historically the "legal opinion" given by the muftī in order to describe its function in legal pronouncements.

2125 _____. "Judicial Organization." In Law in the Middle East (see 2063), pp. 236-78.
Discusses the qādī and the muftī (legal officers), their jurisdictions and roles, and the minor authorities of the courts. Considered also are the criminal (mazālim) courts and the shurṭah (police).

Commercial Law

2126 Aghnides, N.P. Mohammedan Theories of Finance (see 162).

2127 Goitein, S.D. "Commercial and Family Partnerships in the Countries of Medieval Islam." Islamic Studies 3 (1964):315-37.
Discusses legal terminology of business transactions, not from legal handbooks, but from actual legal papers found in the Cairo Geniza of Fāṭimid and Ayyūbid times. A valuable study.

2128 Heffening, W. "Tidjāra." In EI1. Vol. 4, pt. 2 (see 32), pp. 747-51.
This article examines tijārah (trade), mentioning the example of the Prophet and the ḥadīth literature for the legal attitude of Islam. It lists those trade practices that are forbidden and reviews the thoughts of al-Ghazālī, al-Subkī, al-Dimishqī, and Ibn Khaldūn on the subject. Although the article is dated by much new research, it is a good introduction.

2129 Khan, M.S. "Mohammedan Laws against Usury and How They Are Evaded." Journal of Comparative Legislation 2 (1929):233-44.
A study providing examples of the ingenious devices Islamic lawyers employed to legitimize practices otherwise forbidden, such as taking interest.

2130 Klingmuller, E. "The Concept and Development of Insurance in Islamic Countries." Islamic Culture 43 (1969):27-37.
Traces the law's attitude to insurance, from its initial rejection of it to later acceptance of it. Includes an interesting description of Ibn Abidin's (d. 1836) approval of insurance.

2131 Mahmasani, S. "Transactions in the Shariʿa." In Law in the Middle East (see 2063), pp. 179-202.
An informative article on the "general principles relating to ownership, contracts and procedure as laid down by the majority of Muslim jurists."

2132 Mansbach, W. "Laesio Enormis in Muhammadan Law." Bulletin of the School of Oriental and African Studies 10 (1940-42):877-84.
A short examination of the manner in which the Islamic law protects the parties of a sale from excessive loss due, not to fraud, but to error.

2133 Qureshi, Anwar Iqbal. Islam and the Theory of Interest. Lahore: Ashraf, 1946, 189 pp.
A defense of the Islamic prohibition against usury. It portrays the reasons for its prohibition and discusses the disadvantages of allowing interest taking in non-Muslim lands.

2134 Rahman, Fazlur. "Ribā and Interest." Islamic Studies 3 (1964):1-43.
Excessive profit taking in the Qur'ān and tradition is examined in great detail to arrive at some definition of its legal import and limits. Rahman then discusses the Islamic position and its value for modern society. Though he cannot advise the general abolition of profiteering in the present economies, he calls for the reorganizing of Muslim economies in a more cooperative spirit, which would allow the application of the law on the matter of excessive profit taking (ribā).

2135 Udovitch, A.L. "Labor Partnerships in Early Islamic Law." Journal of the Economic and Social History of the Orient 10 (1967):64-80.
An introductory treatment of the problem of partnership investments according to Ḥanafī and Mālikī law. The position of skilled and unskilled labor is discussed, as well as the handling of profits and losses.

2136 _____. "The 'Law Merchant' of the Medieval Islamic World." In Logic in Classical Islamic Culture (see 1596), pp. 113-30.
An essay on Islamic commercial law that shows it to be a practical instrument for the merchant of medieval Islam. Udovitch supports his generalizations by references to the texts of the Geniza records of Cairo.

2137 _____. Partnership and Profit in Medieval Islam. Princeton, N.J.: Princeton University Press, 1970, 282 pp.
A very thorough study of the laws governing partnerships and commenda in medieval Islam, according to the Ḥanafī and Mālikī schools of jurisprudence. Udovitch attempts to demonstrate the versatility of these two legal instruments in the economy of the medieval Muslim world. A technical study.

Inheritance

2138 Abu Yahra, M. "Family Law." In Law in the Middle East (see 2063), pp. 132-78.
An informative article on the legal relations of man and woman, children, and relatives, with emphasis on laws of inheritance.

2139 Coulson, N.J. Succession in the Muslim Family. Cambridge: Cambridge University Press, 1971, 287 pp.
This is the most complete study available on the extremely complex law of inheritance among Muslims. The work touches virtually all possibilities of, as well as impediments to, inheritance. One chapter is devoted to Shīʿī laws on inheritance and another to the effect of more recent reforms on the traditional law of inheritance. There are also indexes of Arabic terms, proper names, countries, and subjects. A technical but clearly written study.

2140 Fyzee, A.A.A. "The Fāṭimid Laws of Inheritance." Studia Islamica 9 (1958):61-69.
A brief discussion of the contents of the Daʿā'im al-Islām by the judge al-Nuʿmān of Fāṭimid Egypt, whose chief rules Fyzee presents in outline form.

2141 Schacht, Joseph. "Mīrāth." In Shorter Encyclopedia of Islam (see 22), pp. 384-88.
Examines inheritance in the Qur'ān and tradition. The article covers in some detail the principles of law of inheritance, notes the major differences of opinion among the schools, and includes a few paragraphs on the Shī'ah and their views.

International Law

2142 Khadduri, M. "International Law." In Law in the Middle East (see 2063), pp. 349-72.
Based on the author's War and Peace in the Law of Islam (see 2143).

2143 _____. War and Peace in the Law of Islam. Baltimore: Johns Hopkins Press, 1955, 321 pp.
The book, concerned with the legal theories supporting jihād (war) and the treatment of dhimmīs (non-Muslims in Muslim lands), discusses the attitude of past Muslim states to conquered and neighboring lands. The chapter on the status of dhimmīs is particularly interesting in relation to the work of Wellhausen (see 146) and Dennett (see 121) on the legal terminology of taxation. Index and glossary of terms.

2144 Kruse, Hans. "The Islamic Doctrine of International Treaties." Islamic Quarterly 1 (1954):152-58.
An analysis of al-Kāshānī's (d. 1191) work on international law, which was the first of two projected articles; the second never appeared. Kruse examines the requirement protecting non-Muslims and discusses briefly amān (pledge of protection).

2145 Liebesney, H.J. "The Development of Western Judicial Privileges." In Law in the Middle East (see 2063), pp. 309-33.
Traces the growth of rights for foreigners on Muslim soil down to the beginning of this century. The final paragraphs assessing the role of the capitulatory rights are of great importance.

2146 Shaybānī, al-. The Islamic Law of Nations. Translated by Majid Khadduri. Baltimore: Johns Hopkins Press, 1966, 311 pp.
A translation of al-Shaybānī's (d. 804) legal work on the law of nations, with a lengthy introduction.

2147 Tritton, A.S. "Non-Muslim Subjects of the Muslim State." Journal of the Royal Asiatic Society (1942):36-40.
A short compendium of the legal opinions of various early legalists in Islam on the legal status of the Christian or Jew under Muslim rule. Tritton arranges the opinions under land, religion, inheritance, marriage, slaves, war, clothes, tribute, and homicide.

Marriage

2148 Abdel Hamid, Ibrahim. "Dissolution of Marriage in Islamic Law." Islamic Quarterly 3 (1956-57):166-75, 215-23; 4 (1957):3-10, 57-65, 97-113.
Covers the legal question of divorce, examined in detail from the husband's and the wife's side, according to all schools of law. Probably the most exhaustive work on the subject in English.

2149 Anderson, J.N.D. "Invalid and Void Marriages in Hanafi Law." Bulletin of the School of Oriental and African Studies 13 (1950): 357-66.
An interesting examination of a legal issue in one school from earliest to modern times that gives a clear illustration of how thought and logic developed in the Islamic law.

2150 _____. "The Problem of Divorce in the Shari'a Law of Islam: Measures of Reform in Modern Egypt." Journal of the Royal Central Asian Society 37 (1950):169-85.
A study of the traditional Islamic law of divorce, on both the husband's and the wife's side, with particular emphasis on Mālikī law. The legal character of laws enacted in the forties in Egypt are compared with the traditional legal attitude.

2151 Heffening, W. "Mut'a." In Shorter Encyclopedia of Islam (see 22), pp. 418-20.
The article examines the basis for the practice of temporary marriage and its acceptability to various schools and touches briefly on Shī'ī views.

2152 Linant de Bellefonds, Y. "Ḥaḍana." In EI2. Vol. 3 (see 20), pp. 17-19.
Discusses child custody by tracing the problem in the various schools of law.

2153 Smith, W. Robertson. Kinship and Marriage in Early Arabia (see 1141).

Penal Law

2154 Anderson, J.N.D. "Homicide in Islamic Law." Bulletin of the School of Oriental and African Studies 13 (1951):811-28.
A detailed discussion, with numerous examples, of the legal nature of homicide, its degrees, and the problem of determination of guilt.

2155 Brunschvig, R. "'Āḳila." In EI2. Vol. 1 (see 20), pp. 337-40.
A study of the institution of 'āqilah (blood money) and an examination of the opinions of the various schools on the payment of compensation for crimes committed. This is a worthwhile article, as very little on the subject is available in English.

2156 Hardy, M.J.L. Blood Feuds and the Payment of Blood Money in the Middle East. Leiden: Brill, 1963, 106 pp.
A study of diyah (compensation) from pre-Islamic times to modern days. Short glossary of terms.

2157 Heffening, W. "Taʻzīr." In Shorter Encyclopedia of Islam (see 22), pp. 589-90.
A valuable article on the extra-Qur'ānic forms of punishment, since very little is available on the subject.

2158 Maydani, R. "Uqubat: Penal Law." In Law in the Middle East (see 2063), pp. 223-35.
A general discussion of penal law (ʻuqūbāt) in Islam and how and to what extent jurists treated it. The various punishments and punishable offenses are briefly noted, as well as criminal responsibility and intent.

2159 Rahman, Fazlur. "The Concept of Ḥadd in Islamic Law." Islamic Studies 4 (1965): 237-51.
A critical investigation into the definition of the term "ḥadd" (limit) as it appears in the Qur'ān and in fiqh (legal) literature. Rahman tries to prove that the Qur'ān offers no basis for the legal theory that "limits of God" (ḥudūd Allāh) signify "punishments of invariable, fixed quantity" (p. 241). His purpose is to find a way to establish an adequate Islamic structure of crime and punishment.

2160 Rosenthal, F. "On Suicide in Islam." Journal of the American Oriental Society 66 (1946):239-59.
The article traces the attitude toward suicide in the Qur'ān and tradition, listing all the reported suicides of the first nine centuries of Islam. The author also cites passages from various Muslim thinkers on the subject. Good bibliography.

2161 Schacht, J. "Ḳatl." In Shorter Encyclopedia of Islam (see 22), pp. 227-28.
Discusses killing as a crime and its punishment.

2162 _____. "Ḳiṣāṣ." In Shorter Encyclopedia of Islam (see 22), pp. 261-63.
Discusses "retribution" in the Qur'ān and the law.

Shīʻī Law

2163 Dodge, B. "The Fāṭimid Legal Code" (see 1497).

2164 Fyzee, A.A.A. Compendium of Fāṭimid Law. Calcutta: Indian Institute of Advanced Study, 1969, 160 pp.
This is a detailed account of Fāṭimid law in Egypt culled from the primary sources and organized under six chief headings. The introduction is of most immediate value as it characterizes Shīʻī law under the Fāṭimids and notes its outstanding figures. This book is particularly valuable since it concerns Twelver Shīʻī law and is based principally on the work of the Fāṭimid judge al-Nuʻmān.

2165 _____. Outlines of Muhammadan Law. London: Oxford University Press, 1955, 509 pp.
A handbook of both Sunnī and Shīʻī law. Provides a historical introduction to the law. See also 2198.

2166 _____. "Shīʻī Legal Theories." In Law in the Middle East (see 2063), pp. 113-31.
Discusses the central problem of the Imām and the rejection of the principle of qiyās (analogy), plus an examination of a very early Shīʻī lawbooks.

Waqf (Religious Endowments)

2167 Anderson, J.N.D. "The Religious Element in Waqf Endowments." Journal of the Royal Central Asiatic Society 38 (1951):292-99.
A study of the basic problem confronting the modern legal reformer when he considers the legal institution of waqf. The article also examines recent legislation on waqf.

2168 Cattan, Henry. "The Law of Waqf." In Law in the Middle East (see 2063), pp. 203-22.
This article defines waqf, drawing an analogy between it and the British law of trusts. Recent changes in the system of waqf in Arab lands are discussed.

2169 "Waqf." Moslem World 4 (1914):173-87.
Although outdated in places, this anonymous article provides a useful introduction to this legal institution.

Miscellaneous

2170 Heffening, W. "Murtadd." In Shorter Encyclopedia of Islam (see 22), pp. 413-15.
"Apostasy," its punishment, and legal effects are discussed briefly.

2171 Hurgronje, G. Snouck. "Islam and the Phonograph." Moslem World 5 (1915):159-65.
What may seem a curiosity is in fact an excellent example of the fatwā (written legal opinion). Hurgronje has translated the legal opinion given by a muftī (legal adviser) on the legality of the phonograph.

2172 Rosenthal, Franz. The Herb: Hashish versus Medieval Muslim Society. Leiden: E.J. Brill, 1971, 212 pp.
Based entirely upon original sources, and well documented, this history of cannabis in the Muslim world (from the twelfth to the sixteenth century) contains a good deal of information on how the law tried to cope with smoking hashish.

2173 _____. Gambling in Islam. Leiden: E.J. Brill, 1975, 192 pp.
Besides much information on games, the work examines the attitude of the sharīʻah condemning gambling. Based on primary sources and well documented.

2174 Rosenthal, F. "Gifts and Bribes: The Muslim View." Proceedings of the American Philosophical Society 108 (1964):135-44.
A succinct discussion of the legal and moral lines dividing the gift from the bribe. Rosenthal follows a variety of views in chronological order from Muḥammad to the twelfth century.

2175 Wensinck, A.J. "Khamr." In Shorter Encyclopedia of Islam (see 22), pp. 243-45.
On wine drinking and the basis for its prohibition in the law. The author has cited many statements on the matter and points out some of the problems in the prohibition of drinking for Muslims.

2176 Zwemer, S.M. "The Law of Apostasy." Moslem World 14 (1924):373-91.
The article is old, but does cover some of the pertinent doctrines and attitudes of Islam toward this error. Footnoting is infrequent, and information tends to be secondhand.

MODERN DEVELOPMENTS OF THE LAW

General Studies

2177 Ahmad, Aziz. Islamic Law in Theory and Practice. Lahore: All-Pakistan Legal Decisions, 1956, 656 pp.
A detailed legal manual offering numerous cases and applications, with chapters on Shīʿī law. The work treats modern application and does not provide a historical discussion.

2178 Anderson, J.N.D. Islamic Law in the Modern World. New York: New York University Press, 106 pp.
An introductory work that first examines the differences between Islamic and Western law, then treats the problems confronting Islamic law today, particularly marriage and inheritance. The final chapter touches on the events of a few decades that have drastically affected the law. Superseded by his Law Reform in the Muslim World (see 2181).

2179 _____. "Law as a Social Force in Islamic Culture and History." Bulietin of the School of Oriental and African Studies 20 (1957): 13-40.
The article emphasizes the practical application of the law as a formative social force in today's world.

2180 _____, and N.J. Coulson. "Islamic Law in Contemporary Cultural Change." Saeculum 18 (1967):13-92.
An extensive discussion by two authorities of the fate of Islamic jurisprudence today. The article is in four parts: the legacy of the historical past; contemporary legal systems in the Muslim world; modern developments in sharīʿah law; and the future of sharīʿah law. The second chapter treats modern systems of law in the old Ottoman lands, India, and Africa. This article is a good introduction to what is happening to Islamic jurisprudence today. Bibliographies.

2181 Anderson, Norman. Law Reform in the Muslim World. London: Athlone Press, 1976, 235 pp.
Representing a lifetime of study on law reform in individual Muslim countries, this study is the best survey on the subject available. The work examines the philosophy and methods of reform, achievements and results, and problems and prospects.

2182 Khadduri, M. "From Religious to National Law." In Modernization of the Arab World (see 549), pp. 37-51.
An essay on the impact of nationalism on the law in Islam. Though brief, the article provides knowledge of the transformation of the law in today's world.

2183 Liebesney, H.J. "Religious Law and Westernization in the Moslem Near East." American Journal of Comparative Law 2 (1953):492-504.
A review of the nature of Islamic law and the effect of Western law on it.

2184 _____. "Stability and Change in Islamic Law." Middle East Journal 21 (1967):16-31.
Liebesney surveys nineteenth-century modernization, particularly in Turkey, and more recent changes (since the First World War) in Iraq, Egypt, and Iran, as well as the influence of English law on Pakistan. He judges these adaptations on the whole as contributing to the flexibility of the legal system in Islamic lands.

2185 Schacht, J. "Problems of Modern Islamic Legislation." In The Modern Middle East. Edited by R.H. Nolte. New York: Atherton, 1963, pp. 172-200.
Schacht compares the task of early jurists confronted with much legal material from non-Islamic sources with the task of modern legislators in Islamic lands who need to synthesize, or reach a balance of some sort between, modern legislation (influenced by various European codes) and the traditional jurisprudence of Islam. Though this subject is one frequently treated, this article is one of the best efforts.

Specific Points of the Law

2186 Anderson, J.N.D. "The Eclipse of the Patriarchal Family in Contemporary Islamic Law." In Family Law in Asia and Africa. New York: F.A. Praeger, 1967, pp. 221-34.
By "patriarchal" the author means the traditional polygamous family with its particular rules of divorce. The article surveys various changes enacted by modern Islamic countries to treat the matters of polygamy and divorce. He suggests these changes have not really gone far enough and so far leave the law quite confused.

2187 _____. "Recent Developments in Shariʿa Law." Muslim World 40 (1950):244-56; 41 (1951): 34-48, 113-26, 186-98, 271-88; 42 (1952): 33-47, 124-40, 190-206, 257-76.
A lengthy and valuable survey of recent changes affecting sharīʿah law regarding marriage and family law, and inheritance and the waqf (endowment).

2188 _____. "Recent Reforms in the Islamic Law of Inheritance." International Comparative Law Quarterly 14 (1965):349-65.
A survey of twentieth-century reforms of the laws of inheritance in Muslim countries of the Middle East, Africa, and Pakistan. Anderson also points out the direction these reforms are taking.

2189 _____. "Reforms in the Law of Divorce in the Muslim World." Studia Islamica 31 (1970): 41-52.
A survey of court decisions and legal enactments on divorce since the early twentieth century in the Islamic lands of the Middle East and Africa.

2190 Esposito, John L. "Muslim Family Law Reform: Towards an Islamic Methodology." Islamic Studies 15 (1976):19-51.
An attempt to show that the origins of Islamic law may provide a historical justification for family law reform and that the traditional sources (Qur'ān, sunnah, qiyās, ijmā', and ijtihād) are fully capable of providing methods of reform.

2191 Schacht, J. "Islamic Law in Contemporary States." American Journal of Comparative Law 8 (1959):133-47.
The article has much to say of interest on Islamic law, in general and in particular, in its treatment of the contemporary legal situation in Saudi Arabia and the manner in which the traditional law and Western legal practices are blended.

Individual Countries

Africa (except Egypt)

2192 Anderson, J.N.D. Islamic Law in Africa. 2d rev. ed. London: F. Cass, 1970, 409 pp.
This work, updated from the 1955 edition, is a study of Islamic law in the former British lands of Africa, where it has had to contend not only with British colonial law but also with the indigenous customary law. The book is organized by countries, with details of cases and circumstances to demonstrate the position of Islamic law. There are eight appendixes, the most interesting of which may be "The Immigrant Muslim Communities." There is also a lengthy glossary of legal terms and a complete index. Though specialized, this is a basic handbook on the subject.

2193 _____. "The Tunisian Law of Personal Status." International Comparative Law Quarterly 7 (1958):262-79.
Anderson discusses the new Tunisian code promulgated in 1956, giving some of its prehistory and then examining its form and content in detail. The article closes with an assessment of the voiced opposition to the code in Tunisia.

2194 Bousquet, G.H. "Islamic Law and Customary Law in French North Africa." Journal of Comparative Legislation and International Law 32 (1950):57-65.
The article treats Tunisia, Morocco, and Algeria and, in a schematic form, discusses the status of Muslim local law in these three countries in the first half of the twentieth century. Bousquet intends to show where and to what extent Islamic law has imposed itself on the peoples of North Africa, and where it has not.

2195 Schacht, J. "Islam in Northern Nigeria." Studia Islamica 8 (1957):123-46.
A survey, in part from firsthand observations, of Islamic law in Nigeria. Schacht depicts the nature of the law in this area, noting the influence of native practices and foreign colonial laws.

2196 Wallis, C. Braithwaite. "The Influence of Islam on African Native Law." Moslem World 11 (1921):145-68, 296-308.
The Fantis of the Gold Coast, the Timnes of Sierra Leone, and the Fulanis of Nigeria are examined. The influence of Islamic law on native law is described by numerous cases and actual situations, many of which were witnessed by Wallis himself.

India, Pakistan, and Bangladesh

2197 Ali, Hamid. "The Customary and Statutory Laws of the Muslims in India." Islamic Culture 11 (1957):354-69, 444-54.
A survey of cutomary and modern statute laws in various areas of India, as they have deviated from Anglo-Muslim law. The article is a helpful introduction to this modern phenomenon in India.

2198 Fyzee, A.A.A. "Muhammadan Law in India." Comparative Studies in Society and History 5 (1963):401-15.
A concise history of Islamic jurisprudence in India covering the period of Muslim domination (1206-1857), the British period (1661-1951), and the republican period (1950-1963). Fyzee characterizes the law and its peculiarities in each period, noting also the reforms or changes instituted in the British period.

2199 _____. Outlines of Muhammadan Law (see 2165).
A textbook of Indian Islamic legal practice. The work is technical, but the large index will lead the reader more directly to the subject matter sought.

2200 Gledhill, A. Pakistan--The Development of Its Law and Constitution. London: Stevens, 1967, 394 pp.
Covers the development of law in Pakistan since the constitution of 1956 and includes the new constitution of 1962. It covers in detail new statutes and the legal procedures of modern Pakistan, using cases as illustrations.

2201 Pearl, David. "Bangladesh: Islamic Laws in a Secular State." South Asian Review 8 (1974):33-41.
A discussion of the principle of secularism as a major basis of the new state of Bangladesh. The author asks how Bangladesh is to pursue its secular goals in light of its inheritance of law from the former united Muslim state of Pakistan.

2202 Saksena, K.P. Muslim Law as Administered in India and Pakistan. Lucknow: Eastern, 1963, 1232 pp.
A lengthy legal handbook of Muslim law as it was administered in the courts of British

India. This work is not meant for casual reading, due to its technical nature, but it is well indexed and any subject of interest can be easily found.

The Middle East

2203 Anderson, J.N.D. "A Draft Code of Personal Law for Iraq." Bulletin of the School of Oriental and African Studies 15 (1953):43-60.
A factual survey of the contents of the 1947 Code of Personal Law in Iraq, in which Anderson points out article by article and section by section what seems of interest in light of Islamic law.

2204 _____. "The Personal Law of the Druze Community." Die Welt des Islams, n.s. 2 (1952): 1-9, 83-94.
A chapter-by-chapter survey of the 1948 Law of Personal Status issued by the community of Druzes in Lebanon. Anderson points out similarities to and differences from the Ḥanafī code. See also 1552-58.

2205 _____. "The Shari‘a and Civil Law." Islamic Quarterly 1 (1954):29-46.
The author is at pains to demonstrate the debt of the modern civil codes of Egypt and Syria to the Islamic law, and provides numerous quotations from the codes to prove the dependence.

2206 Badr, G.M. "The New Egyptian Civil Code and the Unification of the Laws of the Arab Countries." Tulane Law Review 30 (1956): 299-324.
A brief essay on the new civil code promulgated by Egypt in 1948. Badr views this code as a pioneer effort to modernize the civil law, which many other Arab countries have followed.

2207 Hart, P.T. "Application of Hanbalite and Decue Law to Foreigners in Saudi Arabia." George Washington Law Review 22 (1953): 165-75.
Hart, a former U.S. consul-general to Saudi Arabia, provides a most interesting discussion of the relationship between the Muslim religious courts and non-Muslim residents brought before these courts. He also points to elements expected by the average Westerner that are still lacking.

2208 Maktari, A.M.A. Water Rights and Irrigation Practices in Laḥj: A Study of the Application of Customary and Sharī‘ah Law in South-West Arabia. Cambridge: University Press, 1971, 202 pp.
An excellent study detailing the Shāfi‘ī theory of water law, the manner in which it is applied, the techniques of irrigation in Laḥj (located in the People's Democratic Republic of Yemen), the application of customary law plus a chapter on technical terminology relating to water law. Extensive bibliography.

2209 Naqvi, A.R. "The Family Laws of Iran." Islamic Studies 6 (1967):241-65; 7 (1968): 129-63, 265-303, 339-78.
Those parts of the Civil Code of Iran passed in 1967 are here reproduced with some notes and comments.

2210 Safran, Nadev. "The Abolition of the Shar‘ī Courts in Egypt." Muslim World 48 (1958): 20-28, 125-35.
The first part of this provocative article examines the 1956 abolition and the reasons behind it, as well as the popular response. The second part is a review of certain classical doctrines of political structure in Islam. Safran describes the transition of Islamic states from the "shar‘ī state" to the modern national state, concluding that the legists of the sharī‘ah have lost contact with the modern legist and that the Islamic state came to an end with this abolition.

Turkey

2211 ‘Ala Mardin, Ebul. "Development of the Shari‘a under the Ottoman Empire." In Law in the Middle East (see 2063), pp. 279-91.
This treats the various enactments and codes of the nineteenth century under the Ottomans.

2212 Ali, Hamid. "Muslim Law and Modern Turkey." Islamic Culture 12 (1938):119-21.
An extremely brief work in defense of the modern legislators of Turkey, who, Ali believes, have not in their modernism swept away the Muslim quality of the Turks, but rather have built a lasting legal structure for Muslims in Turkey.

2213 Inalcik, Halil. "Law: Sultanic Law (Kanun) and Religious Law (Seriat)." In The Ottoman Empire: The Classical Age, 1300-1600 (see 339), pp. 70-75.
A brief but useful treatment of the various types of kanuns (legal canons), and the relationship between the sulṭān and the qāḍīs (judges).

2214 Onar, S.S. "The Magalla." In Law in the Middle East (see 2063), pp. 292-308.
Deals with the nineteenth-century Ottoman reformed code of law, first from a historical perspective, and then from a structural point of view. The article conveys well the basic rigidity of this code, which led finally to its abolition.

Indonesia

2215 Lev, Daniel S. Islamic Courts in Indonesia--A Study in the Political Bases of Legal Institutions. Berkeley: University of California Press, 1972, 281 pp.
Makes available much material not otherwise in English. Treats the legal system in Indonesia and the persistent tension between Islam and adat in the law as it developed. Glossary of Indonesian Muslim terms and index.

SLAVERY (See also 1920-35)

2216 Arafal, W. "The Attitude of Islam to Slavery." Islamic Quarterly 10 (1966):12-18.
Arafal wishes to demonstrate that Islam, in theory, does not condone slavery. To this end he lists the occasions for the manumission of slaves, as well as other openings to freedom. This article seems typical of what is available on slavery in Islam, a topic that has been little treated by Western scholars.

2217 Brunschvig, R. "ʿAbd." In EI2. Vol. 1 (see 20), pp. 24-40.
A lengthy work on the "slave" in Islam that covers the following subjects: "Before Islam," "The Qur'ān," "The Religious Ethic," "Fiqh (the Law)," "The Practice of Slavery," and "Abolition." The study is a reasonably complete source of information, particularly on the last three topics.

2218 Forand, P.G. "The Relation of the Slave and Client to the Master or Patron in Medieval Islam." International Journal of Middle East Studies 2 (1971):59-66.
Forand shows that in medieval Islam a slave represented a financial as well as an emotional investment. His article investigates a form of slavery in Islam whereby the slave remains tied to the master even after manumission.

2219 Goitein, S.D. "Slaves and Slave-Girls in the Cairo Geniza Records." Arabica 9 (1962): 1-20.
Based on the records of the Jewish community of Cairo in the twelfth century, Goitein notes the occupations of various slaves and their status.

TAXATION

2220 Abd al-Kader, Ali. "Land Property and Land Tenure in Islam." Islamic Quarterly 5 (1969): 4-11.
A good analysis of the nature of land tenure in early Islam, particularly in light of the actions of ʿUmar I and Muḥammad.

2221 Ben Shemesh, A., trans. Taxation in Islam (see 163).

2222 Cahen, Claude et al. "Ḍarība." In EI2. Vol. 2 (see 20), pp. 142-48.
The first, very comprehensive article treats various classes of taxes and is followed by articles on taxes in North Africa under various regimes, the Ottoman Empire, post-Ottoman Egypt, Persia, and India. A good introduction to the systems of taxation in these areas.

2223 _____. "Djizya." In EI2. Vol. 2 (see 20), pp. 559-67.
The introductory article by Claude Cahen on "poll tax" is a good historical treatment of the subject. The article by Halil Inalcik also examines the payment by dhimmīs (protected non-Muslims) of the "poll tax" outside of Turkey. The article on India does not treat the "poll tax" in very great detail, but does indicate the direction of needed research.

2224 Cahen, Claude. "Iḳṭāʾ." In EI2. Vol. 3 (see 20), pp. 1088-91.
This is the best summary of our present knowledge of the land tenure system of Islam. It is a well-balanced assessment, particularly in its refusal to equate this system and European feudalism, and in its cautious treatment of the system under the Saljūqs.

2225 Dennett, D.C. Conversion and the Poll Tax in Early Islam (see 121).

2226 Gibb, H.A.R., and H. Bowen. "Taxation and Finance." In Islamic Society and the West. Vol. 1, pt. 2 (see 338), pp. 1-69.
A valuable study of revenue systems of the Ottoman state, as well as of the provinces under its control, with a special look at Egypt and Syria in the eighteenth century. Since the article is very well documented, it is a good place to begin consideration of taxation under the Ottomans.

2227 Habib, Irfan. The Agrarian System of the Mughal Empire (see 420).
Habib is of the Aligarh school of history, which has contributed much in recent years to the study of Indian history. Of particular interest are chapters 6 to 8, on land assessment, revenue, administration, and royal grants to revenue, which are exhaustively treated and well documented.

2228 Lambton, A.K.S. et al. "Kharādj." In EI2. Vol. 4 (see 20), pp. 1030-56.
Extensive treatment of land tax in the central and western Islamic countries, Iran, Ottoman Turkey, and the Indian subcontinent.

2229 Lambton, A.K.S. Landlord and Peasant in Persia: A Study of Land Tenure and Land Administration (see 72).

2230 _____. "Reflections on the Iqtāʾ." In Arabic and Islamic Studies in Honor of H.A.R. Gibb (see 1492), pp. 358-76.
A good essay on the history of the land tenure system of Persia and its evolution.

2231 Løkkegaard, F. Islamic Taxation in the Classic Period (see 131).

2232 Moreland, W.H. The Agrarian System of Moslem India (see 287).

2233 Shaw, S.J. "Landholding and Land-Tax Revenues in Ottoman Egypt." In Political and Social Change in Modern Egypt (see 733), pp. 91-103.
A study of landownership in Egypt from 1517 to 1798. The chapter investigates the development of the tax-farm land policy system of Ottoman Egypt. He notes that though the system suited the needs of the Ottoman treasury, it ultimately led Egypt to ruin.

2234 Wellhausen, J. The Arab Kingdom and Its Fall (see 146).
This historical study includes an examination of taxes and land revenue (see the index under "tax," "revenue," "land tax," and "poll tax").

2235 Yusuf, S.M. "Land, Agriculture and Rent in Islam." Islamic Culture 31 (1957):27-39.
The article is a defense of Yusuf's strong opposition on religious grounds to the renting or leasing of agricultural lands. He covers the period of the Prophet and early legalists and rulers.

THE ʿULAMĀʾ

2236 Algar, Hamid. Religion and State in Iran, 1785-1906: The Role of the Ulama in the Qajar Period (see 871).

2237 Ashraf, K.M. "The ʿUlamā and the Religious Classes." In Life and Conditions of the People of Hindustan (see 1968), pp. 96-102.
A brief, informative description of various religious classes in Muslim India, both Islamic and Hindu, and their role.

2238 Bulliet, R.W. The Patricians of Nishapur: A Study in Medieval Islamic Social History (see 227).
A detailed study of the so-called patricians of Nīshāpūr of the eleventh century. The first part of the book discusses various aspects of this learned class, their education, relation to rulers, and legal and religious dispositions. The second part treats nine patrician families in particular. A technical work.

2239 Gibb, H.A.R., and H. Bowen. "The Ulama." In Islamic Society and the West. Vol. 1, pt. 1 (see 338), pp. 81-114.
A study of the religious institution of the Ottoman state and its relations with the civil and military authorities. Special consideration is given to the development of this class and its functions, as well as its subdivisions. The article also studies the direction the development of the class took, leading finally to its overthrow.

2240 Hāʾirī, ʿAbd al-Hādī. Shīʿism and Constitutionalism in Iran. Leiden: Brill, 1977, 274 pp.
An important study on the life and thought of Mirzā Muḥammad Ḥusayn Nāʾīnī, a Shīʿī jurist-scholar (mujtahid) who played a significant role along with other Iranian ʿulamāʾ in the constitutional revolution of early twentieth-century Iran.

2241 Heyd, Uriel. "The Ottoman Ulama and Westernization in the Time of Selim III and Mahmud II." In Studies in Islamic History and Civilization. Jerusalem: Hebrew University, 1961, pp. 63-96.
A very informative article on the role of the religious scholars in nineteenth-century Turkey in aiding and abetting modernization. Heyd also looks at the relationship of the ʿulamāʾ to the sulṭāns and other groups, and concludes with an assessment of the effect of westernization on the Islamic character of the Ottoman Empire.

2242 Inalcik, Halil. The Ottoman Empire: The Classical Age, 1300-1600 (see 339).
The fourth part of the book, entitled "Religion and Culture in the Ottoman Empire," is a general discussion of the ʿulamāʾ of the Ottoman Empire. The chapter entitled "The Central Administration" discusses the ʿulamāʾ as a political force.

2243 Keddie, N. Scholars, Saints, and Sufis (see 506).
This includes a collection of essays on the social role of two major religious institutions in Islam since the sixteenth century. The first ten contributions on the ʿulamāʾ or religious scholars and jurists concern: the Ottoman learned hierarchy; the Ottoman ʿulamāʾ and the Tanzimat; the ʿulamāʾ in Musainid Tunisia (nineteenth century); Moroccan ʿulamāʾ, 1860-1912; the nineteenth-century Moroccan scholar al-Nasīrī; ʿulamāʾ of Cairo; the Egyptian ʿulamāʾ and modernization; the basis of power of the ʿulamāʾ in modern Iran; the ʿulamāʾ as an opposition force in Iran; and activism of the ʿulamāʾ in Pakistan.

2244 Nigam, S.B.P. "Nobility, Ulama, and the Crown." In Nobility under the Sultans of Delhi, A.D. 1206-1398. Delhi: Munshiram Manoharlal, 1968, pp. 119-43.
Treats specifically the relationship between the ʿulamāʾ and the Delhi sulṭāns in order to determine the political status of this group of scholars.

2245 Nizami, K.A. "The Ulama." In Some Aspects of Religion and Politics in India during the Thirteenth Century (see 288), pp. 150-73.
This work treats the two classes of the religious scholars in India, giving examples of various outstanding individuals of each class. The office of shaykh al-Islām is discussed, as well as that of judge. This is a helpful introduction to the ʿulamāʾ of medieval India.

2246 Qureshi, Ishtiaq Husain. Ulema in Politics. Karachi: Maʿaref, 1972, 432 pp.
A comprehensive study of the political activities of the learned class in the subcontinent from 1556 to 1947. Chronology of events and glossary of terms. A provocative assessment of the changing role of the ʿulamāʾ in politics affecting Muslims in India.

2247 Sayid, A.L. "The Role of the Ulama in Egypt in the Early Nineteenth Century." In Political and Social Change in Modern Egypt (see 733), pp. 264-80.
A comparative study of the status and role of the religious learned shortly before the government of Muḥammad ʿAlī and during his rule. Sayid concludes that the form of government chosen by Muḥammad ʿAlī and the introduction of nationalism were the beginning of the weakening of the position of the ʿulamā.ʾ

WOMEN IN ISLAM (See also 2857-59)

2248 Abbott, Nabia. Aishah, the Beloved of Mohammed (see 113).

2249 _____. Two Queens of Baghdad: Mother and Wife of Harun al-Rashid (see 220).

2250 _____. "Women and the State in Early Islam." Journal of Near Eastern Studies 1 (1942): 106-26, 341-68.

Explores the role of women during the lifetime of Muḥammad, the first four caliphs and the Umayyads. The study demonstrates that women enjoyed considerable political-religious freedom and influence in Muḥammad's day, but lost ground, especially under the Umayyads. This article is a continuation of the author's "Women and the State on the Eve of Islam," American Journal of Semitic Languages and Literatures 58 (1941):259-84.

2251 Abdul-Rauf, Muhammad. The Islamic View of Women and the Family. New York: Robert Speller & Sons, 1977, 171 pp.

A homiletic, apologetic discourse intended as a guideline for Muslims, particularly those living in the Western world, on sex, the status of women, marriage, and the family. Bibliography.

2252 Celarie, Henriette. Behind Moroccan Walls. Translated by Constance Lily Morris. Freeport, N.Y.: Books for Libraries Press, 1931, 239 pp.

An excellent volume of short story sketches on the lives of Moroccan women as witnessed by Henriette Celarie, the wife of a French officer in Morocco. Index of unusual terms.

2253 Djibar, A. Women in Islam. Translated by J. MacGibbon. Netherlands: Deutsch, 1961.

A hopeful work written by one who expects much from Muslim women in the future. The book is filled with photos and a brief text that indicates new directions in the life-styles of Muslim women.

2254 Fernea, Elizabeth. Guests of the Sheikh. New York: Doubleday, 1965, 346 pp.

The best factual account of the role and position of women in a traditional Muslim (Shīʿī) village in modern-day Iraq.

2255 _____. A View of the Nile. Garden City, N.J.: Doubleday, 1970, 320 pp.

A semifictionalized chronicle of a stay in Cairo and Nubia from 1959 to 1965. This is a revealing book on the social roles accorded men and women in Egyptian society.

2256 _____, and Basima Qattan Bezirgan, eds. Middle Eastern Muslim Women Speak. Austin and London: University of Texas Press, 1977, 402 pp.

A selection of readings by and about Muslim women, past and present, from different regions and different social and economic groups. The volume succeeds admirably in dispelling some basic misconceptions that Western people hold about Muslim women. An essential source for the study of women in Islam. Illustrated.

2257 Fernea, Robert A., and Elizabeth W. Fernea. "Variation in Religious Observance among Islamic Women." In Scholars, Saints, and Sufis (see 506), pp. 385-401.

An important contribution on the women's role in the religious practice of Islam. This husband and wife team write from their own extensive experience and observation in Iraq and Egypt on the participation of women in Muslim religious practices.

2258 Gibb, H.A.R. "Women and the Law." In Colloque sur la sociologie musulmane, 11-14 septembre, 1961. Brussels: Centre pour l'étude des problèmes du monde musulman contemporain, 1961, pp. 233-45.

Examines the rights and duties of women in pre-Islamic times, the Qur'ān, and the actual practice of the law.

2259 Gordon, David C. Women of Algeria: An Essay on Change. Cambridge, Mass.: Harvard University Press, 1968, 98 pp.

A historical survey of the role granted women in Algeria, prior to 1830, during French rule, during the revolution, and finally in the free state of Algeria. Selected bibliography.

2260 Granqvist, Hilma. Birth and Childhood among the Arabs: Studies in a Muhammadan Village in Palestine (see 1864).

An established, though older, study of birth and childhood. It speaks of girls' games and work and their education. It also describes the place women hold at birth.

2261 _____. Child Problems among the Arabs: Studies in a Muhammadan Village in Palestine. Helsingfors: Soederstroem & Co., 1950, 339 pp.

A continuation of the author's former study. Of particular interest are the sections on women's names (pp. 27-39) and the chapter (pp. 134-69) on the value of children.

2262 Hansen, H.H. The Kurdish Woman's Life: Field Research in a Muslim Society, Iraq. Copenhagen: National Museum, 1901, 213 pp.

A detailed study based on observation of the life-styles of Kurdish nomadic women in modern times. The author challenges past conclusions on the position of Kurdish women in their society and attempts a new descriptive definition illustrated in part by veil types. Numerous pictures, drawings, tables. List of Kurdish terms.

2263 _____. "The Pattern of Women's Seclusion and Veiling in a Shiʿa Village." Folk 3 (1961): 23-42.

Based on field research in the village of Sar, this study describes the mundane activities of women and their veiling practices.

2264 Husain, A.F.A. Employment of Middle Class Muslim Women in Dacca. Dacca: Dacca University Socio-Economic Research Board, 1958, 165 pp.
A statistical survey of the background and circumstances of women in present-day Bangladesh. Appendixes give the questionnaires employed in the study plus tables. Not an interpretive work.

2265 Jeffery, Arthur. "The Family in Islam." In The Family: Its Function and Destiny. Edited by Ruth N. Ashen. New York: Harper & Brothers, 1959, pp. 201-38.
Examines many aspects of family life including rights and laws of betrothals, weddings, harem seclusion, polygamy, and divorce.

2266 Korson, J.H. "Dower and Social Class in an Urban Muslim Community." Journal of Marriage and Family 29 (August 1967):527-33.
An American sociologist's report of a study of 1,333 marriages in Pakistan. It examines the function of the mahr, or bride price, paid to the bride in three different levels of society in Karachi.

2267 Layish, Aharon. Women and Islamic Law in a Non-Muslim State. New York: Halsted Press, 1975, 369 pp.
A study based on legal decisions of Muslim courts in Israel. Nine chapters on marriage age, marriage stipulations, polygamy, maintenance, and obedience. A valuable work containing much bibliographical information on the topic plus statistical tables. Glossary and index of Arabic terms.

2268 Levy, Reuben. "The Status of Women in Islam." In The Social Structure of Islam (see 34), pp. 91-134.
An account of marriage, divorce, veiling, and the role of women in the Islamic religion. Most of the material is from primary sources and documented.

2269 Massell, Gregory J. The Surrogate Proletariat: Moslem Women and Revolutionary Strategies in Soviet Central Asia 1919-1929. Princeton, N.J.: Princeton University Press, 1974, 448 pp.
An important study on the impact of the Russian revolution on Muslim women in Central Asia. Massell believes the Soviets gradually came to confront Muslim society by disrupting the traditional role of women in that society. Lengthy bibliography and index.

2270 Mernissi, Fatima. Beyond the Veil: Male-Female Dynamics in a Modern Muslim Society. Cambridge, Mass.: Shenkman Publishing, 1975, 132 pp.
A provocative sociological study of male-female relations with particular reference to Morocco. The treatment of the traditional Muslim view of women and their role in society is not based on careful, critical study. Discussion of male-female dynamics in modern Morocco is based on four hundred letters sent to a counseling service available to Moroccans. Glossary of Arabic terms. Bibliography.

2271 Misra, Rikha. Women in Mughal India (1526-1748 A.D.). Delhi: Munshiram Manoharlal, 1967, 177 pp.
A study of the aristocratic class of women based on material from historical sources. A final chapter discusses the position of the lower classes of women. This is the best work on the topic that is available.

2272 Mukherjee, Ila. Social Status of North Indian Women (1526-1707 A.D.). Agra: Shiva Lal Agarwala & Co., 1927, 172 pp.
A review of the role played by women in the late Middle Ages. Covers birth, marriage, customs peculiar to women, education, widowhood, and prostitution. The author concludes that the life of women was colorless and pathetic.

2273 Papanek, Hannah. "Purdah in Pakistan: Seclusion and Modern Occupations for Women." Journal of Marriage and Family 33 (1971): 517-30.
A sociological introduction to the problems of female segregation in Pakistan and its influence on the participation by women in modern occupations. Also briefly treats the basis and origin of purdah.

2274 Rahmatallah, Maleeha. The Women of Baghdad in the Ninth and Tenth Centuries as Revealed in the History of Baghdad (see 176).

2275 Siddiqi, M. Mazheruddin. Women in Islam. Lahore: Institute of Islamic Culture, 1952, 231 pp.
Examines the ideal role accorded to women in Islam. It laments the non-Islamic deviations and accretions under which Muslim women have suffered. Index.

2276 Smith, Jane I., and Y.Y. Haddad. "Women in the Afterlife: The Islamic View as Seen from Qur'ān and Tradition." Journal of the American Academy of Religion 43 (1975):39-50.
A suggestive study of the effect of authoritative Muslim materials on the position of women. The final comments are especially worth noting for the important influence of Qur'ānic and ḥadīth material in the formation of the role of women.

2277 Smith, Margaret. Rabiʿa the Mystic and Her Fellow Saints in Islam (see 1303).

2278 Sommer, A. van, and S.M. Zwemer, eds. Our Moslem Sisters. New York: Revell, 1907, 299 pp.
This is an unfortunate work that overwhelmingly imposes Western standards in judging the position of women in Muslim society. Some may read it for the stereotypical mold it casts Muslim women into, but this position is scarcely the truth, as other studies have shown.

2279 Sönmez, Emel. Turkish Women in Turkish Literature of the 19th Century. Leiden: Brill, 1969, 73 pp.
A study of the social, economic, and educational position of Turkish women as seen in the prose works of two nineteenth-century Turkish authors, Namik Kemal and Hüseyin Rahmi Gürpinar.

2280 Vreede-de Stuers, Cora. Purda: A Study of Muslim Women's Life in Northern India. Assen: Van Gorcum, 1968, 128 pp.

A very fine sociological study with illustrative case studies on the Muslim institution of purdah (veiling). The author defends the respectability of this institution and its role in Muslim society. She points out that it need not be an obstacle to feminine emancipation. Glossary of Arabic terms and a bibliography.

2281 Young, Katherine K., and Arvind Sharma. Images of the Feminine-Mythic, Philosophic and Human--The Buddhist, Hindu, and Islamic Traditions: A Bibliography of Women in India. New York: New Horizons Press, 1974, 36 pp.

A brief, selective bibliography authored in response to demands of students at Harvard Divinity School working in the area of women in religion. Not annotated.

Art and Architecture

BIBLIOGRAPHIES, INDEXES, ENCYCLOPEDIAS, AND PERIODICALS

BIBLIOGRAPHIES

2282 Creswell, K.A.C. A Bibliography of the Architecture, Arts and Crafts of Islam to 1 January 1960. Cairo: American University at Cairo Press, 1961, 1330 cols. Supplement. January 1960-January 1972. Cairo: American University at Cairo Press, 1973, 366 columns.

The 1961 volume was forty years in the making. It is the most comprehensive single volume of bibliography for Islamic art. Fortunately, it has been supplemented by another volume that contains books and articles published since 1960 as well as a considerable number of Turkish and Slavonic language articles not included in the 1961 volume. The researcher of Islamic art and architecture will find this book to be the most useful and comprehensive bibliographic aid at his fingertips.

INDEXES

2283 Art Index: A Cumulative Author and Subject Index to a Selected List of Fine Arts Periodicals and Museum Bulletins. New York: H.W. Wilson Co., 1929 to date.

Particularly useful for items published since Creswell's Bibliography and its supplement (see 2282) were compiled.

2284 Norgren, Jill. Preliminary Index of Shahnameh Illustrations. Ann Arbor: University of Michigan Press, 1969.

This is a single volume, loose-leaf unpaginated index of illustrations found in the vast majority of extant illustrated manuscripts of the Shāh nāmah of Firdausi. The index proper, preceded by a list of the manuscripts indexed, is primarily useful for those already familiar with the major manuscripts.

2285 Pearson, J.D. Index Islamicus, 1906-1955 (see 6).

ENCYCLOPEDIAS

2286 The Encyclopaedia of Islam (see 20, 32).

An indispensable research tool for art and architecture. A selection of articles appears in this encyclopedia under the appropriate headings.

2287 Encyclopaedia of World Art. 15 vols. New York: McGraw Hill, 1959-1968.

Contains concise entries on numerous aspects of Islamic art and architecture prepared by several outstanding scholars. See also 2351.

PERIODICALS

Periodicals--Other than India. Articles on Islamic art appear frequently in some of the publications listed here, infrequently in others. Although the list is by no means complete, it does identify the periodicals that regular publish important articles on Islamic art in English.

- Ars Asiatiques
- Ars Islamica (1934-1951)
- Ars Orientalis
- Art Bulletin
- Artibus Asiae
- Bulletin of the School of Oriental and African Studies
- Burlington Magazine
- Connoisseur
- Der Islam
- East and West
- Iran
- Journal of the American Oriental Society
- Journal of Glass Studies
- Journal of Near Eastern Studies
- Journal of the Royal Asiatic Society
- Kunst des Orients
- Oriental Art

Periodicals--India

- British Museum Quarterly
- Journal of the Asiatic Society of Bombay
- Journal of the Indian Society of Oriental Art
- Journal of the Oriental Institute
- Lalit Kala
- Marg
- Prince of Wales Museum Bulletin

ART

SURVEYS AND HANDBOOKS RELATING TO ISLAMIC ART AND ARCHITECTURE AS A WHOLE

2288 Dimand, Maurice S. A Handbook of Muhammadan Art. 3d ed. New York: Metropolitan Museum of Art, 1958, 380 pp.
The outgrowth of the extensive collection of Islamic art found at the Metropolitan Museum of Art in New York City. Although based on one collection and exclusively illustrated with examples from that collection, the book remains one of the best available surveys of the various styles found in Muslim painting and in the decorative arts.

2289 Du Ry, Carel J., and Alexis Brown. Art of Islam. New York: Harry N. Abrams, 1970, 263 pp.
The text is simple and straightforward; the photographs are of sufficiently wide scope and good quality to recommend the book on their account alone.

2290 Ettinghausen, Richard. "The Decorative Arts and Paintings: Their Character and Scope." In The Legacy of Islam (see 207), pp. 274-91.
An excellent introductory, interpretive essay on the subject, followed by the author's "The Impact of Muslim Decorative Arts and Painting on the Arts of Europe" (pp. 292-318).

2291 _____. "The Man-made Setting." In Islam and the Arab World (see 36), pp. 57-89.
Ettinghausen's essay sums up many of his thoughts on the character and uniqueness of Islamic art. The essay is accompanied by fifteen pages of photographs illustrating such points as the effect of the environment on Islamic arts, the development of the mosque, and the importance of the Arabic script. The book as a whole is also to be recommended because it is filled with photographs of both well-known and unusual artistic works as illustrations for the other essays.

2292 Fehervari, G. "Art and Architecture." In The Cambridge History of Islam. Vol. 2 (see 30), pp. 702-41.
The emphasis is on a descriptive survey of important objects and monuments. The Islamic art of India and the East is excluded.

2293 Grabar, Oleg. "Architecture." In The Legacy of Islam (see 207), pp. 244-73.
Explores the nature and purpose of Islamic architecture.

2294 _____. The Formation of Islamic Art. New Haven, Conn.: Yale University Press, 1973, 233 pp.
A fundamental study that tries to explain the monuments of the Muslim world from the mid-seventh to the ninth century A.D. The cultural and social background is taken into account while the author explains the formation of a new art. Instead of looking at the monuments as a series of buildings and objects, Grabar groups trends and attitudes of the underlying factors and motivations. He assumes that all explanations are only working hypotheses in need of constant refinement. Enormously stimulating and thought-provoking, with numerous illustrations.

2295 _____. Studies in Medieval Islamic Art. London: Variorum Reprints, 1976.
Previously published articles on a variety of subjects, covering art and architecture. Like Grabar's other works, these essays go far beyond descriptive studies of monuments by taking into account social, ecological, and creative dimensions of culture that figure into the "life" of any individual work of art. Index and plates. See also 2366, 2401.

2296 Grube, Ernst J. The World of Islam. New York: McGraw-Hill, 1966, 76 pp.
This is a pictorial survey of the architecture, painting, and decorative arts of the Islamic world from the seventh century to the eighteenth century, connected by an extended essay. Many illustrations.

2297 Jairazbhay, Rafique A. Art and Cities of Islam. Bombay: Asia Publishing House, 1964, 83 pp.
This small book contains six essays of various length, all of them of interest to anybody concerned with Islamic art. The first two are written for the general public: "Moods and Motivation in Islamic Architecture" and "The Spirit of Muslim Art." The other four essays are devoted to specific problems and are more scholarly. Illustrated.

2298 James, David. Islamic Art: An Introduction. London: Hamlyn, 1974, 96 pp.
A general essay for the newcomer to Islamic art, this book could serve well as a light introduction to the subject. Rather than following the usual chronological sequence, the book gives a very concise historical background and then follows the same divisions used by the World of Islam arts exhibition held in London in 1976: calligraphy, representational art, and architecture. The effect is to stress the unity of the arts of Islam even under the restrictions of time and space. Illustrated.

2299 Kühnel, Ernst. Islamic Art and Architecture. Translated by Katherine Watson. London and Ithaca, N.Y.: Cornell University Press, 1966, 200 pp.
A general survey of the architecture and minor arts of Islam. The author has been successful in covering many areas and time periods, although certain aspects of the subject have been oversimplified. Illustrated.

2300 _____. The Minor Arts of Islam. Translated by Katherine Watson. Ithaca, N.Y.: Cornell University Press, 1971, 255 pp.
This book is an English translation of the second edition of Kühnel's Islamische Kleinkunst (Braunschweig, 1963). The translation is accurate and readable. The text is not organized historically but by material. No aspect of Islamic decorative arts is left out except rug weaving and textiles. The book will be most useful to students or to collectors who are not

very familiar with Islamic art. One has here, in a nutshell, the state of research as of 1963. With illustrations.

2301 Metropolitan Museum of Art. Bulletin. Vol. 33 (Spring 1975, no. 1), 50 pp.
This issue is devoted to the Islamic collection of the museum; decorative arts and painting naturally receive the most attention. The photographs are superb and the price is quite modest. With contributions by Richard Ettinghausen, Marie Swietochowski, Marilyn Jenkins, and Manuel Keene.

2302 Pinder-Wilson, Ralph. Islamic Art. London: Ernest Benn, 1957, 25 pp.
This is a new edition of Cent Planches en Couleurs d'Art Musulman (1928), with major changes in text and plates. The title is too wide for its subject matter, which is confined to Islamic textiles and ceramics. In the text, the sporadic factor of contemporary Byzantine influence is ignored, and the artistic significance of western Islam seems underestimated. The selection of plates, some of which are failures, is unbalanced and unrepresentative. There are neither ʻAbbāsid nor early Fāṭimid lustrewares, nor any of the magnificent early Samarqand or Nīshāpūr pottery.

2303 Rice, David Talbot. Islamic Art. 2d ed. New York: Praeger, 1965, 286 pp. Rev. & updated. London: Thames & Hudson, 1975.
This is an illustrated survey of the art and architecture of Islam. The book is modestly priced and widely used. Unfortunately, the text is often imprecise. In time it goes no later than the seventeenth century; geographically it goes no farther east than Afghanistan.

2304 Rosenthal, Franz. Four Essays on Art and Literature in Islam. Leiden: E.J. Brill, 1971, 121 pp.
Part of this book is a republication of two earlier articles now combined with two new investigations. All four essays are based on statements found in various Arabic texts, which the author skillfully groups according to specific issues of artistic significance. New material is investigated in each article with thoroughness and wide-ranging perspective. Includes a large selection of photographs.

SURVEYS AND HANDBOOKS RELATING TO SPECIFIC COUNTRIES

Egypt and Syria

2305 Mayer, L.A. Saracenic Heraldry: A Survey. Oxford: Clarendon Press, 1933, 302 pp.
A survey, alphabetically arranged by individual, of the ceremonial blazons of sulṭāns, princes, and amīrs primarily of the Ayyūbid and Mamlūk periods (1171-1517) in Syria, Palestine, and Egypt. Each blazon is described, a full bibliography of all objects bearing it is given, and whenever possible a short life of the individual is provided. For the noncollector of blazons the most interesting part of the book is the introduction in which all evidence relating to the use of blazons is concisely examined. With plates.

North Africa and Spain

2306 Burckhardt, Titus. Moorish Culture in Spain. Translated by Alisa Jaffa. New York: McGraw-Hill, 1972, 219 pp.
The translation of Burckhardt's Die maurische kultur in Spanien, this work does not purport to be a comprehensive history of the eight and a half centuries of Hispano-Islamic culture in Spain. Rather, the author has chosen to select certain aspects of "Moorish" culture, which he would prefer to refer to as Arabic or Islamic culture in Spain. The topics selected provide the reader with an overview of the highlights of this culture--literary, scientific, and philosophical achievements--as well as with an acquaintance with the major cities and architectural monuments. The author frequently ties Hispano-Islamic culture into the earlier and contemporary European cultural framework. Numerous figures and illustrations supplement the text. A chronological table and selected bibliography are also included.

2307 Monteguin, François-August de. Compendium of Hispano-Islamic Art and Architecture. St. Paul, Minn.: Hamline University, 1976, 315 pp.
The outline format of this book and the numerous maps and plans enable the reader to gain a quick overview of Hispano-Islamic art. The outline first breaks down the subject matter chronologically by period. Each period is then subdivided into the three uniform headings of introduction, architecture, and decorative arts. An extensive bibliography is included.

2308 Torres, Balbas L. "Al-Andalus. IX Andalusian Art." In EI2. Vol. 1 (see 20), pp. 497-501.
A survey of art and architecture in Spain.

Iran and Afghanistan

2309 Anand, M.R., and K. Fischer. "Afghanistan: Cross-roads." Marg 24 (1970):2-56.
This issue of Marg is devoted to the Islamic art and architecture of Afghanistan. M.R. Anand has written on space, time, and deity; the background of Islamic architecture; color, form, and design in Islamic architecture and the development of Islamic architecture in Afghanistan. K. Fischer has contributed an article on architectural remains in Seistan.

2310 Barrett, Douglas. "The Islamic Art of Persia." In The Legacy of Persia (see 64), pp. 116-47.
A historical survey of the minor arts, with plates.

2311 Godard, André. The Art of Iran. Translated by Michael Heron and edited by Michael Rogers. London: Allen & Unwin, 1965, 358 pp.
A major survey of the arts of Iran including architecture as well as art objects of pre-Islamic and Islamic Iran. The text is authoritative and lucid. With illustrations.

2312 Grabar, Oleg. "The Visual Arts, 1050-1350." In The Cambridge History of Iran. Vol. 5, The Saljuq and Mongol Periods (see 226), pp. 626-58.

Grabar raises stimulating questions concerning three topics: the architecture of the mosque and its implications, the portable objects of art of the twelfth and thirteenth centuries, and painting in the fourteenth century.

2313 Nasr, Seyyed Hossein, and Roloff Beny. Persia: Bridge of Turquoise. London: Thames & Hudson, 1975, 366 pp.

Although not designed as a scholarly text on Islamic art, this book contains spectacular photographs, by Beny, of famous buildings in Iran. Equally important are such chapters as "Light," a photo essay conveying the importance of light and dark contrasts in the aesthetic basis of Persian art. The text is by Nasr.

2314 Pope, Arthur Upham, ed. A Survey of Persian Art from Prehistoric Times to the Present. 12 vols. London: Oxford University Press, 1964-65. Rev. ed. 13 vols.

This is a monumental survey of Persian art that is essential to the study of Islamic art in Iran. The reader must beware of those parts that are now dated or provoked controversy from the outset. It would be wise to read the reviews of this work in Ars Islamica 8 (1941).

2315 Wulff, Hans E. The Traditional Crafts of Persia, Their Development, Technology, and Influence on Eastern and Western Civilizations (see 869).

A book of fundamental importance, extremely useful for the light it sheds on modern Persian crafts. The brief historical surveys in each section of the book are based on secondary sources; the last part of the title is scarcely touched upon. What is truly significant is the coverage of the modern period in which the author writes from personal experience, bringing out the special achievement of the craftsmen, the innovations they introduced, and the changes of technique resulting from foreign influences. A glossary includes the Farsi terms used by the craftsmen themselves for equipment and processes. Black and white plus color plates.

Iran and Afghanistan (Catalogs)

2316 Atil, Esin. Exhibition of 2500 Years of Persian Art. Washington: Smithsonian Institution, Freer Gallery of Art, 1971, 24 pp.

A catalog of an exhibition held at the Freer Gallery of Art in 1971. The objects represent diverse provenances, types, and techniques from the Achaemenid period to the Ṣafavid dynasty.

2317 Pope, Arthur Upham; Phyllis Ackerman; and Eric Schroeder. Masterpieces of Persian Art. New York: Dryden Press, 1945, 204 pp.

A selection of masterpieces of Persian art illustrating different techniques: ceramics, metalwork, textiles, wood, carpets, and the art of the book. This volume records the exhibition of Persian art held in New York in 1940, with some additional items, but it is not just a catalog. The text places the art in relation to the culture of the time, and explains the special features of the art works illustrated.

2318 University of Michigan, Museum of Art. Persian Art before and after the Mongol Conquest, April 9--May 17, 1959. Selected and arranged by Oleg Grabar. Ann Arbor: University of Michigan Press, 1959, 72 pp.

The intent of this exhibition was "to illustrate similarities, if any, and contacts between the artistic expressions of the two periods separated by the Mongol conquest." Remarks are speculative and are treated as an invitation to further research.

2319 University of Texas at Austin, Art Museum. Treasures of Persian Art after Islam: The Mahboubian Collection. New York: Plantin Press, 1970.

This is a catalog of 1,552 items from the Mahboubian collection. Many of the pieces are illustrated, some are in color. The text should be avoided because it is loaded with inaccuracies and untenable assertions. Much of the collection focuses on post-Ṣafavid art of the eighteenth and nineteenth centuries, particularly on lithographs.

2320 Welch, Anthony. Shah ʻAbbas and the Arts of Isfahan. New York: Asia Society, 1973, 15 pp.

A catalog of an exhibition of Persian Islamic art, focusing on one dynasty and one city. The exhibit was sponsored by Asia House Gallery and the Fogg Art Museum. Brief, informative entries have been written for each item.

Turkey

2321 Aslanapa, Oktay. Turkish Art and Architecture. New York: Praeger, 1971, 422 pp.

A comprehensive survey of Saljūq, Turkoman, and Ottoman Turkish art and architecture. Various types of monuments are covered as well as the minor arts such as ceramics, metalwork, glass, miniature painting, carpets, and calligraphy. The writer has a nationalistic bias that leads him at times to overemphasize the ethnic Turkish contributions to art forms used by the Turks. The text is more an encyclopedia of monuments than an analysis of style. There is no clear picture of each building--its space, sequences of space, or complexity of lighting. The chapters on the minor arts are often too scanty to be of value. The book is very well illustrated and contains a great deal of information. Black and white, and color illustrations.

2322 ____. Turkish Arts: Seljuk and Ottoman Carpets, Tiles, and Miniature Paintings. Translated by Herman Kreider. Istanbul: Dogan Kardes Yayinlari, 1961, 147 pp.

This small book presents in color many outstanding examples of three media in which the Turkish artists excelled: carpet weaving, tile making, and miniature painting. The examples illustrated are accompanied by a commentary on their historical, technical, and artistic background. The illustrations are, unfortunately, too small and too indistinct in many instances to be of much value. The drawings of Saljūq carpet patterns, however, are worth looking at.

2323 Ettinghausen, Richard. "The Islamic Period." In Art Treasures of Turkey. Edited by Ekram Akurgal. Geneva and Washington: Smithsonian Institution, 1966.
This catalog is divided into four chronological parts. Ettinghausen's contribution constitutes the fourth part, which is a good introductory essay about the art of the Saljūq, Mongol, Turkoman, and Ottoman periods.

2324 Levey, Michael. The World of Ottoman Art. London: Thames & Hudson, 1975, 152 pp.
Written by a Western art historian, this book attempts to bring the little-known world of Ottoman art within easier reach of the general reader and ordinary tourist. It covers the early and classical periods of Ottoman art as well as the fascinating baroque period.

Arabia

2325 Esin, Emel, and Haluk Doganbey. Mecca the Blessed, Madinah the Radiant. London: Elek Books, 1963, 222 pp.
This is an informative and readable book. There are photographs of buildings, landscapes, and townscapes, including genre scenes and figure groups, as well as works of art of many different kinds. Only one-third of the photographs are of Madīnah and Mecca. Though the photographs are the kernel of the book, a history of the two cities has been added, which sets forth a traditional point of view.

Central Asia

2326 Blunt, Wilfred. The Golden Road to Samarkand. New York: Viking Press, 1973, 280 pp.
The format is a series of tableaux dealing with some world conquerors and travelers who passed through Samarqand: Čingīz-Khān, Friar William of Rubruck, the Polos, Ibn Baṭṭūṭa, Tīmūr (Tamerlane), and Bābur, among others. This book is intended to give the reader a better understanding of Cental Asia. Illustrated.

2327 Rice, Tamara. Ancient Arts of Central Asia. New York: Praeger, 1965, 288 pp.
A brief, well-illustrated survey of the arts of the inhabitants of Transcaucasia, Central Asia, and northwest Persia from the first millennium B.C. through the Byzantine period. Despite the diverse cultural influences on this area and mingling of various artistic traditions, an underlying artistic continuity is often detectable.

India

2328 Goetz, Hermann. The Art of India: Five Thousand Years of Indian Art. 2d ed. New York: Crown Publishers, 1964, 283 pp.
The author insists on a fundamental unity of Indian art, for which he provides a historical and religious background.

2329 Marg 11:3 (June 1958):1.
Special issue devoted to early Mughal art.

2330 Royal Academy of Arts. The Art of India and Pakistan, (Sir) Leigh Ashton, ed.: A Commemorative Catalogue of the Exhibition Held at the Royal Academy of Arts. London: Faber & Faber, 1950, 291 pp.
A commemorative catalog of the exhibition held at the Royal Academy of Arts, London, 1947-1948. With black and white, and color photographs.

2331 Wellesz, Emmy. Akbar's Religious Thought, Reflected in Mogul Painting. London: Allen & Unwin, 1952, 47 pp.
A well-written essay that includes a biography of Akbar, a contrast of the mystical and orthodox trends in Islam, and a historical and stylistic study of Persian, Indian, and Mughal painting.

India (Catalogs)

2332 Asia Society. The Art of Mughal India: Painting and Precious Objects. Edited by Stuart Cary Welch. New York: Harry N. Abrams, 1963, 179 pp.
Intended for the general public.

2333 Binney, Edwin. Indian Miniature Painting from the Collection of Edwin Binney, 3rd: An Exhibit at the Portland Art Museum, Dec. 2, 1973--Jan. 20, 1974. Portland, Ore.: Portland Art Museum, 1974, 202 pp.
Includes brief, general remarks about the paintings, with illustrations.

2334 ____. Persian and Indian Miniatures from the Collection of Edwin Binney, 3rd: Exhibited at the Portland Art Museum, Sept. 28--Nov. 29, 1962. Portland, Ore.: Portland Art Assoc., 1962, 48 pp.
Includes brief, general remarks about the paintings, with illustrations.

2335 ____. Rajput Miniatures from the Collection of Edwin Binney, 3rd. Portland, Ore.: Portland Art Museum, 1962, 132 pp.
Includes brief, general remarks about the paintings, with illustrations.

2336 Elvehjem Art Center. Indian Miniature Painting: The Collection of Ernst C. and Jane Werner Watsen. Madison: University of Wisconsin Press, 1971, 153 pp.
Catalog devoted to an exhibit of miniatures illustrating the major schools and styles of Indian painting. A brief introductory essay precedes each group of entries. Forty-seven entries comprise the Mughal chapter. Approximately one-third of the catalog's total of two hundred seventy-one entries are illustrated.

2337 Ettinghausen, R. Paintings of the Sultans and Emperors of India in American Collections. New Delhi: Lalit Kala Akademi, 1961, 35 pp.
Based on a selection from three American collections of eighteen Indian paintings, mostly from the early Mughal period. Most paintings selected have imperial themes. Mounted illustrations, part color.

2338 Amsterdam. Rijks-Museum, Prentenkabinet. The Indian and Persian Miniature Paintings in the Rijksprentenkabinet (Rijksmuseum). Edited by Hermann Goetz. Amsterdam: Rijksmuseum, 1958, 67 pp.
A catalog of Indian and Persian miniature paintings.

CATALOGS: GENERAL

2339 Colnaghi, P. Persian and Mughal Art. London: P. & D. Colanghi & Co., 1966, 320 pp.
A sumptuous catalog of the exhibition of Persian and Mughal art held at Colnaghi's from 7 April to 20 May 1976. The exhibition contained manuscript paintings ranging from the thirteenth to nineteenth centuries, as well as pottery and objets d'art. The catalog has particularly high quality, full-page color illustrations as well as black and white, although the text is not very helpful.

2340 Ettinghausen, Richard, and Eric Schroeder, eds. Iranian and Islamic Art. Newton, Mass.: University Prints, 1941.
A portfolio of two hundred prints (photographs in black and white) with a special stress on the Islamic period. A map and a catalog are included, but there is no text. This is a group of inexpensive prints that are meant to supplement readings with visual illustrations, and as such are very useful.

2341 Freer Gallery of Art. Art of the Arab World. Edited by Esin Atil. Washington: Smithsonian Institution, 1975, 151 pp.
This is an exhibition catalog of eighty art objects from the permanent collection of the Freer, including Qur'ān pages, ceramics, glass, leather bookbindings, metalwork, book paintings, and a gold bracelet. The pieces date from the eighth to the sixteenth centuries, and their provenance is usually Egypt, Syria, or Iraq. The commentary by Atil is concise and accurate. Her bibliographic references will be particularly helpful for those seeking further reading. Black and white, and color illustrations.

2342 Hayward Gallery. The Arts of Islam. London: Arts Council of Great Britain, 1976, 395 pp.
This is the catalog of the great arts of Islam exhibit held at the Hayward Gallery 18 April to 4 July 1976 for the World of Islam Festival in London. The exhibit was one of the largest in scale held during this century and it not only contained well-known works of Islamic art in the West but also many objects on loan from collections in Muslim countries. The catalog is divided by media and each object is photographed, described, and given a small bibliography of where it has been published. A major bibliography is also at the back of the catalog.

2343 Los Angeles County, California, Museum of Art. Islamic Art: The Nasli M. Heeramaneck Collection: With contributions by Pratapaditya Pal, Katharina Otto-Dorn, Edwin Binney, 3rd, and Mary H. Kahlenberg. Los Angeles: Museum of Art, 1973, 232 pp.
Covers ceramics, metalwork, textiles, and manuscripts. The catalog illustrates an important collection of Islamic art, but the reader must be warned that the text is not altogether accurate. Black and white illustrations.

2344 Welch, Anthony. Catalogue of the Collection of Islamic Art of Prince Sudruddin Aga Khan. 2 vols. Geneva: Chateau de Bellerive, 1972.
A catalog of a private collection of Islamic art on display at the owner's home in Switzerland (Chateau de Bellerive). The text is primarily intended for readers who are not familiar with Islamic art. The collection is a respectable one, the text is accurate and clearly expressed, and the illustrations, many in color, are excellent. The six color maps are stunning. The sumptuous quality of this book expresses the owner's pride in making the world aware of his collection, which is particularly strong in Persian miniatures and drawings, Qur'ānic leaves, and Persian ceramics. The illustrations are contained in both volumes.

FESTSCHRIFTS AND MEMORIALS

2345 American University at Cairo, Center for Arabic Studies. Studies in Islamic Art and Architecture in Honour of Professor K.A.C. Creswell. Cairo: American University at Cairo Press, 1965, 291 pp.
The articles in this volume were collected as a tribute to Creswell by his friends, colleagues, and former students. A bibliography of Creswell's publications is included. Among the articles are a number in English, the more notable of which are: "Foundation-moulded Leatherwork--A Rare Egyptian Technique Also Used in Britain" (R. Ettinghausen); "The Pottery of Byzantium and the Islamic World" (D.T. Rice); and "On Islamic Swords" (A. Rahman Zaky). Illustrated.

2346 Ettinghausen, Richard, ed. Aus der Welt der islamischen Kunst: Festschrift für Ernst Kühnel zum 75. Geburststag am 26. 10. 1957. Berlin: Verlag Gebr. Mann, 1959, 404 pp.
The contributions to this Festschrift are in German, English, French, and Italian. A bibliography of the work of E. Kühnel is included. The reader's attention is directed toward three articles in particular: "New Light on Early Animal Carpets" (Ettinghausen); "Textile Fibers and Near Eastern Designs" (Bellinger); and "The Mamluk Illuminated Manuscripts of Kalila wa-Dimna" (Walzer). Rich in corroborative evidence pertinent to the matters at hand, these articles are very specialized. Illustrated.

2347 Kouymjian, Kickran K., ed. Near Eastern Numismatics, Iconography, Epigraphy and History, Studies in Honor of George C. Miles. Beirut: American University of Beirut, 1974, 428 pp.
A wide-ranging collection of articles of a specialized nature. Perhaps the most useful contribution is that of R. Ettinghausen, "Arabic Epigraphy: Communication or Symbolic Affirmation" (pp. 297-317), in which the author explores

the Muslim attitude concerning inscriptions on art objects and in architecture. With illustrations.

2348 Metropolitan Museum of Art, The. Islamic Art in the Metropolitan Museum of Art. Edited by Richard Ettinghausen. New York: Metropolitan Museum of Art, 1972, 334 pp.
This volume was prepared in celebration of the museum's centennial by the Department of Islamic Art. Most articles are studies of an object or objects in the collection. Other articles are concerned with wider issues of Islamic art for which the collection is a point of departure. The articles vary in quality and in significance.

2349 Princeton Institute for Advanced Study. Archaeologica Orientalia in Memoriam Ernst Herzfeld. Edited by George C. Miles. Locust Valley, N.Y.: J.J. Augustin, 1952, 280 pp.
The articles in this memorial volume are in English, French, and German. The reader is referred in particular to the fine article by Kurt Weitzmann, "The Greek Sources of Islamic Scientific Illustrations." Other articles are equally worthy. Illustrated. See also 2357, 2380.

ENCYCLOPEDIA OF WORLD ART ENTRIES

General Areas

2350 Encyclopaedia of World Art (see 2287).
These articles are on the whole good introductions to the various aspects of Islamic art and architecture and contain good bibliographies for further study. "Islam" (E. Kühnel); "Arabia" (A. Grohmann); "Arabian Pre-Islamic Art" (A. Grohmann); "Ommiad Schools--Painting and Decorative Arts" (O. Grabar); "Abbasside Art: Painting and Decorative Arts" (R. Ettinghausen); "Samanid Art" (U. Scerrato); "Ghaznevid Art" (A. Bombaci); "Tulunid Art" (K. Creswell); "Fatimid Art: Decorative Arts" (M. Marzouk); "Seljuk Art" (M. Alose Catelli); "Moorish Style" (G. Marçais); "Mozarabic Art" (L. Torres Balbas); "Saharan Berber Culture" (J. Galres); "Mameluke Art" (F. Shafiʿi); "Ilkhan Art" (U. Scerrato); "Timurid Art" (E. Grube); "Ottoman Schools" (A. Gabriel); "Safavid Art" (G. Scarcia); "Qajar School" (G. Scarcia); "Rajput School" (H. Goetz); "Moghul School" (H. Goetz); "Indian Art, Moslem India" (J. Auboyer); "Indo-Muslim Schools" (H. Goetz).

Specific Areas

2351 Encyclopaedia of World Art (see 2287).
The following articles relate to more specific aspects of Islamic art and architecture. Iconography: "Images and Iconoclasm, Islam" (R. Ettinghausen); "Human Figure, Islam" (E. Kühnel). Architecture: "Fatimid Art. Architecture" (K.A.C. Creswell); "Abbaside Art. Architecture" (G. Marçais); "Sinan Famous Ottoman Architect" (B.M. Alfieri). Persian Painters: "Behzad" (R. Pinder-Wilson); "Mīr Sayyid ʿAlī" (U. Scerrato); "Rizā-i-ʿAbbāsī" (E. Kühnel); "Ceramics. Islam" (A. Love); "Textiles, Embroidery and Lace" (H. Schmidt); "Tapestry and Carpets. II Carpets" (D. Heinz); "Gold and Silverwork" (R. Ettinghausen); "Glass" (G. Lamm).

CHARACTER OF ISLAMIC ART

2352 Aga-Oglu, Mehmet. "Remarks on the Character of Islamic Art." Art Bulletin 36 (1954): 175-202.
In this article one may read of the author's disagreements with views expressed by other Islamic art hisotrians regarding pre-Islamic civilization in Arabia, the artistic heritage of Islam, attitudes toward luxury in Islam. This article is technical and scholarly. The advanced student will find it essential and stimulating.

2353 Burckhardt, Titus. Art of Islam: Language and Meaning. London: World of Islam Festival Pub. Co., 1976, 204 pp.
A beautifully illustrated book that explores the relationship of Islamic art to Islam and the role of art in Islam. A major part of the book focuses on the spiritual symbolism inherent in Islamic architecture. Discussed in this context are the major sacred architectural monuments as well as the basic form of the mosque. Another theme presented in the book is the ability of Islamic art to embrace a number of diverse artistic styles--those of the nomad and the city dweller, for example--and synthesize them to create a unified style, much as the concept of unity is reflected in the doctrine of Islam.

2354 Ettinghausen, Richard. "The Character of Islamic Art." In The Arab Heritage (see 123), pp. 251-67.
This is a well-known and widely read attempt to define some characteristics of Islamic art. Modifications of some of the views expressed here have been necessary over the years. It is therefore essential for readers of this article to read, as well, the reply article by Mehmet Aga-Oglu (see 2352). Taken together these articles are exemplary of the dialogue by which scholars thrash out points of controversy in order to arrive at conclusions that accord with all of the evidence brought forward on matters of research.

2355 _____. "Early Realism in Islamic Art." In Studi Orientalistici in onore di Giorgio Levi della Vida. Vol. 1. Rome: Istituto per l'oriente, 1956, pp. 250-73.
Despite a predilection for abstract and infinite design, there is an opposite tendency in Islamic art, though to a lesser degree, toward the "realistic" in which movement was the main concern of the artist. In this article Ettinghausen confirms this tendency toward realism by means of painted and carved objects. The examples cited are mostly Fāṭimid (tenth- to twelfth-century Egyptian).

2356 _____. "Interaction and Integration in Islamic Art." In Unity and Variety in Muslim Civilization (see 26), pp. 107-31.
In this essay the author tries to show certain trends and forces in Islam and to illustrate them with examples. He discusses the unity and the diversity of Islamic art.

2357 _____. "The 'Beveled Style' in the Post-Samarra Period." In Archaeologica Orientalia in Memoriam Ernst Herzfeld (see 2349), pp. 72-83.
An examination of the type of ornamentation found at Sāmarrā, which was common there and was copied in other countries in the ninth century, especially in Ṭūlūnid Egypt. The author presents a list of dated objects and monuments from the eleventh, twelfth, and fourteenth centuries that show the continuity in the use of this decoration.

2358 Sourdel-Thomine, J. "Fann." In EI2. Vol. 2 (see 20), pp. 775-78.
A short essay on the idea of Islamic art, which explores the notion of unity and vanity in Islamic art, attitudes toward images and surface decoration, and architectural requirements.

ARCHAEOLOGICAL REPORTS

2359 Bombaci, Alessio. "Introduction to the Excavations of Ghazni." East and West 10 (1959):3-22.
Bombaci summarizes the cultural and artistic background of the Islamic capital of Ghaznī. The most significant part of the article is the catalog of marble sculptures on exhibit in Ghaznī and in the museum of Kabūl.

2360 "Islamic Archaeology." In Archaeology 24 (1971):197-262.
The June issue of Archaeology provides a résumé by acknowledged experts of some current progress in Islamic archaeology in the central lands of Islam. Among the topics covered are Islamic incised glass (Abū al-Farāj al-ʿUsh), Islamic pottery from Susa (M. Rosen-Ayalon); Turkish ceramic art (O. Aslanapa); a shard count at Fusṭāṭ mounds (G. Scanlon); thirteenth- and fourteenth-century mosques in Turkey (A. Kuran); and houses of Siraf, Iran (H. Whitehouse).

2361 Matheson, Sylvia A. Persia: An Archaeological Guide. London: Faber & Faber, 1972, 358 pp.
A handbook that describes the archaeological sites and monuments of Iran from 6000 B.C. to the thirteenth century A.D. As a comprehensive account of finds up to 1970 the book has no rival. The book will be appreciated more by those whose interests lie in archaeology than in the flowering of Islamic art because of the abrupt termination at the end of the Saljūq period. Illustrated.

2362 Scanlon, George T. "Fustat and the Islamic Art of Egypt." Archaeology 21 (1968):188-95.
This article constitutes a summary of the results of the recent excavations of a town that pre-dates Cairo by several centuries, Fusṭāṭ, the ruins of which were later engulfed by Cairo's urban sprawl. Fusṭāṭ flourished from the middle of the eighth century until its demise in A.D. 1168, when it was burned in advance of a foray by a Crusader army sent by the king of Jerusalem. Particularly significant are the conclusions of the author on the continuity of pre-Islamic artistic influences at Fusṭāṭ and the probable Egyptian origins of luster painting on glass and ceramics.

2363 Scerrato, Umberto. "The First Two Excavation Campaigns at Ghazni, 1957-58." East and West 10 (1959):23-55.
This is a preliminary report of the results of excavations the author and his colleague A. Bombaci intend to publish soon. The architectural decoration and pottery are dramatic new evidence for the art of Ghaznī prior to the Mongol invasions.

ARTISTIC EXCHANGES AND TRADE

2364 Ettinghausen, Richard. From Byzantium to Sasanian Iran and the Islamic World: Three Modes of Artistic Influence. Leiden: E.J. Brill, 1972, 69 pp.
The author is concerned in three separate essays with the influence of single elements of classical and Sāsānian art on Islamic art. He discusses three modes of artistic influence: the transfer of forms, the adoption of forms, and the integration of forms. These articles, rich in ideas, will interest those already familiar with Iranian and Mediterranean art. With illustrations.

2365 Gibb, Hamilton A.R. "Arab-Byzantine Relations under the Umayyad Caliphate." Dumbarton Oaks Papers 12 (1958):219-33. Reprint. In Studies on the Civilization of Islam (see 23), pp. 47-61.
Explores the question of whether the Byzantine emperor sent mosaics and craftsmen to the caliphs ʿAbd al-Malik and al-Walīd as stated by some Arabic sources.

2366 Grabar, Oleg. "Islamic Art and Byzantium." Dumbarton Oaks Papers 18 (1964):69-88. Reprint. In Studies in Medieval Islamic Art (see 2295).
The author presents his interpretation of the artistic ideas and forms that Byzantine art, for various historical and geographic reasons, imposed on the early art of Islam. He also tries to show that cultural relations between Constantinople and Muslim art centers continued at later periods. While incorporating Byzantine artistic ideas, early Muslim art and architecture were deliberately made different from what surrounded them, yet made understandable as being uniquely Islamic.

2367 Rice, David S. "The Seasons and the Labors of the Months in Islamic Art." Ars Orientalis 1 (1954):1-39.
This article is intended to show that representations of the seasons and months occur in Islamic art, and that they were borrowed from Christian models in the West during the later

Middle Ages. This study is based primarily on miniature painting and inlaid metalwork from the thirteenth and fourteenth centuries.

2368 Richards, Donald S., ed. Islam and the Trade of Asia (see 177).
Islamic art historians and archaeologists should note J. Michael Rogers' "China and Islam--The Archaeological Evidence in the Mashriq," John Carswell's "Archaeology and the Study of Later Islamic Pottery," and George Scanlon's "Egypt and China: Trade and Imitation."

2369 Rogers, J. Michael. "Evidence for Mamluk-Mongol Relations, 1260-1360." In Colloque International sur l'Histoire du Caire [27 mars--5 avril, 1969] German Democratic Republic: Ministry of Culture of the Arab Republic of Egypt. Köhn: Böhlau, 1974, pp. 385-404.
An important article in which the author has attempted to explain the process by which Persian objets d'art inspired Egyptian art despite a state of conflict between the two opposed spheres of political-religious influence during the period from 1260 to 1360.

ICONOGRAPHY

2370 Baer, Eva. Sphinxes and Harpies in Medieval Islamic Art: An Iconographical Study. Jerusalem: Israel Oriental Society, 1965, 109 pp.
A study of the representation of human-headed birds and quadrupeds, covering the origin of the two motifs, their occurrence in Islamic works of art, and their popularity or lack of it at various times. Representations of these beasts appear on textiles, ceramics, metalwork, and books throughout the Islamic world of the Middle Ages, except, apparently, in Muslim India. Illustrated.

2371 Dodd, Erika C. "The Image of the Word: Notes on the Religious Iconography of Islam." Berytus 18 (1969):35-79.
The author scrutinizes the reasons generally given for the absence of the religious image in Islam. She argues that the art of Islam can be understood and placed squarely within the context of the general history of medieval art: Western Christian, Eastern Christian, and Islamic.

2372 Ettinghausen, Richard. The Unicorn. Washington: Smithsonian Institution, 1950, 209 pp.
The author sets forth the various iconographic forms of the unicorn and the historical setting of this motif, and tries to reconstruct the connotations likely to be found in the mind of a medieval Muslim confronted with a picture of the "animal."

2373 Guest, Grace D., and Richard Ettinghausen. "The Iconography of a Kashan Luster Plate." Ars Orientalis 4 (1961):25-64.
The scene on a plate in the Freer Gallery of Art, Washington, D.C., has been examined by two scholars. They have determined that folk tales and courtly imagery of the period (early thirteenth century) can explain the scene.

2374 Meredith-Owens, G.M. "Fīl." In EI2. Vol. 2 (see 20), pp. 894-95.
Under the heading "Iconography" will be found a concise essay on the depiction of the figure of the elephant in various Islamic art forms. Four plates and bibliography.

2375 Mittwoch, E. "Dhu'l-Fakar." In EI1. Vol. 2 (see 32), p. 959. In EI2. Vol. 2 (see 20), p. 233.
The name of the famous sword that Muḥammad obtained as booty in the Battle of Badr, Muslim iconography represented the sword with two points; "Dhu' al-Fakar" means an attribute of finely engraved swords in general.

2376 Wellesz, E. "Islamic Astronomical Imagery: Classical and Bedouin Tradition." Oriental Art, n.s. 10 (1964):85-91.
A basic study of the famous tenth-century Ṣūfī manuscript of the constellations and signs of the zodiac. Wellesz shows how the illustrations were derived basically from classical tradition yet have interesting differences brought about by the recurring strength of the Arab astronomical tradition.

ARABESQUE--ORNAMENT

2377 Bourgain, J. Arabic Geometrical Pattern and Design. New York: Dover Publications, 1973, 189 pp.
This is a new edition of the plates of the original French book Les éléments de l'art arabe: le trait des entrelacs published in 1879. The 190 linear plates show the basic patterns underlying the geometrical ornament of Islamic art.

2378 Critchlow, Keith. Islamic Patterns: An Analytical and Cosmological Approach. New York: Schocken Books, 1976, 192 pp.
A metaphysical and cosmological analysis of the geometric elements constituting the major patterns in Islamic art. Such an analysis provides clues to understanding the underlying spiritual aspects of Islamic art. Illustrated.

2379 Dimand, Maurice S. "Studies in Islamic Ornament, I." Ars Islamica 4 (1937):293-337.
Devoted to several aspects of Umayyad and early ʿAbbāsid ornament.

2380 _____. "Studies in Islamic Ornament, II: The Origin of the Second Style of Samarra Decoration." In Archaeologica Orientalia in Memoriam Ernst Herzfeld (see 2349), pp. 62-68.
A study of a type of ornament that Herzfeld designated the second style. For fuller details, see E. Herzfeld, Der Wandschmuck der Bauten von Samarra und seine Ornamentik, Berlin: D. Reimer, 1923, pp. 117-82.

2381 Kühnel, E. "Arabesque." In EI2. Vol. 1 (see 20), pp. 558-61.
A clear concise definition of the Islamic form of arabesque.

2382 Landau, Rom. The Arabesque: The Abstract Art of Islam. San Francisco: American Academy of Asian Studies, 1955, 23 pp.
This essay tries to interpret the metaphysical implications of the motif of the arabesque, but it lacks a precise definition of the arabesque.

2383 Shafiʻi, Farid. Simple Calyx Ornament in Islamic Art (A Study in Arabesque). Cairo: Cairo University Press, 1957, 250 pp.
A very thorough, detailed, and meticulous study of one element of Islamic ornament. Illustrated.

ARCHITECTURE

STUDIES RELATING TO ISLAMIC ARCHITECTURE AS A WHOLE

2384 Creswell, K.A.C. "Architecture." In EI2. Vol. 1 (see 20), pp. 608-24.
An excellent summary of the author's Early Muslim Architecture (see 2385) with floor plans and twenty-four plates.

2385 _____. Early Muslim Architecture: Umayyads, Early Abbasids and Tulunids. 2 vols. Rev. ed. Oxford: Clarendon Press, 1969.
This is a comprehensive critical assembly of all the archaeological and textual evidence for the architecture under the Umayyads (vol. 1) and under the ʻAbbāsids, Umayyads of Cordova, Aghlabids, and Ṭūlūnids (vol. 2). The work is essentially a collection of monographs on individual monuments, rather than a history of early Islamic architecture.

2386 _____. A Short Account of Early Muslim Architecture. Baltimore: Penguin Books, 1958, 330 pp.
An abridged version of the monumental Early Muslim Architecture (see 2385). It is too close an adaptation of the earlier work. Fresh evidence has been neglected, such as carved stucco revetments, statuary and balustrades, floor paintings, cross-vaults in masonry and brick, and brick domes; Qasr al-Hayr al-Gharbī and Khirbat al-Mafjar are not mentioned. The plates are excellent; the low cost and portable size of the book commend it.

2387 Hill, Derek, and Oleg Grabar. Islamic Architecture and Its Decoration A.D. 800-1500: A Photographic Survey. 2d ed. Chicago: University of Chicago Press, 1967, 88 pp.
This book deals with the Islamic architecture of the Saljūqs and Mongols, with much less on that of the Sāmānids, Ghaznavids, and others. Grabar has written briefly and deftly on the architectural setting of the decoration and its historical evolution. Unfortunately, there are neither plans nor elevations to help the reader make sense of the photographs that in themselves suffer occasionally from perspective distortion and a failure to indicate scale. The standard of the photographs is lower in the second edition than in the first (London & Chicago, 1964). In conjunction with Grabar's essay these photographs fill a much needed place in studies of the Islamic architecture of Islam.

2388 Hoag, John D. Western Islamic Architecture. New York: George Braziller, 1963, 48 pp.
A brief essay on the Muslim architecture in Syria, Iraq, Egypt, North Africa, Spain, and Turkey, with 137 illustrations and diagrams.

2389 Hoag, John. Islamic Architecture. New York: Abrams, 1977, 424 pp.
A profusely illustrated survey focusing on the evolution of classic Islamic architecture. Those architectural styles or periods that do not follow the mainstream development have been omitted, but without effect on providing the reader with a fairly comprehensive idea of the development of Islamic architecture in the major geographical areas of Islam from the seventh to seventeenth century. The conclusion at the end of each chapter summarizes the characteristics of the discussed buildings. Included is a glossary and a synoptic table that geographically and historically correlates the major architectural monuments.

2390 Mayer, Leo Ary. Islamic Architects and Their Works. Geneva: A. Kundig, 1956, 183 pp.
A basic reference work.

2391 Richmond, Ernest T. Moslem Architecture, 623-1516. London: Royal Asiatic Society, 1926, 159 pp.
This book is concise and authoritative, but it is much in need of revision and should be used only in conjunction with readings that reflect the evidence of more recent research. The majority of the monuments discussed are from Sāmarrā, Jerusalem, and Cairo, with at least one monument from Cordova, Damascus, and Kūfah included. Illustrated.

2392 Seherr-Thoss, Sonia P. Design and Color in Islamic Architecture: Afghanistan, Iran, Turkey. Photographs by Hans C. Seherr-Thoss. Washington: Smithsonian Institution Press, 1968, 312 pp.
This is an excellent picture book with some shortcomings. The scope is narrow. Far too much emphasis has been placed on the Persian architectural tradition, with Turkish architecture being given only a summary coverage. Among the book's virtues: close-up pictures that are particularly outstanding. The descriptions of each photograph are succinct, leaving the pictures to speak for themselves.

2393 Speiser, Werner. Oriental Architecture in Colour: Islamic, Indian, Far Eastern. Translated by W.E. Kessler. London: Thames & Hudson, 1965, 504 pp.
Because the Islamic architecture of Spain and North Africa, with the exception of Egypt, is omitted, the selection of photographs appears to have been capricious. Many of the 112 color plates are marvelous, nonetheless.

STUDIES INVOLVING SPECIFIC AREAS OR COUNTRIES

Egypt, Syria, and Arabia

2394 Becker, Carl. "Cairo." In EI1. Vol. 2 (see 32), pp. 815-26.
Contains a considerable amount of architectural information on numerous monuments. See also 2409.

2395 Brandenburg, Dietrich. Islamische Baukunst in Ägypten. Berlin: Hessling, 1966, 319 pp.
A detailed survey of Islamic architecture in Egypt, from the seventh to midnineteenth century. Numerous plans, sections, and drawings of decorative details, a glossary of architectural terms, and an extensive bibliography make this book a valuable reference work.

2396 Briggs, Martin Shaw. Muhammadan Architecture in Egypt and Palestine. Oxford: Clarendon Press, 1924, 255 pp.
In spite of its title this book is devoted chiefly to architecture in Egypt. Though a standard work since publication, the text is much in need of revision. The treatment is well balanced, good judgment having been used in the selection of monuments representative of those preserved in Cairo of the nearly 240 built before the Turkish Conquest (A.D. 1517). The reader will also find useful chapters on domestic architecture and on craftsmanship. Illustrated.

2397 Buhl, F. "Al-Ḳuds" (see 1907).

2398 Creswell, K.A.C. The Muslim Architecture of Egypt. Vol. 1, Ikhshids and Fātimids; Vol. 2, Ayyūbids and Early Bahrite Mamlūks. Oxford: Clarendon Press, 1952-1959.
A thorough and complete discussion of the Muslim monuments of Egypt to the Mamlūk period. The author takes individual monuments one by one, in chronological order, providing the literary evidence about them, then a minute description and an analysis of original features. Illustrations and bibliography.

2399 Duncan, Alistair. The Noble Sanctuary: Portrait of a Holy Place in Arab Jerusalem (see 1909).

2400 Elisseeff, N. "Dimashk." In EI2. Vol. 2 (see 20), pp. 277-90.
A comprehensive study of one of the most important cities in Islam, including an examination of major architectural units of the city set within the historical context. There are no plans, but seven plates depict the major monuments.

2401 Grabar, Oleg. "The Umayyad Dome of the Rock in Jerusalem." Ars Orientalis 3 (1959): 33-62. Reprint. In Studies in Medieval Islamic Art (see 2295).
The author shows how the first major Muslim attempt at monumental architecture can only be understood in its Umayyad context, both politically and religiously.

2402 Hamilton, Robert William, and Oleg Grabar. Khirbat al-Mafjar: An Arabian Mansion in the Jordan Valley. Oxford: Clarendon, 1959, 352 pp.
A thorough study of an early Umayyad palace. Illustrated.

2403 Hautecoeur, Louis, and Gaston Wiet. Les Mosquées du Caire. 2 vols. Paris: Ernest Leroux, 1932.
A useful introduction to the mosques of Cairo with numerous good photographs illustrating the text. The historical part, written by Gaston Wiet, includes a good study of the social background.

2404 Herzfeld, Ernst. "Damascus: Studies in Architecture." Ars Islamica 9-14 (1942-48).
These articles constitute an excellent survey of approximately eighty monuments in Damascus, which were surveyed by the author between 1908 and 1930. The individual monuments have not been arranged in a strictly chronological order, but have been organized in sections such as the Syrian madrasah (school), the türbe (tomb tower), and the mosque. Some description is given for the general reader, but the emphasis is on analysis and conclusions.

2405 Holod-Tretiak, Renata. "Qasr al-Hayr al-Sharqi: A Medieval Town in Syria." Archaeology 23 (1970):221-31.
This article is a descriptive résumé of the Syrian site that dates from Umayyad times (A.D. 661-750). Judging from ceramic finds, the city flourished in the eighth and ninth centuries and industrial and agricultural activities formed the economic base.

2406 Institut Français de Damas. Les Monuments Ayyoubides de Damas. 4 vols. Paris: E. de Boccard, 1939-1950.
Four indispensable little volumes for the study of the architecture of Damascus during a very prosperous period. All the known facts about each monument are examined: floor plans, cross sections, and details of decoration and plates. The best study on Damascus.

2407 Jomier, J. "Al-Fusṭāṭ." In EI2. Vol. 2 (see 20), pp. 957-59.
A brief but valuable historical survey of the first city to be founded in Egypt by the Muslims (seventh century) and the first place of residence of the Arab governors.

2408 Landay, Jerry M. The Dome of the Rock. New York: Newsweek, 1972, 168 pp.
A study of the Dome of the Rock, its history, and the three faiths that hold that area sacred. Ties the building into the larger history of Jerusalem itself.

2409 Rogers, J.M. "Al-Kāhira." In EI2. Vol. 4 (see 20), pp. 424-41.
A valuable historical survey of the monuments of Cairo, including a map showing the Islamic monuments plus twelve plates. Extensive bibliography. See also 2394.

2410 Russel, Dorothea. Medieval Cairo and the Monasteries of the Wadi Natrun: A Historical Guide. London: Weidenfeld & Nicolson, 1962, 368 pp.
This is one of the best English guides to Cairo. It is well illustrated, mostly from photographs taken by Creswell. Although an amateur, the author possesses a rare firsthand

knowledge of the ancient Coptic and Muslim quarters of the old city. The book describes them in meticulous detail--their history, buildings, tombs, streets, mosques, churches, and other points of interest.

2411 Sauvaget, Jean. Alep: Essai sur le développement d'une grande ville syrienne des origines au milieu du XIX siècle. Paris: P. Geuthner, 1941, 302 pp.
An excellent study of the development of a single city. Sauvaget has studied the physical development of the city of Aleppo using archaeological evidence as his primary material. Through the study of the monuments the author traces the history and role of an important medieval city. This is a scholarly work born of love and devotion to the city and the result is an admirable study.

Mesopotamia

2412 Bell, Gertrude L. Palace and Mosque at Ukhaidir: A Study in Early Muhammadan Architecture. Oxford: Clarendon Press, 1914, 180 pp.
A study of the ʿAbbāsid castle of Ukhaidir discovered by Bell in 1909. This is an excellent monograph for understanding early palace architecture. The book includes studies on the origins of Islamic architecture with maps and a good bibliography. For good illustrations, one should consult Oskar Reuther's Ocheidir (Leipzig: J.C. Hinrichs, 1912), which complements Bell's work. Illustrated.

2413 Massignon, Louis. "Ukhaidir." In EI1. Vol. 4 (see 32), p. 994.
Brief article summarizing the discovery, plan, and dating of this early Islamic palace structure in the Mesopotamian desert. Bibliography includes references to early excavation reports.

2414 Villet, M. "Sāmarrā." In EI1. Vol. 4 (see 32), pp. 131-33.
Brief history of the ʿAbbāsid city of Sāmarrā, followed by a topographical survey of monuments. Bibliography cites archaeological reports.

North Africa and Spain

2415 Bargebuhr, Frederick P. The Alhambra: A Cycle of Studies of the Eleventh Century in Moorish Spain. Berlin: de Gruyter, 1968, 438 pp.
This is a difficult and learned book for which the reader is expected to have a knowledge of Arabic, Hebrew, and Latin poetry, as well as familiarity with medieval Spanish history and Neoplatonic thought. The second part of the book (pp. 89-226) is of prime interest to art historians. Here the author expands on the subject of an eleventh-century origin for the main themes and some of the construction of the Alhambra. Bargebuhr shows that much in the Alhambra can be related to the mythology that throughout the Middle Ages had developed around Solomon, the prophet-king. Illustrated.

2416 _____. "The Alhambra Palace of the Eleventh Century." Journal of the Warburg and Courtauld Institutes 19 (1956):192-258.
The evidence in this article suggests that the main themes and even some of the construction of the Alhambra were eleventh-century work, inspired by the Jewish minister of a Muslim prince.

2417 Bel, Alfred. "Tlemcen." In EI1. Vol. 4 (see 32), pp. 801-5.
Brief historical and cultural survey highlighting the major Hispano-Islamic architectural monuments of the city of Tlemcen, also called Agadir.

2418 Boothe, Louise W. "The Great Mosque of Qairawan." Oriental Art, n.s. 16 (1970): 321-36.
A résumé of the architectural history of the Sidi Uqba mosque at Qayrawan (Tunisia) and its decoration. With photographs.

2419 Brunschvig, Robert. "Tunis." In EI1. Vol. 4 (see 32), pp. 837-44.
Concise historical survey of Tunis, focusing on the city's economical development, physical expansion, and major building phases.

2420 Cenival, Pierre de. "Marrakesh." In EI1. Vol. 3 (see 32), pp. 296-306.
A detailed article on the history of Marrakesh, incorporating the major monuments. The bibliography cites both Arabic and European source materials.

2421 Fikri, Ahmad. La Grande Mosque de Kairouan. Paris: Librairie Renouard, 1934, 167 pp.
A monograph on the first and most important mosque of North Africa. Well documented and copiously illustrated. Bibliography.

2422 Funck-Brentano, C. "Meknes." in EI1. Vol. 3 (see 32), pp. 454-59.
A historical outline of the Moroccan town of Meknes, chosen by Mawlāy Ismāʿīl as his capital after his accession in the 1670s. For approximately fifty years, he sponsored an extravagant building program, which included the construction of a palace, stables, mosque, and madrasah.

2423 Golvin, L. "Ḳalʿat Banī Ḥammād." In EI2. Vol. 4 (see 20), pp. 478-81.
A medieval town in the central Maghreb that was the capital of the Berber dynasty, the Banī Ḥammād. The town experienced a short period of splendor (eleventh century) and the ruins add to our understanding of North African architecture, revealing Egyptian, Iraqi, and Persian influences. A map of the city is provided, plus four plates and bibliography.

2424 Hill, Derek, and L. Golvin. Islamic Architecture in North Africa: A Photographic Survey. With Notes on the monuments and a concluding essay by Lucien Golvin. London: Faber, 1976, 167 pp.
An excellent photographic study by Hill of major monuments in Egypt and the Maghreb, with extensive commentary by Golvin.

2425 Marçais, Georges. L'Architecture Musulmane d'Occident. Paris: Arts et métiers graphiques, 1954, 540 pp.

The basic standard work on Muslim North Africa and Spain. The author covers the monuments of Tunisia, Algeria, Morocco, Spain, and Sicily, from the ninth to the nineteenth century.

2426 Sordo, Enrique. Moorish Spain: Cordova, Seville, Granada. Translated by Ian Michael. New York: Crown Publishers, 1963, 223 pp.

The author examines the achievements of the Moors as seen in the three principal cities of Andalusia. He traces their political history and the progress of their art, primarily architecture and its decorative features. Over half the book deals with Granada. Illustrated.

2427 Terrasse, Henri. L'Art Hispano-Mauresque des Origines au XIII Siècle. Paris: G. van Oest, 1932, 506 pp.

The author examines and describes the monuments of the Umayyad, Almoravid, and Almohad periods in Spain and Morocco. One of the basic books on the subject, it is very useful for its extensive bibliography. Illustrated.

2428 Terrasse, H. "Fās." In EI2. Vol. 2 (see 20), pp. 821-23.

Provides a succinct summary of the major monuments of an important Islamic city of northern Morocco (Fās) stressing the building activity of the thirteenth and fourteenth centuries, when the city along with Granada was one major center of Hispano-Islamic art. Eight plates plus short bibliography.

2429 Terrasse, Henri. "Gharnāṭa." In EI2. Vol. 2 (see 20), pp. 1014-20.

The section on monuments focuses almost entirely upon the Alhambra (near Granada) and offers a good survey of the historical background, architectural composition, and interior decoration of one of Islam's most famous buildings. With plates.

Iran

2430 Ettinghausen, R. "Īlkhāns." In EI2. Vol. 3 (see 20), pp. 1123-27.

A survey of both art and architecture is provided under the section on monuments.

2431 Golombek, Lisa. Timurid Shrine at Gauzur Gah. Toronto: Royal Ontario Museum, 1969, 227 pp.

This book is an attempt to view a large shrine complex of the post-Mongol period in Iran as a total architectural entity that consists of centuries of accretions. This is the only major study of any Tīmūrid monument in a Western language. Originally a doctoral thesis, this study is highly specialized. Illustrated.

2432 Pope, Arthur Upham. Persian Architecture: The Triumph of Form and Color. New York: George Braziller, 1965, 288 pp.

This book traces the development of Persian architecture from the Achaemenid structures of the sixth century B.C. to the Ṣafavid mosques of the early eighteenth century. The text has authority, but the style is sometimes distracting, perhaps because this text is a partly condensed summary of what was written by Pope in A Survey of Persian Art (see 2314). It should be mentioned, however, that this volume also contains the results of some of the later researches made since the survey was published. Abundantly illustrated, both black and white, and color.

2433 Wilber, Donald N. The Architecture of Islamic Iran: The Il-Khanid Period. Princeton, N.J.: Princeton University Press, 1955, 208 pp.

A descriptive catalog of the monuments built in Iran during the thirteenth and fourteenth centuries. The catalog comprises over one hundred entries, chronologically arranged, including inscriptions and some monuments that have now disappeared. Each entry gives a summary description with commentary and a bibliography. There are numerous illustrations, but some of them are too small in format to show details. This is an excellent survey.

Turkey and the Balkans

2434 Aga-Oglu, Mehmet. "The Fatih Mosque at Constantinople." Art Bulletin 12 (1930): 179-95.

The author refutes the common assumptions among contemporary Western art historians that late Turkish mosque style is dependent on Byzantine church style, especially on the domed cross church. He refutes the notion that Haghia Sophia can be considered the direct model for the large domed mosques built after the conquest of Constantinople by the Ottoman Turks.

2435 Deny, J. "Wālide Sulṭān." In EI1. Vol. 4 (see 32), pp. 1113-18.

Discussed is the title borne by the mother of the reigning Ottoman sulṭān. Appearing at the end of this article is a list of buildings erected by certain wālide sulṭāns, attesting to the wealth and power often associated with this title.

2436 Erdmann, Kurt. Das Anatolische Karavansarai des 13 Jahrhunderts. 2 vols. Instanbuler Forschungen, bd. 21. Berlin, Gebr. Mann, 1961, 1:213 pp.; 2:358 plates, 59 floor plans.

Methodically cataloged in this work are 119 Turkish caravansary. Wherever possible, detailed information on dimensions, mason's marks, and construction is provided for each entry, as well as plans. At the beginning of the book, the caravansary are classified according to elements of their plan. In addition to the bibliography for each entry, there is a general bibliography.

2437 Fehervari, G. "Ḥarrān." In EI2. Vol. 3 (see 20), pp. 227-30.

A study of the history and architecture of an ancient city that flourished in medieval Islamic times but whose ruins now lie in the boundaries of modern Turkey. Two plates and bibliography.

2438 Gabriel, Albert. "Dunaysir." Ars Islamica 4 (1937):352-68.
A study of the Great Mosque (601/1204) of Dunaysir, a city that flourished at the beginning of the thirteenth century.

2439 _____. Monuments Turcs d'Anatolie. 2 vols. Paris: Turkish Ministry of Public Instruction, 1931-1934.
A detailed, descriptive, and well-documented account of all the major Islamic monuments of Anatolia. It is a monumental study, and a starting point for all serious studies. A major scholarly account.

2440 Gökbilgin, M. Tayyib. "Edirne, Adrianople." In EI2. Vol. 2 (see 20), pp. 683-86.
A chronological survey of the major monuments of Edirne, Turkey, including the glorious Selimiye mosque designed by the great architect Sinan.

2441 Goodwin, Godfrey. A History of Ottoman Architecture. Baltimore: Johns Hopkins Press, 1971, 511 pp.
A voluminous book on Ottoman architecture with a very large number of plans, sections, and photos. The main theme of the work is to show that there is a uniquely Ottoman style in Ottoman architecture. Many types of buildings are included, but the mosques are the main focus of the book. The buildings are in general studied in chronological order. Though he devotes considerable space to specific monuments, he does not lose sight of the generalization important to any history.

2442 Inalcik, H. "Istanbul." In EI2. Vol. 4 (see 20), pp. 224-48.
A comprehensive study of Istanbul that gives a great deal of information about the important physical structures in the city, but does not stress architectural analysis. Includes a map of the city, four plates, and a massive bibliography.

2443 Kuban, Dogan. Muslim Religious Architecture. Pt. 1 (see 1898).

2444 _____. "An Ottoman Building Complex of the Sixteenth Century: The Sokollu Mosque and Its Dependencies in Istanbul." Ars Orientalis 7 (1968):19-40.
Among the masterpieces of sixteenth-century Ottoman architecture is the Sokollu mosque. The social and architectural importance of the component structures of this mosque and its affiliated buildings are carefully indicated by the author.

2445 Kuran, Aptullah. The Mosque in Early Ottoman Architecture. Chicago: University of Chicago Press, 1968, 233 pp.
This is the first volume of a three-volume study of Ottoman architecture. It takes the reader to A.D. 1506. Pictures, plans, and summary descriptions are provided of ninety-four mosques from the formative period of Ottoman mosque architecture. All but two are within the borders of modern Turkey. Architectural decoration, particularly that of the interior, is only briefly described and scantily illustrated.

2446 Lloyd, Seton, and D.S. Rice. Alanya (ʻAlā'iyya). London: British Institute of Archaeology at Ankara, 1958, 70 pp.
Alanya has remained, perhaps, the least spoiled Saljūq site that can now be found in Asia Minor. This study of its buildings and inscriptions is based on work carried out in 1953. This book is specialized, carefully organized, and quite adequately illustrated.

2447 Rice, David Storm. "Medieval Harran: Studies on its Topography and Monuments I." Anatolian Studies 2 (1952):36-83.
Ḥarrān is a town in southeastern Turkey near the Syrian border. The topography and monuments of the medieval site, dating from the Arab conquest in A.D. 639 until the destruction of the city by the Mongols in A.D. 1260, are researched, incorporating information from Ibn Shaddad's account of Ḥarrān and archaeological excavations by the author.

2448 Riefstahl, Rudolf M. Turkish Architecture in Southwestern Anatolia. Cambridge, Mass.: Harvard University Press, 1931, 116 pp.
This book is a record of monuments, primarily Turkish, in the cities of southwestern Anatolia. Includes a short description of the main characteristics of the monuments and an attempt to indicate the significance of each work in the evolution of Turkish art. Particular stress is laid on the study of decorative features, objects of art, and manuscripts. Woodwork, rugs, and ceramic decoration have been noted. The photographs are excellent. Cities surveyed include Manissa, Birgeh, Tireh, Aydin, Antalya, and Alanya.

2449 Rogers, J. Michael. "The Cifte Minare Medrese at Erzurum and the Gök Medrese at Sivas: A Contribution to the History of Style in the Seljuk Architecture of Thirteenth Century Turkey." Anatolian Studies 15 (1965): 63-85.
This is a very fine comparative study of two magnificent monuments built in Anatolia in the last half of the thirteenth century A.D.

2450 Stratton, Arthur. Sinan. New York: Scribner, 1972, 299 pp.
Historical biography of the great sixteenth-century Ottoman architect and engineer Sinan. Numerous black and white illustrations of his buildings are included, as is a glossary of architectural terms and Turkish titles.

2451 Taeschner, Franz. "Amasya." In EI2. Vol. 1 (see 20), pp. 431-32.
A town in northern Anatolia, Amasya is the site of two important Saljūq period buildings: a mosque, Burmali Minare (1237-1247), and a school, the Gök Medrese (1266-1267).

2452 Ünsal, Behcet. Turkish Islamic Architecture in Seljuk and Ottoman Times, 1071-1923 A.D. 2d ed. New York: St. Martin's Press, 1973, 116 pp.

The scope is more limited than the title suggests: military architecture is excluded as well as the layout of the medieval Turkish town. Bridges and cisterns are not treated adequately, and only the Turkish architecture developed down to 1600 is treated in detail. Furthermore, the Turkish buildings of Syria, Mesopotamia, Egypt, and the Balkans have been omitted.

2453 Vogt-Göknil, Ulya. Living Architecture: Ottoman. London: Oldbourne Book Co., 1966, 192 pp.

The value of this book lies in the illustrations, as the text is factually and intellectually thin. Eduard Widmer is responsible for the very fine photographs.

2454 Yetkin, Suut Kemal et al. Turkish Architecture. Translated by A.E. Uysal. Ankara: Institute of History Publications, 1965, 93 pp.

A comprehensive, clearly organized, and well-documented study, with plates.

India

General Studies

2455 Brown, Percy. Indian Architecture: The Islamic Period. 2d ed. Bombay: Taraporevala, 1943, 140 pp.

The author organizes the material according to dynasties and geographic areas, discussing the main monuments built under the reigns of the various rulers of each dynasty.

2456 Goetz, Hermann. "Persia and India after the Conquest of Mahmud." In The Legacy of Persia (see 64), pp. 89-113.

Historical survey of Indo-Iranian relations beginning first with a background of ancient contacts before focusing on the period from the seventh through the eighteenth centuries. The political and cultural interactions of Persia and India are reflected in the art and architecture of India. Though Persian influences dominated in Indian art, Hindu traditions continued. In his essay, Goetz identifies what he considers to be Persian, Islamic, and Hindu elements in the arts of India.

2457 Hambly, Gavin. Cities of Moghul India: Delhi, Agra and Fatehpur Sikri. London: Elek, 1968, 168 pp.

Describes the reign of the Mughal dynasty from 1526 to 1858 and the architecture and other arts of the period. Contains little about cities or city life. Illustrated.

2458 Volwahsen, Andreas. Living Architecture: Islamic Indian. New York: Grosset & Dunlap, 1970, 190 pp.

In the same series as Living Architecture: Ottoman (see 2453), this book shares its faults and virtues; excellent photographs, not so helpful text.

Specific Studies on Towns and Monuments

2459 Arnold, T.W. "Ḳuṭb Mīnār" In EI1. Vol. 2 (see 32), p. 1168.

A study of a lofty sandstone minaret near the first Indian mosque, dating from A.D. 1193 and located four miles from New Delhi. Three plates.

2460 Brandenburg, Dietrich. Der Tâj Mahâl in Agra: Eine Studie zur Baukunst des Islam in Indien. Berlin: Hessling, 1969, 184 pp.

A detailed study of the Tāj Maḥall, covering aspects not usually found in other works on the building. The author for instance surveys the Islamic grave in India, noting the precursors and prototypes of the Tāj Maḥall. He also includes information on the materials used in its construction and their cost, and the architects and artisans employed. A glossary and extensive bibliography are included. Illustrations.

2461 Burton-Page, J. "Bahmanīs." In EI2. Vol. 1 (see 20), pp. 925-26.

A brief summary of the building activity of the Bahmanī dynasty, which ruled in the Deccan (South India) from the fourteenth into the sixteenth century.

2462 _____. "Bīdjāpūr." In EI2. Vol. 1 (see 20), pp. 1202-4.

A summary of the building activity of the ʻAdīl Shāh Dynasty (sixteenth and seventeenth centuries) at Bījāpūr, a city famous for its Deccan style.

2463 _____. "Dihlī." In EI2. Vol. 2 (see 20), pp. 255-66.

A study of Delhi, India, that examines its history and monuments. No plates, but includes maps, plans, and bibliography.

2464 _____. "Hind." In EI2. Vol. 3 (see 20), pp. 440-52.

A survey of Muslim architecture in India (Hind) that describes the various regional styles of Indian Muslim architecture. No plates, but extensive bibliography.

2465 Carroll, David. The Taj Mahal. New York: Newsweek, 1972, 172 pp.

In the same series as Jerry Landay's Dome of the Rock (see 2408). This beautifully illustrated book seeks to study the Tāj Maḥall in its cultural and historical context.

2466 Hasan, Nurul. "Āgra." In EI2. Vol. 1 (see 20), pp. 252-54.

Examines the major monuments (including the Tāj Maḥall) of one of the capital cities of the Mughal Empire. Bibliography.

2467 "Islamic Architecture." Marg 27 (1974):14-30.

This article is devoted to Islamic architecture in Bangladesh. Contents include Mamlūk style, Ilyās Shahī style, classical phase of architecture in Gaur (Lakhnautī), Ḥusayn Shahī style, Mughal style.

2468 Nath, R. Color Decoration in Mughal Architecture. Bombay: D.B. Taraporevala & Sons, 1970, 82 pp.
Surveys the major modes of decoration evidenced in Mughal architecture--glazed tile, inlay, mosaic, painted, carved stucco--and their use on various architectural elements such as columns, dadoes, pavements, and ceilings. The development of each decorative technique is discussed, including its pre-Mughal traditions. The book includes a bibliography and a glossary of architectural terms. Illustrated.

2469 _____. The Immortal Taj Mahal: The Evolution of the Tomb in Mughal Architecture. Bombay: D.B. Taraporevala & Sons, 1972, 114 pp.
Half the text is devoted to the mausoleums built before the Tāj Maḥall; influences are accounted for. The technical features of the Tāj itself constitute the remainder of the study.

2470 _____. "The Taj Mahal." Marg 22 (1969): 34-55.
Traveler-oriented article on the history, form, engineering achievements, and unique beauty of the Tāj Maḥall. Mention is made at the end of the present sinking problem affecting the future preservation of the building.

2471 Rose, H.A. "Mughal Architecture in India." In EI1. Vol. 3 (see 32), pp. 635-39.
Historical outline of the development of Mughal architecture. Specific buildings are mentioned but not described in great detail. The brief bibliography contains references to more comprehensive bibliographical sources.

2472 Vogel, J.P. Tile-Mosaics of the Lahore Fort. Calcutta: Superintendent Gov't. Printing, 1920, 69 pp.
The chief virtue of this book is the reproduction of 116 panels of tile mosaic from the walls of the Lahore Fort, which contains the palace buildings of the great Moghuls, Jahāngīr and Shāh Jahān. The tile designs are varied and colorful. The representation on the tiles of living beings is a prevailing decorative theme.

2473 Walliullah Khan, Muhammad. Lahore and Its Important Monuments. 2d ed. Karachi: Dept. of Archaeology and Museums, 1964, 91 pp.
The author gives a historical introduction to the city, and then discusses the monuments, one by one.

2474 Yazdani, Ghulam. Bidar: Its History and Monuments. London: Oxford University Press, 1947, 240 pp.
During most of the fifteenth century and the early years of the sixteenth century the city of Bīdar was the capital of the Bahmanī sulṭāns and the chief city of the Muslim Deccan. This book is a comprehensive, thorough, and scholarly treatment of the fort and two great groups of tombs at Bīdar that provided dated or accurately datable monuments for every reign of this Deccani kingdom. One can follow in the style impulses from the north, whence Hindu craftsmen were imported. The continuance of Persian influence and the recurrent use of actual Persian artists during this period is carefully documented.

East Africa

2475 Garlake, Peter S. The Early Islamic Architecture of the East African Coast. Nairobi: Oxford University Press, 1966, 207 pp.
A valuable presentation of the little known Muslim architecture of the East African coast. The author deals with materials and techniques of construction, vaulted structures, applied decoration, mosques, and domestic buildings. The period covered is from the late twelfth to the early eighteenth century, but emphasis is on the medieval period before the coming of the Portuguese. Apparently, the author had no opportunity to visit South Arabia and India to examine evidence that bears on the background to his study. Illustrated.

TYPES OF BUILDINGS AND ARCHITECTURAL FEATURES (ALPHABETIZED BY FEATURE)

2476 Marçais, G. "ʿAmūd." In EI2. Vol. 1 (see 20), pp. 457-59.
A concise survey of the use of the column and capital in Islamic architecture, with drawings.

2477 Creswell, K.A.C. "Bāb." In EI2. Vol. 1 (see 20), pp. 830-32.
Gateways or entrances to mosques, mausoleums, and fortifications are reviewed, with eight pages of plates.

2478 Marçais, Georges. "Bināʾ." In EI2. Vol. 1 (see 20), pp. 1226-29.
A brief discussion on building techniques and materials. The drawings of masonry patterns, arches, vaulting, and transition zones between walls and ceilings are helpful.

2479 Sourdel-Thomine, J. et al. "Burdj." In EI2. Vol. 1 (see 20), pp. 1315-24.
The article is divided into three parts: military architecture in Islamic Middle East (J. Sourdel-Thomine); military architecture in the Muslim West (H. Terrasse); and the tower in Islamic architecture in India (J. Burton-Page). Includes drawings and bibliography.

2480 Marçais, G. "Dār." In EI2. Vol. 2 (see 20), pp. 113-15.
A survey of domestic architecture in Islam.

2481 Sourdel-Thomine, J., and A. Louis. "Ḥammām." In EI2. Vol. 3 (see 20), pp. 139-46.
A general study on the various types of steam baths found throughout the history of Islamic cities (Sourdel-Thomine) and a description of their function (A. Louis). Floor plans and bibliographies.

2482 Husain, A.B.M. "Ḥawḍ." In EI2. Vol. 3 (see 20), pp. 286-88.
A historical survey of the different types of cisterns found in Islamic countries.

2483 Terrasse, H. et al. "Ḥiṣn." In EI2. Vol. 3 (see 20), pp. 498-503.
The article surveys architectural aspects of fortresses found in the Muslim West (North Africa, Spain), Iran, Central Asia, Indonesia, and Malaysia.

2484 Pederson, Johs et al. "Masdjid" (see 1811, 1899).

2485 Diez, Ernest. "Mukarnas." In EI1. Vol. 3 (see 32), pp. 153-54.
A survey of the architectural device used to support or conceal the transition between walls and ceilings. Seven plates.

2486 Marçais, Georges. "Ribāṭ" In EI1. Vol. 3 (see 32), pp. 1150-53.
An analysis of the structure of the fortified frontier outpost.

THE ISLAMIC CITY--ARCHITECTURE (See also 1998-2011)

2487 Brown, Leon Carl, ed. From Madina to Metropolis: Heritage and Change in the Near Eastern City (see 16).
A study of modern Near Eastern cities from Morocco to Afghanistan; composed of essays by historians, sociologists, a demographer, a geographer, a planner, an architect, and an art historian.

2488 Grabar, Oleg. "The Architecture of the Middle Eastern City: The Case of the Mosque." In Middle Eastern Cities (see 33), pp. 26-46.
A thought-provoking survey of the main features of the historical development of the mosque, drawn from both archaeological and literary sources, set forth with the hope of coming to some conclusions about the nature of the Islamic city.

2489 _____. "Cities and Citizens: The Growth and Culture of Urban Islam." In Islam and the Arab World (see 36), pp. 89-116.
Grabar investigates the historical entity of the Islamic city: its strengths and weaknesses and the daily life of its inhabitants. Discusses domestic architecture and the portable arts that appealed to the rich bourgeoisie.

2490 Hourani, A., and S.M. Stern, eds. The Islamic City (see 168).

PAINTINGS, CALLIGRAPHY, AND BOOKBINDINGS

PAINTING

General Studies

2491 Arnold, Sir Thomas Walker. The Old and New Testaments in Muslim Religious Art. London: Oxford University Press, 1932, 47 pp.
The author discusses the circumstances that seem to point to the conclusion that religious forms in Islamic painting derive from representations of similar subjects in Christian painting. Illustrated.

2492 Arnold, Sir Thomas W. Painting in Islam: A Study of the Place of Pictorial Art in Muslim Culture. New York: Dover Publications, 1965, 159 pp.
First published in 1928, this book has proven to be a durable achievement on the subject of figurative representation in Islam and the religious-legal problems of pictorial art. This study is fundamental for an understanding of Islamic art. Illustrated.

2493 Arnold, T.W., and Adolf Grohmann. The Islamic Book: A Contribution to Its Art and History from the VII-XVIII Century. New York: Pegasus Press, 1929, 130 pp.
This is a pioneering work that is still useful despite its age. Grohmann wrote on the early period up to the twelfth century; Arnold wrote on the later period. Illustrated.

2494 Blochet, Edgar. Musulman Painting, 12-17th Centuries. London: Methuen & Co., 1929, 124 pp.
The contents of this book are enormous, but condensed. Blochet believed that Islamic art was derivative and lacked originality. His book has many audacious ideas, disputable parallels, and hazardous conclusions. Nonetheless, it offers many interesting thoughts.

2495 Buchtal, H.; O. Kurz; and R. Ettinghausen. "Supplementary Notes to K. Holter's Check List of Islamic Illustrated Mss. before A.D. 1350." Ars Islamica 7 (1940):147-64.
This is a supplement to the article by Kurt Holter entitled "Die islamischen Miniaturhandschriften vor 1350," which appeared in the Zentralblatt für Bibliothekswesen 65 (1937): 1-34. The two works give the reader an overview and nearly complete listing of all the early Islamic illustrated manuscripts.

2496 Martin, Fredrik R. The Miniature Painting and Painters of Persia, India and Turkey from the 8th to the 18th Century. London: Holland Press, 1971, 156 pp. Reprint of 1912 ed.
Though out of date, this still can be used as a reference work.

2497 Pinder-Wilson, Ralph, ed. Paintings in/from Islamic Lands. Oriental Studies, no. 4. Oxford: Cassirer, 1969, 204 pp.
This book contains ten essays by prominent scholars concerned with the history of Islamic miniature painting in Persia and India. The essays, arranged chronologically, are very specialized studies of manuscripts and of schools of painting. Illustrated.

2498 Rice, D.T. Islamic Painting: A Survey. Edinburgh: Edinburgh University Press, 1971, 185 pp.
Pays more attention to the earlier phases of Islamic painting and to its lesser known branches in Egypt, Turkey, Spain, and North Africa than to the classical period from the fourteenth to the seventeenth century in Persia. Eighty black and white plates, five color plates.

2499 Robinson, B.W. et al. Islamic Painting and the Arts of the Book. London: Faber & Faber, 1976, 322 pp.
A catalog of Arab, Persian, Turkish, and Indian paintings, 157 black and white plates, 44 in color. The articles include: "Fostat Fragments" and "Pre-Mongol and Mamlūk Painting" (E.J. Grube); "Persian and Pre-Mongol Indian Painting," "Illumination and Calligraphy," "Unillustrated Manuscripts," and "Bookcovers and Lacquer" (B.W. Robinson); "Ottoman Turkish Painting" (G.M. Meredith-Owens); and "Indian Painting of the Mughal Period" (R.W. Shelton). Bibliography and indexes.

Studies Relating to Specific Countries or Areas

Arab Painting

2500 Ettinghausen, Richard. Arab Painting. Lausanne: Skira, 1962, 208 pp. Reprint. New York: Rizzoli International Publications, 1977.
The author presents for the first time a concise and lucid history of painting in the Arabic-speaking medieval civilization of Islam reaching from Mesopotamia to Spain. Painting is used in its widest sense and includes frescoes and paintings on wood, paper, parchment, glass, stone mosaic, and pottery. Scholars as well as the general public will gain much by reading this book. Mounted illustrations, some in color.

2501 _____. "Painting in the Fatimid Period: A Reconstruction." Ars Islamica 9 (1942): 112-24.
Drawing on diverse sources, the author suggests a number of styles that probably existed in Syro-Egyptian painting in the eleventh to twelfth centuries. Thus, he suggests a way to fill in some of the gaps in our knowledge about the history of Islamic painting between the Sāmarrā painting of the ninth century and the miniature paintings from 1300 onward.

Persian Painting (Catalogs)

2502 Ettinghausen, Richard. Persian Miniatures in the Bernard Berenson Collection. Milan: Officine Grafiche Ricordi, 1961.
This book is beautifully produced. The 12 color plates are preceded by a short introduction and accompanied by notes explaining their iconography, outlining their historical background, and characterizing their style.

2503 Grube, E.J. The Classical Style in Islamic Painting: The Early School of Herat and Its Impact on Islamic Painting of the Later 15th, 16th and 17th Centuries. Venice: Edizioni Oriens, 1968, 204 pp.
The paintings illustrated here were shown at an exhibition at the Pierpont Morgan Library (New York) in 1968-1969. The accompanying text is a brief essay on the impact of the fifteenth-century school of Persian painting at Harāt on later schools.

2504 Grube, Ernst J. Islamic Paintings from the 11th to the 18th Century in the Collection of Hans P. Kraus. New York: H.P. Kraus, 1972, 291 pp.
This large and handsome publication illustrates all 252 items in the Kraus collection. The catalog is full and thorough, with ample references and annotations.

2505 _____, and Alberta Maria Fabris. Muslim Miniature Paintings from the 13th to the 19th Century, from Collections in the U.S. and Canada: Catalogue of the Exhibition. Venezia: Neri Pozza Editore, 1962, 139 pp.
A collection of mainly Persian and Turkish painting, with 125 plates.

2506 Robinson, Basil William. A Descriptive Catalogue of the Persian Paintings in the Bodleian Library. Oxford: Clarendon Press, 1958, 219 pp.
A catalog of the Persian miniatures in the Bodleian Library of Oxford, classified according to their periods and styles. Each section begins with an account of the development and characteristics of the particular style. There follows a list of the manuscripts found in other libraries and collections in which comparable miniatures are to be found. Illustrated.

2507 Robinson, Basil W. Persian Miniature Painting from the Collections in the British Isles. London: Her Majesty's Stationery Office, 1967, 120 pp.
Catalog of an exhibition at the Victoria and Albert Museum. Illustrated.

2508 _____. Persian Paintings. 2d ed. Victoria and Albert Picture Book, no. 6. London: Her Majesty's Stationery Office, 1965, 18 pp.
This book is a catalog of an exhibition of Persian painting from collections in the British Isles, and is organized according to the various schools of painting and the major styles: the "Metropolitan courty style" and "Provincial style." Illustrated.

2509 Schroeder, Eric. Persian Miniatures in the Fogg Museum of Art. Cambridge, Mass.: Harvard University Press, 1942, 166 pp.
This is a catalog of the thirty Persian paintings in the Fogg Museum and an introduction to the study of Persian painting from the thirteenth to the seventeenth century. Every item described is reproduced on an ample scale in monochrome collotype. Schroeder's date for the Demotte Shāh Nāmah deserves a footnote, since other scholars argue for a date a generation earlier.

Persian Painting

2510 Arnold, Sir Thomas Walker. Bihzad and His Paintings in the Zafarnameh M.S. London: Bernard Quaritch, 1930, 25 pp.
An excellent monograph on the illustrations found in a fifteenth-century manuscript of the Ẓafar Nāmah (Book of Victory), which is a biography of Tīmūr(Tamerlane). The manuscript

contains six superb miniatures (double plates) done by the master of Persian painting, Bihzād.

2511 Barrett, Douglas. Persian Painting of the 14th Century. London: Faber & Faber, 1952, 24 pp.

A small selection of fourteenth-century miniatures, with an introduction followed by color plates and notes. The thesis of this short account is that fourteenth-century painting played an important role in the later development of what can be called classical Persian painting.

2512 Binyon, Laurence. The Poems of Nizami. London: Studio, 1928, 30 pp.

This study centers on the Khamsah of Niẓāmī (British Museum Or. 2265). The text is a study of the characteristics of Persian painting, a life of Niẓāmī and of Shāh Tahmasp (for whose royal library this copy of the Khamsah was prepared), an account of the separate poems of the Khamsah, and a detailed description of each picture. Illustrated.

2513 _____; John Vere Stewart Wilkinson; and Basil Gray. Persian Miniature Painting, Including a Critical and Descriptive Catalogue of the Miniatures Exhibited at Burlington House January--March 1931. London: Oxford University Press, 1933, 212 pp. Reprint. New York: Dover Publications, 1971.

A voluminous and classical study on Persian miniature painting. Following the exhibition at the Burlington House in 1931, the authors felt the need for something permanent that was more than a catalog and therefore produced this invaluable volume. The work is organized according to the chronological development of Persian painting, and each chapter contains an introduction followed by plates and notes. A major study.

2514 Brian, Doris. "A Reconstruction of the Miniature Cycle in the Demotte Shah Namah." Ars Islamica 6 (1939):97-112.

The Demotte Shāh Nāmah is an important example of Persian painting of the fourteenth century. This article lists all the known miniatures (58) of that manuscript in the order in which they belong to the text. Thirty of them are illustrated here. Since the reproductions of the miniatures of the Demotte Shāh Nāmah have not been gathered together in a single publication, this article will be useful in indicating the various places where reproductions had been published as of 1939.

2515 Falk, S.J. Qajar Paintings: Persian Oil Paintings of the 18th and 19th Centuries. London: Faber & Faber, 1972, 63 pp.

This book is a pioneer study of Qājār painting based on the Amery collection, which was acquired by Queen Farah of Iran in 1969. Included are reproductions in color of all the Amery pictures (63), a catalog of the collection giving essential information about each canvas, and biographical notes on artists. Corroborative materials from other collections are reproduced in black and white.

2516 Gray, Basil. Persian Painting. Geneva: Skira, 1961, 191 pp. Reprint. New York: Rizzoli International Publications, 1977.

This survey of Persian painting covers all the major periods and schools. The author emphasizes the emotional intensity of the paintings in a discussion that is scholarly and original in many respects.

2517 Lillys, William, ed. Persian Miniatures: The Story of Rustam. Tokyo and Rutland, Vt.: C.E. Tuttle Co., 1958, 32 pp.

This book illustrates eleven subjects, nine of them as full-page color plates, from the story of Rustam in the Iranian national epic, the Shāh Nāmah.

2518 Robinson, Basil William. Persian Drawings from the Fourteenth to the Nineteenth Century. Boston: Little, Brown & Co., 1965, 141 pp.

The text includes a brief introduction to the major schools of painting, set within the historical framework, followed by a generous number of plates, with notes. The title is a little misleading; "drawings" includes drawings and miniature paintings.

2519 Schroeder, Eric. "Ahmed Musa and Shams al-Din: A Review of Fourteenth-Century Painting." Ars Islamica 6 (1939):113-42.

By analyzing details of early and late fourteenth-century manuscript paintings, the author dates the Demotte Shāh Nāmah in the third quarter of the fourteenth century. He then attributes a number of these miniatures (Demotte) to Shams al-dīn, a pupil of Aḥmad Mūsā, and to painters who were his subordinates. A controversial set of conclusions.

2520 Stchoukine, Ivan. Les peintures des Manuscrits Safavis de 1502-1587. Paris: Librairie Orientaliste Paul Geuthner, 1959, 233 pp.

A basic study of Persian painting during early Ṣafavid times. Illustrated.

2521 _____. Les Paintures des Manuscrits de Shāh ʿAbbās Ier à la fin des Ṣafavīs. Paris: Librairie Orientaliste Paul Geuthner, 1964, 262 pp.

A detailed, comprehensive study of Persian miniature painting under the rule of Shāh ʿAbbās.

2522 _____. Les Peintures des Manuscrits Tīmūrides. Paris: Librairie Orientaliste Paul Geuthner, 1954, 176 pp.

In a precise and scholarly study, Stchoukine gives us a survey of Persian manuscript painting under Tīmūrid rule. The author, an authority and pioneer on the subject of miniature painting, gives a detailed account of the major paintings, discussing style and iconography according to the major "schools" they belong to. Well documented and essential for the student of Persian painting.

2523 UNESCO, Iran. Persian Miniatures-Imperial Library. Preface by Basil Gray and introduction by André Godard. New York: UNESCO, 1956, 25 pp.

This collection is restricted largely to miniatures of the period from the middle of the fifteenth century to the middle of the sixteenth century. Thus, miniatures from the formative period of Persian painting and from the period of final flowering in the late sixteenth and seventeenth centuries are not represented. Gray gives a succinct outline of Persian painting. The value of the book for the public lies largely in its color plates, but the technical quality of some has not been entirely successful.

2524 Welch, Anthony. Artists for the Shah: Late Sixteenth Century Paintings at the Imperial Court of Iran. New Haven, Conn., and London: Yale University Press, 1976, 233 pp.

A study of the patronage and painting of one of the most turbulent periods of Iranian history, this book centers on the work of three masters--Sadiqi Bek, Siyavush the Georgian, and Riza--who are representative of their period and major influences on later generations. Particular attention is paid to the careers of all three men and the relationships between them. From the ample writings of Sadiqi, which deal with his own career and his theories of art, is drawn a biography of this artist. The book is illustrated with sixteen color plates and sixty-eight black and white figures.

2525 Welch, S. Cary. A King's Book of Kings: The Shah-Nameh of Shah Tahmasp. New York: Metropolitan Museum of Art, 1972, 197 pp.

An exciting and scholarly survey of one of the most beautiful manuscripts of Persian painting, known as the Houghton Shāh Nāmah, a product of the court painters of Tabriz about A.D. 1525. Twenty-seven color miniatures of a total of 258 are included in this book as well as one detail color photograph of each of the twenty-seven full-page miniatures. Opposite each miniature is a synopsis of the illustrated story and a note about the artist. Welch provides a clearer description than is available elsewhere of the circumstances of production of a major royal manuscript, and also of the manner in which Persian painters designed their pictures.

2526 _____. Persian Painting: Five Royal Safavid Manuscripts of the Sixteenth Century. New York: George Braziller, 1976, 127 pp.

Everyone interested in Islamic art in general and Persian painting in particular should own a copy of this paperback book. It provides an excellent study copy of color reproductions from five of the most sumptuous books ever produced in Iran.

2527 Wilkinson, J.V.S. The Shah-Namah of Firdausi: The Book of the Persian Kings. Oxford: Oxford University Press, 1931, 92 pp.

Published here are twenty-four illustrations from a magnificent Persian manuscript, painted at Harāt in about A.D. 1430 and now in the possession of the Royal Asiatic Society and on permanent loan to the British Museum.

Persian Painting under Mongol Influence

2528 Ipsiroglu, Mozhar Sevket. Painting and Culture of the Mongols. Translated by E.D. Phillips. New York: Harry N. Abrams, 1967, 112 pp.

This study is based upon four albums of paintings done in Iran under Mongol influence. Illustrated, part color.

Turkish Painting

2529 Atasoy, Nurhan, and Filiz Çagman. Turkish Miniature Painting. Translated by Esin Atil. Istanbul: R.C.D. Cultural Institute, 1974, 107 pp.

Most examples are from the Topkapi Palace Museum and date from the reign of Sulṭān Sulayman the Magnificent and the reigns of his successors to about A.D. 1630. The comments are general and accurate, providing a brief survey of Ottoman book painting. Illustrated.

2530 Esin, Emel. Turkish Miniature Painting. Rutland, Vt.: C.E. Little Co., 1960, 32 pp.

A short introduction followed by a series of twelve plates representing examples of Turkish painting from the sixteenth to the eighteenth century. The author may have gone too far in her view of the Central Asian origin of Turkish painting, but she draws attention to a still underrated source of inspiration.

2531 Yetkin, Suut Kemal. L'ancienne peinture turque du XIIe au XVIIIe siècle. Paris: Klincksieck, 1970, 61 pp.

An outline of Turkish painting, tracing its origins and development. Numerous examples of works and artists are cited, but not always discussed in detail. Illustrated.

Indian Painting

General Studies

2532 Archer, W.G. Indian Miniatures: Color Plates in Collaboration with Madanjeet Singh. Greenwich, Conn.: New York Graphic Society, 1960, 16 pp.

A comprehensive guide to the schools and styles of miniature painting.

2533 Barrett, D., and Basil Gray. Paintings of India. Lausanne: Skira, 1963, 214 pp.

The paintings are written about with sensitivity and insight. The text of this book is scholarly and readable, but it continually notes and uses for argument miniatures that are not reproduced and often not even documented. Illustrated.

2534 Brown, Percy. Indian Painting. 5th ed. Heritage of India. Calcutta: Association Press, 1947, 132 pp.

A historical and descriptive survey of Indian painting. This book is now outdated, and has been superseded by more extensive studies with better texts and reproductions of paintings. Illustrated.

2535 _____. Indian Painting under the Moghuls. Oxford: Clarendon Press, 1924, 204 pp.
The text of this book is detailed, tracing the development of Indian painting during the two centuries of its richest manifestation under the patronage of the Mughal emperors. Illustrated.

2536 Bussagli, Mario. Indian Miniatures. Translated by Raymond Rudorff. Feltham: Hamlyn, 1969, 158 pp.
Primarily a collection of seventy-three color illustrations, each briefly described. The accompanying continuous text summarizes the development of Indian painting.

2537 Hajek, Lubor. Indian Miniatures of the Moghul School. London: Spring Books, 1960, 87 pp.
Catalog of an exhibit of Mughal miniatures held in Prague in 1956. The miniatures, many previously unpublished, were borrowed from Iranian, Indian, and Czechoslovakian collections. The brief text preceding the catalog entries presents a summary of topics relevant to the study of Mughal miniatures. Somewhat distracting is the printing of the text pages to resemble a manuscript, with illustrated margins surrounding the text on each page. Though the fifty-one illustrations include details of some of the manuscripts, they are of mediocre quality. Short bibliography.

2538 Khandalavala, Karl. "Some Problems of Mughal Painting." Lalit Kalā 11 (1962):9-13.
An article primarily concerned with problems relevant to the study of later Mughal miniature painting, such as the presence of inscriptions on works, restoration, and copies of drawings.

2539 Randhawa, Mohinder Singh, and John Kenneth Galbraith. Indian Painting: The Scene, Themes and Legends. Boston: Houghton Mifflin, 1968, 142 pp.
Nearly all the illustrations have never been reproduced before. About a third of the book discusses Mughal painting and its historical background.

2540 Rawson, Philip S. Indian Painting. Paris and New York: Universe Books, 1961, 169 pp.
A lucid, popular approach. A practicing artist himself, the author sees what Indian painters were trying to do and why. He also explores the general cultural background.

2541 Welch, Stuart Cary. Imperial Mughal Painting. New York: George Braziller, 1977, 119 pp.
Discussion of individual rulers as patrons of the imperial Mughal style of miniature painting, followed by forty full-page plates of miniatures with commentary in most cases conveniently printed on the opposite page. A select bibliography is included.

2542 Wilkinson, J.V.S. "Indian Painting." In Indian Art. Edited by Sir Richard Winstedt. London: Sidgwick & Jackson, 1966, pp. 102-50.
An overview of Indian painting that includes pages on the technique, style, and patrons of Mughal painting. Only a few small black and white illustrations are included.

2543 Wilkinson, John Vere Stewart. Mughal Painting. London: Faber & Faber, 1948, 24 pp.
Basically a commentary on a selection of ten miniatures. After a very brief introduction of eight pages, the author presents the miniatures (in color) one by one and discusses them.

Specific Manuscripts

2544 Beach, Milo. "The Gulshan Album and Its European Sources." Bulletin of the Museum of Fine Arts, Boston 63 (1965):63-90.
Article focusing on one of the two muraqqas, or albums, containing Persian drawings executed after European prints, belonging to Jahāngīr and now located in the Gulshan Library, Tehran. Mughal artists sometimes copied motifs and compositions from Western sources, often with unusual results. This article identifies sources for several of the illustrations in the Gulshan album, and notes the major alterations that occurred in the borrowing process.

2545 Krishna, Ananda. "A Reassessment of the Tuti-Nama Illustrations in the Cleveland Museum of Art." Artibus Asiae (1973):241-68.
A detailed reassessment of Leesant Chandra's work on Cleveland's Tutī Nāmah. Krishna disagrees with certain stylistic comparisons, and also points out that some scenes have been overpainted.

2546 Lee, Sherman E., and Pramod Chandra. "A Newly Discovered Tuti-Nama and the Continuity of the Indian Tradition of Manuscript Painting." Burlington Magazine 105 (1963):547-54.
The earliest article dealing with the Cleveland Museum of Art's Tutī Nāmah, or Tales of the Parrot, dated ca. 1560-1568 and displaying both Mughal and non-Mughal stylistic characteristics. Should be read with Krishna's later work on the manuscript (see 2545).

2547 Marek, Jiri, and H. Knizkova. The Jenghis Khan Miniatures from the Court of Akbar the Great. London: Spring Books, 1963, 42 pp.
A selection of illustrations from a variant manuscript of Rashīd al-Dīn's history of the Mongols. The miniatures are typical examples of the Akbar school of the late sixteenth century.

Technique

2548 Ahmad, Jagir. "The Mughal Artist Farrukh Beg." Islamic Culture 35 (1961):115-29.
The author disagrees with many of R. Skelton's attributions of works to Farrukh Beg, especially those in the Bījāpūr style, on the basis of historical evidence.

2549 Chandra, Moti. The Technique of Mughal Painting. Lucknow: U.P. Historical Society, 1949, 108 pp.
A technical survey of the materials, pigments, and methods of painting used by Mughal artists, based on historical texts and the survival of traditional methods among modern artists in India.

2550 Skelton, Robert. "Mughal Painting from the Harivamsa Manuscript." In Victoria and Albert Museum Yearbook. London: Phaidon, 1970, 41-55.
Discussed are six newly acquired illustrated pages from a copy of the Harivamsa, or Genealogy of Hari, which details episodes from the story of Krishna. The Hindu myth miniatures of this particular manuscript were executed about 1590 by Hindu artists, but in the Mughal style.

2551 Welch, S. Cary. "The Paintings of Basāwan." Lalit Kalā 10 (1961):7-17.
An article exploring the artistic refinements exhibited in works attributed to Basāwan, including the artist's interest in the rendering of depth and portrait painting.

Style and Schools

2552 Beach, Milo C. "The Context of Rajput Painting." Ars Orientalis 10 (1975):11-18.
Discussion of Rajput painting within the context of contemporary Mughal and folk painting.

2553 Marek, Jan. "Mughal Miniatures as a Source of History." Journal of the Pakistan Historical Society 11 (1963):195-208.
This article is an excerpt from a book dealing with a selected group of miniatures from Rashīd al-Dīn Faḍl Allāh's chronicle Jāmiʿ al-Tawārīkh. This little-known manuscript, now located in Tehran, consists of 304 leaves and 98 miniatures painted by the major artists of Akbar's time. Marek chose to study 34 of these miniatures that depict a number of events from the history of the Mongols from mythical times to the fourteenth century. Most of the details depicted in these miniatures, such as garments, furniture, and weapons, are patterned after contemporary Mughal examples. This manuscript is thus valuable in documenting life toward the end of the sixteenth century in Mughal India.

2554 Schroeder, Eric. "The Troubled Image: An Essay upon Mughal Painting." In Art and Thought. Edited by K. Bharata Iyer. London: Luzac, 1947, pp. 73-87.
In this short essay the author has attempted to show certain relationships between Mughal painting and the mainstream of Indian art. The citations of the illustrations are badly jumbled in the text; the reader is cautioned to ignore the numbering and to look for each illustration based on the object described.

2555 Skelton, Robert. "Two Mughal Lion Hunts." In Victoria and Albert Museum Yearbook. London: Phaidon, 1969, pp. 33-49.
Two acquired Mughal miniatures dating to the beginning of the seventeenth century serve as sources for information concerning the royal lion hunt, a subject of great antiquity in the Near East. One of the manuscripts depicts the spearing of a lioness by a royal figure, whom Skelton identifies as one of Akbar's sons. In the other manuscript is seen the transportation of a dead lioness from the field, a scene for which Skelton suggests pictorial sources.

2556 Welch, S. Cary, and Milo Beach. Gods, Thrones and Peacocks: Northern India Painting from Two Traditions: Fifteenth to Nineteenth Centuries. New York: Harry Abrams, 1965, 129 pp.
This study tries to set forth the "variety, power and charm of later northwestern Indian miniature painting, as shown in a selection of pictures from several collections, and to trace within the scope of these collections the relationship between two main streams of tradition (Mughal and Rajput); one foreign, the other indigenous." The author attempts to demonstrate that in fact these paintings can seldom be divided according to these two traditions.

Persian Painters and Calligraphers

2557 Ahmad, Ibrahimi Husayni. Calligraphers and Painters: A Treatise by Qadi Ahmad. Translated by V. Minorsky. Washington: Smithsonian Institution, Freer Gallery of Art, 1959, 223 pp.
An interesting historical document that discusses the history of famous calligraphers in the main with brief notes on the artists of the sixteenth century included. Good for an understanding of what was actually considered important in Islamic art circles by the Muslims themselves.

2558 Ettinghausen, Richard. "ʿAbuʿs-Samad." In Encyclopaedia of World Art. Vol. 1 (see 2287), pp. 16-20.
This is the best available résumé in English of the career of ʿAbd al-Ṣamad, a Persian calligrapher and painter of the sixteenth century who was one of the founders of Mughal painting in India.

2559 _____. "Bihzād, Kamāl al-dīn Ustād." In EI2. Vol. 1 (see 20), pp. 1211-14.
A fine summary of the literary evidence regarding one of Persia's greatest painters and the problem of identifying Bihzād's original works. Four plates, extensive bibliography.

CALLIGRAPHY

2560 Deny, J. "Tughra." In EI1. Vol. 4 (see 32), pp. 822-26.
Article summarizing several problems relevant to the study of the tughra, the decorative calligraphic emblem of the Saljūq and Ottoman rulers, including the origin of the word "tughra," the historical development, decorative elements and form, and possible symbolism.

2561 Lings, Martin. The Quranic Art of Calligraphy and Illumination. London: World of Islam Festival Trust, 1976, 242 pp.
Breathtaking plates of various calligraphic styles and different examples of the art of Qur'ānic illumination, drawn from different Islamic regions and dynasties. Each chapter includes text and plates.

2562 Mortiz, B. "Arabia." In EIl. Vol. 1 (see 32), pp. 381-93.
The section on writing contains a number of dated examples, an examination of the various styles, names of famous calligraphers, a summary of papyrus and paper industries, and the artistic development of Arabic writing.

2563 Rosenthal, Franz. "Significant Uses of Arabic Writing." Ars Orientalis 4 (1961): 15-24.
The symbolism of writing in Islam.

2564 Schimmel, Annemarie. Islamic Calligraphy. Leiden: E.J. Brill, 1970, 80 pp.
This book can serve as an introduction to the appreciation of Islamic calligraphy as an art form. The illustrations are well chosen. They represent the entire chronological and geographic range of the art.

2565 Ziyauddin, M. A Monograph on Moslem Calligraphy with 163 Illustrations of Its Various Styles and Ornamental Designs. Calcutta: Kishormahan Santra, 1936, 72 pp.
A survey of the development of Muslim calligraphy, with an introduction to each style of writing accompanied by numerous illustrations. A concise and useful little book.

BOOKBINDINGS

2566 Aga-Oglu, Mehmet. Persian Bookbindings of the Fifteenth Century. Ann Arbor: University of Michigan Press, 1935, 23 pp.
This book deals with the most creative and most advanced period of Persian bookbinding. The catalog includes twenty-two tooled leather bindings, most of which were produced in Harāt, but manuscripts from other centers such as Yazd, Shīrāz, and Iṣfahān have also been included.

2567 Sarre, F. Islamic Bookbindings. Translated by F.D. O'Byrne. London: Trubner & Co., 1923, 167 pp.
The value of this book has been undermined by the poor translation. Particularly where technique is concerned the words have been badly chosen, rendering the text unintelligible.

CERAMIC, TILE, AND STUCCO

GENERAL STUDIES

2568 Atil, Esin. Ceramics from the World of Islam. Washington: Freer Gallery of Art, Smithsonian Institution, 1973, 225 pp.
An excellent catalog of an exhibition of ceramics held at the Freer Gallery. Each object is discussed separately and accompanied by photographs, a full description, and characteristics. Given the scope of the collection, the catalog is a useful handbook for the study of Islamic ceramics. Furthermore, slides of the objects are available for sale with the catalog.

2569 British Museum, Department of Oriental Antiquities and of Ethnography. Guide to the Islamic Pottery of the Near East. Composed by R.L. Hobson. London: Printed by order of the Trustees, 1932, 104 pp.
This catalog is admirably sober and lucid. In the sections dealing with the sixteenth century and later wares it is still not superseded except in detail. Hobson's earlier chapters have been rendered somewhat out of date by recent discoveries and research.

2570 Fehérvári, Géza. Islamic Pottery: A Comprehensive Study Based on the Barlow Collection. London: Faber, 1973, 191 pp.
This book is an illustrative catalog of the Barlow collection, most of which is now distributed in British public collections. It may be used as a guide to identify Islamic ceramics and as a general survey due to the manner in which it is presented. Each piece is described in detail, and 315 black and white photographs and 18 in color have been included.

2571 Grube, Ernst J. Islamic Pottery of the Eighth to the Fifteenth Century in the Keir Collection. London: Faber & Faber, 1976, 378 pp.
Due to the extent of ceramic types represented in the Keir collection, Grube has produced not only a catalog of this material but also a survey of Islamic ceramics. Though the collection includes material from Egypt, Syria, Iraq, and Iran, spanning the major periods and displaying a variety of techniques, Mamlūk, Saljūq, and Egyptian and Syrian blue and white wares are especially well represented. Grube generously cites comparative material in the footnotes, and in both the notes and text uses the Keir material to illustrate certain problems of technique, dating, or decoration important in the study of Islamic ceramics. High quality black and white and color illustrations plus an extensive bibliography ensure this book's reference value.

2572 Lane, Arthur. Early Islamic Pottery: Mesopotamian, Egyptian and Persian. 4th ed. London: Faber & Faber, 1958, 52 pp.
This is the most useful handbook on the subject of early Islamic pottery. The major types are fully described from the technical as well as the stylistic point of view. The illustrations are numerous and representative. The text is exceedingly concise and deceptively simple. The book deserves more documentation and references than the publishers have allowed.

2573 _____. Later Islamic Pottery: Persia, Syria, Egypt, Turkey. 2d ed. Revised by Ralph Pinder-Wilson. London: Faber & Faber, 1971, 133 pp.
This book is a complement and companion to Lane's Early Islamic Pottery (see 2572). It

continues the discussion of the evolution of Muslim ceramics, beginning about A.D. 1300, with the same precision and boldness as the earlier work. With only a few additions to the bibliography and four new color plates, the second edition amounts to little more than a reprint of the first.

2574 _____. The Victoria and Albert Museum: A Guide to the Collection of Tiles. 2d ed. London: Victoria and Albert Museum, 1960, 75 pp.
The two chapters pertaining to the tiles from the Muslim world make it a worthwhile reference.

2575 Marçais, G. "Djiss." In EI2. Vol. 2 (see 20), pp. 556-57.
In this much too brief article on the use of plaster and stucco in Islamic art, the author suggests a Sāsānian rather than a Roman or Byzantine origin for Islamic techniques of the Umayyad period. No bibliography.

2576 _____. "Fakhkhārr." In EI2. Vol. 2 (see 20), pp. 745-48.
A survey of ceramics in Islam, with bibliography.

STUDIES RELATING TO SPECIFIC ASPECTS OF THE ART OR COUNTRIES

Iran

2577 Bahrami, Mehdi. Gurgan Faiences. Cairo: Le scribe égyptien, 1949, 134 pp.
This study of Persian ceramics found at Gurgān (Iran) contributed substantially to what we know of Saljūq pottery. Although many types of Persian ceramics, particularly the lusterware found at Gurgān, were known previously from Rayy and Kāshān excavations, Bahrami found kilns at Gurgān that proved that some types of ceramics were made locally.

2578 Ettinghausen, Richard. "Evidence for the Identification of Kashan Pottery." Ars Islamica 3 (1936):44-76.
The aim of this article is "to establish a Kāshān provenance for a number of pottery types." The author has analyzed a few dated pieces of pottery and has shown that there is a stylistic unity in the works that points to a thirteenth-century Kāshān workshop as their place of production.

2579 Riefstahl, Rudolf M. The Parish-Watson Collection of Mohammadan Potteries. New York: E. Weyne, 1922, 69 pp.
Each specimen is carefully and conscientiously described. A few of the Rakka type pieces are included, but the collection is devoted chiefly to the gorgeous productions of Rayy and Sulṭānabad of the second half of the twelfth and thirteenth centuries.

2580 Volov, Lisa. "Plaited Kufic on Samanid Epigraphic Pottery." Ars Orientalis 6 (1966):107-33.
The author traces the evolution of the style of inscriptions on Sāmānid pottery. Her observations and conclusions are of interest to both amateur and specialist readers. Both the decorative and the philosophical qualities of Islamic epigraphy are discussed.

2581 Wilkinson, C.K. Iranian Ceramics. New York: Asia House, 1963, 145 pp.
This book is the catalog of an exhibition selected by the author and shown in Asia House, New York City. Iranian ceramic art from the fourth millennium B.C. to the nineteenth century is included. Some phases are not shown and others are represented by numerous examples.

2582 Wilkinson, Charles K. Nishapur: Pottery of the Early Islamic Period. New York: Metropolitan Museum of Art, 1974, 374 pp.
This is the final report on excavations carried out by the Metropolitan Museum of Art between 1937 and 1940 and in 1947. The result is a superbly detailed catalog of 827 ceramic objects from nine locations on the Nīshāpūr plain. The author has carefully arranged, codified, correlated, and commented on the enormous range of the finds. Bibliographic entries stop at 1969, omitting important material published more recently. The book is well written. Each item is illustrated with black and white photographs; there are nine excellent color plates.

2583 Yoshida, Mitsukuri. In Search of Persian Pottery. New York: Weatherhill/Tankosha, 1972, 127 pp.
Cannot compare with Lane's (see 2572) scholarly efforts, but interesting for the account of the author's journeys through Iran and his discussion of pottery techniques.

Turkey

2584 Carswell, John, and C.J.F. Dowsett. Kütahya Tiles and Pottery from the Armenian Cathedral of St. James, Jerusalem. 2 vols. Oxford: Clarendon Press, 1972, 1:46 pp.; 2:43 pp.
Volume 1 is a definitive publication on the tiles in the Cathedral of St. James, mostly written by Dowsett. Volume 2, the work of Carswell, is a history of the Kütahya pottery kilns that supplied these tiles.

2585 Lane, Arthur. "The Ottoman Pottery of Isnik." Ars Orientalis 2 (1957):247-82.
This article contains much of the fundamental research behind the author's book Later Islamic Pottery (see 2573). The main part of his discussion is concerned with Isnik and the wares that are attributed to its workshops.

2586 Otto-Dorn, Katharina. Das islamische Iznik. Berlin: Istanbuler Forschungen, 1941, 209 pp.
A survey of the city's monuments that includes numerous plans, sections, and architectural drawings. Also included are chapters on the ceramic production of the city.

2587 Öz, Tahsin. Turkish Ceramics. Ankara: Turkish Press Broadcasting & Tourist Dept., 1954, 49 pp.

This book is important because it is one of the few works published on the subject of architectural decoration on Saljūq and Ottoman monuments in Anatolia. Less space is alloted to lamps and pottery, examples of which were taken primarily from the collections of the Topkapi Museum, the British Museum, the Victoria and Albert Museum, and the Benaki Museum.

2588 Riefstahl, Rudolf M. "Early Turkish Tile Revetments in Edirne." Ars Islamica 4 (1937):249-81.

This article deals with Turkish ceramic art during the period of the emirates, the revival of Turkish ceramic art in the late fourteenth century and after, and blue and white tiles at Edirne made in Syria and Egypt, probably by Persian workmen. Tile revetments in the mosques of Birgeh and Bursa also are examined. Among the author's interesting discoveries is the common identity of the makers of the Edirne and Bursa tiles.

Spain

2589 Frothingham, Alice Wilson. Catalogue of Hispano-Moresque Pottery in the Collection of the Hispanic Society of America. New York: Hispanic Society of America, 1936, 291 pp.

A complete and well-documented survey of the various types of Hispano-Islamic pottery. Each item is described fully, including a technical note. The materials for the history of Spanish luster are so fragmentary and widespread that the general and sectional introductions, with their special bibliographies, are very useful to the student. Illustrations.

2590 _____. Lustreware of Spain. New York: Hispanic Society of America, 1951, 310 pp.

A survey of the historical and technical development of the luster technique in Spain (tenth to eighteenth century) that is complete and reliable. Though she concentrates on the post-Islamic period, the author has given careful attention to the problems of the relationship between the lusterware of Islamic Spain and that of the rest of the Islamic world.

Sculpture

2591 Grube, Ernst. "Islamic Sculpture: Ceramic Figurines." Oriental Art 12 (1966):165-75.

This article deals with figurative representation in the full round, which is very rare in Islamic art. Examples are given of a great variety of media, including glazed clay, cast bronze, glass, ivory, wood, stucco, and stone. So far no extant pottery figurines can with certainty be dated before A.D. 1100. The examples are taken from collections in the Middle East, Europe, and the United States.

2592 Riefstahl, Rudolf M. "Persian Islamic Stucco Sculptures." Art Bulletin 13 (1931):439-63.

The arts of Islam are not particularly inclined to represent human beings. Yet there are many exceptions aside from the religious art, particularly from the periods of Shī'ah hegemony in Fāṭimid Egypt and Ṣafavid Iran. In this article Riefstahl examines figure representation in stucco from Persian examples now in private and public collections in the West. On account of their large size many of these sculptures provide details of Islamic costume. All of Riefstahl's examples seem to have been wall decoration. The author discusses the technique of sculpture and provides a technical description of each piece.

Technique

2593 Caiger-Smith, Alan. Tin-Glaze Pottery in Europe and the Islamic World: The Tradition of 1000 Years in Maiolica, Faience and Delftware. London: Faber & Faber, 1973, 236 pp.

This book contains the results of extensive research on the origin of tin glaze, which made possible the refined and intricate decoration of clay-bodied ware. The author traces the history and development of this single technical process from the ninth century to the present day. A potter himself, he concentrates on a discussion of techniques and their long continuity as well as on the difficulties and problems of the potter. For the Islamicist there are a few chapters dealing with Islamic tin glaze pottery.

TEXTILES, RUGS, SILK, COSTUMES

TEXTILES

2594 Britton, Nancy Pence. A Study of Some Early Islamic Textiles in the Museum of Fine Arts, Boston. Boston: Museum of Fine Arts, 1938, 89 pp.

A catalog of Islamic textiles dating from the eighth to the thirteenth century.

2595 Grohmann, A. "Ṭirāz." In EI1. Vol. 4 (see 32), pp. 785-93.

Discussion of the Islamic institution of the ṭirāz, or presentation of embroidered garments by the Islamic ruler to officials and persons of high rank. Specific literary sources and textiles are cited to illustrate points relevant to the evolution of the institution, changes in decorative design and inscriptional formula on the textiles, and their production.

2596 Serjeant, R.B. "Material for a History of Islamic Textiles up to the Mongol Conquest." Ars Islamica 9-16 (1942-51).

A very important sequence of articles that gather evidence regarding Islamic textiles before the thirteenth century. The ṭirāz system of organizing textile production is examined at Baghdād and provincial towns. Thanks to Serjeant's industry and scholarship, the abundant references in early Arab geographers and historians have been conveniently brought together. Republished as Islamic Textiles: Materials for a History up to the Mongol Conquest, Beirut: Libraire du Liban, 1972, 263 pp.

2597 Victoria and Albert Museum, Department of Textiles. Catalogue of Muhammadan Textiles of the Medieval Period, by Albert F. Kendrick. London: London Board of Education, 1924, 74 pp.

A good introduction to the field of Islamic textiles. Apart from being a catalog with plates and descriptions of a very fine collection, the book includes a brief introductory essay to each section of the book. The major subdivisions of the catalog are Egypt, Syria and Egypt, Sicily, Spain, and China.

2598 Wace, Alan J.B. Mediterranean and Near Eastern Embroideries from the Collection of Mrs. F.H. Cook. 2 vols. London: Halton & Co., 1935.

This catalog includes plates of 120 pieces of embroidery from Morocco to India. The pieces of Greek provenance are the most numerous by far. Some types of embroidery are not represented. Full details are given on materials, stitches, and color. This is the first scientific treatment of embroidery in a major work.

2599 Washington, D.C., Textile Museum. Catalogue of the Dated Tiraz Fabrics, Umayyad, Abbasid, Fatimid, by Ernst Kühnel and Louisa Bellinger. Washington: National Publishing Co., 1952, 137 pp.

The standard work for the study of early Muslim textiles. The text describes each plate separately and gives a technical analysis for each. Since the catalog deals with dated examples, it can be used as a reference and a guide for the study of undated examples. All the textiles described and reproduced here were found in Egypt, mostly in tombs at Fusṭāṭ.

RUGS

General Studies

2600 Bode, Wilhelm von, and Ernst Kühnel. Antique Rugs from the Near East. 4th rev. ed. Translated by C.G. Ellis. Berlin: Klinkhordt & Biermann, 1958, 184 pp.

When it first appeared in 1902 as Vorderasiatische Knupfteppiche, this book was the first comprehensive monograph on the subject. Many new and well-illustrated books have been published recently, but this remains the best introduction to the history of oriental rugs before 1700.

2601 Dimand, M.S., and Jean Mailey. Oriental Rugs in the Metropolitan Museum of Art. New York: Metropolitan Museum of Art, 1973, 353 pp.

This is not a comprehensive inventory of every Oriental rug in the museum, but rather a catalog of important items. The text is absorbing for both the scholar and the amateur. The last section, on the rugs of China and Chinese Turkestan, is the work of Jean Mailey. This book is thought-provoking, but should be read both carefully and critically.

2602 Edwards, Arthur Cecil. The Persian Carpet: A Survey of the Carpet-Weaving Industry of Persia. London: Duckworth, 1953, 384 pp.

This book gives a reliable and adequate account of the weavers as they work at the present time in Persia. The author studied the conditions of the trade and manufacture in each place, as well as traditions, influences, and methods of work that prevail there. No one who is interested in post-Ṣafavid carpets should fail to consult this book. The glossary of technical matters, such as fleeces, croppings, yarns, dyeing, weaving, and marketing, is copious and helpful.

2603 Erdmann, Kurt. Seven Hundred Years of Oriental Carpets. Edited by Hanna Erdmann and translated by May H. Beattie and Hildegard Herzog. Berkeley: University of California Press, 1970, 238 pp.

This book is based on fifty-one articles Erdmann wrote from 1960 to 1964. His aim was not so much to produce a manual or complete history of Oriental carpets as to survey the entire field of study and to clarify some of the complex problems relating to carpets. The book was not written for students but for scholars, dealers, and connoisseurs. In general the author's knowledge and interest are strongest in the western end of his subject, growing sketchier toward the east.

2604 Ettinghausen, R. "Ḳālī." In EI1. Vol. 2 (see 32), pp. 106-11.

A survey of knotted pile carpet in Islamic art.

2605 Kendrick, Albert F., and C.D.C. Tattersall. Handwoven Carpets, Oriental and European. 2 vols. New York: C. Scribner & Sons, 1922.

This book is largely out of date, yet one may still benefit from the numerous clear black and white photographs in volume 2 and from the drawings of hundreds of carpet motifs at the end of that volume.

2606 Landreau, Anthony N., and W.R. Pickering. From the Bosphorus to Samarkand, Flatwoven Rugs. Washington: Textile Museum, 1969, 112 pp.

A catalog of an exhibition at the Textile Museum, Washington, D.C., during the summer of 1969. Illustrated.

2607 McMullan, Joseph V. Islamic Carpets. New York: Near Eastern Art Research Center, 1965, 385 pp.

This is a presentation by the owner himself of a fine collection of Islamic rugs. Besides the "classical" type of rug, the McMullan collection is distinguished for its nomad and village rugs of the eighteenth and nineteenth centuries. Two-thirds of the McMullan rug collection have been added to the collection of the Metropolitan Museum of Art.

2608 Wensinck, A.J. "Sadjdjāda." In EI1. Vol. 4 (see 32), pp. 45-49.
Basically a philological study with no stylistic analysis of the subject, prayer rugs.

Studies Relating to Specific Areas or Countries

Egypt

2609 Washington, D.C., Textile Museum. Cairene Rugs and Others Technically Related, 15th Century-17th Century, by Ernst Kühnel and Louisa Bellinger. Washington: National Publishing Co., 1957, 90 pp.
This catalog deals with a group of rugs that have been identified as products of the Cairo workshop, fifteenth to seventeenth century. Both technical observations and stylistic grounds have helped to support this identification. The authors have explored the rug industry, including its connection to certain rugs not made in Egypt that seem to be related to the Cairene rugs either in pattern, material, or technique. Included are data about spin, weave, and fibers. Illustrated.

North Africa

2610 Gallotti, Jean. "Weaving and Dyeing in North Africa." Ciba Review 21 (1939):738-60.
What remains of the native crafts of weaving and dyeing in Morocco, Algeria, and Tunisia is described and classified. For twelve years the author was inspector of the native arts and industries of Morocco. This article is informative, nontechnical, and well illustrated.

Iran

2611 Aga-Oglu, Mehmet. Safawid Rugs and Textiles: The Collection of the Shrine of Imām ʿAlī at at al-Najaf. New York: Columbia University Press, 1941, 59 pp.
Among the textiles are brocaded silks and velvets, tomb covers, embroideries, and hangings. Two appendixes give useful lists of Ṣafavid weavers and dated textiles. Illustrated.

2612 Briggs, Amy. "Timurid Carpets. Part I, Geometric Carpets. Part II, Arabesque and Flower Carpets." Ars Islamica 7 (1940): 20-54; 11-12 (1946):146-58.
A study of carpet patterns reconstructed from miniatures of the Tīmūrid period.

2613 Edwards, A.C. "Persian Carpets." In The Legacy of Persia (see 64), pp. 230-58.
This essay is primarily a survey of Ṣafavid carpets and their production from the fifteenth to the seventeenth century, as well as the continuation of the carpet industry in post-Ṣafavid times. Some comments on the history and technique of the Persian carpet in general are made at the beginning. Illustrated.

Turkey

2614 Aslanapa, Oktay. "Türk hali sonati. Istanbul: Yabi ve kredi bankasi kültür ve sanat hizmetleri, 1972, 15 pp.
Brief text in Turkish. Short bibliography.

2615 Beattie, May H. "Background to the Turkish Rug." Oriental Art, n.s. 9 (1963):150-57.
A descriptive background to the Turkish rug with technical details referring specifically to Turkish materials and methods. The effects of modern technology on carpet making are discussed.

2616 ______. "Some Rugs of the Konya Region." Oriental Art, n.s. 22 (1976):60-76.
The results of this investigation help fill a gap between the so-called Saljūq carpets and the eighteenth-century Konya-Ladik prayer rugs.

2617 Erdmann, Kurt. Der türkische Teppich des 15. Jahrhunderts. Istanbul: Maarit Basimevi, 1957, 134 pp.
Illustrated.

2618 Öz, Tahsin. Turkish Textiles and Velvets, 14th-16th Centuries. Ankara: Turkish Press, 1950.
This book is based on unedited or previously unavailable archival documents and on pieces of fabrics from the Topkapi Palace Museum and from the Benaki Museum. They have been examined, cataloged and chronologically arranged. Owing to the custom that the garments and robes of deceased sulṭāns were carefully wrapped, labeled, and preserved, the great majority of the fabrics still bear labels saying for whom they were woven and by whom they were worn.

2619 Riefstahl, Rudolph M. "Primitive Rugs of the 'Konya' Type in the Mosque of Beyshehir." Art Bulletin 13 (1931):177-220.
Among the examples of early Islamic carpet weaving are those rugs of the Konya type, a small group of rugs that were formerly in the mosque of ʿAlāʾ al-Dīn in Konya, Turkey, and are now in the Turk ve Islam Asari Muzesi, Istanbul. Riefstahl in this article adds seven examples of this type from those he found in the summer of 1929 in the Eshref Oglu mosque in Beyshehir, Turkey. He subjects these carpets to critical examination as to date, provenance, and quality using the designs of Anatolian Saljūq stone relief carving (twelfth to thirteenth century) and the representations of rugs in Persian miniatures (fourteenth to fifteenth century) as a standard for comparison.

Central Asia

2620 Leix, A. "Turkestan and Its Textile Crafts." Ciba Review 40 (1941):1433-65.
Primarily an examination of twentieth-century production and use of woven, felted, knotted, and embroidered fabrics by the Tajiks, Uzbeks, and the Sarts of Turkestan.

2621 Schürmann, Ulrich. Central-Asian Rugs: A Detailed Presentation of the Art of the Rug Weaving in Central-Asia in the Eighteenth and Nineteenth Century. With a historical review by Hans Konig. London: Allen & Unwin, 1970, 176 pp.

The rugs of Central Asia with the exception of Mongolia are the subject of this book, which presupposes a knowledge of technical details as well as of artistic characteristics of Oriental rugs. Illustrated.

SILK

2622 Becker, Carl H. "Dībādj." In EI1. Vol. 1 (see 32), p. 967.

A brief look at a type of variegated silk cloth or satin. See "Ḳumāsh," in EI2, vol. 5, pp. 373-74.

2623 May, Florence Lewis. Silk Textiles of Spain, Eighth to Fifteenth Century. New York: Hispanic Society of America, 1957, 286 pp.

This book is the first full-length history of Spanish medieval textiles. It combines a profound knowledge of documents with a wide consideration of the surviving fabrics. The notes and bibliography fill a gap in textile research.

2624 Sheperd, Dorothy G. "A Dated Hispano-Islamic Silk." Ars Orientalis 2 (1957):373-82.

A discussion of a fragmentary chasuble that belonged to the Almoravid ʿAlī ibn Yūsūf ibn Tashfīn, who ruled over Spain and North Africa between 1107 and 1143. The chasuble is located in a tiny parish church north of Burgos. An analysis and reconstruction of the silk is offered. This article is a good example of the kind of research that has deepened our understanding of the Muslim art of silk weaving.

COSTUME

2625 Björkman, Walther. "Ḳalansuwa." In EI1. Vol. 2 (see 32), pp. 677-78.

A short piece on a type of cap worn under the turban or alone on the head. See "Libās," in EI2 (see 20).

2626 ____. "Sirwāl." In EI1. Vol. 4 (see 32), pp. 451-53.

Trousers were probably introduced from Persia; the word "sirwāl" is perhaps derived from Old Persian. Included in the article is a discussion of this word's etymology, forms of trousers, the ḥadīth references to the wearing of trousers, by both men and women, and the political significance of the wearing of trousers.

2627 Björkman, W. "Turban." In EI1. Vol. 4 (see 32), pp. 885-93.

The origin, evolution, significance, and symbolism of the distinctive headdress in Islam are dealt with at some length in this article. In addition, variations in form and color are discussed in the context of religion, geography, and history. Names given to these various turban forms are listed and briefly discussed. The bibliography includes pertinent Arabic sources for information relevant to a study of the turban.

2628 Lane, E.W. An Account of the Manners and Customs of the Modern Eygptians (see 762).

See chapter 1, "Personal Characteristics and Dress of the Muslim Egyptians," for a description of the various types of traditional Muslim dress.

2629 Marçais, Georges. "ʿAbāʾ." In EI1. Vol. 1 (see 32), p. 1.

Examines a type of garment that varies in style throughout the Islamic world. See "Libās" in the New Edition.

2630 Mayer, L.A. Mamluk Costume: A Survey. Geneva: A. Kunding, 1952, 119 pp.

This book provides a picture of Mamlūk society as seen in the nature and function of costume. The author's sources: Arabic literary materials, various works of Islamic art, European records of pilgrimages and travels to the Near East, and paintings of Italians who had been in the East. A convenient reference work.

METALWORK, ARMOR, GOLD AND SILVER, COINS, JEWELS, ASTROLABES

GENERAL STUDIES

2631 Barrett, Douglas. Islamic Metalwork in the British Museum. London: Trustees of the British Museum, 1949, 23 pp.

This collection of metalwork contains many important specimens, but lacks certain types of bronzes, particularly Saljūq incense burners in the shape of animals with openwork. Nonetheless, the book serves quite well as a short introduction to Muslim metalwork.

2632 Mayer, Leo Ary. Islamic Metalworkers and Their Works. Geneva: A. Kundig, 1959, 126 pp.

A basic reference work. Illustrated.

2633 Rice, David Storm. "Studies in Islamic Metal Work." Bulletin of the School of Oriental and African Studies 14 (1952):564-78; 15 (1953):61-80; 17 (1955):206-31; and 21 (1958): 225-53.

This is a very original and useful study of Islamic metalwork.

2634 Wiet, Gaston. Catalogue général du Museée arabe du Caire: Objets en Cuivre. Cairo: Imprimerie de l'Institut Français d'archéologie orientale, 1932, 315 pp.

A useful survey of metal objects especially important for those interested in the arts of the Mamlūk period in Egypt and Syria. Illustrated.

SPECIFIC STUDIES

Metalwork

2635 Ettinghausen, Richard. "The Bobrinski 'Kettle,' Patron and Style of an Islamic Bronze." Gazette des Beaux-Arts 24 (1943): 193-208.
In this article a kettle in the Hermitage Museum, Leningrad, is examined for its relative place in the history of Islamic metal production. The kettle is a masterpiece of Saljūq art, revealing in its decorative subject matter some themes that appealed to middle-class taste. Known as the Bobrinski kettle, it is the earliest dated silver inlaid bronze vessel of this period and was made in 1163 by an artist named Mas'ūd ibn Aḥmad at Harāt.

2636 Rice, D.S. Le Baptistère de Saint Louis: A Masterpiece of Islamic Metal Work. Paris: Editions du Chêne, 1951, 26 pp.
A complete and detailed monograph on a single metal object now at the Louvre Museum in Paris. Rice gives a thorough and minute analysis of every single element of the decorative scheme with comparisons and conclusions. Illustrated.

2637 Rice, David Storm. "Inlaid Brasses from the Workshop of Ahmad al-Dhaki al-Mawsili." Ars Orientalis 2 (1957):283-326.
Explores the problem of the so-called Mosul (Mawṣil) school of metalwork and attributes certain works to a single master.

2638 ______. The Wade Cup in the Cleveland Museum of Art. Paris: Les Editions du Chêne, 1955, 36 pp.
An excellent and complete study of a single object. It also sheds much light on our understanding of metalwork in general. Perhaps the most important contribution of the author is his detailed analysis of the inscriptions both of the Wade cup, so called after its donor, J.H. Wade, and of related vessels and the way in which he uses the inscriptions to provide a date. The characteristic feature of this script is the introduction of human beings and animals. For a critique of Rice's book the reader is referred to Richard Ettinghausen's "The 'Wade Cup' in the Cleveland Museum of Art, Its Origins and Decorations," Ars Orientalis 2 (1957):327-66.

2639 Schneider, Laura T. "The Freer Canteen." Ars Orientalis 9 (1973):137-56.
Islamic metalwork with Christian scenes presents us with many problems such as those of patronage, function of the object, and iconographic meaning of the decoration. In this article the large inlaid metal canteen in the Freer Gallery of Art, Washington, D.C., is made the focal point of a stimulating study of these problems.

Armor

2640 Mayer, Leo Ary. Islamic Armourers and Their Works. Geneva: Albert Kundig, 1962, 128 pp.
A basic reference work. Illustrated.

2641 Mayer, L.A. "Saracenic Arms and Armour." Ars Islamica 10 (1943):1-12.
A descriptive survey of Arab arms and armor, with seventeen illustrations.

2642 Robinson, H. Russell. Oriental Armour. London: Herbert Jenkins, 1967, 257 pp.
The author analyzes the origins of Oriental armor, and the armor of Persia, Turkey, the Arab countries, India, Ceylon, China, and Japan. For Islamic armor, the best account remains Mayer's (see 2640).

Gold and Silver Work

2643 University of Michigan, Museum of Art. Sasanian Silver: Late Antique and Early Mediaeval Arts of Luxury from Iran; Catalogue of an Exhibition, Aug.-Sept., 1967. With a historical survey by Martha Carter and an introduction to the art of Sasanian Silver by Oleg Grabar. Ann Arbor: University of Michigan, Museum of Art, 1967, 158 pp.
Grabar's essay attempts to define the art-historical problems of a group of silver objects from American collections. The photographs provide an opportunity for study and comparison. Though sketchy and quite tentative, this essay is an intelligent and penetrating piece of writing. Among the problems defined are: Sāsānian versus post-Sāsānian style; Iranian versus non-Iranian sources; and certain iconographic distinctions with regard to Sāsānian silver. As many as half the pieces in the exhibition are questioned by reliable scholars including Grabar.

Coins

2644 British Museum, Department of Coins and Medals. A Catalogue of the Muhammadan Coins in the British Museum, by John Walker. Vol. 1, Arab-Sassanian Coins, 1941. Vol. 2, Arab-Byzantine and Post Reform Coins, London, 1956.
This work is recognized as a masterpiece of numismatic scholarship. Though intended primarily for specialists, it offers something for the generalist. Introductions to each volume are lengthy, interesting, and filled with information that is difficult to obtain elsewhere.

2645 British Museum, Department of Coins and Medals. Catalogue of Oriental Coins in the British Museum, by Stanley Lane-Poole. 10 vols. Edited by Reginald Stuart Poole. Bologna: Forni, 1967. Reprint of 1875-1890 ed.
A basic catalog of one of the largest collections of Muslim coins.

2646 Mitchell, Michael. The World of Islam: Oriental Coins and Their Values. London: Hawkins Publications, 1977, 511 pp.
A fairly complete historical survey of Islamic coinage in the form of a catalog primarily illustrating the author's collection. The coins are classified geographically and then chronologically. Coins from the major Islamic countries and areas form the bulk of the catalog, though Islamic coins from areas such as East Africa and Southeast Asia are included. Certain

problems associated with Islamic coinage are also dealt with, including Crusader coins, late Byzantine coins, and Viking and Sāmānid coins. Each coin is illustrated, making this book a valuable source for the collector. Also included at the back of the book are appendixes of coin values and weights, and a bibliography.

2647 Plant, Richard. Arabic Coins and How to Read Them. London: Seaby, 1973, 148 pp.
This book is especially adequate for the beginning student of Muslim numismatics who wants to teach himself. There are several exercises at the end of each chapter with keyed answers provided at the end of the book. Hundreds of drawings of coins are provided as illustrations of each point. An eleven-page coin vocabulary is appended.

Jewels

2648 Meen, V.B., and A.D. Tushingham. Crown Jewels of Iran. Toronto: University of Toronto Press, 1974, 159 pp.
Most settings date from the nineteenth and twentieth centuries. Those that are signed are of historical interest. Illustrated.

Astrolabes

2649 Hartner, Willy. "Asṭurlāb." In EI2. Vol. 1 (see 20), pp. 722-28.
An informative survey of the history of the astrolabe including a description of the instrument and the various types; bibliography included.

2650 Mayer, Leo Ary. Islamic Astrolabists and Their Works. Geneva: Albert Kundig, 1956, 123 pp.
A basic reference work. Illustrated.

IVORY

2651 Beckwith, John. Caskets from Cordoba (Victoria and Albert Museum). London: Her Majesty's Stationery Office, 1960, 72 pp.
An excellent and useful short study of the surviving group of ivory caskets from medieval Spain. Although based on the Victoria and Albert collection, objects from other collections are used for comparison. Illustrated.

2652 Cott, Percy B. Siculo-Arabic Ivories. Princeton, N.J.: Department of Art and Archeology of Princeton University, 1939, 68 pp.
The core of this book is the corpus of ivory boxes (nearly two hundred) made in Sicily by Muslim craftsmen during the period of the Norman domination. The text is brief, but reliable. The decorative motifs, ornaments, and animal and human representations are analyzed in detail, many going back to Byzantine or Near Eastern prototypes. Finally, an elaborate, illustrated descriptive catalog gives all the necessary information about each object.

2653 Pinder-Wilson, R. "ʿĀjd." In EI2. Vol. 1 (see 20), pp. 200-203.
An admirable summary of the use made of ivory in Islamic art with emphasis on examples from Egypt, Spain, and North Africa, with illustrations.

GLASS

2654 Lamm, Carl Johan. Glass from Iran in the National Museum, Stockholm. C.E. Fritze, 1935, 21 pp.
A partial catalog of one of the more important Persian glass collections outside Iran. It forms a supplement to what Lamm wrote previously on Persian glass, especially his contribution "Glass and Hard Stone Vessels" in A Survey of Persian Art (see 2314). Illustrations include fifty photographs on eight plates and several hundred drawings.

2655 Lukens, Marie G. "Medieval Islamic Glass." Bulletin of the Metropolitan Museum of Art, n.s. 23 (1965):198-208.
This article explores the art of glass-making in early Islam. Fourteen examples are illustrated, most being of Persian provenance and a few of Syrian origin. The author's conclusions are wisely cautious with regard to stylistic analysis and chronology.

2656 Marçais, Georges. "Fusayfisāʾ." In EI2. Vol. 2 (see 20), pp. 955-57.
Traces the art of mosaic; bibliography, no illustrations.

2657 Oliver, Prudence. "Islamic Relief Cut Glass: A Suggested Chronology." Journal of Glass Studies 3 (1961):8-29.
The author groups twenty-six beakers, bowls, bottles, and ewers of relief cut glass decoration in a sequence ranging from relatively naturalistic treatment to relatively stylized treatment. She dates these pieces from the end of the ninth to the beginning of the eleventh century. This is an interesting, but very speculative, solution to the problem of dating Islamic glass.

2658 Pinder-Wilson, Ralph, and George T. Scanlon. "Glass Finds from Fustat: 1964-71." Journal of Glass Studies 15 (1973):12-30.
A catalog of twenty-six objects of Islamic glass excavated at Fusṭāṭ, an ancient suburb of modern Cairo. The authors have attempted to show that these pieces "offer a more precise chronology of Islamic glass between the eighth and eleventh centuries." Each piece is illustrated quite clearly, but on a very small scale.

2659 Ruska, J., and C.J. Lamm. "Billawr." In EI2. Vol. 1 (see 20), pp. 1220-21.
This short article will provide a good starting point for a study of Islamic rock crystal objects, of which 165 are known to exist, mostly preserved in the treasures of European churches. See also C.J. Lamm's authoritative study Mittelalterliche Gläser und Steinschnittarbeiten aus dem Nahen Osten, 2 vols. (Berlin: D. Reimer, 1929-1930).

GARDENS

2660 Crowe, Sylvia et al. The Gardens of Mughal India: A History and a Guide. London: Thames & Hudson, 1972, 200 pp.

Under the first six Mughal emperors, from Bābur (1526-1530) to Awrangzīb (1658-1707), the paradise garden was transplanted from Persia to India, where it took root and flourished. The authors give accounts of twenty-six gardens, out of more than thirty surviving. This is an elegant, enjoyable, and informative publication. There is a chapter on plant material in the Mughal garden and an appendix on plant names. Illustrated.

2661 Sackville-West, Vita. "Persian Gardens." In The Legacy of Persia (see 64), pp. 259-91.

A delightful essay by a distinguished British novelist.

2662 Wilber, Donald N. Persian Gardens and Garden Pavilions. Rutland, Vt.: C.E. Tuttle & Co., 1962, 239 pp.

A general treatment of Persian gardens that is built around evidence of actual gardens, literary references to gardens, and representations of gardens in Persian miniature paintings. The author examines a Muslim garden tradition that extends from Iran to India.

PLAYING CARDS

2663 Mayer, L.A. Mamluk Playing Cards. Edited by Richard Ettinghausen and Otto Kurz. Leiden: E.J. Brill, 1971, 51 pp.

This is a reedition of an article published in 1939; the number of plates has been increased, so that all the cards are reproduced. This book was found to be full of misinterpretations by Michael Dummett and Kamal Abu Deeb. The reader is referred to their article "Some Remarks on Mamluk Playing Cards," Journal of the Warburg and Courtauld Institutes 36 (1973): 106-28. Mayer's article surprised many when it first came out because no one had suspected that playing cards had been used by Muslims until he published these examples.

WOOD

2664 Culpan, Cevdet. Rahleler Koranständer. Istanbul: M.E.B. Devlet Kitaplari, 1968, 65 pp.

A book on Qur'ān stands in Turkish, with a Germany summary. Illustrated.

2665 Mayer, Leo Ary. Islamic Woodcarvers and Their Works. Geneva: Albert Kundig, 1958, 97 pp.

A basic reference work. Illustrated.

2666 Paulty, Edmond. Catalogue général du Muséé arabe du Caire: Les Bois Sculptés jusqu'à l'époque Ayyoubide. Cairo: Imprimerie de l'Institut Français d'archéologie orientale, 1931, 81 pp.

A catalog of an extraordinarily rich collection of woodwork preserved in Cairo. The catalog covers the pre-Islamic period, early Arab woodcarving, and Ayyūbid woodcarving. Unfortunately, the catalog does not go beyond the year A.D. 1170, which limits its use as a general survey.

Research Aids

PERIODICALS IN ENGLISH ON ISLAMIC STUDIES

ORIENTAL STUDIES IN GENERAL

2667 Acta Orientalia. Societates Orientales Danica, Norvegica, Svedica. Copenhagen. 1923-.

Articles, mostly in English and French, about Islamic and other Oriental studies.

2668 Acta Orientalia. Academiae-Scientiarum Hungaricae. Budapest, 1950-.

Articles on Oriental subjects, mostly in English, French, and German.

2669 Ars Orientalis: The Arts of Islam and the East. Freer Gallery of Art of the Smithsonian Institution and Department of the History of Art of the University of Michigan. Washington and Ann Arbor, 1954-. Plates.

A beautifully produced magazine devoted to all aspects of Oriental art. Supersedes Ars Islamica (see 2690).

2670 Asian Affairs: Journal of the Royal Central Asian Society. London, 1914-. Former titles: Journal of the Central Asian Society (1914-1931), Journal of the Royal Central Asian Society (1931-1969), Royal Central Asian Journal (unofficial name, on cover only), present title (1970-).

The names of this journal and the society that publishes it are somewhat misleading, since the journal covers the study of all Asia (including the Middle East) and is not at all restricted to Central Asia.

2671 Asian and African Studies. Department of Oriental Studies of the Slovak Academy of Sciences. Bratislava, 1965-.

Articles on all aspects of Oriental studies, including Islamic. Most articles in English. "Special attention will be given to mediaeval Turkish history with regard to the expansion of the Ottoman Empire into the Danubian basin and Slovakia" (preface to vol. 1).

2672 Bulletin of the School of Oriental and African Studies. University of London. London, 1917-.

One of the most important of British Orientalist journals. Contains much about the Middle East and the Islamic world.

2673 Folia Orientalia: revue des études orientales. Commission Orientaliste, Centre de Cracovie de l'Académie polonaise des sciences. Krakow, 1959-.

One of the best Orientalist journals. Rich in Semitic, Turkic, and Iranian studies. Articles in English, French, and German.

2674 Journal of the American Oriental Society. New Haven, Conn., 1851-.

Articles and book reviews about all aspects of Oriental studies, including the Islamic.

2675 Journal of the Economic and Social History of the Orient. Leiden: Brill, 1958-.

Embraces all Asia, but the world of Islam forms the largest part in each volume.

2676 Journal of the Royal Asiatic Society of Great Britain and Ireland. London, 18??-.

One of the leading British Orientalist journals. Contains much on Islam and the Middle East.

2677 Mizan. Central Asian Research Centre. London, 1959-1971. Former title: The Mizan Newsletter: A Review of Soviet Writing on the Middle East (1959-1964).

"Mizan reviews the development of Soviet and Chinese relations with Asian and African countries. It also surveys social, political and cultural developments in Soviet Central Asia." The word "mizan" is Arabic for "balance." Published by the editors of Central Asian Review (see 2724).

2678 Oriens: Journal of the International Society for Oriental Research. Leiden, 1948-.

Covering the whole range of Oriental studies, but concentrating on the Middle East. Most articles are in German or English.

2679 The Oriental Collections: Consisting of Original Essays and Dissertations, Translations, and Miscellaneous Papers, Illustrating the History and Antiquities, the Arts, Sciences, and Literature, of Asia. London, 1797-1800. Plates. Ceased publication.
One of the earliest European Orientalist journals, edited by the great British Orientalist Sir William Ouseley. Beautifully printed and illustrated. Most articles deal with Persian literature, although all aspects of Oriental studies are covered.

2680 Orientalia Pragensia. Universita Karlova. Prague, 1960-.
"The Series Orientalia Pragensia will appear within the Acta Universitatis Carolinae approximately once in two years, and it will contain the products of scientific workers concentrated in the Cathedra of philology and history of the Near and Middle East and India and the Cathedra of philology and history of the Far East at the Philosophical Faculty of Caroline University in Prague" (editorial in no. 1). Most articles in English or German.

2681 Orientalia Suecana. Stockholm. 1952-.
All aspects of Oriental studies with emphasis on the Middle East. Articles in English, French, and German.

2682 Rocznik Orientalistyczny. Komitet Nauk Orientalistycznych, Polska Akademia Nauk. Warsaw, 1914/1915-.
One of the best of the scholarly Orientalist journals. Covers all aspects of Oriental studies, but particularly strong on the Middle East. Articles in Polish, English, French, and Russian.

2683 Studia Orientalia. Societas Orientalis Fennica. Helsinki, 1925-.
Articles on all aspects of Oriental studies, including the Middle East. Many articles so long as to occupy a whole number, so that this journal is perhaps more of a monograph series than a periodical. Articles in English, French, and German.

2684 Zeitschrift der Deutschen Morgenländischen Gesellschaft. Leipzig, 1843-1944. Wiesbaden, 1945/1949-. Reprint of early issues. Nendeln, Liechtenstein: Kraus Reprint, 1968.
One of the earliest and most rigorously scholarly of European Orientalist journals, with much about the Middle East and Islam. Most articles in German, but occasionally in English.

ISLAM AND THE MIDDLE EAST IN GENERAL

2685 Abr-Nahrain: An Annual Published by the Department of Middle Eastern Studies, University of Melbourne. Leiden, 1972-.
Learned articles by Australian and other Orientalists about the Islamic and pre-Islamic Middle East.

2686 American Journal of Arabic Studies. Leiden: Brill, 1973-.
"The journal publishes articles and reviews concerning the Arab World, from the pre-Islamic era to modern times. It presents studies dealing with history, geography, political science, sociology, anthropology, applied linguistics, folklore, literature, economics, philosophy, religion, and any other discipline that concerns itself with the Arab World."

2687 Annual of Leeds University Oriental Society. Leiden, 1959-.
"The Annual would be wise if it restricted its purview to the two major fields of Hebrew and Arabic studies . . . and those who wish to keep abreast of modern scholarship in Hebrew and Arabic will know that they can find what they want in the pages of this Annual" (introduction to vol. 1). So far the annual has adhered to its original intention.

2688 Arab Journal. The Organization of Arab Students in the U.S.A. and Canada. New York, 1964-.
Mostly, but not exclusively, about Arab politics, with much about the Palestine problem.

2689 Armenian Review. Hairenik Association. Boston, 1948-.
Numerous scholarly articles about Armenia under Muslim (Ottoman or Iranian) rule and about the history of other Middle Eastern countries seen from the perspective of the Armenian minorities. Turkish readers will object to the presentation of the Armenian-Turkish relations in history.

2690 Ars Islamica. Research Seminary in Islamic Art, Institute of Fine Arts, University of Michigan. Ann Arbor, 1934-1951. Plates. Ceased publication.
A finely produced, illustrated journal dealing with all aspects of Islamic art. Revived in 1954 as Ars Orientalis (see 2669).

2691 Asian and African Studies: Journal of the Israel Oriental Society. Jerusalem, 1965-.
Most articles are about the Arab world.

2692 International Journal of Middle East Studies. Middle East Studies Association of North America. New York, 1970-.
"Publishes articles and reviews concerning the area encompassing Iran, Turkey, Afghanistan, Israel, Pakistan, and the countries of the Arab World from the seventh century to modern times. Spain, Southeastern Europe, and the Soviet Union also are included for the periods in which their territories were parts of Middle Eastern empires or were under the influence of Middle Eastern civilization. Particular attention will be paid to works dealing with history, political science, economics, anthropology, sociology, philology and literature, folklore, comparative religion and theology, law and philosophy."

2693 Der Islam: Zeitschrift für Geschichte und Kultur des Islamischen Orients. Berlin, 1910-.
Most articles are in German, but a significant number are in English. Extremely high level of scholarship.

2694 Islamic Culture: An English Quarterly. Hyderabad, India, 1927-.
The most important scholarly Islamic journal published in India. Scope of articles by leading Indian and foreign scholars is not restricted to India but embraces the whole Muslim world.

2695 Islamic Quarterly: A Review of Islamic Culture. Islamic Cultural Centre. London, 1954-.
Learned articles on all aspects of Islamic culture, with emphasis upon the Islamic religious tradition.

2696 Islamic Studies: Journal of the Islamic Research Institute, Pakistan. Karachi/Islamabad, 1962-.
Articles about Muslim theology, philosophy, law, and political theory, mostly by Pakistani scholars, but not limited to Pakistan.

2697 Israel Oriental Studies. University of Tel Aviv. Tel Aviv, 1971-.
Almost all articles deal with the Middle East, Islamic, and pre-Islamic subject matter.

2698 Journal of Arabic Literature. Leiden: Brill, 1970-.
Critical studies and English translations from Arabic literature. Greater emphasis on modern literature, but classical is also represented.

2699 Journal of the Pakistan Historical Society. Karachi, 1953-.
Covers Islamic history in its widest sense, not restricted to the Indian subcontinent.

2700 Journal of the Regional Cultural Institute (Iran, Pakistan, Turkey). Teheran, 1967-.
"The aim of this journal is to publish scholarly and unbiased articles on all aspects of the religion, history, philosophy, science, literature, arts and crafts, folklore, ethnography, anthropology and sociology of this region" (introduction to vol. 1).

2701 Journal of Semitic Studies. Manchester: University Press, 1956-.
About half the articles deal with Arabic, the other half with the other Semitic languages and literatures that are of interest for the pre-Islamic background of the Middle East.

2702 Merip Reports. Washington: Middle East Research and Information Project, 1970-.
A monthly journal focusing on "the political economy of the contemporary Middle East, the role of imperialism and the popular struggles in the region."

2703 Mid East: A Middle East-North African Review. American Friends of the Middle East. Washington, 1961-1970. Ceased publication. Previous title: Viewpoints (1961-1966).
A rather popular, illustrated periodical designed to acquaint the educated American layman with Islamic and Middle Eastern civilization. Supported the rights of the Palestinians to their own country.

2704 Middle East Forum. Alumni Association of the American University of Beirut. Beirut, 1925-197?. Ceased publication?
Mostly contains articles on the politics of the Middle East by younger Arab scholars. Contains much about the Palestine problem.

2705 Middle East International, Devoted to the Middle East and Its Place in World Affairs. London, 1971-.
Mostly concerned with Arab politics. Sympathetic to the Palestinian cause.

2706 Middle East Journal. Middle East Institute. Washington, 1947-.
"The Middle East Journal, in conformity with the objective of its publishers, The Middle East Institute, takes no editorial stand on the problems of the Middle East. Its sole criterion is that material published be sound and informative, and presented without emotional bias." Covers all aspects of the Middle East with emphasis upon contemporary issues. Includes bibliographies of periodical literature relevant to the Middle East.

2707 The Middle East and North Africa 1972-1973 (see 457).

2708 Middle Eastern Studies. London: Cass, 1964-.
Emphasis is on the recent history of the Middle East. Articles about Palestine tend to be sympathetic to Zionism.

2709 Muslim World: A Journal Devoted to the Study of Islam and of Christian-Muslim Relationship in Past and Present. Hartford Seminary Foundation. Hartford, Conn., 1911-.
A scholarly journal that addresses itself to all areas of Islamic thought, from pre-Islamic times to the present. Includes up-to-date bibliographies of Islamic periodical literature. Former title: Moslem World (1911-1947).

2710 Studia Islamica. Paris: Maisonneuve-Larose, 1953-.
"Offers to the learned public, and not to Islamic scholars only, papers written (preferably in English and in French) by qualified specialists on subjects from all sections of the vast field of Islamic studies."

2711 Studies in Islam: Quarterly Journal of the Indian Institute of Islamic Studies. New Delhi, 1964-.
Articles on all aspects of Islamic studies, mainly, but not exclusively, concerned with Islam in India.

2712 Die Welt des Islams, New Series The World of Islam./Le Monde de l'Islam: International Journal for the Historical Development of Contemporary Islam. Leiden: Brill, 1951-.
Articles in German, English, and French, mostly but not exclusively about recent nineteenth- and twentieth-century developments in Islamic countries. In spite of the name this journal is not really a continuation of Die Welt des Islams (Berlin, 1913-1942?), which was published by the Deutsche Gesellschaft für Islamkunde and contained articles almost exclusively in German.

INDIVIDUAL COUNTRIES AND REGIONS

Arabian Peninsula

2713 Arabian Studies. Middle East Centre, University of Cambridge. London, 1974-.
A new journal devoted specifically to studies of the Arabian peninsula, the motherland of Islam.

Palestine

2714 Journal of Palestine Studies: A Quarterly on Palestinian Affairs and the Arab-Israeli Conflict. Institute for Palestine Studies. Beirut, 1971-.
A periodical published by Palestinian scholars in Lebanon expressing the Palestinian viewpoint, usually ignored in the West. Unemotional factual studies, including analyses of the Hebrew press.

Sudan

2715 Sudan Notes and Records, Incorporating Proceedings of the Philosophical Society of the Sudan. Khartoum, 1918-.
"Exists to promote the collection, exchange and publication of information about the Sudan in every aspect of its history, its people and its institutions, including not only the social but also the natural sciences."

Turkey

2716 Archivum Ottomanicum. The Hague: Mouton, 1969-.
"Concerns itself primarily with Ottoman history and Ottoman philology. However, the editors also welcome articles on subjects related to Ottoman studies in the history and culture of Europe, including in particular Danubian Europe, the Black Sea area and the Caucasus, and in the history and culture of the Arab and Iranian lands, and Byzantium." Most articles in English.

2717 Cultura Turcica. Institute for the Study of Turkish Culture. Ankara, 1964-.
Studies in Turkish culture in its widest sense, embracing Turkey, the former Ottoman Empire and Central Asia. Most articles in English, but some in French or German.

Caucasus

2718 Caucasian Review. Institute for the Study of the USSR. Munich, 1955-1959. Ceased publication.
"Its aim is to acquaint readers in the free world with the historical development and contemporary political, economic, and social structure of the Caucasus" (editorial board).

2719 Studia Caucasica. The Hague: Mouton, 1963-.
Scholarly articles, mostly in English, about the ethnography and linguistics of the Caucasus.

Iran

2720 Indo-Iranica: The Quarterly Organ of the Iran Society. Calcutta, 1946-.
Articles about all aspects of Iranian culture by Indian scholars.

2721 Iran: Journal of the British Institute of Persian Studies. London, 1963-. Plates.
A beautifully produced magazine dealing mainly, but not exclusively, with the art and archaeology of Iran, Islamic and pre-Islamic.

2722 Iranian Studies: Journal of the Society for Iranian Studies. Boston College, Chestnut Hill, Mass., 1967-.
Excellent journal about the classical culture and modern political and economic life of Iran.

2723 Persica: Jaarboek van het Genootschap Nederland-Iran Stichting voor Culturele Betrekkingen. The Hague: 1963/1964-.
Articles on all aspects of Iranian studies in Dutch and English.

Central Asia

2724 Central Asian Review: A Quarterly Review of Current Developments in Soviet Central Asia and Kazakhstan. Central Asian Research Centre, London, 1953-1968. Ceased publication.
"The object of the Central Asian Review is to present a coherent picture of current political, social and material developments in the five Soviet Socialist Republics of Uzbekistan, Tadzhikistan, Kirgizian, Turkmenistan and Kazakhstan as they are reflected in Soviet publications. The selection of material has been made as objective as possible" (introduction to vol. 1). The Central Asian Research Centre "has never swerved from its originally declared intention of presenting an objective picture of developments in Central Asia and of Soviet policies towards the adjoining countries. . . . It is regrettable, but not entirely surprising, that this balanced and seemingly civilized approach should not find favour with Soviet critics. Although Soviet scholars examine the Centre's publications with ever increasing attention and interest, published Soviet reactions to the Centre's activities are still hostile in the extreme" (editorial in vol. 16).

2725 Central Asiatic Journal: International Periodical for the Languages, Literature, History and Archaeology of Central Asia. Wiesbaden, 1955-.
Of great interest for Turkic and Iranian studies.

2726 East Turkic Review. Munich: Institute for the Study of the USSR, 1958-1960. Ceased publication.
"Its purpose is to present analyses of contemporary events and detailed studies of the history and culture of the areas of the Soviet Union inhabited by Turkic peoples."

Afghanistan

2727 Afghanistan: Historical and Cultural Quarterly. Historical Society of Afghanistan. Kabul, 1946-.
Articles, mostly in English (some in French), about the history and general culture of Afghanistan; also of interest to students of Iranian and Indian history.

Indian Subcontinent

2728 Journal of the Asiatic Society of Bangladesh. Dacca, 1956-. Former title: Journal of the Asiatic Society of Pakistan (1956-1971).
Studies dealing mainly, but not exclusively, with Islam on the Indian subcontinent.

2729 Pakistan Philosophical Journal: A Quarterly Organ of the Pakistan Philosophical Congress. Lahore, 1957-.
Perhaps the only Muslim journal in the English language devoted specifically to problems of philosophy. Of special interest are the views of contemporary Muslim philosophers about modern European philosophical trends, such as existentialism or Marxism.

Malaysia and Indonesia

2730 Journal of the Malaysian Branch of the Royal Asiatic Society. Singapore, 1878-. Former titles: Journal of the Straits Branch of the Royal Asiatic Society (1878-1922), Journal of the Malayan Branch of the Royal Asiatic Society (1923-1963).
The most important scholarly journal for the history of Islam in Malaysia and to a lesser extent Indonesia.

2731 Journal of the Oriental Society of Australia. Sydney, 1960-.
Concerned almost exclusively with the Far East and Southeast Asia, which includes Muslim Malaysia and Indonesia. Numerous articles about Indonesia.

HANDBOOKS AND ENCYCLOPEDIAS OF THE ISLAMIC WORLD

ENCYCLOPEDIAS (GENERAL ISLAMIC AND THE MIDDLE EAST)

2732 Adams, Michael, ed. The Middle East: A Handbook (see 449).

2733 Bacharach, Jere L. A Near East Studies Handbook (see 13).

2734 Gibb, H.A.R., ed. The Encyclopaedia of Islam (see 20).

2735 Gibb, H.A.R., and J.H. Kramers, eds. Shorter Encyclopedia of Islam (see 22).

2736 Houtsma, M.T. et al., eds. The Encyclopaedia of Islam (see 32).

2737 Hughes, Thomas Patrick. A Dictionary of Islam, Being an Encyclopaedia of the Doctrines, Rites, Ceremonies, and Customs, Together with the Technical and Theological Terms of the Muhammadan Religion. Clifton, N.J.: Reference Book Publishers, 1965, 750 pp. Orig. pub.: London: W.H. Allen, 1895.
"Still useful. . . . Like The Encyclopaedia of Islam, this volume has articles on a variety of subjects that concern the Muslim's faith, but the articles are much shorter and far fewer subjects are covered" (C.J. Adams in Reader's Guide [see 2794]).

2738 The New Encyclopaedia Britannica. 15th ed. 30 vols. Chicago: W. Benton, 1974.
The new edition of The Encyclopaedia Britannica contains numerous articles on many Islamic subjects prepared by specialists in the various fields of Islamic studies. Particularly useful is the Micropaedia (Ready Reference and Index), which lists topics covered in the Macropaedia volumes and related entries in the Micropaedia. For example, the topics entered under "Islamic mysticism" serve as an outline and guide for the major developments in Islamic mysticism. Indexes and bibliographies. See also 1076.

2739 Ronart, Stephan, and Nancy Ronart. Concise Encyclopaedia of Arabic Civilization (see 49).

2740 Shimani, Yaacov, and Evyatar Lemni. Political Dictionary of the Middle East (see 476).

2741 World Muslim Gazetteer. Karachi: World Muslim Congress, 1964, 563 pp.
A handbook of all the Muslim countries, giving under each entry facts and figures on geography, history, and economics. While the sections on geography and history may still be valid, those on economics are of course out of date. The "Publishers' note" promises a new edition. Statistics of Muslims in non-Muslim countries are wildly exaggerated.

Shīʿah

2742 Amīn, Hassan al-. Islamic Shiʿite Encyclopaedia. 3 vols. Beirut: Slim Press, 1970.
A valuable mine of information about the Shīʿah sect of Islam, dominant in Iran and with large minorities in other Muslim countries. Material is not arranged alphabetically, so the work is difficult to use as a reference book. The English is weak. See also 1225.

BIOGRAPHICAL DICTIONARIES

2743 Beale, Thomas William. An Oriental Biographical Dictionary. Edited by Henry George Keene. New, rev. & enl. ed. Delhi: Manohar Reprints, 1971, 431 pp. Orig. pub. in 1894.

The most valuable work of the kind, with over 4,500 entries. Most are on Indian Muslims, but also included are the most important figures in Iranian, Arab, and to a lesser extent Ottoman history. Each subject's name is given in Arabic script as well as in transliteration. All dates are given in both Christian and Islamic years.

2744 Hill, Richard Leslie. A Biographical Dictionary of the Anglo-Egyptian Sudan (see 797).

2745 Ibn Khallikān. Biographical Dictionary, by MacGuckin de Slane. 4 vols. Paris: Oriental Translation Fund of Great Britain and Ireland, 1834-1871.

The most important biographical dictionary in classical Arabic by the thirteenth-century Iraqī scholar Ibn Khallikān. Mostly biographies of literary men. The entries are in the order of the Arabic alphabet, usually under the first name, not necessarily under the part of the name by which the subject is best known. For example, "Mutanabbī" appears under "Aḥmad." The translator has not changed this arrangement, but has provided an index at the end of each volume. (One index for the four volumes would have been easier to use.) The translator's long introduction, life of Ibn Khallikān (in volume 4), and copious notes are most useful.

HISTORY AND AUXILIARY DISCIPLINES

2746 Philips, Cyril Henry, ed. Handbook of Oriental History (see 42).

By members of the Department of Oriental History, School of Oriental and African Studies, University of London. Contents: "The Near and Middle East" (B. Lewis), "India and Pakistan" (C.H. Philips), "South-East Asia and the (Indonesian) Archipelago" (D.G.E. Hall), "China" (O.P.N.B. Van der Sprenkel), and "Japan" (W.G. Beasley). Of these five sections, section 1 and parts of 2 and 3 are relevant to Islamic studies. Section 1 is divided as follows: the Romanization of words, the Arab-Islamic name, note on place names, select glossary, calendars and systems of dating, and dynasties and rulers. Other sections are divided similarly.

2747 Reychman, Jan, and Ananiasz Zajaczkowski. Handbook of Ottoman-Turkish Diplomatics (see 406).

Dynastic Tables

2748 Bosworth, C.E. The Islamic Dynasties (see 14).

2749 Gomaa, Ibrahim. A Historical Chart of the Muslim World. Handbuch der Orientalistik, 1st division, Ergänzungsband, no. 7. Leiden: Brill, 1972.

"This chart gives a chronological survey in graphical form of the Muslim dynasties and the lands of Islam since 600 A.D. up till the present day. It enables one to see at a glance where a certain dynasty has ruled in the various periods of its existence or by which dynasty one particular part of the world of Islam has been governed in any particular year" (publisher).

2750 Lane-Poole, Stanley. The Mohammadan Dynasties: Chronological and Genealogical Tables with Historical Introductions. Paris: Geuthner, 1925, 361 pp. Orig. pub.: London: Constable, 1893.

The classical work on Muslim royal genealogies, covering the Islamic world from Spain to India. Superseded by C.E. Bosworth's The Islamic Dynasties (see 14).

Chronology

2751 Bīrūnī, al-. The Chronology of Ancient Nations: An English Version of the Arabic Text of the Athār-ul-Bākiya of al-Bīrūnī, or 'Vestiges of the Past,' Collected and Reduced to Writing by the Author in A.H. 390-391, A.D. 1000. Translated and edited by C. Edward Sachau. London: Oriental Translation Fund, 1879, 464 pp.

A most detailed scholarly study of the different calendars used by Muslims, Oriental Christians, Jews, Zoroastrians, and others. Al-Bīrūnī, one of the greatest minds of Islam and of all ages, uses a strangely modern scientific approach. His work is an encyclopedia of comparative religion and Middle Eastern history, ancient and early medieval.

2752 Burnaby, Sherrard Beaumont. "The Muhammadan Calendar." In Elements of the Jewish and Muhammadan Calendars, with Rules and Tables and Explanatory Notes on the Julian and Gregorian Calendars. London: Bell, 1901, pp. 367-508.

A learned study of the theological, historical, and linguistic aspects of the Jewish and Muslim calendars, with methods of calculating dates.

2753 Freeman-Grenville, Grenville Stewart Parker. Chronology of African History. London: Oxford, 1973, 312 pp.

"These historical tables display, in a calendrical fashion, the whole course, so far as it is known, of the principal events and dates in the whole continent of Africa from c. 1000 B.C. until the end of 1971" (introduction). As we might expect from Freeman-Grenville, a distinguished Islamic scholar, a great stress is laid on the part Islam has played in African history.

2754 _____. The Muslim and Christian Calendars (see 19).

2755 Unat, Faik Reşit. Hicrî Tarihleri Milâdî Tarihe Çevirme Kılavuzu [A guide for converting Hijri dates into Christian dates]. Genişletilmiş 4. basīm. Ankara: Türk Tarih Kurumu, 1974, 175 pp.

These conversion tables from Muslim to Christian dates are handier to use than Freeman-Grenville's (see 2753). No knowledge of Turkish is necessary.

Numismatics

2756 Codrington, Oliver. A Manual of Musalman Numismatics. Asiatic Society Monographs, no. 7. London: Royal Asiatic Society, 1904, 239 pp.

"This book is intended for the help of those who, not being Arabic or Persian scholars, would like to know something about the Oriental coins which may come their way" (preface).

LITERATURE

2757 Lang, David Marshall, ed. A Guide to Eastern Literatures. London: Weidenfeld & Nicolson, 1971, 500 pp.

Partial contents: "Arabic Literature" (J.D. Latham), "Persian Literature: Classical and Modern Literature" (A.A. Haidari), "Turkish Literature," (J.R. Walsh), "Indian and Pakistani Literature" (I.M.P. Raeside and R. Russell), and "Indonesian and Malaysian Literature" (E.C.G. Barrett). Each chapter is divided into four sections: historical background, main trends in literature, individual writers, and bibliography. There is a general index at the end of the book. There is no chapter on Central Asian Turkish literature.

INDIVIDUAL COUNTRIES AND PEOPLES

2758 Great Britain, Admiralty, Naval Intelligence Division. Geographical Handbook Series. London, 1943-1946.

Originally restricted to British officials, and still very useful for the history, geography, and ethnography of the countries described, but out of date for politics or economics. It has a slight imperialist bias. The following titles deal with Islamic countries: Algeria, French West Africa, Iraq and the Persian Gulf, Netherlands East Indies, Palestine and Transjordan, Persia, Tunisia, and Western Arabia and the Red Sea.

Saudi Arabia

2759 Riley, Carroll L. Historical and Cultural Dictionary of Saudi Arabia. Historical and Cultural Dictionaries of Asia, no. 1. Metuchen, N.J.: Scarecrow Press, 1972, 133 pp.

"This volume is not intended to be an exhaustive listing, nor should it be viewed as an encyclopaedia. It is intended as a 'ready reference' work which, when used with other bibliographic tools, would prove to be an invaluable source of information. . . . This is certainly the most complete and lucid set of facts and statistics concerning Saudi Arabia yet seen by the editor" (B.C. Hedrich, editor's foreword).

Turkic Peoples

2760 Menges, Karl Heinrich. The Turkic Languages and Peoples: An Introduction to Turkic Studies. Ural-altaische Bibliothek, no. 15. Wiesbaden: Harrassowitz, 1968, 248 pp.

The linguistic parts of this book may be too specialized for the general student, but chapters on the history and ethnography of the Turkic peoples are most interesting for everyone.

2761 Poppe, Nicholas. Introduction to Altaic Linguistics. Ural-altaische Bibliothek, no. 14. Wiesbaden: Harrassowitz, 1965, 212 pp.

Useful for the ethnography of the Turkic peoples. Very rich bibliographical notes. Most useful for the short biographies of leading European Turkologists.

2762 Wurm, Stefan. "Turkic Peoples of the USSR: Their Historical Background, Their Languages and the Development of Soviet Linguistic Policy." Multiplicated copy. London: Central Asian Research Centre; Oxford: Soviet Affairs Study Group, 1954, 51 pp.

A good introduction to the history and ethnography of the Turkic peoples. Easier to use for the beginning student than the more scholarly works by Menges and Poppe (see 2760, 2761).

Indonesia

2763 Crawford, John. A Descriptive Dictionary of the Indian Islands and Adjacent Countries. Oxford in Asia Historical Reprints. Kuala Lumpur and Singapore: Oxford University Press, 1971, 459 pp. Reprint of 1856 ed.

"The Descriptive Dictionary is still of great value well over a century after its publication. It is a mine of statistical and descriptive information, made available in a readily accessible form which was unusual for its time. . . . For the historian the work is invaluable" (M.C. Ricklefs, introduction).

ORIENTALIST INSTITUTES

2764 Ljunggren, Florence, and Charles L. Geddes, eds. An International Directory of Institutes and Societies Interested in the Middle East. Amsterdam: Djambatan, 1962, 159 pp.

Three hundred fifty-one institutions all over the world, arranged alphabetically by country. "The basic scheme of arrangement is as follows: Name of Institute, Address, History, Purpose and Fields of Interest, Administration, Membership, Academic Staff, Degrees Conferred, Meetings, Library, and Publications" (introduction). Somewhat out of date. A new edition would be most welcome.

ARAB GOVERNMENT INSTITUTIONS

2765 Aman, Mohammed M. "Arab States Author Headings." Library Science Series, no. 1. Multiplicated copy. New York: St. John's University, Graduate School of Arts and Sciences, Department of Library Science, 1973, 134 pp.

This work has a much wider usefulness than its stated purpose, and will help not only librarians but all interested students to find the correct Arabic names of all ministries and other government departments of the Arab states. References are given from English and French forms.

PERSONAL NAMES

2766 Khurshid, Anis. Cataloguing of Pakistani Names. Karachi: University, Library Science Department, 1964, 42 pp.

Pakistan does not have a universally accepted system of surnames, as, for example, Iran since 1926 or Turkey since 1935. Hence Pakistani (and Indian) names may appear very bewildering to the student. This short handbook may thus be consulted by the interested student as well as by the librarian for an explanation of the intricacies of Pakistani and Indian Muslim names.

2767 Sharify, Nasser. Cataloguing of Persian Works, Including Rules for Transliteration, Entry, and Description. Chicago: American Library Association, 1959, 161 pp.

This book could be consulted not only by the librarian but also by the general student wishing to be informed about the complexity of Persian names before 1926, when surnames were introduced.

ATLASES OF THE MUSLIM WORLD

THE MIDDLE EAST

2768 Atlas of the Arab World and the Middle East. Introduction by C.F. Beckingham. London: Macmillan; New York: St. Martin's Press, 1960, 68 pp.

Covers the Arab countries, Turkey, and Iran. Clear maps showing all aspects of the modern Middle East, but out of date for political developments since 1960. Excellent historical introduction by Beckingham. Illustrated.

2769 Hazard, H.W. Atlas of Islamic History (see 27).

2770 Oxford Regional Economic Atlas: The Middle East and North Africa. Prepared by the Economist Intelligence Unit Limited and the Cartographic Department of the Clarendon Press. Oxford: Oxford University Press, 1960, 135 pp.

Emphasis on economic development. Very well produced, but out of date, though many data on physical geography (geology, climate, etc.) are still valid.

2771 Reichert, Rolf. A Historical and Regional Atlas of the Arabic World (see 58).

2772 Roolvink, R. Historical Atlas of the Muslim Peoples (see 44).

Individual Arab Countries

Iraq

2773 Sousah, Ahmad. An Illustrated Handbook; or, Iraq in Maps. Baghdad: Ministry of Guidance, 1962, 34 pp.

An excellent pocket atlas of Iraq, each colored map accompanied by a detailed commentary on the opposite page. Maps 1-6 are historical, showing the history of Iraq from the Sumerian to ʻAbbāsid times; maps 9-16 show the physical, economic, and administrative geography of modern Iraq; and maps 17-32 depict individual provinces. This atlas is a must for a foreign visitor to Iraq, but is unfortunately out of print. Let us hope the Iraqī government publishes a new edition (which may need a few minor revisions in the text).

Syria and Lebanon

2774 Khanzadian, Z., and L. Bertalot. Atlas de géographie économique de Syrie et du Liban: Géographie historique, géographie physique, richesses naturelles, commerce et industrie. Paris: Massis, 1926, 87 pp.

A very beautifully produced work, especially the reproductions of the historical maps of the country. For the purpose of economic geography, it is very much out of date. Politically Lebanon has become independent of Syria, and the Sancak of İskandarun (Alexandretta) has been annexed by Turkey. A knowledge of French is not necessary to use the maps, but the student will miss the long introduction glorifying the "mission civilisatrice" of France in the East.

Palestine

2775 Gilbert, Martin. The Arab-Israeli Conflict: Its History in Maps. London: Weidenfeld & Nicolson, 1974, 101 pp.

Excellent clear maps, but the captions clearly show the author's bias: Israel fought a "war of independence" and now conducts "security measures." The Palestinians practice "terrorism."

2776 Vilnay, Zev. The New Israel Atlas: Bible to Present Day. Translated by Moshe Aumann. Jerusalem: Israel Universities Press, 1968, 112 pp.

Beautiful cartography makes this work one of the best atlases of Palestine and thus it cannot be ignored, but the author's Zionist bias should be taken into consideration by the student. The work stresses the Jewish historical claims to the country while playing down any claims the Arabs might also have, although map 23 does show the Muslim holy places and maps 37 and 38 show localities still inhabited by native Palestinians, Muslims, Christians, and Druzes.

Spanish North Africa

2777 Atlas Histórico y Geográphico de Africa Española. Madrid: Dirección General de Marruecos y Colonias e Instituto de Estudios Africanos, 1955, 197 pp.
An atlas of the Spanish possessions in North Africa, northern Morocco, Ifni, and Spanish Sahara, of which only the last one is still under Spanish occupation. No knowledge of Spanish is necessary for use of the fine colored maps. The historical section shows maps of North Africa as a whole, and is not restricted to Spanish territories.

Turkey and the Ottoman Empire

2778 Khanzadian, Z. Atlas de géographie économique de Turquie: Géographie historique, géographie physique, richesses naturelles, industrie, commerce. Paris: Bertalot, 1924, 58 pp.
A very beautiful work, but out of date for economic conditions and for the post-1928 orthography of Turkish place names.

2779 Pitcher, D. An Historical Geography of the Ottoman Empire (see 345).

2780 Tanoğlu, Ali; Sĭrrĭ Erinç; and Erol Tümertekin. Türkiye Atlasĭ: Atlas of Turkey. Istanbul: Istanbul Universitesi, Coğrafya Enstitüsü, 1961, 100 pp.
Eighty-six large colored maps showing the physical, economic, and demographic geography of Turkey, with explanatory notes in Turkish and English. Map 66 gives the minorities according to the 1945 census: Greeks, Armenians, and Jews. Other minorities, like Kurds and Arabs, are ignored.

Iran

2781 Historical Atals of Iran, on the Occasion of the 2500th Anniversary of the Persian Empire. Teheran: University, 1350/1971.
A splendid work, with twenty-nine large colored maps illustrating the history of Iran from 5000 B.C. until the present. Captions on the maps in Persian and English. Historical commentary in Persian, English, and French. A most useful reference work for any student of Iranian history.

2782 Iran, Ministry of Interior. Iran White Revolution: Record of Achievements in Iran in Honour of the First Ten Years of the White Revolution. Teheran: 1973, 197 pp.
A beautifully produced economic atlas of Iran. All captions in Persian and English. "As the wave of inner happiness, joy and deep sense of gratitude spreads all over the country, this publication is issued to briefly portray the achievements of the past ten years" (preface).

CENTRAL ASIA

Soviet Central Asia

2783 Central Asian Research Centre in Association with St. Antony's College (Oxford) Soviet Affairs Study Group. Map of Soviet Central Asia and Kazakhstan. 2d rev. ed. London: 1962, 24 pp.
This is four maps in pocket (43 x 47 cm., scale: 1:3,750,000). "The Map in this folder . . . has been designed and drawn in four separate overlapping sheets for convenience in reproduction. The four Sheets can be accurately joined up to form the complete Map, but each Sheet is in itself, a complete map of the area it represents. . . . The Map . . . is based on a map . . . in the Soviet ATLAS MIRA of 1954. . . . The complete Map has now been brought up to date as far as possible for this present (1962) re-issue" (introduction). "The Gazetteer contains every name printed on the Map including those in the non-Soviet territories of Persia, Afghanistan, Pakistan, Kashmir and China" (introduction to Gazetteer). The only criticism of this excellent work is that all names are given exclusively in their Russian form (in Roman transliteration) and completely ignore the local Turkic or Tajik forms. After all, the constitution of the Soviet Union recognizes the local language as the first official language of each republic.

Chinese Central Asia (Sinkiang Uighur Autonomous Region)

2784 Hedin, Sven Anders. Sven Hedin Central Asian Atlas. Reports from the Scientific Expedition to the North-Western Provinces of China under the Leadership of Dr. Sven Hedin: The Sino-Swedish Expedition, 47, 1, Geography, 1. Stockholm: Statens Etnografiska Museum, 1966.
This contains folding colored maps in a box (size of sheets: 66 x 66 cm., map scale: 1:1,000,000), very detailed, colored physical maps of the different districts of the Sinkiang Uighur Autonomous Region of China, made from the surveys of the great Swedish explorer Sven Hedin. Place names given in both their Chinese and Uigur-Turkish forms. The publishers promise us a three-volume memoir on maps, which will be most welcome.

Afghanistan

2785 Hashimi, Elaine Frances. Afghanistan's Provinces, Cities, Villages, Secondary Schools, and Higher Level Institutions. Kabul: U.S. Agency for International Development Mission to Afghanistan, 1970, 151 pp.
Maps of all provinces of Afghanistan. Captions on the maps in Roman transliteration with diacritics to show the original Persian or Pashto spelling.

SOUTH ASIA (INDIAN SUBCONTINENT)

2786 Davies, Cuthbert Collin. An Historical Atlas of the Indian Peninsula. Bombay: Oxford, Indian Branch, 1949, 94 pp.
Forty-seven very clear maps, each accompanied by a historical commentary on the opposite page. Maps 11-24 deal with the Islamic period in Indian history (eleventh to seventeenth century).

Pakistan

2787 Khan, Farhat-Ullah, and Ali Arshad. West Pakistan in Maps and Statistics; or, Geographical and Economic Atlas of West Pakistan of Today and Tomorrow. Lahore: Feroz & Sons, 1948, 62 pp.
Most of this atlas deals with economics and is out of date now. The physical geography, however, would not have changed.

Bangladesh

2788 Chatterjee, Shiba Prasad. Bengal in Maps: A Geographical Analysis of Resource Distribution in West Bengal and Eastern Pakistan. Calcutta: Orient Longmans, 1949, 105 pp.
"Dr. S.P. Chatterjee's Bengal in Maps is something more than an Atlas of the conventional type: it provides a fairly complete socio-economic picture of contemporary Bengal. . . . His cartographical representations of Bengal depicting the topography, vital statistics and other social and economic data, are in many respects remarkable for their scientific accuracy and meticulous detail" (foreword by S.P. Mookerjee).

INDONESIA

2789 Atlas van Tropisch Nederland. Amsterdam: Koninklijk Nederlandsch Aardrijkskundig Genootschap in samenwerking met den Topografischen Dienst in Nederlandsch-Indië, 1938.
Thirty-one plates of maps (43 cm.). Explanations in Dutch, French, German and English. Since "Tropisch Nederland" has become independent Indonesia many place names have changed; for example, Batavia is now Jakarta.

AFRICA

2790 Boyd, Andrew, and Patrick van Rensburg. An Atlas of African Affairs. Maps by W.H. Bromage. Rev. ed. New York: Praeger, 1965, 133 pp.
Concentrates on political problems (in many cases still unsolved). Each of the sixty-five maps is accompanied by a long commentary. At least half of the maps deal with the Muslim countries of Africa.

2791 Fage, J.D. An Atlas of African History. Bungay, Suffolk, England: E. Arnold, 1958, 64 pp.
Covers North Africa in sixty-two maps. Gives full justice to the role played by the Arabs and Islam in the history of the other parts of the continent.

GAZETTEERS

2792 Lorimer, J.G. Gazetteer of the Persian Gulf, ʻOman, and Central Arabia (see 653).

2793 U.S. Board on Geographic Names. Gazetteers: Official Standard Names Approved by the United States Board on Geographic Names, Prepared in the Office of Geography, Department of the Interior. Washington: U.S. Government Printing Office, 195?, 196?.
Alphabetical lists of all geographical names in different countries in the Roman transliteration used on American maps (or in the original spelling if the local language, e.g., Turkish, is written in Roman characters). References on variant spellings. No information about the places listed except their longitude and latitude. Includes natural features (mountains, rivers, lakes) as well as towns and villages. The following titles deal with Islamic countries: Arabian Peninsula and Associated Islands and Waters, Egypt, Indonesia, Iran, Iraq, Jordan, Libya, Republic of Sudan, Tunisia, and Turkey.

BIBLIOGRAPHIES OF WORKS IN ENGLISH ON ISLAM AND THE MUSLIM COUNTRIES AND PEOPLES

ORIENTAL STUDIES IN GENERAL

2794 Adams, Charles Joseph. "Islam." In A Reader's Guide to the Great Religions. 2d rev. ed. New York: Free Press, 1977, pp. 407-66.
The chapter on Islam (as well as those on other religions by other scholars) is a history of the literature on the subject rather than a bibliography in the strict sense of the term. This makes the work more stimulating to read, although perhaps a little less handy for reference. The compilers have tried to restrict themselves to works in English with the exception of particularly important works in French and German.

2795 Apor, Eve, and Hilda Ecsedy, comps. Hungarian Publications on Asia and Africa, 1950-1962: A Selected Bibliography. Library of the Hungarian Academy of Sciences, East-West Committee of the Hungarian National Commission for UNESCO. Budapest: Akadémiai Kiadó, 1963, 106 pp.
Lists 774 books and periodical articles by Hungarian authors in Hungarian and other languages, including English. All Hungarian titles are translated into English. Of special interest to Islamic studies are numbers 6 to 169 (Near and Middle East), 171 to 222 (India), 277 to 302 (Asian part of the Soviet Union), 563 to 717 (European-Asian relations, mostly about Ottoman Turkish influences on Europe), and 718 to 774 (Africa).

2796 Bibliography of Philosophy. International Institute of Philosophy. Paris: 1937-.
This periodical lists books published in many languages on philosophy. It is particularly useful to the student of Islam because it contains explanatory annotations of books published in Western languages and Arabic that pertain to Islamic theological and philosophical thought. Contains detailed indexes of subjects and authors.

2797 Birnbaum, Eleazer. Books on Asia from the Near East to the Far East (see 1).

2798 De Bary, William Theodore, and Ainslie T. Embree, eds. A Guide to Oriental Classics. New York: Columbia University Press, 1964, 199 pp.
Lists English translations and critical studies of classical Oriental literatures. Contains classified arrangements. Of interest for Islamic studies are section 1 "Classics of the Islamic Tradition" (Maan Z. Madina, pp. 9-35), and "The Poetry of Muhammad Iqbal" (pp. 105-107), a leading modern Indo-Pakistani Muslim poet.

2799 Dobson, William Arthur Charles Harvey. The Contribution of Canadian Universities to an Understanding of Asia and Africa: A Bibliographical Directory of Scholars. 2d ed., rev. & enl. Ottawa: Canadian National Commission for UNESCO, 1967, 160 pp.
A bibliography, arranged alphabetically by author, of 201 staff members of Canadian universities who have published books, articles, or book reviews about Asia and Africa. No annotations.

2800 Fifty Years of Soviet Oriental Studies (Brief Reviews) (1917-1967). Moscow: USSR Academy of Sciences, Institute of the Peoples of Asia: "Nauka," 1968. 27 pamphlets in box.
Bibliographic essays showing the important work produced by Soviet Orientalists. Of special interest to Islamic studies are the following pamphets: Indology: History, Economy and Culture (L.P. Alayev and A.K. Vapha), Central Asia and Kazakhstan (I.S. Braginsky, L.B. Landa, and N.A. Khalfin), The History, Economy and Geography of Turkey (B. Danzig), Soviet Orientology and Studies in the History of Colonialism (N.A. Khalfin), which has much about colonialism in Muslim countries, Turkic Philology (A.N. Kanonov), Archeological Study of Soviet Central Asia (V.M. Masson), Old Iranian Philology and Iranian Linguistics (I.M. Oransky), History of Iranian Studies (I.P. Petrushevsky), The Languages of Southeast Asia, Including Indonesian and Related Languages (Yu. Ya. Plam and Yu. H. Sirk), Afghan Studies (V.A. Romodin), Arabic Studies (Philology) (G. Sh. Sharbatov), History and Economy of the Arab Countries (I.M. Smilyanskaya), Semitics (K. Tsereteli), Study of the History and Economy of the Countries of Southeast Asia, Including Malaysia and Indonesia (V.A. Turin), and Indian Philology (G. Zograf).

2801 International Bibliography of the History of Religions. Leiden: E.J. Brill, 1954. Supplements to date.
Lists books and articles on the various branches of the history of religions, covering materials published from shortly before 1950 to the present. There is an extensive listing of materials on Islam under the following headings: "Pre-Islamic Arabia," "Scriptures," "Theology and Philosophy," "Mysticism," and "History and General." Reviews of books are also listed. Includes index.

2802 Pearson, James Douglas. Oriental and Asian Bibliography: An Introduction, with Some Reference to Africa. London: C. Lockwood, 1966, 261 pp.
More than a bibliography in the strict sense of the term, but describes all the problems faced by the Orientalist librarian, for whom it is an indispensable tool.

2803 The Philosophers Index: An International Index to Philosophical Periodicals. Philosophical Documentation Center. Bowling Green, Ohio, 1967-.
This bibliographical periodical includes subject and author indexes of philosophical works published in Western language periodicals. It is relevant to Islamic studies because it contains listings of books and articles, with brief abstracts, in their respective languages, on Islamic theological and philosophical thought. It is very much up to date.

2804 Quan, L. King. Introduction to Asia: A Selective Guide to Background Reading. Washington: Library of Congress, Reference Department, 1955, 214 pp.
Has 811 entries and long annotations almost amounting to book reviews. Of special interest to Islamic studies are the sections on Pakistan (pp. 112-16), the Near and Middle East (pp. 123-67), Indonesia (pp. 185-89), and Malaya (pp. 189-93).

2805 "Soviet Orientology between the XXV and XXVI Congresses of Orientalists." Multiplicated copy. Moscow, 1963, 87 pp.
A bibliographic essay, classified by subjects; useful in learning about extensive studies carried out by Soviet Orientalists. All titles are given in the original Russian and translated into English. Its major drawback is the lack of an index or table of contents.

Maps and Atlases

2806 Gosling, L.A. Peter. Maps, Atlases and Gazetteers for Asian Studies: A Critical Guide. Foreign Area Materials Center Occasional Publication, no. 2. New York: University of the State of New York, 1965, 27 pp.
Includes the Middle East.

Periodicals

2807 Lewicki, Marian et al. "Katalog Czasopism i Wydawnictw Ciągłych Orjentalistycznych Znajdujących się w Polsce" [A catalog of Orientalist periodicals and serial publications that can be found in Poland]. Multiplicated copy. Lwów, 1933, 81 pp.
An outdated but still useful list of 420 Orientalist journals in all languages, including English. The fact that the catalog lists holdings in Poland is of course irrelevant for the North American student (few of them would have survived World War II, anyway); the list is useful by itself. Most of the journals probably can be found in American libraries.

2808 Pélissier, Roger, and Danielle Le Nan. 2000 revues d'Asie. Edited by Serge Elisseeff. Paris: Bibliothèque nationale, 1964, 474 pp.
A list with bibliographical details, but without critical annotations, of 2,263 periodicals from Asia, arranged by country, and including Muslim countries. These are periodicals in all languages, including English.

ISLAM/MIDDLE EAST/ARAB WORLD

General Bibliographies

2809 American Friends of the Middle East. Catalogue: Specialized Lending Library on the Middle East. Washington: AFME, 1961, 82 pp. Supplement, 1963.
Classified by subject, with short annotations but no index.

2810 American University of Beirut. A Post War Bibliography of the Near Eastern Mandates: A Preliminary Survey of Publications on the Social Sciences Dealing with Iraq, Palestine, and Trans-Jordan and the Syrian States from Nov. 11, 1918 to Dec. 31, 1929. English fascicle edited by Basim A. Faris. Social Science Series, 1. Beirut: American Press, 1932, 248 pp.
Includes 4,699 entries of books and periodical articles arranged alphabetically by author with a limited subject index. No annotations.

2811 Atiyeh, George Nicholas. The Contemporary Middle East, 1948-1973: A Selective and Annotated Bibliography. Boston: G.K. Hall, 1975, 664 pp.
Has 6,491 entries including monographs and journal articles, divided into nine sections: the Middle East, the Arab-Israeli conflict, the Arab countries, the Arabian peninsula, the Fertile Crescent, the Nile Valley, the Maghreb, Turkey, and Iran. Contains full bibliographical data and detailed annotations; indexed by subject and author.

2812 Binder, Leonard, ed. The Study of the Middle East: Research and Scholarship in the Humanities and the Social Sciences: A Project of the Research and Training Committee of the Middle East Studies Association. New York: Wiley, 1976, 648 pp.
Contents: "Area Studies: A Critical Reassessment" (L. Binder), "Islamic Religious Tradition" (C.J. Adams), "History" (A. Hourani), "Anthropology" (R.T. Antoun, with D.M. Hart and C.L. Redman), "Islamic Art and Archaeology" (O. Grabar), "Political Science" (I.W. Zartman), "Philosophy" (S.H. Nasr), "Linguistics" (G.L. Windfuhr), "Literature: (Arabic)" (R. Allen, L. Hanaway, and W. Andrews), "Sociology" (G. Sabagh), and "Economics" (J. Simmons). Not strictly a bibliography, but a collection of bibliographic surveys of literature on each of the above subjects, with a bibliography at the end of each chapter. Much more readable than a straight bibliography.

2813 Bolton, A.R. Soviet Middle East Studies: An Analysis and Bibliography (see 2).

2814 Burke, Jean T. An Annotated Bibliography of Books and Periodicals in English Dealing with Human Relations in the Arab States of the Middle East, with Special Emphasis on Modern Times. Beirut: American University, 1956, 117 pp.
Contains 1,453 entries, classified by subject, with an author index.

2815 Cairo, National Library. Bibliographical Lists of the Arab World. Vol. 1, Algeria (2d ed.), 1963, 134 pp. Vol. 2, Palestine and Jordan (2d ed.), 1964, 482 pp. Vol. 3, Syria. Vol. 4, Lebanon. Vol. 5, Iraq (2d ed.), 1964, 259 pp. Vol. 6, Sudan, 1961, 108 pp. Vol. 7, Al Maghrib (Morocco), 1961, 102 pp. Vol. 8, Tunisia. Vol. 9, Libya, 1961, 51 pp. Vol. 10, Arabian Peninsula, 1963, 179 pp. Cairo: Dar al-Kutab al-Misniyah, 1961-1964.
Each volume is divided into an Arabic and a European language section, with the arrangement differing in different volumes. No annotations. (Vols. 3, 4, and 8 unverified.)

2816 Center for the Study of the Modern Arab World. Arab Culture and Society in Change (see 540).

2817 Erian, Tahany, trans. References Dealing with the Arab World: A Selected and Annotated List. New York: Organization of Arab Students in the U.S.A. and Canada, 1966, 32 pp.
Includes 352 entries, not all of which are annotated.

2818 Ettinghausen, R. A Selected and Annotated Bibliography of Books and Periodicals in Western Languages Dealing with the Near and Middle East, with Special Emphasis on Medieval and Modern Times (see 3).

2819 Heyworth-Dunne, Gamal-Eddine. A Basic Bibliography on Islam. Muslim World Series, no. 4. Cairo: Anglo-Egyptian Bookshop, n.d., 52 pp.
Lists 384 books plus an additional 27 works by the compiler, in alphabetical order by author. Includes a subject index and annotations. Covers the period A.D. 500-1800.

2820 Hopwood, Derek, and Diana Grimwood-Jones. Middle East and Islam: A Bibliographic Introduction (see 4).

2821 Howard, Harry Nicholas. The Middle East: A Selected Bibliography of Recent Works, 1960-1969. 3d printing. Washington: Middle East Institute, 1972, 51 pp. Supplements, 1972-1973.

A classified arrangement with short annotations, but no index.

2822 Howard, Harry N. et al. Middle East and North Africa: A Bibliography for Undergraduate Libraries (see 5).

Contains 1,192 entries, in two sections: classified and alphabetical by author. No annotations.

2823 Ibn al-Nadīm. The Fihrist of al-Nadīm: A Tenth Century Survey of Muslim Culture (see 235).

2824 Jameelah, Maryam, comp. A Select Bibliography of Islamic Books in English. Karachi: Criterion, 1971, 35 pp. Reprint of The Criterion 6, nos. 4-5.

Entries are classified by subject, with author and title indexes. Very valuable annotations. The compiler, an American convert from Judaism to Islam, is very critical of non-Muslim Western Orientalists and of Muslim "modernists."

2825 Kudsi-Zadeh, A. Albert. Sayyid Jamāl al-Dīn al-Afghānī: An Annotated Bibliography (see 509).

2826 Moyer, Kenyon E., comp. From Iran to Morocco, from Turkey to the Sudan: A Selected and Annotated Bibliography of North Africa and the Near and Middle East. New York: Missionary Research Library, 1957, 51 pp.

Classification is by country, and there is no index. The bibliography places some emphasis on Protestant missionary travel literature.

2827 Paret, Rudi. The Study of Arabic and Islam at German Universities: German Orientalists since Theodor Noldeke. Wiesbaden: F. Steiner, 1968, 71 pp.

Informative sketch of leading figures and their contributions. A history of Arabic and Islamic studies in Germany in recent times. Moving description of the difficulties and sufferings of the German Orientalists under the Nazi regime (pp. 45-56). Full names and dates of leading scholars with a critical appraisal of their work. All titles given in English translation only, without the German original. Date, but no place of publication. No indication whether a particular work has been translated into English or any other language. No index.

2828 Penzer, Norman Mosley. An Annotated Bibliography of Sir Richard Francis Burton, K.C.M.G. London: A.M. Philpot, 1923, 351 pp.

A complete bibliography of the writings of one of the greatest of British Orientalists, interested mainly in Islam and the Middle East. Illustrated.

2829 Qubain, Fahim Issa. Inside the Arab Mind: A Bibliographic Survey of Literature in Arabic on Arab Nationalism and Unity, with an Annotated List of English-Language Books and Articles. Arlington, Va.: Middle East Research Associates, 1960, 100 pp.

"This bibliography is divided into two parts: Part I consists of 92 Arabic titles. Part II, a supplement, consists of 145 English titles. The Arabic listings are all books and pamphlets, whereas most of the English titles are articles. The English titles are only briefly annotated. . . . The Arabic material is extensively annotated" (preface).

2830 Sauvaget, J. Introduction to the History of the Muslim East: A Bibliographical Guide (see 7).

Indispensable as an introduction to the sources for Islamic history and secondary scholarship (published before 1964) based upon them.

2831 Sharabi, Hisham Bashir. A Handbook on the Contemporary Middle East: Sectional Introductions with Annotated Bibliographies. Washington: Georgetown University, 1956, 113 pp.

As a handbook, this is somewhat out of date regarding political and economic information, but the bibliographies are still useful. With maps.

2832 Tamim, Suha. A Bibliography of A.U.B. Faculty Publications, 1866-1966. Beirut: American University, 1967, 401 pp.

A complete list of publications (books and articles) by former and present professors of the American University of Beirut, classified by department with an alphabetical list of authors under each department. Middle Eastern and Islamic studies form a large proportion of the publications. There is an index of authors. The entries have no annotations.

2833 U.S. National Archives. Materials in the National Archives Relating to the Middle East (see 499).

2834 Zuwiyya, Jalal. The Near East (South-West Asia and North Africa): A Bibliographic Study. Metuchen, N.J.: Scarecrow, 1973, 392 pp.

There are 3,616 titles arranged by subject, with indexes of authors and titles. Works in European languages and translations from Oriental languages are included. Although there are no annotations, this bibliography is most useful because it gives the full names of most authors, their date of birth, and, if applicable, date of death.

Special Topics

Bibliography of Bibliographies

2835 Geddes, Charles L., ed. American Institute of Islamic Studies Bibliographic Series. Vol. 1, Islam in Paperback, 1969, 58 pp. Vol. 2, An Analytical Guide to the Bibliographies on Modern Egypt and the Sudan, 1972, 78 pp. Vol. 3, An Analytical Guide to the

Bibliographies on Islam, Muhammad, and the Qur'ān, 1973, 102 pp. Vol. 4, An Analytical Guide to the Bibliographies on the Arabian Peninsula, 1974, 50 pp. Vol. 5, Books in English on Islam, Muhammad, and the Qur'ān: A Selected and Annotated Bibliography, 1975, 68 pp. Vol. 6, Islam in Paperback (2d rev. ed.), 1975. Vol. 7, The Arab-Israeli Dispute: An Annotated Bibliography of Bibliographies, 1973. Vol. 8, An Analytical Guide to the Bibliographies on the Arab Fertile Crescent (with a Section on the Arab-Israeli Conflict), 1975, 131 pp. Denver: American Institute of Islamic Studies.

Five of the above volumes (vols. 2, 3, 4, 7, and 8) are bibliographies of bibliographies, perhaps the best available on Islam and the Middle East. Full bibliographic details and long annotations are given under each entry. Students on a limited budget will find Islam in Paperback very useful. The first edition (vol. 1) is out of date, but the second edition (vol. 6) should serve for several years.

Philosophy and Science

2836 Menasce, Pierre Jean. Arabische Philosophie. Bibliographische Einführungen in das Studium der Philosophie, no. 6. Bern: A. Francke, 1948, 49 pp.

A classified arrangement of works in West European languages, including English. With index, but no annotations.

2837 Nasr, S.H., and W.C. Chittick. An Annotated Bibliography of Islamic Science. Vol. 1. Tehran: Imperial Iranian Academy of Philosophy, 1975, 432 pp.

The first of five projected volumes on Islamic science, understood here to embrace the traditional intellectual sciences of Islam. This volume contains 2,770 entries in many Western languages on bibliographies, manuscript collections, reference works, general background (historical, cultural, social, scientific, and intellectual), Islamic education, and biographical and bibliographical studies of Muslim scientists. Most of the entries are not annotated.

2838 Rescher, Nicholas. Al-Farabi: An Annotated Bibliography. Pittsburgh: University of Pittsburgh Press, 1962, 54 pp. Al-Kindi: An Annotated Bibliography. Pittsburgh: University of Pittsburgh Press, 1964, 55 pp.

These are bibliographies of two of the most important Muslim philosophers. Useful for Islamic philosophy in general.

Art and Architecture (See also 2282)

2839 Mayer, Leo Ary, ed. Annual Bibliography of Islamic Art and Archeology, India Excepted. Vol. 1, 1935. Vol. 2, 1936. Vol. 3, 1937. Jerusalem: Divan, 1937-1939.

Each volume is arranged by subject, with an author index, and lists books and periodical articles, with very few annotations.

Numismatics

2840 Eldem, Halil Ethem. Essai d'une bibliographie pour la numismatique musulmane. Ankara: Kitap Yazanlar Kooperatifi, 1933, 64 pp.

Lists 508 titles, 59 in Turkish, the rest in European languages, without annotations.

2841 Mayer, Leo Ary. Bibliography of Moslem Numismatics, India Excepted. 2d enl. ed. Oriental Translation Fund, 35. London: Royal Asiatic Society, 1954, 283 pp.

Includes 2,092 entries in alphabetical order by author, with a subject index. There are very few annotations.

The Crusades

2842 Atiya, A.S. The Crusades: Historiography and Bibliography (see 263).

2843 Harvard University, Widener Library. Widener Library Shelflist: Crusades. Cambridge, Mass.: Harvard University, 1965, 38 pp.

Includes classification schedule, classified listing by call number, alphabetical listing by author or title, and chronological listing. No annotations.

Medicine

2844 Ebied, Rifaat Y. Bibliography of Mediaeval Arabic and Jewish Medicine and Allied Sciences. London: Wellcome Institute of the History of Medicine, 1971, 150 pp.

Contains 1,972 entries, including books and periodical articles. Section 1 lists general works about Arabic and Jewish medicine in one alphabetical author sequence. Section 2 lists works by and about individual Arab and Jewish physicians in chronological order. There are indexes of authors and subjects.

2845 Hamarneh, Sami. Bibliography on Medicine and Pharmacy in Medieval Islam. Veroeffentlichungen der Internationalen Gesellschaft fuer Geschichte der Pharmazie e.v., neue folge, nr. 25. Stuttgart: Wissenschaftliche Verlagsgesellschaft, 1964, 204 pp.

Much wider in scope than its title would suggest, it contains many books about Arab and Islamic civilization in general, with long detailed annotations. Five plates.

Travel Literature

2846 Bevis, Richard W. Bibliotheca Cisorientalia: An Annotated Checklist of Early English Travel Books on the Near and Middle East. Boston: G.K. Hall, 1973, 315 pp.

"A reasonably complete checklist of books reporting at first hand on the Mideast of the Moslem conquest, published in English before 1915" (introduction). Includes translations from European and Oriental languages into English (pp. 235-67).

2847 Weber, Shirley Howard. Voyages and Travels in Greece, the Near East and Adjacent Regions Made Previous to the Year 1801. Catalogues of the Gennadius Library, no. 2. Athens: American School of Classical Studies, 1953, 208 pp. Voyages and Travels in the Near East Made during the XIX Century. Catalogues of the Gennadius Library, no. 1. Athens: American School of Classical Studies, 1952, 252 pp.

These books list 1,206 and 860 entries, respectively, in European languages only. Arranged in chronological order with author and subject indexes at the end of each volume, with some annotations.

Anthropology

2848 Field, Henry. Bibliography on Southwestern Asia. Vol. 1, 1940-1952. Vol. 2, 1953-1954. Vol. 3, 1955. Vol. 4, 1956. Vol. 5, 1957. Vol. 6, 1958. Vol. 7, 1959. Coral Gables, Fla.: University of Miami Press, 1953-1962.

Each volume is divided into two sections: anthropogeography and natural history. Works (books and articles) are listed alphabetically by author within each section, without annotations.

2849 _____. Subject Index to Bibliographies on Southwestern Asia: VI-VII. Vol. 1, Anthropogeography, by Edith M. Laird. Vol. 2, Zoology, by B.J. Clifton. Vol. 3, Botany, by R.C. Foster. Coral Gables, Fla.: University of Miami Press, 1964.

Subject index to the last two volumes of Field (see 2848).

Linguistics

2850 Hospers, J.H., ed. A Basic Bibliography for the Study of the Semitic Languages. Vol. 2, Arabic. Leiden: Brill, 1974, 108 pp.

The scope of this bibliography is wider than its title suggests and includes not only works on Arabic linguistics but studies of the Islamic religion and Arabic literature and cultural history. Classified by subject, with no annotations or index. Volume 1 (1973) deals with the other Semitic languages and is useful for works on the pre-Islamic background of the Middle East.

2851 Sebeok, Thomas A., ed. Linguistics in South West Asia and North Africa. Current Trends in Linguistics, no. 6. The Hague: Mouton, 1970, 802 pp.

A most detailed survey of all the linguistic studies of Arabic, Persian, Turkish, and other languages of the area. Perhaps too specialized for the non-Orientalist student, but worth consulting for literature on the linguistic problems of the Middle East.

Periodicals

2852 Ali, Muzaffar. Periodica Islamica: A Check-List of Serials Available at McGill Islamics Library. Montreal: McGill University, Institute of Islamic Studies, 1973, 28 pp.

An alphabetical list of all periodicals in the McGill Islamics Library, without annotations. Very useful as a list of Orientalist journals.

2853 Ljunggren, Florence, and M. Hamdy, eds. Annotated Guide to Journals Dealing with the Middle East and North Africa (see 545).

2854 Ljunggren, Florence, ed. Arab World Index: An International Guide to Periodical Literature (see 546).

Periodical Articles

2855 Dotan, Uri, comp. A Bibliography of Articles on the Middle East, 1959-1967. Edited by Avigdor Levy. Shiloah Center Teaching and Research Aids, no. 2. Tel Aviv: University, Shiloah Center for Middle Eastern and African Studies, 1970, 227 pp.

Includes 2,902 entries classified by subject. There is an author index, but there are no annotations.

2856 Pearson, J.D. Index Islamicus, 1906-1955: A Catalogue of Articles on Islamic Subjects in Periodicals and Other Collective Publications (see 6).

Women in Islam

2857 Gulick, John, and Margaret Gulick. Annotated Bibliography of Sources Concerned with Women in the Modern Muslim Middle East. Princeton Near East Paper, no. 17. Princeton, N.J.: Princeton University Press, 1974, 26 pp.

Approximately two hundred annotated entries, mostly in English on contemporary works "that are directly relevant to the widespread image of the Middle East as a culture area where the status of women is degraded and the segregation of the sexes is carried to extremes" (introduction). Without index.

2858 Qazzaz, Ayad al-. Women in the Middle East and North Africa: An Annotated Bibliography. Middle East Monographs, no. 2. Austin: Center for Middle East Studies, 1977, 178 pp.

Alphabetically arranged books and articles in English, with lengthy annotations, mainly on position of women in Islam. The selection covers works by both Western and Muslim writers. Subject index.

2859 Raccagni, Michelle. The Modern Arab Woman: A Bibliography. Metuchen, N.J., and London: Scarecrow Press, 1978, 262 pp.

A listing of "all books, articles, reports and dissertations in Western languages, principally English and French, as well as Arabic" (introduction), covering the entire Arab World to 1976. Subject and author index.

Jesus in Islam

2860 Wismer, Don. The Islamic Jesus: An Annotated Bibliography of Sources in English and French. New York and London: Garland Publishing, 1977, 305 pp.

Alphabetical, annotated listing of 726 entries, some of which include lengthy quotations from the sources cited.

INDIVIDUAL COUNTRIES AND REGIONS

Arab Countries

Arabian Peninsula

2861 American Geographical Society. Bibliography of the Arabian Peninsula (see 622).

2862 Heyworth-Dunne, Gamal-Eddine. Bibliography and Reading Guide to Arabia. Cairo: Renaissance Bookshop, 1952, 16 pp.
Contains 146 entries in alphabetical order by author with short annotations. Previously published by the U.N. Food and Agricultural Organization in its Briefing Papers 19 (1951), (FAO/51/9/2062).

2863 Macro, Eric. Bibliography of the Arabian Peninsula (see 634).
Lists 2,380 books and articles in Western and Oriental languages in alphabetical order by author without annotations.

2864 United States of America, Library of Congress, Division of Orientalia, Near East Section. The Arabian Peninsula: A Selected, Annotated List of Books and Articles in English. New York: Greenwood Press, 1969. Orig. pub. in 1951.
Has 719 entries arranged by subject with an author index. Some items are annotated.

Saudi Arabia

2865 Stevens, J.H., and R. King. A Bibliography of Saudi Arabia. Durham, N.C.: Durham University, Centre for Middle Eastern and Islamic Studies, 1973, 81 pp.
Its 1,079 entries include books and articles published between 1900 and 1970, classified by subject without index or annotations.

Yemen

2866 Macro, Eric. Bibliography on Yemen (see 662).

Oman

2867 King, R., and J.H. Stevens. A Bibliography of Oman, 1900-1970. Durham, N.C.: Durham University, Centre for Middle Eastern and Islamic Studies, 1973, 141 pp.
Entries classified by subject without index or annotations.

Syria, Lebanon, and Jordan

2868 Patai, Raphael. Jordan, Lebanon and Syria: An Annotated Bibliography. Behavior Science Bibliographies. New Haven, Conn.: Human Relations Area Files Press, 1957, 289 pp.
Contains 1,605 entries in classified arrangement without index. Useful annotations.

Palestine

2869 Atiyeh, George Nicholas. Jerusalem Past and Present: An Annotated Bibliography in English. New York: Americans for Middle East Understanding (1975), unpaginated.
Jerusalem is the third holy city of Islam (after Mecca and Madīnah). This bibliography lists many works about Palestine in general and is not strictly confined to the city of Jerusalem. Includes Zionist works, usually described in the annotations as "from an Israeli point of view." Divided into eight sections, with a total of 101 entries. No index.

2870 Hussaini, Hatem I. The Palestine Problem: An Annotated Bibliography, 1967-1974. Washington: Arab Information Center, 1974, 81 pp. Reprint. The Arab Israeli Conflict: An Annotated Bibliography. Bibliography series, no. 1. Detroit: Association of Arab-American University Graduates, 1975.
"This annotated bibliography on the Palestine problem attempts to provide the American reader with Arab and non-Zionist perspectives. . . . Its purpose is to familiarize Western readers with the most definitive Arab and anti-Zionist materials, which have not been widely advertised and distributed in the United States. . . . Included in this bibliography are publications from a variety of sources: Palestinian Arabs, Western scholars, journalists and non-Zionist Jews, as well as Israelis" (introduction). Classified by subject. Long annotations. No index.

2871 Khalidi, Walid, ed. Palestine and the Arab-Israeli Conflict: An Annotated Bibliography. Bibliography Series, no. 1. Beirut: Institute for Palestine Studies, 1974, 732 pp.
"The book is divided into nine major parts. . . . It includes entries from six languages: Arabic, English, Hebrew, French, German, and Russian. The focus of this bibliography is on Palestine as a political problem since the problem began to take shape with the rise of Zionism in the latter part of the nineteenth century. But it also includes sources of older historical subjects that the researcher may require for background material" (publisher's prospectus).

2872 Reich, Bernard. Israel in Paperback. Bibliographic Series, no. 2. New York: Middle East Studies Association of North America, 1971, 26 pp.
Very selective. Nevertheless, it includes some works critical of Zionism as well as some publications of the Institute of Palestine Studies in Beirut. Annotations always honestly express the substance of the book, whatever the position of the compiler on the Palestine controversy. Classification is by subject. No index. Addresses of publishers are given. Sections of interest include: Israel and the Arabs (pp. 15-22), the Suez-Sinai crisis of 1956 (pp. 22-23), the June (six-day) war of 1967 (pp. 24-26).

2873 Shulman, Joseph Frank. American and British Doctoral Dissertations on Israel and Palestine in Modern Times. Ann Arbor, Mich.: Xerox University Microfilms, 1973, 25 pp.
Lists 530 entries classified by subject with full bibliographic details and occasional short annotations. There is an index of authors and universities. Sections of interest are: Palestine before 1948 (nos. 1-54), the Palestinian Arabs and minority groups (nos. 366-417), and the Arab-Israeli conflict (nos. 418-530).

Egypt

2874 Coult, Lyman H., Jr., and Karim Durzi. An Annotated Research Bibliography of Studies in Arabic, English, and French on the Fellah of the Egyptian Nile, 1798-1955. Coral Gables, Fla.: University of Miami Press, 1958, 144 pp.
Classified listing of 831 books and articles, with long detailed annotations. Author and subject indexes. Includes two maps.

2875 Heyworth-Dunne, Gamal-Eddine. Select Bibliography on Modern Egypt. Muslim World Series, no. 2. Cairo: Renaissance Bookshop, 1952, 41 pp.
Contains 167 entries in alphabetical order by author. Some annotations are long enough to be considered book reviews.

2876 Ibrahim-Hilmy, Prince of Egypt. The Literature of Egypt and the Sudan from the Earliest Times to the Year 1885 Inclusive: A Bibliography Comprising Printed Books, Periodical Writings, and Papers of Learned Societies, Maps and Charts, Ancient Papyri, Manuscripts, Drawings, etc. 2 vols. Liechtenstein: Kraus Reprint, 1966. Orig. pub.: London: Trubner, 1886-1887.
Attempts to list all works about Egypt in Western languages from the invention of printing to the time of compilation. Alphabetical by author. No annotations. Compiled by the son of the Khedive Ismāʿīl during his exile in Europe.

2877 Lorin, Henri, ed. Bibliographie géographique de l'Egypte. Vol. 1, Géographie physique et géographie humaine, by Henriette Agrel et al., 1928, 472 pp. Vol. 2, Géographie historique, by Henri Munier, 1929, 271 pp. Cairo: Impr. de l'Institut français d'archéologie orientale pour la Société royale de géographie d'Egypte.
The volumes have 6,158 and 2,683 entries, respectively. Books and periodical articles in Western languages, including many in English, are classified by subject. Author index in each volume. No annotations.

2878 Maple, H.L. "A Bibliography of Egypt, Consisting of Works Printed Before A.D. 1801." Multiplicated copy. Pietermaritzburg, 1962, 84.
About 750 entries in alphabetical order by author are listed without annotations.

2879 Pratt, Ida A. Modern Egypt: A List of References to Material in the New York Public Library. Edited by Richard Gottheil. New York: Kraus Reprint, 1969, 320 pp. Orig. pub.: New York: New York Public Library, 1929.
Entries are classified by subject, with an author index. No annotations.

2880 Zaki, Abdel Rahman. A Bibliography of the Literature of the City of Cairo. Cairo: Société de géographie d'Egypte, 1964, 40 pp.
Divided into two sections: Arabic and European languages. Books and periodical articles are included, arranged by subject. No annotations.

Sudan

2881 Hill, R.L. A Bibliography of the Anglo-Egyptian Sudan (see 796).

2882 Jones, Ruth. North-East Africa: General, Ethnography/Sociology, Linguistics. Africa Bibliography Series, vol. 3. London: International African Institute, 1959, 51 pp.
Covers the following countries: Sudan, Ethiopia, Eritrea, and Somalia. Classified by region. Ethnic and linguistic index, author index. No annotations.

2883 Nasri, Abdul Rahman el-. A Bibliography of the Sudan (see 802).

North Africa

2884 Conover, Helen F. North and Northeast Africa: A Selected, Annotated List of Writings (see 61).

2885 Playfair, Robert Lambert. The Bibliography of the Barbary States. Vol. 1, Tripoli and the Cyrenaica. Vol. 2, A Bibliography of Algeria to 1887. Vol. 3, A Bibliography of Morocco from the Earliest Times to the End of 1891. Royal Geographical Society Supplementary Papers. London: Royal Geographical Society, 1889-1893.
These volumes contain 579, 4,745, and 2,243 entries, respectively. Chronological arrangement by date of publication with author and subject indexes. The more interesting works are annotated. There are plans to republish in this series A. Graham and H.S. Ashbee's bibliography on Tunisia (see 2888).

Libya

2886 Hill, Roy Wells. A Bibliography of Libya. Durham, N.C.: Durham University, Dept. of Geography, 1959, 100 pp.
Entries are classified by subject, without index or annotations.

2887 Schluter, Hans. Index Libycus: Bibliography of Libya, 1957-1969, with Supplementary Material, 1915-1956. Boston: G.K. Hall, 1972, 305 pp.
Contains 4,418 entries, classified by subject, with an author index. No annotations.

Tunisia

2888 Graham, Alexander, and H.S. Ashbee. Travels in Tunisia. London: Dulau, 1887, 287 pp.
The bibliography covers pages 211-87. Lists entries in alphabetical order by author with some annotations.

Turkey

2889 Beeley, Brian W. Rural Turkey: A Bibliographic Interpretation. Ankara: Hacettepe University, Institute of Population Studies, 1969, 120 pp.
Books and periodical articles about the sociology of Turkey in different languages, including English. No annotations. Has an interesting introduction.

2890 Birge, J.K. A Guide to Turkish Area Studies (see 79).

2891 Fuller, Grace Hadley. "Turkey: A Selected List of References." Multiplicated copy. Washington: Library of Congress, General Reference and Bibliography Division, 1944, 114 pp.
Has 916 entries of works in European languages (mostly English). No annotations.

2892 Jamesson, J.R. von Reinhold. A Selected and Annotated Bibliography of Basic Books and Monographs in English on Modern Turkey. Rev. ed. Ankara: Türk-Amerikan Eğitim Derneği, 1959, 9 pp.
Short, but very useful for its annotations.

2893 Kornrumpf, Hans-Jürgen. Osmanische Bibliographie, mit besonderer Berücksichtigung der Türkei in Europa. Handbuch der Orientalistik, 1, Abt.: Ergänzungsband, nr. 8. Leiden: Brill, 1973, 1378 pp.
A very extensive bibliography of Ottoman history, with special emphasis on the Balkans. Books and articles in all languages are included with titles in East European and Oriental languages translated into German. There are two sections, one arranged by author and the other by subject. Neither section has annotations.

2894 Michoff, Nicolas Vasilev. Bibliographie des articles de périodiques allemands, anglais, français, et italiens sur la Turquie et la Bulgarie. Sofia: Académie bulgare des sciences, 1938, 686 pp.
"Lists 10,044 articles from 1715-1891, arranged by years" (J.K. Birge, A Guide to Turkish Area Studies [see 79], p. 167). No annotations.

2895 Moran, Berna. Türklerle İlgili İngilizce Yayĭnlar Bibliyographyasi, 15, Yüzyĭldan 18. Yüzyĭla kadar [Bibliography of English publications dealing with the Turks, from the fifteenth century till the eighteenth century]. Istanbul: İstanbul Üniversitesi, Edebiyat Fakültesi, 1964, 176 pp.
Three hundred two English titles in chronological order of publication with full bibliographic description, including location, mostly in British and American libraries. The annotations are in Turkish, but even without them the book is very useful, especially since book titles tended to be very long and descriptive in those days. Included are works about the Middle East not necessarily exclusively about the Turks.

2896 Suzuki, Peter T. Social Change in Turkey since 1950: A Bibliography of 866 Publications. College Park: University of Maryland, European Division, 1969, 108 pp.
"The majority of entries . . . are Western language publications. . . . All non-English titles have been translated into English. Only general works of more than routine interest have been listed. . . . Finally, since it was felt that in most cases the title speaks for itself, annotations have not been provided" (preface).

2897 Tamkoc, Metin. A Bibliography on the Foreign Relations of the Republic of Turkey, 1919-1967, and Brief Biographies of Turkish Statesmen. Ankara: Middle East Technical University, Faculty of Administrative Sciences, 1968, 248 pp.
No annotations, but all Turkish titles translated into English.

2898 U.S. of America, Bureau of the Census. Bibliography of Social Science Periodicals and Monograph Series: Turkey, 1950-1962. Foreign Social Science Bibliographies, P-92, no. 14. Washington, 1964, 88 pp.
"All periodicals and monograph series devoted primarily to the social sciences which were published in Turkey in 1950 or later, and which are available in the Library of Congress. There are 519 publications listed in the bibliography--51 periodicals and 468 serial monographs" (introduction). All Turkish titles translated into English and annotated.

2899 Weryho, Jan Witold. Guide to Turkish Sources. Montreal: McGill University, Institute of Islamic Studies Library, 1973, 24 pp.
A short annotated bibliography of reference works about Turkey (and to a lesser extent Turkic-speaking Central Asia) in Turkish and other languages.

Albania

2900 U.S. of America, Bureau of the Census. Bibliography of Social Science Periodicals and Monograph Series: Albania, 1944-1961. Washington, 1962, 12 pp.
"All periodicals and monograph series devoted primarily to the social sciences which were published in Albania in 1944 or later, and which are available in the Library of Congress. . . . There are 40 publications listed in the bibliography--15 periodicals and 25 serial monographs" (introduction). All Albanian titles translated into English and annotated.

Iran

2901 Bartsch, William H., and Julian Bharier. The Economy of Iran: A Bibliography. Durham, N.C.: Durham University, Centre for Middle Eastern and Islamic Studies, 1971, 114 pp.

"We have tried to include all major English language sources, in addition to a selection of French and Persian sources which we feel are of particular value" (introduction). No annotations.

2902 Browne, Edward Granville. Materials for the Study of the Bābī Religion. Cambridge: Cambridge University Press, 1918, 380 pp.

Bibliography and other materials critically examined by one of the great Western Iranologists. Very sympathetic toward Babism.

2903 Browne, Edward G. The Press and Poetry of Modern Persia (see 860).

2904 Elwell-Sutton, L.P. A Guide to Iranian Area Study (see 68).

2905 Farman, Hafez F. Iran: A Selected and Annotated Bibliography. Washington: Library of Congress, General Reference and Bibliography Division, 1951, 100 pp.

Four hundred twelve entries arranged by subject. Very useful annotations.

2906 Handley-Taylor, Geoffrey. Bibliography of Iran. 5th ed. Chicago: St. James Press, 1969, 150 pp.

Dedicated to the Shāh of Iran and with an introduction by Foreign Minister Ardeshīr Zāhedī. This bibliography does not include any works considered hostile to the Pahlavi regime. Entries are arranged by subject without index or annotations.

2907 Iran, Plan Organization. Socio-Economic Development Plan for the South-Eastern Region: Annotated Bibliography. Rome: Italconsult, 1959.

The 586 items are classified in a very complicated arrangement without a compensating index. In spite of title, the bibliography covers the whole of Iran.

2908 Nawabi, Y.M. A Bibliography of Iran: A Catalogue of Books and Articles on Iranian Subjects, Mainly in European Languages. Vol. 1, Studies on Avesta, Mani and Manichaeism, Old Persian, Pahlavi, Parsis of India and Zoroaster and Zoroastrianism, 1969, 252 pp. Vol. 2, Persian Language and Literature, 1971, 479 pp. Tehran: Iranian Culture Foundation.

No annotations. Volume 1 is now largely superseded by Pearson's Bibliography of Pre-Islamic Persia (see 2909).

2909 Pearson, James Douglas. A Bibliography of Pre-Islamic Persia. Persian Studies Series, no. 2. London: Mansell, 1975, 288 pp.

"An attempt to include all the printed literature available in western European languages" (introduction). Indispensable for the pre-Islamic background of Persia. No annotations.

2910 Pratt, Ida A. List of Works in the New York Public Library Relating to Persia. New York: Public Library, 1915, 151 pp.

A very comprehensive bibliography to the time of publication with exceptions noted as follows: "This list does not include works on the Persian language . . . neither does it include works on Muhammadanism . . . nor Numismatics" (p. 1). There is a special section on Jews in Persia, by A.S. Freidus (pp. 107-18). No annotations.

2911 Ricks, Thomas; Thomas Gouttierre; and Denis Egan. Persian Studies: A Select Bibliography of Works in English. Bloomington: Indiana University, 1969, 266 pp.

Includes books and journal articles. In the case of books, place and date of publication but no publisher given. No annotations.

2912 Schwab, Moise. Bibliographie de la Perse. Paris: Leroux, 1875, 152 pp.

Contains 1,332 books in all languages, including English. No annotations.

2913 Storey, Charles Ambrose. Persian Literature: A Bio-Bibliographical Survey. Vol. 1, Qur'ānic Literature: History and Biography (2 pts.), 1927-1953, 1443 pp. Vol. 2, pt. 1, Mathematics, Weights and Measures, Astronomy and Astrology, Geography, 1958, 192 pp. Vol. 2, pt. 2, Medicine, 1971. London: Luzac.

Attempts to list and give full bibliographic details to all Persian works on the above subjects to the time of compilation. Students unacquainted with Persian may find this work useful because transliterations from Persian into other languages (including English) are included.

2914 Weryho, Jan Witold. A Guide to Persian Reference Sources Available at McGill Islamics Library. Montreal: McGill University, Institute of Islamic Studies Library, 1352/1973, 20 pp.

A short annotated bibliography of reference works about Iran and Afghanistan.

2915 Wickens, G.M.; R.M. Savory; and W.J. Watson, eds. Persia in Islamic Times: A Practical Bibliography of Its History (see 76).

2916 Wilson, Sir Arnold T. A Bibliography of Persia (see 78).

Kurdistan and the Kurds

2917 Behn, Wolfgang. "The Kurds, a Minority in Iran: An Annotated Bibliography." Typescript. Toronto: 1969, 28 pp.

A short work, but very useful for the annotations lacking in other bibliographies of the subject.

2918 Rooy, Silvio van, and Kees Tamboer. "ISK's Kurdish Bibliography, Nr. 1." 2 vols. Multiplicated copy. Amsterdam: International Society Kurdistan, 1968, 658 pp.

The most extensive bibliography of the subject to date, with 9,350 entries. No annotations.

Central Asia

2919 Allworth, Edward. Nationalities of the Soviet East: Publications and Writing Systems (see 970).

2920 Czaplicka, Marie Antoinette. The Turks of Central Asia in History and at the Present Day: An Ethnological Inquiry into the Pan-Turanian Problem, and Bibliographical Material Relating to the Early Turks and the Present Turks of Central Asia. Oxford: Clarendon Press, 1918, 242 pp. Reprint. Amsterdam: Philo Press, 1973.
A very full bibliography with a long introduction, but unannotated. Out of date for the politics of Pan-Turanism, but still valid for the ethnography of the Turkic peoples.

Tajikistan

2921 Belan, V. Tajikistan in Foreign Languages Literature. Vol. 1, 1961-1965, 1969. Vol. 2, 1966-1970, 1972. Dushanbe: Firdousi State Republican Library of the Tajik SSR, Foreign Literature Department.
"A bibliography of Tajikistan in foreign, i.e. non-Soviet languages, comprising books, periodical and newspaper articles and book reviews. The term 'Tajikistan' is taken in its widest sense and includes almost all fields of Iranian studies. I feel most impressed by its comprehensiveness and minute exactness, and even more by the professional integrity of the compiler who has included in it works critical of or even hostile towards the Soviet regime in Central Asia. This excellent work deserves to be better known among Orientalists outside the USSR. Since almost all entries are in European languages, no knowledge of Russian or Tajik is necessary" (J.W. Weryho, "Impressions of Oriental Libraries in the USSR," Library News (McGill University Libraries), pt. 2, 4, no. 1 (1977): 13. Additional volumes are planned.

Afghanistan

2922 Akram, Mohammed. "Bibliographie analytique de l'Afghanistan." Vol. 1, Ouvrages parus hors de l'Afghanistan. Multiplicated copy. Paris: Centre de documentation universitaire, 1947, 504 pp.
Contains 1,956 entries, classified by subject. Mostly English and French works. Author index. Annotations in French.

2923 Bibliographie der Afghanistan-Literatur, 1945-1967. Pt. 1, Literatur in europäischen Sprachen, 1968, 189 pp. Pt. 2, Literatur in orientalischen Sprachen und Ergänzungen in europäischen Sprachen, 1969, 209 pp. Hamburg: Deutsches Orient-Institut.
Includes books and periodical articles. Many of the works are in English. No annotations.

2924 Wilber, Donald N. Annotated Bibliography of Afghanistan (see 112).

Nuristan

2925 Jones, Schuyler. An Annotated Bibliography of Nuristan (Kafiristan) and the Kalash Kafirs of Chitral. 2 vols. Det Kongelige Danske Videnskabernes Selskab, Historisk-filosofisk Meddelelser, 41:3, 13:1. Copenhagen: Munksgaard, 1966-1969.
Volume 2 is subtitled: Selected Documents from the Secret and Political Records, 1885-1900. Volume 1 has not been seen by this compiler.

India

2926 Ahmad Khan, Muin ud-Din. A Bibliographical Introduction to Modern Islamic Development in India and Pakistan, 1700-1955. Dacca: Asiatic Society of Pakistan, 1959, 170 pp.
This M.A. thesis, presented at McGill University, is probably the best bibliography of the subject. Very readable introductions to each section.

2927 Chaudhuri, Sibadas. Index to the Publications of the Asiatic Society, 1788-1953. Vol. 1, 2 pts. Calcutta: Asiatic Society, 1956-1959, 472 pp. Orig. pub. in Journal of the Asiatic Society, 3d series, 22 (1956) and 23 (1957).
A listing of 7,161 entries in alphabetical order by author in each part. Publications of one of the oldest Orientalist learned societies, founded by the great British Orientalist Sir William Jones. Although most of the studies deal with India, there are many on Iran, Central Asia, and Islam in general.

2928 Fürer-Haimendorf, Elizabeth von, comp. An Anthropological Bibliography of South Asia, Together with a Directory of Recent Anthropological Field Work. Vol. 1, To 1954. Vol. 2, 1955-1959. Vol. 3, 1960-1964. Le monde d'outre-mer passé et présent, 4 ser.: Bibliographies, 3, 4, 8. Paris and The Hague: Mouton, 1958-1970.
Contains 12,603 items (books and articles), classified by geographical regions. Includes Pakistan and Muslim regions of India. No annotations.

2929 Sharma, Sri Ram. A Bibliography of Mughal India (see 425).

Punjab

2930 Singh, Ganda. A Bibliography of the Punjab. Patiala: Punjabi University, 1966, 245 pp.
Arranged by author with most entries in English; limited to the Mughal and modern periods of the Punjab. No annotations.

2931 Malik, Ikram Ali. A Bibliography of the Punjab and Its Dependencies (1848-1910). Lahore: Research Society of Pakistan, University of the Punjab, 1968, 309 pp.
Contains 2,259 entries. Arrangement by form of publication: books, government reports, and so on. General index. No annotations.

Pakistan

2932 Abernethy, George L. Pakistan: A Selected, Annotated Bibliography. 4th ed., rev. & enl. Davidson, N.C.: Publications Office, Davidson College, 1974, pp. 50.
Contains English language materials only. Not for the specialist, it "seeks, rather, to meet the typical needs of the general reader, the layman seriously interested in foreign affairs, the busy reference librarian, the teacher and government official for whom Pakistan is a peripheral interest, and a college student working on a term paper" (preface).

2933 Anwar, Mumtaz Ali, and Bashir Ali Tiwana. Pakistan: A Bibliography of Books and Articles Published in the United Kingdom from 1947-64. Lahore: Research Society of Pakistan, University of Punjab, 1969, 102 pp.
Classified by subject. No annotations or index.

2934 Datta, Rajeshwari. Union Catalogue of Government of Pakistan Publications Held by Libraries in London, Oxford and Cambridge. Cambridge: Cambridge University, 1967, 116 columns.
Reproduced directly from typed cards, in alphabetical order by author. Full bibliographic details but no annotations.

2935 Eberhard, Wolfram. "Studies on Pakistan's Social and Economic Conditions, a Bibliographical Note: Working Bibliography Prepared for the South Asia Colloquium, May 1958." Multiplicated copy. Berkeley: University of California, Center for South Asia Studies, 1958, 47 pp.
A list of unpublished theses about the rural sociology of Pakistan (dealing mostly with the Punjab) available in the libraries of the University of the Punjab, Lahore, and the Agricultural College, Lyallpur. Most useful to the social anthropologist interested in Pakistan. Listed alphabetically by villages, with reference to the name of the author. Short annotations give basic data of the locality studied.

2936 Ghani, A.R., comp. Pakistan: A Select Bibliography. Lahore: Pakistan Association for the Advancement of Science, 1951, 339 pp.
"Approximately 9,000 selected references have been collected under eight chapter headings, namely: 1. Making of Pakistan, 2. Geography, Description and Travel, 3. Natural Resources, 4. Peoples of Pakistan, 5. Economy, 6. Industries, 7. Agriculture, and 8. Animal Husbandry. . . . Omits such important subjects as Education, Archeology, Architecture, Languages, Literature, Art, Folklore, etc." (introduction, by Bashir Ahmad). No annotations. No index.

2937 Hodgson, James G., and Irene Coons. "Pakistan: A Bibliography Prepared to Furnish a Background for the Advisory Project with the University of Peshawar." Typescript. Fort Collins: Colorado A. and M. College Library, 1955, 32 pp.
Classified by subject. No index or annotations.

2938 Keddie, Nikki R., and Elizabeth K. Bauer, eds. "Annotated Bibliography for Pakistan: Sociology, Economics, and Politics." Annotated by Stanley Maron et al. Multiplicated copy. Berkeley: University of California, Human Relations Area Files, South Asia Project, 1956, 64 pp.

2939 Khurshid, Anis, and Syed Irshad Ali, eds. Librarianship in Pakistan: Fifteen Years' Work (1947-62). Karachi: University of Karachi, Department of Library Science, 1956, 65 pp.
A bibliography of books and articles about librarianship in Pakistan.

2940 Moid, A., and Akhtar H. Siddiqui. A Guide to Periodical Publications and Newspapers of Pakistan. Karachi: Pakistan Bibliographical Working Group, Karachi University Library, 1953, 60 pp.
Periodicals and newspapers in all languages (mostly English) arranged by subject matter. No index. Each entry gives address, frequency, and subscription rates.

2941 Moreland, George B., and Akhtar H. Siddiqui. Star and Crescent: A Selected and Annotated Bibliography of Pakistan, 1947-1957. Karachi: University, Institute of Public and Business Administration, 1958, 36 pp.
Arranged by subject. No index.

2942 National Book Centre of Pakistan. English Language Periodicals from Pakistan: A Guidelist. Karachi, 1967, 55 pp.
"A bibliographical list of about 400 periodicals published in Pakistan, covering almost all fields of knowledge. The information given for each periodical includes: the title, frequency, date of first issue, address of the publishers and the price. A title index is given at the end" (A.H. Siddiqui, Reference Sources [see 2946], p. 21).

2943 _____. English Language Publications from Pakistan: A Guidelist. Karachi, 1967, 242 pp.
About 2,000 entries, classified by subject. No author index or annotations. List of publishers with their full addresses. "Not a scholarly bibliography" (preface).

2944 Nur Elahi, Khwaja; A. Moid; and Akhtar H. Siddiqui. A Guide to Works of Reference Published in Pakistan. Karachi: University Library, Pakistan Bibliographical Working Group, 1953, 39 pp.
Classified by subject using Dewey numbers. No index.

2945 Pakistan Bibliographical Working Group. The Pakistan National Bibliography, 1947-1961. Fasc. 1, General Works to Islam, 001 to 297. Karachi: National Book Centre of Pakistan, 1972, 79 pp.

Classified by Dewey Decimal classification with full details under each entry. No annotations or index. Islam in Pakistan covers pages 24-79.

2946 Siddiqui, Akhtar H. Reference Sources on Pakistan: A Bibliography. Karachi: National Book Centre of Pakistan, 1968, 32 pp.
Classified by subject with an index of titles. Full bibliographic description of each work is given with excellent annotations. Arranged by subject. No index.

Malaysia and Indonesia

2947 Tregonning, Kennedy G. Southeast Asia: A Critical Bibliography. Tucson: University of Arizona Press, 1969, 103 pp.
Contains 2,058 entries arranged by subject under each country, with a general author index. Concise, critical annotations. Sections relevant to Islam include: Malaysia (pp. 48-65), Indonesia (pp. 66-84), and Sulu (pp. 89-90).

Malaysia

2948 Cheeseman, H.R., comp. Bibliography of Malaya, Being a Classified List of Books Wholly or Partly in English Relating to the Federation of Malaya and Singapore. London: Longmans, Green, for the British Association of Malaya, 1959, 234 pp.
Author index. No annotations.

2949 Pelzer, Karl J. West Malaysia and Singapore: A Selected Bibliography. Behavior Science Bibliographies. New Haven, Conn.: Human Relations Area Files, 1971, 394 pp.
"This is a revised and greatly expanded edition of a volume originally entitled Selected Bibliography on the Geography of South East Asia: Part 3, Malaya" (preface). Classified by subject. Author index. No annotations.

Indonesia

2950 Kennedy, Raymond. Bibliography of Indonesian Peoples and Cultures. 2d rev. ed. Revised and edited by Thomas W. Maretzki and H. Th. Fischer. Behavior Science Bibliographies. New Haven, Conn.: Yale University, South East Asia Studies, 1962, 207 pp.
Classified geographically by islands. No general index or annotations; contains seven maps.

Africa South of the Sahara

General Bibliographies

2951 Cowan, L. Gray. Book List on Africa for Canadians: Liste de livres sur l'Afrique à l'intention des Canadiens. Ottawa: Canadian National Commission for UNESCO, 1965, 28 pp.
English and French works, arranged by topic, not by country. Since there is no author or geographical index, it is difficult to find books about particular African countries. There is very little about Arab North Africa, but quite a lot about Muslim countries south of the Sahara: Senegal, Gambia, Guinea, Mali, Niger, Chad, Somalia. No annotations, but interesting short introductions in English and French before each section.

2952 Ofori, Patrick E. Islam in Africa South of the Sahara: A Select Bibliographic Guide. Nendeln: KTO Press, 1977, 223 pp.
Lists 1,170 books and articles, in European languages, organized by regions. Author index. No annotations.

2953 Zoghby, Samir M. Islam in Sub-Saharan Africa: A Partially Annotated Guide. Washington: Library of Congress, 1978, 318 pp.
A multilanguage work that includes 2,682 entries, mostly annotated, with Library of Congress call numbers, arranged by historical periods, subdivided by subjects. With glossary and subject and author index.

West Africa

2954 Jones, Ruth. West Africa: General, Ethnography/Sociology, Linguistics. Africa Bibliography Series, vol. 4. London: International African Institute, 1958, 116 pp.
Covers, among others, the following countries of interest to Islamic studies: Gambia, northern Nigeria, Mauritania, Senegal, French Sudan (Mali), Niger, Guinea, northern Cameroons, Rio de Oro (Spanish Sahara). Items are arranged by region with ethnic, linguistic, and author indexes. No annotations.

2955 Rydings, H.A. The Bibliographies of West Africa. Ibadan: University Press, for the West African Library Association, 1961, 36 pp.
Fifty titles. Long annotations, sometimes amounting to book reviews. Geographical arrangement. Of special interest to Islamic studies: Mauritania, Senegal, French Sudan (Mali), French Niger, Gambia, and Nigeria. Author index.

Nigeria

2956 Ita, Nduntuei O. Bibliography of Nigeria: A Survey of Anthropological and Linguistic Writings from the Earliest Times to 1966. London: F. Cass, 1971, 273 pp.
Contains 5,411 entries of books and periodical articles with full bibliographic details. This is surely the best and most exhaustive bibliography on Nigeria. It is divided into two sections--works about Nigeria in general and works about specific tribes and ethnic divisions. There are some annotations, an author and an ethnic index, and, most useful for the student of Islamics, an index of Islamic studies (p. 273). A must for any library interested in Nigerian Islam.

2957 Ochai, Adakole, comp. Ahmadu Bello University, Kashim Ibrahim Library, Catalogue of Africana. Zaria, Nigeria: Ahmadu Bello University Press, 1974, 196 pp.

Includes much about northern Nigeria and other Muslim regions of West Africa. All works are listed in alphabetical order by author. No annotations.

Tanzania

2958 Nimtz, August H., Jr. "Islam in Tanzania: An Annotated Bibliography." Tanzania Notes and Records 72 (1973):51-74.

Books and articles from 1911 to the time of compilation. Does not cover literary works, architecture, and local Muslim religious literature. Very useful annotations. Contents include documentary sources, official publications, sources in Arabic and Swahili, published sources in European languages, and unpublished sources in European languages.

South Africa

2959 Hampson, Ruth M., comp. Islam in South Africa: A Bibliography (see 1040).

China

2960 Forbes, Andrew D.W. "Survey Article: The Muslim National Minorities of China" (see 102).

2961 Leslie, Donald Daniel. "Islam in China to 1800: A Bibliographic Guide" (see 103).

2962 Pickens, Claude L., Jr. Annotated Bibliography of Literature on Islam in China (see 104).

Author Index

Subject Index